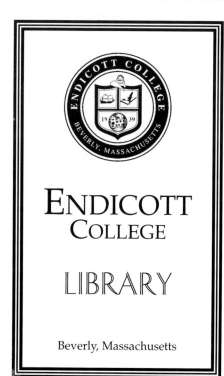

# ATLAS OF COMMUNISM

# ATLAS OF
# COMMUNISM

EDITED BY DR GEOFFREY STERN

**MACMILLAN PUBLISHING COMPANY**

NEW YORK

Copyright © 1991 by Amazon Publishing Limited

US edition published by
Macmillan Publishing Company
A Division of Macmillan, Inc.

Macmillan Publishing Company
866 Third Avenue
New York, NY 10022

Library of Congress Catalog Card Number: 90-19380
Printed in Singapore by Tien Wah Press (PTE.) Ltd
Printing Number
1 2 3 4 5 6 7 8 9 10

Library of Congress Cataloging-in-Publication Data

Atlas of communism / editor, Geoffrey Stern.
p.     cm.
ISBN 0-02-897265-1 : $80
1. Communism—History. 2. Communism—History—Maps. I. Stern,
Geoffrey.
HX36.A87  1991                                         90-19380
335.43'09—dc20                                        CIP

Edited and designed by Toucan Books Limited, London

Maps by ML Design

EDITOR:

**Dr Geoffrey Stern**
Lecturer in International Relations at the London School of Economics. Author
of *Fifty Years of Communism, Marx and the Marxists: 100 Years that Changed
the World* and *The Rise and Decline of International Communism*. Presenter of
News Hour on BBC World Service.

CONTRIBUTORS:

**Dr Terrell Carver**
Lecturer in Department of Politics at the University of Bristol.

**Professor David Childs**
Director of the Institute of German, Austrian and Swiss Affairs at the University
of Nottingham; author of *Honecker's Germany*.

**Dr Margot Light**
Lecturer in International Relations at the London School of Economics; author
of *The Soviet Theory of International Relations*.

**Dr Geoffrey Roberts**
Author of *The Unholy Alliance: Stalin's Pact with Hitler*.

**Dr George Schopflin**
Lecturer in International Relations at the London School of Economics.

**Dr Peter Shearman**
Lecturer in the Department of Government at the Australian National
University.

**Hazhir Teimourian**
Middle Eastern correspondent for *The Times*.

**Richard Walker**
Freelance writer, formerly editor of *Drum* and UN correspondent for the
*Rand Daily Mail*.

**Dr Michael Williams**
Works for the BBC Far Eastern Service.

**Dr Michael Yahuda**
Lecturer in International Relations at the London School of Economics

**The illustrations on pages 1 and 3 show early designs
for the hammer and sickle by Chekhonin.**

# CONTENTS

## DIRECTORY OF MAPS

A Soviet poster of
Karl Marx, published
circa 1920.

# INTRODUCTION

The last two months of 1989 witnessed a series of events unimaginable less than a year before: first the collapse of the Berlin Wall in November, then the 'velvet' revolution in Czechoslovakia and, finally in December, the violent revolution in Romania. As the world entered a new decade, it appeared as if the Communist world was in crisis. But was Communism, whose doctrines had - only ten years before - been the ruling ideology of nearly half the world, simply at a crossroads or was it in terminal decline? The early 1990s, therefore, provide the perfect opportunity to review the history of the movement and to peer into its future, to analyse the breadth of its ideas and to predict the directions which its various supporters may take.

In *The Road to Wigan Pier*, published in 1937, George Orwell noted - somewhat cynically - that in England 'the mere words ''socialism'' and ''communism'' draw towards them with magnetic force every fruit juice drinker, nudist, sandal-wearer, sex maniac, Quaker, ''Nature Cure'' quack, pacifist and feminist'. Beneath this wry comment lies a serious observation. Orwell was writing at the time not as an opponent of the Left, but as a member of it - as a Trotskyist who believed in a Popular Front coalition against Fascism and who would fight in Spain to prove it. But this allegiance had not prevented him from identifying an important truth: that the Left, in Britain as elsewhere,

has always attracted a diverse array of adherents - the self-interested as well as the idealists, the radical chic who alter allegiances as fashions change as well as the committed who stay the course.

This book examines the broad spectrum of left-wing ideas from which 'Communism' emerged. The origins of modern Communism - surveyed in Part One of the book *(The Roots of Communism)* - lie, of course, with the two nineteenth-century German philosophers, Karl Marx and Friedrich Engels. But the problems they sought to address - in particular, the conflict, actual or potential, in organized society between the 'haves' and the 'have-nots' - were scarcely novel. Nor, in a sense, were their proposed solutions. For if 'communism' is taken to mean a form of society without private property, accumulations of personal wealth or ruling caste, and in which rewards for labour are on the basis of some estimation of needs - then it, too, is of ancient lineage. From the time of Plato and even before, philosophers and divines have preached, and in some cases practised, forms of social co-existence that deserve the designation 'communist'. The Jewish Essenes, of which the founder of Christianity was probably one, Saints Benedict and Francis and their followers, and the Diggers of the seventeenth century all practised a kind of communism. And men from the English priest and leader of the Peasants' Revolt, John Ball, in the fourteenth century, through Sir Thomas More, Rousseau, Babeuf, and Godwin, to Saint-Simon, Fourier, Robert Owen and Louis Blanc in the first part of the nineteenth century, all produced plans for a communist organization of society. Marx, with his voracious appetite for libraries and research institutes, was thoroughly familiar with this 'communist' tradition and, though dismissive of much of it, he clearly assimilated many of his predecessors' ideas.

Rousseau, for one, was a noticeable influence. His epigram, 'Man is born free and everywhere he is in chains', has to the modern ear a distinctly Marxist ring about it. And Saint-Simon, too, left his mark: it was from him that Marx derived the notion of a planned economy. From Proudhon Marx 'learned' that 'property is theft' and from Louis Blanc he appropriated the precept, 'From each according to his ability to each according to his need'. His understanding, finally, of the 'class struggle' seems to have been assisted in no small measure by the writings of many of his contemporaries. In fact, Marx's ideas appear to synthesize several different modes of thought - French socialism, German idealist philosophy and British political economy. They do much more than that, however. One important factor, above all, distinguished Marx and Engels from their predecessors - a belief that their prospectus for a communist world was no utopian dream but a scientific endeavour based on a theory of history that was also a guide to the future. As 'historical materialists' they believed that the overall pattern of history was fixed, and that just as the rising bourgeoisie had eventually overthrown feudalism to create capitalism, the rising working class would ultimately destroy capitalism and pave the way for communism. However, as political activists wishing not merely to interpret, but also to change the world, Marx and Engels believed that if they and their followers could tap the revolutionary potential of the working class, history could be 'given a push' - in other words, that they could hasten the revolutionary process.

For all its pretensions to be scientific, Marx's brand of socialism was by no means free of inconsistencies or ambiguities - and these were to become ever more apparent after the death first of Marx in 1883 and then of Engels twelve years later. Marxism's very appeal to a diversity of people - many living in conditions far removed from those of nineteenth-century Western Europe in which the creed first took root - brought its

own problems. In particular, there was the difficulty of securing agreement on the interpretation and political requirements of the theory. The heirs of Marx were bitterly divided, as both evolutionary and revolutionary Socialists laid claim to his mantle. Then the nationalistic passions unleashed during the First World War brought further divisions, leading to a final split, in the wake of the Bolshevik Revolution in Russia of 1917, between the revolutionaries, on the one hand, and reformers, on the other. Many Marxists wanted to have nothing to do with Lenin - the founder of Bolshevism. For them, his organization was too authoritarian, his seizure of power premature, his rule too bureaucratic and his claim to have discovered the blueprint for the socialist transformation of the world preposterous. Russia's revolutionary experience, discussed in Part Two of this book *(The Soviet Experience)*, was, Lenin's Marxist critics claimed, unique, and many of them believed that the strategies and tactics of Bolshevism, both before and after the 1917 Revolution, owed far more to Russian history than to Marxism.

Lenin's Marxist rivals might castigate his approach as unorthodox - but they could hardly ignore him. In the first place, he would not let them. By appropriating the term 'Communist' for his movement, he laid claim to a special status within the Marxist fraternity - he was suggesting that his movement alone held the key to a communist world. Moreover, the facts seemed to be on his side. His was, after all, the first and for some time the only movement to achieve power in the name of Marx. This pre-eminence was ensured in the longer term by the Communist International or Comintern, which Lenin created to promote, co-ordinate and direct Communist activity throughout the world.

It was not until three decades after the revolution in Russia that another country (apart from Mongolia, 'liberated' by the Red Army in 1924) came under Communist control. But this apparent lack of success did little to dampen Communist ardour. The 'crisis' of capitalism in face of the Great Depression, the rise of Fascism and the anti-colonial revolt, all combined to bring a flood of recruits to the Communist cause during the Thirties. Many saw in the events of that decade a vindication of both Marxist theory and Leninist organization. Declining to reflect too closely on the brutal realities of Stalin's 'Socialism in One Country' - with its forced industrialization and collectivization, slave labour and draconian punishments - left-wing sympathizers contrasted the 'successes' of the Stalinist planned economy with the 'failures' of free enterprise.

In reality, Soviet-style Communism was approaching a crisis. Stalin, having completed a bloody purge within his realms, concluded a non-aggression pact with Hitler, Communism's arch-foe, then ordered the Red Army into a number of neighbouring countries, ostensibly to protect them. Though this brought Eastern Poland, part of Finland, the whole of Lithuania, Latvia and Estonia as well as the Romanian provinces of Bessarabia and Bukovina into the Communist arena, the brutality of the Soviet occupation led to a haemorrhage of support. And the movement dwindled to near-insignificance when Stalin called on Communists to abandon resistance to Nazism so as to give Hitler no cause to abrogate his pact with the Soviet Union.

When Hitler himself scuttled the agreement, by attacking the Soviet Union in June 1941, Communist fortunes were at their lowest. The tide was soon to turn, however. Faced with the possibility of Soviet defeat, the world's Communists finally rallied to the anti-Nazi resistance, with in most cases a courage, determination and organizational flair that would later ensure a boost in their political fortunes - though not necessarily along Stalinist lines.

In countries such as China, Indochina, Yugoslavia, Albania and Greece, where the exigences of war forced Communist-led guerrillas to work out strategies largely unaided by Moscow, a new kind of 'Communism' was born - one that was national in orientation. As Communist-style governments-in-embryo appeared in 'liberated' areas, such guerrilla leaders as Mao Zedong, Ho Chi-Minh, Josip Broz-Tito, Enver Hoxha and Markos Vaphiades began preparing for political power.

Yet ultimately, Communist post-war fortunes were the product not so much of domestic as of geopolitical factors, and the global reach of the great powers. Having taken by far the heaviest toll of the war, the Soviet Union felt entitled to the lion's share of the spoils, and with the Red Army in effective control of much of Eastern Europe and East Asia, Moscow was clearly well placed to determine the political destiny of these regions. On the other hand, such a projection of political and military might was bound to create alarm not just among those who were anti-Communist on principle but also among pragmatic observers and politicians fearful of a major tilt in the global balance of power. In Part Three (*Cold War Communism*),

we trace the development of the Communist bloc amid the rival alignments, the threats and counter-threats that characterized the early years of the Cold War.

At first, fearful of a concerted anti-Communist response to the new situation, Stalin discouraged Communists from seizing power. Though Tito and his then client Hoxha rejected Stalin's 'advice' (precipitating a rift that was to lead to Yugoslavia's expulsion from the Moscow-led Communist fraternity), the other Eastern European leaders dutifully adopted 'salami tactics', progressing slice by slice, as it were, to achieve power. First the Communists participated in coalitions on the basis of popular, relatively uncontroversial programmes of reconstruction. Later, their bid for popularity - more difficult to secure in Poland, Hungary and Romania than in Czechoslovakia, Bulgaria and East Germany where Communists had enjoyed considerable pre-war support - took second place to their quest for a hand on the main levers of political and economic power. Only in 1948 were they instructed to seize control - by which time, Yugoslavia excepted, Communist rule in Eastern Europe had become synonymous with Soviet domination.

As in Europe, so in Asia, ideological battle-lines were being drawn at this time. In 1948, the Korean People's Democratic Republic (North Korea) emerged, and the next year Communism scored its greatest triumph since 1917 as the Party swept to power in China, the most populous nation on earth. Unlike the Mongolian People's Republic created twenty-five years earlier and North Korea, the People's Republic of China owed little to the Soviet Union. Indeed, Mao's Nationalist rivals had received far more assistance over the years from Moscow than Mao had ever done. Stalin constantly derided Mao's attempts to give 'Marxism a specifically Chinese stamp' and disparaged him as a 'radish Communist - red outside, white inside'. Nor was Stalin generous when Mao, once in power, sought aid to rebuild his shattered country. Stalin did, on the other hand, offer protection - which Mao was glad to accept, having failed in a secret bid for American backing. Hence, the 'lean to one side' principle which he proclaimed as the basis of China's foreign relations. That principle passed its first test with the outbreak of the Korean War in 1950.

North Korea's attack on the South followed months of serious tension between the peninsula's two contending governments. Though the reasons for Pyongyang's southward thrust are still disputed, its effect was clear: to harden Cold War divisions. As the Communist countries rallied behind the North, China sent 'volunteers', while American-led anti-Communist forces acting under the U.N. banner aided the South. By the time of the armistice in 1953, North Korea's Kim Il Sung was firmly entrenched in power.

For all its violence, the carnage in Korea produced only political stalemate. It was the more prolonged hostilities in Indochina - which began as a revolt against French colonialism - that tilted the balance towards the Communists. With some support from China and other Communist countries, the Vietminh insurgents finally routed the French in 1954, enabling Ho to secure in North Vietnam the Democratic Republic he had first proclaimed (ironically, with U.S. help) in 1945.

Communism now seemed firmly on the ascendent. But its success was questionable. Not long after Hanoi's accession, the Communist 'club' began to manifest the rifts and divisions long simmering beneath the facade of 'fraternal unity'. Indications of what was to come occurred within days of Stalin's demise in 1953, as his newly orphaned heirs began to count the cost of Stalinist rule. It was clear that brutal administrative methods, excessive centralization and bureaucratization had stifled initiative and were slowly strangulating the economy. But how to resolve these problems? The new men in the Kremlin faced an uncomfortable dilemma. If they made only minor adjustments, the system might atrophy, then fall apart. If they tried to dismantle it, they would only undermine their own legitimacy as products of the system. Not surprisingly, they failed to reach any satisfactory accord, and as Stalin's successors vied for power and struggled to come up with an agreed strategy, the Eastern Europeans seized their chance to bid for greater autonomy. At first, Moscow made concessions, but it drew the line in 1956, sending in the tanks when Hungary espoused non-alignment and ended the party's monopoly of power. No sooner was Budapest under control than more problems arose, with a series of ideological and political differences putting Moscow and Beijing on a collision course. By the time Castro's Cuba had forced its way into the Communist 'club' in the early 60s, following a revolution that did not even have Moscow's support, the Communist movement was in disarray. A whole new spectrum of Communist perspectives and policies was emerging, as is shown in Part Four of the book (New Perspectives). No longer could its friends or its foes depict Communism as monolithic.

But still the Communist movement showed a surprising vigour, with its diversity and division proving no obstacle to the expansion of Marxist-Leninist ideas. In the 1970s an increasing number of Third World countries looked to Moscow or Beijing - which were believed to have overcome their legacies of semi-feudal backwardness - to provide both blueprints and assistance for rapid economic development. By the end of the decade, the 'club' had reached its zenith. The second Indochina (Vietnam) war ended in the defeat of American-backed governments, and produced in 1975 two more Communist states, Cambodia and Laos. Then in 1976 Vietnam was united under the red flag. Elsewhere, the withdrawal of British forces from East of Suez, coups in Somalia, Dahomey and Ethiopia and the Portuguese decision to quit Africa allowed the establishment of a number of crypto-Communist regimes of Socialist orientation in the Middle East and Africa. By 1979, Afghanistan, Grenada and Nicaragua could be added to the list.

Many Western alarmists took the Communist claim at face value. In fact, the 'Socialist orientation' among many Third World states turned out to be no more durable than Communist rule in Eastern Europe. As is indicated in Part Five (Reform and Revolution), several developing countries had by the 1990s abandoned Marxism-Leninism. In Eastern Europe the shift away from Marxism-Leninism was even more dramatic. As Communism began to outstrip capitalism in ways never anticipated by Stalin or Khrushchev - in terms, for example, of inflation, unemployment, indebtedness, organized crime and drug addiction - disillusionment spread all too rapidly, and once Gorbachev had given the green light for free elections, most of the formerly Communist countries turned away from Communist rule. Only in Albania, the Yugoslav republic of Serbia and a few Soviet republics did Communists still enjoy a monopoly of power and in none of these places was their position secure. The talk in Eastern Europe was of civil liberties, multi-party democracy and the free market.

So are we witnessing the end of Communism? A number of states, especially in Asia, continue to take pride in flying the red flag, while in such non-Communist countries as the Philippines, El Salvador and even Spain, Communist movements continue to attract adherents by capitalizing on local grievances. This volume assumes that to speak of Communism's demise would be as premature as the Marxist prognosis of the demise of capitalism.

# THE ROOTS OF COMMUNISM

## 1848-1917

The taking of the Panthéon during the June Days, Paris 1848. The disorder of the June Days, brutally suppressed by the government, proved to be the final outburst of the revolution.

# The First Steps

The building in Dean Street, London, where Marx spent five years of his life in dire poverty, is now a luxury restaurant, the Quo Vadis. The building which for many years was the headquarters of the Communist Party of Great Britain, in King Street, London, is now a branch of the Midland Bank. These changes seem to be symbols of the failure of Marxism in the country which Marx thought ripe for a revolution of the type he thought inevitable. Further afield in Milwaukee, USA, considered by the historian Daniel Bell to have been, in 1900, 'the solidest rock of Socialist achievement in America', little remains of the old tradition. Ethnic politics has replaced class politics.

A hundred years after the setting up of the Second Socialist International in 1889, many Marxist regimes and democratic Socialist governments around the world are abandoning their traditional definitions of socialism, embracing instead various elements of the capitalist 'enterprise culture'. In the 1980s the world had become more hostile to Marxism than perhaps at any time since the death of Marx in 1883. And yet it can still be argued, and is argued by many, that Marxism has not failed: rather that a series of historical accidents, false interpretations and the naivety of many self-styled Marxists have all conspired to distort and betray the great legacy.

## Post-Napoleonic Germany

The Germany into which Karl Marx was born in 1818 was a society that was trying to restore the status quo after the traumatic convulsions of the Napoleonic years. The great heroes of the period were Beethoven (who died in 1827), the writers Goethe and Schiller, Thomas Paine, (author of *Rights of Man*), the economists Adam Smith, David Ricardo, the philosopher Immanuel Kant and, for some, the coldly fanatical revolutionaries, Robespierre and Marat. The New world tore itself away from the Old by revolutions, first in America (1776), and then in France (1789), and an unquenchable optimism for the future of mankind was born. It was an optimism of the educated classes, hardly dimmed by the obscenity of the Jacobin terror which had descended on France after the revolution, or by the sweeping imperialism of Napoleon, who had remained a towering hero in the popular French imagination to his death and beyond, as Chateaubriand remembered in his *Memoirs*: 'No man of universal renown had an end similar to Napoleon's ... Eagle that

Adam Smith (1723-90), the influential Scottish academic and economist. His book, *The Wealth of Nations,* was published in 1776.

he was, he was given a rock on the point of which he remained in sunlight until his death, in full view of the world.'

Prussia's crucial role in the defeat of the French allowed it to play a major part in the redrawing of the map of Europe at the peace conferences held in 1815. The Prussian capital, Berlin, would dominate northern Germany from now on and its territorial gains included the city of Trier where Marx was born, close to the border with Luxembourg.

The Prussian government of Frederick William III was determined to nip in the bud any democratic rumblings which smacked of French influence, so political suppression and censorship came to characterize the king's territories in the decades which followed 1815. This need to conform to the traditions of Trier's new rulers had a direct effect on Marx. Both sides of his family had always been devout Jews and many of his ancestors had been rabbis. Despite such ancestry, Marx's father relinquished his faith and became a Christian to safeguard his legal practice, which now operated under the watchful eye of anti-semitic Berlin. In 1824 his children were received into the Protestant church.

The family lived in some comfort and Karl had a good education at the local grammar school. He went on to enrol at the University of Bonn, but the sleepy town provided few

outlets for the energies of young men and the social lives of the students tended to revolve around the taverns and the brothels. This worried Marx senior and Karl transferred to Berlin University in 1836. Before leaving Trier, however, Karl became engaged to 'the girl next door', Jenny von Westphalen.

## Discovering Hegel

The universities still possessed one of the few outstanding areas of Prussian life which remained free from Berlin's oppressive hand. The German philosophers Kant and Fichte had been among the greatest thinkers of the late eighteenth century. Their attempts to resolve the conflicts inherent in their discipline were taken up by Friedrich Hegel, who began his career in Jena and later moved on to Heidelberg. In the year of Marx's birth, Hegel was appointed to the chair of philosophy in Berlin, the most prestigious university in Europe at the time. His books and lectures began to attract large numbers of disciples and even those who did not understand his work were in awe of his reputation. In 1830 he was appointed rector of the university, but cholera swept through Germany during the following year and Hegel was one of its victims.

One of the reasons the Prussian authorities felt comfortable in honouring Hegel was that his system of thought seemed to provide no obvious challenge to the status quo. Indeed, the philosopher's concept of history seemed to justify coercion of the individual by the state, an idea which reflected political reality in Prussia at the time and contained the seeds of later Marxist-Leninist doctrines of the right of the Party to prevail at the expense of individual beliefs.

Hegel believed that mankind had risen from a state of barbarity and that the improvement of human institutions had occurred through a process of continual refinement in which an idea had been opposed by its antithesis and the conflict had led to a synthesis - the Hegelian dialectic. Although he condemned the systematic coercion of a country's citizens as wrong and indicative of political immaturity, Hegel defined the state as the embodiment of the highest level of reason yet achieved. Therefore, in any conflict between the demands of the state and the individual, the former should prevail on the grounds that it personified the most completely rational or progressive ideas applicable to the situation. Such concepts clearly undermined individual decisions and idealistic notions

# The Communist League

The Communist League had its beginnings in a small group of German refugees who were living in Paris in the mid-1830s. They founded the League of the Proscribed, which was republican in sentiment. A more radical clique broke away in 1836 and created the League of the Just, which had a strong connection with the French socialist thinkers of the time. When those French groups rose on 12 May 1839, the League of the Just fought and failed with them. Their leaders, Karl Schapper and Heinrich Bauer, were expelled from France, having been imprisoned there, and settled in London.

From London they began organizing a network which extended across Europe. Each group of members formed a 'community', in turn several communities formed a 'circle', this was then subordinated to a 'leading circle'. Above them all was the 'central committee', which was based in London until 1848. Members were recruited largely through workers' educational societies.

Engels first came into contact with the League of the Just in 1843, when its leading theoretician was Wilhelm Weitling. During the early months of 1846, Marx and Engels, who were based in Brussels at the time, began corresponding with the London group who had, by that time, broken with Weitling because of his violent and apocalyptic vision. Influenced by British trade unionism, the London group had seen the advantages of constant pressure and a gradual approach.

In January 1847 the latter sent one of their leaders, Joseph Moll, to Brussels to talk to the two radicals and a congress was organized in London in June. Engels attended and decisions were taken to change the group's name to The Communist League, to end their conspiratorial approach and to issue a periodical. A second congress was called for the end of the year to be held in London. It opened on 1 December. Marx and Engels dominated the ten days of debate and by the end of the congress, the League had been transformed into their creature. After the congress they both returned to Brussels where Marx began working on the *Communist Manifesto*.

Cologne and was supported by the region's capitalists who chafed against the old Catholic oligarchy who were obstructing their plans for railway construction.

Marx became the editor of the newspaper in October 1842 and many of his contributors were young, radical Hegelians. Some of his own articles analysed debates in the provincial assembly, one of which concerned a bill which aimed to prohibit the local peasants from collecting firewood in the forests. Marx argued that the proposed law was a return to feudalism and wrote eloquently in defence of the peasants. He also espoused the cause of wine-growers on the Moselle River and became involved in an argument with the State Governor. A confrontation with an opposition newspaper led to the accusation that *Rheinische Zeitung* was displaying communist tendencies. As he was not sure what the attack implied, Marx began to investigate the ideas that he was accused of propagating.

Moses Hess was one of Marx's contributors to the newspaper and his first two books had suggested that a revolution was inevitable because of the growing divide between the haves and the have-nots.

But ultimately, he asserted, society would embody harmony and freedom after private property had been abolished. Religion and politics would wither because they were both manifestations of the egoism promoted by greed and envy.

The philosopher Ludwig Feuerbach also attacked religion and his book, *The Essence of Christianity*, published in 1841, was very popular among Marx's friends.

It asserted that 'Man makes religion and not religion man, and that the higher being which man's fantasy creates is nothing but the fantastic reflections of his own being.' Feuerbach saw religious mystification as divisive, wasteful of human energy and a distraction from man's purpose, the study and realization of his own value.

However, later in the 1840s Feuerbach went on to assert that religion was the root of all evil, a point upon which Marx disagreed with him profoundly. But in the course of marshalling his arguments, Feuerbach introduced materialistic arguments into Germany which had been developed in France and Britain during previous centuries and had been unfamiliar hitherto. It was

which contradicted the status quo. It also flew in the face of romantic concepts of human action which emphasized individual choice, which were then at the height of their popularity throughout Europe.

Once Hegel was dead, many of his disciples, particularly the younger and intellectually more vigorous ones, began to shift their ground as their own ideas evolved. But Berlin did not notice these changes at first and promoted young Hegelians to prominent academic positions as they became vacant. But by the mid-1830s, the Prussian government had begun to realize that something was amiss as its proteges began publishing books which contained dangerously radical notions. The first to scandalize the establishment was David Strauss, whose *Life of Jesus* of 1835 called the gospels a collection of Jewish myths and doubted whether Jesus had really existed. The furore which engulfed this book provoked many young Hegelians into a reassessment of their ideas and their discussions drew them together. When Marx arrived in Berlin in 1836, he soon found himself embroiled in these controversies.

Although he joined his new university as a law student, he was drawn to philosophy and was taught by Eduard Gans, one of the few Hegelians who was also a socialist. In 1839 Marx moved on to research his dissertation and was awarded his doctorate in April 1841. His topic involved an analysis of some of the lesser known schools of Greek philosophy, a subject much in favour among Hegelians.

### The Turning Point

During his stay in Berlin, Marx had become involved with a group of young Hegelians known as the Doktorklub. One of Marx's fellow members of the Doktorklub was the theologian Bruno Bauer. Bauer was lecturing at the University of Bonn and Marx joined him in 1841, having been tempted by the possibility of securing an academic post at the university. Marx and Bauer collaborated on a satire which represented Hegel as a closet atheist and an enemy of the church, and all right-thinking people were incensed. Although the satire was published anonymously, Bauer's contribution was hardly a well-kept secret and he lost his job at the university the following spring. Deprived of his friend's influence at the university, Marx stood no chance of academic advancement.

Prussia, meanwhile, had a new ruler. Frederick William IV had come to the throne in 1840 and he looked back to the country's authoritarian past with enthusiasm. Early in 1842, Marx contributed an attack on the state's increased use of press censorship to the *German Yearbook*, which was, needless to say, censored.

During the summer he tried to earn his living through his skill with the pen and the *Rheinische Zeitung* began publishing his articles. This liberal newspaper was based in

*Right:* British economist, David Ricardo, whose *Principles of Political Economy* influenced Marx's thinking. *Far Right:* Pierre Joseph Proudhon, the eminent anarchist writer and agitator, photographed in 1862. Marx bitterly attacked his book *The Philosophy of Poverty* in an article entitled *The Poverty of Philosophy*.

# The Beginnings of Communism

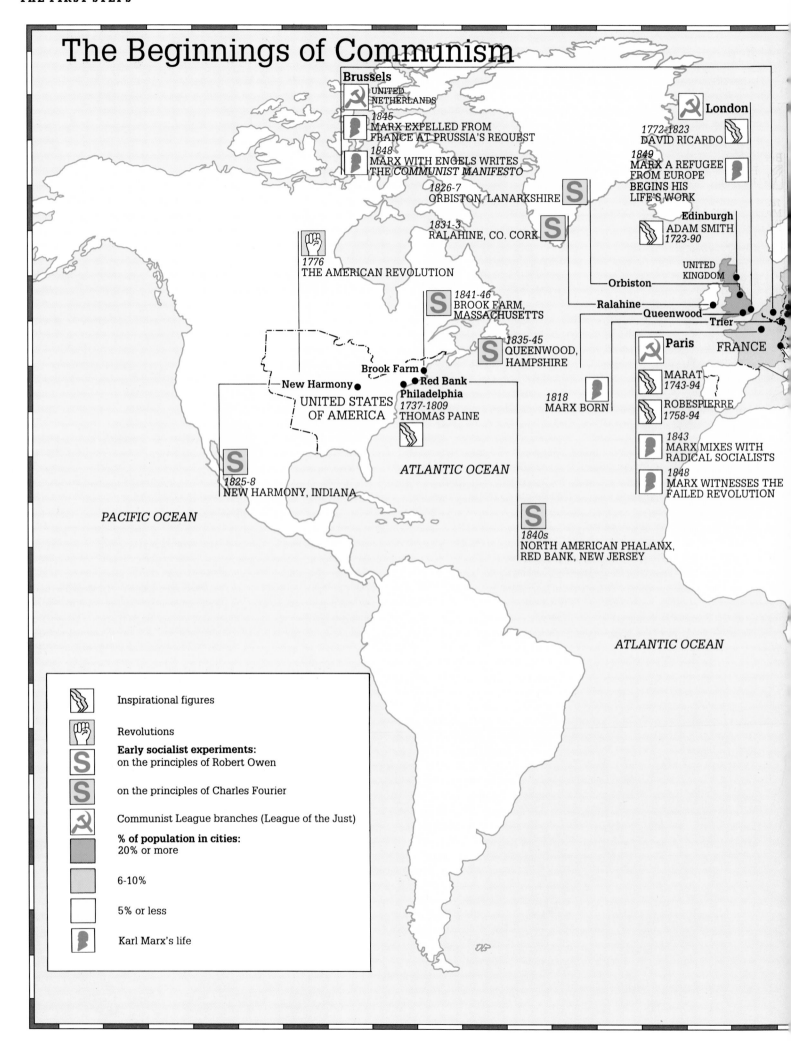

**Brussels**

UNITED NETHERLANDS

*1845*
MARX EXPELLED FROM
FRANCE AT PRUSSIA'S REQUEST

*1848*
MARX WITH ENGELS WRITES
THE *COMMUNIST MANIFESTO*

**London**

*1772-1823*
DAVID RICARDO

*1849*
MARX A REFUGEE
FROM EUROPE
BEGINS HIS
LIFE'S WORK

*1826-7*
ORBISTON, LANARKSHIRE

*1831-3*
RALAHINE, CO. CORK

**Edinburgh**
ADAM SMITH
*1723-90*

UNITED
KINGDOM

Orbiston

Ralahine

Queenwood

Trier

*1776*
THE AMERICAN REVOLUTION

*1841-46*
BROOK FARM,
MASSACHUSETTS

*1835-45*
QUEENWOOD,
HAMPSHIRE

**Paris**

MARAT
*1743-94*

ROBESPIERRE
*1758-94*

*1843*
MARX MIXES WITH
RADICAL SOCIALISTS

*1848*
MARX WITNESSES THE
FAILED REVOLUTION

Brook Farm

Red Bank

Philadelphia

*1737-1809*
THOMAS PAINE

New Harmony

UNITED STATES
OF AMERICA

*1818*
MARX BORN

FRANCE

*ATLANTIC OCEAN*

*1825-8*
NEW HARMONY, INDIANA

*PACIFIC OCEAN*

*1840s*
NORTH AMERICAN PHALANX,
RED BANK, NEW JERSEY

*ATLANTIC OCEAN*

Inspirational figures

Revolutions

**Early socialist experiments:**
on the principles of Robert Owen

on the principles of Charles Fourier

Communist League branches (League of the Just)

**% of population in cities:**
20% or more

6-10%

5% or less

Karl Marx's life

1842
MARX EDITS
*RHEINISCHE ZEITUNG*
Cologne

ARCTIC OCEAN

**Berlin**
HEGEL
*1770-1831*

1836
MARX COMES UNDER
INFLUENCE OF HEGEL

1835
MARX ATTENDS UNIVERSITY

● Königsberg
KANT
*1724-1804*

GERMAN
CONFEDERATION

Bonn
Weimar

**Vienna**
AUSTRIAN
EMPIRE

GOETHE
*1749-1832*
SCHILLER
*1759-1805*

BEETHOVEN
*1770-1827*

SWITZERLAND
**Geneva**

1789
THE FRENCH REVOLUTION

PACIFIC OCEAN

INDIAN OCEAN

through these arguments that he helped to connect Marx with a broader range of European thought which prepared him for the next phase of his life.

## A Meeting of Minds

Early in 1843 the *Rheinsiche Zeitung* was harassed by the Prussian censor and, after the Tsar himself protested about the anti-Russian commentaries of the paper, it was closed down. Marx was so disgusted that he turned his back on his country. Arnold Ruge had already offered him the post of co-editor of the *German-French Yearbook* on a salary that would allow Marx to marry. He and Jenny were married in June and a few months later they left for Paris. Unfortunately, although the monthly publication was intended as a shop window for French and German radicals, Ruge was unsettled by Marx's by now uncompromising revolutionary stance. When the first edition was published it was seized by the Prussian authorities because of its socialist flavour and because it contained articles by Marx, who was now a marked man. At this point Ruge's resolve collapsed. Fortunately for Marx and his wife, they received a large sum from the former shareholders of the *Rheinische Zeitung* as a mark of respect for the successful way he had run the newspaper, trebling its circulation in five months.

Their first child was born, appropriately, on 1 May 1844 and Jenny decided to return to Trier to visit her family for two months. This gave Karl the ideal opportunity to indulge his workaholic nature and he embarked on an orgy of study of classical economics, communism and Hegel.

Later that summer Friedrich Engels arrived in Paris. His contribution to the *Yearbook,* had impressed Marx with its observations that periodical crises of overproduction were the inevitable consequence of a free market and that competition leads to monopoly. They met in one of the most famous Parisian rendezvous, the Café de la Régence, which had been the haunt of celebrities from Benjamin Franklin to the Brothers Grimm. Their immediate rapport led them to collaborate on a book they called *The Holy Family*, which was an attack on Marx's former allies among the Hegelians and a proclamation that communism was the ultimate working class movement.

Engels divided his time between his father's textile mills in Manchester in northern England and Barman in northern Germany. Although Manchester was the centre of the industrial revolution, it still experienced the ebb and flow of trade cycles and Engels witnessed the city's misery during a severe economic downturn, an experience which inspired him to write *The Conditions of the Working Class in England in 1844* during the winter after he met Marx. This classic of socialist literature conjured up a severe indictment of market capitalism:

The house in Dean Street, London where Marx lived in abject poverty, and began work on *Das Kapital.* The building is now a restaurant.

There is an unplanned and chaotic conglomeration of houses, most of them which are more or less uninhabitable... heaps of refuse, offal and stinking filth are everywhere interspersed with stagnant pools. The atmosphere is polluted by the stench and darkened by the thick smoke of a dozen factory chimneys. A horde of ragged women and children swarm about the streets and are just as dirty as the pigs.

It was this awareness of the realities of working class life that Engels brought to their partnership and breathed life into Marx's theoretical wizardry.

Marx, meanwhile, had been contributing to *Vorwarts,* a socialist publication which provoked the Prussian government into pressurising the French into suppression. As a consequence, the Minister of the Interior closed it down and ordered Marx, Ruge and the poet Heinrich Heine to leave France. Marx settled in Brussels where he was to remain for the next three years. He was soon joined by Engels who probably helped him out financially as he could find no way to support himself and his growing family.

In 1846 they published *The German Ideology*, and in the process brought a new term into the left-wing canon. The word 'ideology' was introduced by Destutt de Tracy at the end of the eighteenth century to describe the study of the origins and working of ideas. Marx and Engels manipulated the word to mean the false consciousness of confused or deluded men who believed their ideas to be logical but are in fact the product of their social conditions. This was just the first step in the development of what has come to be called historical materialism.

As individuals express their lives, so they are. What they are, therefore, coincides with their production, both with what they produce and how they produce it. The nature of individuals thus depends on the material conditions of their production.

These arguments were another attack on the Hegelians and Feuerbach who had largely reduced all human ideas to aspects of theology and social consciousness to a variation of religious consciousness. For Marx and Engels, man was a toolmaker and it was his ability to develop his productive capacity which distinguished him from other creatures.

## To The Barricades

By now the two collaborators saw themselves as men of action as well as theorists. They were already members of the League of the Just, a clandestine group of evangelical Communists which had been led by Wilhelm Weitling, a self-educated tailor who had scurried around Europe to avoid prosecution. Marx, with typical arrogance, hijacked the organization at a meeting in the spring of 1846, launching a blistering attack on the unfortunate Weitling. In June 1847 the group's name was changed to The Communist League and in December the two collaborators were charged with drawing up a programme for the group, the process by which they created the *Communist Manifesto*.

Carl Shurz, a German student who knew them at the time, described how Marx dominated such groups.

What Marx said was in fact full of substance, logical and clear. Yet ... anybody who contradicted him he treated with barely concealed contempt. If he disliked an argument he countered with biting sarcasm at the pitiable ignorance of the speaker, or with slanderous insinuations against his motives. I well remember the cutting, contemptuous, I am tempted to say spitting, way in which he uttered the word 'bourgeois'; and he denounced as 'bourgeois', as clear examples of profound spiritual and moral debasement, all who dared disagree with his views.

The ink was barely dry on the newly printed copies of the *Communist Manifesto* before the wave of revolutions in Europe seemed to overtake Marx and Engels. Three weeks after its publication, Paris was in uproar and Louis Philippe had capitulated. In the seesaw of events, tolerant Brussels abruptly ordered Marx out of the city and the newly formed provisional government of France rescinded his exclusion order and welcomed him back to Paris with open arms and encouraging words:

Brave and loyal Marx, the soil of the French Republic is a place of refuge for all friends of freedom. Tyranny has banished you, free France opens her doors to you and all those who fight for the holy cause, the fraternal cause of all peoples.

The possibilities seemed limitless.

# 1848: Year of Revolution

It took just three days' rioting in Paris in late February 1848 to bring down the regime of the 'bourgeois king' Louis Philippe. And from then on a seemingly unstoppable tide of revolution flowed over Europe. It swept across the Rhine into the various small states of Germany, toppling ministries and one king, up into Denmark, across the vast eastern realms of the Habsburg Empire, and down the Italian peninsula. Although Britain - the country that Engels had considered ripe for revolution - failed to fulfill his expectations, it was shaken by troubles in Ireland, and by Chartist agitations for electoral reform. Europe had seen revolutions before - notably the great cataclysm that engulfed France from 1789 onwards. But never before had so many revolts broken out in so many places in the space of so few months.

In fact, however, conditions in Europe had long been building up for such an outburst. Although each of the revolutions had its own characteristics, they also had much in common. Underpinning them all were the democratic aspirations of mostly middle-class liberals and radicals, increasingly impatient with often reactionary regimes, longing for freer, more open societies and a fairer share of political power. Nationalism was another element in the revolutionary mix. In Germany (since 1815 a loose confederation of principalities and kingdoms, dominated by Austria and Prussia) there were growing demands for the petty tyrannies to be merged in one unified democratic state. In Italy, fragmented in a similar way, there were similar calls. And the non-Germanic peoples of the Habsburg Empire longed for at least some measure of autonomy from Vienna.

On top of this were the grievances of the worst-off in town and country, a result of a continent-wide financial slump in the late 1840s, severe unemployment, the squalid conditions of the growing industrial regions, a succession of bad harvests and consequently high food prices. As early as 1842 the German poet Heinrich Heine commented after a visit to the industrial suburbs around Paris on the explosive anger he saw there:

The songs which I heard [the workers] singing seemed to have been composed in hell and had a chorus of the wildest excitement. Really people in our gentle walk of life can have no idea of the demonic note which runs through these songs. One must hear them with one's own ears .... in those enormous workshops where metals are worked and where the half-naked, defiant figures keep time to their songs with the mighty blows which their great iron hammers strike upon the ringing anvil....Sooner or later the harvest which will come from the sowing in France threatens to be a republican outbreak.

The powder was there - it needed only a spark to set it alight.

## February Days in Paris

Events started to come to a head in France in 1847. In many respects, the French were luckier than most in continental Europe at the time. The July Revolution of 1830 had replaced the inept and arrogant Bourbon Charles X with his cousin, the more liberal

'The Citizen King' Louis Philippe riding through a riot-scarred Paris after the July Revolution of 1830. To test his popularity as the new constitutional monarch, he made a successful journey from the Palais Royal to the Hôtel de Ville, the Headquarters of the Republican government.

# 1848 Year of Revolution

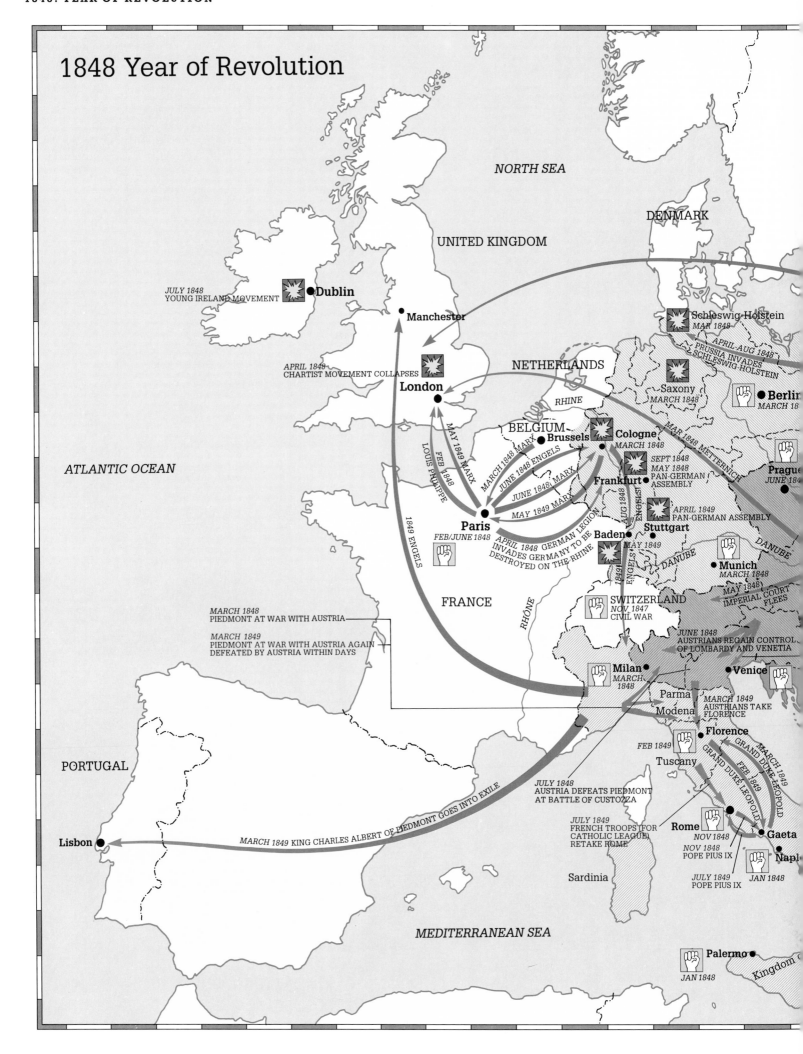

NORTH SEA

DENMARK

UNITED KINGDOM

*JULY 1848*
YOUNG IRELAND MOVEMENT · **Dublin**

• Manchester

*APRIL 1848*
CHARTIST MOVEMENT COLLAPSES
**London**

NETHERLANDS

*RHINE*

ATLANTIC OCEAN

BELGIUM

**Brussels**

*MARCH 1848 MARX*

*FEB 1848*
*LOUIS PHILIPPE*

*MAY 1849 MARX*

*JUNE 1848 ENGELS*

*JUNE 1848, MARX*

*JUNE 1849 MARX*

*MAY 1849 MARX*

**Paris**
*FEB/JUNE 1848*

*1849 ENGELS*

FRANCE

*RHÔNE*

Schleswig-Holstein
*MAR 1848*

*APRIL-AUG 1848*
PRUSSIA INVADES
SCHLESWIG-HOLSTEIN

Saxony
*MARCH 1848*

**Berlin**
*MARCH 18*

*MAR 1848 METTERNICH*

**Prague**
*JUNE 1848*

**Cologne**
*MARCH 1848*

*SEPT 1848*
*MAY 1848*
PAN-GERMAN
ASSEMBLY
**Frankfurt**

*APRIL 1849*
PAN-GERMAN ASSEMBLY

*AUG 1848 ENGELS*

**Stuttgart**

*APRIL 1848* GERMAN LEGION
INVADES GERMANY TO BE
DESTROYED ON THE RHINE

**Baden**
*MAY 1849*

*ENGELS 1849*

*DANUBE*

*DANUBE*

**Munich**
*MARCH 1848*

*MAY 1848*
IMPERIAL COURT
FLEES

SWITZERLAND
*NOV 1847*
CIVIL WAR

*JUNE 1848*
AUSTRIANS REGAIN CONTROL
OF LOMBARDY AND VENETIA

*MARCH 1848*
PIEDMONT AT WAR WITH AUSTRIA

*MARCH 1849*
PIEDMONT AT WAR WITH AUSTRIA AGAIN
DEFEATED BY AUSTRIA WITHIN DAYS

**Milan**
*MARCH 1848*

**Venice**

Parma

Modena

*MARCH 1849*
AUSTRIANS TAKE
FLORENCE

PORTUGAL

**Florence**
*FEB 1849*

Tuscany

*JULY 1848*
AUSTRIA DEFEATS PIEDMONT
AT BATTLE OF CUSTOZZA

*JULY 1849*
FRENCH TROOPS (FOR
CATHOLIC LEAGUE)
RETAKE ROME

*GRAND DUKE LEOPOLD*

*MARCH 1849*

*FEB 1849*

*GRAND DUKE LEOPOLD*

*MARCH 1849 KING CHARLES ALBERT OF PIEDMONT GOES INTO EXILE*

**Lisbon**

**Rome**
*NOV 1848*
*NOV 1848*
POPE PIUS IX

*JULY 1849*
POPE PIUS IX

**Gaeta**

**Naples**
*JAN 1848*

Sardinia

MEDITERRANEAN SEA

**Palermo**
*JAN 1848*

Kingdom

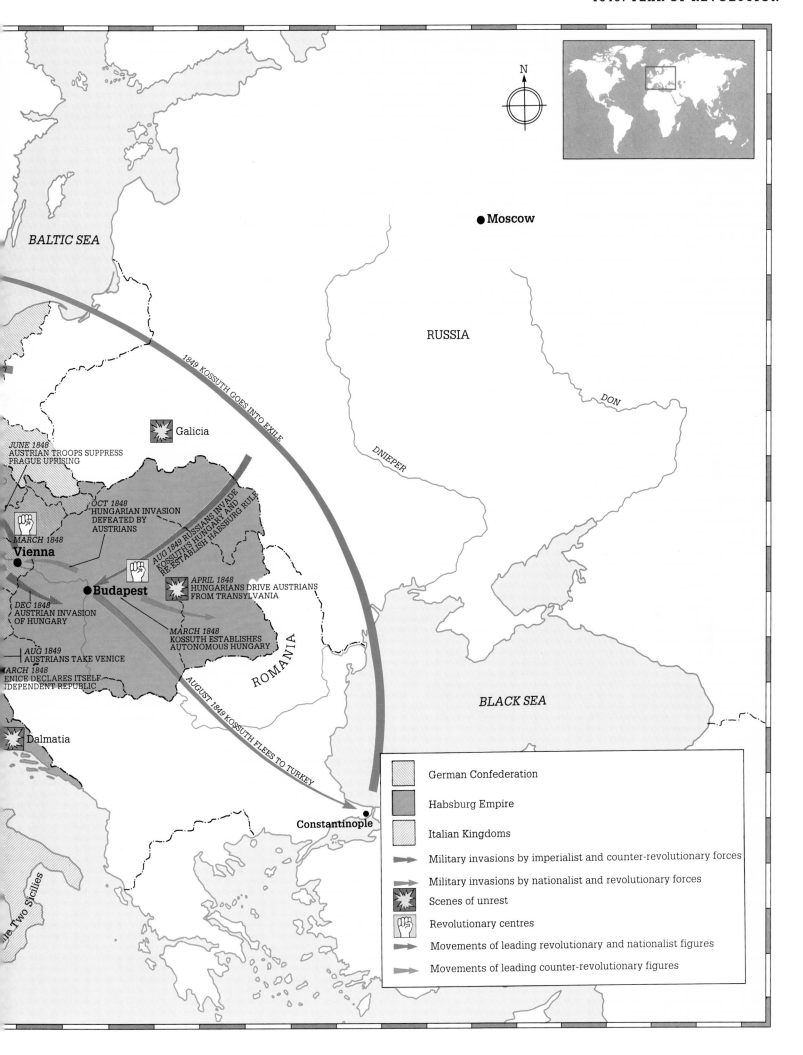

BALTIC SEA

● Moscow

RUSSIA

DON

DNIEPER

Galicia

*JUNE 1848*
*AUSTRIAN TROOPS SUPPRESS*
*PRAGUE UPRISING*

*OCT 1848*
*HUNGARIAN INVASION*
*DEFEATED BY*
*AUSTRIANS*

*1849 KOSSUTH GOES INTO EXILE*

*AUG 1849 RUSSIANS INVADE*
*KOSSUTH'S HUNGARY AND*
*RE-ESTABLISH HABSBURG RULE*

*MARCH 1848*

**Vienna**

**Budapest**

*APRIL 1848*
*HUNGARIANS DRIVE AUSTRIANS*
*FROM TRANSYLVANIA*

*DEC 1848*
*AUSTRIAN INVASION*
*OF HUNGARY*

*MARCH 1848*
*KOSSUTH ESTABLISHES*
*AUTONOMOUS HUNGARY*

ROMANIA

*AUG 1849*
*AUSTRIANS TAKE VENICE*

*MARCH 1848*
*ENICE DECLARES ITSELF*
*IDEPENDENT REPUBLIC*

*AUGUST 1849 KOSSUTH FLEES TO TURKEY*

BLACK SEA

Dalmatia

**Constantinople** ●

e Two Sicilies

| | |
|---|---|
| | German Confederation |
| | Habsburg Empire |
| | Italian Kingdoms |
| → | Military invasions by imperialist and counter-revolutionary forces |
| → | Military invasions by nationalist and revolutionary forces |
| ✴ | Scenes of unrest |
| ✊ | Revolutionary centres |
| → | Movements of leading revolutionary and nationalist figures |
| → | Movements of leading counter-revolutionary figures |

Louis Philippe is satirized by the Republican artist Philipon. 'Poire' (pear) means dimwit.

Louis Philippe of Orléans. He granted a constitutional charter which provided for a Chamber of Deputies, though one elected on a narrow franchise, and opened the country's administration to those best able to profit by the complacent motto of his chief minister of the 1840s, François Guizot: 'Enrichissez-vous!' ('Get rich!'). But in a country where many still had vivid memories of the 1789 Revolution and the subsequent glories of the Napoleonic Empire, the cautious policies of the Orléans monarchy failed to inspire. 'La France s'ennuie' ('France is bored'), proclaimed the Romantic poet and liberal politician Alphonse de Lamartine, encapsulating the feelings of many of his countrymen.

In the summer of 1847 liberal opposition leaders, among them Lamartine, began a campaign for electoral reform, organized around a series of political banquets - ordinary political meetings were banned by the government. The campaign gathered strength, drawing increasing support not only from liberals but also from forces on the radical left. At first the authorities let events take their course. Then they took fright. The culmination of the campaign was to be a banquet in Paris scheduled for 22 February 1848, and at the last moment the government, with the support of some liberal leaders (fearful alike that events might run out of control), agreed to cancel the Paris banquet. It was too late. The radical newspaper La Réforme called on Parisians to carry out plans for a demonstration, and on 22 February thousands gathered in spite of foul weather in the Place de la Madeleine, just a stone's throw from the royal palace of the Tuileries. There was some relatively

small-scale violence - street lamps were smashed, omnibuses overturned - and then the crowds dispersed.

Next day events took a more serious turn. Larger crowds gathered and some demonstrators started to erect barricades. The National Guard, on which the King and his ministers relied to keep control of Paris, added its voice to the calls for reform. Faced with an ever more threatening situation, Louis Philippe dismissed the widely hated Guizot. But this sop failed to appease the crowds. They went on gathering, and that afternoon came an incident that was to turn hitherto peaceful demonstrations into outright revolution. In an encounter between demonstrators and some army troops outside the Foreign Ministry, an unknown soldier panicked and fired a shot, and in the melee that followed some forty demonstrators were killed. That night a cart bearing their bodies was pulled through the streets of Paris. Wild rumours circulated that the government was planning a massacre of workers.

The morning of the 24th dawned and the situation was more dangerous than ever. Overnight more than fifteen hundred barricades had gone up around Paris. As the crowds gathered they were no longer shouting 'Vive la Réforme', but 'Vive la République'. Large numbers began converging on the Tuileries. For the old and far from bloodthirsty Louis Philippe it was too much. He donned disguise, slipped out of the palace, and fled across northern France to Le Havre from where he and his family took ship for England - the first of many casualties of 1848 to seek refuge there. Minutes after the King's escape from the palace, the crowds arrived. They rampaged through the royal apartments, ripping up furniture, stealing clothes and jubilantly tossing the throne into the palace courtyard. From there they swarmed across the Seine to the Chamber of Deputies. Conservative deputies fled, leaving a handful of radicals and liberals. These - led by Lamartine - formed themselves into a provisional government and headed for the Hôtel de Ville, where they were joined by a more radical left-wing group from the Réforme newspaper, who insisted on being included in the government. By midnight Lamartine had proclaimed the republic to rejoicing crowds surging outside.

# The Communist Manifesto

At the end of the Second Congress of the Communist League, held between 29 November and 8 December 1847, Marx and Engels were asked to draw up a document which would summarize the League's agreed postion. It was Engels' idea that it should be called a manifesto and he provided a draft of the document. But its final form was entirely Marx's work. It was published in February 1848, just days before revolution overtook Louis Philippe in Paris.

The Manifesto is divided into four parts. The first and longest is historical and establishes the bourgeoisie as the leading element in contemporary society, indicating how it has 'sprouted from the ruins of feudal society'. The bourgeoisie 'has drowned the most heavenly ecstasies of religious fervour, of chivalrous enthusiasm and philistine sentimentalism, in the icy water of egotistical calculation. It has resolved personal worth into exchange value, and in place of the numberless indefeasible chartered freedoms has set up that single unconscionable freedom - Free Trade.'

The second part of the

The cover of the first German edition of the Communist Manifesto, published in 1848.

Manifesto explains the role of the Communists as the vanguard of the proletariat. Its purpose is the 'formation of the proletariat into a class, overthrow of the bourgeois supremacy, conquest of political power by the proletariat.' They are 'the most advanced and resolute section of the working class parties of every country... they have over the great mass of the proletariat the advantage of clearly understanding the line of

march'. The third part attacks the other schools of socialism: 'The Socialistic bourgeois want all the advantages of modern social conditions without the struggles and danger necessarily resulting therefrom'. And 'Christian Socialism is but the holy water with which the priest consecrated the heart-burnings of the aristocrat.'

The last section is very short but utters a final clarion call: 'The Communists disdain to conceal their views and aims. They openly declare that their ends can be attained only by the forcible overthrow of all existing social conditions. Let the ruling classes tremble at a Communist revolution. The proletarians have nothing to lose but their chains. They have a world to win. WORKING MEN OF ALL COUNTRIES, UNITE!'.

It was greeted with enthusiasm by the few hundred members of the Communist League who were scattered through Europe. But despite their numerical insignificance, the Manifesto marked a turning point because it pointed Socialists away from Utopian idealism and gave them an analytical framework which could lead to practical political solutions.

## Excitement and Reaction

Heady days followed in the French capital, and reforms (many of a socialist hue) poured out. A permanent commission was set up under the socialist Louis Blanc at the Luxembourg Palace to look into the conditions of the workers. The right to work was guaranteed, and National Workshops were instituted to provide jobs and an income for the unemployed. Elections were called for an assembly to devise a new constitution, and they were to be conducted on the basis of universal manhood suffrage.

The city's cafés and public meeting places buzzed with political excitement. Nearly 150 political societies discussed further and yet more exciting reforms. In places the red flag flew alongside the tricolour.

Paris also became a mecca for revolutionaries from all over the continent. Marx (who with Engels had just finished work on the *Communist Manifesto*) was expelled from Brussels by jittery Belgian authorities and arrived in the city in early March at the invitation of the revolutionary government. Engels was there too. Some of the Germans, including Marx's friend, the poet Georg Herwegh, received government support to form a German Legion to help export revolution to Germany. They spent happy days manoeuvring and exercising in the Champs de Mars.

But, despite the revolutionary excitement, signs began to emerge of a conservative backlash. Many in the business and professional classes, in particular, came to regard the heavily subsidized National Workshops as an intolerable burden on the taxpayers. And in the provinces peasants, still the vast majority of the French nation, were less than enthusiastic about the events in Paris. In late April these forces came together to produce a massive conservative victory in the elections for the Constituent Assembly; radicals and socialists won a mere 100 out of 876 seats. A new, more conservative government emerged which easily put down an attempted left-wing coup in May.

Then, in June, the government announced a decision to close all Paris Workshops and to conscript workers between the ages of eighteen and twenty-five registered with them into the army. Others would be sent to the provinces to clear land. This ill-judged move precipitated a massive outburst of popular fury. Barricades went up once more. Crowds even angrier than those in February poured on to the streets, and this time they made careful preparations. Holes were bored between houses within the barricaded sectors of the city to allow the insurgents to move around without going outside. Apparently pregnant women passed unchecked through the streets - in fact they were carrying bags of gunpowder to the insurgents.

But the new government was prepared for more brutal action than Louis Philippe and called in General Eugène Cavaignac, a veteran of wars in France's North African colonies. He bided his time at first, letting the insurgents continue their preparations while he gathered an overwhelming superiority of troops. Then he moved, and four days' bloody fighting followed - the so-called 'June Days'. Artillery hammered at the barricades from near point-blank range. Whole areas of the city were laid waste. A relatively modest four or five thousand rebels were killed at the barricades, but a further three thousand were hunted down after the fighting was over; some were thrown into the Seine to drown, others shot or hanged. Thousands more were sentenced to forced labour or deported to the colonies.

One witness, seemingly impressed more by the aesthetic qualities of the scene than by its sheer human misery, gave all the same a vivid description of the aftermath in one of the places where the fighting had been heaviest:

The Place de la Bastille offered the most terrifying image of chaos. All the trees were felled or twisted by cannon balls; here, houses in ruins or devoured by flames; there, veritable towers of planks, overturned carriages and heaped-up stones; in the midst of all that a people dazed or barely retaining their self-possession in the midst of scenes which surpass the imagination, soldiers asleep from fatigue on the pavements almost under the feet of the people, the fury of the defeated betraying itself despite an affected tranquillity, the disorder of the victors as they opened up a path over the overturned barricades, elsewhere public pity seeking alms for the wounded, and gathering linen to dress their wounds, all came together to present one of those spectacles of a supreme originality, where all the tones of humanity make themselves heard at one time in an admirable disorder....

From now on the forces of reaction were in firm control. In November the Constituent Assembly agreed a presidential-style constitution; a month later Louis Napoleon Bonaparte was elected president by a population yearning for a return to the glorious days of his uncle, the great Napoleon. Two years later he too was to make himself Emperor.

**Fomentation in Germany**

News of the February Days in Paris spread across the continent and produced a wave of sympathetic action. Vienna and Berlin both erupted on 13 March. With the news from Paris but two weeks old, Habsburg archdukes in Vienna - who held the reins of power for the imbecile Emperor Ferdinand I - lost little time in promising constitutional

In 1848 the unemployed, liberals and socialists joined to man the Paris barricades; this is the Rue St Martin. Despite days of street-fighting and ruthless and bloody suppression by the government, here in France the Republic survived. Throughout the rest of Europe counter-revolution triumphed.

Rebellion against the Austrian troops on the Porta Tosa, Milan, 22 March 1848. With the Austrians driven out of Venice and the Bourbons from Palermo, the individual kingdoms could look towards an eventual united Italy under a single national government.

reforms and ousting the hated, arch-reactionary Chancellor Prince Clemens von Metternich, who had dominated Austrian politics for nearly thirty years; like Louis Philippe, he fled to England. In Berlin events were complicated by the young Prussian King Friedrich Wilhelm, who first promised reforms, then on the 18th turned troops on crowds gathered to hear the contents of the reforms. Then he had a change of heart, called the troops off, declared himself in favour of a united Germany and rode through the Berlin streets in the red, black and gold colours of the united German nation. Also in March there were uprisings in, among other places, Cologne (where members of the local Communist League took the lead), Baden, Saxony, among the German-speaking subjects of the Danish Crown in the duchies of Schleswig and Holstein, and in Bavaria (where the ageing and infatuated King Ludwig I was forced to abdicate, while his high-handed, all-powerful mistress, the beautiful Irish-born Spanish dancer Lola Montez was obliged to flee for her life).

At the same time Austria was facing the disintegration of the large non-German parts of its empire. In its north Italian provinces of Venetia and Lombardy, Venice declared itself an independent republic, and the citizens of Milan responded to the news from Vienna with their own 'five glorious days', starting on 18 March. Armed with stones, bottles, some ancient muskets, and pikes and swords purloined from the city's museums and the prop room of La Scala opera house, they drove the Austrian garrison out of the city. The Hungarians, meanwhile, led by the spellbinding nationalist orator Lajos Kossuth, declared themselves an autonomous state linked to Austria only by the Habsburg Crown, and embarked on a wide-ranging programme of reform which included abolishing such feudal hangovers as serfdom and the Hungarian nobles' exemption from taxation.

April dawned and the revolutionary impetus continued. On the 1st, Marx and Engels in Paris issued a seventeen-point appeal on behalf of the Communist League and 'in the interests of the German proleteriat, the petty-bourgeoisie and the peasantry'. They demanded that Germany be proclaimed a republic, one and indivisible, the people armed, princely and other feudal estates nationalized together with the mining and transport industries, national workshops - on the lines of the French ones - established and compulsory

education introduced for children. On the same day Herwegh and the German Legion marched out of the French capital to launch their invasion. Marx dismissed this as 'revolutionary foolery' - and so it proved: the Legion was cut down on crossing the Rhine. A more substantial measure, raising high hopes among nationalists of all hues, came in May when an elected Pan-German Assembly met in Frankfurt to decide a constitution for a united Germany.

### Conservative Backlash

But already - as in France - the tide was turning, although in Germany revolutionary events were to continue well into 1849. In June Marx and Engels, like many of their colleagues in the Communist League, returned to Germany; Marx settled with his family in Cologne, and Engels in Barmen. Chiefly at Engels' instigation, they founded a newspaper, the *Neue Rheinische Zeitung* (New Rheinish Gazette) dedicated to broadly democratic, rather than purely socialist, causes. Despite this moderation, they hit immediate trouble when they came out in heated support of the revolutionaries of the Paris June Days, losing most of their shareholders as a result.

At the same time, the Frankfurt Assembly had become hopelessly bogged down in rancorous disputes about the shape of the new Germany. The chief problem was Austria, with its vast non-German lands. Should it, or should it not, be included? If not, should Prussia be given the leading role? Prussia, meanwhile, had become involved in a futile war against Denmark in an attempt to assert the right of Germany to both Schleswig and Holstein, of which only Holstein belonged to the German Confederation; this ended in August.

As 1848 drew to its close the reactionary tide was flowing with increasing strength. As early as June Austrian troops had put down a Czech uprising in Prague with a brutality akin to Cavaignac's in Paris; further revolts in Vienna were dealt with in similar fashion. In Italy the octogenerian Marshal Radetzky re-established Austrian control over most of Venetia and Lombardy - with the exception of Venice. In November a new, more energetic conservative ministry came to power in Vienna, which brought about the abdication of the Emperor Ferdinand and his replacement by his nephew Franz Josef, who was to remain on the Habsburg throne until the First World War. Elsewhere, Prussian troops put down an uprising in Frankfurt in September, and a now more decisive Friedrich Wilhelm rescinded most of the reforms he had granted in Prussia earlier in the year, and installed a conservative ministry in Berlin.

Hungary still held out - and was to declare itself a completely independent republic in April 1849 with Kossuth as its provisional head of state. But it too was doomed, meeting its fate at the hands of the Russian Tsar Nicholas I. Relieved that his realms had been spared the upheavals of 1848, but worried that the revolutionary spirit

light still prove contagious, he was only too eager to lend a helping hand to his brother emperor in Vienna. A Russian army defeated the Hungarians at Vilagos in August. Kossuth buried the Hungarian crown and fled to Turkey, from where - like so many others - he went on to England.

The Frankfurt Assembly, meanwhile, had also met an inglorious end. In April 1849 it finally resolved its differences in favour of Prussia, offering the imperial crown of a united democratic Reich to Friedrich Wilhelm. He refused it, scorning 'this dog collar with which they want to chain me to the revolution of 1848'. Prussia and Austria pulled out of the Assembly, and the rump that remained moved to Stuttgart where, at Prussia's request, the Württemberg authorities forcibly dissolved it. In May left-wing radicals put up desperate last-ditch fights in Dresden, the Palatinate and Baden, but Prussian troops moved in once more to suppress them - inaugurating a new era of Prussian militarism which would reach its peak under Bismarck.

Two victims of these events had been Marx and Engels, who through all this time had been battling on with the *Neue Rheinische Zeitung*, despite both financial and political difficulties, including its temporary suppression. On 19 May 1849, in what was to be the paper's last issue, they launched a bitter attack on Friedrich Wilhelm. The result was immediate deportation from Prussian territories. Marx made for Paris but there, in the changed political climate, he was no longer welcome. The authorities refused him permission to remain in the capital, though they were prepared to allow him to reside in Morbihan in Brittany, considered one of the unhealthiest parts of France. Wanting to be in a key centre of political activity, and influenced by the fact that his wife was expecting their

fourth child, Marx decided to leave France for London. Engels, meanwhile, had taken part in the armed struggle in south-western Germany, acting as adjutant in a volunteer corps led by the former Prussian lieutenant August Willich in Baden. Then he too made his way - via Italy - to England, where financial pressure forced him to take up an offer from his father to rejoin the family firm in Manchester. For the next two decades one of the twin founders of modern Communism enjoyed the lifestyle of a prosperous capitalist.

## Last Flings in Italy

In Italy and neighbouring Switzerland, revolutionary events had, in fact, preceded those in France and Germany, and were to outlast them. In November 1847 full-scale civil war broke out in the Swiss cantons, between radical forces prepared to fight for sweeping democratic reforms and conservative authorities determined not to grant them.

Then in early January 1848 the people of Palermo in Sicily rose up against the autocratic rule of the Bourbon King Ferdinand II of Naples. By the month's end Ferdinand had granted a liberal constitution, and over the next few weeks the Pope in Rome and the rulers of Tuscany and Piedmont followed suit, anxious to avoid similar disturbances in their own realms. In late March King Charles Albert of Piedmont joined in the revolutionary tide by declaring war on Austria. His armies invaded Lombardy and occupied the independent duchies of Parma and Modena, but in July he was defeated by Marshal Radetzky at Custozza and forced into an armistice.

A lull followed which lasted into the autumn. Then in November came a thoroughgoing revival of revolution. Radical mobs in Rome rose up against Pope Pius IX (who was forced to flee to Gaeta in the kingdom of Naples), assassinated one of his chief ministers, and proclaimed a republic, with the nationalist leader Giuseppe Mazzini (founder of the Young Italy movement) as one of a triumvirate at its head. The new government set about a comprehensive programme of radical democratic reform, akin to that in Paris after the February days. They nationalized Church properties, redistributed land to the peasants, abolished a much-hated tax on flour, and organized elections based on universal manhood suffrage. In February the following year radicals in Tuscany followed suit, driving the Grand Duke Leopold into exile with the Pope at Gaeta. In March Charles Albert of Piedmont joined in by declaring war once more on Austria.

But with the reactionary tide now flowing in full force, the Italians had little chance of long-term success. Charles Albert was the first to go: within days of declaring war, he was defeated and forced into another armistice. Following this second humiliation at the hands of the Austrians he went into

The Sea-Serpent Liberty in a *Punch* cartoon of 1848 threatens to overturn the old ruling classes of Kings and Emperors in their fragile boat. In fact, thanks to a lack of overall co-ordination, little was achieved by the revolutions of 1848 and the old monarchies soon regained control.

# The Chartist Movement

The most serious threat to England's government was the Chartist movement. In London the great Chartist meeting held on Kennington Common on 10 April 1848 pressed for Paliamentary reform.

Disappointed by the failure of the 1832 Reform Act to promote an increase in the number of Radical MPs, the London Working Men's Association was formed in June 1836. Early in 1837 it presented a petition to the House of Commons which espoused six points: universal male suffrage, equal electoral districts, annual Parliaments, the payment of members, a secret ballot and an end to the property qualification for MPs. In 1838 the petition was redrafted as a parliamentary bill by the London Radical William Lovett. It was called the People's Charter, and was launched at a vast open-air meeting in Birmingham on 6 August. The petition was eventually signed by over a million people and debated by

parliament in July 1839. But it was supported by only forty-six members and, although Disraeli spoke on its behalf, it failed.

Its rejection brought calls for a general strike, but its supporters lacked sufficient organization. This feeling of impotence enraged many Chartists but, although many talked wildly, few acted. But on the morning of 4 November 1939, three thousand miners marched on Newport, South Wales, calling for the release of some local Chartists who had been arrested. But their lack of realism and experience was exposed when they were repulsed by a few dozen troops. Twenty-four died, 125 were are arrested and 21 were charged with treason.

In 1842, a second petition was

presented to parliament, this time with over 3 million signatures. Again it was rejected and again a strike was called, this time with greater success. But the movement collapsed a second time with more arrests.

The events of 1848 provoked considerable excitement among the remaining Chartists and another petition was circulated. A meeting was called for 10 April on Kennington Common from where the signatures would be carried by a procession to Parliament. But the government had packed London with troops and special police and, in a compromise deal, the paper was taken to the House in a cab. Despite this, no debate was allowed and the movement finally collapsed.

of Wellington, and an attempted insurrection by the radical Young Ireland movement had been swiftly put down in July. Mazzini summed up the feelings of many disappointed revolutionaries: 'I feel from time to time emotions of rage rising within me at this triumph of brutal force, all throughout the world, over right and justice.'

In fact, the revolutions had never really had a chance. They had never been co-ordinated, occurring in different places at different speeds and times. Furthermore, they had almost all been strictly limited in their aims. In spite of the undoubted anger among many of them, Europe's industrial workers, their rural counterparts and the socialist intellectuals agitating on their behalf, had played only a relatively small part - and only in certain places, such as Paris - in bringing about the revolutions. Here and there, as in France and Rome, there had been attempts to bring about social as well as political change. But the truth was that there were still comparatively few industrial workers in continental Europe in 1848-9. And even these were no match for the middle classes who, as events developed, grew ever more fearful that the revolts would fall into the hands of radical and proletarian elements, and that chaos and terror would follow - as in the first French Revolution. Many who had started out supporting the revolutionary events - even leading them - were later willing to co-operate with the forces of reaction.

And yet the revolutions were not wholly failures. In places reforms won in 1848 remained: the former serfs of Hungary retained their freedom, the Swiss radicals won their civil war. And memories, too, remained that would be an inspiration to future generations of revolutionaries.

Marx, in particular, was quick to read positive lessons from the revolutions of 1848-9. 'With the exception of only a few chapters,' he wrote later, 'every more important part of the annals of the revolution from 1848 to 1849 carries the heading: Defeat of the revolution!' But, he went on, the very violence of the reactionary triumph had polarized class antagonisms, forging the conditions which would favour successful future revolutions:

The revolution made progress ... not by its immediate tragicomic achievements, but, on the contrary, by the creation of a powerful, united counter-revolution, by the creation of an opponent in combat with whom, only, the party of overthrow ripened into a really revolutionary party.

The Paris June Days, above all, he saw as being of crucial importance.

The June defeat has created all the conditions under which France can seize the initiative of the European revolution. Only after being dipped in the blood of the June insurgents did the tricolour become the flag of the European revolution - the red flag!

And we exclaim: The revolution is dead! - Long live the revolution!

exile in Portugal. Then Austrian troops restored Grand Duke Leopold in Tuscany. The Romans, their defences led by the colourful former sea captain Giuseppe Garibaldi, held out for longer. In June French forces (acting on behalf of a league of Catholic states determined to reinstate the Pope in his temporal as well as spiritual powers) laid siege to Rome, and for a month pounded the city with their artillery. It fell on 3 July. Just before the end Garibaldi led a body of troops out of the city to continue the fight in the north - where they were cut down by the Austrians, though Garibaldi was to live on to fight for Italian unification in 1860. Only Venice, which had managed to hold out

since March 1848, remained. Since May it had been under siege by Austrian forces, and was now in the grip of famine and cholera and typhus epidemics. On 22 August it too surrendered.

## Memories That Linger On...

Reaction had triumphed. Throughout Europe the old order seemed re-established - although in places, as in France, in modified form. In Britain demonstrations by the Chartist movement had ended in ridicule in April when a petition for electoral reform was found to contain the forged signatures of, among others, Queen Victoria and the Duke

# Workers of the World

Spreading the call for workers' solidarity: the cover of *The Communist International*, published in Moscow in May 1919 carries the slogan 'Workers of the World Unite!'

In the year following the revolutions Karl Marx was a refugee in London, where he was to remain for most of the rest of his life. While Engels adopted the ways and society of his new country with enthusiasm and success, Marx never lost his sense of shipwreck and loneliness. Although he had contact with British radicals, most of his small circle of friends were Germans or other foreigners. Even with them, he quarrelled easily. In many ways, he was unable to shake his instinctive bourgeois values from his home life, and he was almost entirely dependent on Engels' generosity to maintain them. Politically, Marx was almost unknown in his home country, and he was only tolerated in Britain: he had shied away from personal involvement in political struggle, preferring to follow the route of intellectual conflict. It was only in 1871, after publishing his belated support of the Paris Commune, that he achieved a widespread notoriety which he grimly welcomed: 'I have the honour to be at this moment the best calumniated and most menaced man of London. That really does one good after a tedious twenty years idyll in my den.'

### The Destitute Years

The early years in London were far from idyllic for Marx, his wife Jenny and their four small children. Once they had been evicted from their Chelsea flat in 1850, they were virtually destitute. Jenny described the misery of their situation in a letter to her friend, Joseph Weydemeyer: 'As we did not have the money at the time, two bailiffs came and confiscated all my few possessions - linen, beds, clothes - everything, even my poor child's cradle and my daughters' best toys; they stood there weeping bitterly...we had to leave the house the next day. It was cold, raining and overcast. My husband looked for accommodation for us; when he mentioned the four children, no-one would take us in...'

The family eventually settled at 28 Dean Street in Soho. In the space of five years, the Marxes lost their two small sons Guido and Edgar, and a daughter, Franziska - Marx even had to borrow money to pay for her burial. During this time, he participated in no political activities, since the Communist League had been dissolved in 1852 after the arrest of the leadership of the German section. In England too, the British working movement had lapsed into apathy for a decade after the quelling of the Chartist movement in 1848.

### The Building of Marx's Theory

During this period, Marx started his researches in the reading room of the British Museum, not far from his home. Progress was slow, and for about five years he produced nothing except several articles for the *New York Herald Tribune*: even some of these were written by Engels, although they bore Marx's signature. Eventually, Marx began to set down the results of his intellectual labours in four economic works: *Outlines of a Critique of Political Economy (Grundrisse)* (1858), *Preface to a Critique of Political Economy* (1859), *Critique of Political Economy* (1859) and *Theories of Surplus Value* (1862). His economic theorizing continued during the 1860s, culminating in the publication of the first volume of his celebrated *Das Kapital: Kritik der Politischen Okonomie*, in 1867. This remained the only

# Workers of the World

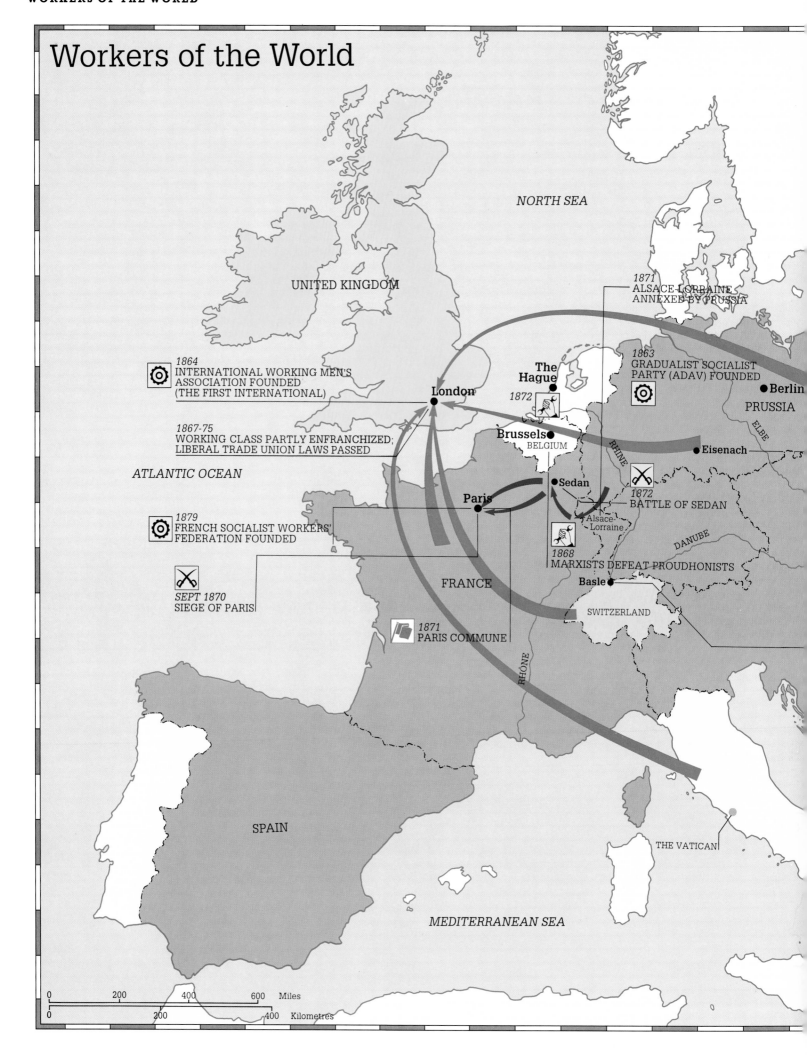

NORTH SEA

UNITED KINGDOM

1871
ALSACE-LORRAINE
ANNEXED BY PRUSSIA

The
Hague

1872

1863
GRADUALIST SOCIALIST
PARTY (ADAV) FOUNDED

Berlin

PRUSSIA

1864
INTERNATIONAL WORKING MEN'S
ASSOCIATION FOUNDED
(THE FIRST INTERNATIONAL)

London

Brussels
BELGIUM

RHINE

ELBE

Eisenach

1867-75
WORKING CLASS PARTLY ENFRANCHIZED;
LIBERAL TRADE UNION LAWS PASSED

ATLANTIC OCEAN

Sedan

1872
BATTLE OF SEDAN

Paris

1879
FRENCH SOCIALIST WORKERS'
FEDERATION FOUNDED

Alsace-
Lorraine

1868
MARXISTS DEFEAT PROUDHONISTS

DANUBE

SEPT 1870
SIEGE OF PARIS

FRANCE

Basle

1871
PARIS COMMUNE

SWITZERLAND

RHÔNE

SPAIN

THE VATICAN

MEDITERRANEAN SEA

0    200    400    600    Miles
0         200         400    Kilometres

*BALTIC SEA*

*1867*
*DAS KAPITAL* PUBLISHED

POLAND

*1869*
GERMAN SOCIAL DEMOCRATIC
WORKERS' PARTY FOUNDED

AUSTRIA-HUNGARY

*1869*
MARXISTS CONFLICT WITH BAKUNIN
AND ANARCHISTS

Countries sending delegates to
the First International

Battle

Workers' associations

Congresses of the First International

The First International persecuted

The First International tolerated

Paris Commune 1871

Franco-Prussian War 1870
(German advances)

*Left:* Delegates at the first congress of the International Working Men's Association held in Geneva in 1866. *Right:* A broadsheet advertising a conference in London. Item nine on the agenda: The Muscovite invasion of Europe, and the re-establishment of an independent Poland.

volume in the study which he was to complete - Engels later edited and published the fragments of volumes two and three.

In these works Marx developed at very great length the outline of Communist theory which he and Engels had put together in the *Communist Manifesto* of 1848.

The first volume simply modified the prevailing economic orthodoxy. Marx attempted to explain the origins and implications of the fact that, in a capitalist society, the wages of the worker had a smaller exchange value than the exchange value of the product; in other words, the product was worth more than the labour put into it. The difference between these values was surplus value, or profit. Since the capitalist controlled the means of production - the factories, mines and land, for example - the worker had to sell his labour to survive, and the capitalist determined the wage level. If workers demanded more, they could always be replaced from the pool of unemployed. Although trade union activity could create some temporary alleviation, wages tended to be set at a traditional subsistence level. This level varied slightly from one industry, skill, or country to another. However, as most people were unable to buy the full range of goods they produced, economic slump tended to follow. Marx then painted a picture of how the capitalist system is doomed by its own success:

Along with the constantly diminishing number of the magnates of capital who usurp and monopolize all the advantages of [the world market], grows the mass of misery, oppression, slavery, degradation, exploitation; but with this too grows the revolt of the working class, a class always increasing in

numbers, and disciplined, united, organized by the very mechanism of the process of capitalist production itself...centralization of the means of production and socialization of labour reach a point where they become incompatible... the knell of capitalist private property sounds. The expropriators are expropriated.

### The Economic Miracle of the 1850s

*Das Kapital* contained a vision that was at once frightening and heroic, based on a mixture of passion, scholarship, observation, and the desire to select facts to fit a theory. However, when it was published in Germany, it was received in utter silence by the critics. The German Marxist journalist Wilhelm Liebknecht burst into tears of disappointment when he read it, prompting Marx to sound off in fury to Engels: 'What does such an ass really want?...Naturally the solutions to the tricky problems of money, etc., are so much shit to Liebknecht since for him these problems do not really exist....'

The economic reality of the 1850s did not fit with Marx's vision. When the 1848 revolutions in Europe petered out, Marx set his sights not on immediate social revolution, but on the beginnings of working men's movements aimed at overthrowing the capitalist economy. Even so, the process was to be much slower than Marx had hoped.

This was just the period when the Industrial Revolution swung into full momentum, and there was an extraordinary economic boom: raw materials were cheap, while prices for manufactured goods rose by around a third. Industrial output of cotton and iron doubled in that decade; railways expanded throughout the continent;

employment grew rapidly, with wages more than keeping pace with inflation; and the standard of living, contrary to Marx's predictions, generally increased. Gold rushes in California, Canada and Australia, and later in South Africa, opened up new economic areas and created new markets, while helping to establish a stable monetary standard, the pound sterling.

With a short lull in 1857, the boom continued throughout the 1860s and 1870s, accompanied by a new surge of labour unrest. When the popular appeal of Marx's International coincided with the rising of the Paris Commune in 1871, it was only through the paradox of governments attempting to contain and control Marxism that labour movements were recognized, and reforms conceded. In England at least, the most liberal trade union laws of Europe were passed between 1867-75, and revolutionary politics became diffused into a liberal scramble for the proletarian vote. As Napoleon III recognized: 'English history speaks loudly to kings as follows: If you march at the head of ideas of your century, these ideas will follow you and sustain you. If you march behind them, they will drag you with them. If you march against them, they will overthrow you!'

### The Conflict with Lassalle

By the time the first volume of *Das Kapital* had been published, Marx's financial situation had improved due to inheritances on his mother's death and on that of his friend, Wilhelm Wolff. He had moved his family to more comfortable quarters in Haverstock Hill in north London. And he had quarrelled violently with Ferdinand Lassalle, who had once regarded himself as Marx's pupil but had since become a leading member of the growing German labour movement. Through this quarrel, Marx probably delayed the growth of Marxism in his native Germany.

Lassalle was a brilliant, flamboyant socialist, and a veteran of 1848 when he had been imprisoned for his activities. Nevertheless, he was rich and successful, with publications that were read throughout Germany - he had once begun an address with the words 'Working men. Before I leave for the spas of Switzerland ....' Both as a scholar and as a social agitator, Marx felt that Lassalle was usurping the position among the German working class that he regarded as his own. The two men differed radically on political tactics and strategy. Lassalle believed in employing reformist tactics to achieve socialism by gradual methods and, to this end, he was prepared to come to an understanding with Bismarck, the great Prussian chancellor, whom he had met several times. Marx regarded Lassalle's approach as a betrayal.

However, it was mainly Marx's personal jealousy that was to goad him into a bitter, open rift. Lassalle was vital to Marx's publishing interests in Germany, and both Marx and Engels felt that Lassalle was hindering this process. Acccording to Franz Mehring, the biographer of Marx, Lassalle was unaware of this resentment for a long time, and always approached Marx 'with an open heart and an outstretched hand'. Marx swallowed his bile in Lassalle's presence, but privately fuelled his contempt of his mixed-race rival in extraordinary letters to Engels: 'This combination of

Jewish and German descent with a basic Negroid background is bound to produce something peculiar. The fellow's importunity is also Negroid.'

Matters came to a head on 23 May 1863, when the Lassallean Socialist Party (ADAV) was founded, with a programme written by Lassalle. Its demands were comparatively modest: universal and equal suffrage, and state aid to be provided for producer-co-operatives. Marx and Engels declared this programme to be full of illusions, believing that there was no possibility of a peaceful transition to socialism in a rigidly conservative country such as Prussia. The following year Lassalle was killed in a manner that was in keeping with his flamboyant lifestyle: in a duel over a love affair. Although Marx was at last invited to take over the leadership of the ADAV, nothing came of it due to his fundamental disagreements.

## The International

On 24 September 1864, a month after the death of Lassalle, the International Working Men's Association was established in London. It was to become known simply as the International, and was regarded by Marx as the culmination of his life's work.

The Industrial Revolution had provided no coherent political organization for the vast new class of working men and women, although there had been several attempts to do so by groups such as the Fraternal Democrats (based on the Chartist movement) and by the Communist League. The main drive for the establishment of the International came from the London Trades Council, a powerful body among the

emerging trades unions, which had called for the British government's armed intervention in Poland's fight for freedom from Russia. The government gave a negative response, claiming that it could move only with help from France. The Council then appealed to French working-class organizations to take action. A meeting was held on 22 July 1863, to express joint British and French working-class solidarity for Poland. By the time the next meeting had been convened on 28 September 1864, armed forces had already crushed the Polish revolt, and in response the meeting was transformed instead into the inaugural meeting of the International Working Men's Association.

A committee of representatives from British, French, German, Italian, Swiss and Polish groups was elected to draw up the rules of the International. Marx, who was at this stage one of the German delegates, was invited to prepare an inaugural address. In an attempt to reach a broad agreement, Marx diluted some of his ideas from *Das Kapital* and included a number of reformist ideals such as Lassalle might have approved, including a recommendation for the development of factory workers' co-operatives. It ended with the ringing slogan from his *Communist Manifesto*: 'Workers of the World, Unite!'

The initial membership and resources of the International, though greatly exaggerated by its enemies, were scanty. The boundless hope for political change it offered to workers across Europe caused the International to be persecuted by nervous governments throughout the German and Austro-Hungarian Empires, in France and in Spain. Condemned by some as a secretive and Jesuitical association, the Pope in turn pronounced it 'the enemy of God and man'.

By the time of the Basle Congress in 1869, it probably had around fifty thousand affiliated trade union members as well as a few thousand individuals; and the fact that the new German Social Democratic Workers Party, established at Eisenach in 1869, declared itself to be a member was a significant political success. The First International was quite successful in increasing the efficacy of strike action, with workers across Europe frequently helping each other financially at times of industrial action. When the builders of Geneva went on strike to reduce their hours from 12 to 10, the mere rumour that the International was involved was enough to persuade the employers to seek negotiations.

## The International in Conflict

The clouds were not long in gathering. The International had to rely on erratic financial contributions, and was also racked by ideological differences which would eventually bring about its downfall. The pragmatic British trades unionists, who enjoyed far more governmental toleration than their European counterparts,

# The Founding Fathers

James Keir Hardie and William Morris represent the two strands of British socialism that were present at its birth and flourish to this day. Hardie, the working-class activist, was the illegitimate son of a Scottish farm servant who taught himself to read and write after being sent to work as a small child. By the time he was a teenager he had been blacklisted by the coal mine owners for his union activities. He went on to help organize the miner's union in Ayrshire. In his twenties he went into journalism. In 1888 he helped found the Scottish Labour Party and was returned to parliament at the general election of 1892 where he was the first labourer to sit in the House of Commons. In 1893 he helped to found the Independent Labour Party, although that was originally more a propaganda group than a

**William Morris (*centre*), artist, craftsman, poet and socialist, surrounded by members of the Hammersmith Socialist League.**

political force. After losing his seat in 1895, he threw all his energy into developing a political party which could rival the Liberal and Conservative parties and bring all the strands

of British socialism together.

William Morris, the Fabian intellectual, was born into a prosperous middle-class family which sent him to Marlborough College and Oxford. After twenty years running the finest design business in Britain, he was converted to Socialism by Hyndman's Democratic Federation. Thereafter he toured the country lecturing on behalf of the cause and on 13 November 1887 he walked into Trafalgar Square side-by-side with George Bernard Shaw, at the head of an unauthorized march which turned into a bloody riot when it was attacked by the police and troops. In 1890 he published *News from Nowhere*, a classic of Utopian socialism. Morris died in 1896, four years before Kier Hardie finally succeeded in founding the Labour Party.

often clashed with strongly Marxist elements. At the Brussels Congress of 1868 there had been a dispute between the Marxists and the French Proudhonists, who had rejected state ownership of the means of production in favour of production co-operatives. The Proudhonists also rejected the principle of forming an alliance with middle-class organizations to achieve specific ends, but they were defeated.

The following year at Basle, the followers of the anarchist Mikhail Bakunin (1814-76) attended for the first time, representing the most extreme form of Proudhonism. Bakunin was regarded by Marx as a dangerous and directionless agitator. The head of police during the rising of the Paris Commune two years later remarked of him in exasperation: 'What a man! On the first day of the revolution he is invaluable, on the second he ought to be shot.' The stage was set for an even greater tussle with the Marxists: Bakunin was not even prepared to support a revolutionary workers' state.

## The Fatal Rift

The outbreak of the Franco-Prussian war in 1870 gravely weakened the International, when it proved powerless to stop the slaughter. It adopted Marx's analysis that Prussia had been forced into a defensive war, but warned against the annexation of Alsace-Lorraine, foreseeing correctly that this would lead to a dangerous alliance of France with Russia. In Germany, the followers of Lassalle supported the war and were opposed by the pro-Marxist figures such as August Bebel and Wilhelm Liebknecht. French military power soon collapsed, and Napoleon III was captured. A republic was proclaimed in Paris, and the International called on Prussia to make an honourable peace. The situation was complicated when the National Guard refused to hand over Paris to the Prussian army, and held an election to set up a democratic civil administration to run the city: the Paris Commune. Although this was not a socialist administration, the ousted government of Adolphe Thiers at Versailles regarded the Commune as a threat to bourgeois society, calling on government troops to attack the Commune. Fourteen thousand Communards were killed or subsequently executed, and the Commune was completely defeated within two months. Following their defeat, over ten thousand members were either transported to New Caledonia or imprisoned.

Marx hailed the uprising of the Commune only in retrospect, in *The Civil War in France*: a thin, vituperative tirade against Thiers, the 'monstrous gnome ... and master in small state roguery'. While it was actually in progress, Marx was either silent, or warned against a seizure of power. Thiers, on the other hand, had no doubt that the International was behind the rising, and a crusade against the organization was launched throughout Europe. Britain and

# Friedrich Engels: Capitalist and Communist

Friedrich Engels was a man who lived two lives simultaneously. As a successful businessman in his father's textile mill he kept regular hours, joined the local choral society, swam, fenced and rode well to hounds. As a revolutionary he wrote the classic *The Conditions of the Working Class in England in 1844,* lived with his mistress and helped to form what became the Communist League with Karl Marx. The profit from the first subsidized the second. Indeed, when he sold his partnership in the textile business in 1869, Engels not only retained enough for his own needs for the rest of his life, he also set up an annuity of £350 for Marx.

Marx and Engels first collaborated on writing a book in 1845 and their informal partnership continued until Marx's death in 1883. The amount that each contributed varied with the book or article, for they even collaborated on some of Marx's journalistic output. Engels tended to specialize in questions of nationalism, warfare, science, business and industrial practice, as well as helping to present their views in the most accessible style. This collaboration continued while Marx was living in London and Engels was in Manchester during the 1850s. Engels also completed the second and third volumes of *Das Kapital* from the

unfinished manuscript and notes after Marx's death.

Thereafter, he became *the* authority on their creed and he did his best to keep their followers on the straight and narrow. This was achieved through an extensive correspondence, a task which was only abandoned when he was striken with cancer.

Despite his personal charm and friendly manner, Engels was the more ruthless of the pair in print. In *Anti-Dühring,* which he wrote in 1878, he destroyed the reputation of a Berlin professor, Karl Eugen Dühring, who threatened their position in the vanguard of socialism. He died in London in 1895.

Switzerland were among the few states not to be drawn in.

Despite this crackdown, the main reason for the decline of the International was due far more to the 'life and death struggle', as Bakunin put it, between the Marxists and the Anarchists. The influence of Bakunin had grown in Italy, Spain, France and French-speaking Switzerland. Marx feared that they would soon take over the International, and sought protection for its General Council by moving it from London to New York in 1872. Defenders of Marx maintain that this decision

was partly a tribute to the rapid development industry and democracy in the USA.

An outraged rump of opposition was left behind to hold a conference in St Imier in Switzerland, at which they declared themselves to be the true representatives of the International - but they were expelled by the 'New Yorkers'. In Philadelphia in July 1876, with only American representatives present, the International was christened formally, and the Workers of the World had lost their first major attempt at political organization across frontiers.

Dwellings of the Manchester cotton workers during the cotton famine, 1862. In 1844, when Engels wrote *The Conditions of the Working Class in England*, there were attempts to see if better housing could be built. The Society for Improving the Conditions of the Labouring Classes was founded; among those who showed interest in the Society was Prince Albert, who displayed his 'model cottages' at the Great Exhibition of 1851.

# France: The Heroic Tradition

At the beginning of 1871 the name Karl Marx was almost unknown outside a small internationally minded group of left-wing revolutionary activists. By the end of the year Marx was famous. The events of the Paris Commune between March and May generated a worldwide 'Red Scare'. The Anglo-Saxon press latched on to the existence of the man in Hampstead who had been preaching revolution for a quarter of a century. For years Marx and his colleague Engels had been pronouncing on class conflicts of all kinds without attracting much local attention. Suddenly they were news. As Marx himself wryly commented, he was becoming 'the best calumniated and most menaced man of London'.

The French revolutionary tradition had always been a source of inspiration for Marx and the early communists. They looked back in admiration on the years of 1789-93 which, despite their bloody terror, they saw as a time of heroic popular revolt, when the people of France took their destinies in their hands, waged violent war on aristocratic privilege and overthrew a reactionary monarchy. The communists regretted the subsequent Napoleonic years of the Directory, Consulate and finally Empire,

which they viewed as a regression to elitism, foreign aggrandizement and general conservatism. But still France's revolutionary tradition continued. It resurfaced, though in limited fashion, in 1830 - when the last of the Bourbons, Charles X, was replaced by his distant cousin, the 'citizen king' Louis Philippe of Orléans - and then again, and much more convincingly, in 1848. For Marx and Engels, the Paris insurrection of June 1848 - the so-called June Days - was a beacon of hope shining from France. It failed, but in it they saw a glorious forerunner of future violent conflicts between proletariat and bourgeoisie that would eventually bring in the socialist millennium.

Then the revolutionary current seemed to vanish, driven underground by the autocratic populism of the Second Empire of Napoleon III that emerged from the events of 1848. It was to emerge once more, and with renewed energy, in 1871.

### The Franco-Prussian War

In 1870 France was facing a political crisis. For over twenty years Napoleon III had ruled with a measure of success. Under him the country had transformed itself from a

basically rural economy into an industrial giant. Industrial output had doubled, foreign trade tripled. French engineers were in demand throughout Europe for their skills in building bridges, railways and such basics as sewerage systems. Within France the foundations had been laid for a modern state education system. But by the late 1860s the tide was turning against Napoleon. At home his populist style of government had alienated conservatives, while attempts at a liberalization of the regime during that decade failed to satisfy the left. An economic slowdown added to the Empire's troubles. Internationally, its position had been weakened by such quixotic adventures as the attempt to impose the Habsburg prince Maximilian as Emperor of Mexico. In addition, trouble was starting to loom on France's eastern frontier.

Since the fiasco of the Frankfurt parliament of 1848-9, Germany had been moving steadily along the road to unification, in the process radically altering the balance of power in Europe. Leading it was Prussia - this 'northern sandbox', as a previous king once disparagingly referred to it; now it was a strongly militaristic state, headed by Wilhelm I and his brilliant chief minister Otto

From the Hôtel de Ville a delegation from the Permanent Committe arrives at the Bastille to persuade the Governor to hand over the fortress to a citizens' militia. The Bastille was the hated symbol of the *ancien régime* and finally fell, in a bloody assualt, to the *Vainqueurs de la Bastille* on 14 July 1789. The symbol of Royal despotism was destroyed.

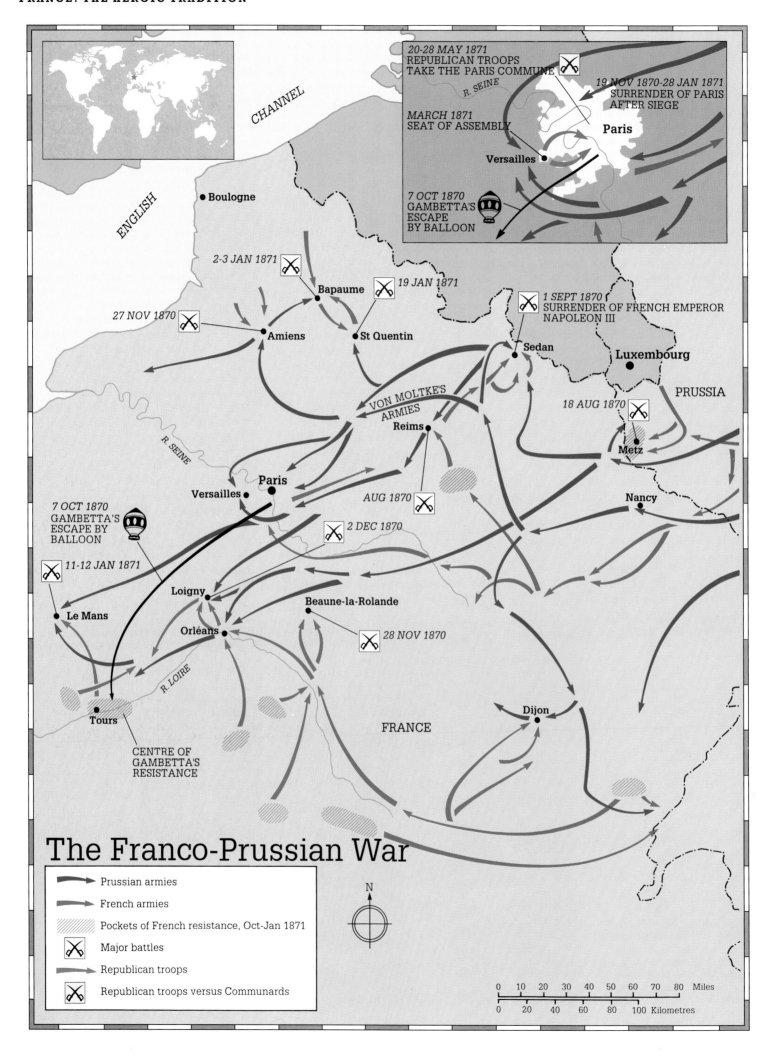

20-28 MAY 1871
REPUBLICAN TROOPS
TAKE THE PARIS COMMUNE

R. SEINE

19 NOV 1870-28 JAN 1871
SURRENDER OF PARIS
AFTER SIEGE

MARCH 1871
SEAT OF ASSEMBLY

Paris

Versailles

7 OCT 1870
GAMBETTA'S
ESCAPE
BY BALLOON

CHANNEL

ENGLISH

● Boulogne

2-3 JAN 1871

Bapaume

19 JAN 1871

27 NOV 1870

Amiens

St Quentin

1 SEPT 1870
SURRENDER OF FRENCH EMPEROR
NAPOLEON III

Sedan

Luxembourg

PRUSSIA

18 AUG 1870

VON MOLTKE'S
ARMIES

Reims

Metz

R. SEINE

Paris

AUG 1870

Nancy

Versailles

7 OCT 1870
GAMBETTA'S
ESCAPE BY
BALLOON

2 DEC 1870

11-12 JAN 1871

Loigny

Beaune-la-Rolande

Le Mans

Orléans

28 NOV 1870

R. LOIRE

Dijon

FRANCE

Tours

CENTRE OF
GAMBETTA'S
RESISTANCE

# The Franco-Prussian War

N

Prussian armies

French armies

Pockets of French resistance, Oct-Jan 1871

Major battles

Republican troops

Republican troops versus Communards

0  10  20  30  40  50  60  70  80  Miles

0  20  40  60  80  100  Kilometres

von Bismarck. In 1866 a North German Confederation was formed, which became a Prussian empire in all but name - the Prussian king was its hereditary head and Prussian deputies dominated the federal Bundesrat. Looking west at the weakened state of France, Bismarck saw a means to complete the work of unification, and a dynastic crisis in Spain gave him his opportunity. In 1869 the Spanish Queen Isabella was forced into exile, leaving a number of possible claimants to her throne; among them was a cousin of the Prussian king. Clearly, Napoleon could not allow the emerging German superstate such an ally to the south. Bismarck manoeuvred him into a declaration of war on 19 July 1870 and then, whipping up German nationalist fervour against French 'aggression', brought the Confederation into the war behind him.

Napoleon had none of the military skills of his uncle and namesake. German armies invaded, and on 1 September boxed a French army into a battlefield at Sedan, near the Belgian frontier, from which it could not escape. The French were defeated and Napoleon was forced to surrender his troops, himself becoming a prisoner of war of the Germans. This humiliation was the death blow to the Second Empire. When news of Sedan reached Paris, crowds poured on to the streets, and on 5 September a republic was proclaimed. No blood was shed: nobody resisted the republican tide. Meanwhile, the Germans pressed on. They sent forces to lay siege to Metz and Strasbourg, while their main armies headed towards Paris, which they reached at the end of September.

Napoleon was gone, but for the time being at least the French were determined to fight on. Soon after the proclamation of the republic, a government of national defence was formed, including as its most dynamic member the radical young republican lawyer Léon Gambetta. He escaped from the now encircled Paris in a potentially lethal coal-gas balloon to organize a new campaign from Tours, but was no more successful than Napoleon. French armies were defeated at battles in the Loire valley and in eastern France; they never managed to penetrate north to relieve Paris. The capital, meanwhile, was in the grip of winter and encroaching famine. Gradually cats, dogs and even rats disappeared off the streets while the zoos were plundered to provide magnificent rhinoceros roasts in restaurants, and elephant joints at 40 francs per pound. For the well-to-do the siege proved no more than an inconvenience, but by December the poor, and especially young children, were dying of starvation at the rate of nine thousand a day.

### The Fall of France

On 5 January 1871 the siege intensified with the opening of a savage bombardment of Paris, and then on the 18th Bismarck achieved his ambition. Amidst the splendour of the Hall of Mirrors at Versailles the Germans, delirious at their armies' victories, proclaimed Wilhelm I Kaiser (Emperor) of a unified Reich. Ten days later, despite the protests of an outraged Gambetta, the French agreed to an armistice - though starving, straggling armies under General Bourbaki in south-eastern France received no word of it, and were driven by German troops over icy passes into Switzerland. One survivor of the retreat the aristocratic republican Henri de Rochefort, described their miserable retreat: 'As there were no leaves on the trees for the men to eat, they tore bark from the trunks and ate it, while the horses gnawed the wood of the gun carriages before falling dead on the road.'

One of the terms of the armistice was that the French should elect a National Assembly with which the new German Reich could negotiate a formal treaty. Elections took place on 8 February, resulting in sweeping gains for the right, and the new Assembly meeting in Bordeaux (the Germans were still occupying Paris) to elect the ageing Adolphe Thiers, a veteran of the years of Louis Philippe, as their chief executive. Humiliation followed humiliation for the French. According to the treaty eventually signed in Frankfurt in March, they were to pay heavy war reparations and lose Alsace and half of Lorraine. As a further twist of the dagger, the Germans were to be allowed to stage a

# Eyewitness

The following account from 'The Suppression of the Paris Commune, 23-24 May 1871' by Archibald Forbes appeared in the *Daily News*, 26 May 1871.

Wednesday. And so evening wore into night, and night became morning. Ah! this morning! Its pale flush of aurora bloom was darkest, most sombre night for the once proud, now stricken and humiliated, city. When the sun rose, what saw he? Not a fair fight - on that within the last year Sol has looked down more than once. But black clouds flouted his rays - clouds that rose from the Palladium of France. Great God! that men should be so mad as to strive to make universal ruin because their puny course of factiousness is run! The flames from the Palace of the Tuileries, kindled by damnable petroleum insulted the soft light of the morning and cast lurid rays on the grimy recreant Frenchmen who skulked from their dastardly incendiarism to pot at countrymen from behind a barricade. How the place burned! The flames revelled in the historical palace, whipped up the rich furniture, burst out the plate-glass windows, brought down the fantastic roof. It was in the Prince Imperial's wing facing the Tuileries Gardens where the demon of fire first had his dismal sway. By eight o'clock the whole of the wing was nearly burned out. As I reached the end of the Rue Dauphine the red belches of flames were bursting out from the corner of the Tuileries facing the private gardens and the Rue de Rivoli: the rooms occupied by the King of Prussia and his suite on the visit to France the year of the Exhibition. There is a furious jet of flame pouring out of the window where Bismarck used to sit and smoke. Crash! Is it an explosion or a fall of flooring that causes this burst of black smoke and red sparks in our faces? God knows what fell devices may be within that burning pile; it were well surely to give it a wide berth.

And so eastward to the Place du Palais-Royal, which is still unsafe by reason of shot and shell from the neighbourhood of the Hôtel de Ville. And there is the great archway by which troops were wont to enter into the Place du Carrousel - is the fire there yet? Just there, and no more; could the archway be cut, the Louvre, with its artistic riches, might still be spared. But there are none to help. The troops are lounging supine in the rues; intent - and who shall blame weary, powder-grimed men? - on bread and wine. And so the devastator leaps from chimney to chimney, from window to window. He is over the archway now, and I would not give two hours' purchase for all the riches of the Louvre. In the name of modern vandalism, what means that burst of smoke and jet of fire? Alas for art; the Louvre is on fire independently. And so is the Palais-Royal and the Hôtel de Ville, where the rump of the Commune are cowering amidst their incendiarism; and the Ministry of Finance, and many another public and private building besides.

I turn from the spectacle sad and sick, to be sickened yet further by another spectacle. The Versaillist troops collected about the foot of the Rue Saint-Honoré were enjoying the fine game of Communist hunting. The Parisians of civil life are caitiffs to the last drop of their thin, sour, white blood. But yesterday they had cried *Vive la Commune!* and submitted to be governed by this said Commune. Today they rubbed their hands with livid currish joy to have it in their power to denounce a Communist and reveal his hiding place. Very eager at this work are the dear creatures of women. They know the rat-holes into which the poor devils have got, and they guide to them with a fiendish glee which is a phase of the many-sided sex. *Voila!* the braves of France returned to a triumph after a shameful captivity! They have found him, the miserable! Yes, they drag him out from one of the purlieus which Haussmann had not time to sweep away, and a guard of six of them hem him round as they march him into the Rue Saint-Honoré. A tall, pale, hatless man, with something not ignoble in his carriage. His lower lip is trembling, but his brow is firm, and the eye of him has some pride and defiance in it. They yell - the crowd - 'Shoot him; shoot him!' - the demon women most clamorous, of course. An arm goes into the air; there are on it the stripes of a non-commissioned officer, and there is a stick in the fist. The stick falls on the head of the pale man in black. Ha! the infection has caught; men club their rifles, and bring them down on that head, or clash them into splinters in their lust for murder. He is down; he is up again; he is down again; the thuds of the gunstocks on him sounding just as the sound when a man bats a cushion with a stick. A certain British impulse, stronger than consideration for self, prompts me to run forward. But it is useless. They are firing into the flaccid carcass now, thronging about it like blowflies on a piece of meat. His brains spurt on my boot and plash into the gutter, whither the carrion is bodily chucked, presently to be trodden on and rolled on by the feet of multitudes and wheels of gun carriages.

victory march down the Champs-Elysées. The novelist Flaubert, writing after the fall of Paris, summed up the anguish of many of his countrymen:

The capitulation of Paris... has plunged us into an indescribable state! It's enough to make you want to hang yourself from rage! I am angry that Paris has not burned to the last house, leaving no more than a great black space. France is so low, so dishonoured, so debased, that I long for her to disappear completely.

On 15 March Thiers entered Paris to confront its outraged citizens. Having endured the winter siege, they were in no mood to accept a 'dishonourable' peace, let alone one engineered by a man whom they considered as little more than a monarchist in republican guise. (Marx was later to give his own pungent view of Thiers: 'A master in small state roguery, a virtuoso in perjury and treason, a craftsman in all the petty stratagems, cunning devices, and base perfidies of parliamentary party-warfare.') Revolution was in the air. The Paris National Guard in particular was a source of danger, outnumbering the regular troops at Thiers' disposal. In the small hours of 18 March, he surreptitiously moved in some regular troops to disarm the Guard. But the Paris radicals were vigilant. Crowds poured on to the streets and violent conflicts ensued, during which two generals were lynched. Thiers hastily pulled his troops, as well as all government offices, out of Paris to Versailles, where the National Assembly was also meeting. He then started gathering forces for a renewed onslaught on the capital.

## Solidarity Versus Patriotism

From London, meanwhile, Marx had been taking a keen interest in the events across the Channel. No sooner was the Franco-Prussian War declared than he drafted a statement in English on behalf of the General Council of the International Working Men's Association. It was swiftly translated into German, French, Russian and other languages, printed and widely distributed. In it Marx faced a dilemma. He supported solidarity by the working class of both France and Germany against a 'fratricidal feud' concocted by the 'governments and ruling classes of Europe'. However, he was also forced to recognize that working-class Germans would respond to a war of national defence against a French army. Similarly the French workers could hardly be expected to allow an invasion by the Prussian army, however heartily they might reject the undemocratic regime of Napoleon III or question the existing distribution of property.

Marx's difficult task as an international Communist was to counsel German workers to resist the waves of German nationalism and anti-French hysteria. At the same time, though, Germany must resist successfully to prevent the reactionary Napoleon III from triumphing. An ideal outcome would have been, on the one hand, defeat for Napoleon leading to the creation in France of a radical republic influenced by the proletariat; and, on the other, a decisive rejection by the Germans of Bismarck's militarism, permitting the workers to take over the political high ground. One thing Marx and Engels did not want was failed revolutionary outbreaks, leaving a trail of ultra-radical martyrdoms, but allowing conservatives in both countries to triumph, and causing working-class organizations to sink under waves of repression. Unhappily for Marx and Engels, this was more or less what transpired.

In a Second Address from the General Council issued after the proclamation of the republic in France, Marx modified his line. He now urged the world, and especially Prussia, to recognize a moderate republic in France. Aware of the dangers of revolutions only half-accomplished, he warned against what he considered to be senseless French republican resistance against the Germans. The extraordinary events that were to follow the signing of the Frankfurt treaty would take him completely by surprise.

## The Commune

In Paris the revolutionary leaders had responded to Thiers' withdrawal by setting up their own government. On 26 March elections were held under the auspices of the National Guard for a popular assembly, later named the Commune de Paris after a similar revolutionary body established in 1792. The resulting assembly was dominated by the left. It included a scattering of manual workers and members of the Socialist International, though most of the Communards were poorer artisans, tradesmen, shopkeepers, radical intellectuals and professional men. Other similar communes were set up in Lyon (where the Russian anarchist Bakunin was active), Marseilles and Toulouse, but these were quickly suppressed.

At first the Paris Commune raised millennial expectations. In its 'Declaration to the French people' issued in April, it proclaimed a whole new departure for the French nation:

Once again Paris labours and suffers for the whole of France, for which it prepares, by its combats and its sacrifices, intellectual, moral, administrative and economic regeneration, glory and prosperity.... It is the end of the old government and clerical order, of militarism, of bureaucracy, of exploitation, of financial speculation, of monopolies, to which the proletariat owes its bondage, the country its misfortunes and disasters.

In fact the Commune proved a political ragbag, rent between differing left-wing groups, its military defences badly organized, unco-ordinated and doomed to defeat. It initiated some measures to introduce, for example, free and secular primary education, and made attempts to improve the lot of workers and artisans.

But soon events degenerated into a reign of terror akin to that of the 1789 Revolution. On 2 April government forces - including French prisoners of war whom Thiers had begged Bismarck to release - began their assault on Paris.

It was to prove a long, bloody, suburb-by-suburb, street-by-street battle, lasting until the end of May. Inside Paris, the need to defend the revolution led the Communards to form a Committee of Public Safety, and a period of increasing suppression of all dissent followed. Hostages were taken, and many of them (including later the Archbishop of Paris) shot.

When on Sunday, 21 May, the government forces reached the centre of Paris, their arrival seemed a welcome deliverance to many Parisians, as the writer Edmond de Goncourt remembered:

*Above:* Léon Gambetta, one of the founders of the Third Republic, escaped from Paris on the maiden flight of Nadar's new balloon, the *Barbès*.
*Left:* The *Neptune* in the Place Saint Pierre, Paris 1870. The aeronaut and photgrapher Nadar broke the Prussian blockade of Paris by the use of balloons. The *Neptune* carried the first messages out of the besieged city.

The German Army at Fort Issy, Paris 1871. The superior military might of the Prussians under Count von Moltke led to the surrender of Napoleon III and victory over France. The treaty of Frankfurt, signed on 10 May 1871, ceded Alsace and most of Lorraine to the Germans.

There were acute food shortages during the Commune. This French cartoon shows Parisians queuing for rats that emerged from the sewers.

The call to arms was sounding all over Paris, and soon, drowning the noise of the drums and the bugles and the shouting and the cries of 'To arms!', came the great, tragic, booming notes of the tocsin being rung in all the churches - a sinister sound which filled me with joy and sounded like the death-knell of the odious tyranny oppressing Paris.

There followed *la semaine sanglante* (bloody week), in which the brutality on both sides reached a terrifying peak. All that represented culture and privilege in Paris - the Tuileries palace, the Palais-Royal, the Hôtel de Ville, the Mazarin and Louvre libraries, even the cathedral of Notre Dame - were looted and set alight by mobs. Haphazard arrests and shootings, carried out by both sides, accompanied the chaos. As the government troops slowly gained control, they inflicted ferocious reprisals. On 28 March their commander was able to proclaim that 'Paris is liberated. Today the struggle is over: order, work and security will be reborn.' But the brutal cost at which he had won this victory was such that even the London *Times* of 1 June was forced to deplore it:

The crimes of the insurgents have surpassed the most gloomy forebodings of what would be accomplished under the Red Flag.... [But] it seems as if we were destined to forget the work of these maddened savages in the spectacle of vengeance wreaked upon them. The wholesale executions inflicted by the Versailles soldiery, the triumph, the glee, the ribaldry of the 'Party of Order', sicken the soul.

Around twenty thousand people were executed by Thiers' soldiers, with the Municipality of Paris alone paying for the burial of seventeen thousand corpses. Thousands more were imprisoned or sent in cattle trucks and penal ships into lifelong exile in Africa and New Caledonia. Hundreds of socialists who managed to escape these reprisals fled from France, many of them finding refuge in England.

## The Legacy

For Marx, who had watched the unfolding of events with close attention, the episode was of crucial significance. 'History has no comparable example of such greatness,' he proclaimed in his classic pamphlet *The Civil War in France,* issued directly after the crushing of the Commune. 'Its martyrs are enshrined forever in the great heart of the working class.' He regretted that an enterprise so clearly doomed to failure had taken place, but saw it none the less as genuinely revolutionary, and hence an inspiration for international Communism. He argued that armed action by workers - as seen during the Commune - should only be undertaken with extreme care, but that revolutionary fervour where it arose was a potent force for Communists to use. It has been held against Marx that in his pamphlet he was not an objective historian of the Commune, but that was not his intention.

Marx believed that the Commune was important for the political lesson it contained for the future of Communism. In his view even highly democratic institutions were a mere sham so long as the 'producers' in the economy were 'enslaved' by capitalists and other exploiters, the owners of factories, mines, railways and similar sources of wealth. In the Commune he saw an attempt to institute a 'social republic', the political form in which class rule by the bourgeoisie or 'possessing classes' would be abolished. It was, he held, a body of municipal councillors chosen by universal suffrage, acting as legislative and executive at the same time. Thinking into the future, Marx suggested that such communes would be the political form by which every town and village would govern itself, and he envisaged these local communes sending delegates to district and national represen-tative bodies. Under such a constitution the opportunity for repressive state power would be destroyed and a nation would be able to achieve true unity because the legitimate functions of government would be restored to the people.

The legacy of the Commune - as well as the example of its savage repression - was indeed to prove an inspiration to future generations of revolutionaries. Lenin was to declare the Commune 'the greatest working-class uprising of the nineteenth century'. A Bolshevik veteran of the Russian Revolution later recalled: 'In....grave moments we said, "Look, workers, at the example of the Paris Communards and know if we are defeated, our bourgeoisie will treat us a hundred times worse." The example of the Paris Commune inspired us and we were victorious'. In some respects too, the local councils or 'soviets' that sprang up throughout Russia and its territories during the revolution of 1917-18 were similar to the Paris Commune.

What Marx could not foresee, however, was that the apparatus of decentralized government, with its mass participation of the 'armed people', was never destined successfully to overthrow conservative forces. Lenin and the bolsheviks were to claim that an elite party, taking upon itself the burdens of a centralized government, provided the only correct solution to safeguarding the success of the revolution.

Marx's *The Civil War in France* was essentially an obituary for the Commune's failure. Heroes do not always succeed, and indeed their heroism may derive from their tragedies. The heroic tradition of the French Revolution bears these characteristics, and Marx's analysis of the Commune represented an attempt to snatch future victory from the jaws of past defeat.

# Germany Takes the Lead

Europe after the Commune was a different world from the continent in which the young Marx and Engels had grown to maturity. Bismarck's ruthless determination to forge a united Germany from the minor principalities and political fragments which constituted the heart of Europe transformed international politics and the economic prospects of a country which was now run from Berlin by an authoritarian, Prussian bureaucracy.

In France, the repression which followed the massacres of 1871, that turned even membership of the International into a criminal offence, gave Thiers the confidence to pronounce one of the many premature obituaries of socialism in 1877 when he said, 'Nobody talks of socialism any more, rightly. We are rid of it.' It would be years before the working class of France would be able to organize itself effectively, and never again would it be in the vanguard of the movement.

## Socialism Takes Root in Germany

The failure of socialism was predicted with less confidence in Germany, where the rapid industrialization of the 1860s had created a much larger urban proletariat than was yet known in France. The first working-class leader to take advantage of this changing situation was Ferdinand Lassalle, who formed the German General Workers' Association on 23 May 1863. As a former member of the Communist League, Lassalle agreed with Marx and Engels on many points. However, he was more a reformer than a revolutionary, and he was prepared to side with Bismarck if it would gain him an advantage, particularly over unification.

Then, in 1869, the Social Democratic Workers' Party was founded by Wilhelm Liebknecht and August Bebel, who were at one with Marx in their desire to align themselves with the bourgeoisie and against the unification of Germany under Prussian leadership. However, once the empire had been proclaimed and unification was an accomplished fact, there was little to divide the Party and the Association.

The boom years of the 1870s saw the development of a skill shortage in Germany which gave workers a strong position from which to conduct their negotiations with employers. This led to a rash of strikes as trades unions began to flex their muscles. As a result, the imperial administration had no compunction in fostering the growth of industrial cartels; these were not only a means of sustaining economic growth but balanced the industrial equation with groups of capitalists which could match the power of the developing unions.

The growing self-confidence of the German working class also expressed itself in political activity, now given its first opportunity to flourish because Germany's imperial constitution gave voting rights to all men over twenty-five years old in elections to the national Parliament, the Reichstag. In the second election under the new system, in 1874, the moderate success of the workers' representatives in attracting 6 per cent of the electorate alarmed Bismarck, who took their potential for provoking social unrest very seriously. Accordingly, police and judicial harassment were increased.

In a move to consolidate their position and protect themselves against official aggression, the Association and the Party held a joint meeting at Gotha in 1875 in which they sank their remaining differences and agreed on a joint programme. Although Lassalle had died in 1864, those who still adhered to his views were in the majority and the manifesto of the merged party, which at first took the name Sozialistische Arbeiterpartei Deutschlands (Socialist Workers' Party of Germany), was pragmatic in its aims. It called for, amongst other things, universal male suffrage, a progressive income tax, free elementary education, state inspection of industrial premises and freedom of association. The new party, which changed its name to the Sozaildemokratische Partei Deutschlands (Social Democratic Party of Germany) in 1890, decided to fight for its stated aims 'by every lawful means'.

The new party emphasized its appeal to the electorate in the 1877 elections by taking 9 per cent of the vote. Although this gave the socialists only a dozen MPs, Bismarck concluded that he must act decisively to head off any further growth in the party's popularity. The attempted assassination of the Emperor the following year offered him the occasion he needed to try to whip up public hysteria against the 'red menace', despite the fact that he knew that socialists had nothing to do with the plot.

The Reichstag resisted his attempts to manipulate it for his own ends, and rejected his anti-socialist legislation by a vote of 243 to 60. But another attack on the Emperor gave Bismarck a further opportunity. A general election was called and those liberals who had rejected his measures lost seats heavily, while the socialists' share of the vote dropped to 7.5 per cent. Bismarck now had the Reichstag dancing to his tune, and his anti-socialist bill was passed by 221 votes to 149. It outlawed all social democratic organizations and virtually all unions. On the other hand, it did allow social democrats to participate in pre-election campaigns and to sit in the Reichstag. It was this lifeline which ensured the party's survival during the following twelve years of repression.

## The Years in the Shadows

The years which followed had a decisive and long-lasting effect on the character of German social democracy. The party was left in the odd position of being illegal at local level while its representatives operated quite openly in the Reichstag.

This pushed the party in two conflicting directions simultaneously. The persecution of the paid functionaries by the authorities left the leadership of the party and the formulation

## Wilhelm Liebknecht

Wilhelm Liebknecht belonged to the generation of socialism which was electrified by the events of 1848 and went on to build the foundations of the new movement. The February Revolution was over when he arrived from Switzerland, so he travelled on to Baden where he tried to foment an insurrection. Instead he spent eight months in jail before he was allowed to return to Geneva. However, that was not far enough for the Prussian government, who leaned on the Swiss. Liebknecht moved on to London, where he worked with Marx and Engels in the Communist League for thirteen years and was a correspondent for a German newspaper. Berlin finally relented in 1862 and the exile returned. But Bismarck now dominated the Prussian horizon and was determined to undermine anything which smacked of socialism. In 1865 he had Liebknecht expelled from the city; but the growth of socialism could not be halted so easily. Even the ban of 1878 was only a temporary impediment. It was these years of clandestine activity which proved the effectiveness of Liebknecht's evolutionary approach which used books and pamphlets instead of guns and barricades. By the time of his death in 1900 the German Social Democrats were firmly set in the gradualist mould that he had developed.

'Fritz', the largest steel-beating steam hammer in the world at the Krupp works. The booming steel industry of the 1870s allowed the Krupp factory at Essen to dominate the town and the workforce. The huge gun used against Paris in the Franco-Prussian war was manufactured by the Krupp works.

of its future policy in the hands of a group of parliamentarians. Their accumulating experience reinforced their pragmatic attitudes, as did their growing electoral support during the 1880s.

The rank-and-file membership, on the other hand, could only meet clandestinely - a situation which was bound to encourage a conspiratorial approach. The leaders of the party recognized this danger and distributed a broadsheet which implored their members: 'Do not let yourself be provoked! ... Resist all

August Bebel (1840-1913), the co-founder of the German Social Democratic Workers' Party.

attempts to lure you into secret societies and insurrection! Hold fast to the watchword which we have so often repeated to you: Our enemies must perish at the hand of our legality.'

Such reassurances and appeals to a bright future in which their enemies would inevitably be vanquished were needed to sustain ordinary members through these dark years. The most eloquent reassurances were found in Marx's analysis of capitalism, which predicted the collapse of the system through its own internal contradictions. Such conclusions were a lamp of hope for most German working-class activists during the 1880s, and their rhetoric became increasingly Marxist as the decade passed.

Bismarck, meanwhile, was not letting the grass grow under his feet and sought to outmanoeuvre the socialists by promoting bills in the Reichstag to lay the foundations of a welfare programme that was formerly the cornerstone of the Social Democrats' manifesto. In 1883 the Reichstag passed a sickness insurance scheme which awarded benefits to workers who were unable to earn their living as a result of illness; two-thirds of the cost of the scheme was met by workers' contributions and one-third by those of employers. In 1884, a bill was passed which created an industrial injuries compensation scheme funded by employers. Bismarck's third scheme, which provided pensions for the elderly and infirm, was enacted by the

Reichstag in 1889 and drew funding from workers, employers and the state.

In spite of all these attempts to buy off the working class and drive a wedge between them and the socialists, the number of Social Democratic voters increased during the 1880s, once the early days of repression were passed. In the Reichstag election of 1887 they polled 763,000 votes, over twice the size of their support in 1874.

### The Birth of the Second International

The situation of French workers improved as the Commune receded into the past. Most of its leaders had been pardoned by 1879 and a complete amnesty was issued the following year. A French socialist party, the Parti Ouvrier Français, was founded at a conference in Marseilles in 1879 after the Marxists managed to outmanoeuvre the other factions involved, including the anarchists. The party's leading light was Jules Guesde, who visited Marx in London and gained his blessing for the new organization. But it was only three years before factionalism, which remained a strong feature of French politics until the 1960s, produced a large breakaway group which formed its own party, the Fédération des Travailleurs Socialistes de France. It was led by Paul Brousse, who distrusted the revolutionary thrust of Marx and Engels and preferred a more accommodating approach to the larger, well-established parliamentary

# Socialism in the German Reich 1871-1918

SWEDEN

DENMARK

NORTH SEA

BALTIC SEA

NETHERLANDS

Lübeck
*1901*

Hamburg
*1897*

Bremen
*1904*

ELBE

ODER

VISTULA

Hanover
*1899*

Magdeburg
*1910*

Berlin
*1883*

**S** FIRST SOCIAL SECURITY LAW PASSED
*1889*
OLD AGE PENSIONS INTRODUCED
*1890*
SAD LARGEST PARTY IN
GERMANY WITH 20% OF VOTES

Essen
*1907*

Halle
*1890*

SAD FOUNDED **S**

Cologne
*1893*

Leipzig

**A** *1863*
*1909*

Dresden
*1903*

Breslau
*1895*

RUSSIAN EMPIRE

BELGIUM

RHINE

Erfurt
*1891*

Eisenach
*1869*

Gotha
*1875*

Jena
*1905*
*1911*
*1913*

Chemnitz
*1912*

ADAV FOUNDED

Frankfurt
*1894*

Mainz
*1900*

Mannheim
*1906*

Nuremberg
*1908*

Paris
*1889*
SECOND INTERNATIONAL
SET UP

Stuttgart
*1898*
*1907*

SECOND INTERNATIONAL MEETS

DANUBE

Munich
*1902*

AUSTRO-HUNGARIAN MONARCHY

FRANCE

**S** Zürich
*1880*

**S** St Gallen
*1887*

SECRET CONGRESS OF SAD

SWITZERLAND

SECRET CONGRESS OF SAD

ITALY

| | | |
|---|---|---|
| ● **Breslau** *1895* | | Significant Social Democrat conference |
| **A** ADAV | | Allgemeine Deutsche Arbeiterverein (ADAV) (General German Workers's Association) |
| **S** SAD | | Sozialistische Arbeiterpartei Deutschlands (SAD) (Socialist Workers's Party of Germany) |

N

0   100   200   300 Miles

0   100   200   300   400 Kilometres

parties. As other left-wing groups coalesced around individual leaders French socialism presented a highly fragmented picture, especially when compared to the Germans.

The centenary of the French Revolution fell in 1889 and people from all over the globe were drawn to the celebrations in Paris. The group led by Brousse proposed a congress to be held in July. They were supported by the British Trades Union Congress, who really wanted only union representatives to attend. The Germans wanted all socialists to come and tried to reconcile the different French factions. But the Marxists led by Guesde would not compromise and set about organizing their own event. Both opened on Sunday, 14 July, the hundredth anniversary of the storming of the Bastille. Since dozens of other groups were in Paris at the time, these two were hardly noticeable.

The rivalry between the two factions was intense although allegiances were frequently a consequence of friendships rather than political stance. Delegates drifted from one location to the other, and anarchists infiltrated both in an attempt to encourage further chaos. But as the days went by, the Marxist Congress became the dominant venue, attracting their hero's daughter, Eleanor Marx-Aveling and her two brothers-in-law, as well as most of the important socialist leaders of Europe. Over four hundred delegates from more than twenty countries were recognized, and the proceedings lasted for a week.

Motions were passed agitating for an eight-hour day in factories; standing armies were condemned in favour of national defence by 'peoples in arms'; and May Day was designated as an international holiday which would demonstrate the worldwide solidarity of workers on behalf of their demands. This last proposal developed from an idea on which the American Federation of Labour had agreed a few months before. The French and Austrians took the motion seriously, and their actions the following year led to strikes and clashes with the police.

## A New Programme

Back in Germany, Wilhelm II had inherited the imperial throne. This weak and intemperate young man was determined to assert his independence and he chose to achieve that by making life so uncomfortable for Bismarck that he would resign. The German Chancellor was already having problems getting the anti-socialist laws renewed by the Reichstag. One group of liberals wanted a slightly more lenient attitude, while the conservatives wanted tougher measures. Neither side would budge; as a result the motion for renewal was not passed and the law lapsed. The Social Democrats were liberated by default and could function freely again. Bismarck finally resigned in March 1890, and at first the Emperor tried to cast himself in the guise of a protector of the working classes. A Workers' Protection Bill was soon

The German empire, set up in 1871, dominated Europe. This *Punch* cartoon of 1884 shows Bismarck manipulating the emperors Alexander III of Russia, Wilhelm of Prussia and Franz-Joseph of Austria.

on the statute book, but when the recipients of his great magnanimity showed no sign of gratitude Wilhelm soon tired of the role.

The first result of the Social Democrats' new freedom was a massive increase in support in the national elections of February 1890, in which 1,427,000 votes were cast in their favour. This gave them thirty-five seats in the Reichstag and made them the largest party. Now that they could meet openly, they decided to hold a congress in Erfurt to revue the party's programme. The draft of the new proposals was sponsored by Liebknecht and Bebel but was really the work of Karl Kautsky and Eduard Bernstein. The introductory section, drafted by Kautsky, was concerned with principles that were rigidly Marxist. The practical proposals were the work of Bernstein and concerned the improvement of workers' economic and social conditions, equal rights for women, the secularization of schools and freedom of association.

This dichotomy between revolutionary theory and reformist practice was never put to the test before the First World War because the Reichstag did not function like the British Parliament at the end of the nineteenth

century. The German assembly was much closer to Westminster during the seventeenth century, when Charles II's ministers were appointed by him and only reported to Parliament. After the election of 1898, the German government might have to recognize that the Social Democrats were a major force in the Reichstag with fifty-six seats and over 2 million voters, but Wilhelm chose his own ministers quite independently and that situation did not change until the collapse of the empire.

The last decade of the nineteenth century saw the emergence of the German Social Democrats from the shadows of repression into the limelight of electoral success. But the imperial constitution divorced the party from the exercise of power and the consequences of practical actions. This allowed it to wallow in Marxist rhetoric without examining the consequences of the postures which it had adopted. Preoccupied with lecturing capitalists about the contradictions of their position, it never got round to disentangling its own. Only the inescapable realities of August 1914 would expose its illusions. Until then, its leaders could bask in the glow of being the world's leading socialist party.

# Russia: An Empire in Crisis

'Your Majesty has 130 million subjects. Of them, barely more than half live, the rest vegetate.' This description of the country in 1898 by the chief minister, Count Witte, confirms an impression of tsarist Russia that is still popular today. Russia was, on the one hand, a land where over three-quarters of the population scratched a living from the soil during the summer and often starved through the six months of winter. On the other hand, it was a country so rich in cultural achievement that the early years of Tsar Nicholas II's reign were known as the 'Russian Renaissance'. This was the land of the composers Borodin, Rimsky-Korsakov, Rachmaninov, and Tchaikovsky and the writers Turgenev, Gorky, Chekhov, Tolstoy and Dostoevsky: artists of world stature who gave the educated classes of Europe an unforgettable picture of the brutal contradictions of their country.

## Town and Country

Russia was a feudal society until 1861, when Tsar Alexander II emancipated 22 million serfs. Although this act allowed the peasants to acquire two-thirds of the land they had previously worked, and thereby gave them greater personal freedom, it failed to bring them the certainty of food. In most cases, they were unable to meet the annual redemption dues demanded by the government to cover the compensation given to the nobles for the loss of their land. Like the nobles, for whom compensation was insufficient to clear what they already owed, the peasants fell heavily into debt. In 1872 a commission which had been established to investigate the lot of the peasantry reported that, in the case of one region, 'anyone who looks at it from the outside might well think that the district had been ravaged by the enemy, so pitiful has it become'.

As a result, increasing numbers of peasants left the countryside to seek a better life in the towns. Industrialization did not really arrive in Russia until the last decade of the nineteenth century, considerably later than in the rest of Europe. When it did, however, there was steady growth in mining, manufacturing and railway construction: between 1891 and 1902 around 17,000 miles of railway track were laid.

Most of the investment capital came from government sources or overseas investors, a fact which encouraged the interests of Russia's tiny middle class to converge with those of the government. Although the urban working class was highly concentrated, it too

A cartoon from *Nagaechka,* 1905; the woman in chains is Russia, the two-headed dog the reactionary press, the spider the bureaucracy, and the men on the right the Peasant Assembly and the 'New Life'.

was very small, badly paid and forbidden from forming unions. In many ways, the labour situation in Russia at the end of the nineteenth century resembled that of England at the beginning. Although the state was beginning to regulate the growing industrial system, introducing restrictions on the employment of children and basic legislation for wages and working conditions, there were in reality few factory inspectors, with little power to enforce the law.

'Autocracy, orthodoxy and nationalism' - the slogan espoused by Tsar Nicholas I in the first half of the nineteenth century - was an apt description of the policies adopted by his successors. Even the Tsar-Liberator Alexander II, who established a degree of local self-government in the *zemstvos,* or councils, of 1864, refused to adopt a proper constitution. As with his emancipation of the serfs, any early hopes that he had aroused were soon dashed.

The most articulate opposition to the autocracy came from the intelligentsia: disaffected members of the nobility (or, in a few cases, the middle class) with either liberal or socialist inclinations. But since there were no facilities for expressing political demands and dissent was ruthlessly suppressed, opposition political organizations were driven underground. As a result, a tradition developed in Russia of using terrorism in an effort to force political change.

In 1881 Alexander II was assassinated in St Petersburg by a terrorist's bomb. His son and successor, Alexander III, proclaimed in his accession manifesto that he would rule 'with faith in the power and right of autocracy'. Six feet four inches tall and with a manner of speaking which, according to one court official, 'gave [him] the impression of being on the point of striking you', Alexander III increased the level of repression in the country. The press was heavily censored and hundreds of dissidents were sent into exile in Siberia. Political opposition to the regime was pushed even further underground, where it was often penetrated by the Tsar's ubiquitous secret police. This inevitably encouraged another traditional feature of Russian politics - the tendency to conspiracy.

When Alexander III died in 1894 his son, Nicholas II, stuck to his father's rather than his grandfather's principles and saw no need for a more liberal regime. The empire he inherited was a multi-national, multi-lingual one, whose 130 million subjects included Balts, Jews, Germans, Georgians, Armenians, Uzbeks and Tartars, as well as Slavs. One of the devices adopted by the government to control overt political dissent was to encourage violent nationalism. The Jews (who were forced to live in the Pale of Settlement on the periphery of the Empire) were the victims of a series of vicious pogroms, to which the authorities turned a blind eye. One of the worst started on Easter Day 1903, when a mob ran riot in the town of Kishenev in Bessarabia, murdering forty-five Jews and destroying six hundred houses; the police did not intervene until the end of the following day. In other areas, such as the young Stalin's native Georgia, the government continued its policy of Russification - enforcing, for example, the use of the Russian language in schools.

Nicholas II was a monarch of unlimited autocratic power invested in him by a political system that had barely altered in centuries. He controlled nominations to the Council of State, composed of sixty members drawn not only from ministers, but also from members of the imperial family and their friends. This opened the way for personalities such as Grigori Rasputin, a Siberian peasant turned seer, who was appointed to the Council in 1905. Under such conditions, government tended to be ineffectual. One member of the Council described its workings in 1901:

There is nothing consistent, considered or firmly directed. Everything is done spasmodically, haphazardly, under the influence of the moment, in accordance with the intrigues of this or that person, or the lobbying of those crawling out from their different corners in quest of fortune. The young Tsar is filled more and more with contempt for the organs of his power and begins to believe in the beneficent force of his absolute power, asserting it sporadically, without preparatory debate.

Nevertheless, there were few signs in the first years of the twentieth century that the empire was in crisis. In addition, most of the criteria that would have encouraged Marx to predict a revolution were missing. The landed nobility was newly poor but passive; the peasantry was dispirited but personally loyal to the Tsar; the small urban working class resembled a displaced branch of the peasantry rather than a labour movement; the middle class was small and bound to the government by financial incentives; and the government, if ineffectual in policy-making, was strong in its powers of repression.

## The Russo-Japanese War of 1904-5

The first shock to the Tsar was the war that broke out between Japan and Russia, as the two powers tried to control the eastern corner of the dying Chinese empire. Under the pretext of Chinese attacks on the Russian-built and owned Chinese Eastern Railway, the Russians had occupied virtually the whole of Manchuria in 1900. As a result of angry concern in London, Washington and Tokyo, the Russians reluctantly announced their respect for Chinese sovereignty over Manchuria in 1902, and agreed to withdraw their troops.

The focus of the crisis then moved to Korea, which Japan had taken over in 1895. At first, the Japanese proposed that the Russians should recognize Japanese interests in Korea in exchange for Japanese recognition of Russian rights in Manchuria. The Tsar would not confirm Russia's agreement to such a scheme, and in 1903 began to assemble troops along the Yalu River on the Korean frontier. The Japanese decided that attack was the best form of defence and, on 27 January 1904, Japanese destroyers torpedoed three Russian battleships in Port Arthur, the strategic Russian port on the Chinese coast. Japanese troops then laid siege to the port and, after several months, forced the Russian garrison to surrender. It was a humiliating defeat, made all the more painful because the Russians despised the Japanese as an inferior race. The war ended, as it had begun, with a naval engagement. Within forty-five minutes, the Russian Baltic Fleet, having steamed halfway round the world to get there, was almost annihilated at the Battle of Tsushima on 27 May 1905. Under the terms of the peace treaty, which was concluded in September 1905, Russia had to give up Port Arthur and evacuate Manchuria.

## The Russian Revolution of 1905

When the war first broke out, it had seemed that it might bolster further the Tsar's authority. Patriotic fever gripped many sections of Russian society. But Russian defeats simply disillusioned moderate Russians and spurred on the more revolutionary. In July 1904 Vyascheslav Plehve, the Minister of the Interior, was killed

---

# Rasputin: Siberian Peasant turned Seer

The great personal tragedy of Tsar Nicholas and his wife was that their only son and heir suffered from haemophilia - a condition which prevents the blood from clotting and which can turn an everyday bruise into the source of excruciating pain. As the young Tsarevich, Alexis, lay dying in October 1912, his mother Alexandra cabled to Rasputin, a holy man who was believed to possess extraordinary healing powers, to pray for his life. Alexis survived, and Rasputin's role cemented his influence within the imperial household. Rasputin became the Tsarina's spiritual adviser and intimate confidant. When the Tsar became Commander-in-Chief and went to the front during the First World War, the Tsarina was left to direct domestic affairs and Rasputin's power grew even greater.

A peasant from Siberia, the mystical Grigori Efimovich Rasputin (1871?-1916).

Naturally, this elevation to power for the son of a Siberian horse dealer caused deep resentment. The 'mad monk' was uneducated, licentious and physically filthy. According to the French ambassador, Paleologue, he 'carried with him a strong animal smell, like the smell of a goat'. His table manners were appalling and he delighted in shocking St Petersburg society with descriptions of the sex life of horses.

In 1916 several aristocrats decided to assassinate him to save the monarchy from further scandal. At first, they tried poison but, when he appeared unaffected, Prince Yusupov shot him. Even then, Rasputin did not die and had to be shot a second time. According to legend, his body was then put in a bag and thrown into the River Neva. When it was recovered, it appeared that he had gone on struggling even after being thrown into the water. The Empress was heartbroken at his death and he was buried at the royal palace at Tsarskoe Selo.

# The Empire in Crisis 1880-1905

N

Finland
1905
NATIONALIST DEMANDS

1905
NAVAL MUTINIES

1881
ASSASSINATION OF ALEXANDER II

1905
COUNTER-REVOLUTIONARIES MASSACRE
CINEMA-GOERS WITH FIRE

Kronstadt
St. Petersburg
(Leningrad)

1905
STRIKES

Estonia

Latvia

Lithuania

GERMANY

**Moscow**

Kazan

Tomsk

Omsk

**Lodz**
**Warsaw**
Poland

1905
NATIONALIST
DEMANDS

1905
STRIKES AND DEMONSTRATIONS LEAD
TO MASSACRE OF BLOODY SUNDAY

1905
STRIKES

AUSTRO-HUNGARIAN
EMPIRE

Kishinev

1903

Odessa

1905
NAVAL MUTINIES

ROMANIA

1905

SERBIA

MONTENEGRO

BULGARIA

**Sevastapol**

1905
STRIKES

ARAL SEA

CASPIAN
SEA

ALBANIA

BLACK SEA

Georgia

GREECE

1905
MUTINY ON
BATTLESHIP
POTEMKIN

**Krasnovodsk**

OTTOMAN EMPIRE

MEDITERRANEAN SEA

AFGHANISTAN

PERSIA

EGYPT

RED
SEA

INDIA

ARABIAN SEA

BAY OF
BENGAL

0       200    400      600  Miles

0    200   400  600   800  Kilometres

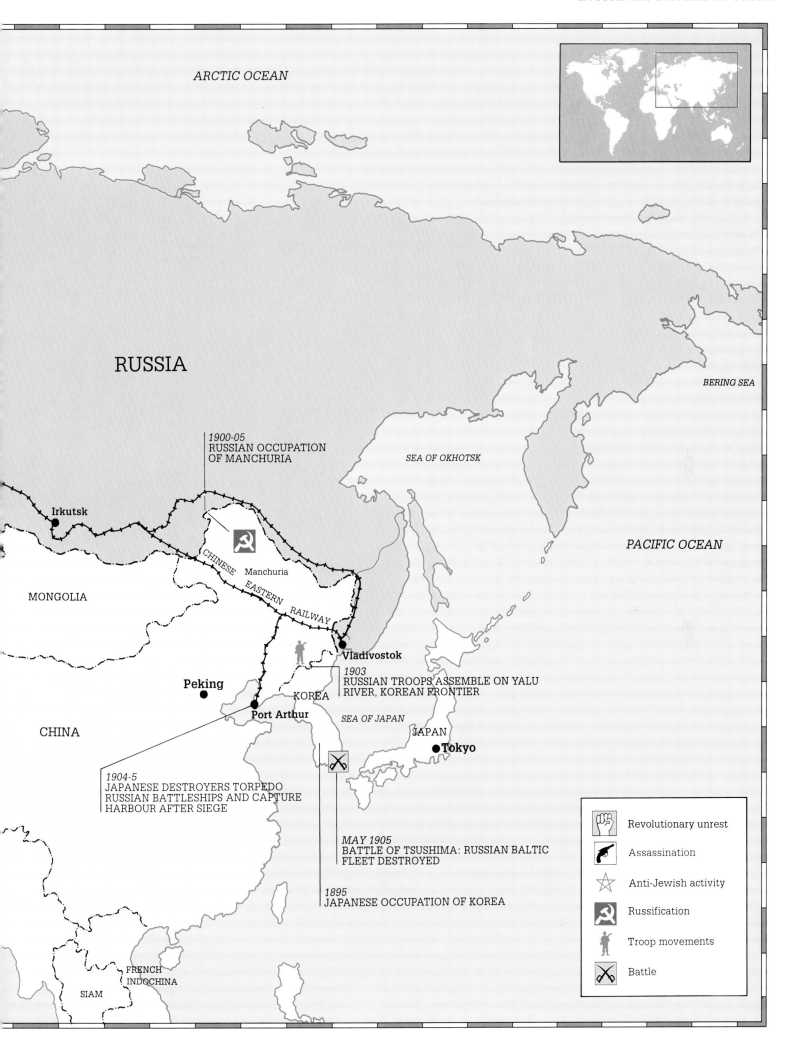

*ARCTIC OCEAN*

**RUSSIA**

*1900-05*
RUSSIAN OCCUPATION
OF MANCHURIA

Irkutsk

*SEA OF OKHOTSK*

*BERING SEA*

*PACIFIC OCEAN*

CHINESE EASTERN RAILWAY

Manchuria

MONGOLIA

Vladivostok

*1903*
RUSSIAN TROOPS ASSEMBLE ON YALU
RIVER, KOREAN FRONTIER

Peking

KOREA

CHINA

Port Arthur

*SEA OF JAPAN*

JAPAN

Tokyo

*1904-5*
JAPANESE DESTROYERS TORPEDO
RUSSIAN BATTLESHIPS AND CAPTURE
HARBOUR AFTER SIEGE

*MAY 1905*
BATTLE OF TSUSHIMA: RUSSIAN BALTIC
FLEET DESTROYED

*1895*
JAPANESE OCCUPATION OF KOREA

FRENCH
INDOCHINA

SIAM

Revolutionary unrest

Assassination

Anti-Jewish activity

Russification

Troop movements

Battle

by a bomb. There was turmoil in the towns. In January 1905, workers at the giant Putilov arms factory in St Petersburg went on strike for a minimum wage and an eight-hour day. They were led by an Orthodox priest called George Gapon, who had originally been recruited by the police to form tame, non-political unions. Gapon soon became a political figure in his own right, however, spreading the strike to factories around the city. He then decided to lead a mass march to present a petition to the Tsar, calling for an end to the war, the introduction of full civil liberties, universal suffrage and the abolition of direct taxes.

On Sunday, 9 January, a crowd of almost three hundred thousand people made their way peacefully to the square in front of the Winter Palace. Some of them were singing the imperial anthem and carrying portraits of the Tsar. When the marchers ignored two orders to disperse, the soldiers fired into the crowd and the Cossacks charged. Gapon, who disappeared into hiding, described 'the swords lifting and falling, the men, women and children dropping to the earth like logs of wood, while moans, curses and shouts filled the air'.

It was officially admitted that 130 people were killed and several hundred wounded, although the figures were probably several times higher. Whatever the death count, however, the events of 'Bloody Sunday' did more than anything else to undermine the allegiance of the masses to the Tsar.

Trotsky and his wife Alexandra Sokolovskaya in Siberia, 1902. In 1897 they had founded the South Russia Workers' Union. The following year, Trotsky was arrested for organizing the workers, jailed and sentenced to four years in Siberia.

There were a few half-hearted attempts to repair the damage. Financial compensation was to be offered to the families of the victims. A commission was to investigate the grievances of the workers. There was to be constitutional reform, although nothing that would threaten the principle of autocracy. None of these measures stemmed the tide of discontent, however, that rose throughout the spring and summer. In June there was a new

wave of strikes, stretching from the Russian-ruled Polish city of Lodz, in the north-west, to Odessa in the south. On 14 June the crew of the Black Sea Fleet's newest battleship, *Potemkin*, refused to eat some bad meat they had been served, attacked their officers and raised the red flag. There were mutinies on other ships, too, later in the month.

It was against this background of escalating disorder that on 6 August, a law was passed that provided for a freely elected assembly, or Duma, to be formed of delegates from all over Russia. It soon became apparent, however, that the institution was fatally flawed. It was to have consultative status only, and virtually excluded urban workers and the intelligentsia. A second law made the universities independent corporations free of police supervision, which provided the liberals and revolutionaries with venues where they could debate freely. One of the ideas discussed was a general strike.

In September strikes broke out in Moscow, and by October they had spread to many parts of the empire. They hit most sectors of the economy, from transport to textile mills and from printers to bakeries. Electricity and water were cut off in the big urban centres. There were clashes in Moscow between the strikers and their counter-revolutionary opponents, the 'Black Hundreds', who fought back rather like the fascist squads of Italy two decades later. Meanwhile the first soviet, or council of workers' representatives, made its appearance in St Petersburg. It was here, in what was to become one of the great

The Russian people demonstrate against their government in the streets of Moscow, 1905. The first banner reads 'Workers of the world unite!'. After the events of 'Bloody Sunday', when more than a hundred people were shot by the army as they demonstrated peacefully outside the Winter Palace in St Petersburg, a wave of strikes and riots swept the country to protest against the autocratic regime of the Tsar.

A cartoon from the fourth issue of *Burya* ('Storm'), 1906, in which the defeated Tsarist army is returning from the Russo-Japanese War. The crushing military defeat was used by the satirical journals to spur on revolutionary fervour against an incompetent government who used soldiers to fire on the workers.

institutions of the Russian Revolution, that Leon Trotsky first unleashed his brilliant oratory on the people of Russia.

In an attempt to stem the rising tide of revolution the Tsar called on Count Witte, a man of mildly liberal sentiments, to try to find a solution. He also issued a manifesto on 17 October which guaranteed freedom of conscience, speech, assembly and association, broadened the electorate and declared that all future legislation would be subject to the approval of the Duma. Although the manifesto succeeded in calming the more moderate sections of those wanting reform, it did little to placate the revolutionaries.

The empire lurched towards civil war. In one incident in Tomsk, on 20 October, counter-revolutionaries set fire to a theatre where a revolutionary meeting was in progress, killing over two hundred people. The Jews, who were traditional scapegoats in times of unrest and who included some of the most prominent revolutionaries such as Trotsky, were particularly vulnerable to the wrath of the counter-revolutionaries. Pogroms broke out all over the empire. The worst, late that month in Odessa, claimed more than five hundred lives.

There were mutinies at the naval bases in Kronstadt and Sevastopol, a series of violent peasant uprisings, and nationalist demands for autonomy in Poland and Finland. From St Petersburg the soviet issued a manifesto designed to cripple the state by denying it tax revenue. The Tsar was determined, however, that there should be no more concessions. The leaders of the soviet were arrested and replaced.

In Moscow there was a call for a general strike and an armed rising, backed by the soviets of the two cities, the Social

Democrats, the Socialist Revolutionaries and various labour unions. The revolutionaries used urban guerrilla tactics against government officials and troops, and succeeded in gunning down the head of the Moscow secret police in his home. But the authorities, sensing that more and more people were getting weary of the continuing disorder, moved with great determination against the revolt and had crushed it by the end of the year.

### The Rallying of the State

The Tsar never reconciled himself to the Duma, and only reluctantly agreed to the principle of limited 'universal' suffrage passed in December, declaring that 'God alone knows how far people will go with their fantastic ideas!' Nor did Witte, who claimed 'I have a constitution in my head, but as to my heart....'

The elections to the first Duma were boycotted by the left, but even so 30 per cent of its delegates were workers and peasants. This proportion was greater than in any other European parliament, and so alarmed the Tsar that he immediately drew up plans to dissolve the Duma at the first opportunity. Unaware of this sentence of death, the first Duma met in the Winter Palace on 26 April 1906, the glittering retinue of the Tsar and his court on one side of the throne room, the Duma on the other. The dowager empress Maria Feodorovna was drawn repeatedly to look at certain faces, 'so much did they seem to reflect an incomprehensible hatred for us'. Deadlock was soon apparent, with the cabinet unwilling to allow any legislative power to the Duma. In July the new chief minister, Stolypin, dissolved the Duma.

Over the next few years the Russian regime seemed to stabilize itself, at least on the surface. The number of participants in strikes fell dramatically as the country tired of anarchy: from 1.8 million strikers in 1906, the number fell to around 46,000 in 1910. Stolypin's land reforms created millions of small, and conservative, peasant landowners by freeing them from the village communes which had been introduced at the time of the emancipation of the serfs in 1861.

The political success of this manoeuvre was confirmed by a run of good harvests betweeen 1906 and 1911. Through the personal influence of the imperial Romanov family, Russia was able to negotiate loans for industry from French, British, Austrian and Dutch banks. The railway network was expanded and the vast Trans-Siberian Railway, one of the most daring railway projects ever attempted, was completed before 1914. The mining of coal and iron broke new records.

The election of the second Duma in 1907, which was not boycotted by the left this time, went almost unremarked, although it resulted in two-fifths of the elected deputies being socialists. Like the first and indeed the third and fourth Dumas, the parliament was dispersed and the Social Democratic deputies were deported to Siberia. As Lenin left Russia for Geneva in 1907, he announced: 'An era of counter-revolution has begun; and it will last some twenty years, unless tsardom is in the meantime shaken by a major war.'

The Russian Revolution of 1905 had failed. But it came to be seen by many of its leading participants as the great rehearsal for 1917, and an influence on events elsewhere: in the next few years there were revolutions in Turkey (1908), Persia (1909), Mexico (1910) and China (1911).

# Nationalism Overwhelms the Left

No government in 1914 intended its sabre-rattling gestures to erupt into a full-blown war. Many conflicts over the previous twenty years had been resolved by diplomacy or limited to local hostilities: few people really expected August 1914 to be any different. When the Archduke Franz Ferdinand of Austria and his wife were assassinated in Sarajevo, European governments presumed that Austria would settle the matter with Serbia without involving them. But when the Austro-Hungarian Empire actually declared war on the tiny Balkan state and provoked Russia into a show of Slav solidarity, statesmen throughout Europe were alarmed. The news that the Tsar had mobilized his armies caused even the bombastic Kaiser Wilhelm II to fly into a panic: 'Frivolity and weakness are to plunge the world into the most dreadful war, whose ultimate aim is the destruction of Germany. For I have no doubt left: England, France and Russia have agreed among themselves ... to use the Austro-Serbian conflict as an excuse for waging a war of extermination against us.'

These events, as depicted in old newsreels, are frequently accompanied by scenes of enthusiastic German crowds lining the streets as their troops march off to war. Such footage undoubtedly captures the mood of the moment, but there was another side to German public opinion which is not recorded on film. The elections to the Reichstag conducted in 1912, for example, gave 61 per cent of the vote to those parties which were clearly anti-militaristic. The Social Democrats, the SPD, gained 35 per cent; the Catholic Centre Party gained 14 per cent; while the Progressives captured another 12 per cent. However, although these parties were antagonistic to the military establishment, Germany had been at peace with its neighbours for a generation, and these pacific sentiments had never been tested against the nationalistic fervour often released by the threat of war.

## The Confusion of the Left

The SPD was a leading member of the Second International and had repeatedly spoken out against militarism. On 25 July 1914, three days before the Austro-Hungarian Empire declared war on Serbia, the SPD issued a statement denouncing any forthcoming conflict and asserting that the workers would be used as cannon fodder by a ruling class which had exploited and despised them in peacetime. The statement ended with the cry, 'Down with War! Long live international brotherhood!'

Despite such seemingly unequivocal public statements, the SPD had only one foot in the pacifist camp. Like their mentors, Marx and Engels, its leaders tried to differentiate between 'just' and 'unjust' wars. Just wars were those which advanced the cause of revolutionary ideals or national liberation, such as the American War of Independence and the struggles of the Poles against their Russian overlords. Many German socialists had held that it was 'just' to defend Prussia against the French emperor in 1870, but that once France had been defeated at Sedan and the German government began to advance claims to Alsace-Lorraine, it became 'unjust'. The more complicated issue of how German socialists should react to a declaration of war on Russia, given their antagonism towards the Tsar and their sympathy for the Russian peasantry, was never resolved by the SPD. The guidelines issued in 1891 by August Bebel, the joint chairman of the party, fudged the issue in a flourish of patriotism. 'The soil of Germany, the German fatherland, belongs to us the masses, as much as and more than to the others. If Russia, the champion of terror and barbarism, went to attack Germany to break and destroy it ... we should be as much concerned as those who stand at the head of Germany.'

More fudging took place at the meeting of the Second International in Stuttgart in 1907, where a declaration was made that 'though wars are ... inherent in the nature of capitalism ... the International is not able to lay down the exact form of working-class action against militarism at the right place and time, as this naturally differs in different countries.' This left the SPD and other socialist parties free to take any action they thought fit. It also left them at the mercy of events, without any prepared position.

The Congress of Copenhagen in 1910 was slightly more practical but still abandoned a motion calling for a general strike in the event of war. Instead, it urged member parties to vote against war credits, demand compulsory arbitration and work for general disarmament.

With such inadequate guidance, it is not surprising that the executive committee of the SPD should be hesitant when faced with the complications of the summer of 1914. They were quick to condemn Austria's demands of Serbia as 'the most brutal ... ever presented to an independent state'. But Russia, which they loathed, sided with the small Balkan state with which they were sympathetic. In the end, the Russian mobilization on 30 July decided the matter, for that allowed them the face-saving gesture of calling the war a defensive one.

In addition, the declaration of a state of emergency the following day circumscribed their opportunity for legal opposition to war preparations. Simultaneously, those in government circles began courting them. Even the Kaiser went to the Reichstag on 4 August to proclaim, 'I know parties no longer, I know only Germans.' In such an atmosphere, it was difficult for the SPD to assert their independence.

Their immediate problem was a vote on war credits. At a meeting called to resolve the issue, 78 out of 92 SDP deputies wanted to vote in favour because, they argued, hostilities had been forced on Germany. Although personally opposed to the appropriations, the chairman of the group, Hugo Haase, read the formal statement to the Reichstag which declared that the party would not betray its fatherland in its hour of need.

Signing the treaty of Brest Litovsk, 3 March 1918. The Bolshevik and German delegates had met in 1917 to discuss the terms of peace. Lenin was impatient to end the war but Trotsky resigned his post as Foreign Minister in protest at the Bolsheviks' yielding to Germany's demands.

This decision had critical consequences for the International. The immediate reaction of other parties was one of disgust: the radical socialist Paul Lensch called it 'the evisceration of the International'. And, with the collapse of the best-organized voice in the socialist set-up, other parties fell into line behind their national governments in order to kill their fellow workers. In the longer term, this cowardice in the face of adversity, as they saw it, led Lenin and the other Bolsheviks to their ruthless domination of the Third International - in an attempt to avoid such compromises in the future. After 4 August 1914, the parliamentarians and the radicals took different paths; only occasionally over the next sixty years did their aims coincide.

## Down the Slippery Slope

Once the SPD had capitulated, they were drawn into approving a war in which Germany's role was soon far from defensive. The German Chiefs of Staff were preoccupied with the idea of avoiding a war on two fronts. They believed that their army had to defeat its enemy in the west, France, with the greatest possible speed so that it could then turn to counter the might of its eastern foe, Russia. Bearing in mind the example of 1870 and the improvements in transport and communications since then, the generals estimated that France would be beaten in six weeks. To realize this goal, the German troops had to attack through neutral Belgium, which had rejected a clumsy offer of post-war reparations in compensation for any damage caused by the passage of the army.

The violation of Belgian territory consolidated French opinion and silenced any qualms felt by the socialists. The same was true in Britain, where Belgian neutrality had been a cornerstone of the country's foreign policy. Only in Russia did the social democrats fail to fall into line immediately.

The twelve social democrat representatives who sat in the Duma issued an ambiguous statement about defending 'the cultural treasures of the people from attack, either from abroad, or inside the country', and then walked out of the Tauride Palace without casting their vote. Yet, in Lenin's mind, they were all tarred with the same brush, and he urged all 'true' socialists to sever their ties with the Second International.

Meanwhile, fighting on the Western Front was not going according to plan. The German thrust into France started to run out of steam as it approached Paris, partly because the troops were beginning to tire. On 22 August six German divisions unexpectedly found themselves face-to-face with two divisions of the British Expeditionary Force, part of the highly trained regular army. After one day of bloody conflict the two sides separated, beginning a series of manoeuvres which ended on 14 September, when the exhausted German soldiers dug in and mounted machine guns to protect their lines. They quickly discovered that they were able to repulse almost any attack and, in this accidental manner, discovered the characteristic tactic of the next four years - trench warfare.

To a generation of senior commanders who had learnt their lessons in mobility in 1870 and rehearsed them during the Boer War, this war of attrition was almost incomprehensible; millions of lives were lost in futile attempts to gain yards of barren ground. Attack after attack, and repeated artillery barrages, destroyed the soil structure and turned the front line into a morass.

## A Change of Heart

Despite a suffocating censorship, which prevented news photographers from reaching the front and forbade French publications from printing any pictures of the dead, word of the enormity of what was

happening began to seep back to Berlin and London. Many social democrats, who had been moved to vote for war credits in their first flush of patriotism, regretted their earlier enthusiasm. By 1915 the number of dissidents in the SPD had swelled to twenty and when they too voted against war credits, the party expelled them.

A far from inconsequential group, the rebels included the former party chairman, Haase. Together with their supporters outside Parliament, during April 1917 they formed the Independent Social Democratic Party of Germany in the town of Gotha. Other prominent members included the radicals Rosa Luxemburg and Karl Liebknecht, as well as the orthodox Marxist Karl Kautsky.

While this new party opposed militarism and imperialism in word and deed, the majority of the SPD in the Reichstag acquiesced in the conduct of the war: a process which was preparing them for their role in post-war Germany.

In Britain, those who had opposed entry into the war were quicker to form an opposition group - the Union of Democratic Control, set up in September 1914. This organization, composed primarily of liberal pacifists, was joined by the Independent Labour Party, which had been formed by socialists and trade unionists in 1893. Ramsay MacDonald, later to become Britain's first Labour Prime Minister, was the most prominent politician in the group. With the Labour Party taking much the same path as the SPD in Germany, the UDC was, for some time, the only organized form of dissent. Across the Atlantic, before the USA entered the war, such liberal pacifism was much more respectable; indeed, Woodrow Wilson was elected to the presidency on the understanding that he would keep his country out of the war. He was supported in this stance by many trade unionists and socialist intellectuals. However, Wilson changed tack and in April 1917 declared war against the Central Powers. The Socialist Party of America remained opposed to involvement in the conflict and, despite a not unexpected wave of nationalistic fervour at this time, increased its popularity.

By 1917 the war in Europe was no longer confined to uniformed combatants and whole populations were involved. Airships were being used to bomb Britain, while long-range artillery shells were reaching the suburbs of Paris. Lloyd George had become the British Prime Minister and had taken unprecedented powers of coercion and direction of the economy to stave off a collapse caused by the German submarine blockade. Britain's naval blockade of Germany, in its turn, was slowly squeezing the population into starvation and society into collapse. Russia's primitive economy had already failed and the Tsar, having seriously mismanaged the war effort, was forced to resign. The old order was drowning in a great blood-letting. It was now only a matter of months before the unthinkable happened and the revolutionaries took power.

Tsar Nicholas II (1868-1918), the last tsar of Russia, gives the troops his blessing while on one of his visits to the front during the First World War. He and his family were executed in 1918.

# War and the Second International

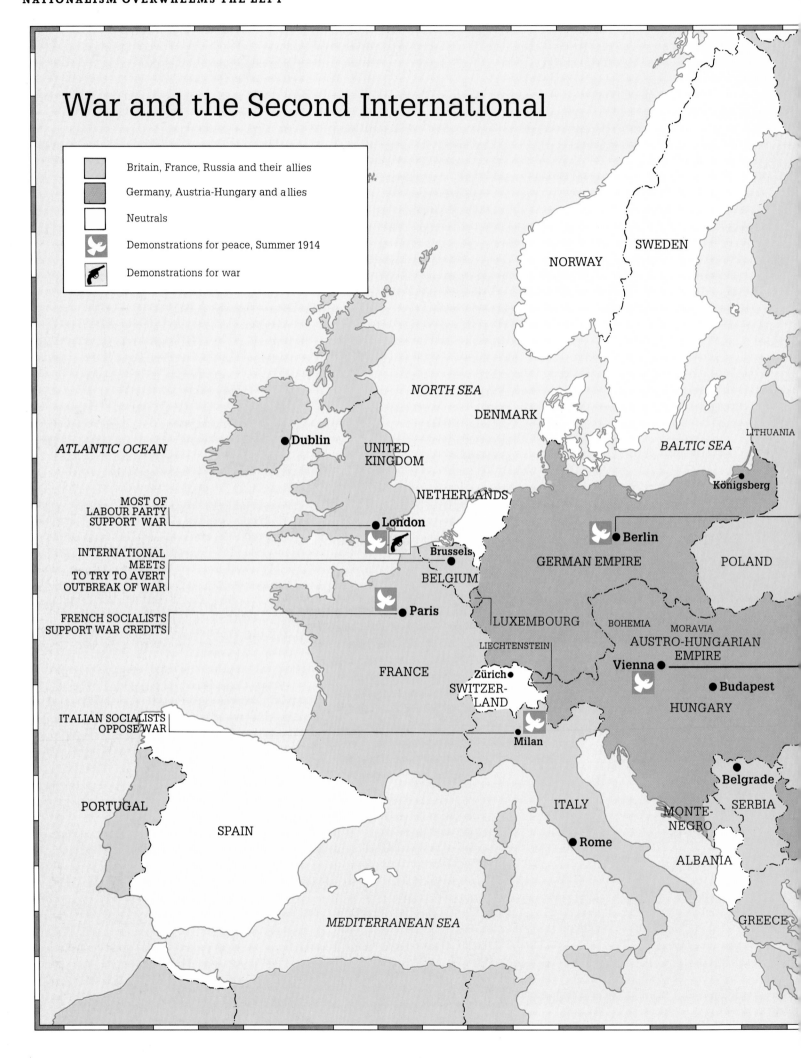

Britain, France, Russia and their allies

Germany, Austria-Hungary and allies

Neutrals

Demonstrations for peace, Summer 1914

Demonstrations for war

NORWAY

SWEDEN

NORTH SEA

DENMARK

ATLANTIC OCEAN

Dublin

UNITED KINGDOM

BALTIC SEA

LITHUANIA

Königsberg

NETHERLANDS

MOST OF LABOUR PARTY SUPPORT WAR

London

Berlin

GERMAN EMPIRE

POLAND

Brussels

INTERNATIONAL MEETS TO TRY TO AVERT OUTBREAK OF WAR

BELGIUM

LUXEMBOURG

BOHEMIA

MORAVIA

FRENCH SOCIALISTS SUPPORT WAR CREDITS

Paris

LIECHTENSTEIN

AUSTRO-HUNGARIAN EMPIRE

FRANCE

Zürich

SWITZER-LAND

Vienna

Budapest

HUNGARY

ITALIAN SOCIALISTS OPPOSE WAR

Milan

PORTUGAL

SPAIN

ITALY

Belgrade

MONTE-NEGRO

SERBIA

Rome

ALBANIA

MEDITERRANEAN SEA

GREECE

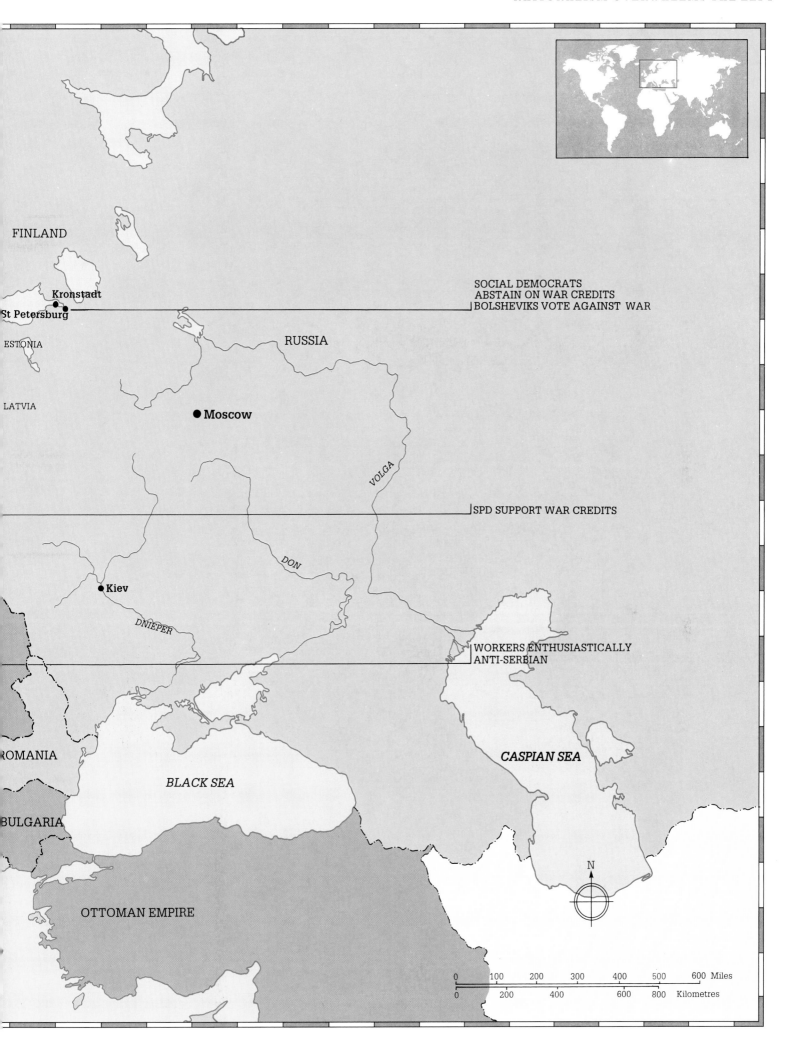

FINLAND

Kronstadt

St Petersburg

ESTONIA

LATVIA

RUSSIA

● Moscow

VOLGA

DON

● Kiev

DNIEPER

SOCIAL DEMOCRATS
ABSTAIN ON WAR CREDITS
BOLSHEVIKS VOTE AGAINST WAR

SPD SUPPORT WAR CREDITS

WORKERS ENTHUSIASTICALLY
ANTI-SERBIAN

ROMANIA

BULGARIA

BLACK SEA

CASPIAN SEA

OTTOMAN EMPIRE

N

| 0 | 100 | 200 | 300 | 400 | 500 | 600 Miles |
|---|---|---|---|---|---|---|
| 0 | 200 | 400 | | 600 | 800 | Kilometres |

The old and the new in a Russian poster of 1919. On the left, the Tsarist army: "What they fought for before", and on the right, the Red Army: "What they fight for now".

# The Architects of Revolution

ВЫШЕ ЗНАМЯ МАРКСА ЭНГЕЛЬСА ЛЕНИНА и СТАЛИНА!

Heroes of the Revolution: Marx, Engels, Lenin and the new man, Stalin who, even before Lenin's death, was concentrating power in his own hands.

The ever-optimistic Karl Marx never really believed, before 1871, in the immediate possibility of revolution in Russia. That year he stated in an interview in the *New York Herald* that 'there is a revolution coming in Russia, slowly, but surely'. Even at the beginning of the twentieth century, Russia seemed the least ready of all the countries of Europe for a Marxist revolution. Development of industry had scarcely begun. The industrial working class, which Marxist theory maintained would make the revolution, was very small, with the peasantry accounting for some 80 per cent of the population.

Why then did a revolution take place in Russia? And why was it a socialist revolution when there were other revolutionary parties in Russia with many more members than the Bolsheviks? The answers lie partly in the social, economic and political changes that took place in Russia after 1861 and partly in the way in which the revolutionary movement and political parties developed in Russia. But the most important immediate causes of the events of 1917 lay in the suffering and despair that resulted from the First World War.

### Revolutionary Movements

In January 1917, the three men who were to become the heroes of the Bolshevik Revolution were far from the centre of events. Trotsky was working in New York as a journalist and lecturer. Stalin - who had forsaken a theological seminary in his native Georgia to become a revolutionary outlaw - was in exile, fishing, hunting and reading in the ice-bound wilderness of Siberia. And Lenin was in Switzerland, so unaware of the events about to unfold that he was assuring young Swiss socialists that, even though he would never witness a second Russian revolution, they - the younger generation - most certainly would.

Throughout most of the nineteenth century, there were two distinct views within the Russian intelligentsia about the Russian empire and its role in the world. The Westerners believed that Russia was backward and needed to modernize along Western lines. The Slavophiles, on the other hand, believed that Russia was a unique society with its own model of progress and development. By the 1870s, this intellectual debate had given rise to two different revolutionary movements.

### The Champions of the Peasants

The populists (Narodniki) were Slavophile by inclination, believing that the peasants could be liberated through education and enlightenment. In the 1870s, these revolutionaries carried their message addressed 'to the people' of the villages. But the peasants refused to be persuaded; they distrusted the townspeople and turned them over to the police instead. The populists then turned to terrorism, forming first an organization called Land and Liberty and then another called the People's Will. It was this latter organization which, in 1881, succeeded in assassinating Tsar Alexander II. But it failed to change the nature of the regime, and repression merely increased under the new Tsar. Lenin's own brother, Alexander, was executed in 1887 for his part in a plot to assassinate Tsar Alexander III with a bomb concealed in a medical encyclopedia. In the words of Winston Churchill, the execution of his elder brother deflected the 'broad white light', with which Lenin saw the world, 'through a prism: and the prism was red'.

Throughout the nineteenth century, the revolutionary epicentre of Russia was held to be the countryside, rather than the towns. Many of the peasants were still heavily behind in their redemption payments for the land they had acquired at the time of emancipation in 1861. And, in many cases, the new arrangements had left them with less land to work than before. In 1902 a group of populists formed the Socialist Revolutionary Party (SR), with a programme based on the village commune, a primitive form of socialism which already existed and functioned effectively in Russia. The SRs wanted a democratic republic in which land was to be divided among the peasants and worked in common. Factories and workshops, similarly, would become co-operative undertakings. To achieve these ends, the Socialist Revolutionaries continued to believe in terrorism.

### The Heroes of the People

At the turn of the century, the Russian Social Democratic Labour Party - the ancestor of the Bolsheviks - was just one of a number of revolutionary groups in Russia, and would have been considered less significant than the Socialist Revolutionary Party. Its chief theoretician was Georgi Plekhanov (1856-1918), the son of a minor landowner. Plekhanov had begun his revolutionary career as a populist, believing in terrorist tactics. While living in western Europe, however, he turned to Marxism, and developed an admiration for western European social democracy which he wanted to see introduced into Russia. Although he did not return to his homeland until 1917, Plekhanov made important contributions to Communist theory and practice, being the first native Russian to write a positive exposition of Marxism as it applied to Russia. In this essay, called *Our Differences*, he attacked the populist movement and envisaged a gradual development of social democracy as the industrial working class expanded with the industrial base.

Although his influence was at first confined to a small group of exiles in Switzerland, where he had co-founded a Marxist group known as Liberation of Labour, Plekhanov's ideas gradually infiltrated intellectual circles in Russia. By the 1890s, students had carried the Marxist credo to the factories and some towns. One of the followers of Plekhanov was a young lawyer called Vladimir Ilyich Ulyanov, who was to be known as Lenin. He had been expelled from university for taking part in a socialist demonstration. By 1895 Lenin had formed a secret group in St Petersburg which preached the ideas of Marx to factory workers. The police caught up with him, and he was banished to Siberia for three years.

While Lenin was in exile, differences developed in the left-wing groups between the so-called 'economists' and those who were more politically orientated. The economists emphasized the use of strikes against employers in the battle to improve wages and working conditions; while the others advocated a broader strategy aimed primarily at political change. In an attempt to find some common ground, a secret meeting was held in Minsk in 1898. It was here that the Russian Social Democratic Labour Party (RSDLP) was born.

Many of the delegates were arrested immediately after the meeting, and those who escaped arrest fled abroad. From then until the Revolution of October 1917, most of the leaders of the RSDLP spent more time in exile than in Russia. They were joined by Lenin on his release from Siberia. In 1900, in Switzerland, Lenin invited Plekhanov to join the editorial committee of a new journal, called *Iskra* (spark) after a phrase used by an early nineteenth-century revolutionary group: 'A spark will start a big blaze. ' With them were Vera Zasulich, a veteran of revolutionary activity; Paul Axelrod, a pioneer of Russian Marxism; Martov (Julius Tsederbaum), who was to lead the Mensheviks in the St Petersburg soviet in 1905; and Alexander Potresov, who put up most of the money. Thus, for a time, the Russian underground movement revolved around the editorial board of a small journal that constantly shifted its offices, from Stuttgart to Munich to Geneva to London.

It was not long before each of them had fallen out with the ruthless, power-seeking Lenin; 'this is the stuff of which the Robespierres are made,' claimed Plekhanov. The struggle for power was, quite naturally, carried out within the framework of political argument: over the structure and organization of the Russian Social Democratic Labour Party. Should the party, like its brothers in western Europe be open to all, a mass, democratic working-class party that agitated, campaigned in elections and worked with the unions? Or should it consist of a small, highly motivated, revolutionary elite: a vanguard leading the working class? Lenin set out his arguments for a vanguard party in a celebrated essay entitled 'What Is to Be Done?' (1902).

Although most of the others had strong reservations about Lenin's views, they did not oppose him at first, so strong was the desire for unity. It was only at the Second Congress of the party in 1903 that matters came to a head. Lenin had hoped that, through his domination of the *Iskra* group, he would be able to gain a majority and thus capture the party. The group split at various sessions throughout the Congress, and Lenin was outvoted at first on an issue defining party membership. It was not until the twenty-seventh session of the Congress, when a group of Jewish delegates had walked out after being defeated on a separate issue, that Lenin managed to win a majority of 24 to 20 in a vote over the composition of *Iskra*'s editorial board. From that moment onwards, those who supported Lenin called themselves - rather tenuously - the Bolsheviks, or majoritarians, and dubbed their opponents the Mensheviks, or minoritarians. When Lenin held the Third Congress of the party in London in April 1905, it was not recognized by the non-Bolshevik factions.

For the next twelve years, this party in exile was racked by fierce controversy. There were disputes over whether land should be nationalized or distributed to the peasants, and over the use of armed robberies, counterfeit roubles and marriages of convenience to the rich to help swell party funds. And there were considerable misgivings when in 1912, Lenin called a conference of Bolsheviks in Prague and proclaimed his faction the true party.

But, even though it might have appeared that the party was destroying itself, the years in the wilderness did, in fact, prepare the Bolsheviks for the situation in Russia in 1917; and they did influence many of the policies that lay at the heart of the Soviet experience after that date. The Bolsheviks remained a conspiratorial body based on the principle of democratic centralism - that is, democratic election to positions within a strict hierarchy of control and responsibility, together with freedom of discussion up to the point at which a policy decision was reached, after which all dissent had to cease. The Bolsheviks also remained a revolutionary party, who believed that they could race Russia through the Marxist theory of history, which presupposed an industrially advanced society, a large urban proletariat and a dominant bourgeoisie. The Mensheviks, on the other hand, adopted an 'evolutionary', gradualist view of the way in which socialism would occur in Russia and advocated co-operation with the bourgeois parties in the struggle against autocracy.

### The Bourgeois Revolutionaries

After the 1905 Revolution the liberals, who had been pressing the Tsar for a constitution and democratic reform, formed themselves into political parties. The Octobrists, on the right wing, were named for their acceptance of the October Manifesto in which the Tsar had promised limited reform. The more radical liberals, who believed that the Duma should be transformed into a parliament modelled on Westminster, called themselves the Constitutional Democratic Party and were popularly known as the Kadets. Although the Tsar had no sympathy for the views of the Octobrists and Kadets, both parties were tolerated. Both participated in the elections to the Duma - elections that were boycotted by the Marxist parties and the SRs. And, when the monarchy finally fell in February 1917, the members of the provisional government belonged predominantly to these two parties. To some people's way of thinking, this was the bourgeois revolution that Marx had predicted.

The existence of revolutionary movements undermining the monarchy and of political parties pressing for reform indicated the necessity of change if Russia was to avoid revolution. But it was the First World War that brought matters to a head. And it was the attitude of the Bolsheviks to this war that, to a large extent, enabled them to take power.

### The First World War

By 1914 there was so much industrial unrest and social dissatisfaction in Russia that it was clear to many people that the government might not survive a major war. Nevertheless, as conflict between the Triple Entente, consisting of Russia, Britain and France, and the Triple Alliance, consisting of Germany, Austro-Hungary and Italy, became increasingly inevitable, some of the Tsar's advisers suggested that a war might in fact

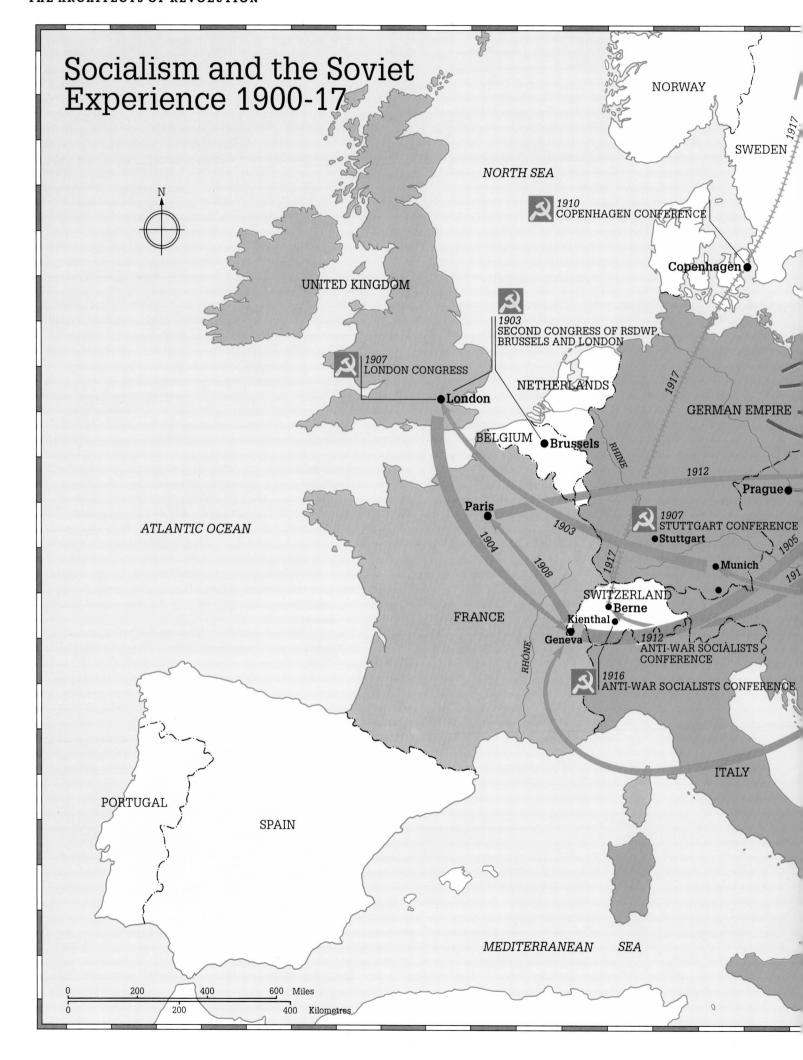

# Socialism and the Soviet Experience 1900-17

NORWAY

SWEDEN

*NORTH SEA*

*1910*
COPENHAGEN CONFERENCE

Copenhagen

UNITED KINGDOM

*1903*
SECOND CONGRESS OF RSDWP,
BRUSSELS AND LONDON

*1907*
LONDON CONGRESS

NETHERLANDS

GERMAN EMPIRE

London

BELGIUM  Brussels

*RHINE*

*1912*

Prague

Paris

*ATLANTIC OCEAN*

*1903*

*1907*
STUTTGART CONFERENCE

Stuttgart

*1904*

*1905*

*1908*

Munich

*1917*

SWITZERLAND

*1916*
ANTI-WAR SOCIALISTS CONFERENCE

FRANCE

Berne

Kienthal

*1912*
ANTI-WAR SOCIALISTS
CONFERENCE

Geneva

*RHÔNE*

ITALY

PORTUGAL

SPAIN

*MEDITERRANEAN    SEA*

0        200        400        600    Miles
0            200            400    Kilometres

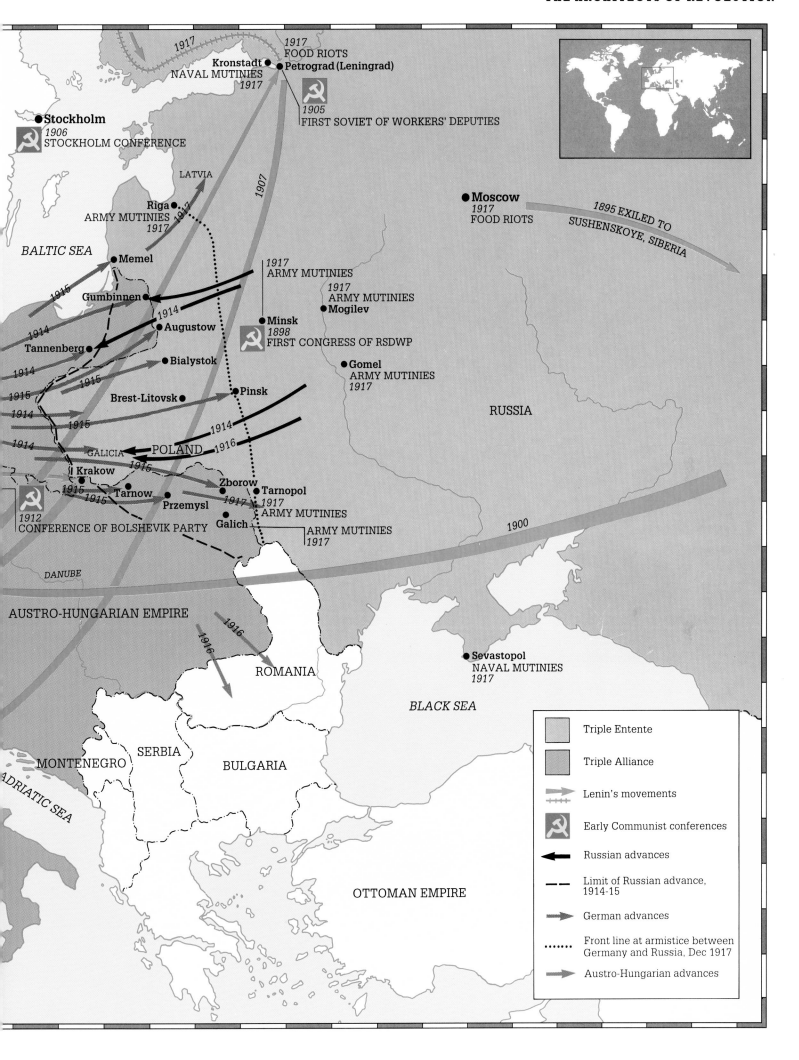

1917
FOOD RIOTS

Kronstadt
NAVAL MUTINIES
1917

Petrograd (Leningrad)

1905
FIRST SOVIET OF WORKERS' DEPUTIES

Stockholm
1906
STOCKHOLM CONFERENCE

LATVIA

Riga
ARMY MUTINIES
1917

1917

BALTIC SEA

Memel

1915

Gumbinnen

1914

1917
ARMY MUTINIES

1917
ARMY MUTINIES

Mogilev

Moscow
1917
FOOD RIOTS

1895 EXILED TO
SUSHENSKOYE, SIBERIA

Tannenberg

1914

1914

1915

Augustow

Bialystok

Minsk
1898
FIRST CONGRESS OF RSDWP

RUSSIA

Brest-Litovsk

1915

Pinsk

Gomel
ARMY MUTINIES
1917

1914

1915

1914

POLAND

1914

1916

GALICIA

Krakow

1915

1915

1915

Tarnow

Przemysl

Zborow

Tarnopol
1917
ARMY MUTINIES

1917

Galich

ARMY MUTINIES
1917

1900

1912
CONFERENCE OF BOLSHEVIK PARTY

DANUBE

AUSTRO-HUNGARIAN EMPIRE

1916

1916

ROMANIA

Sevastopol
NAVAL MUTINIES
1917

BLACK SEA

MONTENEGRO

SERBIA

BULGARIA

ADRIATIC SEA

OTTOMAN EMPIRE

Triple Entente

Triple Alliance

Lenin's movements

Early Communist conferences

Russian advances

Limit of Russian advance,
1914-15

German advances

Front line at armistice between
Germany and Russia, Dec 1917

Austro-Hungarian advances

# The End of the Romanovs

After Tsar Nicholas II had abdicated at Pskov on 15 March 1917 he returned to his family at Tsarskoe Selo. The family and their servants who remained were under house arrest. Their guards were young, poorly trained and rude. Kerensky visited them a number of times to question the Tsar and Tsarina about their previous conduct.

Petrograd, meanwhile, was in turmoil as the Bolsheviks sought to overthrow the provisional government. To protect the Romanovs, Kerensky moved them to Tobolsk in Siberia during August on a train marked 'Japanese Red Cross'. The new home was the former governor's mansion. Now they were guarded by disciplined troops who protected them from any unrest. But it soon became clear that the townspeople sympathized with the Romanovs and smuggled food and clothing to them. The Tsar's four daughters occupied themselves by enacting French plays and by reading and sewing.

After the Bolshevik Revolution, their circumstances changed slowly until the money for their guards' wages dried up. In January 1918 the family were put on soldiers' rations. The Tsarina retreated increasingly into religion. A new commissar arrived on 22 April with orders to return them to Moscow. The Tsarevich was now too ill to be moved so his father, mother

The deposed Tsar with his family during their imprisonment in the remote town of Tobolsk, Siberia, August 1917.

and sister Marie went ahead. But their train was intercepted at Ekaterinburg, where the rest of the family joined them a few weeks later. Their guards were now factory hands who enjoyed being disrespectful.

On 4 July they were replaced by ten polite, quiet members of the Cheka, the secret police. Their leader, Yurovsky, woke the royal family at midnight on the night of 16 July and told them they had to flee. When they assembled in the basement they were shot.

industry formed a War Industries Committee which took over supply and distribution. Although the government was reorganized in 1915, it failed to improve the economic situation. The Duma had scarcely met since the war began - it was easier to rule by executive decree. When a meeting was finally called in August 1915, its members demanded more popular representation. Tsar Nicholas II's simple response was to suspend the Duma indefinitely.

In September 1915, the Tsar made another mistake; he took over supreme command of the army from Grand Duke Nicholas and left the conduct of domestic affairs to the Tsarina and her disreputable and unpopular adviser, Rasputin. While the Tsar became personally identified with the failures of the army, dissatisfaction mounted at home. There were acute food and fuel shortages; prices rose; strikes occurred more and more frequently; and troops deserted from the front, joining the strikers at home or foraging for food in the countryside by looting from the peasantry.

Although some territorial gains were made in 1916, the war had reached a stalemate by the end of the year. The entire social and economic structure of Russia was on the brink of collapse; society was demoralized and overwhelmed by war-weariness.

## The Eve of Revolution

Nicholas II was out of touch with events at home. The Tsarina and Rasputin meddled in the work of the government, while the liberals became increasingly frustrated by their inability to improve the situation. Not surprisingly, demands for political change became increasingly articulate.

On 23 February 1917 troops were sent to put an end to food riots and demonstrations in Petrograd, which had begun on the anniversary of Bloody Sunday. Instead of crushing the demonstrators, the soldiers joined them in their calls for 'Bread and Freedom'. On his return to Petrograd on 2 March, the Tsar was stopped by the revolutionaries and forced to abdicate in favour of his brother, Grand Duke Michael; Michael refused the crown, however, and the rule of the Romanov dynasty came to an end after more than three hundred years. The imperial family was arrested and a temporary committee of the Duma formed a provisional government, pending the drafting of a constitution and the election of a Constituent Assembly.

This might well have been the beginning of constitutional democracy in Russia. But the prerequisite for the success of any government in 1917 was the extrication of Russia from the war. The provisional government failed to do this. Lenin was the only political leader who understood how important peace was to the people of the Russian empire. It was this, and his ability to persuade the Bolsheviks to his way of thinking, that enabled the Bolsheviks to take power in the October Revolution and to establish a Soviet state.

provide a rallying point for his increasingly unpopular regime.

At first this argument proved convincing. When war broke out, there was a surge of popular unity in Russia and industrial unrest ceased. The *zemstvos,* or local councils, united in a loyal union under Prince Lvov, and a patriotic Union of Municipalities was formed. The name of the capital, St Petersburg, was deemed too German and was changed to Petrograd; in the city there were demonstrations in support of the Tsar and his allies. Most European members of the Second Socialist International, who had previously voted against participating in any future imperialist war, patriotically supported their respective national governments. Lenin, on the other hand, was alone in calling on socialists to 'turn the imperialist war into civil war'; it was an appeal which, at the time, seemed doomed to lose support for the Bolsheviks in Russia as well as solidarity with the international socialist movement.

Russia was not well prepared for a war, however, and the initial popular patriotic fervour soon turned to discontent. In 1914

and 1915 the Russians were defeated at Tannenburg in East Prussia, and in Galicia, with heavy losses. During the first ten months of the war 3.8 million men were lost; by 1917, this figure had risen to 8 million, out of a total of 15 million soldiers who had by then been mobilized. However, the strategists of the First World War measured defeat and victory not in terms of human losses but in pieces of territory. As Russia was driven out of the Balkans and Poland, refugees from the enemy-occupied areas and from the front flooded into central Russia, causing a housing crisis, food shortages and price rises.

The army was poorly equipped for an offensive war, and the military command was divided by mutual distrust. By the end of 1915, some regiments had no rifles and others had their artillery rationed to four shells per gun a day. Britain, France and the United States began to send supplies. But Russia also suffered from inadequate communications and there was no provision for putting the economy on a wartime basis. In June 1915 the first serious strikes occurred. At the same time, the leaders of trade and

# The Russian Revolution

In 1906, in St Petersburg, the British ambassador had a grim premonition: 'Should the peasantry, excited by socialist and anarchist agitators, be led on...and should the working classes simultaneously rise in the towns, there will be a catastrophe such as history has rarely witnessed.'

Russia, however, was to experience not one revolution but three in the first two decades of the twentieth century. The first, in the wake of the country's defeat in 1905 in the Russo-Japanese War, failed, but proved to be a useful practice run. The second erupted in February 1917 as a direct result of the costly, mismanaged and vastly unpopular First World War; the Tsar was toppled and a Provisional Government established. The third revolution, which broke out amidst the mounting chaos of the disintegrating Russian empire, established Bolshevik rule in Petrograd in October 1917. It is this third revolution, the one that brought the Bolsheviks to power, that is generally known as the Russian Revolution.

The provisional government established by the moderates in March 1917 quickly declared freedom of speech and assembly, a universal franchise and an immediate amnesty for political prisoners. But, once these had been achieved, the government did not really know what to do next; there was no detailed political programme. The government had the grudging support, however, of the main left-wing parties - the Mensheviks and the Socialist Revolution-aries, who were supported by the peasants - so long as they were allowed to impose their policies on it. Lenin and the Bolsheviks, however, were determined to destroy the provisional government and refused to participate. At the same time self-elected councils, or soviets, of workers' and soldiers' deputies sprang up all over the country, as they had done in 1905.

### The Return of Lenin

Lenin had not anticipated the February Revolution. At first, like the Mensheviks, he had believed that a prolonged period of capitalist development was needed before Russia would be ready for a socialist revolution. But he had also long believed in a policy of 'national defeatism', in which the sabotage of a country's war effort by her own countrymen could precipitate a revolution. He had believed, too, that the proletariat could instigate the 'bourgeois-democratic' revolution (in this case, the February Revolution) and move straight on to a

One of the first sessions of the Petrograd soviet of workers' and soldiers' representatives, held at the Tauride Palace in April 1917. Soviets were formed all over the country after the February Revolution.

socialist revolution. On 16 April (or 3 April, according to the pre-revolutionary Julian calendar), Lenin returned secretly from exile in Switzerland, arriving at Petrograd's Finland Station.

He immediately prepared the Bolsheviks to profit from the chaos and seize political power. In his *April Theses*, he insisted that the war would end only if capitalism was overthrown - thereby appealing to the deep war-weariness in the country. He called for the expropriation of all estates, giving the peasants the right to redistribute the land - thus stealing some of the thunder from the Socialist Revolutionaries. And he claimed that all political power should be vested in the soviets, which should also control production and distribution - thereby appealing to the supporters of the Mensheviks and the Socialist Revolutionaries, who dominated the soviets.

By this time, the provisional government had already implemented so many democratic policies that even Lenin admitted

Rioting on the streets of Petrograd in July 1917. Riots became widespread throughout the country during the power struggle that followed the downfall of the Romanov dynasty.

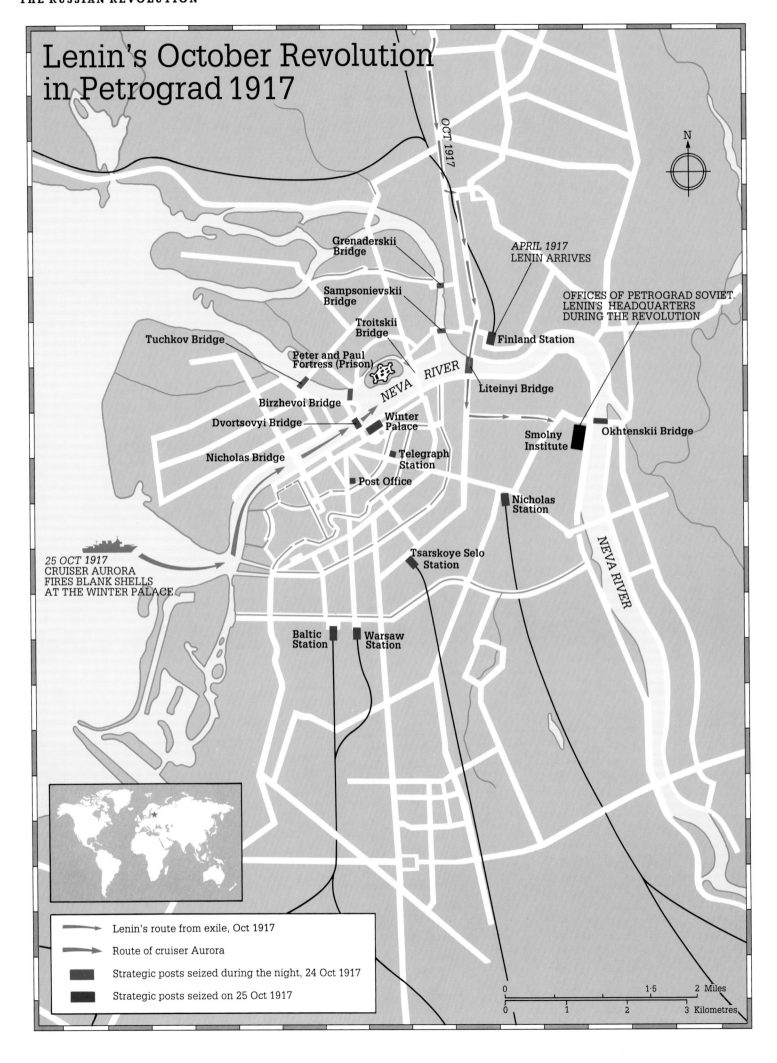

# Lenin's October Revolution in Petrograd 1917

N

Grenaderskii
Bridge

Sampsonievskii
Bridge

*APRIL 1917*
LENIN ARRIVES

OCT 1917

OFFICES OF PETROGRAD SOVIET.
LENIN'S  HEADQUARTERS
DURING THE REVOLUTION

Troitskii
Bridge

Tuchkov Bridge

Peter and Paul
Fortress (Prison)

Finland Station

NEVA  RIVER

Birzhevoi Bridge

Liteinyi Bridge

Dvortsovyi Bridge

Winter
Palace

Smolny
Institute

Okhtenskii Bridge

Nicholas Bridge

Telegraph
Station

Post Office

Nicholas
Station

*25 OCT 1917*
CRUISER AURORA
FIRES BLANK SHELLS
AT THE WINTER PALACE

Tsarskoye Selo
Station

NEVA  RIVER

Baltic
Station

Warsaw
Station

Lenin's route from exile, Oct 1917

Route of cruiser Aurora

Strategic posts seized during the night, 24 Oct 1917

Strategic posts seized on 25 Oct 1917

| 0 | | 1·5 | 2 Miles |
|---|---|---|---|
| 0 | 1 | 2 | 3 Kilometres |

A public holiday rally in Petrograd Palace Square, April 1917. The banners read 'Hail Socialism' and 'Hail Democratic Republic', perhaps anticipating the success of the Bolshevik revolution later that year.

that the country had become the freest in the world. But it had not held elections, which would have given it legitimacy and public support, nor had it addressed the most serious grievances of the February Revolution. Despite the fact that the war had been a major cause of that revolution, the provisional government announced in March that it would honour its international obligations and continue fighting.

Agrarian reform, another urgent demand, was delayed pending the postponed election of a Constituent Assembly. Reluctant to wait, the peasants began seizing the landowners' estates spontaneously. Despite morale-boosting tours of the front by Alexander Kerensky, the only Socialist Revolutionary founder member of the provisional government, the largely peasant army began to desert in vast numbers.

In June, pressed by the Allies and propelled by a vain attempt to distract attention from the deteriorating domestic situation, the government launched an offensive against the Germans. It was a disaster. The Russian soldiers were reluctant to advance and, when the Germans counter-attacked, they retreated in disarray. For the Bolsheviks, however, it was yet another opportunity to exploit; they simply stepped up their propaganda for peace.

The Bolshevik Party had grown in size from twenty thousand members in February to a hundred thousand by July.

Although it was still much smaller than either the Mensheviks or the Socialist Revolutionaries (SRs), it was far better organized. In line with Lenin's strategy the Bolsheviks had infiltrated, and were now gaining control of, many local soviets and factory workers' committees. They had also established party cells in military units. However, the provisional government counter-attacked. Kerensky accused Lenin of being a German agent and arrested many of

the leading Bolsheviks; Lenin fled to Finland.

With the Bolsheviks apparently defeated, the right now attempted a counter-revolution. The new Commander-in-Chief, General Kornilov, planned to march on Petrograd in order to destroy both the Bolsheviks and the soviet. Bolshevik-led workers poured into the streets to defend their capital, and the provisional government, which had earlier disbanded the Bolshevik Red Guards, now distributed rifles to them. Although the general never reached Petrograd, it appeared to many that the Bolsheviks had saved the revolution from military dictatorship. Once again they had benefited from the turn of events, and by October

their membership had surged to two hundred thousand.

In September, Lenin decided that it was time for the Bolsheviks to seize power. The provisional government had set a date in November for elections to the Constituent Assembly, and he realized that the Bolsheviks would probably not win a majority of the seats. If he wanted a socialist revolution to succeed, therefore, it would have to take place before November. Trotsky, who had recently joined the Bolsheviks, insisted that that they should wait until the Second Congress of Soviets had met in October, so that power could be transferred from the provisional government to the soviets,

Vladimir Ilich Ulyanov (Lenin), the imperious leader of the Bolshevik party. After the February Revolution in Petrograd, he returned from Geneva and began his attack on the provisional government.

# Witness to the Revolution

John Reed was the leading radical journalist of his time in America. Born into a wealthy, West-Coast family, he displayed no political affiliations before he graduated from Harvard, although he contributed to many college publications. He joined *The American Magazine* in 1911, a best-selling monthly with strong radical allegiances. Affected by the attitudes of the staff, Reed moved to the left and joined *The Masses* in 1914 and began speaking at strike meetings. That year he visited Pancho Villa in Mexico and his reports on the revolution won him fame in America. His eye-witness reports on the First World War increased his reputation. In 1917, he and his wife, Louise Bryant, arrived in Petrograd in time to observe the Revolution at first hand.

**The Russian edition of *Ten Days That Shook the World,* published in Moscow in 1923.**

He became a close friend of Lenin and helped write Soviet propaganda. When he returned to America he was tried for sedition but was never convicted. He published *Ten Days That Shook the World* in 1919, an account of the Revolution that has never been surpassed. In an introduction to the book Lenin wrote: 'With the greatest interest and with never slackening attention I read John Reed's book ... Unreservedly do I recommend it to the workers of the world. Here is a book which I should like to see published in millions of copies and translated into all languages.'

Later that year Reed escaped from America using a forged passport and eventually reached Moscow while the FBI was still seeking him at home. But he caught typhus and died in 1920. He was buried in the Red Square as a hero of the Revolution, an unprecedented honour for an American.

where the Bolsheviks had a majority. Accordingly, Lenin resurrected his slogan of 'All Power to the Soviets!' Other Bolsheviks felt so strongly that an armed uprising in October would be premature that they leaked the plans to the press. But the provisional government was so confident of the loyalty of the armed forces that it took no action to suppress the Bolsheviks.

That confidence was misplaced. Many soldiers already felt that they owed more allegiance to the Petrograd soviet than to the government. At the beginning of October, the Petrograd soviet formed a Military Revolutionary Committee (MRC), of which Trotsky was chairman, to defend the revolution and to control the armed forces around Petrograd. Trotsky then fanned a rumour that the Petrograd garrison was to be sent to the front and that the capital and the Second Congress of Soviets were under threat from counter-revolutionaries. This ensured that the garrison would support the MRC, which organized the Bolshevik coup.

## The October Revolution

Wednesday, 25 October was the day chosen by the MRC of the Petrograd soviet to overthrow the moderate provisional government of Alexander Kerensky. There were, however, disagreements among the revolutionaries up until the last moment. On the night of 24-25 October, the majority of the MRC and the Bolshevik Central Committee argued simply in favour of uniting the socialist parties against the Kerensky regime at the Soviet Congress, which was due to meet in the Smolny Institute on the following day. But Lenin, having come out of hiding to join the MRC on the upper floors of

the Smolny, was impatient for an immediate uprising in order to present the Congress with the soviet revolution as a *fait accompli*. His scheme was finally agreed by the Bolshevik Central Committee in the early hours of 25 October. The plan, arranged and controlled by Trotsky, was for up to 25,000 troops to occupy the key points of the city. The MRC was to capture the Mariinsky Palace and to disperse the Council of the Republic. The surrender of the Kerensky cabinet in the Winter Palace would then be demanded. If the ministers refused to give themselves up, the palace would be shelled from the Peter and Paul Fortress and from the cruiser *Aurora*, anchored in the Neva.

In the end it was a bloodless revolution. The legendary 'storming' of the Winter Palace was more like a house arrest, since most of the troops defending the palace had already surrendered, hungry and dejected. The only damage to the imperial residence during the whole affair was a chipped cornice and a smashed window on the third floor.

## The First Days of Revolution

On the evening of 25 October, the Second All-Russian Congress of Soviets, in which the Bolsheviks commanded a majority of nearly two-thirds, proclaimed the transfer of all power throughout Russia to the soviets of workers', soldiers' and peasants' deputies. The revolution had been accomplished. In Trotsky's words, the dissenting Mensheviks were consigned to the 'dustheap of history'. The Congress in turn elected an All-Russian Central Executive Committee to deal with soviet affairs between congresses. It also elected a Council of People's Commissars under the chairmanship of Lenin, which was

to become the effective government of Russia for the next few years.

But winning power in Petrograd was not enough. The Revolution had to be extended to the rest of Russia and Bolshevik power had to be consolidated. Hundreds of Bolshevik commissars were sent to towns throughout the country, and Military Revolutionary Committees were established in Moscow and other cities to maintain public order and to guard against counter-revolution.

At first here was remarkably little armed opposition to the Bolsheviks. On 27 October the Council of People's Commissars had declared an end to the war and proposed immediate negotiations to secure a democratic peace. Moreover, it had adopted a decree which provided for all land to be distributed to the peasants. Nevertheless, the process of seizing political power was not as speedy in the provinces as it had been in Petrograd. In towns and villages all over the country local soviets, often consisting predominantly of members of the other socialist parties, took charge of political affairs. The Bolsheviks only gradually managed to win control of those soviets in which they did not already have a majority.

## The Political Coup

The provisional government had set 12 November as the date for elections to the Constituent Assembly. In eliciting support for the Bolshevik takeover, Lenin had stressed that his party alone could ensure that the long-awaited elections actually took place. He now decided to honour this promise, even though it seemed unlikely that the Bolsheviks would receive the popular mandate they desired.

The elections took place as planned on 12-13 November. Of the 707 delegates elected, 175 were Bolsheviks, 40 were left-wing SRs, 16 were Mensheviks, 17 were Kadets and 370 were SRs. The Bolsheviks had won less than 25 per cent of the vote, and the Socialist Revolutionaries, who had the overwhelming support of the peasantry - the largest section of Russian society - had an absolute majority. It was a crushing vote, and one which presented the Bolsheviks with a dilemma, for Lenin and his colleagues had no intention of handing over power.

When the Assembly met on 5 January 1918, the Bolsheviks proposed that it should adopt a Declaration of the Rights of Toiling and Exploited People, by which it would effectively abdicate power in favour of the Congress of Soviets. When the Assembly refused, the Bolsheviks and the left-wing SRs walked out. Before the Assembly could reconvene the next day, the All-Russian Central Executive Committee accused the Assembly of being a cover for counter-revolution and dissolved it. There was little public protest at this political coup, and even less when the Third Congress of Soviets declared itself in sole control. The opposition now realized that force was the only means of removing or restraining the Bolsheviks.

# The Civil War

It is ironic that a revolution which had promised peace should plunge the country into a bloody civil war, in which hundreds of thousands were killed in battle and as many as 25 million may have died through disease and famine brought on by the war.

During its course, the Bolsheviks extended their power throughout the country and, under the demands of the war, abandoned many of the original principles of the revolution. In many ways, the Soviet state was forged in the Civil War.

### From Peace to War

It was the signing of the promised peace that acted as a catalyst for war. Immediately after the October Revolution, the Bolsheviks had proclaimed a Decree on Peace, which proposed an end to the First World War without annexations or indemnities. Russia's allies, however, refused to recognize the new regime and were not interested, in any case, in suing for peace. The Bolsheviks therefore ignored the wartime Allied agreement that there should be no separate peace and began to negotiate with Germany.

There could have been few more unprepossessing sites for a peace conference than the snow-bound border town of Brest Litovsk. Here, some of Europe's most powerful diplomats negotiated with men who, until recently, had been prisoners of their own government. Russia was on her knees; many of her soldiers had, in Lenin's words, 'voted for peace with their feet', deserting the army in order to share in the division of the landed estates. 'To carry on a revolutionary war, an army is necessary, and we do not have one. It is a question of signing the terms now, or of signing the death sentence of the Soviet government three weeks later.' Peace, however, could be achieved only on German terms. When the treaty was signed on 3 March 1918, Russia agreed to the annexation by Germany of most of the lands that had been occupied by German forces, including Poland, the Baltic states and part of the Ukraine. Russia had compromised its commitment to a peace without annexations and lost more than a million square miles and 60 million people.

The peace had several immediate effects. Russia's original allies feared that the collapse of the Eastern Front would enable Germany to concentrate on the Western Front, and were therefore prepared to aid, at first, any group in Russia which would resist Germany and, later, any group which would fight the Bolsheviks. These included tsarist

officers, left-wing Socialist Revolutionaries who objected to the peace, and nationalists. One of the promises of the Bolshevik campaign before the Revolution had been the right of all nations to self-determination, thus winning the support of the national minorities within the Russian empire. Lenin hoped that once they had been given the right to independence, they would opt for integration within a free union of socialist nations. After the Revolution, the Bolsheviks therefore recognized the independence of Poland, Finland, Estonia, Latvia and Lithuania, all previously part of the empire. However, it was less easy to contemplate the independence of other border areas in the south and east, since this was where the anti-Bolshevik armies were forming. Self-determination became both a contributory and complicating factor of the Civil War: when the Bolsheviks ceased to honour their promises, nationalist leaders turned to the foreign-backed counter-revolutionary forces

known as the Whites. But the Whites were, more interested in restoring the empire than in harnessing nationalism, and many disillusioned leaders transferred their allegiance back to the Bolsheviks.

### The Battle Lines are Drawn

Gradually a motley band of monarchists, landlords, industrialists and socialists who were opposed to Bolshevik rule made its way to Rostov-on-Don in the south to join the three thousand tsarist officers who had fled after the October Revolution. Called the volunteer army, they recruited soldiers locally in the areas where they fought. But, with so many ambitious generals and politicians, there was no unity of purpose or command. Other White armies were formed in the Volga area, in Siberia and in the north.

Initially, the Red Army too consisted of volunteers, but it was similarly ill-equipped and ill-disciplined. At the time of the

## The Polish Dream

Independent Poland had been born at the end of the First World War out of the collapse of Russia, Germany and Austro-Hungary. Under Head of State Joseph Piludski, Poland was determined to push back her frontiers to include estates that had been lost at the end of the eighteenth century. Piludski dreamed of a chain of independent buffer states with the Ukraine as the central link, to minimize the Soviet threat. The White Army was deaf to such ideas, which would have reduced the Empire to a Muscovy rump. By 1920 the Whites had been driven back to the Black Sea, and Piludski decided to invade.

An agreement was made with the Ukrainian Nationalist, Petlyura, in which Piludski would support a Ukrainian nationalist regime if Poland's territory in the Ukraine were returned. The alliance was initally successful, with Polish and Ukrainian troops capturing Kiev, but the advance had overstretched the hastily improvised army of Piludski. Kiev was re-captured by the Red Army and the Poles were pushed back to the Vistula. This time the Bolsheviks were overstretched,

Trotsky did not follow the Russian leaders' belief that the Poles would hail the Red Army as their liberators. In this poster he is crushing Polish reactionaries.

and by October 1920 they were routed from an advance on Warsaw. Both sides were now ready for peace. The Treaty of Riga was signed the following

year, in which Poland retained large areas of disputed territory, but lost the Western Ukraine and Belorussia. Her borders were to remain fixed until 1939.

# The Revolutionary Civil Wars 1919-22

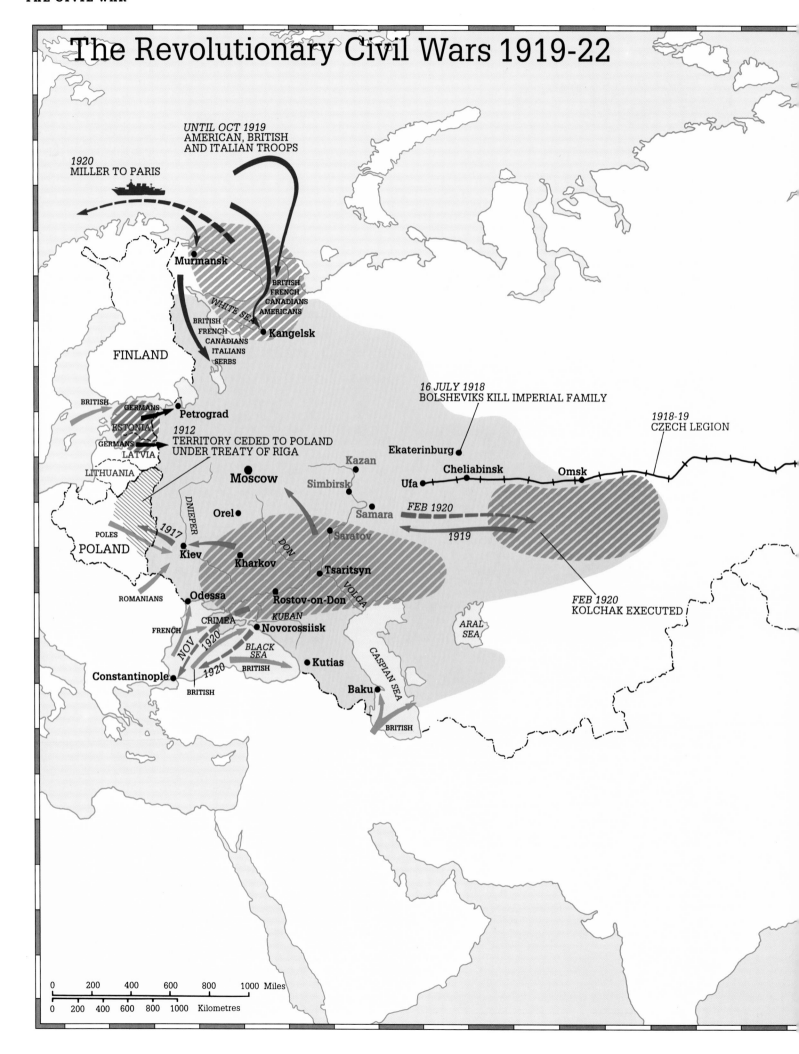

*UNTIL OCT 1919*
AMERICAN, BRITISH
AND ITALIAN TROOPS

*1920*
MILLER TO PARIS

**Murmansk**

*WHITE SEA*

BRITISH
FRENCH
CANADIANS
AMERICANS

BRITISH
FRENCH
CANADIANS
ITALIANS
SERBS

**Kangelsk**

FINLAND

BRITISH

GERMANS

ESTONIA

**Petrograd**

*16 JULY 1918*
BOLSHEVIKS KILL IMPERIAL FAMILY

*1918-19*
CZECH LEGION

GERMANS

LATVIA

LITHUANIA

*1912*
TERRITORY CEDED TO POLAND
UNDER TREATY OF RIGA

**Ekaterinburg**

**Cheliabinsk**

**Omsk**

*Kazan*

**Moscow**

*Simbirsk*

**Ufa**

*DNIEPER*

**Orel**

*Samara*

*FEB 1920*

*1917*

*Saratov*

*1919*

POLES

POLAND

**Kiev**

**Kharkov**

*DON*

**Tsaritsyn**

*FEB 1920*
KOLCHAK EXECUTED

ROMANIANS

**Odessa**

*VOLGA*

**Rostov-on-Don**

*ARAL
SEA*

*KUBAN*

CRIMEA

FRENCH

*NOV
1920*

**Novorossiisk**

*BLACK
SEA*

*NOV
1920*

BRITISH

**Kutias**

*CASPIAN
SEA*

**Constantinople**

BRITISH

**Baku**

BRITISH

0   200   400   600   800   1000 Miles

0   200   400   600   800   1000   Kilometres

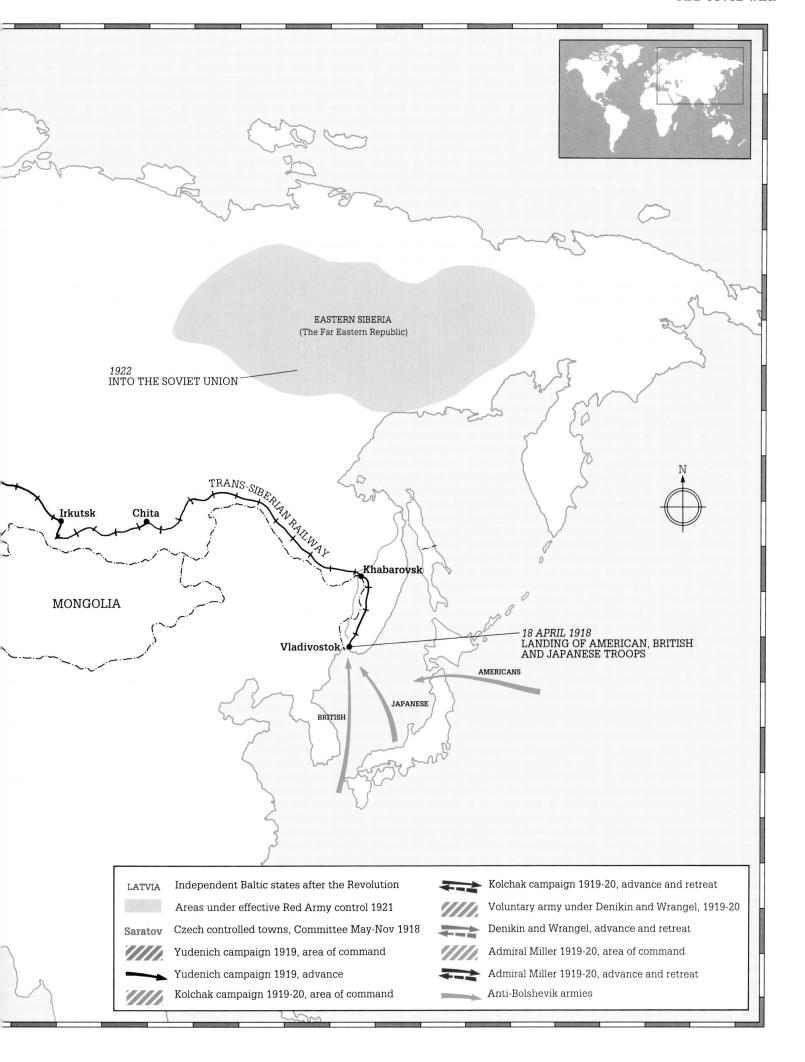

EASTERN SIBERIA
(The Far Eastern Republic)

*1922*
INTO THE SOVIET UNION

TRANS-SIBERIAN RAILWAY

Irkutsk    Chita

MONGOLIA

Khabarovsk

N

Vladivostok

*18 APRIL 1918*
LANDING OF AMERICAN, BRITISH
AND JAPANESE TROOPS

AMERICANS

JAPANESE

BRITISH

| LATVIA | Independent Baltic states after the Revolution | | Kolchak campaign 1919-20, advance and retreat |
|---|---|---|---|
| | Areas under effective Red Army control 1921 | | Voluntary army under Denikin and Wrangel, 1919-20 |
| **Saratov** | Czech controlled towns, Committee May-Nov 1918 | | Denikin and Wrangel, advance and retreat |
| | Yudenich campaign 1919, area of command | | Admiral Miller 1919-20, area of command |
| | Yudenich campaign 1919, advance | | Admiral Miller 1919-20, advance and retreat |
| | Kolchak campaign 1919-20, area of command | | Anti-Bolshevik armies |

Trotsky reviewing troops of the Red Army during the Civil War. Initially ill-disciplined and badly equipped, the Red Army became a powerful military organization under Trotsky's leadership. After he introduced conscription the army grew from 7,000 soldiers to some 5 million in three years.

Revolution there had only been seven thousand Red Guards but in April 1918 Trotsky became Commissar for War and started to create an army from scratch. He introduced conscription and compulsory military training for all people aged between eighteen and forty. Under him, discipline was tightened, ranks were reintroduced and the election of officers terminated. Former tsarist officers were re-employed - to such an extent that, in 1918, more than three-quarters of the officers in the Red Army had served the old regime. The Bolsheviks had by now abandoned their original antipathy to a standing army, and by 1920 there were 5 million men under arms.

Complicating the war, but not influencing its outcome, was the intervention of the Allied forces. In April 1918 Japanese and British forces landed in Vladivostok. They were joined in August by American forces. With the exception of one British battalion in Omsk, however, and a few Japanese forces at Lake Baikal, most of the soldiers remained at the coast and were not involved in combat, nor did they become involved in the tangled politics of the conflict.

On 13 April 1918 Trotsky's ill-fed Red Army defeated the volunteers under General Kornilov, and for a while the Bolsheviks believed they had settled the Civil War. In fact it had hardly begun.

### The Civil War

In the spring and summer of 1918 the White armies had a string of successes. In May the Bolsheviks tried to disarm Czech soldiers who were travelling on the Trans-Siberian Railway. Within two weeks, the Czechs had taken several major towns and were soon in control of the whole of the line. As they moved eastwards across Siberia from Cheliabinsk to Vladivostok, they gave assistance to anti-Bolshevik forces. These forces then moved back westwards towards the Volga, capturing Kazan, Simbirsk and Samara, where on 8 June they helped the local Socialist Revolutionaries to overthrow the Bolsheviks and set up a rival government, called the Committee of Members of the Constituent Assembly. It was while the White forces were besieging Ekaterinburg (now Sverdlovsk) that the Bolsheviks executed the Tsar and his family, who were held captive there, claiming that they needed to eliminate this powerful rallying symbol of the White Army.

With the Whites at Kazan, only a few hundred miles east of Moscow, another threat to the Bolsheviks came from the south. In April 1918 General Denikin had taken over command of the volunteer army and withdrawn his forces from Rostov-on-Don to the River Kuban on the Black Sea. Supported by General Krasnov, the new leader of the Don Cossacks, he began to march north in June, aiming to join forces with the White Army which was moving west from Siberia. Within three weeks he had swept the Bolsheviks from the whole of the North Caucasus area. By the late summer, it seemed as if the defeat of the Red Army was only weeks away. But on 10 September, Kazan was recaptured and Simbirsk, Lenin's birthplace, fell two days later. For Lenin, who was recovering from an attempt on his life, the seizure of Simbirsk was 'the most health-giving and best bandage for my wounds'. In October, Stalin prevented the Whites from taking Tsaritsyn (renamed Stalingrad in 1942 to honour his achievement). Admiral Kolchak, who had proclaimed himself leader of the various anti-Bolshevik groups in Siberia and supreme leader of all Russia, was foiled in his attempt to meet up with Denikin's troops from the south, and was forced to retreat.In 1919 Kolchak regrouped and advanced on Moscow from Omsk with 120,000 men - only to be driven back by the Red Army. In May, however, General Denikin

## Nestor Makhno and the Ukraine

Of all the theatres of war during this period, the Ukraine was the most important and the most complex. It lay between the Bolshevik's area of control in the north, and the White strongholds in the south. Furthermore, most of the Empire's mineral wealth was here, and the rich black soil yielded most of the grain for the whole country. The Bolsheviks were naturally unwilling to grant independence to such a favoured region. There was no certainty that an independent Ukrainian government would allow fighting armies criss-crossing its land.

Under the terms of the Brest Litovsk treaty of March 1918 much of the Ukraine had been ceded to Germany. When the Central powers collapsed, French forces landed at Odessa and left-wing nationalists briefly took control. In February 1919, the Red Army captured Kiev, which prompted the French to withdraw from Odessa.
The struggle for power in the Ukraine was far from over, however.

Rivals for political power in the region included left- and right-wing nationalists, and numerous groups of anarchists. Some groups were little more than robber bands, terrorizing the countryside, while others were more tightly organized. One of the most formidable was led by the anarchist Nestor Makhno.

Nestor Makhno was one of the most extraordinary characters of the Civil War. He was an eastern Ukrainian peasant who became an anarchist, and was jailed for his activities. After the February Revolution he was released from life imprisonment and organized a group of Partisans to fight against General Skoropadsky, the German puppet governor of the Ukraine. True to his anarchist principles, he was opposed to all state authority. His commanders were all elected, and anyone wanting to join his forces was accepted without reservation.

Suprisingly in the light of such principles, his movement was very disciplined, and grew to a formidable and well-organized army of around 40,000 men. In the areas under his control, the basic form of social organiz-ation was local self-administration by peasant and worker soviets. The idea was that local soviets would federate on a local, regional and national level, but supreme power would remain local.

There were times when Makhno controlled extensive parts of the Ukraine, fighting alternatively for or against the Bolsheviks with the slogan, 'Beat the Whites until they're red, beat the Reds until they're black!'

Denikin's defeat was due almost as much to Makhno's forces as to the Red Army. However, Makhno refused to incorporate his men into the Red Army, or to subject himself to Bolshevik rule. In August 1921 he abandoned Russia and crossed the frontier into Romania with the tatters of his forces. Like many Russian exiles, Nestor Makhno eventually settled in Paris, where he died in abject poverty in 1944.

A Russian poster of the 1920s. Agitational art (agit-prop) posters appeared on the streets to inform and educate a semi-literate population.

The German artist Käthe Kollwitz responded to the Russian call for help during the drought in the Volga Basin in 1921 by producing this stirring poster 'Help Russia' to encourage aid.

War was won, and the unsuccessful attack on the Red Army in June 1920 by Denikin's successor, General Wrangel, was little more than an epilogue.

Throughout the war, the White forces had been divided by more than political differences. They were also separated by thousands of miles, with Kolchak in Siberia, Denikin in the south and Yudenich in Estonia. The strength of the Red Army lay in its ability to control the centre, countering one thrust from the periphery before shifting its forces to counter the next. Although they came very close to it in the summer of 1918 and in October 1919, the White forces never quite succeeded in converging.

## The Forging of the Soviet State

Profoundly modified by the Civil War, which had encouraged the development of a monolithic state, Russian socialism was becoming increasingly remote from the notions of a socialist society sketched out by

Marx and Engels. In particular, there was the economic system that Lenin established soon after his seizure of power. War Communism, as it was known, was a means of mobilizing the resources of the state very quickly in order to cope with the demands of war. Free enterprise was abolished; and land, banks, shipping and foreign trade were all nationalized; by 1920 all factories employing more than ten workers were nationalized too. To deal with the shortages brought on by war a food commissariat was established, which requisitioned grain from the richer peasants and distributed it to the towns. As Lenin admitted, 'To get bread - that is the basis of socialism today.'

Another aspect of increasing state control was the institution of the Red Terror. In July 1918, the Left Socialist Revolutionaries, who had objected so vehemently to the peace treaty with Germany, rose against the Bolsheviks. On 6 July they assassinated Count Mirbach, the German ambassador, in the hope of precipitating a war between Germany and Russia; later the same day they occupied the main post office in Moscow, only to surrender shortly afterwards. Then, in September, a Socialist Revolutionary called Fanny Kaplan very nearly succeeded in assassinating Lenin.

The main effect of these events was to intensify the suppression of political opposition. From a position of initial tolerance towards opponents, the Bolsheviks became increasingly ruthless. Felix Dzerzhinsky, the head of the secret police or Cheka, who had been arrested briefly by the Socialist Revolutionaries during their insurrection, claimed on his release that 'We exist on a basis of organized terror, which is an absolutely essential element in revolution.' In 1922 the Cheka reported that it had carried out 12,733 executions between 1918 and 1922.

advanced northwards again, seizing Kiev, Kharkov and Odessa and gaining control of much of the Ukraine. In October he captured the town of Orel and was within about 200 miles of Moscow. The third threat came from the north-west where, in May, General Yudenich regrouped the anti-Bolshevik forces in Estonia. His advance on Petrograd was at first very successful, and by October, his forces were close enough to the city to see the dome of St Isaac's cathedral. Then, just as it seemed that the Soviets were about to lose both Petrograd and Moscow, Trotsky returned to save the capital. 'Like fresh reinforcements arriving ... Trotsky's presence on the spot at once showed itself,' wrote one eye-witness. General Yudenich himself described the Red Army fighting back with 'heroic madness'.

By the end of the year the Whites were in retreat on all fronts. General Yudenich's army no longer existed; General Denikin, who had been driven out of Orel, was attempting in vain to defend Rostov-on-Don; and Admiral Kolchak, the supreme leader of all Russia, was a prisoner of the Bolsheviks. The Civil

Lenin's funeral procession in Red Square, Moscow, January 1924. The struggle for power had devloped during Lenin's illness in 1922. Stalin, always the master tactician, stage-managed the funeral and went on to win control of the party machine.

# Europe: The Lights That Failed

The badge of an officail of the OGPU (the State Security Agency), dating from 1927. The portrait in the middle is of Felix Dzerzhinsky, the head of the Cheka or Russian Secret Police.

By the beginning of 1917, the war of attrition being waged in Europe was exhausting civilians as well as soldiers. Russia was on the brink of collapse. Britain had abandoned its traditional *laissez-faire* attitudes and was being run by directives issued from a war cabinet of five men. The French army, after the butchery of the Battle of Verdun, was lurching towards a mutiny which would eventually affect fifty-four divisions. In Germany, the Allied blockade was causing widespread malnutrition, as the German Crown Prince pointed out in his memoirs:

As early as the beginning of the year 1917... war-weariness was already very great. I also saw a great and menacing change in the streets of Berlin. Their characteristic feature had gone; the contented face of the middle-class man had vanished; the honest hard-working hourgeoisie, the clerk and his wife and children, slunk through the streets, hollow-eyed, lantern-jawed, pale-faced and clad in threadbare clothing that had become too wide for their shrunken limbs. Side by side with them jostled the puffed-up profiteer and all the other rogues.

The stress of confronting the political realities of the war had merely emphasized the long-held differences of political perspective among German Social Democrats. By 1917 they had split into three factions. To the left was a small revolutionary group led by Karl (son of Wilhelm) Liebknecht

and Rosa Luxemburg. Their uncompromising stand against the war had already led to prison sentences. Until January 1916 they were known as the International Group; after that date they were called the Spartacists, after the slave uprising against the Romans. In the middle were the parliamentary radicals who had been driven by their consciences to vote against a war loan in the Reichstag at the end of 1915 - for which they had been ostracized by the rest of the party. As anger over the conduct of the war grew, this group gradually increased in number until, at the beginning of 1917, they broke away and formed their own Independent Social Democratic Party. Within three months they claimed 120,000 members, which meant that they had almost as many active supporters as the third group - the rump of the Social Democrats whom Lenin called the 'social patriots'.

The effect on socialists everywhere of the abdication of the Tsar and the inauguration of a new regime in Russia during March 1917 was electric. The British Prime Minister of the time, David Lloyd George, later wrote, 'The shock that came from Petrograd passed through every workshop and mine.'
The example of the Russian soviets undoubtedly had its effect in Germany, where unrest was spreading. Riots and looting broke out in Königsberg in May 1917.

Only weeks later, a further cut in the bread ration provoked serious strikes in Berlin, Leipzig, Magdeburg, Halle and Braunschweig, involving about three hundred thousand workers. In Leipzig the strike was organized by a workers' council, the first such council to appear in Germany and an obvious link with Petrograd.

Although the Independents had taken no part in launching these strikes, individual members of the group lent their assistance in prolonging them.

The members of the SPD and the official trade union leaders, on the other hand, refused to condone such a threat to the war effort. Philipp Scheidemann, the former co-chairman of the party and a future prime minister, called them, rather oddly, 'a most serious danger to peace'.

Now that the radical wing of the socialists had decamped to form its own organization, the SPD's desire for respectability could flourish without being constantly reminded of its radical past. Such revisionism was made explicit at the party's first war-time congress, held at Wurzburg in October 1917. August Winnig, a trade unionist from Hamburg, suggested: 'It was our historical error to

believe before the war ... that we should achieve something through a revolutionary ideology. A working class whose progress is guaranteed by organizational and parliamentary work will never let itself be persuaded to risk a revolution.'

## Countdown to Chaos

The autumn of 1917 witnessed the complete collapse of the Russian war effort, the success of the Bolsheviks' bid for power and their arrival at the peace negotiations with Germany in Brest Litovsk just before Christmas. When it became obvious that the German government was trying to impose a punitive settlement, the indignation of radical shop stewards in Berlin led them to organize a strike which called for a fair treaty and a universal franchise in the country. On 28 January four hundred thousand workers downed tools. They were followed by a further hundred thousand the next day. Although the Berliners remained solid, sympathetic action in the rest of the country was sporadic and the action was called off after a week. When the harsh Brest Litovsk Treaty was sent to the Reichstag for ratification, four members of the SPD voted for it. The rest either abstained or absented themselves for, although they could not disregard German working-class opinion, they did not wish to offend the government or the military authorities.

With American troops pouring on to the European battlefields, but with only one front to contest, the German High Command under General von Ludendorff made one last desperate effort to break through on the Western Front before being outnumbered. Although the Germans forced the British and French to retreat, no decisive advantage was gained. On 8 and 14 August, separate attacks by the French and the British using large formations of tanks - a new tactic invented by the British - shattered the German lines. The stalemate was at an end and the German army was soon in full retreat.

The effect of these defeats on both military and civilian morale was catastrophic. In September, Ludendorff lost his nerve and told the Kaiser and his advisers that the army needed an armistice within twenty-four hours in order to avoid a disaster; he also advised that a broader-based government was necessary. Chancellor von Hertling was forced to resign and was replaced by a liberal aristocrat, Prince Max of Baden, who was supported by a coalition which included two leaders of the SPD.

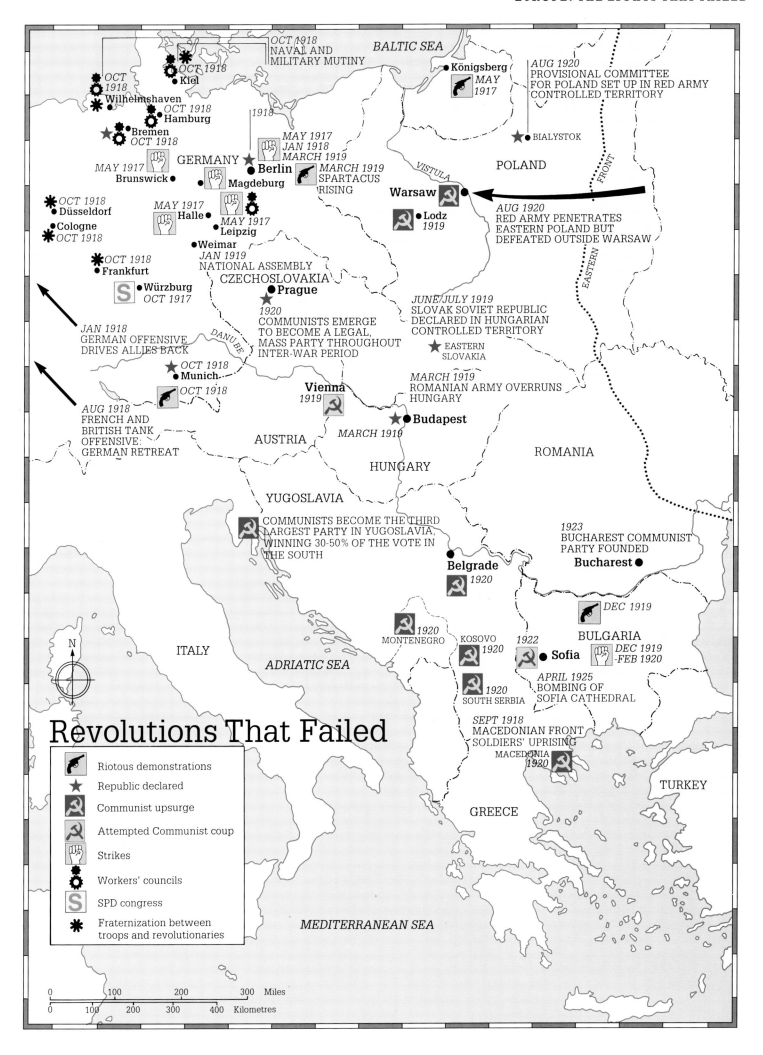

# Revolutions That Failed

*OCT 1918*
NAVAL AND
MILITARY MUTINY

*OCT 1918*
*OCT 1918*
Kiel

*OCT 1918*
Wilhelmshaven

*OCT 1918*
Hamburg

*1918*

Bremen
*OCT 1918*

**Königsberg**
*MAY 1917*

*AUG 1920*
PROVISIONAL COMMITTEE
FOR POLAND SET UP IN RED ARMY
CONTROLLED TERRITORY

BIALYSTOK

*MAY 1917*
GERMANY
*MAY 1917*
JAN 1918
MARCH 1919
**Berlin**

Brunswick

Magdeburg
*MARCH 1919*
SPARTACUS
RISING

POLAND

**Warsaw**

*AUG 1920*
RED ARMY PENETRATES
EASTERN POLAND BUT
DEFEATED OUTSIDE WARSAW

*OCT 1918*
Düsseldorf

*MAY 1917*
Halle

Cologne
*OCT 1918*

*MAY 1917*
Leipzig

Lodz
*1919*

Weimar

*OCT 1918*
Frankfurt

*JAN 1919*
NATIONAL ASSEMBLY
CZECHOSLOVAKIA

**Prague**

*JUNE/JULY 1919*
SLOVAK SOVIET REPUBLIC
DECLARED IN HUNGARIAN
CONTROLLED TERRITORY

S Würzburg
*OCT 1917*

*1920*
COMMUNISTS EMERGE
TO BECOME A LEGAL,
MASS PARTY THROUGHOUT
INTER-WAR PERIOD

EASTERN
SLOVAKIA

*JAN 1918*
GERMAN OFFENSIVE
DRIVES ALLIES BACK

DANUBE

*OCT 1918*
Munich

*OCT 1918*

**Vienna**
*1919*

*MARCH 1919*
ROMANIAN ARMY OVERRUNS
HUNGARY

*AUG 1918*
FRENCH AND
BRITISH TANK
OFFENSIVE:
GERMAN RETREAT

AUSTRIA

**Budapest**

*MARCH 1919*

HUNGARY

ROMANIA

YUGOSLAVIA

COMMUNISTS BECOME THE THIRD
LARGEST PARTY IN YUGOSLAVIA,
WINNING 30-50% OF THE VOTE IN
THE SOUTH

Belgrade
*1920*

*1923*
BUCHAREST COMMUNIST
PARTY FOUNDED
**Bucharest**

ITALY

*1920*
MONTENEGRO

KOSOVO
*1920*

*1922*

*DEC 1919*

BULGARIA

ADRIATIC SEA

**Sofia**

*DEC 1919*
-FEB 1920*

*1920*
SOUTH SERBIA

*APRIL 1925*
BOMBING OF
SOFIA CATHEDRAL

*SEPT 1918*
MACEDONIAN FRONT
SOLDIERS' UPRISING

MACEDONIA
*1920*

TURKEY

GREECE

MEDITERRANEAN SEA

N

### Legend

|  |  |
|--------|-------------|
| 🔫 | Riotous demonstrations |
| ★ | Republic declared |
| ☭ | Communist upsurge |
| ☭ | Attempted Communist coup |
| ✊ | Strikes |
| ⚙ | Workers' councils |
| S | SPD congress |
| ✳ | Fraternization between troops and revolutionaries |

0    100    200    300   Miles

0   100   200   300   400   Kilometres

# Rosa Luxemburg

Rosa Luxemburg at a Spartacus League rally. The Spartacists joined the German Communist Party in December 1918. Luxemburg and Karl Liebknecht were killed during the Berlin Revolt of 1919.

Rosa Luxemburg was born in 1871 in eastern Poland but moved to Germany in 1898 so that she could throw herself into the fight for socialism. Her intellectual gifts brought her success as a speaker and a writer. In 1906 she published a pamphlet, *The Mass Strike,* which analysed this weapon and demonstrated how its use had been refined in Russia between 1895 and 1905. In 1913, her book *Accumulation of Capital* extended Marxist analysis of imperialism and consolidated her position as Germany's leading left-wing theoretician.

Early in 1914, her criticism of the army and the Kaiser landed her in court. She was sentenced to a year in prison but allowed bail pending an appeal. This, failed and she was imprisoned the following year. Released in February in 1916, she was taken into 'protective custody' within months and remained in jail until after the end of the war.

Released in November 1918, she immediately joined Karl Liebknecht and the Spartacist radicals. This group, who were to turn themselves into the German Communist Party, were led by those who could speak well but lacked organiz-ational ability. Rosa realized this and her analysis in *Rote Fahne*, the group's daily newspaper, published shortly before she was murdered, remains the accepted judgement on the reasons for the failure of the January 1919 rising in Berlin.

Negotiations over an armistice were conducted by letter between the Prince and the American President, Woodrow Wilson, but the Kaiser refused to accede to the demand that he abdicate.

On 28 October, the admirals ordered the battleships of the German fleet that were anchored at Kiel and Wilhelmshaven make a suicidal attack on the British navy. With peace negotiations in the wind, the sailors refused to move. Although they were arrested, the mood spread ashore and sailors began making republican speeches. Troops sent to suppress the trouble went over to the rebels and, on 3 November, sailors' councils were elected and the red flag was run up.

The leadership of the SPD now saw its opportunity to prove how useful it could be to the establishment. It despatched Gustav Noske, soon to become the German Defence Minister, to placate the sailors. However, the news of what had happened in Kiel inspired others and, by 6 November, the ports of Bremen and Hamburg were controlled by workers' and soldiers' councils. The following day a crowd of fifty thousand strode through conservative Munich led by Kurt Eisner,

a fiery Independent, and pro-claimed a Bavarian republic. Cities all over Germany followed the same path, as soldiers and police fraternized with the revolutionaries. In Berlin, on the morning of 9 November, Prince Max resigned as Chancellor and forced the Kaiser to abdicate as well. Friedrich Ebert, the leader of the SPD, replaced the Prince and the party were at last in the seat of power. That afternoon, Scheidemann proclaimed the establishment of the republic from the balcony of the Reichstag. Two hours later the red flag was raised over the royal palace by Karl Liebknecht, the Spartacist leader.

## The High Tide of Revolution

The SPD and the Independents immediately agreed to co-operate to form a government of six commissars, with three from each party. The arrangement was confirmed by a large meeting of workers' and soldiers' representatives the next morning. This, in turn, elected fourteen soldiers and fourteen workers to be the executive committee of the revolution. That evening Ebert came to an

arrangement with the army which would allow the orderly retreat to German territory decreed by the armistice. At first the High Command agreed to recognize the soldiers' councils, but as the days passed they made a concerted effort to erode their power. Germany might have possessed the trappings of a revolution, but beneath the surface the established framework of the civil service, the army and the major industrialists survived.

The six commissars were confronted by enormous changes which had to be implemented at breakneck speed. Millions of men needed to be demobilized and integrated into an economy which was already in tatters. On 12 November they made a start by abolishing martial law and censorship, re-establishing pre-war industrial laws, implementing the eight-hour day, the secret ballot and universal suffrage for all citizens over the age of twenty.

Three days later the unions came to an important agreement with the employers' organization, which the Spartacists denounced as a betrayal of the revolution.

## A Bloody End in Berlin

The first response by the right wing came on 6 December. Some senior Foreign Office officials paid a group of thirty soldiers to invade a meeting of the twenty-eight-strong Executive Committee of the revolution and arrest them in the name of the government. One member resolutely chased them off, but a few hours later another group of soldiers invaded the Chancellery to proclaim Ebert president - a move which would discredit him in the eyes of the left. When a meeting of Spartacists, which was being held in the north of Berlin, heard rumours of these events, they immediately marched on the centre of the city. Their route was barred by troops loyal to the government and, when someone in the crowd fired a shot, the soldiers panicked and unleashed a burst of machine-gun fire which killed sixteen Spartacists. Although the instigators of this cruel farce were later caught, its object of releasing the potential for conflict among the socialists was effective and the Spartacists never trusted Ebert again.

Ten days later, a congress of representatives of the workers' and soldiers' councils was convened in Berlin. It voted overwhelmingly for parliamentary democracy and against the Spartacists' demands for a dictatorship of the proletariat. The revolutionary left seemed to be losing ground to their more moderate comrades.

On 23 December another farcical incident occurred which precipitated the tragic climax of the German revolution. About a thousand sailors from Kiel, who were camped in the royal palace, were asked to leave by the government. They agreed on condition that they receive all the back pay owing to them. But when confusion arose over handing back the keys to the palace, they surrounded the Chancellery and cut its

A procession of armed members of the Spartacus League prepare to confront and fight the Freikorps in Berlin, January 1919.

Spartacist sympathizers protect themselves behind barricades made from rolls of newspaper during the street-fighting in Berlin.

telephone lines. Troops arrived that night to defend the government ministers and began firing artillery shells into the royal palace where the sailors had returned. Ebert was horrified and a ceasefire was arranged. But the damage to the Chancellor's reputation had been done, and the three Independent members of the cabinet resigned.

The only Independent remaining in a prominent position was Emil Eichhorn, Berlin's chief of police. After he had tried to intercede on behalf of the sailors on 24 December, the state authorities, who were all members of the SPD, decided to sack him: this decision was announced on 3 January. Two days later seven hundred thousand people took to the streets in protest at the decision and the group of shop stewards who had organized the strike a year before called for the people to rise and depose the government. They were joined by the Spartacists, despite Rosa Luxemburg's misgivings, but few other groups were prepared to fight.

The government decided to use the volunteer groups of ex- officers and NCOs, the Freikorps, to supress the roving bands of armed but ineffectual militant left-wingers who were roaming the streets of Berlin. This disciplined but ultra right-wing force soon scattered the opposition through an indiscriminate use of force. On 13 January the leaders of the Spartacists, Luxemburg and Liebknecht, were found and handed over to the Freikorps. Their heads were smashed in with rifle butts and then they were shot, and their bodies thrown into the river. Those who had perpetrated the murders were tried by military courts, only to have the charges quashed. Some went on to achieve high office under Hitler.

### The Final Judgement

Lacking popular support or the determined organization which had taken power in Russia, other self-proclaimed socialist republics in Bremen and Bavaria soon faded out. An adverse election result in Munich pursuaded Kurt Eisner to accept the inevitable, but on the way to the new

assembly he was murdered by a demented monarchist. This outrage incensed the left in Berlin and a general strike was called on 2 March. Street-fighting broke out on a much larger scale than in January, and twelve hundred people died as the Freikorps were allowed to run rampant. The new national assembly, meanwhile, had been established in the city of Weimar to protect the delegates from the rioting in the capital.

Despite their bloody defeat in Berlin, Communists throughout Europe saw new hope in the establishment of a Soviet republic in Hungary in March 1919. Punitive demands from the victorious Allies had forced the Prime Minister of the provisional government to resign in favour of the socialist left wing; they then formed an alliance with the Communists whose leader, Béla Kun, proclaimed a Soviet republic. He went on to announce a programme of wholesale nationalization, the distribution of arms to the workers and the formation of his own Red army. But his attacks on religious

Cheers Noske! - the workers have been disarmed. Noske, the Social Democratic Minister of the Interior, living up to his acceptance speech: 'someone has to be the butcher'.

observance and failure to redistribute the large estates alienated the peasants, while the mismanagement of the economy and the liberal use of what he was pleased to call 'Red Terror' alienated all but his most devoted followers. What was left of his diminishing prestige vanished almost entirely as the Romanian army over-ran large areas of the country. After only 133 days the Hungarian Soviet state collapsed, although Kun escaped to Moscow where he became a member of the Comintern.

While it lasted, however, the temporary success of the Communists in Hungary inspired the left in other fragments of the former Austro-Hungarian Empire. But these ephemeral attempts at revolution were no more successful. More substantial was a *coup d'état* in Munich, which was also inspired by events in Hungary. A Soviet republic was proclaimed on 6 April, but those who controlled it lasted only a week. Then another, more determined group of revolutionaries emerged to arm the workers. But the city ran short of food and the arrival of the Freikorps spelled the end. As in Berlin, the streets were soon running with blood.

Several years later, one of the revolutionary trade union leaders from Berlin, Richard Muller, wrote a history of the unsuccessful German revolution. His judgement on its final stages in Munich might well be applied to many of those who became caught up in the events which followed Germany's defeat. 'The declaration of the Soviet republic [on 6 April] was nothing but miserable and unscrupulous play acting at revolution by political pushers and coffee-house scribblers, who became intoxicated by their own words and could not find their bearings in the confusion of revolutionary events.'

Lenin had held out great hopes for Germany, since its highly organized proletariat conformed to Marx's prescription for a pre-revolutionary situation. However, its failure only confirmed his belief, and that of his colleagues in Moscow, that a disciplined organization backed by a loyal army was the only way to win a revolution and successfully sustain it.

# Socialism in One Country

The wave of 1929 and 1930, the size of a good river Ob, drove a mere fifteen million peasants, maybe even more, out into the taiga and tundra. But peasants are a silent people, without a literary voice, nor do they write complaints and memoirs...this wave poured forth, sank down into the permafrost, and even our most active minds recall hardly a thing about it.

So wrote Alexander Solzhenitsyn in 1973 of the liquidation of the wealthier Russian peasants, known as kulaks, who perished in their millions on thousand-mile journeys to work camps or resettlement areas in the wilderness. This liquidation was part of a vast social experiment by which Stalin hoped to drag Russia into the industrial twentieth century. He achieved his goal, but at an incalculable human cost. It has been argued that Stalin's totalitarian dictatorship constituted a terrible perversion of the Marxist-Leninist tradition, a perversion which lasted for thirty-five years, destroyed an estimated 60 million lives, strangled the economy and stifled political development and the arts. It cast a shadow over the rest of the Eastern bloc, from which some countries have not yet emerged three decades after the death of its perpetrator.

### The Building of Soviet Russia

By the end of the Civil War, it had become clear that the Communists' hopes of spontaneous revolutions occurring across Europe would not be realized immediately. There seemed no alternative but to construct socialism in Russia alone.

More than six years of war and civil war had left the economy in ruins, making the immediate priority one of reconstruction. After the revolution, land had either been seized directly by the peasants or distributed among them by the village soviets; industry had been nationalized. The harsh exigencies of the Civil War had resulted in economic centralization and the forced requisitioning of food - Lenin's War Communism. This system was extremely unpopular with the peasants, who responded by sowing less grain. As a result, food shortages became even more acute; industrial output fell drastically and further aggravated the economic consequences of an Allied blockade.

In March 1921 sailors from the naval base at Kronstadt, which had provided some of the most loyal revolutionary shock troops in 1917, mutinied against the Bolsheviks. They demanded an end to the Bolshevik monopoly of power and more freedom for

Stalin and his daughter, Svetlana, visiting a farm in 1934. A few months later Sergei Kirov (centre), a potential rival, was assassinated. Svetlana herself, when an adult, defected to the West.

the workers and peasants. Although the rebellion was soon suppressed, Lenin realized the need to placate the peasants and to promote economic recovery. Under the New Economic Policy (NEP), the 'commanding heights' of the economy, such as transport, finance and mining, remained in the hands of the state, but a limited return to capitalism was permitted in trade, agriculture and small-scale manufacturing. The requisitioning of land was replaced by a graduated tax in kind, and peasants were allowed to sell off their surplus, to rent extra land and to employ labour.

### The Struggle for Power

As long as Lenin was alive, he was the undisputed leader of the Russian Communist Party. The Menshevik and Socialist Revolutionary parties had been increasingly harassed during the Civil War, and by 1922 they had ceased to exist. But, as opposition groups outside the Bolsheviks were suppressed, they began to proliferate within the party instead. This alarmed Lenin, who believed that such divisions demon-strated a weakness that could be exploited by enemies of the Soviet Union when the NEP was introduced. At the Tenth Party Congress, in 1921, Lenin persuaded his colleagues to

ban the formation of factions, on pain of expulsion from the party.

Although it represented a compromise of Bolshevik principles, the NEP was very successful for a time, allowing the economy to recover almost to pre-war levels. It did not, however, produce the rapid industrialization necessary for the Soviet Union to catch up with the rest of Europe. Furthermore, left-wing Bolsheviks believed that it favoured the peasants at the expense of the workers (the initials NEP, they said, stood for the 'New Exploitation of the Proletariat'). It seemed to be reintroducing many of the unwelcome phenomena of capitalism: social classes were reappearing, for example, and unemployment became common. When Lenin died, the question of whether the NEP should continue became a major issue in the struggle for his succession.

Lenin's 'Decree on Party Unity' was the instrument that enabled Stalin, then Commissar of Nationalities and one of five members of the ruling Politburo, to eliminate his rivals - first politically, then physically. By the time his political colleagues had begun to fear him, he was too powerful to dislodge. In his role as General Secretary of the Central Committee - a post to which he was appointed on 3 April - he controlled the agenda of the Politburo, and was also

*Opposite:* Covers of *USSR in Construction* from the 1930s. This propaganda magazine, issued in several languages, expounded the Soviet achievements in industrial growth during that period.

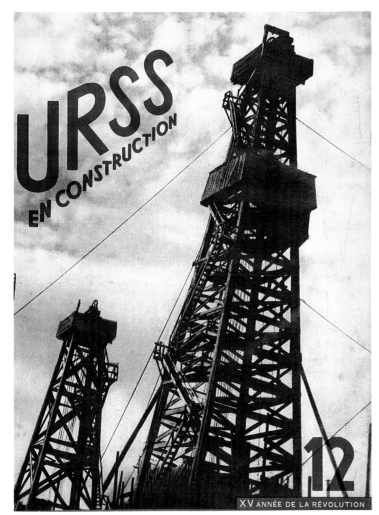

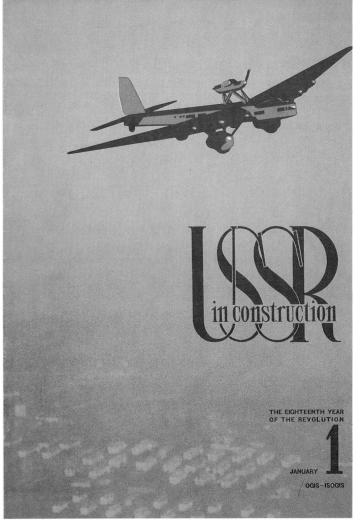

# The Soviet Union 1922-39

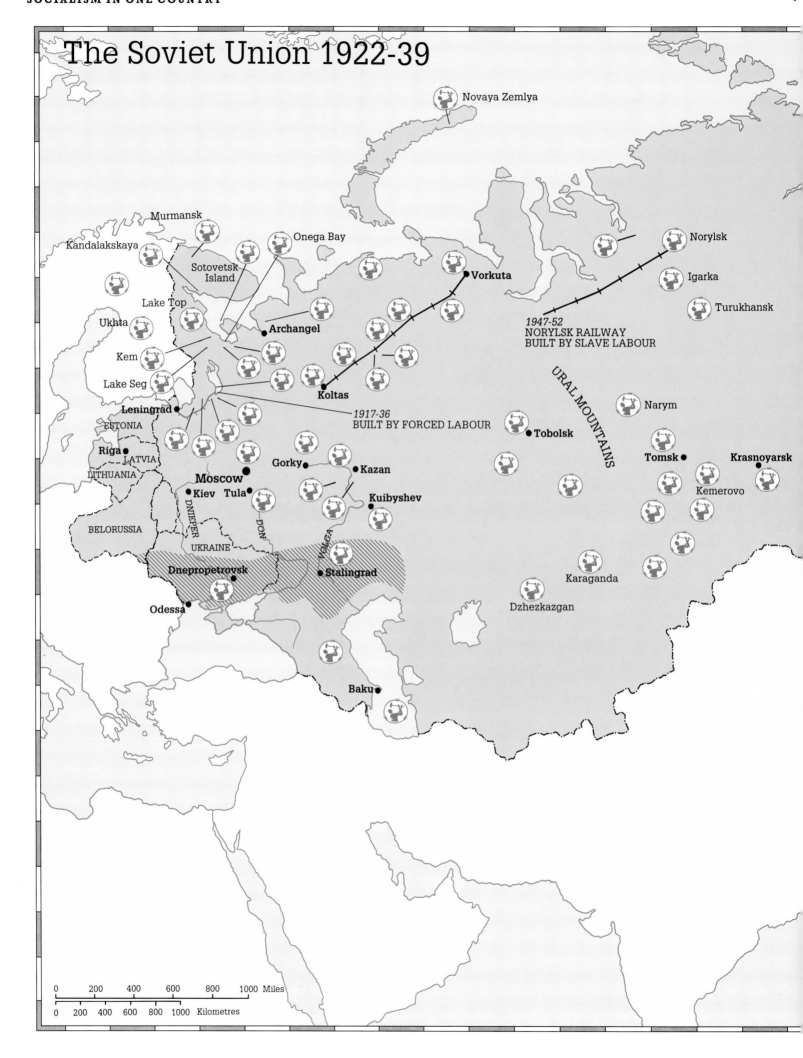

Novaya Zemlya

Murmansk

Kandalakskaya

Sotovetsk Island

Onega Bay

Lake Top

Ukhta

Kem

Lake Seg

**Archangel**

**Vorkuta**

**Norylsk**

Igarka

Turukhansk

*1947-52*
NORYLSK RAILWAY
BUILT BY SLAVE LABOUR

Koltas

*1917-36*
BUILT BY FORCED LABOUR

**Leningrad**

ESTONIA

**Riga**

LATVIA

LITHUANIA

**Moscow**

**Kiev** **Tula**

**Gorky**

**Kazan**

**Kuibyshev**

U R A L   M O U N T A I N S

Narym

**Tobolsk**

**Tomsk**

**Krasnoyarsk**

Kemerovo

BELORUSSIA

DNIEPER

DON

VOLGA

UKRAINE

**Dnepropetrovsk**

**Stalingrad**

Karaganda

**Odessa**

Dzhezkazgan

**Baku**

| 0 | 200 | 400 | 600 | 800 | 1000 Miles |

| 0 | 200 | 400 | 600 | 800 | 1000 Kilometres |

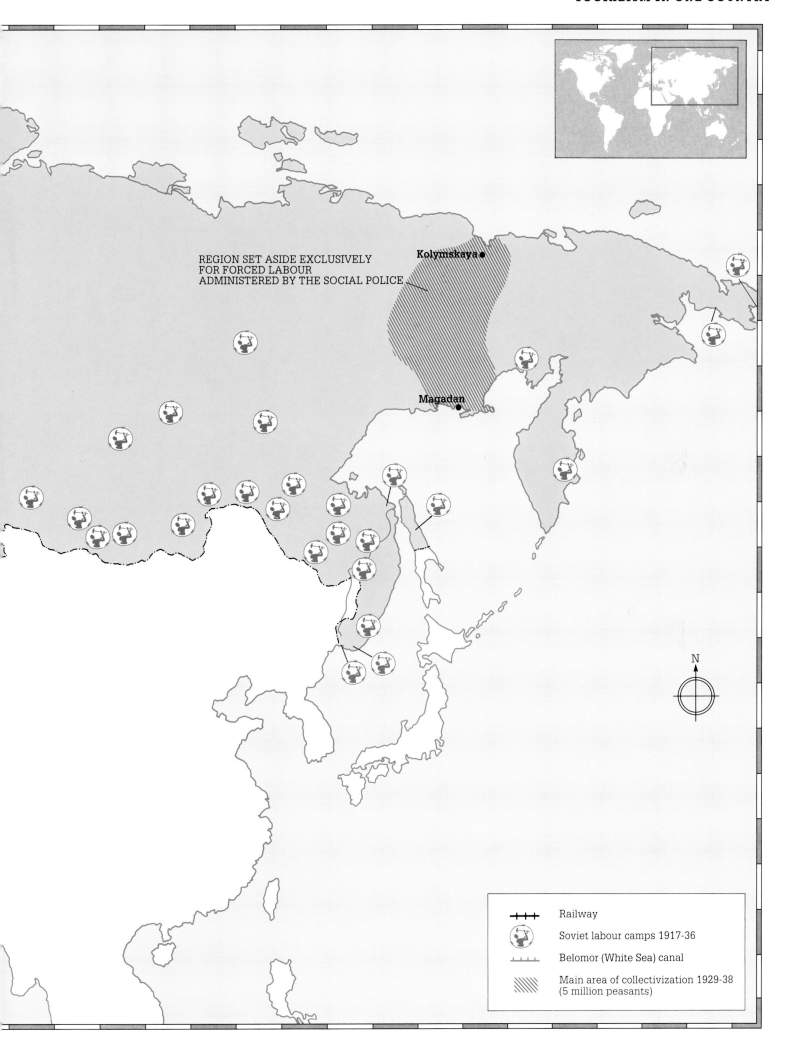

REGION SET ASIDE EXCLUSIVELY
FOR FORCED LABOUR
ADMINISTERED BY THE SOCIAL POLICE

Kolymskaya●

Magadan
●

N

Railway

Soviet labour camps 1917-36

Belomor (White Sea) canal

Main area of collectivization 1929-38
(5 million peasants)

responsible for the appointment, promotion and demotion of party functionaries; this enabled him to ensure that important posts were filled by his supporters. Less than two months after Stalin's appointment, Lenin suffered the first of several strokes which were gradually to remove him from the political scene. Nevertheless, after his second stroke in December 1922 he warned of Stalin's ambition: 'Comrade Stalin, having become General Secretary, has concentrated an enormous power in his hands; and I am not sure that he always knows how to use that power with sufficient caution.'

Despite these misgivings, Stalin was permitted to control so many of the levers of power that, during Lenin's lingering and ultimately fatal illness, he virtually ruled the country. In 1923 he had formed a coalition, or triumvirate, with Zinoviev and Kamenev against Trotsky. Lenin died on 21 January 1924 - to universal mourning. Through skilful stage management, Stalin made sure that he was at the forefront of the funeral ceremonies. For example, he was one of the leaders who carried Lenin's coffin and stood in the guard of honour at the bier.

Lenin had left neither a successor nor a means of choosing one. The first issue dividing the leading contenders - Stalin, Trotsky, Zinoviev, Kamenev and Bukharin - was whether socialism could be built in one country, or whether, as both Lenin and Trotsky had previously believed, the revolution had to be 'permanent' and spread geographically before socialism could be constructed in any one country. In the autumn of 1924, in a pamphlet entitled *Problems of Leninism*, Stalin contradicted an assertion he had made earlier in the year and claimed that a proletarian revolution could build socialism in one country: that the Russian Revolution was self-sufficient. Despite his superior intellectual gifts and organizational talents, Trotsky was an inferior tactician, possibly erring in underestimating Stalin's influence. When, in 1925, the Fourteenth Party Conference accepted the switch from traditional Bolshevism to national Communism, Trotsky, whose radical views were no longer fashionable, became increasingly isolated.

Stalin then turned against Zinoviev and Kamenev, who had begun to oppose the NEP and to fear the power Stalin had accumulated. They tried to form an alliance with Trotsky but the 'united opposition', as they were called, fell foul of the decree on party unity. All three lost their seats in the Politburo, and in 1927 they were expelled from the party. Zinoviev and Kamenev promptly recanted their views and, although reinstated into the party, became victims of Stalin's purges in the following decade. Trotsky was exiled to Alma Ata in Kazakhstan and then deported from the country in 1929. In 1940 he was murdered at his home in Mexico City by Stalin's agents, who drove an alpine axe through his skull.

For the moment, Stalin could declare: 'Now, at the end of 1927, in connection with

# Stakhanov and the Shock Brigades

During industrialization, labour productivity increased rapidly. Although harsh discipline was partly responsible (absenteeism was defined as one day's absence from work without an approved reason, and incurred dismissal), the rise in productivity was also the result of increasing use of machinery. However, 'shock brigades' also contributed to the success of the Five Year Plans, with party members announcing 'there are no fortresses the Bolsheviks cannot storm!'

The most famous 'shock worker' was Andrei Stakhanov, a coalminer in the Donbass. With the aid of two assistants, he allegedly hewed 102 tons of coal in a single shift in 1935, instead of the average seven tons. 'Stakhanovism' was enthusiastically taken up by the party to induce workers to increase productivity. Those who succeeded were rewarded with extra pay and better living conditions, while failure led to disgrace and punishment. Inevitably, standards were soon raised to reflect the achievements of Stakhanovism. This made such

Anatoly Shurikhin's photograph of Magnitka in the course of construction, 1932. It was one of the earliest industrial complexes of the first Five-Year Plan.

campaigns very unpopular and shock workers soon ran the risk of being beaten or even killed by their colleagues. After Stalin's death Stakhanovism fell into disrepute. Stakhanov died a lonely alcoholic in 1977, leaving a sceptical public to wonder whether he had ever achieved anything like the exceptional feats attributed to him in his youth.

new difficulties, the opposition have again begun to issue cuckoo cries of the "ruin" of the revolution... but you all see, comrades, that the revolution lives and flourishes, and it is certain other people who perish.'

## The Collectivization of Agriculture

In his campaign against the 'united opposition' Stalin was supported by the 'right-wingers' Bukharin, Rykov and Tomsky, who favoured a continuation of the NEP. However, once the 'left-wing' Bolsheviks had been defeated, Stalin decided to adopt some of their policies and to abandon the NEP. He then used the same tactics so successfully employed against the left to eliminate his own right-wing supporters.

In 1929, Stalin propelled Russia into her second major revolution. He imposed a series of highly centralized five-year economic plans aimed at building a heavy industrial base. By then, the peasants who had supported the Bolsheviks during the Civil War had begun to turn against them. The land redistribution programmes of 1917 had not, in fact, contributed to efficient agricultural production, and many small farms had reverted to subsistence cultivation. With the new economic policy, agricultural production increased, but many peasants refused to sell grain to the towns, partly in order to drive up the price. This led to a critical shortage and to Stalin's drastic remedy.

Rapid industrialization implied changes in agricultural policy. Part of the new industrial workforce had to come from the farming sector. And although this meant that fewer people were available to grow the food for the towns, they would have to supply even more than they had done before in order to create the surplus needed to invest in industry.

The way in which these aims were accomplished was by enforced collectivization. From 1928, farmers were forced to pool their resources and to work their land in common. The state set targets and prices, and compulsorily purchased most of what was produced. Though each collective farm household was allowed a small plot and some personal livestock for private cultivation, Soviet agriculture has still never recovered from the harm that collectivization inflicted.

As collectivization proceeded apace, Stalin embarked on the liquidation of the kulaks, or richer peasants. Because kulaks were said to be the 'sworn enemies of the collective farm movement', their property was appropriated and they were deported to remote parts of the country; millions died in transit or in exile. Among the victims were many non-kulak peasants of modest means. Rebellious villages were compelled to hand over their crops at gunpoint. Stalin justified the repression by calling it an unavoidable part of collectivization. 'When the head is off,' he claimed, 'one does not mourn the hair.'

The number of collectives rose from 4 per cent of all farm holdings in 1929 to 58 per cent at the end of March 1930. Many peasants reacted to this intrusion into their life and livelihood by slaughtering their livestock and destroying their grain and equipment; it has been estimated that, between 1929 and 1933, half of Russia's 34 million horses were killed. Alarmed by reports of the destruction and fearing that the peasants would refuse to sow summer crops, Stalin publicly blamed local officials for the speed and excesses of collectivization, accusing them of being 'dizzy with success', and the campaign came to a temporary halt in March 1930.

Within weeks, more than half the peasants had left the collectives. The campaign was renewed in the summer, however, and by the end of 1931, a quarter of a million collectives had been formed from 20 million individual farms.

The new farms were inefficient; the machinery and transport were inadequate, and the state often took an excessive quota of grain - including some that was intended for the peasants' personal consumption and seed grain for their animals. As a direct result, there was a terrible famine in 1932-3, in which about 6 million are estimated to have died from starvation or disease. Yet, no attempt was made to help those who were starving, and until the late 1980s the famine was never mentioned in the Soviet press.

### Forced Industrialization

In June 1930, over a year after the introduction of the first five-year plan, Stalin announced: 'We are on the eve of our transformation from an agrarian into an industrial country.' The essence of this and subsequent economic plans was, first, that all industrial production should be planned from the centre, and, second, that the attaining (or surpassing) of production targets should dominate the entire political and economic life of the Soviet Union.

The first plan, deemed to have been completed in four years at the end of 1932, concentrated on capital goods rather than consumer goods - a characteristic feature of the Soviet economy. The second plan (1933-37) consolidated and expanded the projects launched during the first - with such success that, unobserved by the outside world, Russia's industrial power was catching up with Germany's. By the time of the 'Great Patriotic War', which interrupted the third consecutive five-year plan (1938-42) in 1941, the annual growth rate was about 9 per cent and industrial output had trebled. The industrial workforce had grown from 4.3 million in 1928 to 11.6 million in 1937. Many new industries (some of them vital for defence) had been set up; traditional industrial areas such as Moscow, Leningrad, Donets Basin and the Urals had been expanded; and new ones had been established in formerly backward republics, such as Kazakhstan. In addition many prestige projects, such as the Moscow metro,

had been launched. In some ways, Russia had achieved in just over a decade what the industrialized nations of Europe had taken over two centuries to gain.

These achievements seemed all the more astonishing as the rest of the world was suffering a severe economic depression. Industrial growth, however, was achieved only at the cost of decreasing personal consumption - and hardship. During the course of this transformation, Stalin had departed even further from traditional Marxism than had Lenin; for whereas he shared with Marx and Lenin a belief in public ownership, he differed in the degree of force and human suffering that he was prepared to inflict in attaining it.

### The Purges

Although Stalin was in undisputed control of the party by 1930, his drive for absolute power was not yet satisfied. In fact he needed no lessons from Hitler - whose bloody purge of the Nazi Brown Shirts in 1934 impressed him - on how to be rid of ambitious subordinates. Soon he acted out on a grand scale a scenario he had outlined to Kamenev years before: 'To choose one's victim, to prepare one's plans minutely, to slake an implacable vengeance, and then to go to bed.'

In December 1934 Sergei Kirov, a rising star in the party and a potential rival, was assassinated - almost certainly at Stalin's instigation. Stalin used this as a pretext to eliminate past opponents and potential future rivals in the party, the army and the secret police. Most of the Bolshevik old guard, including Zinoviev, Kamenev, Rykov and Bukharin, were arrested, interrogated, exhibited at 'show trials', and sentenced either to death or to a lengthy sojourn in a labour camp after their 'confession' to crimes of which they were frequently innocent. Wave upon wave of arrests followed. Millions were executed, imprisoned without trial, tortured to obtain false confessions, or sentenced to decades in labour camps. In 1930 there were already some 750,000 in

the camps, working as forced labour for the security police; by 1941 the number had risen to an estimated 8 million.

No one was sacrosanct or safe, with the party itself particularly badly hit. Some 70 per cent of the Central Committee and over 90 per cent of the delegates to the Seventeenth Party Congress in 1934 did not reappear at the Eighteenth Congress in 1939, many having perished during the purges. The Red Army also suffered severely, the officer corps being virtually decimated. Ironically, among the last of the prominent 'victims' was the principal assassin, N.I. Ezhov, the chief of the secret police (NKVD), together with some of his chief henchmen. As Beria took charge of the NKVD all of his opponents fell at a stroke, including Kedrov, a retired Bolshevik, whose desperate letter from prison illustrated the complete incomprehension of the party faithful at such events: 'Boundless pain and sorrow press and convulse my heart. Neither the party nor the Soviet government will allow such a cruel and irremediable injustice to be committed.... I deeply believe that truth and justice will triumph. I believe, I believe.' Kedrov was exonerated by the Supreme Court, but Beria had him shot, nevertheless. By 1939, the wave of arrests and deportations had begun to abate. At the Eighteenth Party Congress Stalin declared there had been 'grave mistakes', but that 'its results, on the whole, were beneficial'.

Of all the cruel ironies of the 'great terror', three stand out. First, in 1936, the Soviet Union adopted the Stalin constitution, 'the most democratic constitution in the world', granting universal franchise. Second, the purges and show trials discredited the Soviet Union in the eyes of the world at the very time when Stalin was most intent on negotiating a collective security treaty against Nazi Germany. Third, when Hitler attacked the Soviet Union in June 1941, thousands of army officers and experts in military science gaoled on trumped-up charges during the purges, had to be released from labour camps in order to defend their country against its real enemies.

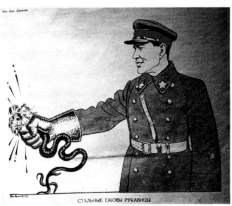

*Above: Yezhov's Steel Glove* by Efimov, 1938. During Yezhov's time as head of the secret police the terror of the purges was at its most intense. *Left:* In Boris Efimov's cartoon, *Fatherland* (1938), Trotsky (far right) and fellow defendants are eating from the Gestapo trough. They had been accused of being Gestapo agents.

# The Comintern

When the forty-four delegates to the first congress of the Communist International assembled in the Kremlin on 2 March 1919, they must have thought that their time had come. Their hosts were the leaders of the world's first successful proletarian revolution. A wave of strikes and revolutionary uprisings was already engulfing Germany, Austria, Hungary and Italy. Within weeks, Soviet republics were proclaimed in Budapest, on 21 March, and in Munich, on 7 April. In the middle of April, the French Black Sea Fleet mutinied. On 1 May, the streets of Paris were the scene of bloody fighting between socialist demonstrators and the police. This was followed by a series of bitter strikes in Leipzig, Eisenach and Erfurt. The Communist International, or Comintern, had good reason to proclaim: 'Before the year is out, the whole of Europe will be Soviet.'

The driving forces behind the foundation of the Comintern were, of course, Lenin and the Bolshevik leadership who hand-picked most of the delegates from among émigré groups in residence in Russia. They saw the organization as the revolutionary key to the political and economic upheavals which seemed about to overwhelm Europe. Schooled in the pre-revolutionary factional in-fighting of the radical left, they believed that the Comintern should be organized so that it could provide disciplined and determined revolutionary leadership - in contrast to the reformist labour and social democratic parties of the socialist Second International, which had capitulated to nationalistic pressures in the first days of war in 1914. Indeed, one of Lenin's aims in holding the congress, which proclaimed itself to be the Third International, was to counter the claims of the Second International, which was still trying to present itself as the voice of the left.

During February the rival organization had held a conference at Berne in Switzerland, which appeared to be a determined attempt to re-establish its pre-war position. However, the meeting was rent by recriminations against the German Social Democrats over their vote for war credits in 1914; many other parties, particularly the French, had seen this as a betrayal of the International's principles. Heated discussions on this topic, as well as a debate about events in Russia, hindered moves by the delegate parties to reassert their hegemony over the left, and the task of reconstructing the Second International in the post-war world was passed to a committee. This allowed Lenin to grab the initiative.

The civil war rages on as Lenin presides over the first meeting of the Communist International, or Comintern, in the Kremlin, 2 March 1919. The congress claimed to be the Third International, and its aim was to promote revolution throughout Europe.

The aims of the Bolshevik leadership were evident in the text of the Comintern's manifesto, written by Trotsky:

'If the First International predicted the future course of development and indicated the roads it would take, if the Second International rallied and organized millions of proletarians, then the Third International is the International of open mass struggle, the International of revolutionary realization, the International of Action.'

## The Years of Disappointment

These revolutionary expectations were quickly confounded. Germany's 1918 'November Revolution', which ousted the Kaiser, failed to develop beyond the stage of a democratic republic. The Soviet republic in Munich was easily crushed, as was a Communist-led uprising in Vienna two months later. The Soviet republic established in Hungary, under the leadership of Béla Kun, survived for only 133 days.

By the time of its second and much more representative congress in July-August 1920, all the Comintern had to show for its revolutionary efforts was a catalogue of defeats and a modest improvement in the motley band of left-wing representatives who had proclaimed its foundation the previous year. Of the 167 voting delegates, 40 per cent were Bolsheviks, while most of the rest represented only small revolutionary groups. Although there were important delegations from the French, Italian and German socialist movements, these were split into factions and many of their representatives were excluded from voting.

The second congress, like the first, was dominated by the Bolsheviks, whose credentials, as the only currently successful revolutionary party, were impeccable. As the source of the Comintern's money and organizational resources, and as the wielder of the biggest block of votes, their power was irresistible. After a succession of failures by other parties to take and retain power in various countries in recent months, the Moscow leadership was determined to foster the establishment of Communist parties in its own mould. That meant creating bodies of disciplined cadres which were politically and ideologically united, and organized according to Lenin's theory of democratic centralism. These would be parties which would readily accept Comintern - and hence Bolshevik - leadership and directives.

The bolshevization process began at the second congress with the promulgation of the 'Twenty-one Conditions for Admission to the Communist International'. Among these conditions was the stipulation that henceforth all affiliates to the Comintern had to accept its resolutions and decisions as binding. Equally important was the insistence that affiliates purge themselves of all 'reformist' and 'centrist' elements - that is, of everyone who disagreed with Bolshevik policy.

The focus of Moscow's hopes for revolution centred on Germany. Here the split with the Social Democrats had led to the emergence of a Communist Party with a mass membership and mass influence. Moreover, the country was still in a state of turmoil, following its defeat at the hands of the Allies.

In March 1921 the German Communists seized on a mounting wave of working-class unrest and declared an armed insurrection. But the 'March Action' was a disastrous failure. Within a fortnight the insurrection had fizzled out, leaving thousands in prison and resulting in a massive decline in membership.

### The Years of Consolidation

This defeat dashed Moscow's hopes for immediate revolutionary advances. At its third congress in the summer of 1921, the Comintern initiated a review of tactics. The policy of the 'revolutionary offensive', as exemplified by the March Action, was discarded in favour of the 'United Front' tactic. Outright hostility to social democrats was replaced by a policy of co-operation in defence of working-class interests. In this way, the Comintern sought to infiltrate popular working-class movements while undercutting political support for the mainstream labour and social democratic parties. Needless to say, the social democrats were not very keen on this idea, and Comintern appeals to the remnants of the Second International for joint political action generally fell on deaf ears.

These tactics formed the basis of Comintern politics for most of the 1920s. But although the United Front period was one of consolidation for the Comintern, it was not one of growth. During the seven years after 1921 membership dropped by half, and by 1928 there were no more than half a million Comintern adherents outside Soviet Russia. Nowhere did the Communists supplant social democrats as leaders of the labour movement and of the working class.

On the other hand, the Comintern did achieve a degree of organizational stability. The Bolsheviks gradually purged it of opposition to their leadership and policies, although not without a struggle. An elaborate and tightly controlled structure of central institutions, regional bureaux, local agents and various political, cultural and trade union front organizations was established. By the end of this period the faction-ridden local parties had evolved into disciplined agents of Comintern policy and directives.

The process of bolshevization was accompanied by a merging of Comintern and Soviet foreign policy interests. This development was heralded by article 14 of the twenty-one conditions, which stated that 'each party desirous of affiliating with the Communist International should be obliged to render every possible assistance to the Soviet Republics in their struggle against

counter-revolutionary forces'. By 1927 this injunction had hardened into Stalin's dictum that 'An internationalist is one who is ready to defend the USSR without reservation, without wavering, unconditionally; for the USSR is the base of the world revolutionary movement, and this revolutionary movement cannot be defended and promoted unless the USSR is defended.' Wherever Soviet and Comintern interests clashed, it was the former that took precedence. Any dissent was quickly silenced, either by an appeal to internationalist duty or, failing that, by expulsion from the movement. The popular image of Communists as agents of Soviet foreign policy, which became established at this time, was not the whole truth, but it did have a considerable basis in fact.

### Foreign Adventures

Throughout its history, the Comintern emphasized the European dimension and the importance of the industrialized countries of the West, which Marx had predicted would be in the vanguard of revolutionary action.

However, some effort was also put into fomenting revolution in the rest of the world, particularly in Asia. At its second congress, the Comintern adopted a series of positions on the 'national and colonial question'. Communists in Asia and elsewhere were directed to immerse themselves in the struggle for national independence and to form alliances with movements for colonial freedom.

In line with Marxist-Leninist theory, revolution in the colonial world was seen as a two-stage process. First there would be a bourgeois revolution against imperialist rule, and then there would be a socialist revolution.

This misguided premise wasted years of effort and almost brought the revolutionary struggle in China to an end. By the mid-1920s the Chinese Communist Party had, under Comintern direction, established an alliance with the Guomindang, China's Nationalist Party. But when the army of the two groups advanced north and defeated many local warlords in an attempt to create the bourgeois society urged by the Comintern, the Nationalists betrayed their

## Rewriting History

Cutting, rearranging and retouching the photograph above, taken in 1925, has erased five members of the group from history. The 'edited' version (right), was published fourteen years later.

Repressive regimes throughout history have tried to suppress information. The Soviet authorities added a new twist by inventing new storylines to explain old events. History was given a new face under Stalin as patriots became traitors and former heroes of the revolution became enemies of the people. By the mid-1930s, this revision of the past had become an industry.

However, it was not just a matter of words. Inconvenient photographs reminded citizens that Trotsky, Kamenev and other revolutionary leaders had been closer comrades of Lenin than Stalin ever was. These irrefutable reminders required the highest skill of the retouchers as large groups of victorious Bolsheviks were transformed into more intimate gatherings.

# The Comintern

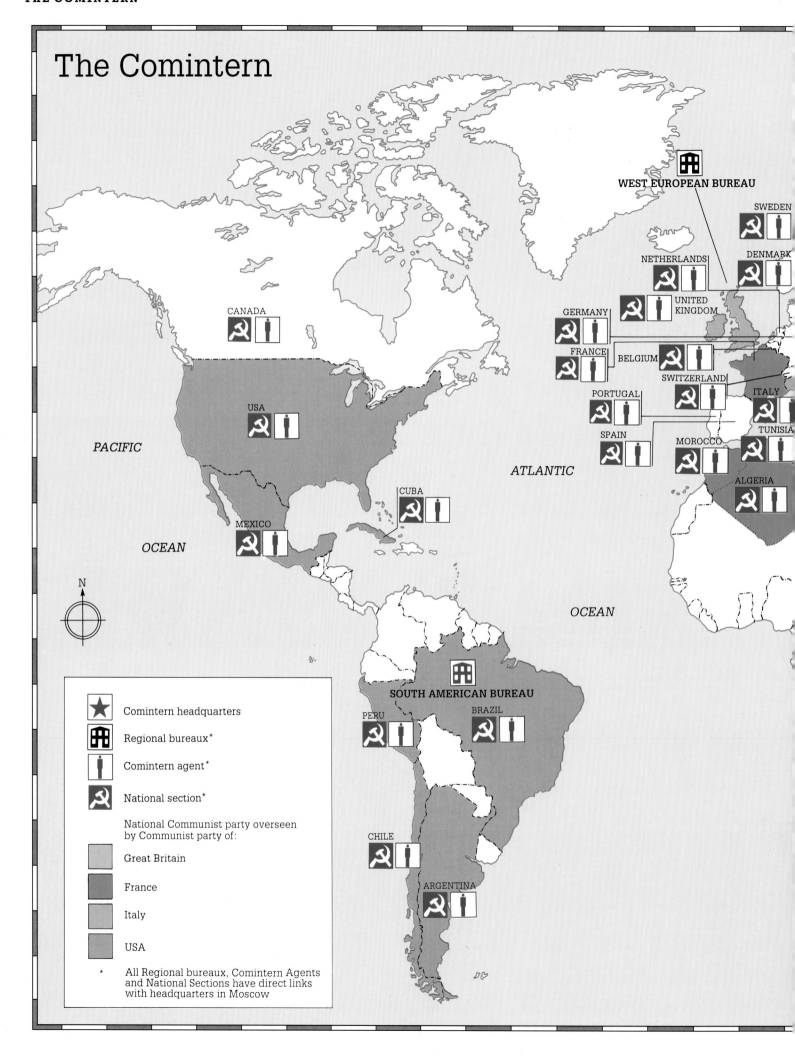

WEST EUROPEAN BUREAU

SWEDEN

DENMARK

NETHERLANDS

UNITED KINGDOM

GERMANY

FRANCE

BELGIUM

SWITZERLAND

ITALY

PORTUGAL

SPAIN

MOROCCO

TUNISIA

ALGERIA

CANADA

USA

CUBA

MEXICO

PACIFIC

OCEAN

ATLANTIC

OCEAN

N

SOUTH AMERICAN BUREAU

PERU

BRAZIL

CHILE

ARGENTINA

Comintern headquarters

Regional bureaux*

Comintern agent*

National section*

National Communist party overseen by Communist party of:

Great Britain

France

Italy

USA

*   All Regional bureaux, Comintern Agents and National Sections have direct links with headquarters in Moscow

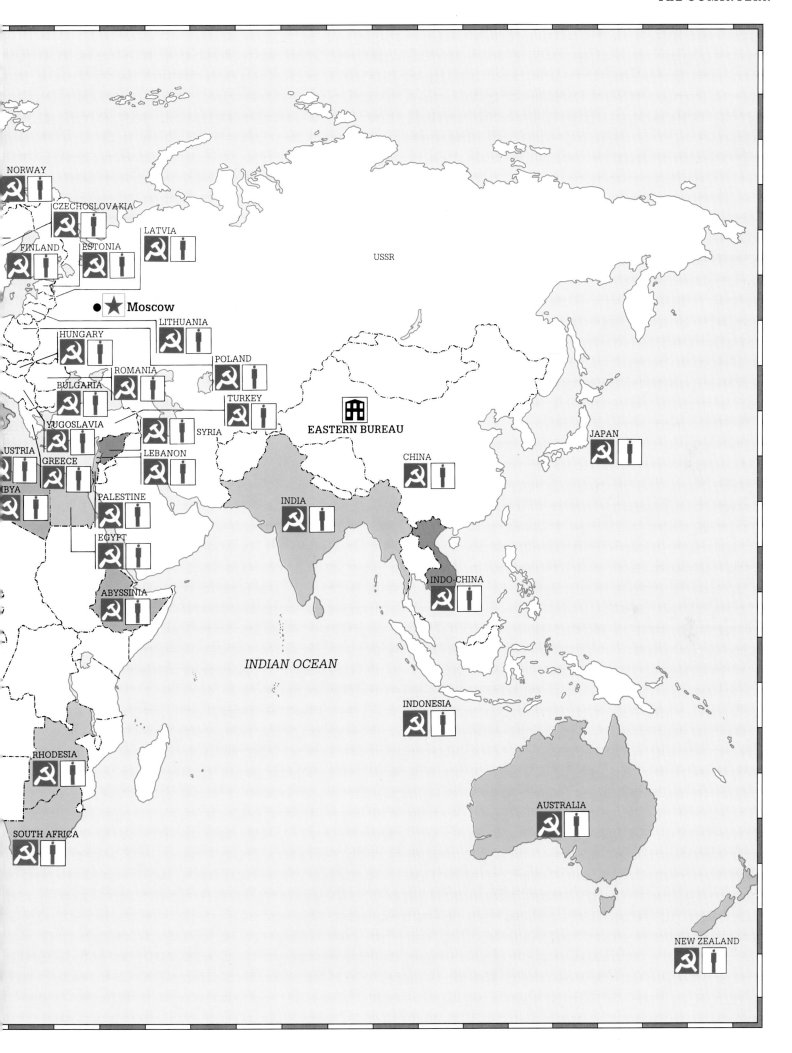

NORWAY

CZECHOSLOVAKIA

LATVIA

FINLAND    ESTONIA

USSR

● ★ Moscow

LITHUANIA

HUNGARY

ROMANIA          POLAND

BULGARIA

TURKEY

YUGOSLAVIA        SYRIA

AUSTRIA           LEBANON

GREECE

IBYA          PALESTINE

EGYPT

ABYSSINIA

EASTERN BUREAU

CHINA

INDIA

JAPAN

INDO-CHINA

INDIAN OCEAN

INDONESIA

RHODESIA

AUSTRALIA

SOUTH AFRICA

NEW ZEALAND

Ernst Thälmann, leader of the Communist Party of Germany speaks at an open-air meeting in 1932. Industrial Germany had the earliest and most advanced workers' movement inspired by Marx.

allies and tens of thousands of workers were murdered on the streets of Shanghai.

By the end of the 1920s it had become obvious that the United Front policy had failed. While the total membership of parties affiliated to the Comintern stood at just over 1.7 million, 1.2 of whom lived in the Soviet Union, membership of the reformist Labour and Socialist International stood at over 6.6 million, with over 26.4 million voters supporting them worldwide.

## A Slight Miscalculation

After its concern to defend the Soviet Union, the Comintern's greatest preoccupation was with Germany and its mass of loyal Communist voters. In 1928 Moscow and the Comintern adopted a new mood of confrontation with the reformist left, which too had its greatest power base in Germany. The Communists were urged to attack the Social Democrats, who in June 1928 had formed their first government in the Reichstag for eight years.

The summer of 1928 seemed to mark a new level of stability for Germany after the economic turmoil of the previous decade. The currency was firm and full employment seemed in sight. Fifteen months later, the Great Depression was underway and Germany's economy was in ruins. The flight from industrial investment and currencies after the October 1929 crash in New York drained the German economy of capital and raised unemployment to 3 million in less than a year. The Social Democrats fell from power in March 1930, ceding their leadership to a minority right-wing coalition with Heinrich Brüning as chancellor. As soon as the socialists asserted their independence and defeated Brüning in the Reichstag,

he called an election - in which support for the Nazis soared from 800,000 to 6.5 million. Although the Communist vote also increased dramatically - by well over a million to more than 4.5 million - Hitler was the major beneficiary of this crisis of German capitalism. His nationalistic rhetoric served to capture the mood of an increasingly despairing population.

Despite this sudden support for the extreme right, the Comintern was jubilant because the Social Democrats had lost votes.

A magazine for the loyal Communist voters in Italy. The Italian Communists attracted a strong following in the early 1920s and at the time of the Popular Front (1935-39), but they were never able to attain power.

The electoral result persuaded the Comintern that the attacks on Social Democracy had made the difference, and only encouraged it to persist. Most Communists dismissed Hitler's success as a flash in the pan. Meanwhile, the Social Democrats had little alternative but to support Brüning as a lesser evil than Hitler.

The economy of the country continued to sink, so that by April 1932 there were officially six million unemployed; and the real wages of those with jobs had fallen in value by a third since 1929. At this moment a presidential election became due. The weak and ineffectual leaders of the Social Democrats could not decide on a candidate, despite their position as Germany's largest party. In the face of Hitler's strong candidature they were forced to support the re-election of the current President and veteran commander from the First World War, Hindenburg, who made no secret of his contempt for them.

Six weeks after swearing at his inauguration to uphold the constitution, Hindenburg dissolved the Prussian Parliament quite illegally, declared a state of emergency and ejected the local Social Democrats from office. Their leaders did nothing more than wring their hands in anguish.

The Communists, meanwhile, blind to the danger from the right, were jubilant that their greatest enemy had been humiliated in this way and pressed on with Moscow's policy. In the national elections which followed on 31 July, the Communists again increased their support and registered over 5.2 million votes. Ernst Thälmann, the German party leader, was summoned to Moscow to attend an executive meeting of the Comintern. Such was his prestige at that moment that he was invited to give the opening speech.

Germany was by now in a state of a perpetual parliamentary crisis. Hitler had a strong enough following in the Reichstag to destroy governments, but without Hindenburg's acquiescence he was unable to form one. Another election was called for 6 November and Nazi support dropped. The combined vote of the left exceeded that of the Nazis by 1.5 million but, rather than promote the left, Hindenburg finally ceded the Chancellorship to Hitler on 30 January 1933. Many were appalled, and spontaneous mass demonstrations took place in most major German cities, but their leaders were either too timid to act, in the case of the Social Democrats, or too interested in attacking their neighbours, as in the case of the Communists.

The Reichstag was destroyed by fire within a month of the Nazis taking power, giving Hitler the excuse he needed to suppress opposition to his government. Communist leaders were jailed on trumped-up charges, deputies were expelled from Parliament and Communist party property was confiscated.

In the years to come, thousands of party members died in concentration camps. Much of what followed can be blamed on the Communist Party's unquestioning support for the Comintern.

# The Popular Front

European politics during the twenty years between the two world wars was a battleground between right and left in which the Communists found themselves on the losing side time after time. Those ruling elites which had held the reins of power during the nineteenth century, and continued to control events until the end of the First World War, were horrified by the fate of the Tsar and the destruction of the old order in Russia. In their determination to hold on to their position, they were prepared to form alliances with any group which would keep the Communists at bay. It was this panic which gave the Fascists their chance.

Fascism was a movement dedicated to promoting the undisputed authority of a charismatic leader behind whom the people would unite in a disciplined mass. Its members had no use for democracy, rational analysis or the individual rights for which so many had campaigned during the nineteenth century; their way to the top would follow the path of violence, intolerance and an undisguised appeal to the irrational.

An authoritarian stance such as this appealed to many anxious citizens in the turmoil which followed the First World War. Mussolini, who had given Fascism its name in 1919, was the first to take advantage of the situation when he swept to power in Rome in 1922. Hitler's opportunity came in 1933 in the economic depression which followed the Wall Street Crash and a political stalemate in the German Parliament. By 1932, the country's national income was 40 per cent lower than it had been in 1929 and a third of the working population was unemployed.

Fascism in the rest of Europe suffered from a shortage of charismatic leaders. Even in Spain, it was not the Falange, the Spanish Fascist party, which led the attack on democracy but the army. Although the Fascists lacked a precise idea of what they wanted to do when they achieved power, they knew clearly what they were against - Communism. After becoming Chancellor on 30 January 1933, Hitler acted quickly to suppress first the Communist Party and then the Social Democrats.

### From the Ashes of Catastrophe

The Communist International's response to these attacks on the most highly organized working-class movement in Europe was to execute a spectacular U-turn. Revolutionary socialism was shelved in favour of the aim of peace, progress and democracy. Priority was given to the formation of anti-Fascist

'Who is the most important man in the world?' asks this election poster for the National Socialist Party from 1932. It is an example of the political propaganda that was used to persuade the German people that only Hitler and the Nazi system could restore their country's greatness.

alliances with a range of democratic forces. Communists posed as the champions of bourgeois freedom and as patriots who would do anything to defend their country.

The first moves came after a belligerent right-wing demonstration in Paris early in 1934. On the afternoon of 6 February, a large crowd assembled in the Place de la Concorde while a debate on a vote of confidence in the French government was being conducted in the Chamber of Deputies on the other side of the River Seine. As more and more people gathered, the demonstration got out of hand and scuffles broke out. Once darkness had fallen, the police decided to meet force with force and twice opened fire on the crowd.

Meanwhile, across the river the deputies were giving the Radical Prime Minister, Daladier, a resounding vote of confidence. Despite this, France woke the next morning to find that their Premier, intimidated by the mob, had resigned. Four days later, thirty-two left-wing intellectuals, who had been alarmed by this show of right-wing strength, issued an appeal to the working class to 'bar the route of Fascism', calling on the Socialist Party and the Communists to sink their differences and come together in 'a spirit of conciliation'.

Such an appeal was necessary because these two bulwarks of the left had frequently seemed to be more interested in attacking each other than the parties of the right. The same had been true in Germany where, in the last election before Hitler achieved power, the combined vote of the Social Democrats and the Communists had exceeded that of the Nazis by a comfortable margin - and yet they had succumbed. Now the intellectuals cited the 'terrible experience' of Germany as 'a lesson'. The Communists called for a one-day general strike on 12 February; amid general surprise, the leadership of the Socialists called on their members to support the strike and suggested that peaceful demonstrations be held. On the 12th, the supporters of the two groups assembled at different points and only joined forces on the march. Observers watched the two factions with anxiety as they approached one another. But their meeting provoked only an exchange of smiles and handshakes rather than insults.

Even now the leaders of both parties were suspicious, and it was July 1934 before they signed a pact to combat the growing threat of French Fascism. Then, in October, the leader of the Communists, Maurice Thorez, attended a committee formed to co-ordinate the activities of the two parties and demanded 'the alliance of the middle classes'. The next day he addressed a public meeting and called for a 'rassemblement populaire'. The next morning the Communist daily newspaper, L'Humanité, called for a front populaire, and a new rallying cry was born.

The initial aim of the French Popular Front was to organize mass protests and demonstrations against Fascism and in defence of French democracy. The greatest of these took place on 14 July 1935, Bastille Day, when the leaders of the Communists, Socialists and Radicals marched together in Paris while other demonstrations of solidarity, during which crowds sang the 'Marseillaise' and the 'Internationale', took place all over

# The Popular Front

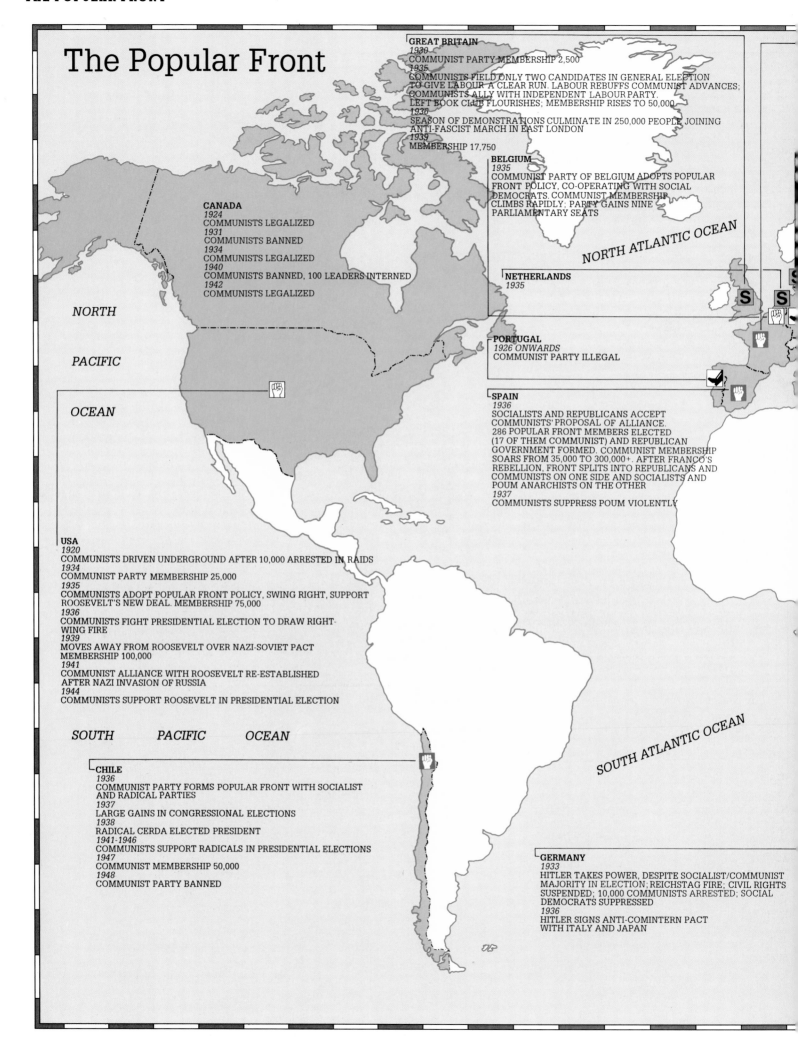

**GREAT BRITAIN**
*1930*
COMMUNIST PARTY MEMBERSHIP 2,500
*1935*
COMMUNISTS FIELD ONLY TWO CANDIDATES IN GENERAL ELECTION TO GIVE LABOUR A CLEAR RUN. LABOUR REBUFFS COMMUNIST ADVANCES; COMMUNISTS ALLY WITH INDEPENDENT LABOUR PARTY. LEFT BOOK CLUB FLOURISHES; MEMBERSHIP RISES TO 50,000
*1936*
SEASON OF DEMONSTRATIONS CULMINATE IN 250,000 PEOPLE JOINING ANTI-FASCIST MARCH IN EAST LONDON
*1939*
MEMBERSHIP 17,750

**BELGIUM**
*1935*
COMMUNIST PARTY OF BELGIUM ADOPTS POPULAR FRONT POLICY, CO-OPERATING WITH SOCIAL DEMOCRATS. COMMUNIST MEMBERSHIP CLIMBS RAPIDLY; PARTY GAINS NINE PARLIAMENTARY SEATS

NORTH ATLANTIC OCEAN

**NETHERLANDS**
*1935*

**CANADA**
*1924*
COMMUNISTS LEGALIZED
*1931*
COMMUNISTS BANNED
*1934*
COMMUNISTS LEGALIZED
*1940*
COMMUNISTS BANNED, 100 LEADERS INTERNED
*1942*
COMMUNISTS LEGALIZED

*NORTH*

*PACIFIC*

*OCEAN*

**PORTUGAL**
*1926 ONWARDS*
COMMUNIST PARTY ILLEGAL

**SPAIN**
*1936*
SOCIALISTS AND REPUBLICANS ACCEPT COMMUNISTS' PROPOSAL OF ALLIANCE. 286 POPULAR FRONT MEMBERS ELECTED (17 OF THEM COMMUNIST) AND REPUBLICAN GOVERNMENT FORMED. COMMUNIST MEMBERSHIP SOARS FROM 35,000 TO 300,000+. AFTER FRANCO'S REBELLION, FRONT SPLITS INTO REPUBLICANS AND COMMUNISTS ON ONE SIDE AND SOCIALISTS AND POUM ANARCHISTS ON THE OTHER
*1937*
COMMUNISTS SUPPRESS POUM VIOLENTLY

**USA**
*1920*
COMMUNISTS DRIVEN UNDERGROUND AFTER 10,000 ARRESTED IN RAIDS
*1934*
COMMUNIST PARTY MEMBERSHIP 25,000
*1935*
COMMUNISTS ADOPT POPULAR FRONT POLICY, SWING RIGHT, SUPPORT ROOSEVELT'S NEW DEAL. MEMBERSHIP 75,000
*1936*
COMMUNISTS FIGHT PRESIDENTIAL ELECTION TO DRAW RIGHT-WING FIRE
*1939*
MOVES AWAY FROM ROOSEVELT OVER NAZI-SOVIET PACT MEMBERSHIP 100,000
*1941*
COMMUNIST ALLIANCE WITH ROOSEVELT RE-ESTABLISHED AFTER NAZI INVASION OF RUSSIA
*1944*
COMMUNISTS SUPPORT ROOSEVELT IN PRESIDENTIAL ELECTION

*SOUTH     PACIFIC     OCEAN*

**CHILE**
*1936*
COMMUNIST PARTY FORMS POPULAR FRONT WITH SOCIALIST AND RADICAL PARTIES
*1937*
LARGE GAINS IN CONGRESSIONAL ELECTIONS
*1938*
RADICAL CERDA ELECTED PRESIDENT
*1941-1946*
COMMUNISTS SUPPORT RADICALS IN PRESIDENTIAL ELECTIONS
*1947*
COMMUNIST MEMBERSHIP 50,000
*1948*
COMMUNIST PARTY BANNED

SOUTH ATLANTIC OCEAN

**GERMANY**
*1933*
HITLER TAKES POWER, DESPITE SOCIALIST/COMMUNIST MAJORITY IN ELECTION; REICHSTAG FIRE; CIVIL RIGHTS SUSPENDED; 10,000 COMMUNISTS ARRESTED; SOCIAL DEMOCRATS SUPPRESSED
*1936*
HITLER SIGNS ANTI-COMINTERN PACT WITH ITALY AND JAPAN

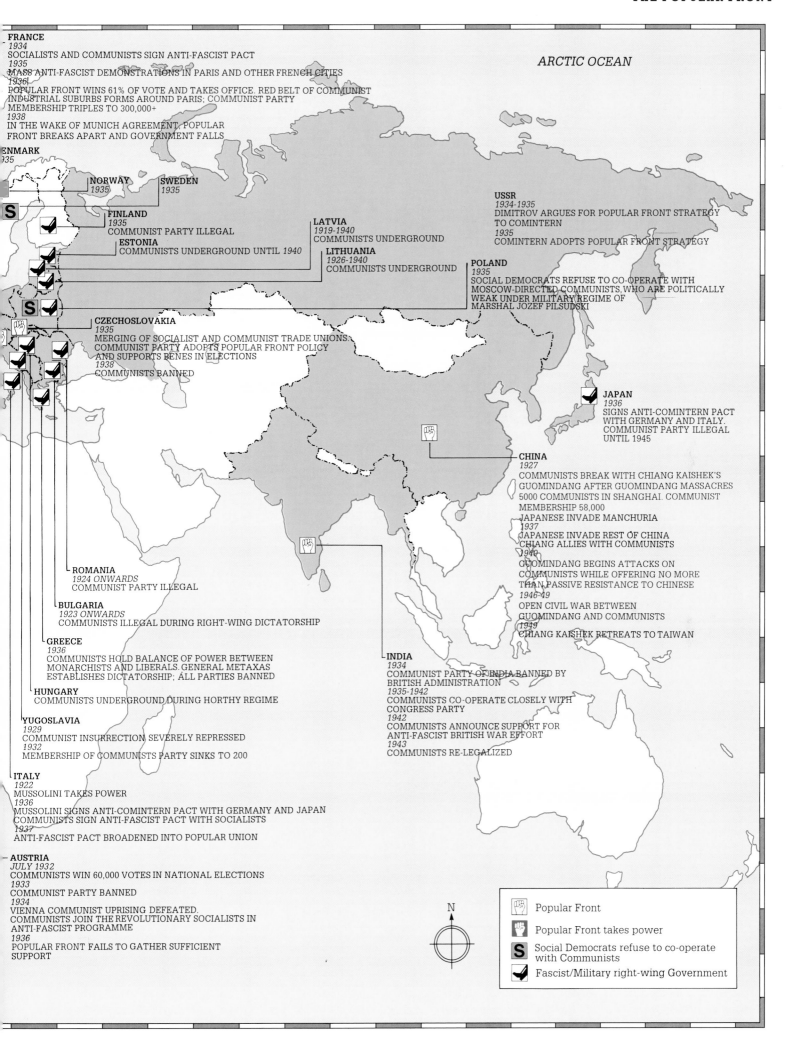

**FRANCE**
*1934*
SOCIALISTS AND COMMUNISTS SIGN ANTI-FASCIST PACT
*1935*
MASS ANTI-FASCIST DEMONSTRATIONS IN PARIS AND OTHER FRENCH CITIES
*1936*
POPULAR FRONT WINS 61% OF VOTE AND TAKES OFFICE. RED BELT OF COMMUNIST
INDUSTRIAL SUBURBS FORMS AROUND PARIS; COMMUNIST PARTY
MEMBERSHIP TRIPLES TO 300,000+
*1938*
IN THE WAKE OF MUNICH AGREEMENT, POPULAR
FRONT BREAKS APART AND GOVERNMENT FALLS

**DENMARK**
*1935*

**NORWAY**
*1935*

**SWEDEN**
*1935*

**FINLAND**
*1935*
COMMUNIST PARTY ILLEGAL

**ESTONIA**
COMMUNISTS UNDERGROUND UNTIL *1940*

**LATVIA**
*1919-1940*
COMMUNISTS UNDERGROUND

**LITHUANIA**
*1926-1940*
COMMUNISTS UNDERGROUND

**CZECHOSLOVAKIA**
*1935*
MERGING OF SOCIALIST AND COMMUNIST TRADE UNIONS.
COMMUNIST PARTY ADOPTS POPULAR FRONT POLICY
AND SUPPORTS BENES IN ELECTIONS
*1938*
COMMUNISTS BANNED

**USSR**
*1934-1935*
DIMITROV ARGUES FOR POPULAR FRONT STRATEGY
TO COMINTERN
*1935*
COMINTERN ADOPTS POPULAR FRONT STRATEGY

**POLAND**
*1935*
SOCIAL DEMOCRATS REFUSE TO CO-OPERATE WITH
MOSCOW-DIRECTED COMMUNISTS, WHO ARE POLITICALLY
WEAK UNDER MILITARY REGIME OF
MARSHAL JOZEF PILSUDSKI

**JAPAN**
*1936*
SIGNS ANTI-COMINTERN PACT
WITH GERMANY AND ITALY.
COMMUNIST PARTY ILLEGAL
UNTIL 1945

**CHINA**
*1927*
COMMUNISTS BREAK WITH CHIANG KAISHEK'S
GUOMINDANG AFTER GUOMINDANG MASSACRES
5000 COMMUNISTS IN SHANGHAI. COMMUNIST
MEMBERSHIP 58,000
JAPANESE INVADE MANCHURIA
*1937*
JAPANESE INVADE REST OF CHINA
CHIANG ALLIES WITH COMMUNISTS
*1940*
GUOMINDANG BEGINS ATTACKS ON
COMMUNISTS WHILE OFFERING NO MORE
THAN PASSIVE RESISTANCE TO CHINESE
*1946-49*
OPEN CIVIL WAR BETWEEN
GUOMINDANG AND COMMUNISTS
*1949*
CHIANG KAISHEK RETREATS TO TAIWAN

**ROMANIA**
*1924 ONWARDS*
COMMUNIST PARTY ILLEGAL

**BULGARIA**
*1923 ONWARDS*
COMMUNISTS ILLEGAL DURING RIGHT-WING DICTATORSHIP

**GREECE**
*1936*
COMMUNISTS HOLD BALANCE OF POWER BETWEEN
MONARCHISTS AND LIBERALS. GENERAL METAXAS
ESTABLISHES DICTATORSHIP; ALL PARTIES BANNED

**HUNGARY**
COMMUNISTS UNDERGROUND DURING HORTHY REGIME

**YUGOSLAVIA**
*1929*
COMMUNIST INSURRECTION SEVERELY REPRESSED
*1932*
MEMBERSHIP OF COMMUNISTS PARTY SINKS TO 200

**ITALY**
*1922*
MUSSOLINI TAKES POWER
*1936*
MUSSOLINI SIGNS ANTI-COMINTERN PACT WITH GERMANY AND JAPAN
COMMUNISTS SIGN ANTI-FASCIST PACT WITH SOCIALISTS
*1937*
ANTI-FASCIST PACT BROADENED INTO POPULAR UNION

**AUSTRIA**
*JULY 1932*
COMMUNISTS WIN 60,000 VOTES IN NATIONAL ELECTIONS
*1933*
COMMUNIST PARTY BANNED
*1934*
VIENNA COMMUNIST UPRISING DEFEATED.
COMMUNISTS JOIN THE REVOLUTIONARY SOCIALISTS IN
ANTI-FASCIST PROGRAMME
*1936*
POPULAR FRONT FAILS TO GATHER SUFFICIENT
SUPPORT

**INDIA**
*1934*
COMMUNIST PARTY OF INDIA BANNED BY
BRITISH ADMINISTRATION
*1935-1942*
COMMUNISTS CO-OPERATE CLOSELY WITH
CONGRESS PARTY
*1942*
COMMUNISTS ANNOUNCE SUPPORT FOR
ANTI-FASCIST BRITISH WAR EFFORT
*1943*
COMMUNISTS RE-LEGALIZED

*ARCTIC OCEAN*

Popular Front

Popular Front takes power

Social Democrats refuse to co-operate
with Communists

Fascist/Military right-wing Government

N

France. These joint events were so successful that the alliance continued in order to fight the 1936 general election.

Meanwhile, a radical reassessment of Comintern strategy and tactics was taking place following the disaster in Germany. The new Comintern leader, Georgi Dimitrov, was a key figure in this policy review. He argued that the German debacle demonstrated the dangers of divisive conflict within the left, and that the continuing Fascist threat necessitated a new strategy and tactics. Dimitrov's struggle against a discredited but entrenched policy continued through 1934 and 1935. It was war and the destruction of democracy that were on the horizon, not world revolution, he told the Comintern.

Dimitrov's new approach was supported by the French, who were already revising their tactics at home. More importantly, Dimitrov also got the backing of the Soviet leadership, who were beginning to realize the extent of the threat which Fascism posed to the movement. Dimitrov's triumph over the conservative opposition was celebrated at the last and most famous of the Comintern's

congresses - the seventh - in the summer of 1935. The wisdom of this change of stategy was only confirmed by the anti-Comintern pact signed by Japan and Germany in 1936.

### The Popular Front Takes Office

The French general election in April 1936 marked the high point of enthusiasm and success for the Popular Front, which gained an absolute majority of the seats in the Chamber of Deputies - 378 out of 618. Most spectacular of all was the advance of the Communists, whose representatives increased from 11 to 72 and whose vote doubled to almost 1.5 million. Party membership increased from under a hundred thousand to over three hundred thousand. This change of fortune extended into local government, and the famous 'Red Belt' of Communist municipalities around Paris was established at this time.

The Popular Front took office on a wave of euphoria under the leadership of the Socialist Léon Blum. Many of its supporters expected more than just a parliamentary

victory. A series of factory occupations swept across France in what became the largest strike movement in the history of the republic. With such public support, the Chamber passed radical legislation which transformed France. From now on the workers would have collective bargaining rights, paid holidays and a forty-hour week.

Despite this atmosphere the Communist Party declined to join the government, even though they were urged to do so by their Popular Front partners. Why the party refused ministerial responsibilities has never been revealed; it may have been for the sound tactical reason of not wanting to provoke the French Right, or perhaps the Comintern leadership in Moscow decided that joining an essentially reformist government, however progressive, was going too far.

Absence from office did not, however, prevent the Communists from playing an important role in the running of the country, particularly during the early days of Blum's premiership. In the summer of 1936, for example, the Communist Party was crucial in defusing the strikes which followed the electoral victory. Conciliation was a new role for a party which had built its reputation in the 1920s on industrial militancy.

But the success of the Popular Front was short-lived. The ailing French economy was unable to sustain an extensive programme of social reform as well as rearmament, a policy which received support also from the Communists. Within two years the high hopes that had greeted the victory of 1936 had crumbled. Problems at home were compounded by differences within the coalition over foreign policy. The Communists campaigned for a militant anti-Fascist stance in foreign affairs, including an alliance with the USSR; many Socialists adhered to their movement's traditional pacifism. While others, particularly among the Radicals, pursued appeasement with the aim of a peaceful settlement with Hitler. The issue of whether or not France should support the Republican side in the Spanish Civil War was a particular source of conflict. The final demise of the French Popular Front came in November 1938, in the wake of the Munich Agreement, when the Radicals split from the Socialists and Communists and formed a government with the right.

Outside France, the Comintern's Popular Front strategy met a different fate. Nowhere, apart from Spain, China and Chile - where there was a short-lived Popular Front government, did the Communists achieve the kind of advance registered in France. In Britain the Communists' attempt to affiliate to the Labour Party was repeatedly rebuffed. Indeed, the Labour Party took strong disciplinary action against any member who co-operated with them. On the other hand, British Communists did score a number of successes in other areas. In the intellectual and cultural sphere, the Left Book Club reached a membership of fifty thousand. A campaign to send aid to Republican Spain

# Georgi Dimitrov: Leader of the Comintern

Georgi Dimitrov, the architect of Comintern policy during the Popular Front period, was leader of the Communist International from 1935 until its dissolution in 1943. Dimitrov was a Bulgarian Communist who came to work in the Comintern apparatus in 1923. In the early 1930s he headed the West European Bureau of the Comintern in Berlin. Arrested by the Nazis in 1933 and charged with setting fire to the Reichstag, he conducted his own defence at a trial later that year. Dimitrov's clashes with Goering during the trial made headlines all over the world. Acquitted of all charges he was allowed to return to the Soviet Union in 1934.

In Moscow he quickly gained the confidence of Stalin who accepted his advice that a radical change in Comintern policy was required. Dimitrov's brilliant presentation of the new, anti-Fascist policy at the seventh congress of the Comintern in 1935 confirmed his position as the organization's leader. During the latter 1930s hundreds of members of the Comintern and foreign Communists in exile became victims of Stalin's purges. Dimitrov tried, unsuccessfully, to use his status as leader of the Comintern and confidant of Stalin to save many of them.

After the Second World War Dimitrov returned to Bulgaria, becoming Prime Minister of the new people's democracy in 1946. He died in 1949.

Anti-Nazi propaganda, in the form of a political photo-montage by the German artist John Heartfield. Georgi Dimitrov is being cross-examined by Goering during the trial for his alleged involvement in the Riechstag fire in Berlin in February 1933.

Communist leader Jacques Duclos (right) and pacifist writer Roman Rolland in earnest conversation at a Popular Front rally in Paris, 1936. The Communist Party chose not to join the government after the Popular Front's election victory in April 1936.

raised the present-day equivalent of £50 million. The British party also had an important role in organizing some of the biggest demonstrations of the 1930s against unemployment. Finally, there was the anti-Fascist movement, which in October 1936 mobilized a quarter of million people to block a march by Oswald Mosley's Blackshirts through the predominantly Jewish section of London's East End.

In the United States the party's role in fashioning and popularizing the social and ecomonic reforms of President Roosevelt's New Deal administrations went unacknow-ledged in public. American Communists provided much of the energy, enthusiasm and organizational skill for the various public works and welfare movements which buttressed Roosevelt's popular support, but got little of the credit. Indeed, in 1936 the American Communist Party deliberately contested the American presidential elections in order to draw the fire of right-wingers away from President Roosevelt. Party membership, however, grew from twenty-five thousand in 1934 to a hundred thousand in 1939 (though how many were bona fide members and how many were agents of the FBI has never been revealed). In the trade union movement, the Communists formed part of a centre-left coalition which organized millions of unskilled and semi-skilled workers and fought some of the fiercest labour battles of the 1930s.

Similar stories of the Popular Front can be recounted for other parts of the world - Canada, Australia, New Zealand, India,

Belgium, the Netherlands, Scandinavia, parts of Asia and Latin America, Czechoslovakia and other eastern European states. In many countries, of course, the Communists had to work underground - Nazi Germany, Italy, Japan and elsewhere; any attempt to form a Popular Front in these countries would have been much too dangerous.

The Comintern's Popular Front period came to an abrupt end with the signing of the

A triumphant Léon Blum holds a miner's lamp aloft during the July celebrations to mark the Popular Front's victory in the French general election of April 1936. The new government transformed working conditions in France.

Nazi-Soviet pact of August 1939 and the outbreak of the Second World War a week later. Within six weeks the strategy of anti-Fascist unity and defence of democracy had been abandoned. The Comintern and its member parties swallowed the Soviet line that the war was imperialist, that the working class had no interest in its outcome, and that the main culprits were Britain and France, not Nazi Germany. But this second U-turn did not go unopposed. In Britain, for example, the party's General Secretary, Harry Pollitt, resigned in protest.

For the next two years the Comintern abstained from the anti-Fascist struggle. Only with the German attack on the Soviet Union in June 1941 did the Comintern try to revive the Popular Front, this time under the guise of national fronts against Hitler and the Nazis. However, it was the Communists' role in the armed resistance to the Nazi occupation of Europe which positioned them for power in the post-war period.

After the German surrender, Communist parties participated in national unity governments in most European countries, including France and Italy. The Comintern itself had been abolished in 1943 and its demise met with no resistance from its member sections. During the days of the Popular Front, Communist parties had acquired a taste for independence and the latitude to devise policies to suit their own countries. In this experience lay the roots of the post-war collapse of the Communist movement as a monolithic international political force.

# The Spanish Civil War

The most celebrated painting of the Spanish Civil War. *Guernica* painted by Pablo Picasso depicts the destruction of the Basque town after bombing raids carried out by German aircraft in support of the Nationalist army. It was first exhibited at the World Exhibiton in Paris in 1937.

No cause galvanized the Communist movement more than that of the defence of Republican Spain during the 1930s. The struggle was seen as being crucial in the fight against Fascism. It was also viewed as an arena for a unique experiment in the politics of the Popular Front. The Comintern considered Republican Spain to be a transitional stage between capitalism and socialism - a 'democracy of a new type'. Ultimately the movement saw Spain as a socialist prize. However, in the short term, that aim was strictly subordinated to the objective of winning the Civil War.

The Spanish Civil War was not, on the other hand, merely a repeat of the struggles between right and left seen in the rest of Europe; the conflict possessed its own local dimensions which were deeply rooted in the turbulent history of modern Spain. The feudal society which had run Spain for centuries collapsed with the arrival of Napoleon's army in 1808. The fall of the monarchy destabilized the country and, although the Bourbon family were eventually restored to the throne, the following sixty-eight years witnessed a relentless power struggle between a conservative clergy and a liberal army. Only in 1876 was a constitutional monarchy established which gave Spain some political stability.

The late nineteenth century saw the industrial revolution cross the Pyrenees, and give rise to the growth of an urbanized working class. The constitution of 1876 had promised universal male suffrage, but the people found that their votes counted for little because the established parties struck deals which circumvented the wishes of the electorate. The frustration of the growing working class found release in the formation of two trade unions: the Confederación Nacional de Trabajo, or CNT, which was inspired by anarchism, and the Unión General de Trabajadores, or UGT, which was Marxist. Many of these workers lived in the north-east of the country in the Catalonian region which surrounds Barcelona. Catalan nationalists wanted more autonomy from Madrid, and the mingling of their movement with that of the workers turned Barcelona into a cauldron of radical ferment which many Spaniards renamed the 'city of bombs'.

Another ingredient added to the Spanish pot at the end of the nineteenth century was the sudden loss of the remnants of the country's empire in the Americas and Asia, including Cuba, the Philippines, Guam, Hawaii and Puerto Rico at the end of the Spanish-American war of 1898. With many other European states carving up Africa, the Spanish sought to salve their bruised pride by staking a claim to the nearest corner of the Dark Continent. In 1904, they came to an arrangement with the French which divided Morocco into spheres of influence. Unfortunately for the Spanish, the fierce nomadic tribes of the interior refused to acquiesce to this arrangement;

within five years, forty thousand troops were tied down in Morocco. When the government tried to call up more reservists from north-east Spain, a general strike precipitated a week of riots in which 120 people died and fifty churches were burnt down. Order was only restored by bringing the army on to the streets and back into the centre of political life.

The years which followed were marked by the assassination of political leaders, violent strikes and plots by army officers. The climax came in 1921 when the Spanish suffered a humiliating defeat at the hands of Moroccan tribesmen; the enquiry into the affair revealed gross incompetence and corruption in the army. However, before the parliamentary report castigating the general staff could be published, General Primo de Rivera staged a coup.

Although he left King Alfonso XIII as Spain's nominal ruler, the general was the country's *de facto* dictator for seven years. Rivera's own wayward decisions undermined his position, however, and after he had incensed the judiciary, the army, the financial community and the liberal middle class, the King felt strong enough to insist on his retirement.

## The Republic

At first King Alfonso tried to rule with the disregard for democracy shown by Rivera, but when he allowed local elections to proceed, popular discontent overflowed and

# The Spanish Civil War

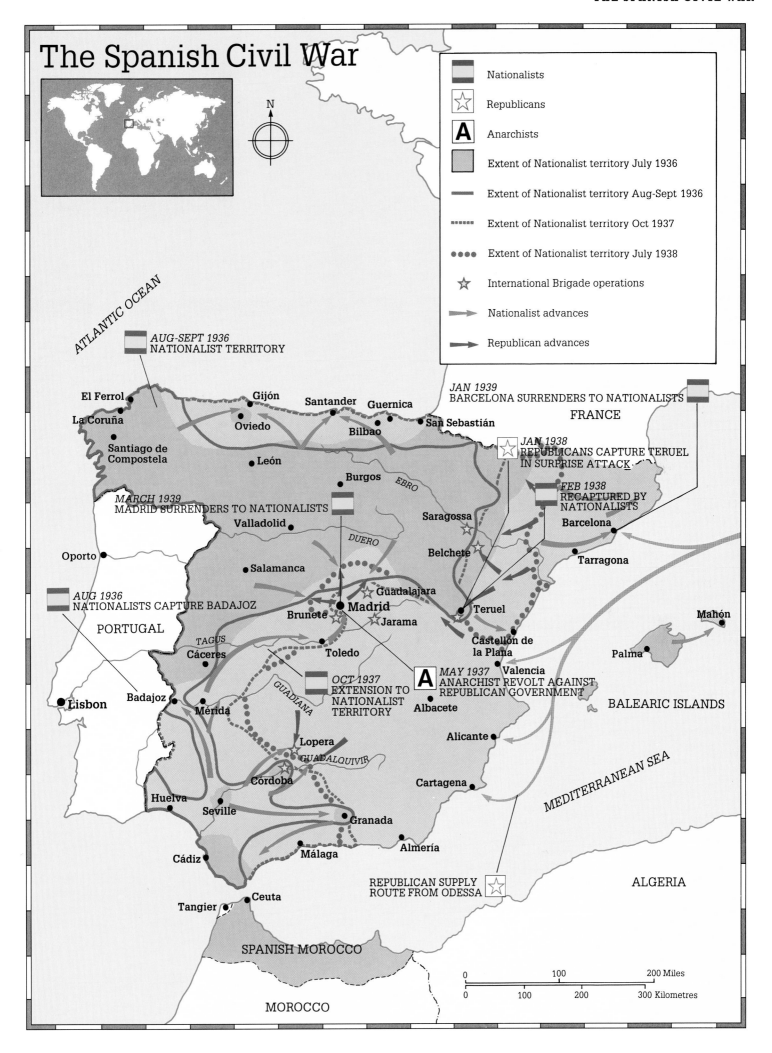

forced him to abdicate, creating the republic. Unfortunately the people were not mollified by this change and Spain remained, in the words of a former Prime Minister, General Berenguer, 'a bottle of champagne, about to blow out its cork'.

Spain was soon divided into two armed camps. To the right was the National Front, with the army and the Church at its heart, accompanied by a small group of Fascists, the Falange. To the left was the Popular Front, which was an amalgam of socialists, Communists, Republicans and anarchists. To the horror of the right, the Popular Front won a clear majority in the general election of 16 February 1936, although the ministers of the new government were taken entirely from the Republican Party. Instead of both sides accepting the result, the poll only led to further violence and bloodshed. In the first four months of the new Parliament there were, according to the political leader of the Catholics, Gil Robles, 269 political murders and 341 strikes; 10 newspaper offices were wrecked and 160 churches were burnt down. The stage was set for the Civil War.

The final spark came in the early hours of 13 July as all of Spain seethed with rumours of a right-wing coup. That morning Calvo Sotelo, a parliamentary leader of the right, was awakened in his Madrid apartment by members of the security forces. Telling his family he was being taken to police headquarters, his captors led him to a waiting car. A quarter of a mile down the road one of his guards shot Sotelo in the back of the neck. The body was dumped at a local cemetery without identification. The crime was discovered the following day, and early on the morning of the 15th came the signal

for the anticipated right-wing insurrection.

The rising began on 17 July in the city of Melilla in eastern Morocco; its leaders, a group of officers in the Army of Africa, declared a rebellion in the name of General Franco, the Chief of the General Staff - at that time Governor of the Canary Islands. Their example was followed by military units all over Spain, particularly in the north-west and south. Reactions were, however, confused; many officers sided with the legitimate government and refused to participate. Crews in the navy mutinied against their officers, many of whom were then shot before the men contacted the Admiralty in Madrid to assert their loyalty.

The situation was further complicated by the poor standard of communications in Spain in 1936, which left many communities bewildered about the course of events. Only the use of radio overcame these problems; General de Llano's success in rallying Andalusia to the Nationalist cause through such novel means, after he had captured the local radio station in Seville, was not lost on Spaniards or on foreign observers.

In the middle of all this confusion, both sides began terrorizing their local opponents. In many cities that had fallen into the hands of the rebel forces in Andalusia in the south and Castille in the north, tens of thousands of people were shot, frequently for no reason. Most famous of these victims was Spain's greatest poet of the time, Garcia Lorca, who had no interest in politics and whose only crime was that his sister had married a socialist mayor.

Two months after the fighting began, the crisis provoked the formation of a new government led by the socialist Largo

Caballero. His cabinet included five socialists and two Communists, who were later joined by four members of the anarchist CNT. The shift to the left - the government included only three ministers from the Republican Party - reflected the importance of the armed workers and peasants who had defended eastern Spain, including all the major cities and urban areas, from occupation by the forces of the National Front.

The influence of outsiders now began to be felt as Franco's Army of Africa marched towards Madrid; they had reached the mainland only because Germany had provided the planes for the first major airlift of troops in history. Now the disciplined columns easily brushed aside the ill-armed and inexperienced militiamen defending the road to the capital from the south. However, the government had allies too, and Russian aircraft and tanks arrived in the nick of time.

Franco's forces launched their attack on Madrid on the morning of 8 November and many citizens expected the city to be overrun within hours. The Army of Africa was, however, not trained in street-fighting, while many of the militiamen were now in their element. The advance ground to a halt as the two armies fought in hand-to-hand combat through the university campus.

Both sides had now been joined by foreign reinforcements. Over forty thousand volunteers fought in the Comintern-organized International Brigades, and the arrival of the first unit on 8 November raised the morale of the Republican defenders. Nazi Germany's Condor Legion had joined the nationalist army two days earlier and was well armed with tanks and aircraft. The Germans saw the conflict as a useful arena in which to test new tactics and technology, and Madrid experienced some of their first experiments in the use of incendiary bombs on civilian populations.

Fortunately, the first winter of the war saw more humane innovations brought to the battlefield as José Trueta, the chief surgeon of Barcelona's General Hospital, developed new ways of treating wounds. When combined with another innovation of the Republican army, the mobile, front-line hospital, the number of post-combat deaths from infected wounds dropped dramatically.

Despite the German intervention, it was clear to Franco and his fellow generals that, after two weeks of fighting, advancing into the centre of the city might cost them their entire army. So both sides dug trenches and waited. This successful defence of the capital secured the future of Republican Spain, at least for the time being.

### The Larger Picture

Outside Spain, the Comintern organized an impressive international campaign in support of the Republic. Its optimism about revolutionary prospects in Spain was raised by the radical measures taken by the government following the military revolt. The big agricultural estates were broken up

# Stalin on the Spanish Civil War

In December 1936 Stalin sent a message to the socialist Prime Minister Largo Caballero. It is a rare example of direct intervention by Stalin in matters that would normally be dealt with via the Comintern. It also illustrates the broad political approach of the Comintern and the USSR to the winning of the civil war in Spain.

Here are four pieces of friendly advice which we submit to you:

1. Attention should be paid to the peasants, who are of great importance in an agrarian country like Spain. It would be good to issue decrees dealing with agrarian questions and taxation, which would meet the peasants' interests. It would also be good to draw peasants into the army, or to form them into partisan detachments in the rear of the fascist armies.

Stalin urged the Comintern to help supply the Republicans with arms during the Civil War.

Decrees favouring the peasants could facilitate this.

2. The urban petty and middle bourgeoisie must be attracted to the Government side or, at least, given the possibility of taking up a neutral attitude favourable to the Government, by protecting

them against attempts at confiscation and assuring to them as far as possible freedom of trade, otherwise these groups will follow fascism.

3. The leaders of the Republican Party should not be repulsed; on the contrary, they should be drawn in, brought close to the Government, persuaded to get down to the job in harness with the Government... This is necessary in order to prevent the enemies of Spain from presenting it as a Communist Republic, and thus avert their open intervention, which represents the greatest danger to republican Spain.

4. An opportunity might be found to state in the press that the Spanish Government will allow nobody to interfere with the property and legitimate interests of foreigners in Spain who are citizens of countries which do not support the rebels.

and the land distributed among the peasants. Large elements of industry and financial institutions were taken into public ownership. A new infrastructure of popular democracy began to emerge.

The role of the Spanish Communist Party in this programme was crucial, and with every reorganization of the crisis-ridden government its influence increased; party membership jumped from under fifty thousand to over a quarter of a million. The Communists were the best-organized and most disciplined force within the army. Their role in the conduct of the war was underpinned by Soviet aid and by the Soviet military advisers that accompanied it.

The absolute priority which the Communists gave to winning the war brought them into frequent conflict with the anarchists and with some of the socialists, who were more concerned with social reform than with the menacing military forces at the gates of Madrid. These divisions on the left weakened the Republican camp, but the Communists were ruthless in eradicating opposition to their policy. In 1937, fighting broke out in Barcelona between Communist groups and those of the Partido Obrero de Unificación Marxista (POUM) - a group allied to Trotsky. With the Soviet secret police aiding the communist struggle, POUM was crushed and its leader, Andrés Nin, murdered.

Such behaviour was justified on the grounds that the POUM were Fascist agents conspiring against the Republican government and sabotaging the war effort. These accusations were as spurious as those levelled against the victims of Stalin's purges, for with Soviet aid to Spain came the politics of Stalin's Great Terror, the Soviet secret police playing a prominent role in seeking out and liquidating what Stalin deemed the 'enemies' of the Republican cause.

The Republic's conduct of the war was severely hampered by the decision of Great Britain and France to form a non-intervention

# The International Brigades

The organization of a force of international volunteers to help the Republican army in Spain was first suggested at a meeting of the Comintern on 26 July 1936 after foreigners had begun to arrive at the battlefront on their own initiative. Dimitrov, the leader of the Comintern, expressed his enthusiasm for the proposal and Stalin gave it his backing because it would rid him of the large numbers of Communist refugees living in

Moscow. These émigrés would lead the brigades and the volunteers would be recruited from foreign parties, who were given quotas to fill.

As volunteers of different nationalities arrived they were organized into groups based on language. The Eleventh Brigade was the first to reach Madrid on 8 October, the day the Nationalists attacked. The sight of a battalion of Germans with a section of British machine-

gunners marching up the Gran Via while the city was under heavy artillery bombardment transformed the mood of the Madrilenos who had assumed that defeat was a matter of time. Although this Brigade only numbered 1900 men, they and the Twelfth Brigade, who arrived on 12 November, exhibited such courage, discipline and determination that they inspired their Spanish comrades who fought Franco's forces.

committee to block supplies to either side in the conflict. France, for example, closed the critical supply route across its border three times during the course of the Civil War. Yet repeated efforts to get Germany and Italy to stop supplying Franco failed abysmally, although both countries claimed adherence to the arms embargo.

The Soviet Union also agreed to the policy at first. But in October 1936, amid mounting Comintern concern, Moscow declared that it would only refrain from supplying arms to the same extent as other great powers. Given the undisguised participation of Germany and Italy, this resolution gave the USSR carte blanche to aid the Republicans, and Soviet arms began to flow into Spain just in time to play their crucial role in the defence of Madrid.

## The Noose Tightens

Their failure to capture the capital caused the Nationalists to adopt a more cautious strategy and they chose to extend their territory gradually by attacking individual

pockets of government resistance. The coastal area facing the Bay of Biscay and centred on Bilbao, the home of Basque nationalism, was taken in the summer of 1937. The Asturian coalfields to the west followed in October. Franco was now in a position to concentrate all his efforts in the east of the country.

As the military situation worsened, so did the Republic's political problems. One uneasy Republican coalition succeeded another, but these successive reorganizations soon led to a situation where only the Communists and their closest allies remained united.

In the spring and early summer of 1938 the Nationalist army made a concentrated effort to drive a wedge between Barcelona in the north-east and the remainder of Republican Spain by breaking through to the Mediterranean coast. With the best artillery and bombers that Germany could supply, they soon overcame an army in which half the men did not even have a rifle. By the end of July, Franco had secured a section of coast seventy miles long.

After a series of indecisive but bloody attacks and counter-attacks, Franco launched what proved to be the decisive strike on Catalonia just before Christmas 1938. The exhausted and poorly armed Republicans were no match for the Nationalist army's tanks and bombers, and Barcelona was captured a month later. Nearly half a million Spaniards managed to escape across the border into France.

The final act of the drama came two months later when Republican forces in Madrid turned on each other as Communists fought anti-Communists. The fighting lasted for five days, and any chance of further resistance to Franco's Nationalists collapsed. Fighting finally came to an end on 31 March 1939. Some half a million people had died in the Spanish Civil War, which had lasted for just under three years.

For the Spanish Communists, their defeat at the hands of Franco's army marked, for the lucky ones, the beginning of nearly forty years in exile - for the less fortunate death at the hands of either Franco's or Stalin's execution squads.

TRUSTFUL TONY:
"JUST TO DISCOURAGE CHEATING, I'LL WEAR A STRAIT-JACKET AND LET YOU BOYS PLAY MY HAND FOR ME."

Hitler    Mussolini    Eden  Stalin  Blum

**NON-INTERVENTION POKER**

*Non-Interventon Poker* by David Low, January 1937. British Foreign Secretary Anthony Eden and French Prime Minister Léon Blum turn a blind eye to the breaking of the non-intervention agreement.

# The Nazi-Soviet Pact

On the morning of 22 August 1939, Popular Front sympathizers and Communists the world over woke to read newspaper headlines which shattered all their illusions. Late the previous night, Berlin had announced that the Foreign Minister, Joachim von Ribbentrop, was flying to Moscow 'to complete the negotiations' for a non-aggression pact with the Soviet Union. The *New York Times* called it 'a German bomb'. French diplomats admitted that they were astounded. The British *Daily Express* claimed that the announcement 'exploded the European diplomatic situation'. With every newspaper full of speculation about war and an imminent attack on Poland by the German army, it was clear that the generals could now proceed without risking a counter-attack by the Red Army.

Obedient party organs desperately tried to put a brave face on the situation by standing the truth on its head. 'Soviets' Dramatic Peace Move To Halt Aggressors', cried the British *Daily Worker*. Some fellow travellers such as the French philosopher, Jean-Paul Sartre had made excuses: 'To keep hope alive one must, in spite of all mistakes, horrors and crimes, recognize the obvious superiority of the socialist camp.' But, whatever the willing pens of party drones might write, many of the most diligent activists could feel only disgust; the leading British Marxist theoretician John Strachey was only one among many who resigned

from the party in a wave of revulsion, as the country in which they had invested all their faith was revealed as having feet of clay. Perhaps the shock was all the more intense among those who, for many years, had suppressed their doubts about Stalin and Stalinism in the belief that the Soviet Union was the only hope against Germany's expansionist ambitions and the Nazi's vicious domestic persecution.

## An Accommodating Relationship

Much of the shock expressed around the world arose because many people had taken the mounting war of words between Moscow and Berlin at face value. Yet only a decade or so earlier they had established a *modus vivendi* based on common interest. After years of civil war, Moscow needed technical assistance and money to rebuild the industrial fabric of the Soviet republics. Germany, on the other hand, needed land where it could evade the provisions of the Versailles Treaty and rebuild its armed forces. These needs led to the construction deep within Soviet territory of German arms factories where new weapons (including lethal gases) could be built and tested. The aircraft manufacturer Junkers built a plant near Moscow. New munitions factories went up and by 1926 were making three hundred thousand shells a year, which were shipped back to Germany.

The two countries also had something else in common - their resentment of Poland. Both had lost territory to the government in Warsaw and both were merely biding their time before taking revenge. As early as 1922 the head of the German army, General von Seeckt, who later did his best to destroy the Communists in China, had seen the writing on the wall.

Poland's existence is intolerable, incompatible with the survival of Germany. It must disappear and will disappear through its own internal weaknesses and through Russia - with our assistance. For Russia, Poland is even more intolerable than for us; no Russian can reach agreement with Poland.

Soviet-German mutual assistance tailed off and then stopped in the wake of Hitler's rise to the Chancellorship in 1933. And although for a time Maxim Litvinov, Commissar for Foreign Affairs since 1930, was willing on the basis of *realpolitik* to maintain a tolerable coexistence with Nazi Germany, his offer was spurned and he soon came to favour an alliance with France and Britain to contain any German threat. Yet throughout this troubled period Moscow kept open its channels of communication to Berlin, sometimes engaging in secret, though usually pointless, diplomatic discussions. However, after Czechoslovakia had been betrayed by Britain and France at Munich,

*Far left:* An anti-Russian cartoon published in Germany in 1937 before the short-lived peace pact of 1939.
*Left:* The German Foreign Secretary von Ribbentrop is welcomed to Moscow by Stalin for the signing of the non-aggression pact.

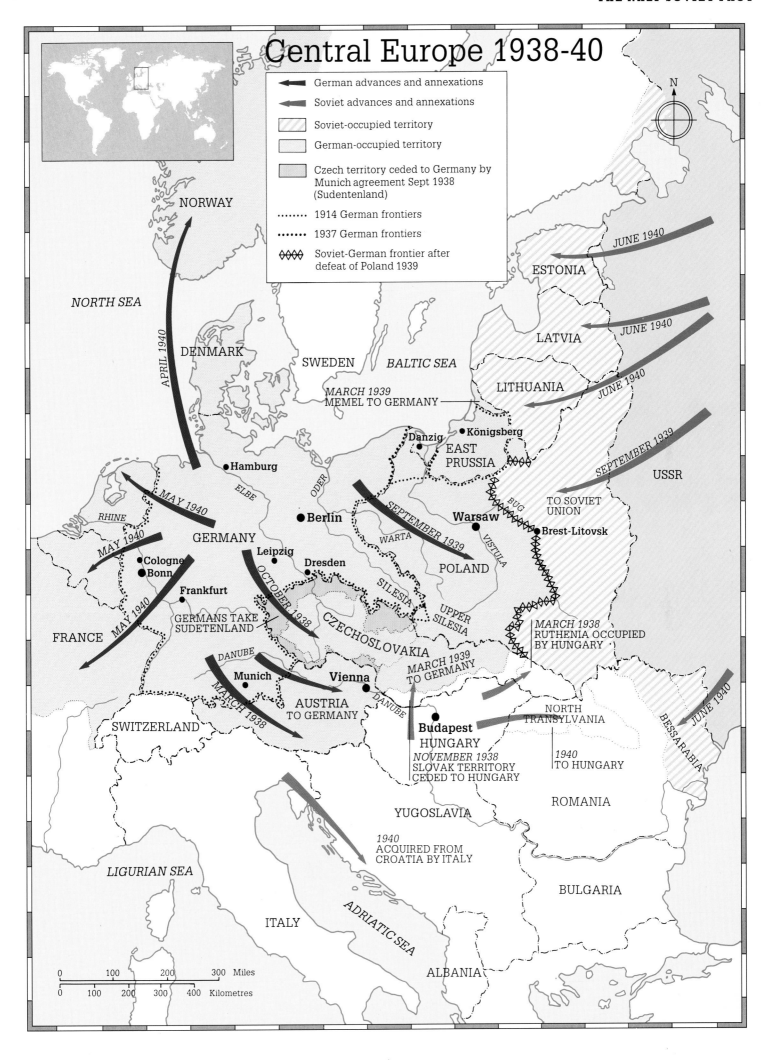

# Central Europe 1938-40

German advances and annexations

Soviet advances and annexations

Soviet-occupied territory

German-occupied territory

Czech territory ceded to Germany by
Munich agreement Sept 1938
(Sudentenland)

1914 German frontiers

1937 German frontiers

Soviet-German frontier after
defeat of Poland 1939

N

NORWAY

*NORTH
SEA*

APRIL 1940

DENMARK

SWEDEN

*BALTIC SEA*

ESTONIA

JUNE 1940

LATVIA

JUNE 1940

LITHUANIA

JUNE 1940

*MARCH 1939
MEMEL TO GERMANY*

Danzig

Königsberg

EAST
PRUSSIA

SEPTEMBER 1939

USSR

Hamburg

ELBE

ODER

MAY 1940

Berlin

SEPTEMBER 1939

Warsaw

BUG

TO SOVIET
UNION

MAY 1940

GERMANY

Leipzig

WARTA

Brest-Litovsk

Cologne
Bonn

Dresden

SILESIA

VISTULA

OCTOBER 1938

POLAND

Frankfurt

GERMANS TAKE
SUDETENLAND

CZECHOSLOVAKIA

UPPER
SILESIA

*MARCH 1938
RUTHENIA OCCUPIED
BY HUNGARY*

MAY 1940

RHINE

FRANCE

DANUBE

MARCH 1939
TO GERMANY

Munich

Vienna

*MARCH 1938*

AUSTRIA
TO GERMANY

DANUBE

Budapest

HUNGARY

NORTH
TRANSYLVANIA

*JUNE 1940*

BESSARABIA

SWITZERLAND

*NOVEMBER 1938
SLOVAK TERRITORY
CEDED TO HUNGARY*

*1940
TO HUNGARY*

ROMANIA

YUGOSLAVIA

*1940
ACQUIRED FROM
CROATIA BY ITALY*

BULGARIA

*LIGURIAN SEA*

ITALY

*ADRIATIC SEA*

ALBANIA

| 0 | 100 | 200 | 300 | Miles |
| 0 | 100 | 200 | 300 | 400 | Kilometres |

there was a reordering of political priorities in Moscow. Britain and France no longer seemed that attractive as potential partners in alliance.

A few weeks later, at the anniversary celebrations of the Revolution, Stalin and the Prime Minister, Molotov, in their speeches hinted at a change in attitude towards the Nazis. Soon they began negotiating a new trade agreement, and on 10 March 1939, Stalin in a speech to the Eighteenth Congress in Moscow, held out a barely concealed olive branch to Berlin. Five days later, Germany over-ran what was left of Czechoslovakia after Munich; it was now obvious that Hitler's next target would be Poland.

### Bear and Snake Lie Down Together

Although London lacked the means to intervene directly should an invasion of Poland take place, Chamberlain offered Warsaw a guarantee of assistance. On 3 April the German High Command were ordered to proceed with the plan to invade Poland, and a week later Hitler signed the order for detailed preparations.

Meanwhile, Litvinov was soon travelling around Europe trying to organize a grand alliance against Germany. But on the very day that he was speaking to the British government, Moscow was also making a discreet approach to Hitler - its diplomatic dialectics underscored by what seemed a lack of enthusiasm in London and Paris for an alliance with the Soviet Union. Then on 3 May, Litvinov, a Jew, was sacked and Molotov replaced him.

The Germans made an immediate response to Litvinov's dismissal. The press was told to tone down its attacks on the Soviets, who duly noted the shift. On 6 May Hitler asked to be briefed on the Soviet political, military and economic position. When Chamberlain announced to the House of Commons on 24 May that he might soon be in a position to conclude an agreement with the Soviet Union, Berlin hastened to outmanoeuvre him. Under cover of trade negotiations, Germany pressed its suit on the Kremlin.

The economic agreement was signed in Berlin on 19 August by two senior trade officials representing the two governments. The non-aggression pact which would follow could not yet be divulged since, although the wording of the document which would be published had been agreed, the secret protocols had still to be concluded - and such negotiations needed participants with the highest authority.

The German delegation arrived in Moscow at 11 am on the 23rd and by the afternoon were locked in talks. During an adjournment, direct telephone conversations took place between the Chancellery and the Kremlin, and the talks were concluded that evening. The details which were announced to the world seemed relatively innocuous: 'Both High Contracting Powers obligate themselves to desist from any act of violence, any aggressive action, and any attack on each other, either individually or jointly with other Powers.' The pact was to last for ten years, and prolonged automatically for another five, unless either of the two parties notified the other of its objection. It took effect from the moment of signing.

The secret protocols were another matter, and apportioned part of eastern Europe into spheres of Soviet and German influence. Stalin received Finland, Latvia and Estonia, as well as northern Romania in the Balkans;

Hitler got Lithuania; and Poland was split in two. By 7 pm on the 24th, Ribbentrop was back in Berlin.

Seven days later the German forces, who had been delayed until the pact was signed, crossed the Polish border. On 17 September, Soviet forces moved in to occupy their portion of the spoils. Under the terms of the pact, Warsaw came under Soviet control; but the Germans concluded that possession of the capital would be to their own advantage, and so they arranged another session with the Soviets, swapping it for Lithuania. This exercise in *realpolitik* was so offensive to outsiders that even Pope Pius XII, not given to public expressions of political disgust, was shocked into describing Poland as being 'crucified between two thieves'.

### The Winter War

The possibility of open conflict with the Western allies moved one step closer when the Soviet Union attacked Finland on 30 November 1939. With a border located only twenty miles from Leningrad and an anti-Soviet government in power, this country of only 4 million people looked like an easy target. Soviet diplomats had demanded the use of a coastal strip as a base from which to defend Leningrad, but the Finns had refused to believe Moscow's assurances that the soldiers would leave at the end of the war.

Western magazines were soon full of pictures of gallant soldiers on skis giving 'Uncle Joe' a bloody nose. Stalin's slaughter of the officer corps of the Red Army during the purges of the 1930s had destroyed its ability to wage war effectively, and the invasion by the Soviet 7th and 13th armies foundered in a morass of fear and incompetence. A Finnish observer described the Soviet troops as being 'genuinely terrified of any notification being made of their capture, as they had been warned that, should they surrender, dire retribution would fall on their families ... with only a few exceptions, all ranks refused to return to the Soviet as exchanged prisoners of war. They are confident of being instantly shot.'

During December and January, the poorly equipped Finns held the line of scattered blockhouses which became known to the world's press as the Mannerheim Line, after the general who had insisted that the defences were built in the late 1930s. Then the Finnish army went on the offensive, scoring its first victory by attacking across the frozen River Tolvajarvi. Familiarity with the heavily wooded terrain allowed the Finns to outmanoeuvre the Red Army successfully.

After two months, Stalin, furious at the humiliation which he had suffered in the eyes of the world, ordered a massive assault on the Mannerheim Line which after two weeks' intense fighting, broke forcing the Finns to retreat. With few reserves to fall back on, they had little alternative but to negotiate a ceasefire. The peace treaty was signed in Moscow on 3 March 1940.

## Toeing the Comintern Line

When Britain declared war on Germany on 3 September 1939, the British Communist Party supported the government's action. The party's General Secretary, Harry Pollitt called it a 'just' war, and the *Daily Worker* lauded Churchill as a man who could unite the country against Hitler. But on 23 September the notion that this was a 'just' war had to be disavowed when the Comintern representative arrived with new instructions for the CPGB from Moscow.

The present war is an imperialist and unjust war for which the bourgeoisie of all the belligerent States bear equal responsibility. In no country can the working class or the Communist Parties support the war. The bourgeoisie is not conducting war against fascism as Chamberlain and the leaders of the Labour Party pretend. War is carried on between two groups of imperialist countries for world domination. The international working class may under no conditions defend Fascist Poland, which has refused the aid of the Soviet Union and repressed other nationalities. The division of States into fascist and democratic States has now lost its former sense. From this point of view the tactics must be changed. The tactics of the Communist Parties in the belligerent countries in this first stage of the war is to operate against the war, to unmask its imperial character. The Communist Parties have fought against the supporters of Munich because these have prevented a real anti-fascist front with the participation of the Soviet Union in order to be able to carry on a robber war.

The war has fundamentally changed the situation. Where the Communist Parties have representatives in Parliament these must vote against war credits. It must be made clear to the masses that war will bring them nothing but new troubles and misery. In the neutral States we must unmask the Governments which maintain the neutrality of their own countries but support the war of other countries and operate on their profits, as, for example, the Government of the United States has done with regard to the war between Japan and China. The Communist Parties have to take on everywhere the offensive struggle against the treacherous policy of Social Democracy. The Communist Parties which acted contrary to these tactics must now immediately correct their policy.

The Germans were punctilious in their observance of the non-aggression pact while the Red Army was engaged in Finland. Indeed, their attitude put considerable strain on their relationship with Italy. A few days after the Soviet attack, Italians were demonstrating in the streets while their press denounced the unprovoked assault and sided with the Finns. Mussolini's government then began working out ways in which Italy could send aid to the defending army, but was informed by Germany that such assistance could not be shipped across its territory. Such was the strength of the Italian reaction that the Duce sent Hitler a personal letter and the reply was carried to Rome by the German Foreign Minister, Ribbentrop. Only then was the crisis in relations between the Axis powers defused.

## The Snake Strikes

The German attack on Norway and Denmark on 9 April 1940 caused a cooling in relations with the Soviet Union, although Berlin could not afford to allow any major antagonism with Moscow to develop now that its armies were fully committed in the west. However, Germany's successful expansionism caused Moscow to assert its claims to territories along the lines of the non-aggression pact. During June and July of that year it exerted heavy political and military pressure on the Baltic states, and proceeded to incorporate them into the Soviet Union. Claiming territory in northern Romania was a more delicate matter because the area contained vast oilfields which the German leadership also coveted. For this reason Molotov made sure that Berlin knew exactly what the Soviets intended before they advanced in the Balkans and that the Germans did not object.

Events in the west now had their effect on Soviet-German relations. The capitulation of France on 22 June 1940 left Britain isolated in its resistance to Germany and in its vigorous rejection of the vaguely worded peace offer Hitler made in the Reichstag on 29 July. Two days later, in a meeting with his most senior military staff, Hitler expressed bewilderment at Britain's intransigence and concluded that the British must be hoping to manoeuvre the Soviet Union into an alliance against Germany, which would mean fighting a war on two fronts. This was a horrifying prospect after Germany's experience in the First World War.

Ten days later Hitler, in another meeting with his military leaders (at which Franz Halder, the Chief of Staff of the German army, took extensive notes), pointed out that the capitulation of Britain might take another two years, and speculated: 'Britain's hope lies in Russia and the United States.... Russia is the Far Eastern sword of Britain and the United States .... Russia is the factor on which Britain is relying the most. Something must have happened in London! ... With Russia smashed, Britain's last hope will be shattered.... Decision: Russia's destruction must therefore be made a part of this struggle.... The sooner

*Top:* Polish soldiers, taken prisoner by the German Army, march through Warsaw after a gallant defence of the city. *Above:* In David Low's cartoon, *Just in Case There's Any Mistake*, Great Britain makes clear her attitude to German aggression against Poland.

Russia is crushed the better.' Their attack was set for the spring of 1941.

The decision of 31 July had immediate consequences for the secret protocols of the pact. Although Hitler had raised no objections to Soviet intentions towards Romania just a few weeks before, there was now every reason to head off the Red Army's incursion into the Balkans - for the oilfields were going to become of vital importance to both parties. The goodwill of Finland was also necessary if Germany wanted to attack the Soviet northern flank. Berlin therefore concluded secret negotiations with both Finland and Romania to provide military assistance. Late in September 1940, without notifying Moscow beforehand, units of the German army appeared in these countries, effectively blocking any hopes of further Soviet expansion.

Then, on 27 September, in Berlin, Germany, Italy and Japan signed the Tripartite Agreement, which apportioned spheres of influence to the parties involved. Understandably the Soviets were by now thoroughly alarmed at what appeared to be a re-emergence of the anti-Comintern Pact, and although it was suggested to Molotov at

a meeting in Berlin that Moscow might wish to append its signature to the Agreement, this in no way allayed the Soviet Union's growing fears. Meanwhile, preparations for the German attack, scheduled for the following spring, were still proceeding without a hitch.

Ironically, Stalin who had agreed that war was inevitable and had been advised by Soviet and British intelligence when Germany would attack, was not prepared for Operation Barbarossa when it came. On the night of 21-22 June 1941, Stalin's forces were literally caught napping and some units were overwhelmed by the might of the Wehrmacht even before they had time to dress. Ill-informed, poorly led and low in morale as a result of Stalin's purges, the Red Army suffered one defeat after another. Many important bridges were captured intact, while hundreds of Soviet planes were destroyed on the ground. Moscow had learnt the hard way about Hitler's duplicity. Four years later a defeated Germany became a divided country, and it was nearly half a century before the Soviet Union was prepared to discuss reunification with the nation which had mauled the hand of peace extended towards it.

# China: The Long March

According to classical Marxist theory, China was not ripe for revolution in the first half of the twentieth century. Its population was primarily poor, rural and illiterate - the antithesis of the Marxist-Leninist politicized proletariat. Life was centred around the village, which in turn depended on a local market town for selling the peasants' produce. Methods of transportation and communication were extremely primitive over much of the Chinese interior. It was the genius of the Chinese Communist Party, and of Mao Zedong in particular, to turn the Marxist formula for revolution on its head and transform a chaotic countryside and the goodwill of the peasants into the party's greatest allies.

## The Seedbed of Change

The Chinese imperial system, virtually unchanged for 2000 years, had long been in decay. Repeated encounters with the West, especially since the mid-nineteenth century, had manifestly disproved the imperial claim both to universal sovereignty of the civilized world and to moral and technical superiority, while the whole fabric of Chinese life was threatened by the innovations and concessions forced on them by the West after the Opium Wars of the 1840s. After the failure of the anti-foreign Boxer Rising in 1900, resistance to Western ideas seemed to crumble and as traditional ideas and institutions were modernized, the agents of revolution began to organize.

On 9 October 1911 a group of revolutionaries blew themselves up as they were preparing a bomb in a basement in the city of Wuchang in central China. When the local police arrived, they found a list of local radicals whom they proceeded to round up. Rather than be led away to an uncertain fate, the radicals decided to fight; at this point the provincial governor and his army commander both fled. On 12 October the province of Hupei declared its independence, and within a month most of the other provinces had followed suit. Many of those who issued these declarations were the leaders of local assemblies and solid members of the bourgeoisie, who were more concerned to further their interests through greater provincial autonomy than to promote democracy. The Chinese empire was beginning to disintegrate.

The court in Beijing responded to this flush of republican fervour by summoning the country's leading general, Yuan Shikai, to lead the army against the rebels. Yuan, however, insisted on negotiating. The rebels' first move was to offer him the presidency if he changed sides. The Emperor's abdication was published on 12 February 1912, and a month later Yuan was inaugurated. He remained in charge of China until his death in June 1916. As the army had remained united only by its loyalty to Yuan, the summer of 1916 saw it fragment into factions seeking regional power. For the next twelve years these forces, and those of bandits who grabbed territory amid the subsequent anarchy, dominated China, even though foreign governments recognized a nominal Beijing regime. It was in the middle of this political chaos that three thousand students staged a mass demonstration in the capital on 4 May 1919.

The students were moved by nationalist sentiments and were particularly incensed by Japan's growing stranglehold on Manchuria, China's most resource-rich province, since the Russo-Japanese war of 1904-5. One consequence of the demonstration was a rapid growth of interest in new ideas to save China from complete collapse. Marxism was one of the novel introductions - its rejuvenating effect on Russia had not gone unnoticed.

However, the seeds of this new idea fell on relatively stony ground. The *Communist Manifesto* was not translated in full into Chinese until 1920; the first volume of *Das Kapital* did not appear in Chinese until 1930. Out of a population of about 400 million, the first Congress of the Communist Party of China, held in Shanghai in July 1921, could muster only thirteen men to represent fifty-three members.

Party membership developed slowly and by the start of 1925 there were still only a thousand people in it. This failure to develop encouraged the Soviet Union to look elsewhere for allies, and in January 1923 the Soviets signed a pact with the Nationalist leader, Sun Yat-sen, and his party, the Guomindang. Sun had carved out a sphere of influence based on the southern port of Guangzhou (Canton), and he needed Moscow's money to finance an army that would extend his power and protect him from the surrounding warlords. Encouraged by Moscow, the Communists and the Guomindang formed a united front to destroy the warlords, to unify the country and to curtail foreign interference.

## Sun Yat-sen: The Father of Modern China

As China's first great republican leader, Sun Yat-sen is revered by both Communists and Nationalists alike. He was born near Macao in 1866 and attended various village schools until he was thirteen, when he joined his brother in Hawaii. He continued his education here before moving to Hong Kong to study medicine.

In 1894 he returned to Hawaii where he organized the Society to Restore China's Prosperity, a secret group of little importance in itself. However, he conceived a plan for a rising which would be funded by overseas Chinese and aided on the ground by the aggressive skills of the Chinese mafia, the Triads. This alliance continued clandestinely for decades and did much to undermine the Nationalist cause among the native Chinese. Sun slipped into Canton in to lead the planned rebellion but he was betrayed in October 1895 and was lucky to escape with his life.

In 1896 he travelled to London where he found lodgings in Gray's Inn Place. On 10 October he visited the Chinese legation under an assumed name, thinking that he would be safe. But he was betrayed and when he returned the next day he was taken prisoner. A week passed before he managed to bribe the legation's porter into taking a note to his friends. 'I was kidnapped into the Chinese Legation on Sunday, and shall be smuggled out from England to China for death ... O! Woe to me!' But when the Foreign Office and *The Times* were both informed of this infraction of international law, neither did more than hesitate. Only when *The Globe* got wind of the story was firm action taken by the Foreign Office to rescue Sun, who was turned into an international celebrity overnight as a result of all the publicity. Sun was forced to travel the world for the next fifteen years, during which time he founded another group, the Alliance Society, in Tokyo. Meanwhile, his views were becoming popular among China's growing student population and when the last emperor finally abdicated in 1912, Sun was offered an important position in the new government. Political in-fighting, however, forced him into exile again.

His Society now changed its name to the Guomindang and steadily increased its power. In 1923, a Soviet diplomat resident in Shanghai recommended that Moscow should give Sun the financial backing he needed in return for future territorial concessions. Sun reorganized the Guomindang on more disciplined lines; but he died of cancer in March 1925, before he could launch the planned joint attack with the Communists on the warlords who dominated rural China.

Mao Zedong (standing) presides over the first meeting of the Chinese Communist Party in this revolutionary painting. The party was formed in 1921 when it had just fifty-three members and its growth was slow - by 1925 there were only a thousand members.

They created a military academy to promote their cause and placed a young officer called Chiang Kaishek (sometimes today called Jiang Jieshi) in charge. His second-in-command, Zhou Enlai, was one of the few founding members of the Communist Party who had studied abroad. The third key figure for the future was a young party member called Mao Zedong, who was despatched to Hunan to soften up the opposition and to create a sympathetic underground organization, in case the army needed to pass through the province on its way north. Mao was so successful in his task that he was elected to the Central Executive of the Guomindang on his return. In March 1925, however, Sun Yat-sen died and the death knell of co-operation was sounded.

Within a year, factional conflict within the Guomindang propelled Chiang into effective control of the party. In July 1926 the long-postponed attack on the warlords began and the success of the campaign surprised even some Nationalists. Although China was strewn with hundreds of petty rulers, seven major warlords dominated the country. In less than a year, three of them were defeated and the combined army of the Nationalists and Communists controlled much of the rich eastern seaboard. It was at this point that Chiang showed his hand.

In the spring of 1925 the Communists had led a successful strike in Shanghai, and within a few months their membership had soared to thirty thousand. As the liberating army approached in March 1927, the workers under Zhou Enlai's leadership rose and took over the city. Chiang had already shown his hatred of the left wing within his own party, and now the Communists had a power base to rival his own. He decided to use his strong ties with organized crime to deadly effect. On the morning of 12 April, at the sound of a solitary bugle, heavily armed gangsters turned on the workers, murdering thousands. Zhou, with an $80,000 price on his head, managed to escape.

**The First Soviet**

As the cities of the east became increasingly unsafe for the Communist Party, many of their number decided to take to the countryside. Mao was instructed to provoke an uprising in the central province of Hunan, but when that failed he retreated to the isolated hills of the Jinggangshan, on the border of Jiangxi province, which became a centre of Communist activity. It was here that Mao learned the skills of guerrilla warfare, which he owed more to the expertise of two local bandits and his continual reading of a Chinese classic, *The Water Margin*, than to any Marxist text.

In May 1928 Mao welcomed Zhu De, an ex-bandit who had joined the party and was to become one of its greatest generals. Together they played cat and mouse with the Nationalist forces and created the strategy which would become the model for rural revolutionary groups for generations to come. A few years later Zhu described their plan of action: 'The enemy advances, we retreat; the enemy camps, we harass; the enemy tires, we attack; the enemy retreats, we pursue.'

Communist troops also displayed great discipline in their relationship with the local people and, although they dispossessed rich landowners and frequently executed them, the land was redistributed to the peasants. They also impressed the local merchants with their honesty, which contrasted sharply with the behaviour of the Nationalist troops, who were frequently described as little more than bands of thieves. By January 1929 the Communists had attracted so many recruits that they were unable to feed them in Jinggangshan. As a result, they had to move their troops to what became the Central Soviet Area in southern Jiangxi and neighbouring Fujian. By 1932 the region under their control encompassed thirty-five counties and held 3 million people. It was at this point that Stalin, through the Comintern, imposed two of his agents upon them and

The Japanese army entering Hangzhou in December 1937. The Soviet Union sent pilots and warplanes to help the Chinese, but superior Japanese airpower destroyed city after city.

things started to go wrong. Mao was the first to stress party discipline to his troops. 'Political power comes from the barrel of a gun,' he claimed, 'but the party must always control the gun and the gun must never control the party.' He was now hoist by his own petard. Stalin's two agents, Li De and Bo Gu, held Mao in total contempt for they assumed, quite falsely, that he was an uneducated peasant. As they were the emissaries of the Comintern, their status in the Jiangxi soviet gave them the authority to dictate policy; they used this power to exclude Mao from the Central Committee. Their training in Moscow was based on European warfare, and their inclination was to stand their ground and to fight Chiang in set-piece battles. This strategy played into the hands of the Nationalists, who were able to command a much larger pool of reserves and who soon acquired their own European-trained adviser.

Late in 1933 Adolf Hitler, recognizing in Chiang someone as fervently anti-Communist as himself, sent General von Seeckt, one of his most able tacticians, to aid the Nationalists. Von Seeckt began building blockhouses and pillboxes on a vast scale, slowly encircling the Soviet territory and cutting it off from outside supplies. Within a year the Communists had lost sixty thousand men and 58 per cent of their territory. They had no alternative but to break out.

## The Great Snowy Mountains

Mao's army had been marching for eight months when they reached the remote province of Sichuan. They were now beyond the range of their Nationalist enemies, but their greatest struggle was yet to come. Across the path lay the Snowy Mountains, which climbed to heights the troops had never encountered before.

Mao chose to tackle Jiajin Mountain, a pass which rises to 14,000 feet and is snow-bound even in the first week of June when they began to climb. The way up was very deceptive because the gradient was easy, although it seemed to go on for ever. All the soldiers were briefed on the dangers of the snow and cold and of walking at high altitudes. They were instructed to walk steadily without pausing, to eat well before starting, and to wear what protective clothing they had. But some of the marchers, frightened by the altitude, believed that they had to whisper because of the lack of oxygen. Others, not realizing how exhaustion could catch up with them in the thin air, sat down for a breather and could not get up again. They froze to death where they were.

Some of the cooks suffered particularly badly because they insisted, against orders, on carrying their heavy woks and supplies of rice on their backs. Some of those in the Third Army tried to prepare fresh ginger and hot pepper soup to revive their exhausted comrades when they reached the top. But trying to work at 14,000 feet, where water boiled at a low temperature because of the weak air pressure, resulted in two of them dropping dead as they handed out the soup.

Once they had reached the summit, the quickest way down was to slide, and several marchers careered off the track and over the cliffs which lined the path. Others held hands to stop themselves from falling. Even the leaders of the march suffered. Lin Biao collapsed several times and only reached safety with the aid of his bodyguards. Mao had great difficulty because he did not have a padded jacket and his cotton trousers were soon soaked from by the snow. At one point he stopped to encourage the men and could only get moving again with the help of one of his bodyguards. The weather conditions were appalling: fog alternated with storms and Zhou Enlai developed a cough which turned into a near fatal lung infection some weeks later.

Twelve days after they had begun the ascent, the troops reached the far side of the mountains on 14 June. As they emerged from their ordeal and entered the small village of Dawei, they came face-to-face with a second Communist army which was searching for them. Both sides were taken by surprise and shots were exchanged before they realized that they were facing friends. That night, despite their exhaustion, they celebrated with a great rally. Mao made a speech in which he talked of unity and the need to travel north to attack the Japanese. Soldiers danced, sang and drank all night, relieved that they were still alive.

### The Long March

Starting on 16 October 1934, the People's Liberation Army marched westwards. They were split into two columns a few miles apart, flanking a central group which contained the commanders, the sick and the bearers, who carried everything from sections of printing presses to office chairs. Under orders from the Soviet agents, the soldiers were told little about their destination; accustomed as they were to a regular flow of information about their objectives from their commanders, the

# The Long March 1934-5

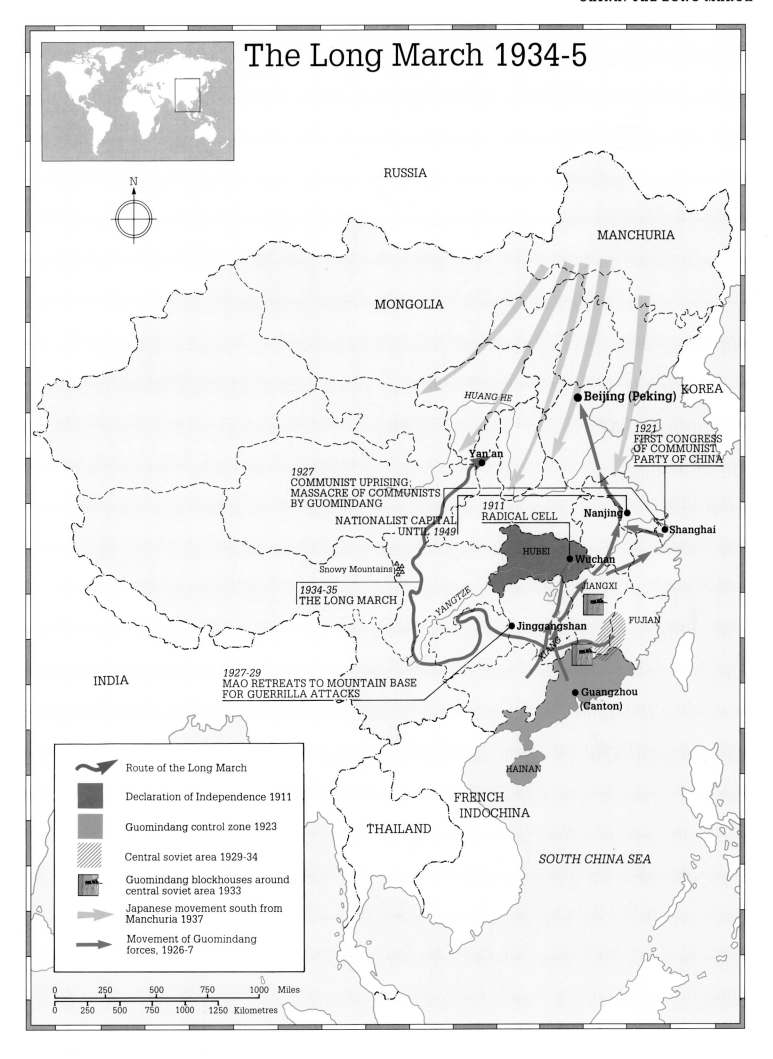

RUSSIA

MANCHURIA

MONGOLIA

KOREA

*HUANG HE*

● Beijing (Peking)

Yan'an

*1927*
COMMUNIST UPRISING;
MASSACRE OF COMMUNISTS
BY GUOMINDANG

*1921*
FIRST CONGRESS
OF COMMUNIST
PARTY OF CHINA

NATIONALIST CAPITAL
UNTIL *1949*

*1911*
RADICAL CELL

Nanjing ●

● Shanghai

HUBEI

Wuchan ●

Snowy Mountains

JIANGXI

*1934-35*
THE LONG MARCH

FUJIAN

*YANGTZE*

Jinggangshan ●

*XIANG*

*1927-29*
MAO RETREATS TO MOUNTAIN BASE
FOR GUERRILLA ATTACKS

INDIA

● Guangzhou
(Canton)

HAINAN

Route of the Long March

Declaration of Independence 1911

Guomindang control zone 1923

Central soviet area 1929-34

Guomindang blockhouses around
central soviet area 1933

Japanese movement south from
Manchuria 1937

Movement of Guomindang
forces, 1926-7

FRENCH
INDOCHINA

THAILAND

*SOUTH CHINA SEA*

0   250   500   750   1000  Miles

0   250  500  750  1000  1250  Kilometres

N

**9 7**

newer recruits became anxious and confused. The army marched at night to avoid detection by Chiang's aircraft. Much of the route was over very rough terrain; many lost their footing in the darkness and plunged to their deaths. They encountered little resistance at first because Zhou Enlai had come to an accommodation with a local warlord. Furthermore, Chiang's intelligence section was so incompetent that it was a month before it realized that the enemy had slipped away. However, once the alarm had been raised, the Communists were soon located since their route was dictated by the mountain ranges in their path.

Chiang rushed his troops to the Xiang River, for there was only one point where the Communists could cross. Even so, if the baggage bearers had not been so slow the Communists might have slipped away again. Instead, the crossing turned into a six-day battle in which about fifteen thousand of the marchers were lost. Six weeks after eighty-six thousand men and woman had set out, the columns contained no more than thirty thousand, for many of the fresh recruits had already slipped away or been lost in skirmishes.

All this time Mao, who was recovering from an attack of malaria, was being carried on a stretcher. Two of his wounded companions were commanders who had been among his critics back in Jiangxi. Their constant conversations on the journey turned them into supporters of Mao and against the two agents from Moscow who were dictating strategy. Supported by these allies, Mao was invited to a Military Commission meeting on 11 December, his first in two years. His authoritative analysis of the army's situation was accepted by all commanders, and that of Moscow's agents ignored. Other meetings during the next weeks confirmed Mao's *de facto* position. Stalin had lost his hold on his Chinese comrades.

The Communists had broken Chiang's radio codes and their information about the Nationalist positions was therefore quite detailed. The Military Commission decided to head further west to avoid Chiang's army of four hundred thousand. Discussions were now dominated by those party members who would figure prominently in Chinese history for decades to come. Lin Biao was the commander of the elite First Army Group; Deng Xiaoping was the editor of *Red Star*, the army's newspaper; and Liu Shaoqi was in the Politburo.

Mao now wanted to head north-west, but he blundered into eight regiments of some of the Nationalists' best troops. The Communists had no alternative but to wheel round in an enormous circle to the south-east to avoid them; only then could they head north to their final home - Yan'an in the far north-west. To reach their destination, the army had to cross the high passes of the Snowy Mountains dressed only in the light uniforms they had worn in the subtropical conditions of the Jiangxi soviet. Beyond the mountains, the troops saw what they took to

US Ambassador Marshall sipping tea with Mao (second from left) in Yan'an, 1945. At the end of the war, President Truman sent Marshall to negotiate between the Guomindang and the Red Army to try to prevent a total Communist takeover.

be grasslands covered by wild flowers. In fact, the wasteland was a marsh which took over five days to cross and claimed hundreds of lives as troops wandered from the indistinct path or sat down to rest and were sucked into the mud. By the time the army reached Yan'an, after marching and fighting for six thousand miles, fewer than four thousand soldiers were left alive - but news of their exploits was beginning to spread. Soon they would be part of a legend which would inspire an army to win a revolution.

### The Road to Victory

In July 1937 a new factor entered the Chinese equation. This was the Japanese army, which thrust south from Manchuria and over-ran the majority of China's largest cities within two years. In achieving this victory, the Japanese cut Chiang off from his main source of revenue - the eastern business community - and destroyed his finest regiments. The threat from the Japanese also forced Chiang to conclude an alliance with the Communists, who were recognized as having their own area of operations in the north. This agreement lasted until 1941 when, under the growing weight of mutual suspicion, hostilities between the Chinese factions were resumed.

The invasion was a godsend to the Communists, since many peasant recruits joined in order to flee from Japanese atrocities. Mao's precept of exemplary behaviour - the party must be like 'fish' in the 'water' of the people - was beginning to pay off; as was the fact that the party's leaders did not live in fine houses like warlords but in caves cut into the cliff faces of Yan'an. In three years party membership soared from forty thousand to eight hundred thousand and the army soon had half a million troops. To ensure that this vast mass of new recruits understood the party's intentions and beliefs, Mao insisted that they undergo an intensive programme of re-education and wrote many of the texts himself. These were the years when Mao Zedong thought became the basis of Chinese Communism.

Once the Japanese had been defeated, the American General Marshall put much effort into reconciling the Communists and the Nationalists; on 10 October 1946, an agreement was concluded. However, Chiang's forces attacked within weeks, and the Civil War began in earnest. The cat-and-mouse tactics developed fifteen years earlier by Mao and Zhu were now transacted on a monumental scale.

During the first half of 1947, the Nationalists were tempted to over-extend their supply lines. The Communists counter-attacked throughout 1948 and, during the course of their encircling movements, captured vast quantities of weapons. The final blow was delivered late in 1948 at the Battle of Hwai-Hai in north-eastern China, where an entire Nationalist army surrendered and its commanding officer committed suicide.

Such victories were assisted by knowledge gained from Communist intelligence agents planted in the Nationalist camp. General Fei, Chiang's Assistant Chief of Staff, was actually a Communist spy and all the Nationalist battle plans and troop movements were known to Mao's commanders in advance.

The Nationalist camp was now completely demoralized and a delegation was sent to try to negotiate a ceasefire. Since General Fei was part of the Nationalists' six-man team, Mao was able to outmanoeuvre them at every turn.

The final thrust came a few weeks later when the Communists staged an amphibious attack across the Yangtze River. The defending Nationalist, General Tai, instructed his troops not to fire on the advancing boats and within three days Nanjing, the Nationalists' capital, had fallen. The People's Liberation Army swept on south towards the Indochinese border through a region demoralized by hyper-inflation and rampant corruption. Even those who had begun as Chiang's most solid supporters were not sorry to hear Mao proclaim the establishment of the People's Republic of China from the Gate of Heavenly Peace on 1 October 1949.

# The Great Patriotic War

The Russian counter-offensive began in November 1942, encircling Stalingrad and the besieged German 6th army. They surrendered in February 1943.

'Perhaps you think we bled and starved for the collective farms, Stalin, the Cheka [political police] and the party bosses? Of course not. We fought for Russia and the prospects of a new life.' With these words a Russian guard in a forced labour camp explained to a German prisoner the depth of his people's commitment during the Second World War. This patriotic fervour had been encouraged since 1931, when Stalin urged the Soviet people to greater efforts in the battle to industrialize, warning them that they would be defeated if they did not overtake capitalism within ten years. In the summer of 1941, that defeat loomed over them as - despite the best efforts of the Commissar for Foreign Affairs, Molotov, to keep the Nazi leadership happy - the German armies scythed through the Soviet countryside and threatened the very heart of Russia.

The first warning the Red Army received of the impending battle was when six thousand shells landed on their positions at 3 am on 22 June. Local commanders were so shocked that they radioed the news back to their headquarters without taking the elementary precaution of encoding their signals. Within hours German tanks had breached the inadequate Soviet defences, and by noon vital sections of their line had fallen to the invading forces.

The German success was achieved through a combination of intense concentration of firepower on three fronts and complete surprise. Despite warnings of the imminent attack from both British and Soviet intelligence, Stalin had failed to reinforce his front line. Now the German

army, the Wehrmacht, was throwing most of its armoured divisions forward to attack the Red Army at its most vulnerable points. Meanwhile the German air force, the Luftwaffe, was destroying most of the Soviet airfields, fuel dumps, tank parks and transport network in the battle zone. According to one German lieutenant, 'The Russian defences might have been a row of glass-houses.'

By the evening of the first day one German armoured group was twenty-five miles inside

### От БРИТАНСКОГО НАРОДА

### К ПОБЕДЕ! МЫ С ВАМИ

A poster by the English artist Reginald Mount illustrating the aid (in the form of tanks) given to the Red Army by Great Britain.

Soviet territory, and the units in the vanguard of the attack were motoring along open roads. The pockets of resistance left behind by this rapid advance did not capitulate, however, as the Germans had come to expect from their experience in Poland, the Low Countries and France; the fierce and unpredictable nature of the counter-attacks caused the invaders considerable problems and unexpected losses.

The delay caused by these sporadic attacks in the German rear gave the Soviet leaders the brief respite that they needed, and although the military leadership was weak, the party's command of Soviet industry enabled whole factories to be shipped to the east, beyond the reach of the German guns. Since factories had been established deep in the Russian interior during the 1930s, such transfers could be grafted on to an existing transport and communications network.

## The Rout of the Red Army

By the middle of July 1941 the Wehrmacht was pushing forward on a front which stretched from a point close to Odessa on the Black Sea to Narva on the Gulf of Finland, only a hundred miles short of Leningrad. Such successes looked impressive in Berlin, but the commanders at the front were anxious because the resistance of the Soviet forces was undiminished and their co-ordination was unimpaired.

Meanwhile, the Wehrmacht hesitated as a conflict developed between Hitler and his generals. The majority of the German

# The Soviet Union at War

FINLAND

RUSSIA

N

Leningrad

EXTENT OF OFFENSIVE
18 NOV 1942

ESTONIA

VOLGA

LATVIA

Moscow

Minsk

OFFENSIVE
AUTUMN 1942

DON

OCT-NOV 1942
BATTLE OF STALINGRAD

EASTERN
POLAND

Kiev

Stalingrad

EASTERN
GALICIA

DNIEPER

BUKOVINA

UKRAINE

OFFENSIVE
JULY 1943

BESSARABIA

CASPIAN
SEA

OMANIA

Bucharest

MARCH 1944

BLACK SEA

BULGARIA

TURKEY

| | Occupied Russia, Oct 1939-Dec 1940 |
| | German troops |
| | German advances |
| | German frontlines |
| | Russian troops |
| | Russian advances |
| | Russian frontlines |
| | German territory, 8 May 1945 |
| | British troops |
| | Advance of Allied forces |
| | American troops |
| | Liberated by British and American troops before May 1944 |

| 0 | 100 | 200 | 300 | 400 | 500 | 600 | Miles |

| 0 | 200 | 400 | 600 | 800 | Kilometres |

general staff wanted to launch a concentrated assault on Moscow, the hub of the Soviet railway system as well as the capital, but Hitler was intent on capturing Leningrad in the north and the Ukraine in the south. When Hitler insisted, the general staff did their best to frustrate his intentions without breaking their oaths of loyalty.

On 8 August, after several weeks' delay, the northern flank of the Wehrmacht turned towards Leningrad and a month later was on the outskirts of the city. Proclamations were posted in the city in an effort to rally the defenders. 'The enemy is at the gates of Leningrad! Grave danger hangs over the city. The success of the Red Army depends on the heroic, valiant, and firm stand of each soldier, commander, and political worker, and also on how active and energetic the assistance given to the Red Army by us Leningraders is.'

As the Germans closed in for the kill, they found themselves involved in street-fighting; it soon became obvious that the loss of men and machines needed to conquer the city would not be worth the territory gained. On 16 September the general staff ordered the Panzers to withdraw so that a circle of guns could be established around the city. The long siege of Leningrad began.

Hitler's thrust into the Ukraine was much more successful and the German armour was able to surround the city of Kiev, which was defended by a garrison of three-quarters of a million men. The Soviet commander, Marshal Budenny, had been appointed because Stalin found him congenial. Stalin's confidence, however, had been misplaced for the Marshal proved unable to organize one of the Red Army's last major concentrations of manpower. While the Germans were manoeuvring to encircle the city, Budenny did nothing. On 13 September Stalin was forced to relieve him of his

command but the situation was irretrievable. On the 18th the German trap snapped shut and five days of slaughter followed. Despite an absence of fuel, ammunition and a co-ordinated command structure, the Red Army hung on. It was only a matter of time, however, before the defenders capitulated, and by the end of September, six hundred thousand men were being herded away to forced labour and death in German concentration camps.

The German army was now free to drive home what it believed to be the last nail in the Soviet coffin: the capture of Moscow. In the first week in October, the German armoured divisions broke through the thin screen of ill-equipped troops which shielded the Soviet capital. The German commanders concluded that Stalin would soon give up. In their elation they missed two critical changes in the situation: the first fall of snow, on 7 October, and a change in the command of the defensive forces. Marshal Zhukov, 'Stalin's fireman', had arrived.

As the weather deteriorated, the German tanks began to churn up the soggy dirt roads, making travel difficult for the supporting groups of troops and supplies, which slowed the entire advance. Zhukov now played one of his strongest cards - a tank brigade entirely equipped with the revolutionary new T-34 tanks. At dusk on 11 October, as the freezing ground allowed them to move freely, the brigade attacked the 4th Panzer roup. The German gunners watched in horror as their shells bounced off the Soviet tanks, which sliced up the Panzer column into manageable portions that were soon destroyed.

As the temperature dropped, the engine oil and guns froze solid. With no winter clothing, the German troops were dying of hypothermia or were in hospital with frostbite. The Red Army, on the other hand, was now coming into its element, and in

early November it began to transfer units from its Far Eastern command after its spy network in Tokyo had reported that the Japanese intended to attack American bases to the south.

## The Red Army Retaliates

The troops from Siberia were the best equipped and trained in the Red Army and their first appearance on the battlefield on 17 November, with their white, quilted uniforms and effective automatic weapons, caused a frozen and demoralized German infantry division to flee in panic. On the night of 4-5 December, the Wehrmacht was rocked by a massive counter-attack which continued to pummel its positions for three months. But because Hitler insisted they must not retreat, very little ground was conceded.

While the German and Soviet armies were locked in battle in front of Moscow in the worst weather for 140 years, the Japanese attack on Pearl Harbor tranformed the conflict. America seemingly forgot a generation of anti-Communist propaganda and joined Britain in sending supplies to the Soviet Union.

The Soviet Union entered 1942 having lost half of its industrial capacity in the west, while its relocated factories in the east had as yet made little contribution to the country's economy. Despite this basic weakness, the poor state of the German forces during the winter encouraged the Red Army to launch three major spring offensives, all of which failed and caused large numbers of men and weapons to be lost in the process.

The depleted Soviet units in Russia and the Ukraine were in no state to withstand the fresh onslaught unleashed by the Wehrmacht at the end of June. The open plains were the perfect ground for the German armour, as it wheeled south-east through the industrial

Victorious Soviet soldiers fly the Red Flag over the Reichstag in Berlin, 1945. The Great Patriotic War, which lasted for four years, saw the loss of 20 million Russians.

# Surviving the Siege of Leningrad

Vera Inber, poet and wife of a Leningrad doctor lived in Leningrad with her husband throughout the siege. In 1948 she published her war-time diary.

By December 1941 there was a shortage of coffins in the city: 'Each day, eight to ten bodies are brought [to the mortuary] on sleighs. And they just lie on the snow. Fewer and fewer coffins are available ... So the bodies are wrapped in sheets, in blankets, in tablecloths, sometimes even in curtains ... The mortuary itself is full. Not only are there too few lorries to go to the cemetry, but more important, not enough petrol to put in the lorries ... and the main thing - there is not enough strength left in the living to bury the dead.'

Vera Inber, standing among the ruins of Leningrad, 1943.

The weakness of the living was caused by starvation. Vera Inber's daily help went to the baker's shop. On the way there she saw a man 'laughing, crying, clutching his head as he walked along'. When she reached the shop she understood why: 'The bread ration has been increased, and this man was one of the first to learn about it. The radio doesn't work for lack of current, the newspapers are only posted on the walls every second or third day. Therefore, people only learned that the bread ration had gone up when they were at the counter ... Everyone is radiant ... Manual workers now receive 250-300 grammes, white-collar workers 250 grammes.' Before this most people had only received 125 grammes per day.

major Soviet attack. However, in the north the siege of Leningrad was relieved and the Germans were forced to withdraw from their most threatenting positions close to Moscow.

## The Tide Turns

In due course, Soviet industry recovered its momentum after its transfer east, and by the spring of 1943 the Red Army was receiving large quantities of munitions. Germany, on the other hand, was having production problems with its new tank, the Panther. By July, however, it had built sufficient numbers to use them on a fresh battlefield surrounding Kursk, about 120 miles north of Kharkov.

Soviet intelligence kept Marshal Zhukov fully informed of the plans for the attack, and a sophisticated defence with massive fire-power was designed. Despite the deployment of nine of the Wehrmacht's finest armoured divisions, the tank battle ended in a Soviet victory. At this point the initiative on the Eastern Front passed from German hands.

Local engagements forced the Germans to retreat steadily, and by January 1944 nearly two-thirds of the Soviet territory occupied by the Wehrmacht had been liberated. This was followed by the great attack which came on 22 June, just two weeks after the Normandy landings - now the Germans were stretched over two fronts. Within weeks the Red Army had returned to the Soviet Union's 1941 frontiers in Poland, but their supply lines had become stretched. As Soviet troops halted just short of Warsaw the Polish resistance, which was loyal to the right-wing government in exile in London, rose against the Germans; by 6 August the Poles controlled most of the capital. The Red Army delayed their advance long enough for the Germans to eliminate largely the leadership of the Home Army, a group which would have opposed his post-war plans for Poland. In the meantime, the Red Army was being beaten back along the Baltic coast; and when they did try to enter Warsaw, on 16 September, they were repulsed.

Stalin now turned his attentions south and used the Red Army to take control of the Balkans, and the Red Army reached the Danube on 5 October. Both sides now prepared themselves for the final battle. The Soviet attack was unleashed on 12 January and broke through the defensive lines in Poland within thirty-six hours. Within eight days they were on German soil, but their caution gave the Nazi leadership another respite. Only on 16 April did the Red Army deliver the final blow from the east, which carried them through to Berlin; here they received the white flag of surrender on May Day.

No Soviet citizen can forget the losses of the Second World War. In the wake of Stalin's 'Terror' at least another 20 million people were slaughtered and much of the Soviet Union was devastated. It was to protect themselves against further depredations from the west that the Russians erected the cushion of satellite states to the east of their country which was to remain until the leaders of the Great Patiotic War were in their graves.

region of the Donets Basin towards Rostov and down the valley of the River Don. Unlike the situation in 1941, the advance met only occasional stubborn resistance; the Germans did not seem to realize that they were being nudged in one direction as the Red Army tried to buy time through conceding territory.

The Germans were elated by their success and Hitler told his Chief-of-Staff, General Halder, that 'The Russian is finished.' By the evening of 23 August they had reached the railway bridge at Rynock, which straddles the River Volga about ten miles north of Stalingrad. That night the Luftwaffe bombed the city and destroyed the suburbs of wooden houses in a spectacular fire, but the attack which followed made slow progress against determined resistance. As the German armour edged closer to the city centre, its advance ground to a halt. Soviet soldiers and snipers played a deadly game of hide-and-seek with the enemy among the rubble; in response, the German commanders poured all their reserves into the battle in an attempt to crush the Soviet people.

Zhukov, meanwhile, was holding his reserves back until, on 19 November, he unleashed half a million infantrymen, 900 T-34s, 230 regiments of field artillery and 115 regiments of Katyusha rocket launchers against a forty-mile-wide front. Even the Germans had never managed to amass such concentrated firepower, and the relentless counter-attack slowly encircled the German 6th Army. Neither side wanted to concede an inch, and both armies suffered appallingly from the cold, the lack of food and medical supplies. The Russians did, however, know the terrain better than the Germans and were able eventually to cut their supply and communications lines. On 1 February the surviving trapped units of the Wehrmacht finally surrendered after a five-month siege of the city, thereby giving the Red Army what was probably its greatest victory of the war.

The defeat at Stalingrad dealt a savage blow to the morale of German civilians, but the army soon recovered and within weeks was involved in a pitched battle for the city of Kharkov in the Ukraine, where it defeated a

'The Big Three', Churchill, Stalin and Truman, shaking hands and smiling jovially at the meeting at Potsdam in July 1945. During the meeting they had established the principles of allied control of Germany immediately after the war.

# The Secret Armies

The citizens of Europe were stunned by the speed and scale of the German advances during the spring of 1940. In a matter of a few weeks, the German army had achieved mastery of lands stretching from the Baltic to the Bay of Biscay. From this moment until their liberation, those in occupied Europe had to decide whether to resist or to collaborate with the Axis powers.

This situation put the Communists, particularly in eastern and central Europe where the national parties had long been forced to work underground, in a very special position. For having learnt to live without the reassurance of mass approval and the compromises which that entailed, they found this position as a beleaguered minority surrounded by aggressive opponents the perfect training for the occupation. While traditional political groups floundered, the Communists flourished, once they were free to play a role. Such freedom did not come immediately, for while Stalin insisted on adhering rigorously to the Molotov-Ribbentrop pact of August 1939 he ordered Communists to stay their hand. The orders were, however, revised after Germany invaded Russia in June 1941.

The pact had few repercussions in Hungary, Romania, Bulgaria or Yugoslavia, where the party was an insignificant minority in the early days of the war. However, in Italy, the pact obstructed the party's desire for collaboration with other anti-Fascist groups, and in Poland and Czechoslovakia, where the need to resist the German invaders surfaced earlier than in other countries, it isolated the Communists from their fellow citizens. This had serious long-term consequences in Poland, where most people identified the Soviet Union as their enemy once Stalin's troops occupied the east of their country in line with the terms of the pact.

The greatest confusion was experienced in France as the repercussions of one of the most humiliating defeats in the country's history became clear. By the end of June 1940, the French were completely demoralized and bewildered. But as a consequence of the country's traditional admiration of strong military leaders, the disciplined behaviour of the German army of occupation appealed to many. Indeed after July, when the British navy attacked its French counterpart - which had refused to hand itself over to the Allies - and killed over a thousand sailors, it was Britain that came to be seen as the enemy.

French politicians, meanwhile, were too busy fighting each other, as they had done

Yugoslavia's Communist Party leader, Tito (right), in the mountains where he organized the National Liberation Army's guerrilla war against the Germans.

throughout the history of the republic, to create a resistance movement. It was in this atmosphere that the Communists demanded their due under the Soviet-German pact and for a short time operated openly, even though they were vigorously suppressed in Germany and other countries of central Europe. However, the party machine clung to its subservience to Moscow and the Comintern's directives, and *L'Humanité*, the Communists' daily paper, denounced the first sporadic acts of sabotage as 'provocations'. German soldiers were identified as 'workers in uniform', while the City of London was continuously vilified, as was General de Gaulle, leader of the French government in exile in London. For those Europeans regarding it as only a matter of time before the British were overwhelmed, resistance was in any case regarded as dangerous and futile.

The following winter was well advanced before this attitude began to change. The first break came in the Netherlands, when attacks on Jews in Amsterdam provoked resistance to the Dutch branch of the SS. When German police were attacked, the occupying authorities immediately arrested 425 young Jews, expecting the anti-Nazi incidents to subside.

To everyone's surprise, the Communist Party called a series of wildcat strikes and a one-day protest on 25 February 1941. The strike was completely successful and the Germans were alarmed. They moved in ruthlessly, killing civilians, imposing a curfew and deporting a thousand strikers. Overt resistance collapsed, but a spark had been ignited which would raise the Dutch underground.

## A Balkan Imbroglio

Hitler made his first serious mistake when on 6 April he launched the German invasion of Greece and Yugoslavia; this was in support of Mussolini, whose army was hopelessly bogged down. Hitler's contempt for the Balkan peoples led him to underestimate their spirit. Furthermore, the ruthless attacks on the population which he encouraged crystallized their feeling that they had nothing to lose by resisting: their treatment would be barbaric whatever they did.

Guerrilla bands soon took to the mountains while the Germans and their Hungarian, Bulgarian and Italian allies held the towns, ports and lines of communications. The initial confusion among the Yugoslavs began to be resolved during the summer as two sets of allegiances emerged. One was a group of royalists who called themselves Chetniks, while the other consisted of Communists led by Josip Broz, who soon became known by the codename Tito. Trained in Moscow in the 1930s, he had run Communist supply trails across the border from France during the Spanish Civil War until he returned to Yugoslavia to lead the party.

For the first few months, both groups were content to organize without provoking the enemy and to consolidate their arms supply. But on 22 June 1941, after the surprise German attack on the Soviet Union, the Comintern sent Tito a desperate message to attack and harass the Germans whatever the consequences. On 5 July, the Communist Partisans distributed a leaflet written by Tito in which he called the nation to arms: 'Now is the time, the hour has struck to rise like one man in the battle against the invaders... killers of our peoples. Do not falter in the face of any enemy terror.' Attacks on the Germans began immediately. In August Montenegrin nationalists began their own campaign against the Italians, and the occupying forces began to realize that they might have a serious and protracted struggle on their hands.

The first concerted Axis campaign was launched in September 1941, based on the tactics employed by General von Seeckt in China against Mao Zedong and Zhu De. One hundred thousand well-equipped and trained troops, supported by tanks and aircraft, attacked in a pincer movement and tried to surround the guerrillas. Tito's disciplined groups immediately dispersed and slipped through the advancing lines. The poorly led royalists, who were already more interested in killing Communists than Germans, were badly mauled.

### The German Recruiting Corporal

The turning point of the war came in 1942. The German manpower shortage on the Eastern Front became acute and British penetration of German air space, through bombing raids of increasing size, was beginning to disrupt German arms production. The remedy was Hitler's decree, issued on 21 March, that labour would now include 'hired workers and war prisoners'. This one act, which was a cover for press-gang tactics, did more than any other to enlist the populations of the occupied countries into the secret war against the Germans. When anyone at all might be abducted and transported to work in Germany in a forced labour camp, everyone had a strong personal reason to resist.

Despite the Germans' inadvertent recruiting drive for the resistance movements, these organizations were numerically insignificant in much of western Europe. They were largely supplied by the Special Operations Executive based in London, which was starved of resources by the traditional British military establishment

Palmiro Togliatti, leader of the Italian Communist Party, broadcast resistance messages to Italy.

which resented its methods and its challenge to the established pecking order in Whitehall. As late as 1942, SOE had only five light aircraft with which to supply all of France. In these circumstances it is not surprising that it chose to curtail deliveries to the Communist resistance network in France, the Front National, when it realized that these forces were concerned as much with political events after the liberation as with speeding its arrival.

Because their network was penetrated by German counter-intelligence and eventually run by them, SOE's incompetence in the Netherlands managed to compromise

virtually all guerrilla activity of whatever political complexion in that country from March 1942 until October 1943. In Belgium over a dozen rival resistance groups were in existence, of which the Communist Front de l'Indépéndance was just one.

The only guerrilla groups operating in occupied Europe in 1942 which did more than merely irritate the Germans were Tito's Partisans. The territory in which they operated lay astride some of the German supply routes into North Africa and close to Germany's allies in south-eastern Europe. They were also an affront to Nazi Aryan pride, being both Slavs and Communists. To rid themselves of these offensive groups, the Germans stepped up their Balkan operations in January 1942 and diverted divisions which were badly needed in the battle for Moscow. Tito was slowly driven south, but discipline was maintained and the Partisans always retained their coherence as a fighting force.

Quite where Tito was getting his money to pay for supplies is not clear, for he was receiving no support from Moscow. The British, whose regional SOE office in Cairo was scarcely a model of efficiency, kept sending their supplies to the Chetniks, who were already beginning to co-operate with the occupying armies. The Partisans, meanwhile, managed to halt the German advance for a few weeks at the end of April and create a breathing space for themselves. However, Axis attacks resumed with renewed force in May and the Partisans retreated slowly through the mountains of western Bosnia towards Montenegro. Despite these mixed fortunes, Tito's men and women attracted large numbers of new recruits, largely because they were the only group providing effective resistance to the hated armies of occupation.

By the end of December 1942, the Germans began to realize that the Partisans were no mere local group of bandits and that in Tito

## The Liberation of Northern Italy

The final Allied offensive to liberate those areas of Italy still in German hands began on 5 April 1945. The Americans were worried about Communist influence in the north and tried to discourage their local groups from participating. But the Italian Communist Party realized that their moment had come. On 10 April they issued Directive No. 16 which began, 'Partisan formations will attack and eliminate Nazi-Fascist head-quarters and effect the liberation of cities, towns and villages'. And that was exactly what happened.

When the Allies entered Bologna, they found the 'Red citadel' already under partisan

control. The attack by American and Brazilian units into the Po Valley was helped by the Communists, who crippled the attempts of the Germans to retreat. The port of Genoa was saved from destruction when workers rose and overwhelmed well-armed German troops. When the commanding German general threatened to bombard the city with artillery, the workers proved how well they had learned from the SS by counter-threatening to execute a thousand prisoners. He surrendered the next day.

Milan followed immediately, causing Mussolini to scurry from the city. Turin's insurrection on 26 April was quite bloody,

but Venice escaped serious damage when the German commander struck a bargain with the partisans. The climax to the partisans' campaign arrived when they seized Mussolini and his entourage. After some confusion among the partisans, the Duce and his mistress, Clara Petacci, were executed.

The $90 million treasure that Mussolini was alleged to be travelling with was never traced, but rumours suggested that it found its way into Communist coffers. General Cadorna commented that it was 'impossible to keep a minute check on the book-keeping of the myriad patriot formations during the feverish liberation period.'

# Secret Armies

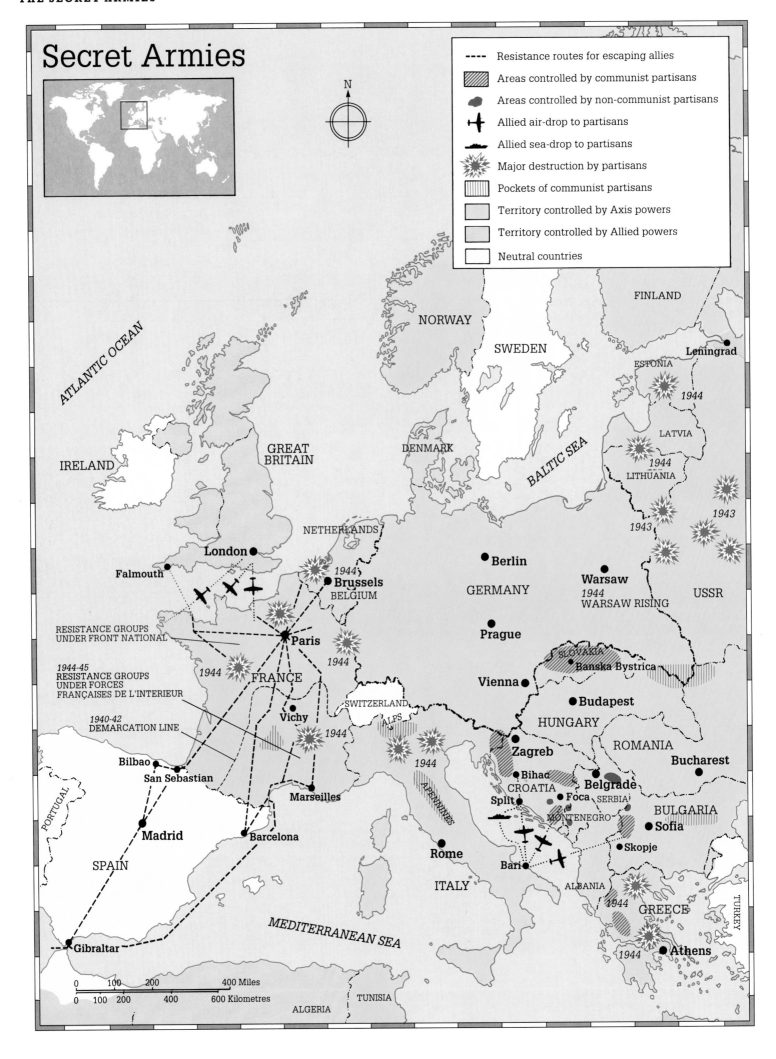

**Legend:**

- - - - - Resistance routes for escaping allies
- Areas controlled by communist partisans
- Areas controlled by non-communist partisans
- Allied air-drop to partisans
- Allied sea-drop to partisans
- Major destruction by partisans
- Pockets of communist partisans
- Territory controlled by Axis powers
- Territory controlled by Allied powers
- Neutral countries

ATLANTIC OCEAN

N

NORWAY

SWEDEN

FINLAND

Leningrad

ESTONIA

1944

LATVIA

1944

LITHUANIA

1943

IRELAND

GREAT BRITAIN

DENMARK

BALTIC SEA

1943

NETHERLANDS

Berlin

GERMANY

Warsaw

1944
WARSAW RISING

USSR

London

Falmouth

1944

Brussels

BELGIUM

Prague

SLOVAKIA

Banska Bystrica

RESISTANCE GROUPS
UNDER FRONT NATIONAL

Paris

1944

FRANCE

Vienna

Budapest

HUNGARY

ROMANIA

1944-45
RESISTANCE GROUPS
UNDER FORCES
FRANÇAISES DE L'INTERIEUR

1944

SWITZERLAND

ALPS

Vichy

1944

Zagreb

1944

Bihac

CROATIA

Belgrade

SERBIA

Bucharest

1940-42
DEMARCATION LINE

Bilbao

San Sebastian

APENNINES

Split

Foca

MONTENEGRO

BULGARIA

Sofia

Madrid

Barcelona

Marseilles

Rome

Skopje

SPAIN

ITALY

Bari

ALBANIA

1944

GREECE

TURKEY

PORTUGAL

Gibraltar

MEDITERRANEAN SEA

1944

Athens

0    100    200         400 Miles
0  100  200        400      600 Kilometres

ALGERIA    TUNISIA

they were facing one of their most formidable opponents. Hitler reinforced his troops in the area and turned it into a separate command. Simultaneously, it dawned on the Allies that their previous assumptions about the Balkans had been mistaken and that the Partisans, not the Chetniks, were the group to support.

Further south, in Greece, SOE had been more successful in identifying the most effective fighting groups. British agents landed by submarine early in 1942 were able to supply and organize highly successful attacks on the rail network, which was carrying German supplies to the Mediterranean.

Sandwiched between Greece, Yugoslavia and the sea, Albania presented another chaotic mixture of competing guerrilla groups who were more interested in overcoming one another than in defeating the Italian forces of occupation. The latter had invaded the country in 1939 and retained control of the cities, leaving the countryside to its enemies. Only after Mussolini's fall from power did the Albanians make a concerted effort to evict their oppressors.

## The Tide Turns

The overthrow of the Duce and the coming to power of the Badoglio government on 25 July 1943 grabbed headlines around the world. But it was the new leader's announcement of Italy's surrender on 8 September which transformed the military situation in southern Europe, and possibilities now opened up for Communist groups in the Balkans.

The German High Command, however, had made plans for such an eventuality as early as 1941. Everywhere that the Italian army was to be found, the Wehrmacht moved in swiftly to fill the vacuum, confiscate weapons and deny any advantage to the guerrillas.

The German army entered areas formerly controlled by the Italians in Yugoslavia the day after the surrender. However, their units were too far from the Adriatic port of Split to win the race against Tito's Partisans, who stripped the city of all Italian weapons.

In Greece, the sudden power vacuum precipitated all-out war between the rival guerrilla groups, which the Germans exploited by inflicting wholesale slaughter on the countryside. The violence of their onslaught was so great that by December 1943 the Communists had to agree a truce with their Republican rivals so that they could protect themselves.

Amidst the political chaos which marked Italy's abrupt withdrawal from the conflict, the Badoglio government did its best to avoid the internecine warfare which scarred Greece. In this it was helped by the traditions of the Italian Communist Party, which favoured compromise with other parties and emphasized its independence from Moscow. Instead, the party spent its venom on the German forces which continued to occupy Italy. This strategy transformed its position, and membership exploded from five thousand in 1943 to

A Communist election cartoon of 1951 appeals to the French electorate to vote for a party that offers bread, peace and liberty, unlike the so-called 'de Gaullists' who wereonly interested in rearmament.

1.6 million in 1945. Its Garibaldi brigades spearheaded the campaign against the Germans and established the party in the mind of the Italian public as a defender of national pride. In some parts of the country, notably the Po Valley, it was able to liberate large areas before the Allied armies arrived.

The story of Communist resistance fighters in France was very different from that of their comrades south of the Alps - because they had three enemies, not one: the Germans, de Gaulle and the Allied High Command. They were consistently successful in mounting attacks on the first, but their political enemies outmanoeuvred them while Eisenhower's generals starved them of weapons.

In complete contrast, by the summer of 1944 the predominantly Communist guerrillas of the Balkans had sucked in a million Axis troops, who were sorely needed on other fronts as the Red Army drove westward. The vanguard of the Soviet forces reached the Yugoslav border on 8 September and liberated Belgrade in a joint operation with the Partisans. In the eastern Balkans, few Communist guerrilla groups were formed and the liberation of Bulgaria and Romania, as well as Czechoslovakia, Hungary and Poland, was largely the work of the Red Army.

The Wehrmacht delayed its withdrawal from the Balkans until the last moment, and then left in haste. The sudden power vacuum in Greece again precipitated war between the Communist and Republican guerrillas. The Communists commanded forces of about a million men in a population of 7 million, and Greek public opinion in 1944 was strongly in their favour. Only Churchill's commitment of the British army to fight against the Communist guerrillas prevented their rise to power.

The closing stages of the Second World War witnessed a change in the image of the various Communist parties throughout Europe. Communist regimes were imposed on Poland, Hungary, East Germany, Bulgaria and Romania under the umbrella of the liberating Red Army, as Moscow built a barrier between itself and future Western aggression. But in Yugoslavia, Albania, Greece and Italy the party had harnessed nationalist sentiment in the struggle against the occupying Axis forces. Allied politicians and generals had managed to thwart a similar achievement in France; but they could not prevent the Front National guerrillas from winning the respect of a large section of the French electorate, who supported the Communists in large numbers for a generation after the war ended.

Extolling the virtues of Capitalism over Communism: vice-president Richard Nixon makes his point to an unusually subdued Nikita Khrushchev, Moscow 1959.

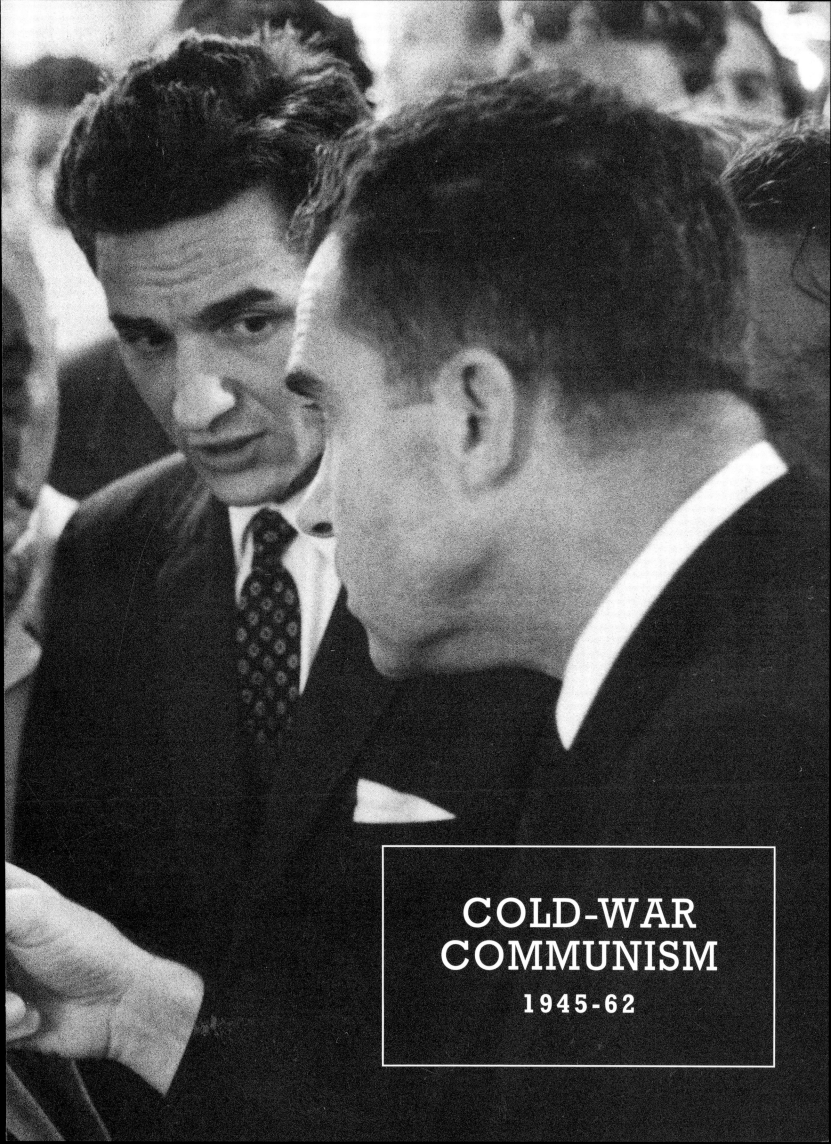

COLD-WAR
COMMUNISM

1945-62

# The Cold War

The first days of May 1945 were a time of joy in much of western Europe; crowds danced in the street and cheered their leaders, while complete strangers embraced in secluded doorways. But even while the flags were waving and the bells were ringing to celebrate the end of the war, the ghost of Adolf Hitler cast a shadow across the proceedings. The prediction that Hitler had made - that the Western democracies would come to realize that their real enemy was based in Moscow - was shortly going to be proved true.

The defeat of Germany not only removed a totalitarian regime from the world; it also destabilized central Europe by removing the region's dominant country from the international scene: at least for the moment. The division of the spoils was agreed at the Yalta Conference - the last meeting of Roosevelt, Churchill and Stalin - in February 1945. At the meeting, which also endorsed plans for the establishment of the United Nations, the dying Roosevelt conceded to Stalin's demand for a post-war Europe split into spheres of influence. The Soviet leader undoubtedly saw this as a way of protecting his country from a repeat of the surprise attack of June 1941. Furthermore, Russian expansionism had been a central plank in the country's foreign policy long before the Bolsheviks came to power; and the differences which would soon emerge between America and the Soviet Union were

rooted in a time that long preceeded the post-war euphoria.

Tsarist Russia, which was autocratic, suspicious of foreigners and steeped in an elaborate, ritualistic religion, had been the antithesis of America's democratic, puritanical and fiercely competitive society in the late nineteenth century. During the fifty years which preceded the Tsar's abdication, millions of his subjects had sailed west to the land of opportunity. But the regime's downfall in 1917 had altered Washington's attitude and the United States became the first country to recognize Kerensky's provisional government. This enthusiasm did not last long. Relations turned sour when the Bolsheviks took over in the October Revolution, and the United States was one of the last of the major powers to exchange ambassadors with the new government.

The spark of resentment was fanned into a flame of hatred by American alarm at Bolshevik rhetoric, which proclaimed world revolution and the extinction of the very system - capitalism - that had made America rich. In addition, many of America's first generation immigrants had only just escaped from the repressive regimes of central and eastern Europe. They and their children encouraged Washington to oppose a regime which seemed intent on reimposing the restrictions they had only recently escaped. With such an ingrained legacy of antagonism, it is hardly surprising

that the two countries should have become estranged once the immediate task of destroying Nazi Germany had been successfully completed.

## A New Broom

On 12 April 1945 a new figure entered the international scene: Harry S. Truman. With only eighty-two days' experience as Vice-President, he took the oath of office after Roosevelt died and was catapulted into a situation for which he had received no training. Truman had spent his first forty years in a small town in the mid-west of America, much of it as an unsuccessful businessman. He did not enter national politics until he was fifty-one, when he was elected as a senator for Missouri. Despite an unfortunate association with a corrupt political machine in his home state, in Washington he built a reputation for honesty and came to public notice as the leader of a congressional committee investigating waste and mismanagement in the defence industry. But, prior to the day he was made President, he had acquired no experience of decision-making in government.

Within months of his elevation he had facilitated the writing of the United Nations Charter in San Francisco, helped end the war in Europe and met Stalin at Potsdam. But his most important decision - and one that would affect international relations for

The President of the United States John F. Kennedy (far right) inspects the Wall from the viewing platform at the Brandenburg Gate during his visit to Berlin in 1963. The East German authorities covered the arches with red cloth so that the East Berliners could not see the President nor he see into East Berlin.

generations to come - was to drop atomic bombs on Hiroshima and Nagasaki. The knowledge that, in the final analysis, the United States was prepared to use such cataclysmic weapons to defend its interests had a profound effect on East-West relations in the years ahead.

Stalin, meanwhile, was doing his best to fill the vacuum left in eastern Europe by Germany's defeat. At Yalta he had manipulated Churchill and Roosevelt into accepting a Communist puppet regime in Poland. To ease the process, he incorporated a few representatives of the group which had spent the war exiled in London, but it soon became obvious that, with the Red Army camped in the country, Poles had no alternative but to toe Moscow's line. By the beginning of 1948, Hungary, Romania and Bulgaria had followed Poland's path into satellite status. Czechoslovakia's situation was somewhat different since Edvard Benes, who had been President of his country when the Nazis took over in 1939, was allowed to return as the head of a coalition government. However, that only meant that the Soviet subversion of his country took a little longer, and by 1948 Stalin was dictating precisely how Czechoslovakia would be run.

The British government, first under Churchill and then under the Labour leader Clement Attlee, was the first to raise the alarm about these developments - at a time when Truman was more concerned with 'bringing the boys back home' and demobilizing his forces. But Britain's economic plight was dire and in 1947 the Foreign Secretary, Ernest Bevin, made it plain to the Americans that his government was no longer able to finance anti-Communist operations such as those in Greece, and that the United States would have to take up the reins.

## A World Divided

Truman responded to this challenge in a special emergency address to a joint session of Congress on 12 March 1947, in which he proclaimed the determination of the United States to help 'free peoples' resist 'attempted subjugation by armed minorities or by outside pressure'. This became known as the Truman Doctrine and has remained a cornerstone of American foreign policy ever since. Congress immediately voted for an appropriation of $400 million to support this policy. It was also generous in its funding of the French effort to contain Ho Chi Minh's army of liberation in Indochina - a commitment which eventually led to America's disastrous, direct involvement in the Vietnam War over a decade later.

Both houses of Congress were controlled by the Republican Party at this time, and the swing of the political pendulum after the liberal Roosevelt years encouraged the American right during the late 1940s. Popular magazines, such as the *Saturday Evening Post* and *Readers' Digest,* contained many articles attacking as Communist any

# The McCarthy Witch-hunts

Joseph McCarthy became a senator in 1946 when anti-Communist hysteria was beginning to infect American politics, but he attracted little notice until in February 1950 he attacked the State Department, claiming that it was 'infected' with Communists. He backed his claim with a piece of paper which he said listed 205 known Communists working for the Department. Under pressure from journalists, he later changed his story about the list.

Undaunted, McCarthy began making outrageous attacks on some of the most prominent men in Washington. However, once Eisenhower had been elected President in November 1952 the mood changed. When McCarthy attacked the army late in 1953, the White House let television

Senator Joseph McCarthy (centre) receives an award from his supporters in recognition of his battle against Communism.

cameras into the investigation and Americans saw McCarthy in close up for the first time. A few months later, McCarthy was censured for his behaviour by a vote in the Senate and his popularity collapsed. He died of alcoholism in 1957.

political system which endorsed nationalization, social ownership or even the welfare state. One group of politicians and military officers took another viewpoint and urged that the United States 'rollback' Soviet power in Europe.

The policy which eventually prevailed was first described by an American diplomat, George F. Kennan, in an article published in the influential journal *Foreign Affairs.* He advocated a stategy of containment, steering a course between abject surrender and outright war. The policy involved opposing Soviet expansionism at every turn, wherever it appeared around the globe: confronting every thrust with an equal counter-thrust. Such an approach required a worldwide intelligence network and it can hardly be a coincidence that the article appeared in 1947, the year in which Truman created the Central Intelligence Agency (CIA).

Ironically, the black-and-white vision of good and evil that characterized America's virulent anti-Communism, and which was deeply rooted in the American puritan tradition, was being mirrored in Moscow during 1947 by Stalin's favourite theorist of the moment, Andrei Zhdanov. Of course, Zhdanov inverted the moral postures of the two protagonists in the global contest by describing the Soviet Union as peace-loving and progressive, while the United States was reactionary and imperialistic.

In fact, any vision which encouraged the view that the international community was divided into two, almost-warring camps suited the purposes of powerful vested interests within each of the two countries. In the US, what President Eisenhower, who succeeded Truman in 1953, would call 'the military-industrial complex' needed the business which only Washington could

provide. Such a vision also suited Truman, because he needed an argument to counter the deep-seated isolationism which had characterized American foreign policy before the Second World War and which now threatened to reappear in a Republican congress. In the Soviet Union, Stalin needed to encourage discipline and self-sacrifice to rebuild the country's economy after the devastation of the war. If the Soviet media could induce a siege mentality by portraying the Americans as Germany's successor in their threat to Mother Russia, then the people might work as hard as they had during the war.

## A Contest of Wills

Truman's first major salvo in the Cold War - a phrase first used in this context by the veteran American statesman Bernard Baruch - was the Marshall Plan, a massive aid programme designed to boost the economy of western Europe and to stave off the rise of Communism by reducing poverty. When America, Britain and France attempted to extend the revival to their sectors of occupied Germany, Stalin responded by blockading Berlin. After the war the former capital had been divided into four zones of occupation, like the rest of the defeated country. In June 1948 the Western powers removed the barriers between their sectors throughout what was now West Germany and reformed the currency. Stalin claimed that this violated their treaty obligations and used it as an excuse to close the roads to Berlin, which lay deep in the Soviet sector. But this ploy to test Western resolve and starve two million citizens into submission backfired. The three Western powers mounted a round-the-clock airlift of food and

# The Cold War

GREENLAND

NETHERLAND

ICELAND

NORWA

GERMAN DEMOCRATIC REPUBLIC
*FROM 1955*

DENMARK

FEDERAL REPUBLIC
OF GERMANY
*FROM 1955*

UK

CANADA

BELGIUM

ROMANIA
*UNTIL 1958*
RED ARMY PRESENCE

*1968*
PARTIAL WITHDRAWAL FROM MEMBERSHIP

FRANCE *TO 1974*

BULGARIA
NO RED ARMY PRESENCE

1ST FLEET

AZORES

UNITED STATES OF AMERICA

ALBANIA
*1961*
WITHDRAWS FROM
COMECON

PORTUGAL SPAIN

6TH FLEE

MIDWAY

*1968*
WITHDRAWS FROM WARSAW PACT

2ND FLEET

MOROCCO

PACIFIC OCEAN

ALGERIA
*1961*
PRO-COMMUNIST REGIME
AFTER INDEPENDENCE

HAWAII

PUERTO RICO

GUINEA
*1960*
SEKOU TOURÉ PRO-COMMUNIST
LEADER AFTER INDEPENDENCE

CUBA
*1962*

MISSILE CRISIS
*FROM 1972*

GHANA
*1957*
KWAME NKRUMAH PRO-COMMUNIST
LEADER AFTER INDEPENDENCE

PANAMA

N

Member of Warsaw Pact (1955)

Member of Council for Mutual Economic Assistance
(Comecon) (founded 1949)

Member of Nato (founded 1949)

Member of Middle East Treaty Organization
(founded 1955; renamed Central Treaty
Organization 1959; disbanded 1979)

Member of South East Asia Treaty Organization
(founded 1955)

Member of ANZUS (founded 1951)

Balkan Pact 1953/54

Ring of US nuclear and major bases

US fleets

Cold War trouble spots

Soviet aid and intervention

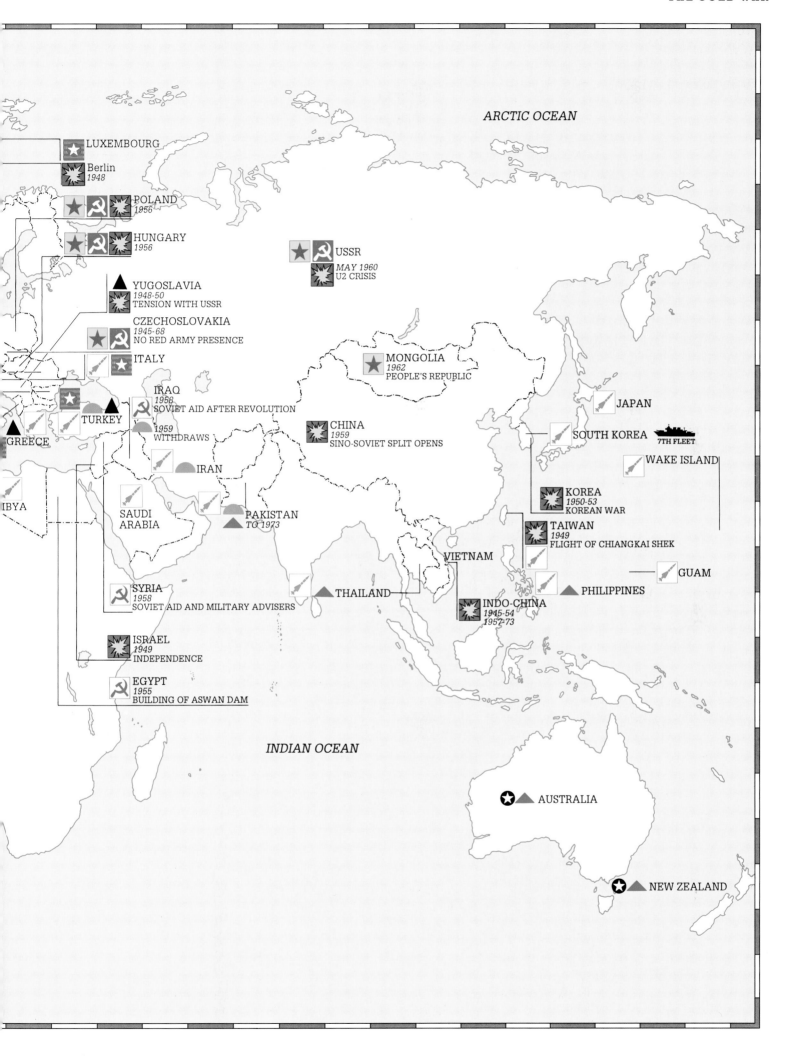

ARCTIC OCEAN

LUXEMBOURG

Berlin
*1948*

POLAND
*1956*

HUNGARY
*1956*

USSR

*MAY 1960*
*U2 CRISIS*

YUGOSLAVIA
*1948-50*
*TENSION WITH USSR*

CZECHOSLOVAKIA
*1945-68*
*NO RED ARMY PRESENCE*

MONGOLIA
*1962*
*PEOPLE'S REPUBLIC*

ITALY

IRAQ
*1958*
*SOVIET AID AFTER REVOLUTION*

JAPAN

TURKEY
*1959*
*WITHDRAWS*

CHINA
*1959*
*SINO-SOVIET SPLIT OPENS*

SOUTH KOREA

7TH FLEET

GREECE

WAKE ISLAND

IRAN

IBYA

KOREA
*1950-53*
*KOREAN WAR*

SAUDI
ARABIA

PAKISTAN
*TO 1973*

TAIWAN
*1949*
*FLIGHT OF CHIANGKAI SHEK*

VIETNAM

GUAM

SYRIA
*1958*
*SOVIET AID AND MILITARY ADVISERS*

THAILAND

PHILIPPINES

INDO-CHINA
*1945-54*
*1957-73*

ISRAEL
*1949*
*INDEPENDENCE*

EGYPT
*1955*
*BUILDING OF ASWAN DAM*

INDIAN OCEAN

AUSTRALIA

NEW ZEALAND

The famous 'kitchen debate' on Capitalism versus Communism between Khrushchev and Vice-President Nixon at an American exhibition in Moscow, 1959.

supplies into the city and, after 272,000 flights in 321 days, the blockade was lifted.

The experience of overcoming the blockade reinforced the commitment of Western politicians to the creation of an alliance which would co-ordinate their military response to what they saw as the Soviet threat. In April 1949 the representatives of Belgium, Britain, Canada, Denmark, France, Iceland, Italy, Luxembourg, the Netherlands, Norway, Portugal and the United States met in Washington and signed the North Atlantic Treaty. Once the agreement had come into force the following July, all the signatories were bound to a system of collective defence.

Meanwhile, on the other side of the world, the Chinese Communists were about to achieve victory over a nationalist army led by Chiang Kaishek and supported by America. Despite warnings by experienced 'China hands' in the US State Department about the extent of corruption among the Nationalist leaders and Chinese support for the Communists, any suggestion that Washington should recognize Mao's government was engulfed in a wave of denunciations from the American right.

The emotional reactions generated among American politicians and the press to this sequence of events were orchestrated by Senator Joseph McCarthy. He used smear tactics and wild accusations, based on information fed to him by the head of the Federal Bureau of Investigation (FBI), J. Edgar Hoover, to attack anyone in public life who showed any left-wing sympathies.

It was in this atmosphere, and in the knowledge that the Soviet Union had already exploded its first nuclear device, that news of the Russian-supported North Korean attack on the US-backed South was received in June 1950. America immediately stepped into the breach and, because the Soviet Union

was boycotting the United Nations Assembly at the time, managed to persuade the Security Council to send a 'peace-keeping force' to liberate South Korea. Led by General MacArthur, the force swept through into the North and seemed to be heading for the border with China. Such a threat forced a reluctant Beijing to join the struggle, and the UN troops were driven back. The conflict subsided into a stalemate which ended in a ceasefire agreed in 1953.

Despite Truman's departure from office in 1952, the incoming Eisenhower administration followed the pattern set by its predecessor. In Moscow, however, a new chapter opened when Stalin died the following year. Unfortunately the Soviet Politburo seemed unclear about the direction their new policies should take. Such doubts were not felt by citizens of the Soviet satellite states, who wanted to be free of Soviet domination. East Germany experienced a major uprising in 1953, while Bulgaria and Czechoslovakia also endured strikes and demonstrations. In Hungary the Kremlin imposed a reformist Prime Minister, Imre Nagy, to the consternation of the hard-line party leader, Mátyás Rákosi. Eventually, the conflict between the two men split the party and helped to precipitate the 1956 uprising, which was suppressed by the Red Army.

## Eyeball to Eyeball

In Moscow, Nikita Khrushchev gradually consolidated his hold on power at home, and in 1955 sought to stabilize the Soviet position in eastern Europe by fashioning a military alliance - the Warsaw Pact - incorporating all the European Communist parties save Yugoslavia. At the same time he signed an agreement with the other occupying powers to withdraw from Austria and approved the abandonment of Soviet bases

in Finland. But his room for manoeuvre was severely curtailed by the armed action in Hungary, which was viewed with deep hostility in the West. By the end of the 1950s, any hint of a thaw in the Cold War had evaporated as Moscow again sought a confrontation over Berlin. East Germans were using the ease of travel within the city to slip away to the West without a permit. Khrushchev insisted that all links between West Berlin and the rest of West Germany must be severed. The West, however, stood firm and the tanks of both sides were soon facing one another across the dividing line between the two halves of the city. Three years later, in 1961, the East Germans tried to staunch the loss of skilled workers by sealing off East Berlin through the construction of a wall along the dividing line and guarding it with mines and troops.

Khrushchev, meanwhile, had met the new American President, John F. Kennedy, in Vienna and had decided that such a youthful and inexperienced leader could be bullied into giving ground. With Cuba under Fidel Castro, the Kremlin gained its first ally in the Western hemisphere and decided to take advantage of the island's proximity to the coast of the United States by installing ballistic missiles. Contrary to Khrushchev's calculations, Kennedy did not back down. Soviet technicians were forced to remove the weapons when the Kremlin realized that the White House was apparently prepared to face a nuclear holocaust rather than concede. The Cuban missile crisis was undoubtedly the climax of the Cold War. Anyone who read the headlines or listened to news broadcasts knew that they were staring annihilation in the face. No leader of either side has dared provoke such a confrontation since, the two camps preferring to test their weaponry and resolve through surrogate states around the world. After 1962, the Cold War was conducted by proxy.

# The Curtain Falls

When Winston Churchill declared, in a speech given in Fulton, Missouri in 1946, that an 'iron curtain' had descended across Europe, he implied that Communist rule was an alien system imposed by Moscow on a democracy-loving eastern Europe. Although this has been a commonly held view, it oversimplifies the sequence of events which took place in the different countries within the region after Hitler's defeat and it obscures the pre-war political reality in the area.

Of those countries which became Soviet satellites in the late 1940s, only Czechoslovakia had established a vigorous democratic tradition before the Nazis took over. And in that country, after the Soviet forces had withdrawn in 1945, the Communists were able to form a coalition administration after winning the largest share of the votes cast in a free election. It was partisan warfare, not Soviet bayonets, that won power for the Communists in Yugoslavia and Albania. While before 1939, countries such as Poland and Hungary were run by regimes almost as autocratic, if not as ruthless, as the one based in Berlin.

In fact, the collapse of the Austro-Hungarian Empire in the dying days of the First World War had destabilized those lands which had been administered from Vienna, and throughout the inter-war years many central, southern and eastern European countries were prey to civil strife, territorial disputes, coups and counter-coups. The Second World War merely increased the devastation and dislocation which had become endemic to the region and intensified the population's desire for a radical break with the past.

Once the Red Army had swept to victory, the Soviet net was at first cast with a delicate hand. Moscow-trained agents, many of whom were nationals of the country to which they travelled, were despatched to convey the Kremlin's message and to give assistance to those Communists who had survived Nazi rule. Fearing that a precipitate transition to one-party control would provoke a counter-revolution, endangering Soviet security in the process, Stalin insisted that the Communist takeover should be a gradual one, concealed, if possible, behind a smokescreen of apparently legal moves.

## Stalinism in Stages

The transformation of a country into a Soviet puppet was achieved in several stages, defined by the British historian Hugh Seton Watson as 'genuine coalition, bogus coalition

*Top:* The fascist ex-Prime Minister of Hungary, Lazlo Bardossy, faces the firing squad in Budapest, 1946. *Above:* The rigid Stalinist Rákosi (seated second left), forcibly seized power for the Communists remarking that he had cut away his opponents 'like slices of salami'.

and monolithic bloc'. During the first stage, the Communists were prepared to bid for popular support, share power with other parties and permit a free press, some elections and parliamentary debates - so long as the Ministry of the Interior, which controlled both the civilian and secret police, was in Communist hands.

During the 'bogus coalition' phase, the party would remove any powerful political opponents, penetrate the country's political, economic and cultural organizations,

and enlarge the role of the secret police. Other parties were allowed a fitful existence; the press was controlled to some degree; and the courts were still permitted to exercise partial autonomy. In the final phase, all institutions came under direct Communist control and the local party danced to Moscow's tune.

The rate at which each country was transformed into a client state varied. The first stage was very brief in Romania and Bulgaria and virtually non-existent in Poland

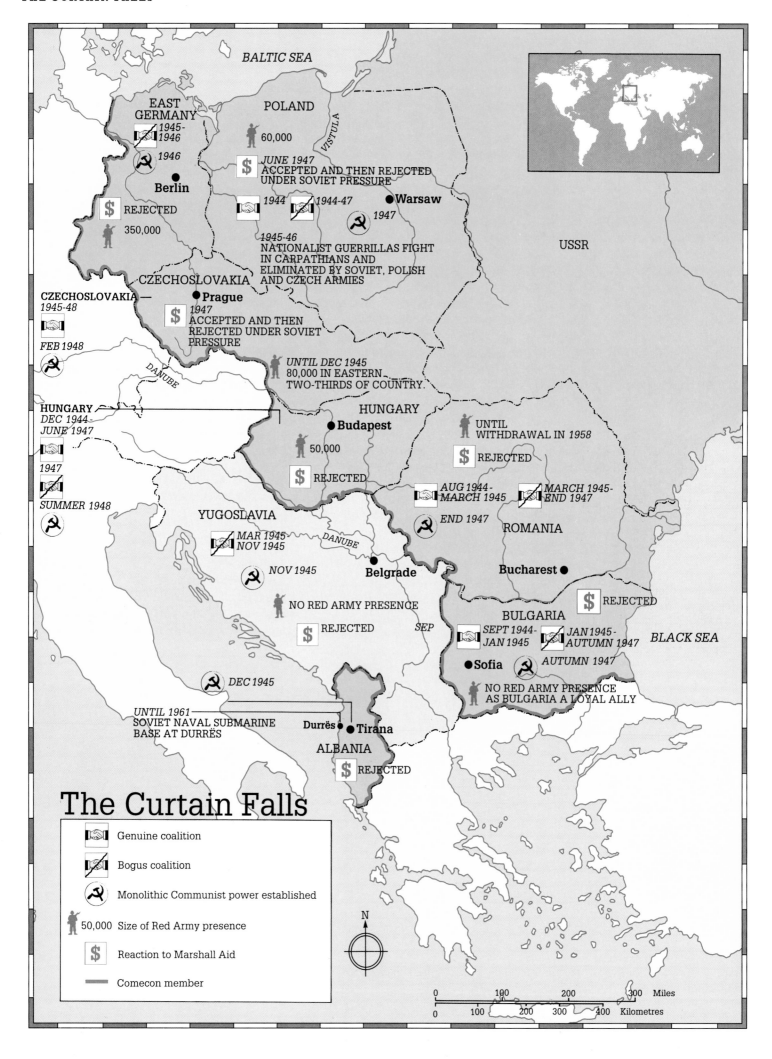

BALTIC SEA

EAST
GERMANY
*1945-1946*

*1946*

● Berlin

**$** REJECTED

350,000

POLAND

60,000

**$** *JUNE 1947*
ACCEPTED AND THEN REJECTED
UNDER SOVIET PRESSURE

*1944*  *1944-47*

● Warsaw

*1947*

*1945-46*
NATIONALIST GUERRILLAS FIGHT
IN CARPATHIANS AND
ELIMINATED BY SOVIET, POLISH
AND CZECH ARMIES

USSR

CZECHOSLOVAKIA
● Prague

*1947*
ACCEPTED AND THEN
REJECTED UNDER SOVIET
PRESSURE

CZECHOSLOVAKIA —
*1945-48*

*FEB 1948*

DANUBE

HUNGARY
*DEC 1944*
*JUNE 1947*

*1947*

*SUMMER 1948*

*UNTIL DEC 1945*
80,000 IN EASTERN
TWO-THIRDS OF COUNTRY.

HUNGARY
● Budapest

50,000

**$** REJECTED

*UNTIL
WITHDRAWAL IN 1958*

**$** REJECTED

*AUG 1944-*
*MARCH 1945*

*MARCH 1945-*
*END 1947*

*END 1947*

ROMANIA

● Bucharest

**$** REJECTED

YUGOSLAVIA

*MAR 1945*
*NOV 1945*

*NOV 1945*

DANUBE

● Belgrade

NO RED ARMY PRESENCE

**$** REJECTED

*SEP*

BULGARIA

*SEPT 1944-*
*JAN 1945*

*JAN 1945-*
*AUTUMN 1947*

BLACK SEA

● Sofia

*AUTUMN 1947*

NO RED ARMY PRESENCE
AS BULGARIA A LOYAL ALLY

*DEC 1945*

*UNTIL 1961*
SOVIET NAVAL SUBMARINE
BASE AT DURRËS

Durrës ●   ● Tirana

ALBANIA

**$** REJECTED

# The Curtain Falls

Genuine coalition

Bogus coalition

Monolithic Communist power established

50,000 Size of Red Army presence

**$** Reaction to Marshall Aid

Comecon member

N

0    100    200    300   Miles

0   100   200   300   400   Kilometres

and Yugoslavia. In Czechoslovakia and Hungary, on the other hand, the democratic period lasted long enough for free elections to be held and for the Communists to be threatened by the vagaries of political life. Although in retrospect the transitional nature of the second stage was obvious, Communists in some countries hoped that it might become permanent and allow them some freedom from Soviet domination. But in Poland, Hungary, Romania, Bulgaria and Yugoslavia it lasted little more than a year. In Czechoslovakia it was avoided entirely as the country moved from a genuine coalition to a puppet regime as a result of the Prague coup of February 1948.

The Kremlin's path to the domination of eastern Europe had been smoothed by the Nazi administration which had preceded it. It was Hitler's minions rather than the victorious Red Army or local Communists who had prepared the ground. The elites which had held sway in the inter-war years had been weakened, demoralized and, in some cases, murdered.

### Three Paths to Power

In Hungary the Social Democrats were tolerated until 1944, when the Germans over-ran their former ally. The party leaders were arrested and few returned from the concentration camps. Those who did were no match for the Communists, despite their popular support. National elections were held in November 1945; much to the Communists' astonishment they were soundly beaten by the Smallholders' Party, a coalition of centre and right-wing groups. The Smallholders gained 57 per cent of the vote while the Communists could only manage 17 per cent - the same level of support as the Social Democrats. The Smallholders realized that the key to retaining power was the Ministry of the Interior, but they came under extreme pressure from the Soviet Union, whose army was occupying the country, to concede the post to a Communist or at least a sympathizer. Eventually the post fell to Ferenc Erdei, the leader of the Marxist faction of one of the peasant parties.

The campaign to oust the Smallholders was orchestrated by the Communists' leader, Mátyás Rákosi, who used any means he could, including fraud and intimidation, to discredit the ruling party. Because the Smallholders were a politically expedient grouping of parties, it was relatively easy for the Communists to sow the seeds of dissent within their ranks. Rákosi's first target was the right wing of his opponents, and to this end he managed to manoeuvre the Prime Minister into dismissing their leader, Dezsö Sulyok. But the key event was the discovery of a 'conspiracy' in which the Smallholders were implicated; much of the 'evidence' was extracted by torturing those already in jail. The Secretary-General of the Smallholders was arrested by the Soviet secret police on the grounds that he had

---

## A Soviet Sandbagger

In 1943, the NKVD (secret police) were anxious to undermine the morale of the German forces still occupying the Soviet Union. So they flew one of their agents, Nikolai Khokhlov, into Belorussia. His task was to assassinate Wilhelm Kube, the barbaric commissar who ruled the region. Khokhlov's German was so good that he managed to pass himself off as a security officer, which enabled him to move freely around Minsk. He found out that Kube had acquired a taste for the local 'blondies', who looked quite Aryian. One had already been approached by the NKVD and she agreed to attach a limpet mine to the underside of Kube's bed. The commissar was killed and Khokhlov made his escape by hitching a lift on an SS troop carrier. He went on to fight behind German lines until the summer of 1944 when he retired to his Moscow appartment to enjoy his substantial salary of 1500 roubles a month.

In March 1945, the NKVD flew him to Bucharest where he languished for four years doing nothing except organize black-market deals for his own profit.

His 'cover' was an electrical equipment store, which he ran. Not known for his enthusiasm for celibacy, Khokhlov soon began an affair with a Romanian woman, whom he married in April 1946. This gave him the advantage of a Romanian passport.

In October 1949 he was recalled to Moscow but was given no specific tasks. So he found himself another girlfriend and married her as well, never having divorced the Romanian woman he left behind in Bucharest. Wife number two, who was very religious, managed to persuade him to try to leave ther service, but the KGB ignored his requests. He wiled away the his time by attending college until the summer of 1951, when he was sent on a trip around western Europe to check how easy it was to get visas and open bank accounts. Then, in March 1952 was he recalled to more lethal pursuits: the murder of a Russian émigré with a fountain pen which had been turned into a gun. But Khokhlov'chickened out', confessing that he had lost his nerve. To his surprise, he was not thrown into prison.

Towards the end of 1953 he

was given another 'hit': a leading anti-Communist émigré whom he was to kill with a silenced pistol concealed in a packet of twenty cigarettes. But Khokhlov had other ideas and gave himself up to his intended victim in Frankfurt. The local CIA officers did not believe his story until he showed them the gun. However, from that point they co-operated fully and rounded up the rest of the group which had been sent to West Germany to support Khokhlov. Two German accomplices were taken a week later. They were followed by an Austrian contact, who in turn led on to a senior Soviet agent. However, the leader of the circuit was too astute to be taken and he slipped away and returned to Moscow.

Khokhlov was flown to the United States where he worked on the lecture circuit promoting the anti-Soviet message, which annoyed the NKVD. In 1957 he was foolish enough to return to Europe and his former masters poisoned his coffee with radio-active thallium. CIA doctors saved his life, although his body did develop brown stripes in the course of the treatment.

---

been involved in attacks on Soviet soldiers, and was whisked out of the country.

By 1947 the Communists were ready to face another electoral contest, and this time the bloc which they led won 65 per cent of the vote. In the autumn, they moved against the non- Communist groups in Parliament and the following year the Social Democrats were eliminated through a shotgun merger with the Communists. The last remnant of opposition, the People's Democratic Party, was dissolved in 1949. Now the Communists had the floor to themselves.

In Poland, the pre-war aristocracy had disappeared during the war, with over one-third of the intelligentsia perishing as well. Of the 1.2 million inhabitants of Warsaw, 800,000 had been killed in the fighting of 1939 and the uprisings of 1943 and 1944. Altogether the country had lost 6 million people, or 20 per cent of its population. By 1945 the national minorities had been almost eliminated and the population was predominantly young, female and poor. Even if the Communists had not taken over, a power vacuum would have existed.

When a coalition government dominated by the Communists assumed power in 1945, it had to cope with severe shortages of basic necessities and with sporadic guerrilla warfare. The armed resistance seems to have been provoked by the arrogant and brutal behaviour of the Soviet Security

Corps, the NKVD; it managed to alienate a population which, after five years of Nazi domination, would have co-operated with any administration that treated it with decency and humanity. In the chaos of the immediate post-war period, some of these guerrillas managed to hold out for several years in areas such as the Carpathian Mountains and were finally eliminated only by the combined operations of the Soviet, Polish and Czech armies.

A referendum was held in June 1946 to determine the form and constitution of the state, but as a result of the intimidation of the opposition, the ideas decreed by Moscow were adopted by a comfortable margin. The Communists saw the Polish Peasant Party, led by Stanislaw Mikolajczyk, as the most serious threat to their position. Fraud and violence were used against them, including the murder of one their leaders. This campaign of terror intensified towards the end of 1946, during the run up to the first election under the new constitution, which was held in January 1947. The Communists won the election easily and the Peasant Party was all but eliminated.

As early as 1943 the Czechoslovak leader in exile, Edvard Benes, had signed an agreement with the Soviet Union, effectively offering Stalin a considerable influence over the country's future. This was Benes's response to the trauma of Munich, which had convinced him that Stalin was more trustworthy than the Western democracies. When the country was liberated, the Red Army occupied two-thirds of it and the Americans the remainder. Both armies withdrew on 1 December 1945.

The Communists enjoyed considerable support in the country; in the free elections of 1946 they gained 38 per cent of the poll and became the largest party in the new Parliament. Klement Gottwald, the Communist leader, became Prime Minister. Events outside Czechoslovakia now played a part, for Stalin was incensed by the exclusion of Communists from the new governments formed in France and Italy in the spring of 1947. As a result, his relatively relaxed attitude to his comrades in Prague hardened, since he did not want Czechoslovakia, which was beginning to show signs of dissatisfaction with Communist rule, to escape from his grasp as well.

To ensure against this eventuality, the party began to reinforce its influence in the civil service, the unions and the police. From the start the Communists' political partners in the ruling coalition objected to this, and demanded proper parliamentary control over the Ministry of the Interior. Matters came to a head in February 1948 when the non-Communists in the government insisted that the minister stop packing his department with henchmen; when he ignored the demand, his critics resigned in protest. Mobs organized by the party were then used to lay siege to the premises of non-Communist organizations and publications; tanks appeared in the street and the Communists seized control. One morning a month later, the Foreign Minister, Jan Masaryk, was found

Cover of the magazine *GDR in Construction*. After the war East Germany's economic resourses were mercilessly exploited by the Soviet Union.

dead beneath his office window in very suspicious circumstances. President Benes died in the following June, and the Communist takeover was complete.

## Stalin's Helping Hand

In each of these three examples, the Communist tactic that opponents found the most difficult to counter was penetration of the civil administration. Every state needs a relatively compliant bureaucracy, but the Communists saw it simply as a vehicle for their own ambitions. Even when they

suffered an electoral defeat, their strength in the bureaucracy would still enable the Communists to influence decisions. And, in the Ministry of the Interior, they saw a great opportunity for exploiting its natural supervisory role within the state.

Such behaviour was considered legitimate because the Communists regarded all other political organizations as enemies who had to be destroyed, rather than opponents with whom to disagree. They harassed their rivals, mounted intense propaganda campaigns, claimed a monopoly of anti-Fascist virtue and denounced all their opponents as reactionaries. In the uneasy climate of the time, their forceful strategy offered a degree of certainty.

The Soviet Union, meanwhile, made sure that its agents did not fail through a lack of resources. From the very outset, the local Communists had privileged access to cars, technology, newsprint and money at a time when they were in very short supply throughout Europe. The interim Soviet administrations ensured that their local allies were given the best facilities. They even used the Soviet secret police, the NKVD, to neutralize awkward opponents.

On the international front, Western politicians gradually realized that any reassurances issued by Stalin about democratic freedom in the East were worthless, and that Churchill's pessimism had been justified. This mood was reinforced by the eruption of the civil war in Greece and the behaviour of Communist parties in western Europe. At the eleventh hour, the Western powers finally drew together to confront the Stalinist menace.

The proclamation by President Truman in March 1947 that the United States was prepared to counter Communist expansion throughout the world preceded the granting of substantial aid to Greece and Turkey. This was followed in June by the Marshall Plan, through which the USA offered money throughout Europe in an attempt to promote the market economy. The Soviet Union rejected the proferred aid and forced Poland and Czechoslovakia to follow, despite their interest in participating. To compensate, the Kremlin put together its own package for its satellites, and the division between the two halves of Europe was further reinforced.

The dramatic climax to this first stage of the Cold War centred on Berlin and the blockade, which lasted eleven months. But even in less obvious ways, the Iron Curtain - a mined and heavily guarded strip of no man's land stretching from the Baltic to the Black Sea - had a damaging effect on the countries of the East. They were not merely cut off from their neighbours to the West; they were also detached from much of their own past and traditions. The Kremlin treated all these countries as if they were alike and expected gratitude in response. In reality, the only way in which Stalin's rigid system could be imposed was by using very high levels of coercion. It was this, above all, which characterized the Stalinist monolithic bloc.

# The Forest Detachments

Although the European war ended in May 1945, many Poles refused to accept the Communist regime imposed by Moscow. A large number were survivors from the pre-war Polish army who had acquired arms from the Allies and the retreating Germans. Despite an amnesty, which allowed about 44,000 underground fighters to resume a normal life in August, over 30,000 hard-core activists refused to concede defeat. Many were members of a group known as the National Armed Forces, which had strong ties with Fascists, who had flourished during the German occupation. Bands of criminals and deserters soon joined them. Units of between 600 and 800 men, equipped with machine guns, light artillery and military transport, took to eastern Poland where vast forests and the Carpathian Mountains were

ideal for guerrilla warfare.

Communist officials, civil servants and the police were the prime targets of what became known to the people as the Forest Detachments. On 4-5 August 1945, for example, a group of 250 men swept into the town of Kielce in seven lorries, captured the key points and stormed the prison, releasing 376 inmates. A similar attack in September 'sprang' 292 prisoners from the jail in Radom.

According to the Polish government they killed over 10,000 people, most of whom died during the period between November 1945 and July 1946 when the fighting was at its most intense. In some regions where the people gave the partisans considerable support, the party itself had to go underground to protect its members from assassination.

A report to the Central

Committee in December 1945 concluded that 'Party work in some districts such as Kozienice, Sandomierz and Pinczow encounters immense difficulties ... due to the marauding bands ... [in Pinczow] Party activity literally exists only in conspiracy. It is impossible because of the intense terror of the bands ... to conduct activity in the terrain. In Zawierce district our Party has been unable to expand since as a result of the activity of the bands, five of our commune committees were forced to suspend activity.'

To combat this threat, a special Internal Security Corps was created and five infantry divisions of the Polish army were thrown into the struggle. These overwhelming numbers were eventually successful and by the spring of 1948 the anti-Communist underground had been wiped out.

# The Communist Fringe

With his tanks rumbling towards Berlin, Stalin saw the Yalta Conference of February 1945 as an exercise in *realpolitik*, in which the deserving victors could carve up the spoils as compensation for the havoc and destruction left in the wake of Nazi imperialism. However, he had no love for his opposite numbers at the negotiating table:

Perhaps you think that because we are allies of the English we have forgotten who they are and who Churchill is .... Churchill is the kind who, if you don't watch him, will slip a kopek out of your pocket. And Roosevelt? Roosevelt is not like that. He dips his hand in only for bigger coins.

Yet such cynicism did not stop him making deals or honouring them, just as he had scrupulously honoured his pact with Hitler which had been signed in August 1939. As far as Stalin was concerned, Greece was a British satellite; and having given the Greek Communists little support at a critical point in the civil war, he instructed them to cease their resistance struggles, even if they were within sight of victory.

Europe was a tense continent in the post-war years. With the Red Army encamped at its centre, a civil war raging in Greece, strong Communist parties operating within Italy and France, and Soviet satellites being established as far south as the Aegean, no one could be certain of Stalin's next move. Communist hegemony had already been established in Poland and Hungary, and democracy was collapsing in Czechoslovakia; few politicians could feel certain of their grip on power. Yet it was in this charged atmosphere that Marshal Tito made his historic choice and decided to go it alone. By encouraging the Yugoslavs to develop their own form of Communism, Tito seemed to be throwing down the gauntlet in front of Stalin. However, as he later pointed out, it was a matter of survival rather than provocation. For him, the clash arose out of 'Russian attempts to enslave our country economically and make it into a colony'.

## Tito's Yugolsavia

Tito possessed a charisma which was as powerful among Yugoslavs as that of Stalin was among his own people: a characteristic which helped unite all Yugoslav Communists behind him. He was also a man of vision, with a degree of subtlety unusual among his fellow Communist leaders at the time. Furthermore, having lived in Moscow during the 1930s and eluded Stalin's firing squads

and prison camps - something that so many other exiled Communists had failed to do - he possessed a strongly developed sense of self-preservation. Such qualities did not, however, prevent him from indulging in imperialist fantasies of a Pan-Balkan federation, comprising Albania, Bulgaria, Romania and maybe even Greece, as well as his own country.

Such a grand design made Stalin suspicious, and he vetoed any plans for a grouping which might create an embarrassingly powerful threat to his southern flank in the future. Tito responded by purging known Soviet agents in the Yugoslav party, a move which made a showdown inevitable. Stalin, who was incensed by such 'insubordination', demanded that the 'healthy elements' among the Yugoslav party combine to eject their 'undemocratic' leader from his post, and seems to have been surprised when his command was not obeyed. His only recourse was to expel the Yugoslavian party from the Cominform - an information bureau created in 1947 to link the CPSU to those European Communist parties enjoying a share in government - and to ensure that the ambitions of other would-be independent spirits who might take 'separate roads to socialism' were sharply curtailed.

Amid a wave of arrests, Wladyslaw Gomulka, the General Secretary of the Polish Communist Party and the country's deputy Prime Minister, was seized, together with six other ministers, and imprisoned. In Bulgaria the acting Prime Minister, Traicho Kostov, a party member for thirty years, was arrested and executed for 'having been an agent of the Bulgarian police since 1942'. Six out of the country's nine Politburo members were dismissed. In Hungary László Rajk, the Foreign Minister, was tried and executed as a 'Fascist spy'. Few eastern European party officials felt safe from Stalin's paranoia, but Enver Hoxha, the Albanian leader, was a notable exception. He received Stalin's backing in resuming full sovreignty over a country that had been a virtual Yugoslav satellite until 1948. And, indeed, Hoxha's lingering resentment and fear of his larger Communist neighbour explains in part Albania's strong attachment to Stalin and Stalinism, which far out-lasted that of any other eastern European power.

Despite Yugoslavia's geographical distance from the Soviet Union, Stalin came very close to invading Yugoslavia in 1949 and was reported to have threatened, 'I will shake my little finger, and there will be no more Tito.' Indeed, the situation looked

The changing face of Belgrade: portraits of Lenin and Stalin come down, and only Tito's remains as Yugoslavia drifts away from Moscow.

particularly grim since Yugoslavia could expect no other country to lift a hand to save it, given Tito's aggressive anti-Western stance at the time. However, it was one thing for Stalin to use Soviet troops already stationed in countries such as Poland or Romania to threaten the local leaders; it was quite another to contemplate their use in an invasion of a mountainous country such as Yugoslavia, whose partisan forces had sustained a determined and unbeaten resistance to Hitler.

By the time the Red Army might have been ready to undertake such a risky campaign - an opportunity which would certainly not have occurred before 1951 - Yugoslavia had escaped from its isolation. In April that year, President Truman risked the censure of right-wing Republicans and anti-Communists by promising the country economic assistance. In June, the chief of the Yugoslav General Staff visited Washington and signed an agreement for the purchase of arms. In July, Britain, France and the US combined to offer Tito a loan of £50 million 'to aid Yugoslavia to maintain its independence in the face of growing Soviet pressure'. After Truman had proved his determination to commit American forces to back up the country's policy in Berlin and then Korea, Stalin's usual caution in foreign affairs returned, and he declined to initiate another

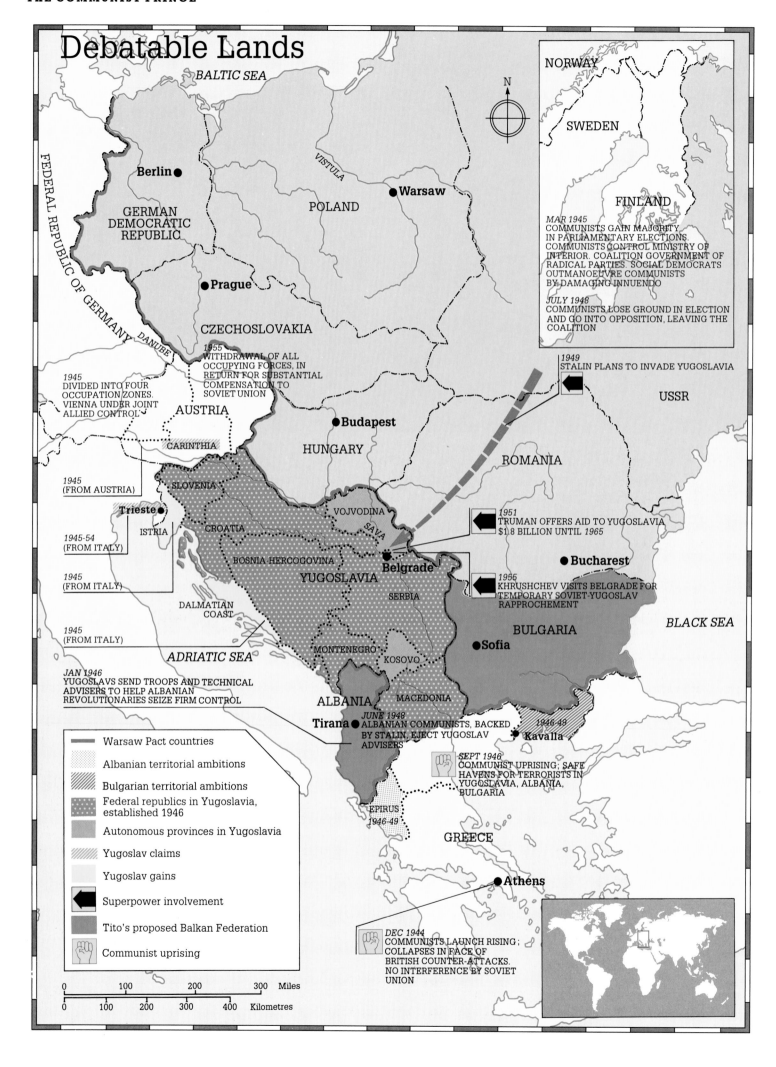

# Debatable Lands

*BALTIC SEA*

**Berlin** ●

GERMAN
DEMOCRATIC
REPUBLIC

FEDERAL REPUBLIC OF GERMANY

**●Prague**

POLAND

●**Warsaw**

VISTULA

CZECHOSLOVAKIA

DANUBE

*1955*
WITHDRAWAL OF ALL
OCCUPYING FORCES, IN
RETURN FOR SUBSTANTIAL
COMPENSATION TO
SOVIET UNION

*1945*
DIVIDED INTO FOUR
OCCUPATION ZONES.
VIENNA UNDER JOINT
ALLIED CONTROL

AUSTRIA

CARINTHIA

*1945*
(FROM AUSTRIA)

SLOVENIA

**Trieste**●

ISTRIA

*1945-54*
(FROM ITALY)

*1945*
(FROM ITALY)

CROATIA

DALMATIAN
COAST

*1945*
(FROM ITALY)

*ADRIATIC SEA*

BOSNIA-HERCOGOVINA

YUGOSLAVIA

VOJVODINA

SAVA

**Belgrade**●

SERBIA

MONTENEGRO

KOSOVO

*JAN 1946*
YUGOSLAVS SEND TROOPS AND TECHNICAL
ADVISERS TO HELP ALBANIAN
REVOLUTIONARIES SEIZE FIRM CONTROL

ALBANIA

MACEDONIA

**Tirana** ●

*JUNE 1948*
ALBANIAN COMMUNISTS, BACKED
BY STALIN, EJECT YUGOSLAV
ADVISERS

NORWAY

SWEDEN

FINLAND

*MAR 1945*
COMMUNISTS GAIN MAJORITY
IN PARLIAMENTARY ELECTIONS.
COMMUNISTS CONTROL MINISTRY OF
INTERIOR. COALITION GOVERNMENT OF
RADICAL PARTIES. SOCIAL DEMOCRATS
OUTMANOEUVRE COMMUNISTS
BY DAMAGING INNUENDO

*JULY 1948*
COMMUNISTS LOSE GROUND IN ELECTION
AND GO INTO OPPOSITION, LEAVING THE
COALITION

*1949*
STALIN PLANS TO INVADE YUGOSLAVIA

USSR

**Budapest**

HUNGARY

ROMANIA

*1951*
TRUMAN OFFERS AID TO YUGOSLAVIA
$1.8 BILLION UNTIL *1965*

●**Bucharest**

*1955*
KHRUSHCHEV VISITS BELGRADE FOR
TEMPORARY SOVIET-YUGOSLAV
RAPPROCHEMENT

*BLACK SEA*

BULGARIA

●**Sofia**

*1946-49*
**Kavalla**

*SEPT 1946*
COMMUNIST UPRISING; SAFE
HAVENS FOR TERRORISTS IN
YUGOSLAVIA, ALBANIA,
BULGARIA

EPIRUS
*1946-49*

GREECE

●**Athens**

*DEC 1944*
COMMUNISTS LAUNCH RISING;
COLLAPSES IN FACE OF
BRITISH COUNTER-ATTACKS.
NO INTERFERENCE BY SOVIET
UNION

N

## Legend

— Warsaw Pact countries

Albanian territorial ambitions

Bulgarian territorial ambitions

Federal republics in Yugoslavia,
established 1946

Autonomous provinces in Yugoslavia

Yugoslav claims

Yugoslav gains

◀ Superpower involvement

Tito's proposed Balkan Federation

Communist uprising

0    100    200    300 Miles
0  100 200 300 400 Kilometres

armed confrontation. Tito had survived.

After Stalin's death, a short note from Tito was found on his desk: 'Comrade Stalin, I request that you stop sending terrorists to Yugoslavia to kill me. We have already caught seven men, one with a revolver, another with a grenade, the third with a bomb, etc. If this does not stop, I will send one man to Moscow and there will be no need to send another.' As the new Soviet leadership established itself in Moscow in 1953, Tito's Yugoslavia pursued its own, hesitant road to socialism, with a foreign policy at first coming under NATO's aegis and then increasingly emphasizing the country's common interest with the many newly independent countries, such as India, Indonesia and Egypt, which refused to join either of the two armed camps of the Cold War. Yugoslavia became a founder member of what came to be called the 'non-aligned nations'. In the post-Stalinist world of eastern Europe, Tito's example looked like a useful model to the uncertain leadership of countries such as Poland and Hungary. In 1955 the Soviet Politburo even made moves of reconciliation, and Khrushchev went to Belgrade to apologize for Yugoslavia's expulsion from the Cominform, blaming the decision on Stalin and Beria, his chief of secret police. However, the inconsistency of Soviet foreign policy under the new leader soon became apparent. Tension between the two countries re-emerged and Yugoslavia distanced itself farther from the Soviet camp.

### The Eastern Balkans

Until 1944, the Romanian government had been a loyal ally of Nazi Germany - although the compact was very unpopular in the country, even among right-wing politicians. But on 23 August a successful *coup d'état* overthrew the Antonescu dictatorship. It was organized by those close to King Michael, in collaboration with a group of army officers; and it was backed by a coalition known as the National Democratic Bloc which was dominated by two parties, the National Peasants and the National Liberals. The Communists (of which there were but a few hundred in the country) and the Social Democrats had a very small stake in the alliance. As the rising coincided with the Red Army's breakthrough in Moldavia, the disruption hampered the German army's ability to resist and made a major contribution to its defeat.

In October that year, the Communists seceded from the governing coalition and set about disrupting it, aided and abetted by the administration which had been established by the occupying Soviet forces. The divisive tactics which were used in Hungary were also applied in Romania, as the Communists attempted to play one faction off against another. They persuaded minor or retired politicians to form breakaway parties which disrupted old alliances and confused the national political

scene. The pressure on the provisional government mounted at the end of February 1945, when King Michael was harassed into dismissing the leader, General Radescu, in favour of Dr Petru Groza, a non-Communist but a nominee of the party.

Although the Soviets had driven out the Nazis, their popularity was only temporary, particularly since they managed to frustrate the calls for elections until November 1946. These tactics were used to give the miniscule party time to establish itself in the local administrations and the security forces. Despite this period of grace, the two major parties were so dominant that the Communists were able to win the election only through employing intimidation, violence and gross fraud.

Once their victory was proclaimed, the Communists used the same tactics as in neighbouring countries gradually to eliminate their political opponents. By the end of 1947 they were in a strong enough position to force the King to abdicate, and on 30 December the Romanian People's Republic was proclaimed. A further set of national elections was held three months later and seats were 'won' by a few nominal opposition groups as window-dressing to placate Western politicians.

The government soon moved to adopt Soviet practices; but it was so incompetent and provoked such steadfast opposition that this potentially rich country rapidly sank into poverty, and the party's position was maintained through fear and intimidation.

*Top:* A portrait of Klement Gottwald (centre), President of Czechoslovakia, and the obligatory icons of Marx, Engels, Lenin and Stalin, look down on the delegates of the Ninth Congress of the Czechoslovakian Communist Party in 1949. *Above:* A hero's welcome: Albanian leader Enver Hoxha greets his Chinese counterpart and staunch ally, Zhou Enlai.

The Kremlin used Romania as a source of raw materials, and vast quantities of iron ore, coal, oil and grain were exported to sustain Soviet industry and its workers. By the mid-1950s, it was a colony in all but name.

Events in Bulgaria followed a very similar course to those in Romania, with the country's leaders favouring Nazi Germany during the Second World War while the people were generally pro-Soviet. In March 1941 the government signed the anti-Comintern pact, and allowed the German forces to use Bulgaria as a base from which to mount operations against Greece, Yugoslavia and, later, the Soviet Union.

In 1942 a coalition of underground political groups led by the Communists formed the Fatherland Front in 1942 to organize sabotage and to prepare the country for a revolutionary insurrection. The date was set for September 1944. But, by the late summer of that year, with the Red Army approaching and a rising threatened at home, the government was trying to wriggle out of its commitment to Germany. Its first move was to announce that it had withdrawn from the war; then, on 1 September, it proclaimed its strict neutrality. This was not enough for the Kremlin, and the Bulgarian government was forced to declare war on Germany the following day. This did not stop the Fatherland Front from proceeding with the planned rising, which had been scheduled that very day. Within a week the Front was in control and, by the end of October, Bulgaria signed an armistice with the Allies.

After the victory came the bloody retribution. The trials began in December, and on 2 February 1945 the three regents who had acted for King Simeon, who was still a child, twenty-two ministers, sixty-eight Members of Parliament and eight former royal advisers were executed. The trials continued, and by the late spring 2680 people had been sentenced to death.

An election had been scheduled for the summer, but when the Communists tried to pressure their partners in the provisional government into not standing against their own candidates, six ministers resigned, while Britain and America protested, and the election was postponed. A Soviet diplomat visited the capital, Sofia, to try to dissuade members of the broad coalition of the provisional government from resigning, but he failed. The succeeding administration was composed purely of the radical groups from the Fatherland Front.

In September 1946, a referendum on the monarchy was held, and 92 per cent of the population voted for a republic. Elections followed on 27 October and Georgi Dimitrov, a veteran Communist who had spent many years in the service of the Comintern became Prime Minister. Britain recognized the government in February 1947, and the USA followed suit in October. Acceptance by the United States lasted for a mere two years, as details of the political manoeuvres and deaths endemic to Communist rule in the region leaked to the West.

## Tito: Marshal of Yugoslavia

Josip Broz, the only son of a poor peasant, transformed his country from a loose collection of jealous states into a federation which played an important role in international politics in little more than twenty years.

Born in 1892, he started work at the age of thirteen as an apprentice locksmith. He travelled north into Bohemia and Germany in the years prior to the First World War, getting jobs as a metal worker and becoming involved in trade union activity. After being drafted, he was decorated for bravery before being captured by the Russians. When he returned to Yugoslavia in 1920 he had been converted to Communism. He rose through the ranks of the Party during the 1920s but was arrested in 1928 and sentenced to five years. On his release he assumed the pseudonym Tito and travelled through Europe, ending up in Moscow.

In 1936 he went to Paris, where he was resonsible for organizing the flow of volunteers who wished to join the International Brigades in Spain. He returned to Yugoslavia in 1937 to organize his own country's contribution to the Spanish conflict. The survivors of this group formed the nucleus of the partisans with which he attacked the Germans in 1941. Towards the end of the war he asserted his independence from all the great powers, a path he followed once the fighting was over. He annoyed the West by trying to seize Trieste and then refused to obey Stalin's orders. But after Stalin's death, the new Soviet leaders went out of their way to heal the breach and a delegation led by Khrushchev paid an official visit to Belgrade in June 1955.

Tito, meanwhile, had been changing the Yugoslav constitution which, in its first form, was closely modelled on its Soviet counterpart. The revised version abandoned centralism and turned the republic into a federation of the five major Yugoslav nationalities. His foreign policy in the 1950s led him to join the leaders of India and Egypt in forming a group of twenty-five non-aligned nations which denounced imperialism and attacked apartheid in South Africa. Meanwhile, his leadership at home gave his country unprecedented peace and stability.

As in the other Soviet satellites, so in Bulgaria Stalin's death led to a relaxation of the totalitarian system. Attempts were made to resuscitate the Fatherland Front, and some politicians who had been smeared in the late 1940s were rehabilitated. Bulgaria was admitted to the United Nations in December 1955 and in 1959 the United States restored diplomatic relations.

### The Three That Got Away

Partisan activities in Greece during the Second World War established the Communists as a powerful force within the country. But they failed to seize power at the crucial moment in October 1944 as chaos followed the Germans' retreat. Churchill offered Stalin a free hand in Romania and Bulgaria in return for Western hegemony in Greece.

Nevertheless, in December the local Communists launched a rising in Athens, which collapsed in the face of determined British counter-attacks. The Soviet Union remained aloof throughout.

Another Communist rising took place in September 1946 and this time their forces took to the hills for three years, waging a successful guerrilla campaign. But they became caught up in the conflict between Tito and Stalin. When the Yugoslav border was closed to them and their supply and communication lines were broken, they had to give up and go into exile.

Austria followed the pattern of Germany and was divided into four zones of occupation in 1945, with the status of Vienna being similar to that of Berlin in that it was operated under joint control. The Communists made little headway in their sector, since Marshall Aid laid the foundations for a viable democracy, and in 1955 the Soviets were content to withdraw their troops in line with the other occupying powers, in return for substantial Austrian compensation.

Finland seemed ripe for a Soviet-backed Communist takeover when the war ended. It was a former part of the Russian Empire, had recently been invaded by the Red Army, and was an important buffer territory on the Soviet border. Moreover, it had been an ally of Germany, and it possessed a radical working class. But it remained outside the Soviet camp, partly because of the incompetence of the party leadership in Finland, and partly because Stalin was content to allow it to remain neutral.

Most of the pre-war leaders of the Finnish Communist Party had fled across the border on the outbreak of war with the Soviet Union in 1941. Not only had they lost touch with their supporters; they had also learnt that, to survive Stalin's paranoia, it was better not to cause trouble. This approach was completely inappropriate in the fluid political situation in Finland after the war.

As in Czechoslovakia, the Communists of Finland enjoyed a measure of popular support, and after the elections of March 1945 they formed the largest group in Parliament. They managed to secure the Ministry of the Interior as part of a coalition of radical parties, but their opponents on the far right and within the Social Democrats did not allow the Communists to manipulate them. Instead, they used the same tactics of pressure and innuendo against the Communists as the Communists used themselves. Consequently, in the elections of July 1948 the Communists lost ground and decided to go into opposition rather than remain in the coalition. They would not return from the political wilderness until the 1960s.

# Germany Divided

With the end of the Second World War in sight by the spring of 1945, it was obvious to everyone that Germany would pay a heavy price for defeat. Even Hitler realized that a united country could not survive such a catastrophe. 'If the war is lost, this nation will also perish. This fate is inevitable,' he prophesied a month before his suicide.

The process of dividing the old Germany had already begun in earnest in the shattered Black Sea resort of Yalta in the early days of February 1945. The ageing leaders of Britain, the US and the Soviet Union had gathered here in the mellow winter sunshine to formulate a joint approach to the post-war world. Some of the most radical proposals - such as those of redrawing the pre-war boundaries of Poland and of breaking Germany into separately administered zones - had originally come from the Americans. Roosevelt had to contend with a 6 million-strong Polish community in the United States, but he felt that they would accept the loss of territory in the east to the Soviet Union so long as Poland received compensation in the form of valuable land which had formerly been part of Germany. Silesia, Pomerania and part of East Prussia, which were rich in raw materials and agricultural land, were proposed, but the details were not finalized.

The post-war division of central Europe was eventually agreed at Potsdam at the final conference of the war-time allies in July 1945. Stalin now presented the West with a *fait accompli* in Poland which neither the new American President, Truman, nor Churchill was in a position to contest. It was agreed that the Soviet zone of occupied Germany should cover the forty thousand square miles formed from the states of Mecklenburg, Thuringia, Brandenburg, Saxony-Anhalt and Saxony. The remaining territory to the west, which was about the same size as the United Kingdom, was divided into British, French and American zones.

The Soviet zone contained advanced industrial and engineering plants which were strong in optics, office equipment, vehicles, chemicals, textiles and consumer goods of all kinds. It also possessed the remnants of a once-thriving agricultural community. By 1945, most of its large towns had been reduced by bombing to piles of rubble which were haunted by emaciated figures who survived as best they could while living in the cellars beneath the ruins. Only the smaller cities, such as Magdeburg and Leipzig, were still intact. However, rather than try to put the region back into working order, the first job for the Soviet occupying forces was to strip from the factories what remained of the heavy industrial plant and to ship it back home to replace what the Germans had destroyed.

## The Well-Organized Democracy

The Kremlin was well prepared for this moment and arranged for groups of selected Communist émigrés to establish a power base in the vacuum left by the fleeing Nazi administration. They moved in behind the Red Army as it advanced, armed with lists of Communists and other likely sympathizers in those areas which had once possessed strong left-wing traditions. Non-Communists were usually selected as mayors, but with party members placed in key positions as 'technical experts'. The police force was also rebuilt, using former German troops who had been 're-educated' at 'anti-Fascist schools' for prisoners of war and then placed under party supervision.

A young man is shot dead behind the East Berlin side of the Wall while trying to escape to the West. When the city was divided by the Wall, Herr Willy Brandt, Mayor of West Berlin, broadcast to the people of East Berlin and told them, 'You cannot be held in slavery for ever.'

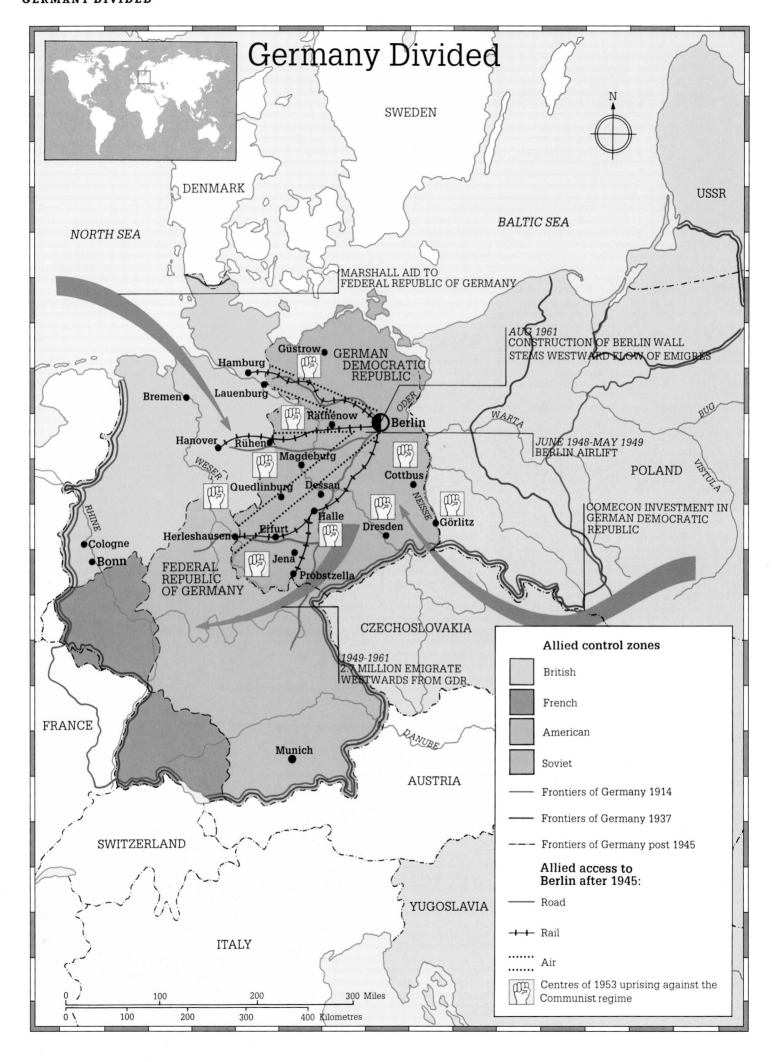

# Germany Divided

SWEDEN

DENMARK

NORTH SEA

BALTIC SEA

USSR

MARSHALL AID TO
FEDERAL REPUBLIC OF GERMANY

Güstrow

GERMAN
DEMOCRATIC
REPUBLIC

*AUG 1961*
CONSTRUCTION OF BERLIN WALL
STEMS WESTWARD FLOW OF EMIGRÉS

Hamburg

Lauenburg

ODER

Bremen

Rathenow

Berlin

WARTA

BUG

Hanover

Rühen

WESER

Magdeburg

*JUNE 1948–MAY 1949*
BERLIN AIRLIFT

POLAND

VISTULA

Quedlinburg

Dessau

Cottbus

RHINE

Halle

NEISSE

COMECON INVESTMENT IN
GERMAN DEMOCRATIC
REPUBLIC

Cologne

Herleshausen

Effurt

Dresden

Görlitz

Bonn

Jena

Probstzella

FEDERAL
REPUBLIC
OF GERMANY

CZECHOSLOVAKIA

*1949–1961*
2.7 MILLION EMIGRATE
WESTWARDS FROM GDR

FRANCE

DANUBE

Munich

AUSTRIA

SWITZERLAND

YUGOSLAVIA

ITALY

## Allied control zones

British

French

American

Soviet

Frontiers of Germany 1914

Frontiers of Germany 1937

Frontiers of Germany post 1945

## Allied access to Berlin after 1945:

Road

Rail

Air

Centres of 1953 uprising against the
Communist regime

0      100      200      300 Miles

0   100   200   300   400 Kilometres

By the end of 1945, almost 60 per cent of the police in the Soviet zone were party members.

The Potsdam communiqué had announced that 'It is not the intention of the Allies to destroy or enslave the German people. The Allies want to give the German people the chance to prepare itself to rebuild its life on a democratic and peaceful basis.' Consequently, in the summer of 1945 the Soviet authorities licensed four parties to compete for the electorate's allegiance: the Social Democrats, the Christian Democrats, the Liberal Democrats and the Communists. However, the real power lay in the hands of the Soviet military administration. It set about implementing the policy of denazification agreed at Potsdam, and by 1948 520,000 people had lost their jobs as state employees. Most of them had been replaced by party members or sympathizers.

The first major reform carried out in the Soviet zone during the autumn of 1945 was the redistribution of land. The 7000 people who owned the large estates were dispossessed without compensation, and their 8500 square miles were distributed among the 560,000 citizens who applied. When the leaders of the Christian Democrats objected to the lack of compensation they were dismissed by the Soviet administration.

Many of the Social Democrats in the East were much further to the left than their fellow party members in the West. They were also acutely conscious that it had been their quarrels with the Communists prior to 1933 that had opened Hitler's way to power. When the Communist leader, Wilhelm Pieck, called for the two parties to form the Socialist United Party of Germany, or SED, in order to strengthen the left after the Communists in Austria and Hungary had failed at the polls, the Social Democrats in the Soviet zone acquiesced. Their fellow members in the West vigorously rejected the move, however. On 20 April 1946 the 679,000 members in the Soviet zone joined the 619,000 of the Communist party.

The first important test of the new super-party came in October that year when elections were held in the Soviet zone. The SED romped home with 4.6 million votes against 2.3 million cast for the Christian Democrats. However, the political situation in the East was complicated by the anomalous position of Berlin, which had retained a unified administration and electoral system as a result of its special status. Here, the SED was challenged by the Social Democrats of the West who had rebuilt the party in the city to confront their former colleagues who were now in league with the Communists. Despite substantial support from the Soviet administration, the SED was heavily defeated, even in the Soviet sector of the city.

## A City Under Siege

The Soviet reponse was to make it virtually impossible for newly elected officials to work in the city hall, which was located in the Soviet sector. Petty harassment gradually increased in intensity. Towards the end of 1947, a People's Congress movement was initiated in the Soviet-occupied zone. At its first meeting in Berlin in December, it proclaimed that the movement was an all-German affair, despite the fact that the main protagonists were the SED and the only delegates from the Western zones were Communists. When this move to counter the growing cohesion in the Western zones failed, the Soviet authorities began impeding access to Berlin. Military trains were stopped or diverted; canal traffic was halted for days at a time; and when Marshal Sokolovskii walked out, taking the remaining Soviet staff with him, the Allied Control Council ceased to function . On 5 April 1948, a Soviet fighter buzzing a British airliner made a fatal error which killed fourteen people.

In the face of this increasing pressure, the Western Allies made a move which only deepened the divisions between them and the Soviets. On 20 June the Reichsmark was replaced by the Deutschmark in the three Western zones; this effective devaluation reduced the cost of German exports and helped to propel the Western zones towards the economic transformation of the 1950s. However, the Soviets had already closed all surface routes into the former capital; the Berlin blockade had begun.

Air transportation skills had developed considerably during the Second World War as airborne troops, armour and supplies became commonplace. But no one had ever tried to supply a city by plane before, let alone one containing over 2 million people. Coal, food, drugs, milk and even Christmas trees had to be airlifted into Tempelhof Airport before the Kremlin relented. At its peak, Operation Vittels was landing one aircraft every five seconds and, by April 1949, was able to deliver 13,000 tons of supplies in one day.

Throughout the summer of 1948 and into the autumn, the pressure on Berliners was sustained in the city's corridors of power.

The president of the police force, a Soviet appointee, was dismissed by the city assembly for disobeying instructions, but he refused to leave his post. Another police force was formed, therefore, based in sectors of the city under Western control. On 23 August, the members of the assembly arrived at the city hall for a regular meeting and found the building overflowing with a mob brought there in Soviet trucks. When the postponed meeting was reconvened on 6 September, the scene was replayed and the chairman of the assembly announced that it would meet henceforth in the British sector. When, three days later, Western generals sought a compromise to end the feuding, three hundred thousand Berliners met near the Brandenburg Gate and then marched to the building where the meeting was being held, to insist that they would rather endure than captitulate.

The determination of the Berliners to resist was critical to the success of the Western relief operation. The city's one remaining electricity generating station was in the Soviet sector, and the power was cut within days of the start of the blockade. The citizens were lucky that the winter proved a mild one, for it was not until 4 May 1949 that the Soviets admitted defeat and called off the travel restrictions.

## One Country, Two States

The dividing line between the two Germanys had now been clearly drawn. In the same month that the blockade came to an end, a new constitution was introduced in the Western states - drafted by their eleven regional Parliaments. The first elections for a West German Parliament in the new provisional capital, Bonn, were scheduled for 14 August. The Soviet response was to call a third People's Congress. This adopted a recently drafted constitution for the Eastern zone, which would henceforth be known as the German Democratic Republic, or GDR.

# Crossing the Wall

Once the first rolls of barbed wire were strung along the dividing line between East and West Berlin, escape from the east of the city was on the agenda. The first occurred within twenty-four hours when a family of three swam across the Teltow Canal and one wriggled through the wire behind the ruins of the Reichs Chancellery building. Forty-one people managed to escape during the first night.

The first of the border guards to make a break was Conrad Schumann, who jumped over a few inadequate strands of wire on 15 August and hoped that his former comrades would not shoot him in the back as he ran headlong towards a waiting crowd in the West.

But perhaps the most famous escape attempt was one that failed. Within weeks, the barbed wire was being replaced by a more permanent barrier built with breeze blocks and concrete. Seventeen-year-old Peter Fechter and a friend decided to go over the wall close to Checkpoint Charlie. After hiding in a disused building, they dashed for the wall. Peter's friend managed to climb over the two-metre obstacle, evade the barbed wire on the top and slide down the other side in a hail of bullets without being hit. Peter, however, was not so lucky and he fell back. He was surrounded by *Vopos*, who stood and did nothing for an hour while he slowly bled to death. Meanwhile, a crowd had gathered across the Wall and their fury mounted as they realized what was happening.

Mass demonstrations followed and Soviet soldiers and diplomats were stoned. West Berliners could not understand why the Americans would not send in their tanks and anti-American feeling had a hold on the city for some years.

# Walter Ulbricht: The Grey Fox

Walter Ulbricht was the ultimate grey *apparatchik* who created the dreary regime of East Germany. He was born in 1893 in Leipzig, the eldest son of socialist parents, and joined the Communist Party as soon as it was formed. He soon discovered that he was a poor public speaker but a skilful organizer, a talent which brought him steady promotion within the party. A visit by a Soviet official led to a training course in Moscow and a job with the Comintern. He returned to Germany in 1925.

Ulbricht escaped the police and went underground after the Nazi crackdown of 1933. Later he got away to Paris where the surviving German Communists had located their headquarters. In 1937 he was called to the Kremlin to answer to the Comintern's Central Committee, but he avoided being purged. He was given a job in Moscow the following year.

Ulbricht returned to Germany

Walter Ulbricht (right), the architect of the German Democratic Republic, entertains Khrushchev during his visit to Berlin in 1959. Two years later he ordered the building of the Berlin Wall.

on 30 April 1945, charged with creating a native administration in the Russian Zone. He became Deputy Chairman of the party and controlled communications with the Soviet army.

However, Ulbricht had to wait until 1960 and the death of Wilhelm Pieck before he

achieved undisputed control of East Germany. Unfortunately, the country's economy began to slip during the 1960s from its position as one of the world's ten richest and in 1971 Ulbricht was finally forced to step down in favour of Erich Honecker. He died two years later.

In October Congress turned itself into a two-house Parliament in Potsdam, and elected Wilhelm Pieck, a leader of the Spartacist rising, as President of the new state.

The Soviets, however, still wished to retain the appearance of a democracy at work, even if the reality was very different. Only eight of the eighteen ministers in the new government were members of the SED but, as in other Eastern bloc states, this group kept its hands firmly on the levers of power by maintaining a tight control on the security forces, the economy and the media. In order to avoid a repeat of the embarrassing election results in Berlin, voters were presented with a single national list of candidates from what was called the anti-Fascist bloc. On election day, the voters collected their ballot papers and were permitted only to delete the names of candidates of whom they disapproved.

In West Germany, industrial production had risen by 50 per cent during the second half of 1948 and by another 25 per cent during 1949, as hundreds of millions of dollars of Marshall Aid flowed into the country. Confronted by this economic success, the Kremlin had little alternative but to stop stripping the GDR's factories of machinery and to introduce its own economic package. A programme of nationalization, collectivization of agriculture and heavy industrial investment was rapidly effected. The other trappings of Stalinism were imported as well, with the creation of a new state security service and an increase in the armed forces. Many people found the

heavy hand of Stalinism intolerable, however, and the GDR lost many of its most skilled workers who slipped away to the West. More than 182,000 left in 1952 alone.

Stalin's death in March 1953 raised hopes that the SED might adopt a fresh approach and on 9 June the 'New Course' was inaugurated. This admitted 'a string of mistakes', reversed some nationalization and promised increased civil liberties. Workers in heavy industry were offered nothing, and when the trade union newspaper *Die Tribune* defended the government's attitude on 16 June, some three hundred thousand people took to the streets of over 270 towns and cities throughout the GDR. When the demonstrations were almost over, the Soviet army proclaimed a state of emergency and combined with the People's Police to clear the streets without, it would appear, any loss of life. But the next day the demonstrators reappeared in Magdeburg and Halle-Merseburg; some carried placards bearing political slogans, including a demand for free elections. The security forces lost control and there were many casualties. The fighting revealed the emptiness of claims by the SED that it was a workers' party and that the GDR was a workers' state. That year, more than 330,000 left for the West.

Despite 'the rising', the New Course continued, and increases in wages and pensions were announced. The SED also proclaimed that 'if large numbers of workers do not understand the party's position, then it is the party which is at fault, not the workers'. Between July and October 1953, many rank

and file members were interviewed and later expelled or forced to resign because they had 'no political education or party resolve'. Over 70 per cent of trade union officials were sacked. Despite this removal of 'dead wood' and the commitment of many senior party officials to a more liberal attitude, the party's leader, Walter Ulbricht, and a small group of followers were committed Stalinists who were determined to bide their time. They had to trim their sails after Khrushchev's attack on Stalin at the Twentieth Party Congress of the Soviet Party in Moscow in February 1956. But during 1957 they managed to oust many of the leading reformers, who frequently ended up in jail.

Ulbricht's moment finally arrived once Khrushchev had won the power struggle in the Soviet Union and added the premiership to his portfolio in March 1958. Following a series of militarily-related Soviet space triumphs, including the launch of Sputnik, Khrushchev had decided on a much more aggressive stance towards the West. He strengthened Soviet forces in the GDR throughout the summer, and on 27 November he sent the leaders of the three other occupying powers in Germany an ultimatum. If they did not quit Berlin within six months, he would come to a unilateral agreement with the GDR which would transfer the powers of granting access into East German hands. When the deadline passed and the Western powers had conceded nothing, Khrushchev had to find another way of sustaining his pressure.

Meanwhile, the increased tension made all the more acute by Ulbricht's move to collectivize the remaining private farms was driving many more in the East to escape westwards. By April 1961, the stream of refugees had turned into a flood. On 25 July 1961 the new American president, John F. Kennedy, announced that the United States regarded the presence of Western troops in Berlin and their rights of access as non-negotiable. Khrushchev had two alternatives: to seal off West Berlin and the flood of refugees, or to go to war.

At a meeting of the Warsaw Pact countries in Moscow a week later, Ulbricht urged the sealing of the border. He got his wish. During the night of 12-13 August, units of the security police, factory militias, border troops, the People's Police and Soviet troops stationed near Berlin, all under the control of Erich Honecker, Ulbricht's 'heir apparent', erected barbed-wire fences and improvised walls along the border between East and West Berlin. The underground railway still connected the two halves of the city, so stations which lay to the east were sealed; anyone trying to escape was liable to be shot.

By the time Ulbricht had got his way, over 2.7 million East Germans had fled to the West. The Wall helped to revive the GDR's economy by stemming the haemmorhage of talent. But it also sealed the growing anger and frustration of the East German people. This finally exploded under the country's leaders and destroyed their power in 1989.

# The New Order in China

Mao Zedong waves to the crowd from the Gate of Heavenly Peace, Tiananmen Palace, Beijing during the National Day Parade, October 1958.

'The Chinese people have stood up! Ours will no longer be a nation subject to insult and humiliation.' With these words, Mao Zedong declared the establishment of the People's Republic of China from Beijing's Gate of Heavenly Peace on 1 October 1949. These were sentiments of national independence rather than international brotherhood. For, although the familiar Communist rhetoric about international solidarity laced many public speeches, members of the Chinese Politburo were keenly aware that Stalin's policies had frequently been counter-productive and that it was Chinese strategy and courage which had carried the day. As Mao pointed out in a later speech: 'The Chinese revolution won victory by acting contrary to Stalin's will... If we had followed...Stalin's methods the Chinese revolution couldn't have succeeded. When our revolution succeeded, Stalin said it was a fake.'

Nevertheless, despite the distrust of foreigners born of a hundred years of interference in their country by the great powers, the Chinese leadership was in desperate need of outside assistance. To transform a country which had been crippled by hyper-inflation under the Nationalists and scarred by decades of civil conflict, and which possessed a largely illiterate population, required aid and injections of skill. Mao and Zhou Enlai's aversion to Moscow had led them to sound out Washington early in 1949, despite America's massive aid programme to the Nationalists. Mao had been a fan of America's own revolutionaries since he was a teenager, but the United States administration of 1949 was in the grip of Cold War hysteria and therefore unlikely to make an imaginative change of policy. As far as the Truman government was concerned, all Communists were tarred with the same brush. Ironically, it was this attitude that cemented Communist unity and forced Mao to negotiate with Stalin.

When Mao led the Chinese delegation to Moscow in December 1949 it took two months of hard bargaining to produce a thirty-year Sino-Soviet treaty which granted China trade concessions and a $300 million loan spread over five years. In return, Beijing conceded that Stalin would continue to exert influence in Manchuria and Sinkiang; that Port Arthur and Dairen would remain for the time being under Soviet occupation and that the 'independence' of the Mongolian People's Republic (once integral to China) would be maintained. All those sitting round the table might have been Communists, but the issues that they were discussing were national priorities.

## The Road to Socialism

Mao had defined his brand of Communism in a slightly different way from that of his northern neighbours. Lenin had advocated a 'democratic dictatorship of workers and peasants'. Mao, who was influenced by the radical but non-Marxist Chinese intellectuals who had preceded him, believed that those

# The New Order in China 1949-60

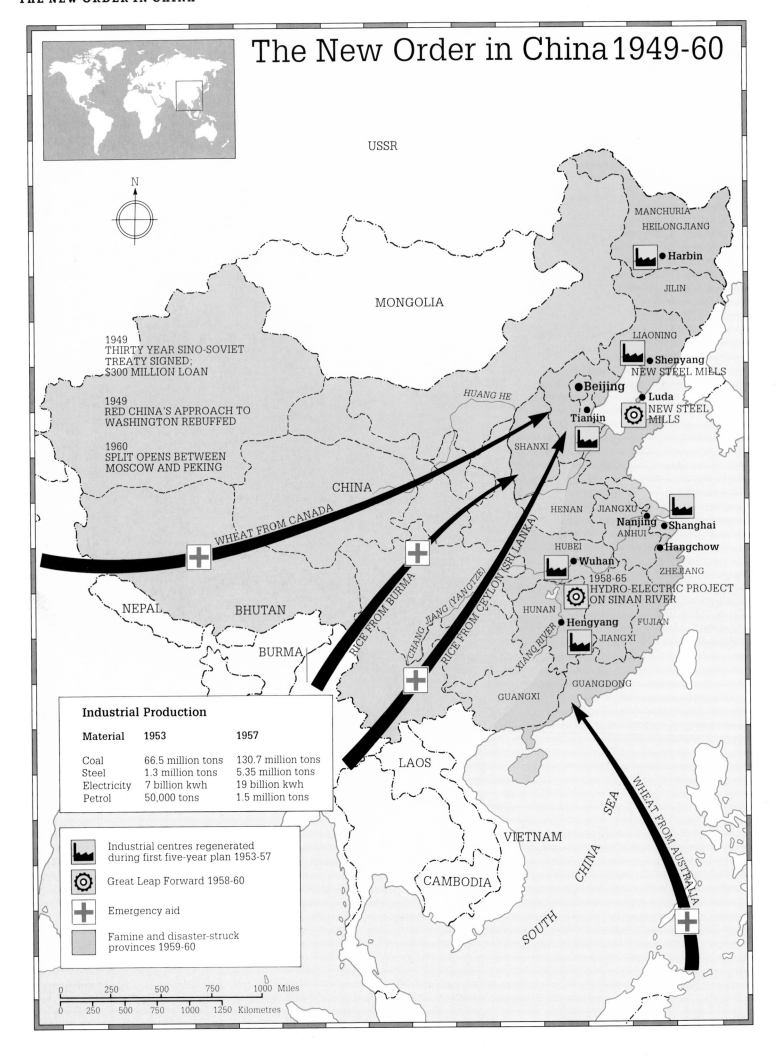

USSR

MONGOLIA

MANCHURIA
HEILONGJIANG

Harbin

JILIN

LIAONING

Shenyang
NEW STEEL MILLS

Beijing

Luda
NEW STEEL
MILLS

Tianjin

SHANXI

HUANG HE

1949
THIRTY YEAR SINO-SOVIET
TREATY SIGNED;
$300 MILLION LOAN

1949
RED CHINA'S APPROACH TO
WASHINGTON REBUFFED

1960
SPLIT OPENS BETWEEN
MOSCOW AND PEKING

CHINA

HENAN    JIANGXU

Nanjing
ANHUI

Shanghai

Hangchow

HUBEI

ZHEJIANG

Wuhan
1958-65
HYDRO-ELECTRIC PROJECT
ON SINAN RIVER

WHEAT FROM CANADA

RICE FROM BURMA

CHANG JIANG (YANGTZE)

RICE FROM CEYLON (SRI LANKA)

HUNAN

Hengyang

FUJIAN

XIANG RIVER

JIANGXI

NEPAL

BHUTAN

GUANGDONG

BURMA

GUANGXI

## Industrial Production

| Material | 1953 | 1957 |
|---|---|---|
| Coal | 66.5 million tons | 130.7 million tons |
| Steel | 1.3 million tons | 5.35 million tons |
| Electricity | 7 billion kwh | 19 billion kwh |
| Petrol | 50,000 tons | 1.5 million tons |

LAOS

SOUTH CHINA SEA

WHEAT FROM AUSTRALIA

VIETNAM

CAMBODIA

Industrial centres regenerated
during first five-year plan 1953-57

Great Leap Forward 1958-60

Emergency aid

Famine and disaster-struck
provinces 1959-60

| 0 | 250 | 500 | 750 | 1000 Miles |
| 0 | 250 | 500 | 750 | 1000 | 1250 Kilometres |

businessmen who had relied on their own initiative and local money, the national capitalists, could be used to help the revolution. On the other hand the bureaucratic capitalists, that is those who owned businesses set up on government initiative during the nineteenth century and funded by foreign money, could not be trusted. Mao defined the workers as 'masters', who were joined in their dictatorship over the landlords and the bureaucratic capitalists by the peasants, the petty bourgeoisie and the national capitalists. These four groups were defined as 'the people' and were represented on the new Chinese flag by four small stars.

This vision of the people was not seen as immutable, however. The Chinese leaders thought that they could rebuild the country's social structure. Their first move was to get the economy back on a more stable footing. A combination of austerity measures, balanced budgets, currency reform and price controls brought inflation under control. Large-scale industry, foreign-owned property and banks were expropriated. Railways and roads were restored and an expansion programme was started.

A new deal in education was another top priority. Most of the 4.5 million party members were no more than semi-literate, and most had never seen such everyday twentieth-century objects as cars, light bulbs and buses until they liberated the cities from Japanese or Nationalist rule. It is hardly surprising that Mao had warned them about being seduced by the 'sugar-coated bullets of the bourgeoisie'. He needed them to form the basis of the new administration that the party would use to reshape China.

In some respects, the structure adopted for the national government differed little from that of other non-Communist countries. A state council, presided over by the premier, supervised a series of ministries which controlled local government and special agencies. On the other hand, all debate in China was conducted by the party. The Congress was the formal decision-making body, but met only infrequently: one was held in 1945, with others following in 1956, 1969, 1973, 1977 and 1982. Each Congress in turn elected a Central Committee, which varied in size: the Seventh Party Congress in 1945, for example, named 77 regular and alternate members to the Central Committee; the Ninth, in 1969, named 279. The Central Committees met more frequently than the Congress in 'plenary sessions' or 'plenums'. Since the Committee was too unwieldy to make day-to-day decisions, it elected a Politburo. This was where the real power lay.

One of the first questions that the party had to face once it had taken power was how to deal with those people whom it defined as 'counter-revolutionaries' - the landlords and Nationalist officials who had sustained Chiang Kaishek: they were handed over to the people. It was claimed that 80 per cent of the population participated in the mass accusation meetings which began in February 1951. Mass executions took place in sports stadia and public meeting places. It was no coincidence that this rooting out of internal enemies took place during the Korean War when China's Communists feared an alliance between internal and external 'counter-revolutionaries'.

In addition, land reform reinforced party control of the countryside. Peasants were organized into 'speak bitterness meetings' to denounce and then lynch landlords and their henchmen. This unleashed a great deal of latent violence and an estimated 2 million victims died. Some survivors 'gained merit' through their zeal in denouncing class enemies or in helping to run campaigns; they were described as 'positive elements', and many joined the party. Over a third of China's farmland changed hands in the process.

Late in 1951, the party launched the 'three and five anti- campaigns', against corrupt bureaucrats and businessmen respectively. The first purged about 150,000 party officials at and above county level by attacking three weaknesses: lax attitudes to counter-revolutionaries, job aggrandizement and corruption. The second destroyed the independence of those businessmen who had remained in mainland China, attacking them on five counts: bribery, tax evasion, stealing state property, cheating on government contracts and stealing government economic data. In 1956, businessmen 'voluntarily' handed over their assets to the state, creating a 'windfall' which may have amounted to US$1.7 billion.

Despite the party's success in overturning thousands of years of tradition and in reorientating Chinese society in just a few years, Mao was not satisfied. Once the land reform programme was complete, the party organized what were called 'mutual aid teams' - groups of four to ten households which would co-operate in raising agricultural production. These would then be developed into 'Agricultural Producers' Co-operatives' of between a hundred and three hundred households, which would function as collective farms. By moving gradually, the Chinese hoped to avoid the disastrous collapse in agricultural yields caused in the Soviet Union by forced collectivization. But resistance by the richer peasants and the inability of the poorly educated, lower party cadres to implement the policy led a group within the Politburo, which included Liu Shaoqi, Zhou Enlai, Chen Yun and the party's Rural Work chief, Deng Zihui, to suggest a pause in the programme. Some collectives were even dissolved.

Mao would have none of this, however, and, on 31 July 1955 he delivered his speech 'On the Co-operative Transformation of Agriculture', in which he threw his weight behind a more radical programme and denounced his Politburo colleagues as 'tottering behind the masses like women with bound feet'. He set a target of 1.3 million collective farms for the country, and by the end of 1958 the programme was largely complete. The pragmatists were silenced for the moment, but a split was developing in the party that would have disastrous consequences for China during the Cultural Revolution of the late 1960s.

Party rule tightened further after the nationalization of businesses and the collectivization of agriculture. City dwellers were tied to their workplaces by residents' permits, ration coupons for food and clothing, and the right to housing, education, medical care and pensions. Because they were not allowed to travel the peasants were tied to their land, but they lacked the social safety net provided in the cities. Even their produce was compulsorily purchased by the government at fixed prices.

However, despite the growing weight of the party during the 1950s, the Chinese people seemed grateful for what it did achieve and appeared to give their support.

Peasants eating their family meal together at home. Attempts to reduce private and family life failed.

# Zhou Enlai: China's Moderate Marxist

Zhou Enlai was the oil on the troubled waters of the Chinese Communist Party from the time it was founded in 1921 until the time he died in 1976. His charm and evident humanity earned him a special place in the hearts of the Chinese people that was unparalleled and which led to spontaneous public demonstrations of disgust when he was not given the state funeral that the people expected.

Unlike the other Chinese leaders of his generation, he travelled extensively. After studying in France, he returned to China and co-operated with the Nationalists. But after he organized a workers' rising in Shanghai, the Nationalists betrayed their former allies and he barely escaped with his life.

In 1928 he attended the Comintern's Sixth Congress in Moscow and was elected to the Executive Committee. Back in China he went underground and then joined Mao, taking over political control of the southern Soviet. But during the Long March he recognized Mao's superior judgement and never again questioned his decisions.

Zhou's negotiating skill had already become evident before the Communist victory in 1949. This led to his appointment as Foreign Minister and during the 1950s and 1960s his successes on the international stage transformed China's prestige and gave it an influence out of proportion to its economic strength. Finally, in the aftermath of the Cultural Revolution, Zhou worked hard, although he was dying of cancer, to reinstate those disgraced leaders he knew China would need after he and Mao were dead.

---

Prostitution, drug addiction and infanticide, which had been endemic in the poorest areas for generations, were eliminated, as was unemployment. The first five-year plan, which ran from 1952 to 1957 and to which the Soviet Union contributed 156 major industrial plants, tens of thousands of experts and hundreds of thousands of blueprints, achieved annual growth rates of over 10 per cent. At last the poor, who had formed 60 per cent of the population before the Revolution, could look to the future with hope.

The Hungarian uprising of late 1956 appalled Mao, and on 27 February 1957 he delivered a speech 'On the Correct Handling of Contradictions Among the People', which advocated a flexible approach to criticism.

Marxists should not be afraid of criticism from any quarter. Quite the contrary, they need to temper and develop themselves and win new positions in the teeth of criticism and in the storm and stress of struggle. Fighting against wrong ideas is like being vaccinated - a man develops greater immunity from disease as a result of vaccination. Plants raised in hothouses are unlikely to be hardy. Carrying out the policy of letting a hundred flowers bloom and a hundred schools of thought contend will not weaken, but strengthen the leading position of Marxism in the ideological field.

The pragmatic group within the leadership had tried to stop Mao from presenting his ideas and Liu Shaoqi, the second most powerful figure in the party, was pointedly absent when the speech was made. However, by late April the party press had fallen into line behind the chairman and even Liu was calling for 'blooming and contending'.

Encouraged by these liberalizing gestures, staff at Beijing University, officials within the unions and even members of the army put their thoughts on paper. Even Mao had not expected the trenchant comments that were published, and the policy was soon reversed. When Mao's speech appeared in print on 18 June, additions had been made indicating that 'fragrant flowers' of criticism had to be distinguished from 'poisonous weeds'. The line was drawn in such a way that no fundamental criticism of the party or its road to socialism would be acceptable. This was just the first of a series of radical thrusts by Mao - all of which failed.

## A Great Leap into the Dark

From the summer of 1957 onwards, Mao became increasingly anti-intellectual. In October of that year he attended the fortieth anniversary celebration of the Russian Revolution in Moscow. Mao was suspicious of Khrushchev's reforms, and on his return he promoted a new drive that depended on a group previously untainted by Soviet revisionism - the Chinese peasantry.

The winter of 1957-8 witnessed the amalgamation of many collectives as the government attempted to pool their labour for the construction of irrigation projects; as many as 60 million peasants were involved. In the following spring there were calls for this restructuring of the workforce to be made permanent. For Mao, the peasants were the country's great hope because they were 'poor and blank': 'Poor people want change, want to do things, want revolution. A clean sheet of paper has no blotches, and so the newest and most beautiful words can be written on it, the newest and most beautiful pictures can be painted on it.'

Grand rhetorical gestures took the place of sensible planning. A move to 'cartize' the south - that is, to replace carrying poles with wheeled carts - was launched although the south still lacked the roads to carry the new vehicles. The 'four pests' - rats, flies, mosquitos and sparrows - were to be eliminated, but when it was realized that sparrows helped to control other pests, bedbugs were substituted as the fourth pest. In industry, technicians and experts were denounced as intruders in the production process, and workers and managers were ordered to join together. The ministries in charge of production were decentralized.

Backyard steel furnaces were promoted as the means of providing the metal necessary to manufacture China's agricultural machinery, and 60 million peasants, were enrolled to work in them. But the steel produced was useless. With the countryside drained of labour, the grain harvest rotted in the fields. Meanwhile, the collective farms were amalgamated into huge communes and the people were asked to produce 'more, faster, better, and more economically'. This was China's Great Leap Forward.

The bubble burst in the autumn. If the reports of a wonderful harvest were true, why was everyone's rice allowance being cut? Whatever was said in public, political manoeuvring was going on behind the scenes. In the summer of 1959 it finally surfaced.

Peng Dehuai, one of the commanders of the Long March, had been Minister of Defence since 1949. In April 1958 he had criticized Mao for launching the Great Leap Forward without proper consultation. In July 1959 the Politburo met at Lushan. Mao tried to put a brave face on the economic difficulties, but Peng criticized him severely in committee and circulated a letter trying to rally support for his own position. Feeling threatened, Mao launched a counter-attack and said he would step down if Peng's letter were not withdrawn. Peng was forced to resign amid accusations that he was a 'rightist'. This alarmed the soldiers who had been enlisted to supervise production in the communes. Worried that they too might be labelled 'rightists', they redoubled their efforts to make the communes work, but with disastrous results; in the three terrible years that followed, as many as 25 million people may have died as famine stalked the land.

This catastrophe was compounded by the consequences of a war of words between Beijing and Moscow. China was becoming increasingly resentful of Soviet foreign policy which seemed to put Soviet national concerns well above those of revolution in general and China's revolutionary ambitions in particular. Certainly, having maintained a discreet silence over China's brutal suppression of a revolt in Tibet, reoccupied by Beijing in 1950, Moscow slowly tilted towards India in its various border skirmishes with China in the early 1960s. A verbal confrontation conducted in the press of each country during the spring of 1960 escalated into a thinly disguised slanging match between Mao and Khrushchev. The result was that the Soviet Union turned off the supply of aid and recalled all its technicians, together with their blueprints.

During the early 1960s, Mao kept out of the limelight. Pragmatists such as Deng Xiaoping and Liu Shaoqi reinstated more rational policies and China slowly regained its economic momentum. But Mao was only biding his time. After the twenty years of the war of liberation in which his unorthodox decisions had saved the party, he could no longer accept that he might be wrong. The stage was set for the final tragic act of his life - the Cultural Revolution.

# The Korean War

The second atomic bomb had just been dropped on Japan, and the end of the Second World War was only days away when a pair of American army colonels were given thirty minutes to make a fateful choice. The officers scrutinized a small-scale map of Korea, noted the location of the capital Seoul, and drew a line just to the north of it, along the 38th Parallel of latitude. In so doing, they unknowingly delineated the battleground for the first war to be fought between major armies of Communism and the West.

## Dividing a People

The United States had left the defeat of the Japanese armies in Korea to the Soviet Red Army, but with victory suddenly in sight, perspectives and priorities were greatly altered. The War Department put it to the Russians that the USA should share in the occupation of Korea. One of the officers, future Secretary of State Dean Rusk, pointed out that there was nothing the Americans could do if the Russians chose to ignore this proposal, but the Kremlin did not demur. The Red Army swept up to the 38th Parallel, and halted. It was another month before the first Americans reached Seoul.

The Americans arrived in September 1945 to find the population deeply demoralized. After centuries of isolation as the 'Hermit Kingdom', Korea had endured thirty-five years of cruel colonization by Japan, which in modernizing the country, and making it a part of their war machine, had sought to obliterate its language and culture, even to the extent of bulldozing palaces and temples. Some rich Koreans had collaborated and prospered, while guerrilla bands continued to fight the occupier from the hills. Now the old social order was under challenge from a younger generation passionately resentful of past humiliation.

The US commander, General John R. Hodge, was a military man with no pretence to political sophistication, and without even a competent interpreter, yet under instructions to 'create a government in harmony with US interests'. At first General Hodge listened to the warnings of the defeated Japanese as to the 'pernicious Communist influences' among the Korean guerrillas who had fought against them. As a result, he permitted the Japanese to retain responsibility for the maintenance of law and order - to the chagrin of the local people. He disregarded the cross-section of leading nationalists and resistance fighters who might have formed a credible, democratic leadership, allowing a

A group of South Koreans stand guard at the 38th parallel in 1948. The line of latitude marked the frontier between Communist North Korea and the South Korean Republic.

conservative, landowning local legislature to emerge. Furthermore, it was backed by a bureaucracy heavy with men who had held office under the Japanese. As leader, the Americans pinned their faith on Syngman Rhee, an egotistical septuagenarian who had spent most of his adult life in the USA. Rhee was a virulent anti-Communist and this, combined with his easy familiarity with things American, was sufficient for the US forces to overlook his controversial reputation. Under Rhee there was widespread unrest, and increasing dependence upon a repressive national police organization inherited intact from the Japanese.

In the north, the Russians did things in reverse. Their choice of leader was Kim Il Sung, a thirty-three-year-old revolutionary nationalist who had been battling the Japanese for a dozen years, and with a cadre of resistance fighters they built upon a network of 'people's committees' to create a centralized Soviet-style system. Opponents could choose liquidation or flight to the South, and by 1947 all political opposition had been eradicated with a thoroughness far surpassing that of the South.

The two Koreas, each led by an autocratic demagogue and each a caricature of its sponsor nation, now formalized their division. In August 1948, the flag of a new

Republic of Korea was hoisted over Seoul and Rhee was installed as President after elections boycotted by the left and marred by a wave of violence. The North duly responded by declaring its own Democratic People's Republic. Rhee pressed the Americans for heavy arms and vowed to reunify the country by force, but the USA was becoming disenchanted with its protégé, and saw no sense in promoting civil war where it sought only containment. The Red Army had already withdrawn from the North, and in June 1949 the Americans also completed withdrawal of their occupation forces, leaving five hundred advisers.

## Invasions

The two regimes were like snarling dogs let off the leash by rival masters, but one dog had sharper teeth. The North Korean army was better equipped, better led and vastly more motivated than its counterpart in the South. There was a year of border skirmishing, then on 25 June 1950 a force of perhaps ten thousand Northern troops, supported by about fifty T-34 tanks, broke through and headed for Seoul. Rhee's army fled helter-skelter along quagmired roads before Kim's mustard-yellow battalions. Within two days, Seoul had fallen.

# The 'Great Leader'

Zhou Enlai with Kim Il Sung, head of the Korean government delegation which visited China in 1958.

Kim Il Sung joined the Korean Communist Party when he was nineteen and spent the 1930s in China fighting the Japanese. He led a Korean unit within the Red Army during the Second World War and was made Supreme Commander of the Korean People's Army when Soviet forces overran Pyongyang, the ancient capital of the country.

Korea became a bone of contention between East and West after the war and their forces of occupation established sympathetic regimes within their own zones as in Germany. A new constitution was drafted for the North in 1948 and Kim was appointed Prime Minister. He became Party Chairman the following year.

Soviet aid promoted North Korean development during the 1950s. But after the Sino-Soviet split financial support was withdrawn, and the country's growth began to falter during the 1960s. Kim's regime became increasingly repressive and the cult of his personality began to resemble Stalin's. From time to time gestures of reconciliation were made between the two Koreas, but they never came to anything the North became increasingly isolated from both East and West.

The news stunned the Truman administration, which was still smarting from the 'loss' of China and absorbed with fears of a global Communist conspiracy. Without even waiting for the approval of Congress the President committed American forces to the fight and made the fledgling United Nations turn into an unprecedented international crusade. The USA at the time dominated the UN, which was being boycotted by the Soviet Union over its refusal to seat Communist China, and so, with no risk of a veto, the Americans were able to put the UN's imprimatur on a 'police action' under General Douglas MacArthur, the victor in the war against Japan.

The first troops flown from soft occupation duty in Japan performed woefully. On 5 July, a token force of a few hundred was brushed aside fifty miles south of Seoul; then an infantry division broke ingloriously at the approach of the T-34s. 'Bug-out fever' - the urge to bolt at the first squeak of a tank track - took hold as the image of a remorseless, fanatical enemy grew. Compounding the panic were Southern guerrilla groups who were liable to strike from the rear; sometimes posing as refugees, they would then pull guns and grenades from their bundles. The troops sought refuge in racist callousness - Koreans became 'gooks'.

With reinforcements pouring in, the US and remaining Rhee forces made a last stand around the south-eastern port of Pusan, and it was here, on 28 August, that the first British unit arrived in a somewhat grudging response to the US/UN call for support. Air strikes on the North Korean supply lines relieved the pressure, then MacArthur turned the war around with a spectacularly daring amphibious assault on the west coast at Inchon, with the intention of cutting off the enemy. An armada of 260 ships from ports in Japan negotiated treacherous tides to land seventy thousand US troops almost unopposed, and then the beleaguered garrison burst forth in all directions from the Pusan perimeter. After only eleven days the Stars and Stripes was hoisted over Seoul's shattered Capitol building (only to be hastily replaced by the blue UN colours).

MacArthur was now in full cry, and let the momentum carry his forces across the 38th Parallel and deep into North Korea. The Northern capital, Pyongyang, was taken on 19 October, and a week later some units reached the Yalu River, the border with China. While newspaper headlines celebrated victory, strategists concluded that only scattered pockets of resistance remained. On 24 November - Thanksgiving Day - MacArthur launched a drive intended to mop up what remained of the enemy, and to 'bring the boys back by Christmas'. Traditional turkey dinners were distributed to his troops, and in the thrill of the chase no heed was paid to warnings from Beijing, or to pilots' reports of unidentified formations 'swarming all over the countryside'.

Four Chinese armies totalling about 130,000 men had crossed the Yalu by night and taken up enveloping positions. Now they attacked. Lightly armed, and relying upon 'human wave' tactics and an unnerving din from bugles, whistles and rattles, they swept all before them. Three South Korean divisions fled, abandoning their equipment, while the US 8th Army scattered through the cold and wintry hills; its 2nd Division alone lost three thousand men in a six-mile 'death ride' through an enemy-held pass. Some honour was retrieved by disciplined Marines trapped to the east, who courageously fought their way through blizzards and frozen rivers to a sea evacuation. As well as being harried from the north, the retreating forces had to fight their way back through guerrillas and regrouped North Korean units, who proved to be far from a spent force.

## The War Against China

The American Secretary of State, Dean Acheson, called the rout the worst defeat of US arms in a hundred years. President Truman talked of using the atomic bomb, and the British Prime Minister, Clement Attlee, flew to Washington to dissuade him. Instead, the US air force pounded the North with conventional bombs. The Communists retook all of their territory and crossed the Parallel to capture Seoul for the second time in six months. But in the raging snowstorms of late January their primitive back-packing supply lines reached their limits of endurance, and they were pushed back out of the capital. The winter weather was almost as great a killer as their enemy's immense superiority in firepower: unable to light fires because they would be spotted by US planes, the Chinese often had to sleep in the open, without blankets, in temperatures as low as minus 30 degrees; as a result they suffered fierce frostbite. In mid-1951, stalemate was reached with the battle lines straddling the Parallel. It was during this phase that a British battalion, the Gloucesters, made a heroic stand on the Imjin River, north of Seoul. Britain's force numbered about twelve thousand, making it the largest of sixteen minor contributors to the UN cause; all were US allies, with the British Commonwealth most prominent, along with Turkey and the Philippines.

MacArthur was sacked in April. He had been openly rebellious in pressing for unlimited - that is, nuclear - war on China, even when the panic was over, and although immensely popular with the American public he deeply alarmed the country's allies. Following secret diplomacy, the Soviet UN ambassador, Jacob Malik, now proposed a ceasefire. Battlefield talks between the US and a North Korean-Chinese delegation began on 10 July 1951, but made no progress, even though Mao Zedong had been warned by his commander Peng Dehuai that the war was unwinnable.

The North was now relentlessly pounded

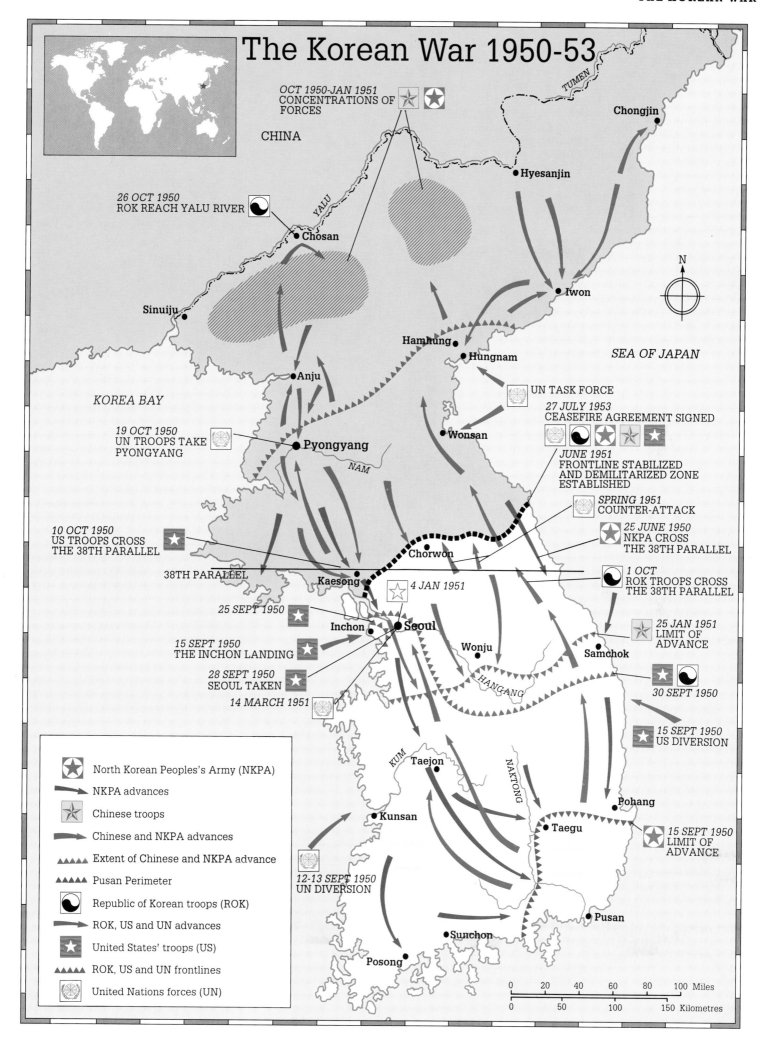

# The Korean War 1950-53

OCT 1950-JAN 1951
CONCENTRATIONS OF
FORCES

CHINA

Chongjin

Hyesanjin

TUMEN

26 OCT 1950
ROK REACH YALU RIVER

Chosan

YALU

Iwon

N

Sinuiju

Hamhung

Hungnam

SEA OF JAPAN

KOREA BAY

Anju

UN TASK FORCE

27 JULY 1953
CEASEFIRE AGREEMENT SIGNED

19 OCT 1950
UN TROOPS TAKE
PYONGYANG

Pyongyang

NAM

Wonsan

JUNE 1951
FRONTLINE STABILIZED
AND DEMILITARIZED ZONE
ESTABLISHED

SPRING 1951
COUNTER-ATTACK

10 OCT 1950
US TROOPS CROSS
THE 38TH PARALLEL

25 JUNE 1950
NKPA CROSS
THE 38TH PARALLEL

Chorwon

38TH PARALLEL

Kaesong

1 OCT
ROK TROOPS CROSS
THE 38TH PARALLEL

4 JAN 1951

25 SEPT 1950

Inchon

Seoul

Wonju

25 JAN 1951
LIMIT OF
ADVANCE

Samchok

15 SEPT 1950
THE INCHON LANDING

HANGANG

28 SEPT 1950
SEOUL TAKEN

30 SEPT 1950

14 MARCH 1951

15 SEPT 1950
US DIVERSION

KUM

Taejon

NAKTONG

Pohang

North Korean Peoples's Army (NKPA)

Kunsan

Taegu

NKPA advances

Chinese troops

15 SEPT 1950
LIMIT OF
ADVANCE

Chinese and NKPA advances

Extent of Chinese and NKPA advance

Pusan Perimeter

Pusan

Republic of Korean troops (ROK)

ROK, US and UN advances

12-13 SEPT 1950
UN DIVERSION

Sunchon

United States' troops (US)

ROK, US and UN frontlines

Posong

United Nations forces (UN)

| 0 | 20 | 40 | 60 | 80 | 100 Miles |

| 0 | 50 | 100 | 150 Kilometres |

from the air and sea, forcing the inhabitants to live underground. North Korea's piston-engined Yak fighters had been shot out of the skies in the first weeks and, apart from a brief spell when the first MIG-15 jets appeared in late 1950, American F-86 Sabres enjoyed such air superiority throughout the war that the other side could operate only by night. Bombing campaigns with evocative names - 'Operation Strangle' and 'Operation Insomnia' - now blasted the interior, and ports such as Wonsan were reduced to rubble by the most sustained naval bombardment in history. The peace talks bogged down over the issue of prisoner repatriation, which the US insisted must be voluntary. While US charges of Communist 'brainwashing' became a major issue in the West, less was said about the appalling conditions in UN prison camps. Communist charges of germ warfare became a further issue in the spring of 1952. These were never proved, but the growing perception of Korea as a 'dirty' war, and the corruption of the Rhee dictatorship, were causing general disillusionment.

That summer massed bombers struck the North's vital dam and power complexes, blacking out the country, and Pyongyang was pounded, strafed and napalmed as never before. Another winter set in, jamming guns, immobilizing equipment and freezing the morphia needed by the wounded. By night, the brightly illuminated talks site at Panmunjom could be seen for many miles along a front where more than 2 million troops were dug in like the armies in First World War Flanders. The Communists kept digging until their defences incorporated almost 800 miles of tunnels and 3500 miles of trenches. US troop morale slumped.

It took the election of a new US President, Dwight D. Eisenhower, and the death of Stalin before agreement could be reached on an exchange of sick and wounded prisoners, but ground fighting for negotiating advantage intensified. In May 1953 Americans bombed irrigation dams and swept away much of the North's rice crop. By mid-June only Rhee stood out against a settlement, which he tried to sabotage by causing chaos through a mass breakout of close to thirty thousand Communist prisoners. This failed to stop an armistice being signed on 27 July 1953, after two years and seventeen days of

tortuous negotiations. The artillery kept firing with passionate intensity right up to the 10 pm ceasefire.

In a war of firepower against manpower, the US put Chinese and North Korean deaths at 1.5 million. If this seems incredible, there are Chinese sources which put it even higher. The civilian slaughter was worst of all - at least 2 million died, probably 3. The treatment of Korean by Korean was savage, and atrocities were commonplace. American reliance on massive bombing and its policy of scorched earth retreat exacted a terrible civilian toll. As for the Americans themselves, out of more than 1.3 million who served in the war, 54,246 died and 33,629 were listed as killed in action. The South Korean army suffered even heavier casualties. Battle deaths among other UN forces totalled 3194, of whom 686 were British.

## The Consequences

The Korean War spurred massive Western rearmament and the girding of the NATO alliance. To Winston Churchill, that was its only worth. The US military budget soared from $15 billion to $50 billion. The CIA was unleashed. US policy had been based upon the conviction that the Kremlin was behind the war, though it now appears certain that Kim Il Sung acted on his own. Soviet involvement was minimal, and when it did begin to provide China with supplies from late 1951, it charged for them. Beijing's resentment was a factor in the subsequent split of the Communist world. China became a world power in its own right, and the hard lessons of the war were absorbed - though not by America. Confused over the failure to conquer a peasant enemy, Americans looked for enemies within: thousands of civil servants, academics, writers and entertainers, were purged in anti-Communist witch-hunts. Korea was to lead directly to the tragedy of Vietnam in the following decades, since the US had learnt nothing about the limitations of overwhelming firepower.

The war stimulated the world economy, with a cost in inflation deferred until much later. Japan benefitted from serving as launchpad for the UN effort, being rehabilit-ated as a Western ally and set on the path of economic recovery. Chiang Kaishek and the

Chinese Nationalists were saved by the war, which brought Taiwan, their retreat, under the US defence umbrella.

The Soviet Union quickly resumed its United Nations seat; there are suspicions that it may have intentionally stayed away, aiming to show up the world body as an American tool, and content to let both the US and the UN become bogged down in the war. After Korea, the UN changed out of recognition as a mass of emergent Third World countries came to dominate its debates. North Korea became a latter-day Hermit Kingdom under the idiosyncratic cult leadership of Kim Il Sung, who was distrustful even of Beijing. Syngman Rhee was overthrown in 1960, and died in exile in Hawaii. His going provided no relief from repression at the hands of successive military governments, indulged by the US as bastions against Communism yet ultimately fostering great industrial growth and material success. To a Western public that once shivered over horror comic images of crazed Asiatic hordes, the Korean War became a very muddled memory, sustained mainly by the comforting T series *MASH,* with its cast of lovable eccentrics drawing upon the self-doubt and anti-war sentiments of a time that had yet to come.

## The Atomic Threat

It will never be known how close the United States came to using the atomic bomb during the Korean War, but it maintained the threat throughout the conflict. By the outbreak of the war, the US had bombs to spare - 455 against an estimated 25 in the Soviet arsenal. China's early success led President Truman to state publicly, on 30 November, that resort to the bomb was under 'active consideration', but General MacArthur had been privately pressing for its use before that. The general persisted with ever more lurid schemes. In an interview, published after his death, he said that he had wanted to drop 'between thirty and fifty atomic bombs' on China, and to seal off the Korean peninsula with 'a belt of radioactive cobalt'.

In the spring of 1951 bombs were stocked on Okinawa in Japan for a possible strike against Manchurian bases, and the first tactical nuclear weapons were available for use. During a halt in the peace talks, the US made its enemy sweat through simulated atomic bombing missions, each frighteningly realistic until the moment of impact - when the bomb proved to be a dummy.

It is generally believed that President Eisenhower threatened China with the bomb when he took office. It is known that he discussed specific battlefield targets and came to agree with his Secretary of State, John Foster Dulles, 'that somehow or other the taboo which surrounds the use of atomic weapons would have to be destroyed'. After that, the peace talks moved quickly to a successful conclusion, and mankind was allowed time for the taboo to take greater hold. Perhaps that was Eisenhower's intention in going to the razor's edge.

President Syngman Rhee, an embarrassing ally for the United States, visits the front during the Korean War.

# The Khrushchev Years

Russian leaders mourn Stalin, 1953. Beria and Malenkov (third and fourth from left) soon lost their posts. Khrushchev remained as Secretary General.

Stalin left no obvious successor and no mechanism through which the party could choose one on his death in 1953. The purges had eliminated any serious political rivals. Among the survivors, his technique of playing one off against another meant that his legacy to the party leadership was one of mutual suspicion and distrust.

The provisional arrangement agreed immediately after his death put a troika of senior party officials at the head of the country: Beria, Malenkov and the Foreign Minister, Molotov. The funeral arrangements were placed in the hands of Nikita Khrushchev, one of the country's most capable organizers. This collective leadership did not survive for long, however, because their jealousy of one another soon got the upper hand.

The first to suffer a demotion was Malenkov, who was relieved of his post as First Party Secretary on 14 March. But the first to disappear was Beria, the People's Commissar for Internal Affairs. His control of the secret police, whose writ had run almost without check under Stalin, made Beria a danger to all his colleagues.

No one in the Soviet Union, no matter how senior their position in the party, had been safe from trumped-up accusations and a rap on the door at the dead of night. Indeed, it is quite clear from the Soviet press that Stalin had been planning another purge in late 1952, and that a campaign had been gathering pace which bore a very strong resemblance to the events of 1937. This operation ceased abruptly a few weeks before Stalin's death, and the coincidence has given rise to speculation that the stroke which carried him off might well have been induced by those at the top who wished to avoid the fate of their predecessors in the 1930s.

Beria was arrested in late June, but his detention was not announced to the party until the evening of 9 July in a series of closed meetings held throughout the country. The news was published in *Pravda* the next day. In the months that followed, the press contained many stories attacking the former secret police chief. Meanwhile, his nominees within the Soviet Union began losing their posts, as did others in East Germany and Korea with whom he had maintained close contact. Beria and his closest associates in the Ministry of the Interior were tried in

## The U2 Incident

In August 1960, Francis Gary Powers, a former American Air Force pilot who had been hired by the CIA for $30,000 a year, was put on trial in a Moscow courtroom. He had been shot down over Sverdlovsk in Central Russia on 1 May while flying an extraordinary spy plane, code named the U2. The CIA had assured President Eisenhower that this aeroplane was capable of eluding Soviet radar and rockets by flying at over 60,000 feet.

The reconnaissance flights had begun in June 1956 and Powers had been one of the first pilots to sign up to undertake these missions But the Americans received their first shock within days when Khrushchev protested privately about the flights. This meant that Soviet radar could track the planes, which was beyond the capabilities of American military technology.

After this blow, every flight had to be approved in every detail by President Eisenhower before it was allowed to take off. Even if the Soviets knew what was happening, they were

Gary Powers, the pilot of the ill-fated U2 reconnaisance plane, after his capture by the Russians. He served two years of a ten-year prison sentence.

protesting discreetely and, Washington reasoned, they had no way of bringing down the aircraft.

However, Washington had underestimated Soviet expertise, and Powers barely escaped with his life after his plane was hit by one of the first SAM missiles. In his haste to eject Powers forgot to arm the self-destruct switches in the cockpit and a triumphant Kremlin was able to parade both the pilot and the wreckage of his spy plane to the world's press.

This May Day success was a gift to Khrushchev, who was due to meet Eisenhower on 16 May in Paris for a much-trumpeted summit. The meeting turned into a humiliation for the President and helped Khrushchev in his long-running battle with the 'hawks' in the Politburo as the General Secretary demanded a complete apology from the Americans.

Powers was convicted of espionage and sentenced to ten years in prison. But in February 1962 he was exchanged for Rudolf Abel, a KGB agent caught by the Americans.

# The Khrushchev Years

N

*1953*
CENTRAL COMMITTEE MEETING:
KHRUSHCHEV PILLORIES SOVIET
AGRICULTURAL PERFORMANCE

*1956*
TWENTIETH PARTY CONGRESS
KHRUSHCHEV CRITICIZES STALIN

*JUNE 1956*
TITO ARRIVES TO GENERAL
RAPTURE; MOLOTOV SACKED

U N I O N   O F   S O V I E T

Ural Mountains

KAGANOVICH TO THE URALS

MOLOTOV BECOMES AMBASSADOR
TO OUTER MONGOLIA

Krasnoyarsk ●

● Moscow

Petropavlovsk ●    ● Omsk    ● Novosibirsk

*1957*
KHRUSHCHEV SURVIVES
ATTEMPTED COUP

MALENKOV MANAGES POWER STATION
IN EAST KAZAKHSTAN

● Stalingrad
(RENAMED
VOLGOGRAD IN *1961*)    ● Chelkar

KAZAKHSTAN
*1955*
LEONID BREZHNEV BECOMES
FIRST PARTY SECRETARY

*OCT 1964*
KHRUSHCHEV SUMMONED FROM
CRIMEAN HOLIDAY TO FACE
DISMISSAL IN MOSCOW

ARAL
SEA

BLACK SEA

GEORGIA

CASPIAN

SEA

● Tashkent

TURKEY

*1955*
SECURITY SERVICE MEMBERS
PUT ON MASS TRIAL

AFGHANISTAN

MEDITERRANEAN SEA

IRAQ

IRAN

SAUDI ARABIA

INDIA

ARABIAN SEA

0    200    400    600   Miles

0   200   400   600   800   Kilometres

SOCIALIST REPUBLICS

OUTER MONGOLIA

MONGOLIA

CHINA

PACIFIC OCEAN

JAPAN

Virgin Lands region of North Kazakhstan

Waste and abandoned lands temporarily cultivated during Virgin Lands campaign

----- Boundary of Kazakhstan SSR

# Khrushchev's Secret Speech

The official programme of the Twentieth Party Congress had already ended when Khrushchev made his secret speech. Delegates, including some representing foreign Communist parties, were admitted by special pass. The reason for the secrecy was probably fear of the effects of the revelations. The intention was that delegates would inform members of their local organizations who would tell others. The contents of the speech would thus be filtered gradually to ordinary people. A foreign delegate leaked the contents of the speech, however, and it was published abroad and broadcast back.

Khrushchev's denunciation of his former leader was a merciless attack on Stalin's egoism and his 'absolutely insufferable character'. To the shock and consternation of the delegates, he read out a hitherto unknown letter from Lenin to Stalin complaining of rude and offensive behaviour to his wife Krupskaya, who was herself a senior party official. Khrushchev revealed that 70 per cent of the Central Committee of the Seventeenth Congress had been arrested and shot after 'accusations against them were fabricated'. He exposed the irregularities and the 'inexplicable and mysterious' events which preceeded and followed the murder of Kirov in 1934, which Stalin used as the starting point of the purges. And within those remarks were strong hints that Stalin himself might well be implicated in the murder. Khrushchev even went so far as to mention such un-persons as Trotsky and his followers, who he dismissed as a threat to the party by the middle of the 1930s but a quite inadequate reason for a campaign of mass arrests.

Such an uncompromising attack must have come as a profound shock to those present who were accustomed to Stalin being discussed in terms of unstinted praise. In the days to come, this ripple of anguish spread throughout the Soviet Union as the rest was read to closed meetings of the party. It is an indication of the anxiety that was generated about the revelations that Khrushchev waited five years before he attacked Stalin again and that such attacks were stifled after he fell from power.

December and then shot. The secret police ceased to be a ministerial responsibility and was supervised henceforward by the Committee for State Security, or KGB.

## The Thaw

During the summer of 1953 there were many indications that the hold of the secret police on Soviet life was to be relaxed. All those sentenced to jail terms of less than five years for political crimes were given amnesty, and those who had been sentenced to internal exile were allowed to return home. In the periodical *Znamya,* the writer Ilya Ehrenburg attacked the party's regimentation of literature, while the critic W. Pomerantsev was allowed to suggest in *Novy Mir* that honesty was more important than loyalty to the party. The most famous book published under the party's 'New Course' was Ehrenburg's *The Thaw,* whose title became a synonym for destalinization.

The New Course was also reflected in the running of the economy. On 8 August, Malenkov - still the Prime Minister - announced a new consumer goods programme to the Supreme Soviet. Three weeks later, a full session of the Central Committee was called which lasted four days. The chief item on the agenda was Soviet agricultural policy. Khrushchev had been responsible for this topic within the Politburo during 1950, and he made the keynote speech. Instead of the usual fawning panegyric on the successes of the system, which had been essential under Stalin, Khrushchev's speech was a catalogue of failures: the land used for growing potatoes was less than half the area used before the war; there were 3.5 million fewer cows on the country's farms compared to 1941; and only 5 per cent of the country's agricultural experts worked on the farms. Motions were passed approving an increase in farm prices, the cancellation of the debts of collective farms and the sending of a hundred thousand experts from their offices into the fields.

The September session also had wider effects. Announcements on policy changes had previously been made by state officials; party representatives now took their place. The authority of the party over the state apparatus was re-established. The session was also a crucial stage in Khrushchev's rise to power: he was officially appointed First Secretary of the Central Committee. Within weeks he had used this new-found power to dismiss the Leningrad Party Secretary, who was a close supporter of Malenkov.

The New Course was given the limelight at the anniversary celebrations of the October Revolution on 7 November 1953, but by the following autumn it was becoming apparent that the approved measures were failing. Controversy over the consumer goods programme had split the leadership, with Malenkov, Mikoyan (the Minister of Trade), Kosygin (deputy chairman of the Council of Ministers) and Bendiktov (Minister of Agriculture) on one side, and Khrushchev, Bulganin (Minister of Defence) and Marshal Zhukov (deputy Minister of Defence) on the other. In September 1954 Khrushchev stressed that priority should be placed on heavy industry in the Soviet economy.

Malenkov's fall from grace was signalled by the trial of a former Minister of State Security, Viktor Abakumov, who had been part of the Malenkov faction. Abakumov and three associates were sentenced to death for arresting innocent party members and intellectuals, and torturing them to get confessions. A report of the trial appeared in the Soviet press on 24 December 1954 - the same day that Khrushchev's interview stressing heavy industry was published. Malenkov resigned as Prime Minister six weeks later. He was replaced by Marshal Bulganin, although he remained on the Praesidium, the new name for the Politburo.

Under Bulganin, military leaders were propelled into senior positions within the government. Eleven new marshals were installed in the armed forces and there was a call for a revision of the official history of the Second World War. The new members of the government also emphasized the need for a collective leadership, and Khrushchev was rebuffed for issuing orders without consulting his colleagues.

## Stalin in the Dock

The party leadership continued to attack the bureaucratic overmanning of the various Soviet ministries during 1955, and substantial cuts were made in staff numbers. Tens of thousands of party officials throughout the country were replaced by younger people. In Kazakhstan, the First Party Secretary was replaced by Leonid Brezhnev. A large trial of members of the Georgian Security Service was staged in September; for the first time, officials were rehabilitated who had been disgraced during the purges of the 1930s. However, these revisions were as nothing compared with what was about to occur at the Twentieth Party Congress.

The first session was scheduled for 14 February 1956. That morning everyone in Moscow knew that something sensational was about to happen because the masthead of *Pravda* had changed - Stalin's head had disappeared from its customary place alongside Lenin's. When the fifteen hundred delegates filed into their places to listen to Khrushchev's keynote speech no one could have failed to notice that Stalin's portrait had been removed from the wall. In a session open only to Soviet party members - called just before midnight on 24 February - Khrushchev spent four hours attacking Stalin with a savagery which left many of his listeners in a state of shock. Stalin's behaviour after 1934 had, he claimed, resulted in the imprisonment and execution of many innocent party stalwarts - for which there was no excuse.

Although the Congress is remembered for this turning point in Stalin's reputation in his own country, it also initiated other profound changes. A new tolerance was accorded to 'different roads to socialism' and many quotations from the classics of Marx, Engels and Lenin were used to justify the ways in which different countries could take different paths to the same end. Even the idea of peaceful co-existence with capitalist countries was endorsed. Party historians were requested to re-examine the past and discard the 'falsifications' promulgated under Stalin; the rehabilitation of increasing numbers of victims of the purges was encouraged;

Nikita Khrushchev visits Washington for talks with President Eisenhower in 1959 as relations between the Soviet Union and China deteriorate further.

and the devolution of power to the republics was promoted. But, above all, the industrial and agricultural failures of the past were exposed and bureaucratic inflexibility castigated.

## The Pendulum Swings Back

Khrushchev emerged from the Congress with his stature in the country at a new high. During the spring and summer of 1956 the movement for reform reached its first peak. On 2 June, Tito arrived in Moscow to a rapturous welcome. Molotov, who in 1948 had signed the Cominform resolution expelling Yugoslavia, was sacked the same day. Four days later another old Stalinist, Kaganovich, was also dismissed.

Events outside the country now took a hand, however, as the effects of the destalinization programme were felt in eastern Europe. The turmoil in Poland and Hungary gave the old guard the opportunity to turn on those who had deposed them. Kaganovich returned to the government on 22 September, while Molotov was rehabilitated on 22 November in the wake of the Hungarian rising. By the end of December, Stalinism itself seemed on the point of rehabilitation. Even Khrushchev felt compelled to praise the dead leader. It was in this mood that a session of the Central Committee was called for 13 February, with economic reform on the agenda.

Khrushchev made the main speech, criticizing the centralization of the economy. His proposals to devolve economic planning to regional authorities were not accepted immediately, and when his speech was published on 30 March 1957 it was described as a document for discussion. The debate began immediately in the Soviet press, and tens of thousands of letters were published in newspapers throughout the

country. The effect of the controversy was to align provincial leaders, who stood to gain from decentralization, behind Khrushchev.

Early in June, Bulganin and Khrushchev visited Finland and Khrushchev's enemies had an opportunity to plot their downfall. At a session of the Praesidium starting on 18 June Khrushchev was attacked. By the 21st, his dismissal was on the agenda, but he insisted that he was appointed by the full 255 members of the Central Committee and that only they could sack him. Marshal Zhukov then came to his aid by supplying army aircraft to ferry the provincial leaders to Moscow in the shortest possible time. At first the momentum stayed with Khrushchev's enemies: Malenkov, Molotov, Kaganovich and their supporters. But the provincial leaders steadfastly supported the First Party Secretary and the manoeuvres rebounded on his attackers. By the end of the session it was they who were forced to resign.

By the autumn of 1957 Khrushchev looked as though he was in an unassailable position, but he lacked Lenin's intellect and organizational flair and also Stalin's murderous ambition. The First Secretary had survived because the campaign for decentralization was popular with the Central Committee. Many of his subsequent reforms proved far less attractive to his colleagues and in the end he paid the penalty for a plethora of 'hare-brained schemes'.

## Decline and Fall

The first opportunity for Khrushchev to demonstrate his talents on a world stage came at the fortieth anniversary celebrations of the Revolution. Party leaders attended from all over the world, and the opening speech was made by Mao Zedong. A declaration was agreed which emphasized

the unity of the movement and condemned deviations from 'the universal truth of Marxism-Leninism'. Such a position directly contradicted the policy which Khrushchev had advocated at the Twentieth Party Congress in February 1956, and his continued support for countries outside the Communist fold alienated the Chinese leadership and Mao in particular.

On the other hand, Khrushchev's initiatives in assisting Third World countries changed the status of the Soviet Union on the international scene in a permanent way and encroached on areas which had formerly been considered Western preserves. When Soviet influence penetrated Latin America, this expansion of the Cold War alarmed the Americans. It also damaged Khrushchev's prestige at home when Soviet aid was supplied to unstable and inexperienced regimes where coups and counter-coups wrote off millions of roubles of aid. However, the greatest loss of face which Khrushchev suffered internationally came from the Cuban crisis. But these foreign debacles would not have undermined his position at home if his domestic policies had been more successful.

The Soviet Union's most serious problem concerned the supply of food. Agricultural productivity was low because those who worked the land had no incentive to do better. Khrushchev's solution was to endorse the dramatic but ill-considered 'virgin lands project', which involved ploughing up the steppes of northern Kazakhstan, southern Siberia and south-east Russia and sowing grain. The first results in 1954 were spectacular, as millions of acres were put into productive use and 10 million extra tons of grain were harvested. But the soil was poor, the equipment inadequate and transportation rudimentary. By the early 1960s the land had become a gigantic dustbowl and the productivity of the older agricultural areas, starved of investment, had fallen. The harvest was so poor in 1963 and 1964 that large quantities of grain had to be imported.

Then there were Khrushchev's attempts to improve the administrative efficiency of the country. The decentralization scheme which had kept him in power soon proved to be fraught with inefficiences and corruption. In 1962 he introduced his final and most catastrophic change: he separated the party and the administration into agricultural and industrial sectors. Since each sector had its own staff, the number of officials at every level doubled and the whole system collapsed in confusion.

By 1964, Khrushchev's policies had turned against him even those who had voted for him in 1957. Although he insisted on the party's control over policy, he kept interfering with spur-of-the-moment decisions on complex military, political and economic issues, which frequently backfired. On 13 October 1964 he was summoned back from holiday to a meeting of the Praesidium and told to clear his desk. The palm of Leonid Brezhnev was about to grasp the Soviet Union.

# Unrest in Eastern Europe

The Twentieth Congress of the Communist Party of the Soviet Union in 1956 affected the socialist movement throughout the world. Nowhere were its repercussions more pronounced than in Poland and Hungary, although the political skills of the leadership in the two countries led to quite different consequences, particularly in the short term. The cohesive and determined response of the liberal wing of the party in Warsaw kept Soviet tanks off the streets and the bloodshed to a minimum. The heroic but unsuccessful rising in Budapest, on the other hand, will be remembered for generations.

The seeds of dissent were sown in Poland in 1954 when Colonel Jozef Swiatlo, the deputy head of the section of the secret police which monitored the party elite, defected to the West with a number of incriminating documents. Swiatlo's revelations were broadcast by Radio Free Europe, a station based in Munich and

Armed soldiers guard the Communist Party headquarters in Warsaw after allegations of irregularites in the general election of 1947.

## Radio Free Europe

In the chaos of the Hungarian uprising, the beleaguered citizens looked to foreign radio stations for reliable news of their country. While many tuned in to the BBC World Service or Voice of America, some listened to Radio Free Europe. This station had been set up in Munich in 1951 to beam propaganda to eastern Europe. It was funded openly by the American government, but extra covert monies were channelled to it by the CIA, a situation which was only revealed to the American Congress in 1971. The broadcasters were émigrés who made no secret of their anti-Communist attitudes.

During the Hungarian uprising, Radio Free Europe lost all sense of proportion in its attempts to incite Hungarians to fight in the streets and seriously misled them about any outside help that might materialize. False reports of a UN delegation led many Hungarians to assume that a force similar to that which fought in Korea would soon appear at their sides.

In the aftermath of the fighting, Radio Moscow continued to attack RFE for months for its complicity in the revolt. Budapest Radio broadcast messages expressing its gratitude to the BBC for not having stooped to 'extremism'. Even in Washington, officials realized that the station had gone too far and stricter controls were imposed on the émigrés. It was noticeable that Radio Free Europe showed greater restraint during the Czechoslovak crisis of 1968.

funded by the CIA. They attracted an audience of millions in Poland because they confirmed everything that the people had suspected - the arbitrary arrests, the trumped-up charges and the luxurious life-style of the elite at a time when the people were barely making ends meet. Even the elite was shocked to discover that its comings and goings were under surveillance. The party leader, Boleslaw Bierut, was forced to admit the truth of the allegations at a meeting of the Central Committee held on 25 January 1955; he then had to arrest members of the secret police and move their boss, the Minister of the Interior, to a new government post. The loss of face by Bierut, a devoted disciple of Stalin, gave the reformers among the leadership a boost and undermined the authority of the secret police. The Polish press began to print guarded criticisms of the excesses of the regime. Then, in August, *Nowa Kultura* published *Poem for Adults* by Adam Wazyk, whose 'odes to construction' and other such confections had made him a favourite of the leadership. The bitterly sardonic tone of its many verses contrasted the Communist dream with Polish disillusionment:

The dreamer Fourier prophesied so beautifully
that the waters of the sea would flow with lemonade
and was this what happened?
They drink the sea water
and cry, 'This is lemonade'
and stumble home in silence
to vomit
to vomit.

The poem unleashed more criticism and prepared the ground for Khrushchev's bombshell of the night of 24 February 1956.

Within days of the end of the Twentieth Congress in Moscow, the Polish Party newspaper, *Trybuna Ludu,* published an attack on Stalin's cult of personality which, it said, had produced a 'blind faith in the omniscience of one man'. Radio Warsaw proclaimed that 'each person can realize that he has not only the right but the duty to express his opinions'.

In the midst of this ferment, the party leader Bierut died on 12 March. Khrushchev invited himself to the Central Committee meeting called for 20 March to elect a new First Secretary, but was politely shown the door by the Poles. One of the first acts of the new leader, Edward Ochab, was to announce that Wladislaw Gomulka, the former First Secretary who had been jailed at the height of Stalin's crackdown on eastern Europe in 1950, and others were to be released.

### Spring in October

The new Polish leader toured Silesia to meet the workers and was so shocked at what he found that he ordered an immediate 15 per cent pay rise for the miners. But discontent was not confined to the pits, and the anger finally boiled over in Poznan. Discontent had been building up in the ZISPO locomotive works for years as wages had fallen. A meeting held on 23 June despatched a delegation to Warsaw, but only two of its five demands were met. Early on the morning of the 28th the workers' anger erupted,

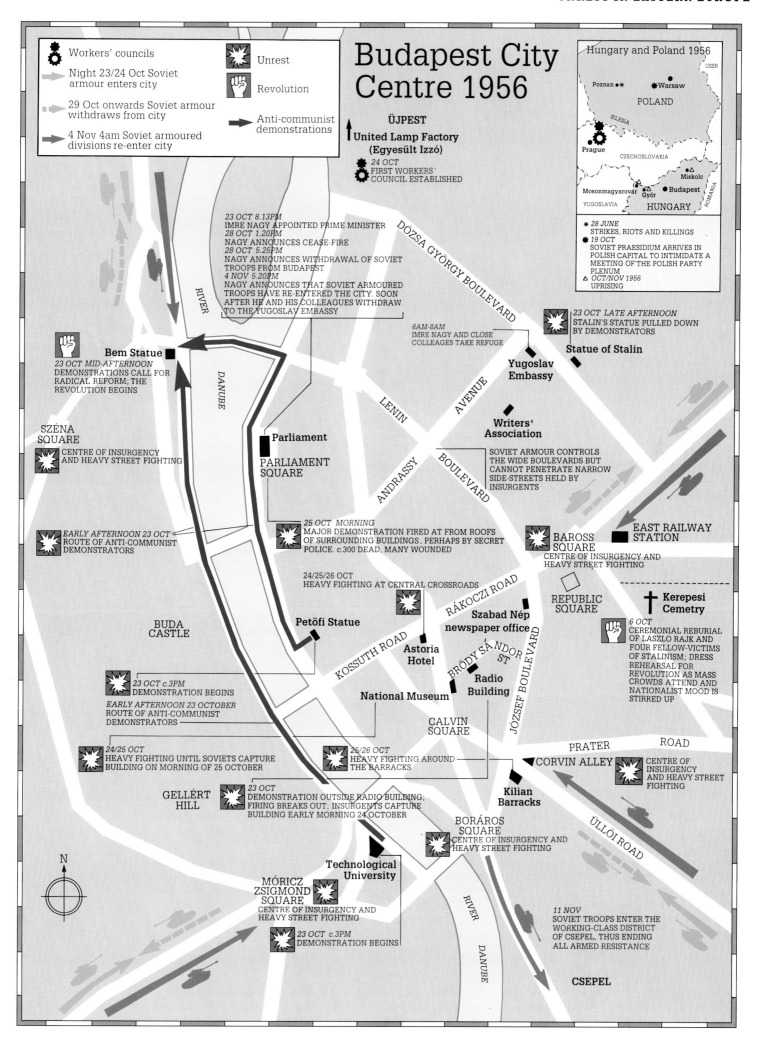

# Budapest City Centre 1956

**Workers' councils**

**Night 23/24 Oct Soviet armour enters city**

**29 Oct onwards Soviet armour withdraws from city**

**4 Nov 4am Soviet armoured divisions re-enter city**

**Unrest**

**Revolution**

**Anti-communist demonstrations**

### Hungary and Poland 1956

POLAND
USSR
Poznan
Warsaw
SILESIA
Prague
CZECHOSLOVAKIA
Miskolc
Mosonmagyaróvár
Győr ● Budapest
YUGOSLAVIA
HUNGARY
ROMANIA

**★ 28 JUNE** STRIKES, RIOTS AND KILLINGS
**★ 19 OCT** SOVIET PRAESIDIUM ARRIVES IN POLISH CAPITAL TO INTIMIDATE A MEETING OF THE POLISH PARTY PLENUM
**△ OCT/NOV 1956** UPRISING

**ÜJPEST**
**United Lamp Factory (Egyesült Izzó)**
**24 OCT** FIRST WORKERS' COUNCIL ESTABLISHED

*23 OCT 8.13PM* IMRE NAGY APPOINTED PRIME MINISTER
*28 OCT 1.20PM* NAGY ANNOUNCES CEASE-FIRE
*28 OCT 5.25PM* NAGY ANNOUNCES WITHDRAWAL OF SOVIET TROOPS FROM BUDAPEST
*4 NOV 5.20PM* NAGY ANNOUNCES THAT SOVIET ARMOURED TROOPS HAVE RE-ENTERED THE CITY. SOON AFTER HE AND HIS COLLEAGUES WITHDRAW TO THE YUGOSLAV EMBASSY

DÖZSA GYÖRGY BOULEVARD

*6AM-8AM* IMRE NAGY AND CLOSE COLLEAGES TAKE REFUGE

**23 OCT LATE AFTERNOON** STALIN'S STATUE PULLED DOWN BY DEMONSTRATORS
**Statue of Stalin**

**Yugoslav Embassy**

**Bem Statue**
*23 OCT MID-AFTERNOON* DEMONSTRATIONS CALL FOR RADICAL REFORM; THE REVOLUTION BEGINS

RIVER
DANUBE

**Writers' Association**

LENIN
ANDRASSY
AVENUE
BOULEVARD

SOVIET ARMOUR CONTROLS THE WIDE BOULEVARDS BUT CANNOT PENETRATE NARROW SIDE-STREETS HELD BY INSURGENTS

**SZÉNA SQUARE** CENTRE OF INSURGENCY AND HEAVY STREET FIGHTING

**Parliament**
**PARLIAMENT SQUARE**

*EARLY AFTERNOON 23 OCT* ROUTE OF ANTI-COMMUNIST DEMONSTRATORS

*25 OCT MORNING* MAJOR DEMONSTRATION FIRED AT FROM ROOFS OF SURROUNDING BUILDINGS, PERHAPS BY SECRET POLICE. c.300 DEAD, MANY WOUNDED

**BAROSS SQUARE** CENTRE OF INSURGENCY AND HEAVY STREET FIGHTING

**EAST RAILWAY STATION**

**REPUBLIC SQUARE**

**† Kerepesi Cemetery**

24/25/26 OCT HEAVY FIGHTING AT CENTRAL CROSSROADS

RÁKOCZI ROAD

**Szabad Nép newspaper office**

**BUDA CASTLE**

**Petöfi Statue**

KOSSUTH ROAD
BRÓDY SÁNDOR ST
JÓZSEF BOULEVARD

**Astoria Hotel**

**Radio Building**

*6 OCT* CEREMONIAL REBURIAL OF LASZLO RAJK AND FOUR FELLOW-VICTIMS OF STALINISM; DRESS REHEARSAL FOR REVOLUTION AS MASS CROWDS ATTEND AND NATIONALIST MOOD IS STIRRED UP

**National Museum**

*23 OCT c.3PM* DEMONSTRATION BEGINS
*EARLY AFTERNOON 23 OCTOBER* ROUTE OF ANTI-COMMUNIST DEMONSTRATORS

**CALVIN SQUARE**

PRATER ROAD

**CORVIN ALLEY** CENTRE OF INSURGENCY AND HEAVY STREET FIGHTING

*24/25 OCT* HEAVY FIGHTING UNTIL SOVIETS CAPTURE BUILDING ON MORNING OF 25 OCTOBER

*25/26 OCT* HEAVY FIGHTING AROUND THE BARRACKS

**Kilian Barracks**

**GELLÉRT HILL**

*23 OCT* DEMONSTRATION OUTSIDE RADIO BUILDING; FIRING BREAKS OUT; INSURGENTS CAPTURE BUILDING EARLY MORNING 24 OCTOBER

ÜLLÖI ROAD

**BORÁROS SQUARE** CENTRE OF INSURGENCY AND HEAVY STREET FIGHTING

**Technological University**

N

**MÓRICZ ZSIGMOND SQUARE** CENTRE OF INSURGENCY AND HEAVY STREET FIGHTING

RIVER
DANUBE

*11 NOV* SOVIET TROOPS ENTER THE WORKING-CLASS DISTRICT OF CSEPEL, THUS ENDING ALL ARMED RESISTANCE

*23 OCT c.3PM* DEMONSTRATION BEGINS

**CSEPEL**

and sixteen thousand marched to the centre of Poznan waving banners which proclaimed their economic concerns. The sight of such a protest was so electrifying that people poured on to the streets to support them, and by 10 am about a third of the city's population was demonstrating in front of the city hall. The demonstration turned into an attack on the city jail and the offices of the security police. Many died when the latter fired into the crowd. The trouble subsided only when special security units of the army appeared.

The party leadership and the press were outraged at first, but the reformist wing of the increasingly divided party realized that compromise might be wiser than confrontation and made their influence felt when the Poznan demonstrators were brought to trial in September. In a virtually unprecedented move, the state prosecutor refused to use evidence gained through torture; most of the defendants were released and their remarks reported.

The Kremlin was now thoroughly alarmed, and as 19 October approached - the day on which the party plenum was expected to elect Gomulka as First Secretary - Soviet tanks and troops moved towards Poland. The border guards and the special security units of the army loyal to the reformists were put on the alert and refused to stand down when, on the day of the plenum, most of the Soviet Praesidium flew to Warsaw. For a time it looked as if there might be a bloody confrontation between Soviet and Polish units. But Khrushchev backed down, having suffered the humiliation of a fruitless negotiation with Gomulka, whose return to the party leadership he had tried to prevent.

The new leader was given support from unexpected quarters. From outside the country, both the Chinese and the Yugoslav Communists gave him their fraternal blessings. The Catholic hierarchy also gave him their support and even Radio Free Europe saw him as a liberating influence. They were soon to be disappointed for Warsaw's growing sense of vulnerability in face of West Germany's rapid military and economic advance, combined with Gomulka's own growing doubts about the wisdom of freeing his volatile people from past restrictions, led to a 'retreat from October'. By the end of the 1950s many of the rights which the liberals thought had been won had been slowly eroded and Poland returned to a more orthodox Communist position.

### The Hungarian Prelude

The excitement in Warsaw and Poznan had its effect across the border in Hungary, and inflamed an already volatile situation. Mátyás Rákosi had been in power since 1947 and his enthusiasm for the subtleties of eliminating those who stood in his way was exceeded only by Stalin himself. Indeed, those who succeeded Stalin were so

A Russian soldier lies dead on a street in Budapest after the Soviet invasion of the city. The Red Army achieved their goal of suppressing the Hungarian Revolution of 1956.

embarrassed by the Hungarian leader that they summoned him to Moscow in June 1953 and told him in no uncertain terms that his behaviour had jeopardized the success of Communism in his country. The breakneck speed of industrialization had to slow down, the terror had to end and Rákosi had to step down as Prime Minister, although he could remain as First Secretary. His replacement was to be Imre Nagy, who had achieved popularity with the Hungarian people just after the war when, as Minister of Agriculture, he had distributed the large estates among seven hundred thousand peasants.

Within a week, in his first speech as Prime Minister, Nagy made an uncompromising attack on the Stalinists in Hungary, accusing them of bringing the country to the point of collapse. 'The targets of the stepped-up plan exceed our abilities in many respects,' he complained. 'Their implementation would exhaust our resources of energy and hinder the growth of the material basis of prosperity.' After years of nodding acquiescence in all levels of Hungarian society, such a denunciation of official policy rocked the socialist state to its foundations. Rákosi could do little but bide his time.

At a meeting of the Central Committee on 1-3 October 1954, the party came close to accepting Nagy's reformist measures; on 20 October he published an article which opened up the debate to a wider public and exposed the rift within the party. Early in the New Year, however, Rákosi's patience paid off when Nagy had a minor heart attack and was ordered to rest by his doctor. The demotion of Malenkov in Moscow on

8 February removed Nagy's strongest supporter and opened the way for a resurgence of Stalinism in Budapest.

At the Central Committee meeting on 2-4 March 1955, Imre Nagy was denounced as a nationalist and as someone hostile to the dictatorship of the proletariat. The following month he was ousted from the premiership and later expelled from the party. But the Pandora's Box had been opened, and Hungary's intellectuals vowed that it would not be closed again and subjected Rákosi to a barrage of criticism throughout 1955.

In the wake of the CPSU's historic Twentieth Party Congress, with its uncompromising anti-Stalinist message, Rákosi's authority waned. By the summer, the Kremlin had realized that it must act to avoid greater problems later, and Rákosi was ordered to step down on 18 July. His replacement, Ernö Gerö, lacked any qualities of leadership, however, and Hungary seemed to be sinking into chaos. It was at this stage that the spark of Poznan illuminated the growing chorus of dissent.

## A People's Revolution

By autumn 1956, the pressure for a public reburial of László Rajk had become irresistible and the ceremony was attended by well over a hundred thousand mourners. On 14 October, Nagy was reinstated as a party member. The following week, a number of student meetings called for a demonstration on the 23rd in support of their 'Polish brothers' and the government agreed. The Politburo then lost its nerve and withdrew its permission, but it was too late - a massive crowd surged on to the streets.

As the day passed, their numbers swelled. As they moved towards Parliament Square, the crowd heard reports of a radio address by Gerö in which he accused them of being nationalists whose only aim was chaos. Most of the people then set off for the radio station where, despite their anger, they sent a small delegation into the building to argue their case. When their representatives failed to return, the crowd became restive and began to push forward. The five hundred political police defending the building tried using tear gas to clear the crowd, but the wind was blowing in the wrong direction. One nervous policeman then fired his machine gun, and a few demonstrators fell to the ground. The crowd's mood was transformed into fury, and stones and petrol bombs were soon flying. The revolution had started.

From the very first hours, the insurgents had access to hand weapons since many policemen and soldiers sided with them and opened the armouries. By the evening the fighting had spread throughout Budapest and barricades had been thrown up. Early the next morning, the government called on Nagy to return as Prime Minister and institute a reform programme - but the measures were too little and too late. Soviet tanks were brought on to the streets and were content, at first, merely to threaten action; some crews

Three years after the Soviets' death blow to the twelve-day-old Hungarian revolution, Kadar (second from right) welcomes Khrushchev to Budapest for the Hungarian Communist Party Congress of 1959.

even fraternized with the citizens. But in the confused situation the Russians were fired upon, and in response they turned their weapons on the insurgents.

On the afternoon of 24 October, a Soviet tank pulled up outside the offices of the Central Committee and out jumped two members of the Praesidium, Mikoyan and Suslov. They had come to insist that Gerö was fired and replaced by János Kádár, a reform-minded, though pro-Soviet Communist. By the time that Kádár had been installed as First Secretary, early the following afternoon, the struggle had spread throughout the country and people were forming revolutionary soviets to run their towns and villages. Provincial radio stations were commandeered, and it was soon evident that the people were winning control of their country. Soon the party newspapers and the national radio stations ended their condemnation of the insurgents and began speaking for the revolution.

Kádár's first move was to broadcast to the nation, urging calm. He was followed by Nagy, who promised to form a new coalition government and to negotiate the removal of the Soviet troops. These commitments were honoured, and Mikoyan and Suslov were able to return to Moscow having completed an agreement with the new leaders. Moscow Radio broadcast very complimentary reports on the revolution. But the fighting still continued and, amid the confusion of the street-fighting, it became evident that well-armed right-wing groups had infiltrated the city to settle old scores. A group of young policemen defending the headquarters of the Greater Budapest Communist Federation were shot. A self-appointed national revolutionary council, based at Györ in the

north-west of the country, then announced that it would refuse to recognize the Budapest government unless Soviet troops left the country immediately.

Opinion in Moscow began to turn against the revolution. On 1 November, Nagy proclaimed that Hungary would henceforth be a multi-party and neutral state which would withdraw from the Warsaw Pact. Soviet troops had, meanwhile, withdrawn from Budapest. On Sunday, 4 November at 5 am they returned and at 5.30 Nagy addressed the nation on the radio: 'Today at daybreak Soviet forces started an attack against our capital, obviously with the intention of overthrowing the legal Hungarian democratic government. Our troops are fighting. The government is in its place.' By the evening most of the city was in the hands of the Red Army, but it was a hollow victory. Despite threats and intimidation, guns could not make the people work, even if they were forced to return to their factories. For a time the workers' soviets kept essential services going. Nagy and other ministers decided to take sanctuary in the Yugoslav Embassy. Kádár, who was now little more than a Soviet puppet, gave the group a guarantee of safe conduct - but they were arrested by the Red Army just a few hundred yards down the road. Nagy and three colleagues were hanged in secret eighteen months later. On 11 December the entire Central Workers' Council of Greater Budapest was arrested.

Thousands were arrested and many died. But conditions never quite reverted to the oppression experienced under Rákosi. Indeed, the speed with which Hungary achieved its independence of Moscow in 1989 was a legacy of 1956.

# The Cuban Missile Crisis

The confrontation that brought the world to the brink of nuclear war began on the morning of 16 October 1962, when the United States confirmed that the Soviet Union had stationed on the island of Cuba missiles that were capable of striking into the American heartland. The crisis lasted thirteen days, and ended on 28 October when the Soviet Prime Minister, Nikita Khrushchev, agreed to back down. The missiles were removed.

In a sense, the crisis had been growing ever since January 1959, when Fidel Castro and a small band of guerrillas seized power in Havana after a two-year insurrection against the notorious dictatorship of Fulgencio Batista. The victory of the charismatic young lawyer-revolutionary was immensely popular with most Cubans, who cheered lustily when he told them in his first speech: 'What greater glory than the love of the people? What greater prize than those thousands of waving arms, so full of hope, faith and affection towards us?'

The orientation of the new government was uncertain, and its subsequent development along classical Marxist-Leninist lines was due as much to prevailing Cold War attitudes as to the radical nationalism of its inexperienced leader, as he admitted in 1961:

Sometimes, in the mountains, between fighting, I'd think of what would happen when we won, how we would have a new party and fight for the people's needs....we could only think of politics in the old way, without realizing it was not such a good way....I'm a middle-class man with middle-class ideas, many ideas learned in school and never matched against life.

Cuba was a Caribbean slum subject to the whims of American big business (and crime syndicates), and Castro had long since made clear his hopes of improving the lot of its 10 million people. At his trial after an abortive attack on an army barracks in 1953, he listed six 'problems' that needed solving: land, industralization, housing, unemployment, education and health. Later, while campaigning in the mountains of the Sierra Maestra, he set as his priorities an end to mass illiteracy, agrarian reform and an economic policy geared to domestic needs.

The United States was accustomed to treating Cuba as a virtual colony, and throughout the twentieth century had intervened when necessary to prop up pro-American dictatorships. Thus it supported Batista until the revolutionaries swept down from the mountains in triumph, and Castro demonstrated his strength by calling a general strike that paralysed the country. Relations with the revolutionary government were poor from the start. When Castro visited the United States after his first two months in power he was seen briefly by Vice President Richard Nixon, who decided there and then that he was a Communist.

Cuba depended upon its sugar exports to the United States, so the Eisenhower administration threatened to cut back imports as a warning against moves to nationalize American interests. The Soviet Union was at first wary of interfering in America's back yard, but in February 1960 it agreed to take Cuban sugar in exchange for the farm and industrial machinery that Cuba needed, but had been unable to purchase on credit from US firms. In June, Cuba's US-owned oil companies refused to refine Soviet crude oil shipments, and then the US acted on its threat to cut the sugar quota. Cuba became an issue in the American presidential elections, with Republicans and Democrats vying in their expressions of concern. In October President Eisenhower instituted an embargo on all trade with Cuba, and the Soviets stepped up aid, including military assistance. All US property on the island was nationalized.

### The Bay of Pigs

In November 1960, when John F. Kennedy succeeded as US President, Castro welcomed his victory - but nothing came of the gesture. Ever since the Nixon meeting the CIA had been under orders to plot Castro's removal, and assassination attempts had been made. Cuba told the United Nations that an invasion was imminent, but this was strongly denied by US ambassador Adlai Stevenson, who had been purposely kept in the dark.

On 15 April 1961 two B-26 aircraft, painted in Cuban colours by the CIA, tried to knock out Cuba's small air force with bombing attacks. 'What they can't stand is that we have made a socialist revolution in the very nostrils of the US,' Castro declared next day,

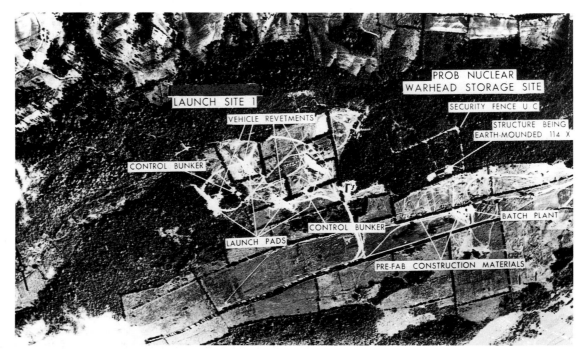

Photographic evidence of an intermediate ballistic missile site under construction in Cuba, 1962, taken by United States Air Reconnaissance. The missile crisis became the world's first brush with the possibility of a nuclear war.

# The Cuban Missile Crisis

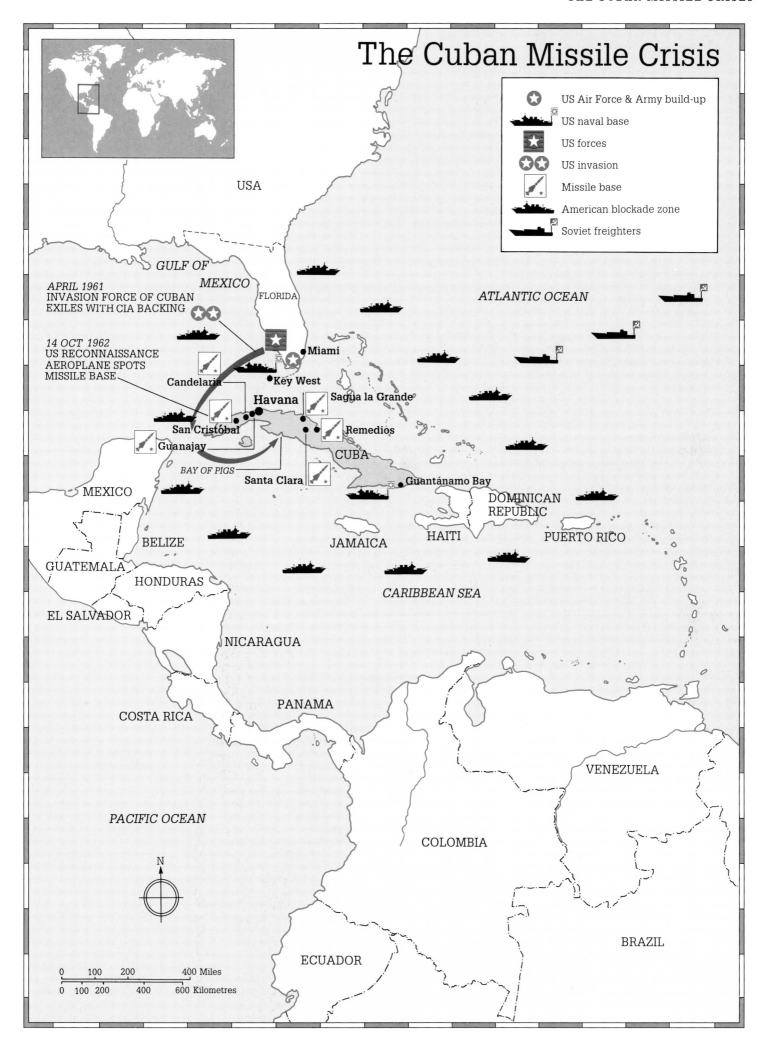

**Legend:**
- US Air Force & Army build-up
- US naval base
- US forces
- US invasion
- Missile base
- American blockade zone
- Soviet freighters

USA

GULF OF MEXICO

FLORIDA

ATLANTIC OCEAN

APRIL 1961
INVASION FORCE OF CUBAN
EXILES WITH CIA BACKING

14 OCT 1962
US RECONNAISSANCE
AEROPLANE SPOTS
MISSILE BASE

Miami

Candelaria

Key West

Havana

Sagua la Grande

San Cristóbal

Remedios

Guanajay

CUBA

BAY OF PIGS

Santa Clara

Guantánamo Bay

MEXICO

DOMINICAN
REPUBLIC

BELIZE

JAMAICA

HAITI

PUERTO RICO

GUATEMALA

HONDURAS

CARIBBEAN SEA

EL SALVADOR

NICARAGUA

PANAMA

COSTA RICA

VENEZUELA

PACIFIC OCEAN

COLOMBIA

N

BRAZIL

ECUADOR

0    100    200        400 Miles

0  100 200     400     600 Kilometres

at the funeral for those killed. It was his first public reference to the revolution as 'socialist', rather than nationalist or 'humanitarian'. Two days later about fourteen hundred anti-Castro exiles, equipped and trained by the CIA at bases in Nicaragua and the Dominican Republic, landed in the Bahia de Cochinos - the Bay of Pigs - in Las Villas province. The CIA had predicted that their appearance would spark a popular uprising, but it had underestimated the extent of Castro's support. The invaders never advanced beyond the beach, and almost all were captured within forty-eight hours, eventually to be released in exchange for American baby foods and medicines.

For Castro, the message was simple: the US was not going to accept his regime, and Moscow was his only lifeline. In December 1961 he proclaimed himself a Marxist-Leninist, thereby increasing the moral obligation of the Soviets to render assistance. There was probably another reason. Absolute power in the hands of a single individual, without formal government institutions to take the blame for any failures, was less attractive than a Communist system, which enabled him to enlist Soviet support to defend the revolution while maintaining his own dominant position.

## The World on the Brink

Placing nuclear missiles in Cuba - just ninety miles off the Florida coast - was Khrushchev's brainchild, and Castro had to be persuaded that it would be the best deterrent against further US attack. Right after the Bay of Pigs fiasco, Khrushchev had vowed to give Cuba 'all necessary assistance in beating back armed attack', but it was seemingly not until April 1962 that he first offered to provide missiles. From July, Soviet troopships and arms freighters clogged Cuban ports, and it was estimated that as many as forty thousand Soviet troops arrived. In August, a high-flying American U-2 spy plane spotted SAM anti-aircraft missile sites. Early in September, when Kennedy warned that 'the gravest issues would arise should offensive missiles be discovered in Cuba', the Soviets insisted that they were arming Cuba 'exclusively for defensive purposes'.

The crisis began on 16 October, when Kennedy was awakened with the news that a U-2 had obtained hard photographic evidence of the existence of sites for medium-range ballistic missiles at San Cristobal, in the north-west of Cuba. Such missiles would be capable of hitting targets across much of the US. It was assumed, though not confirmed, that the missiles were being armed with nuclear warheads.

The President assembled a special committee of fifteen close advisers in the White House. It was agreed that the Soviets had broken an unwritten rule of the Cold War - that neither side should attempt to establish military bases within the other's sphere of influence. A majority, the President among them, at first favoured an air strike on

# The Cult of 'Che' Guevara

Ernesto Guevara de la Serna's great political achievement was to die at the right moment. In life he was a respected leader of Fidel Castro's guerrilla band, but was little known outside Cuba.

Born in Argentina and trained as a doctor, his travels through South America turned him into a Marxist. In 1954 he witnessed the overthrow by the CIA of a popular, progressive regime in Guatemala and acquired his nickname. In Mexico he joined the group led by the Castro brothers, which was training for a guerrilla campaign in Cuba.

After their victory he spent six years as a prominent member of the Havana government and published a number of books. In 1965 he disappeared and the CIA became very apprehensive. In the autumn of 1966 he travelled secretly to Bolivia, where he trained and led a group of guerrillas. The CIA were soon on his trail and they spared no expense in tracking him down. A special group of the Bolivian army was trained and equipped and on 8 October 1967 they surrounded and massacred the guerrillas. 'Che' Guevara was captured after being wounded but was executed immediately. To prove he was dead to the outside world, his corpse was photographed. It was this image that inspired many followers around the world.

---

the missile sites, and invasion plans were also drawn up. US forces in the Caribbean were strengthened, and civilians prepared for evacuation from Guantanamo Bay, a US base on Cuba itself, which Castro had not hitherto dared to remove. Cuban intelligence picked up enough clues to expect the worst. The island was placed on alert, and Castro's closest comrade, Che Guevara, took command of forces on the west of Havana, near most of the missile sites.

On 22 October, Kennedy broke his silence with a broadcast that was carried by every American TV and radio station. He revealed the existence of the missile sites, and declared a naval blockade of Cuba. While the world held its breath, a girdle of aircraft carriers and other warships was slung around the island, and all approaching ships were subject to inspection.

Emotions around the world ran high, and reactions were mixed. In London, more than a hundred people were arrested

outside the US Embassy, and the famous philosopher and anti-nuclear campaigner Bertrand Russell denounced the blockade as an act of war. 'Within a month, you will all be dead to please American madmen,' he protested, and he cabled both Kennedy and Khrushchev, urging them to meet. Khrushchev's first response was unbending and belligerent: Soviet ships would defy the blockade and proceed to Cuba. But he surprised his advisers, and deftly mixed his signals, by taking them to the Bolshoi Theatre that night to see an opera - performed by an American company.

The first days of the blockade passed with no confrontation. Then, on 25 October, American warships closed on the *Marucla*, a merchant ship carrying a mixed cargo, with a dozen trucks lashed on deck. The *Marucla* was boarded by an unarmed party from the U.S.S *Joseph P. Kennedy*, a destroyer named after a brother of the President who had been killed in the Second

Second only to Fidel Castro in the Cuban revolution of 1959, the Argentinian-born revolutionary Ernesto 'Che' Guevara became Minister of Industry in Cuba in 1963.

Fidel Castro speaks to the United Nations in 1960 and is warmly applauded by Khrushchev and the leaders of Communist satellite countries. The Cold War in general and the Cuban missile crisis in particular served only to increase Cuba's dependency on Russian economic and technical support.

fortnight earlier had obtained the first evidence of the existence of missiles. It was also said that Castro pressed the firing button on the SAM battery that shot him down.

With the pressure mounting on Kennedy to order a counter-attack, his brother, Attorney-General Robert Kennedy, met the Soviet ambassador to Washington and made an offer in the form of an ultimatum. It was a promise not to invade Cuba, tied to confirmation that the missiles would be removed and the launch sites dismantled. The Americans also wanted a UN inspection team to confirm that the missiles had been removed. If the Soviets refused, war was inevitable, the President's brother made clear. While Washington slept, the Soviet leaders met in the Kremlin. At 10 am on 28 October, Khrushchev's reply arrived. He accepted the terms. The missiles would go. The news was celebrated around the world, and in Cuba people rejoiced in the streets.

## Aftermath

Castro had never been consulted. He sulked, and refused to receive the Soviet ambassador in Havana. So the deputy Prime Minister, Anastas Mikoyan, was despatched from Moscow at the head of a high-level delegation. Mikoyan managed to mend the rift at the price of a very generous trade agreement, by which the Soviets agreed to pay more for Cuban sugar and provide more aid. Castro said no to UN inspectors: it was the one gesture of defiance left to him.

For Castro the crisis confirmed his precarious position, demonstrably outside the Soviet's nuclear umbrella, with an implacable superpower adversary intent on undermining his position by every means short of war. There was no option but to tighten ties with Moscow. In 1971 Cuba became the only state in the Western hemisphere to join Comecon, the Eastern bloc attempt at a Common Market.

The missile crisis forced the Soviet Union to adjust its foreign policy. The Foreign Minister, Andrei Gromyko, stressed how the destinies of people everywhere were dependent upon Soviet-US relations, and how necessary to world peace co-existence between socialism and capitalism had become. Communist factions hostile to Moscow gleefully pounced upon this. To Albania, as to China, the Kennedy-Khrushchev agreement was an act of cowardice and the concept of peaceful co-existence a sell-out to imperialism.

Early in 1963 Kennedy removed American missiles from Turkey and Italy, and also some from Britain. A nuclear test ban treaty was signed between the superpowers, and a 'hot line' was installed between the White House and the Kremlin.

To Kennedy the outcome seemed a major victory, enhancing his own and America's image around the world. Yet some regarded the outcome as an American defeat, since Castro remained entrenched with the US pledged not to invade.

World War. The cargo was inspected without incident and the vessel allowed on its way. Soon it became apparent that the blockade was being respected, and that captains bound for Cuba were allowing their cargoes to be inspected.

### The Breaking Point

The crisis persisted. Work on the missile sites was nearly complete, with Soviet troops dug in around them, and IL-28 bombers were being assembled from components that had already arrived in Cuba. These planes were capable of carrying out a nuclear strike.

The negotiations became stealthy. The Americans slipped Castro a message, in which it was suggested that he was being used as a Soviet pawn. Time was running out, the message warned, but it ended with a promise that the US would not invade Cuba if the missiles were withdrawn. In Washington, a senior KGB official approached an American journalist, John Scally, and made a similar offer: if America agreed not to invade Cuba, the missiles would be removed and the Soviets would undertake never to reinstate such weapons.

On 26 October, Khrushchev sent a long, rambling cable message to Kennedy, in which he maintained that the situation would immediately change if Kennedy gave an assurance that there would be no attack on

Cuba, and removed the blockade. Next day, he added a further demand: the removal of American missiles from Turkey. Then tensions were brought to breaking point when a U-2 flying reconnaissance over Cuba was brought down and its pilot, Major Rudolf Anderson, killed. It was Anderson who a

South American cartoonist, Aldor, depicts Khrushchev and Mao using the Trojan Horse (Castro) to gain entry to Kennedy's fortress.

A Russian tank in the streets of Prague, 1968.
The attempt to transform Czechoslovak society
within the bounds of socialism came to an
abrupt end with the invasion of the Red Army.

# The Monolith Cracks

In the autumn of 1964, the Soviet Praesidium met while Nikita Khrushchev was on holiday by the Black Sea; it summoned him back to Moscow and sacked him. He was replaced by the triumvirate of Leonid Brezhnev, Alexei Kosygin and Nikolai Podgorny, who believed that a period of consolidation was required after the erratic policies that Khrushchev had pursued had caused his comrades so many problems. The recent dangerous confrontations with the United States had brought the Soviet Union no credit and no strategic advantages. The Partial Nuclear Test Ban Treaty, which had been signed in 1963 by Britain, the US and the Soviet Union, was seen as a pointer to the way ahead; its terms outlawed the testing of any weapons in the atmosphere, outer space and under water, and in addition it limited the size of underground test explosions.

The following years were marked by the gradual extension of treaties with the West. In 1968, after China and France had exploded hydrogen bombs, Washington and Moscow tried to contain further expansion of the 'nuclear club' by signing the Non-Proliferation Treaty. In 1970 West Germany and the Soviet Union signed the Moscow Treaty, which recognized the post-war European borders. And in 1971 West Germany joined Poland in signing the Warsaw Treaty, which recognized the integrity of the modern Polish state. That same year, the Quadripartite Treaty recognized the special status of Berlin and guaranteed access from the West. This arrangement appeared to provide a permanent solution to 'the German problem', and both states, East and West, were admitted to the United Nations.

## Communist Versus Communist

Much of the momentum behind the Kremlin's desire to humour the West came from their anxieties about Beijing. Mao Zedong had been quite happy to travel to Moscow in 1957 to attend the fortieth anniversary celebrations of the Revolution and to acknowledge the Kremlin's leadership. But, by May 1964, the Chinese were refusing to participate in a congress of the world's Communist parties and had published the text of a vitriolic attack that had been made on them by the Soviets. Many commentators had blamed Khrushchev for what looked like a personal feud between him and Mao, but the differences between the world's two greatest Communist powers went much deeper than this.

Presidents Nixon and Brezhnev shake hands after signing SALT 1 in Moscow, 1972. The two superpowers had begun talks on strategic arms limitations in 1969.

Beijing increasingly saw Moscow as 'revisionist', while the Kremlin accused the Chinese of being too dogmatic. The changing relationship between the USA and the Soviet Union only seemed to confirm Beijing's analysis. But beneath these insults lurked nationalist ambitions that Communism was supposed to supersede. As the 1960s progressed, the disagreements between the two powers increasingly dwelt on disputes which had arisen during the nineteenth century. These rivalries also had their effect on the rest of the Communist world, as pro-Moscow and pro-Beijing factions disputed control of the various national parties.

After the troubled times of the Khrushchev era, eastern Europe gave the Kremlin few problems in the mid-1960s. To the south-east, Romania began to develop an independent line in foreign policy, first under Gheorghiu-Dej and then under Nicolae Ceausescu. This apparent assertion of national autonomy was applauded in the West as further evidence of the break-up of the 'Soviet empire', but few commentators on the situation looked too closely into Romanian domestic policy, which was modelled on Stalin's use of terror. Such orthodoxy gave the Politburo under Brezhnev little cause to worry.

Meanwhile, the Soviet Union was applying the other lesson it had learned from the Cuban missile crisis: that large armies are not enough to guarantee success in superpower confrontations. Vast sums of money were ploughed into developing intercontinental ballistic missiles and, later, multiple warheads. The Soviet navy underwent a massive expansion so that it would have the capacity to counter any

future marine blockade which the United States might try to impose. Spy satellites were developed which could orbit above the US and Europe to provide detailed information about troop movements and weapon deployment.

## The Prague Spring

As the decade approached its end, trouble in Czechoslovakia provoked the last old-style Soviet military intervention in eastern Europe. During the 1950s, the Prague government had been able to placate its people with economic growth and a rise in the standard of living. This was achieved because its factories were able to make goods which were scarce through the rest of eastern Europe at prices those markets could afford. However, as a result of the gradual industrial rejuvenation of the other eastern European countries, their factories could produce the goods for themselves, and the Czechs fell on hard times.

Economic problems combined with a sudden re-emergence of national feelings soon provoked political dissent. In January 1968 the party leader, Antonin Novotny, was forced to resign as First Secretary; in March he gave up the presidency and his place was taken by Alexander Dubcek. But the radical approach that the new leader took to solving his country's malaise - attacking the party's central control of the economy, ending censorship and allowing opposition groups to be formed - alarmed the Kremlin. Other members of the Warsaw Pact joined in the chorus of disapproval, fearful that the virus of reform would spread and infect their own fragile regimes.

When the troops of five eastern European nations invaded Czechoslovakia on the night of 20-21 August 1968, Dubcek urged his countrymen not to resist. He then co-operated with conservative elements within his own party, as well as the Kremlin, to weed out dissidents in order to avert more Soviet repression. But mass demonstrations continued through the winter following the invasion; when the Soviets demanded that stronger measures be implemented, Dubcek felt unable to comply and handed over power to Gustav Husak.

Like 1848, 1968 saw a brushfire of discontent rage across Europe. Roadblocks and riots filled the streets of Paris and Berlin, while students occupied university and college buildings throughout western Europe. The crowds were usually formed by young students whose common cause was fuelled by their anger over the American role in Vietnam. However, although they knew what they disliked, there was little structure or co-ordination between the different groups, and the protests disintegrated into disaffection. The most extreme students, particularly those in Germany, then turned to urban terrorism - but they were never able to attract widespread support.

In 1969, the confrontation between the Soviet Union and China - which had been developing over the past few years with acts of provocation along their common border and accustions from both sides - erupted into open conflict over the border territory along the Ussuri River. However, neither wanted the skirmishes to escalate into a full-scale war and within months they began the process of negotiating an end to the dispute by diplomatic means.

Nationalistic overtones also affected the Vietnam War. Since it shared a border with North Vietnam, China was clearly in the best position to sustain its Communist neighbour. Nevertheless, it was mainly Soviet aid which helped to keep Hanoi supplied. Chinese and Vietnamese rivalry went back many centuries and Communism did not seem able to heal the rift, even though the Vietnamese guerrilla tactics that were employed against the Americans were much closer to Mao's model for revolutionary struggle than to Lenin's - based as they were on a rural campaign rather than on the creation of an urban proletariat.

American involvement began in the late 1940s when the US started to finance French attempts to regain control in their colony of Indochina, which during the Second World War had been occupied by the Japanese. However, after the French defeat at Dien Bien Phu in 1954, America was slowly but steadily sucked into the war. President Johnson's commitment of American units to the fighting in the 1960s upped the stakes further, and Moscow's aid to the North increased. No matter how hard they tried, the Americans and their South Vietnamese allies were unable to gain the upper hand, and eventually Washington had to admit defeat. Yet, despite the intensity of the fighting, detente was always treated as a separate issue during this period and there was never any question that a direct Soviet-American confrontation would develop.

## The Moscow Honeymoon

Despite the substantial rearmament programme which was adopted by the US and the Soviet Union during the 1960s, and the confrontation between East and West in Vietnam, tension had eased sufficiently by the end of 1971 for a broad agreement to be reached between the two superpowers. When President Nixon announced on 12 October that he would be visiting Moscow - after years of denouncing the hyperbole surrounding summit meetings - commentators assumed that important negotiations were under way. On 10 April, after some major commercial contracts had been concluded, Britain, the US and the Soviet Union signed a treaty banning biological weapons. But the climax to the process came in late May 1972 during the first visit by an American president to Moscow: Nixon and Brezhnev signed the Strategic Arms Limitation Treaty, or SALT 1.

The Americans were the target of friendly gestures from both Communist superpowers in 1972. With substantial numbers of troops committed to their common border, China and the Soviet Union wished to keep the White House happy. As a result President Nixon visited Beijing, as well as Moscow, during that year in a display of friendship which completely contradicted the 'reds-under-the-bed' rhetoric upon which he had built his career twenty years before.

In the long term, China was the one to gain the most from these friendly overtures, because they ended America's implacable opposition to its entry into the United Nations and several other international organizations, such as the Olympic movement. Ambassadors were finally exchanged in 1979 and Ronald Reagan's venomous and widely publicized anti-Communist rhetoric of the early 1980s largely ignored China's existence.

## Other Paths to Socialism

During the 1970s, the Communist parties of western Europe sought to channel the disaffection of their electorates with the consensus of the centre parties; they revised their programmes in a direction which took its cue from the Prague Spring. This caused considerable dismay in Moscow, and Brezhnev called for a congress which would re-establish solidarity of purpose; in reality, this meant a reacceptance of the Kremlin's domination of the movement. To Moscow's dismay, the meeting in East Berlin in 1976 actually cemented the bond between parties of the West and created a new grouping, of which the most powerful parties were those of France, Italy and Spain. Journalists soon named this phenomenon 'Eurocommunism', and by the end of the Berlin congress the Soviet delegation was forced to accept that each party had the right to a 'free choice of different roads' to socialism.

Despite the criticism which had been levelled at Khrushchev for wasting financial aid on the Third World, the Kremlin under Brezhnev was unable to refrain from similar entanglements, even though it did adopt a more cautious approach and tried to concentrate on governments that were avowedly Marxist. In 1969 it began supporting South Yemen. In 1974 a Marxist group toppled Emperor Haile Selassie in Ethiopia. The 1970s also saw the collapse of Portugal's colonial empire, and Marxist governments achieved power in its two most

A military parade in Addis Ababa, Ethiopia, in 1978 celebrates the fourth anniversary of the revolution. President Mengitsu's anti-Chinese declaration was welcomed by the Soviet delegate.

# The Monolith Cracks

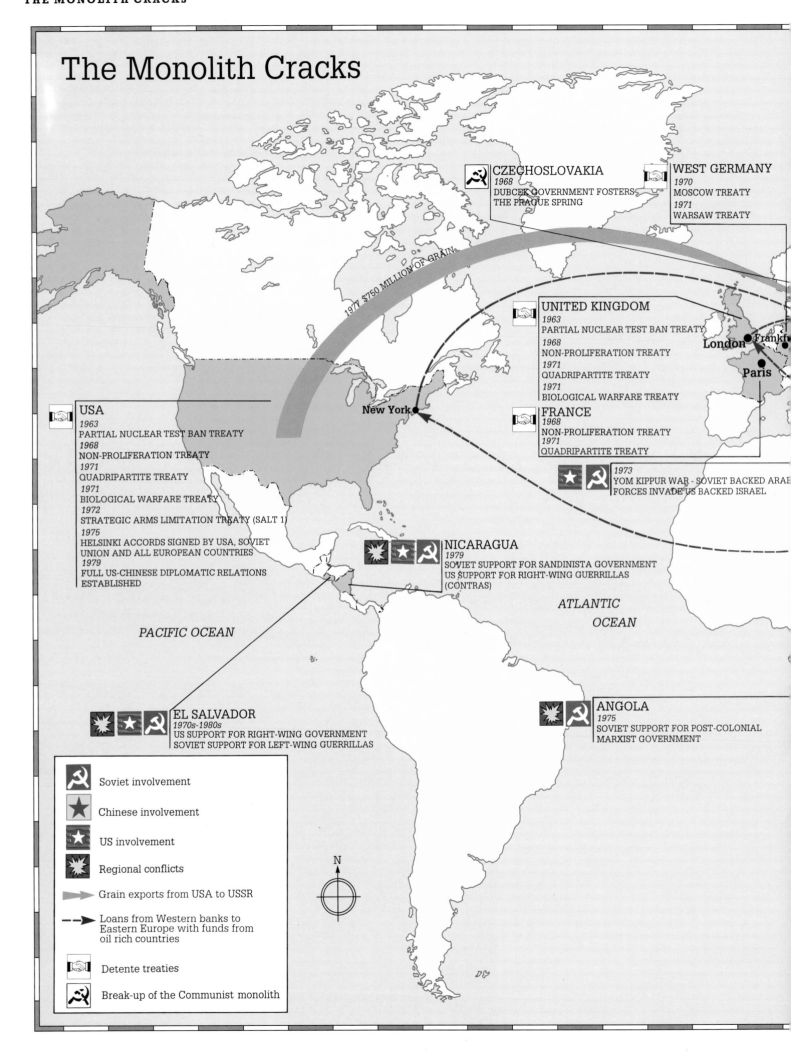

**CZECHOSLOVAKIA**
*1968*
DUBCEK GOVERNMENT FOSTERS
THE PRAGUE SPRING

**WEST GERMANY**
*1970*
MOSCOW TREATY
*1971*
WARSAW TREATY

**UNITED KINGDOM**
*1963*
PARTIAL NUCLEAR TEST BAN TREATY
*1968*
NON-PROLIFERATION TREATY
*1971*
QUADRIPARTITE TREATY
*1971*
BIOLOGICAL WARFARE TREATY

**FRANCE**
*1968*
NON-PROLIFERATION TREATY
*1971*
QUADRIPARTITE TREATY

**USA**
*1963*
PARTIAL NUCLEAR TEST BAN TREATY
*1968*
NON-PROLIFERATION TREATY
*1971*
QUADRIPARTITE TREATY
*1971*
BIOLOGICAL WARFARE TREATY
*1972*
STRATEGIC ARMS LIMITATION TREATY (SALT 1)
*1975*
HELSINKI ACCORDS SIGNED BY USA, SOVIET
UNION AND ALL EUROPEAN COUNTRIES
*1979*
FULL US-CHINESE DIPLOMATIC RELATIONS
ESTABLISHED

*1973*
YOM KIPPUR WAR - SOVIET BACKED ARAB
FORCES INVADE US BACKED ISRAEL

**NICARAGUA**
*1979*
SOVIET SUPPORT FOR SANDINISTA GOVERNMENT
US SUPPORT FOR RIGHT-WING GUERRILLAS
(CONTRAS)

**EL SALVADOR**
*1970s-1980s*
US SUPPORT FOR RIGHT-WING GOVERNMENT
SOVIET SUPPORT FOR LEFT-WING GUERRILLAS

**ANGOLA**
*1975*
SOVIET SUPPORT FOR POST-COLONIAL
MARXIST GOVERNMENT

*1977 $750 MILLION OF GRAIN*

London  Frankf
Paris

New York

*PACIFIC OCEAN*

*ATLANTIC*

*OCEAN*

N

**Legend:**
- Soviet involvement
- Chinese involvement
- US involvement
- Regional conflicts
- Grain exports from USA to USSR
- Loans from Western banks to Eastern Europe with funds from oil rich countries
- Detente treaties
- Break-up of the Communist monolith

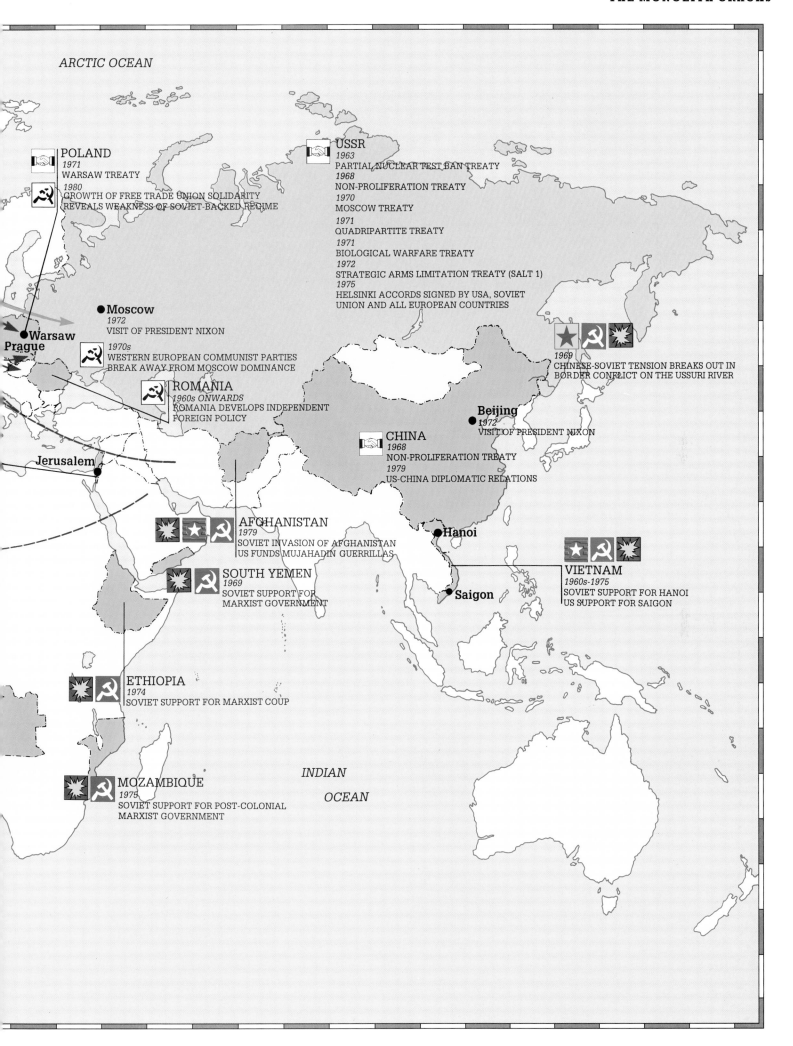

ARCTIC OCEAN

POLAND
*1971*
WARSAW TREATY
*1980*
GROWTH OF FREE TRADE UNION SOLIDARITY
REVEALS WEAKNESS OF SOVIET-BACKED REGIME

USSR
*1963*
PARTIAL NUCLEAR TEST BAN TREATY
*1968*
NON-PROLIFERATION TREATY
*1970*
MOSCOW TREATY
*1971*
QUADRIPARTITE TREATY
*1971*
BIOLOGICAL WARFARE TREATY
*1972*
STRATEGIC ARMS LIMITATION TREATY (SALT 1)
*1975*
HELSINKI ACCORDS SIGNED BY USA, SOVIET
UNION AND ALL EUROPEAN COUNTRIES

● Moscow
*1972*
VISIT OF PRESIDENT NIXON

● Warsaw
Prague

*1970s*
WESTERN EUROPEAN COMMUNIST PARTIES
BREAK AWAY FROM MOSCOW DOMINANCE

ROMANIA
*1960s ONWARDS*
ROMANIA DEVELOPS INDEPENDENT
FOREIGN POLICY

*1969*
CHINESE-SOVIET TENSION BREAKS OUT IN
BORDER CONFLICT ON THE USSURI RIVER

● Beijing
*1972*
VISIT OF PRESIDENT NIXON

CHINA
*1968*
NON-PROLIFERATION TREATY
*1979*
US-CHINA DIPLOMATIC RELATIONS

Jerusalem ●

AFGHANISTAN
*1979*
SOVIET INVASION OF AFGHANISTAN
US FUNDS MUJAHADIN GUERRILLAS

● Hanoi

VIETNAM
*1960s-1975*
SOVIET SUPPORT FOR HANOI
US SUPPORT FOR SAIGON

SOUTH YEMEN
SOVIET SUPPORT FOR
MARXIST GOVERNMENT

● Saigon

ETHIOPIA
*1974*
SOVIET SUPPORT FOR MARXIST COUP

INDIAN

OCEAN

MOZAMBIQUE
*1975*
SOVIET SUPPORT FOR POST-COLONIAL
MARXIST GOVERNMENT

# The Space Race

The Soviet Union's greatest victory over the United States occurred on 4 October 1957 when the world's first artificial satellite, Sputnik 1, was launched into space from the Baikonor Cosmodrome in Soviet Central Asia. A month later they put up a capsule, containing a dog, that weighed six times as much and went twice as far from the earth's surface. The world was astonished and the Pentagon was dumbfounded. American assumptions about the Kremlin's capabilities were turned on their head overnight.

Khrushchev treated his technological victory as a personal triumph and was even more jubilant when Yuri Gagarin made the first manned space flight on 12 April 1961, little more than three weeks before the Americans launched Alan Shepherd. The Soviet programme continued to upstage the Americans for some years and achieved another spectacular first in June 1963 when Valentina Tereshkova piloted Vostock 6 to become the first woman in space.

During the 1960s, the Americans invested vast sums in their own programme and gradually overhauled the

Cosmonaut Yuri Gagarin (1934-68), the first person to orbit the earth, in the cabin of the spacecraft Vostock 1. This first manned space flight was made in April 1961 and was regarded as a great technological victory for the Soviet Union.

Soviet team. And although the Americans finally got to the moon first in July 1969, the Soviets concentrated on long flights, working towards a space station. This gave them an unassailable lead in space medicine, a discipline which will be critical in the industrial exploitation of space. They also pioneered the exploration of deep space during the 1960s, making the first landing on another planet, Venus, using an unmanned vehicle in 1965.

After the US Apollo programme to land men on the moon ended in December 1972, the Americans seemed to lose interest in space. But the Soviet programme continued to send Soyuz craft into orbit, and their effort culminated in the Salyut Space Stations, which continued to orbit the earth throughout the 1970s and 1980s. One of their goals was the creation of new materials which are impossible to manufacture on earth. This new industrial phase began in 1990.

important former territories in Africa, Angola and Mozambique.

To counter Soviet influence, the United States spent large sums of money supporting South Africa's attempts to subvert both regimes. The same pattern of a Cold War by proxy was adopted in Nicaragua. The reverse situation, in which the White House propped up a weak regime which was being undermined by left-wing guerrillas, could be found across the border in El Salvador. Arrangements of this sort seemed safe to the American government after the long nightmare of Vietnam.

## SALT Goes Sour

Six weeks after the SALT treaty was signed in May 1972, Washington sold Moscow $750 million worth of grain at bargain prices. The deal raised hackles in the American Congress, however, and caused politicians to table amendments to the enabling act which had to be passed to allow the deal to proceed. The question of human rights in the Soviet Union was raised and Senator Henry Jackson commented: 'Fifty years ago, Lenin promised the Soviet people bread and freedom. If American farmers are to provide the bread, is it too much to ask that the Soviet leaders provide their own people a measure of freedom?' The grain was not used to make

bread, however. Instead it was turned into animal feedstuffs in order to satisfy the growing demand throughout the Soviet Union for meat.

Detente was further damaged by the Yom Kippur War of October 1973. The White House suspected that the Kremlin had prior knowledge of the Arab attack, which it had not passed on in the manner described in their newly signed agreements. Henry Kissinger and Andrei Gromyko, who were responsible for the foreign policies of their respective countries at the time, tried to maintain the momentum of the process of co-operation; but, once Nixon had resigned after Watergate, much of Washington's enthusiasm evaporated.

After the first meeting of the 35-nation Conference on Security and Co-operation in Europe (CSCE), the Helsinki accords were signed on 1 August 1975. The section on human rights eventually came to damage East-West relations more than it helped them, particularly under President Carter. The end of the 1970s witnessed little progress on detente and, although SALT 2 was signed, it was never ratified by the United States Congress.

Although the Soviet leaders were relatively conservative in their approach, and although the admissions of the East Berlin congress of 1976 were bound to cause problems,

they had no desire to return to Stalinist terror in their running of eastern Europe. Reforms and greater consultation were introduced into the workings of Comecon and the Warsaw Pact, which gave the countries of eastern Europe a greater say in the direction of policy. And in order to pay for new technology and training, as well as food, they were also encouraged to seek loans from Western financial institutions, particularly during the late 1970s when banks were awash with money from the newly rich oil-producing countries.

Poland took advantage of this freely available capital to invest thousands of millions of dollars in new factories and industrial plant which, it believed, could be paid for in the future when the new facilities would be producing goods to sell in the West. But the projects were poorly co-ordinated and the economic promise was never realized. In its desperation to repay the vast sums which it owed the West by the end of the 1970s, food, raw materials and fuel were sold abroad - and this caused acute shortages at home. Finally, in the summer of 1980, a doubling of the price of better quality meat provoked the strikes which led to the occupation of the Gdansk shipyards and the formation of Solidarity.

Despite the expectations of its members and of most outside observers, the union survived for fifteen months before the army crackdown led by General Jaruzelski, who imprisoned most of its leaders and proclaimed that the organization was dissolved. The Polish leadership had persuaded the Kremlin that the Red Army was not needed and that it could handle its own problems. The West reacted sharply to this suppression of trade union rights, even though Reagan and Thatcher were both leading anti-union crusades at the time in their own countries.

The final blow to East-West relations came with the invasion of Afghanistan by the Red Army in December 1979, when Moscow claimed that the Kabul government had invited their involvement in the war against the mujahidin guerrillas. The move was planned by the two generals who had master-minded the invasion of Czechoslovakia, but the similarity ended there. Where the jungles of Vietnam had defeated the Americans, the mountainous terrain of Afghanistan defeated the Soviet forces. As with the Americans, their equipment was not designed to cope with the landscape. And, although they did not suffer casualties on the same scale as the Americans, they eventually had to leave with the conflict unresolved.

Like the regimes which had preceded it, that of Brezhnev created as many problems in its closing years as it had solved when it began. With Soviet leaders ageing rapidly and a crusading Ronald Reagan waiting in the wings, the icy blast of a second Cold War chilled the international climate. Only when Mikhail Gorbachev appeared on the international stage did goodwill return.

# The Brezhnev Era

The collective leadership which succeeded in October 1964 aimed for political stability, particularly since their own careers had been at the mercy of Stalin and the caprice of Khrushchev. In this, the First Secretary of the party, Leonid Brezhnev, the Chairman of the Council of Ministers (Prime Minister), Alexei Kosygin, and the Chairman of the Praesidium of the Supreme Soviet (President), Nikolai Podgorny, were perhaps too successful, for the triumvirate which they established succumbed only to the natural processes of ageing. Significantly, no widespread purge of Khrushchev's former supporters followed their takeover, and little fresh blood was allowed to percolate to the party's upper echelons for some considerable time.

During 1965, Kosygin launched a drive towards major economic reforms. He attempted to link wages to productivity and prices to demand, and he tried to transfer the authority for decision-making to the factory level. But, despite support from Podgorny, he was unable to overcome the immovable deadweight of the party *apparatchiks* whose power was dependent on the survival of the top-heavy bureaucracy which ran the economy. This failure helped to shift the balance of power at the top towards Brezhnev, and his title was changed to General Secretary at the Twenty-third Party Congress, in March-April 1966: a move which emphasized that he was now the first among equals.

On the other hand, Brezhnev did not try to oust his fellow leaders, and Kosygin remained at his post until his death in December 1980. Podgorny remained the country's President for over a decade and retired in 1977. Only then did Brezhnev have himself pronounced President as well as head of the party. By that point, however, the change was largely irrelevant, for he had already suffered his first stroke and those who wanted to succeed him were already manoeuvring for position. Yet, despite Brezhnev's steady, almost lifeless hand on the tiller of the ship of state, his navigational skills were no greater than those of Khrushchev. He too failed to negotiate the problems of putting more food on the Soviet family table. And where Khrushchev's years were stained by the Hungarian invasion, Brezhnev's were similarly marked by the suppression of the Prague Spring and the ultimately disastrous invasion of Afghanistan.

On the other hand, the stability which the triumvirate brought to the Soviet Union did create a situation in which steady progress could be made in the supply of consumer

Leonid Brezhnev became the fourth leader of the Communist Party of the Soviet Union since the 1917 Revolution. He failed to solve the country's economic and agricultural problems, but he did give the Soviet Union military parity with the United States.

goods, even if the display of products in the shops still lagged behind demand. In 1965, only 24 per cent of Soviet households possessed a television and 11 per cent a refrigerator. By 1982, 91 per cent of homes had a television and 89 per cent a fridge. Washing machines were found in only 21 per cent of homes in 1965, while 70 per cent had them by 1982. However, such indications of quantity reveal little about quality, and no one in the Soviet Union was surprised when a report revealed that exploding colour televisions were the commonest cause of domestic fires.

It was harder to satisfy the desire of every Soviet citizen to own a car and, given the low cost of Soviet public transport, this was not considered a high priority. Nevertheless, private car production trebled in the 1970s and, by the end of the Brezhnev era, was running at over a million a year. Waiting lists for the vehicles were still measured in years, however, even though the cost of each car was the equivalent of almost four years' wages for the average skilled worker.

Housing was another area in which substantial progress was made during the Brezhnev era. Until the late 1950s, the state was happy to set a goal of 'a roof over the head for every inhabitant', which meant one room per family and a shared kitchen and bathroom. Now new housing laws were

enacted, which doubled housing construction and set a target of providing a self-contained flat for each family. The size of each apartment also gradually increased, and by the early 1980s each Soviet citizen had an average of 30 per cent more space to himself or herself than in the mid-1960s. However, such standards still compared poorly with countries such as West Germany, where the average citizen has over twice as much space as his Soviet counterpart.

### The Consequences of Education

One reason why the Soviet leadership failed to deliver consumer goods to its citizens with greater speed was the size of its defence budget. Khrushchev had cut spending on armaments; but after the Soviet humiliation during the Cuban missile crisis Moscow decided that the country needed to be able to confront the American armed forces on an equal footing, if it was going to maintain its high profile on the international scene.

By the 1970s, the Soviet Union was spending a much higher proportion of its GNP on armed forces than the United States, and many of the country's most skilled craftsmen and best-educated technicians were employed in the arms industry, with its considerable export potential. The availability of such a skilled pool of

# The Brezhnev Years

N

**1974**
*SOLZHENITSYN EXPELLED FROM SOVIET UNION TO WEST GERMANY*

**Helsinki** ●

● **Leningrad**

**1972**
*BLOODY SUPPRESSION OF DEMONSTRATIONS FOR A FREE CATHOLIC CHURCH*

● Riga

LITHUANIA

Kaunas ●
● Vilnius

**Moscow**

● Gorky

● Omsk

● Lvov

● Kiev

UKRAINE

DNIEPER

DON

**1980**
*ANDREI SAKHAROV SENT TO INTERNAL EXILE*

USSR

ARAL SEA

*WESTERN TOURISM BRINGS HARD CURRENCY AND DISSIDENT CONTACTS WITH WEST*

*BLACK SEA*

GEORGIA

CASPIAN SEA

**1968**
*INVASION OF CZECHOSLOVAKIA*

TURKEY

ARMENIA

● Tashkent

*MEDITERRANEAN SEA*

IRAQ

IRAN

AFGHANISTAN

**1979**
*INVASION OF AFGHANISTAN*

SAUDI ARABIA

INDIA

*ARABIAN SEA*

| 0 | 200 | 400 | 600 | Miles |
| 0 | 200 | 400 | 600 | 800 | Kilometres |

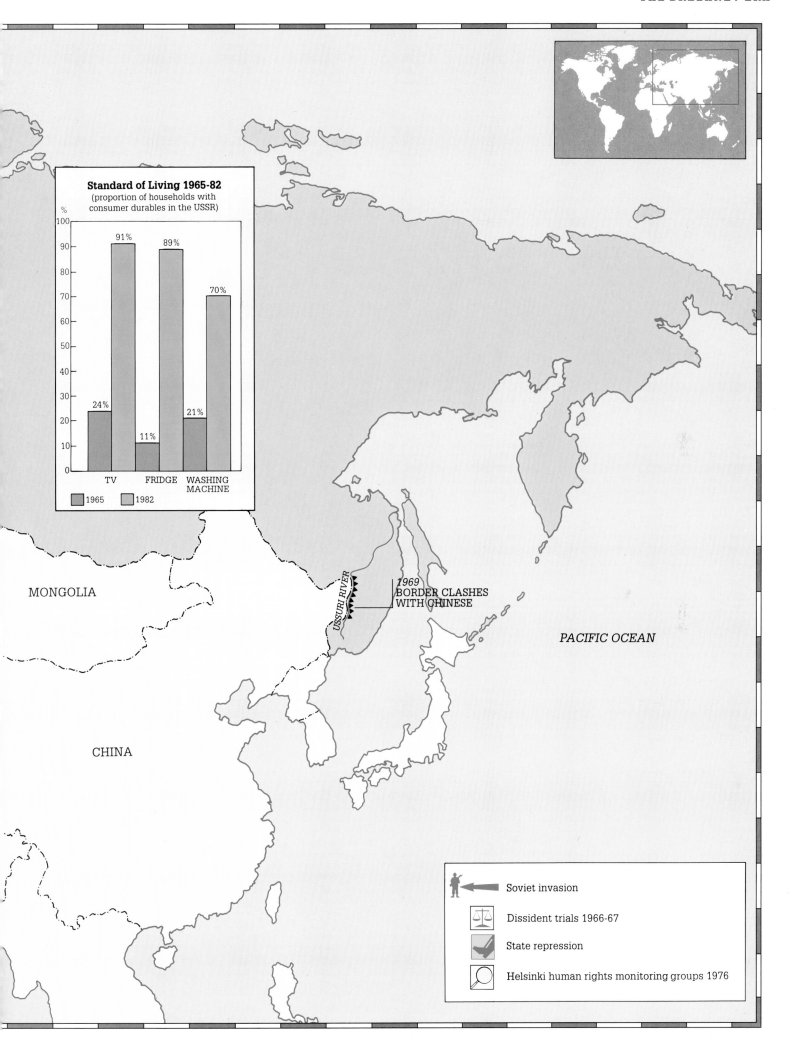

## Standard of Living 1965-82
(proportion of households with consumer durables in the USSR)

%
100
90 — 91%
80 — 89%
70 — 70%
60
50
40
30
24%
20 — 21%
11%
10
0
TV      FRIDGE   WASHING
                 MACHINE

■ 1965    ■ 1982

MONGOLIA

CHINA

*USSURI RIVER*

*1969*
BORDER CLASHES
WITH CHINESE

*PACIFIC OCEAN*

Soviet invasion

Dissident trials 1966-67

State repression

Helsinki human rights monitoring groups 1976

Mujahidin rebels in
Afghanistan capture a Russian
T-72 tank intact, 1980.
The lightly armed rebels using
guerrilla fighting tactics outmanoeuvred the Soviets' huge
firepower.

labour was largely the result of educational reforms introduced in the 1920s when the curriculum was revised to ensure that practical work was combined with a high level of scientific and technical knowledge. The idea of educationalists such as Nadezhda Krupskaya was that science should no longer be taught as a series of abstract experiments but as part of industrial and agricultural practice.

As Stalin's stranglehold on the country had tightened, however, these educational ideals had gone the way of other innovations of the Revolution, and in 1934 examinations and traditional forms of discipline were reintroduced. Only in 1958 were these conservative methods challenged, when Khrushchev launched a package of reforms which looked to Krupskaya for inspiration. 'Our general education schools suffer from the fact that we have taken over very much from the pre-revolutionary gymnasiums, whose purpose was to give their pupils a certain amount of abstract knowledge, sufficient to receive the matriculation certificate,' he pointed out in a speech made in August 1958. It was an indication of the conservatism of the collective leadership which took over in October 1964 that one of their first decisions was to abandon Khrushchev's initiative and return to the old, narrowly pedagogical ways.

Despite these shifts in emphasis, the educational level among Soviet citizens and their leaders was rising. Meanwhile, the government increasingly made use of the ideas of experts in the academy of sciences and in the universities, while the public was allowed at least a symbolic role in the political process by being encouraged to air

their views in the press. However, the important decisions were still taken by those at the top, and the process of decision-making in the Praesidium, which returned to its old title of the Politburo in 1966, remained as secretive as ever.

### Crime and Punishment

In 1977 a new constitution was adopted, enshrining in Article 6 the central role of the party. It declared that the party was 'the leading and guiding force of Soviet

Andrei Gromyko, the Soviet Foreign Minister
from 1957 until 1985. One of the 'old guard', he
was replaced when Gorbachev came to power.

society and the nucleus of its political system, of all state organization and public organizations'. Part of this power was dispensed through the *nomenklatura*, a system bequeathed by Stalin which listed which key appointments were in the gift of a closely knit corps of loyal party functionaries. With such power went access to a range of privileges not available to the average citizen.

For the Soviet leaders, however, the rising levels of education within the population led to a greater awareness of the rest of the world and of the limitations of their own country. While the Kremlin did not want a return to Stalinist repression, it clearly felt that a line had to be drawn somewhere. The levels of official tolerance were indicated in the year following the triumvirate's rise to power by the trial of Andrei Sinyavsky and Yuri Daniel, who were prosecuted and imprisoned for allowing their work to be published abroad without official sanction. In addition, those who refused to conform to the approved conventions were expelled from the creative unions and deprived of the opportunity to publish, perform or exhibit their work. Such disapproval led dissident writers to participate in *samizdat*, literally self-publication, in which authors circulated underground multiple carbon copies of their books and articles.

This clandestine culture thrived until 1971 because the intelligentsia chose to work within the law: Article 190 of the Soviet Criminal Code legislates against 'the distribution of false information which slanders the Soviet state and social system'. If, therefore, an author could prove that his information was accurate, he could avoid

# Dissidence in the Brezhnev Era

There were probably never more than about three thousand dissidents, and they did not form a coherent group with an agreed platform. Solzhenitsyn, for example, was a traditional Russian nationalist, while Roy Medvedev was a Marxist and Andrei Sakharov was a liberal. They were predominantly intellectual and, despite their small numbers their effect was astonishing. They captured the imagination of the West, and Western governments supported them to put pressure on the Soviet government. But perhaps their most valuable effect was on the future leaders of the Soviet Union.

Political dissent became vocal when writers Andrei Sinyavsky and Yuri Daniel were arrested in

Alexander Solzhenitsyn was expelled from Russia in 1974.

1965 for producing anti-Soviet propaganda. Dissidents attempted to use Soviet law to secure better civil rights and,

after the signing of the Helsinki Final Act, they formed groups to monitor Soviet compliance with the human rights clauses.

Nationalism is a potent dissident cause in a country with more than a hundred different nationalities. In the 1970s many dissidents campaigned for the return of the Crimean Tartars, deported by Stalin on the pretext that they had collaborated with the Germans, exonerated in 1967 but not allowed to return to the Crimea. Religious dissent also became common in the 1970s, particularly by Baptists, Catholics and Jews.

The authorities clamped down on all dissidents, however, no matter how prominent, particularly when detente came to an end and there was nothing left to lose in East-West relations.

being jailed. This meant that every case which was brought to trial involved a dispute about the accuracy of the published material: a situation which extended the length of the case, tied up KGB resources and brought the Soviet Union into disrepute abroad.

In 1970 the KGB, under Yuri Andropov's direction, managed to restrict the publication of *samizdat* materials by introducing a number of new procedures, which included committing dissidents to psychiatric hospitals, forcing them into exile or revoking their citizenship while they were on trips abroad. However, the problem could not be eliminated entirely because contact with Western publishers was increasingly facilitated by the growth of tourism. This had become ever more important in Moscow's drive for foreign currency to pay for the Western technology needed to raise the quality of Soviet consumer goods. Several joint projects were launched, including the building of the Togliatti car plant by Fiat. But the electronic components which Soviet industry needed were embargoed by Western governments on the grounds that they might be used for defence purposes.

### The Brezhnev Doctrine

For over a decade, Soviet-American relations were managed so as to avoid any confrontation which might escalate into a repeat of the Cuban missile crisis. Even when US planes bombed North Vietnam's main port of Haiphong while Kosygin was in Hanoi, the Soviet Union chose to ignore the provocation. Similarly, when the Warsaw Pact armies invaded Czechoslovakia, American politicians might have made their disapproval known; but no one seriously suggested that the Pentagon should despatch forces to protect the reformers in Prague.

Moscow justified its interference in the affairs of its neighbour in terms which came to be called the 'Brezhnev doctrine'. It was first expressed five weeks after the invasion of Prague in the pages of *Pravda* by Sergei Kovalev, who claimed: 'World socialism as a social system is the common achievement of the working people of all countries, it is indivisible, and its defense is the common cause of all Communists'. Brezhnev expressed the same sentiment when he spoke in Poland on 12 November 1968. He claimed that a threat to the cause of socialism in one country was 'a threat to the security of the socialist commonwealth as a whole - this is no longer merely a problem for that country's people, but a common problem, the concern of all socialist countries'.

This attempt to contain all potential conflicts between the two superpowers faltered when Jimmy Carter arrived at the White House in January 1977. His preoccupation with human rights led him to communicate directly with dissidents in the Soviet Union, which was denounced by the Kremlin as interference in internal affairs. Nevertheless, both sides were still sufficiently committed to arms limitation talks to reach agreement on SALT 2. The US Senate never ratified the agreement and when the Red Army over-ran Afghanistan, detente was at an end. Soon people were talking of a 'Second Cold War'.

### The Kremlin's Vietnam

Moscow had always maintained cordial relations with Kabul, even when the Afghan monarchy was running the country. In July 1973 a member of the royal family, Mohammed Daoud, staged a successful coup and proclaimed a republic. The Kremlin welcomed the change at first,

but as Daoud consolidated his position he became increasingly autocratic and the Kremlin turned to the People's Democratic Party of Afghanistan (PDPA), a Marxist group. In April 1978 a prominent member of the group was murdered, and the size of the subsequent demonstration took Daoud's government by surprise. They immediately arrested the group's leaders, but the crackdown provoked a rising by sympathetic commanders in the army. The coup was so effective that many people in Kabul did not know it was going on; rebel tanks were even flagged down by traffic policemen and told to keep out of the way of taxis. Daoud was deposed in less than twenty-four hours.

However, the PDPA government which assumed power lacked coherent leadership and the two major Marxist-Communist groups within it were at odds - with bloody consequences. Meanwhile, intensely anti-Soviet guerrilla units - the mujahidin - were infiltrating the country from Pakistan. In one incident, a provincial town was over-run and the families of Soviet military advisers were sought out, beheaded and their bodies hacked to pieces.

As the situation in Afghanistan grew more chaotic, the Soviet forces became increasingly involved in the fighting. In late 1979, with no end in sight, the Kremlin decided on a massive intervention. On 24 December, units of the elite Guards Airborne Divisions landed at Kabul Airport together with a unit of the *spetsnaz* - the Soviet equivalent of the SAS. They attacked the palace of the country's Marxist President, Hafizullah Amin, and shot him on the 27th. That night, the main body of Soviet troops took over government buildings in the capital. Two days later, two motorized rifle divisions crossed the border and joined up with the divisions which had flown in.

The operation was masterminded by Generals Yepishev and Pavlovskiy, who had organized the invasion of Czechoslovakia. The leaders of the mujahidin rebels did not roll over and co-operate, however; and the puppet regime which the Kremlin installed was intensely unpopular. Furthermore, the White House reacted with unexpected virulence and began channelling aid, via Pakistan, to the rebels, in whom it had hitherto shown no interest. Brezhnev's last important act had embroiled his country in a conflict it could not win, but from which it could not withdraw without humiliation. The man who had come to power as part of a move to avoid reckless brinkmanship had entangled the Soviet Union in its greatest misadventure.

Leonid Brezhnev died on the morning of 10 November 1982. He was so heavy that, when his coffin was raised, the bottom fell out and his corpse crashed to the floor. The widespread corruption which had marked the closing years of his regime had even touched his family, and his daughter Galina was accompanied to the funeral by two well-dressed KGB minders. The cool touch of Yuri Andropov was already apparent.

# The Prague Spring

Czechoslovakia in mid-1967 appeared to the outsider as a perfect reflection of President and party chief Antonin 'Frozen Face' Novotny: the most stolid, stable and dependable of Moscow's servants. In fact, Novotny was losing face fast, and a stimulating experiment in Communist self-reform was soon to begin - so stimulating, in fact, that it was to take an invasion by Warsaw Pact forces to quash it.

## The Fall of Novotny

Under Novotny, who owed his position to the purges of the early 1950s, destalinization had proceeded with glacial slowness. But in 1963, a major economic crisis, combined with a sudden upsurge of national feeling among Slovak Communists, led the President to dismiss several leading politicians, to topple Stalin's massive statue from its perch above Prague, and to introduce a belated programme of political and cultural reform. Change was most evident among the young, who had taken to rock music, jeans (they called them *texasski*) and long hair. By the mid-1960s, Prague was hosting an international jazz festival and had gained a reputation as the hippy capital of eastern Europe. Dramatists such as the biting satirist Vaclav Havel had critic Kenneth Tynan toasting Prague as the theatre capital of Europe. It was legal once more to read the writings of Franz Kafka in his native land - though the circumstances remained Kafkaesque, for all of this was happening in what remained a one-party state, staunchly loyal to Moscow, and ever ready to crack down on the over-adventurous who agitated for more fundamental change.

Unfortunately, Stalin's economic legacy had been less easy to jettison than his statue. Czechoslovakia, once celebrated for its glassware, ceramics, shoes, textiles and other consumer goods, had been designated as the arsenal and machine shop of eastern Europe, and was sinking under the load. Predictions of spectacular economic growth had been so dashed by grotesque central planning, inefficient management, lack of incentive and poor allocation of scarce capital that it became proper to criticize 'the cult of the plan' while waiting in the ever-lengthening food queues. After long debate, partial economic reform, dubbed 'market socialism', was introduced at the start of 1967 - only to be sabotaged by party bureaucrats fearful of losing their powers. The economic woes were most keenly resented by the Slovaks, a sensitive minority of 4 million in the poorer eastern third of the country,

who had not attained the sort of autonomy the Communists had promised in 1948, and who were still smarting over the executions and purges of the Stalin era. Though closely related, Czechs and Slovaks had been politically separate for a thousand years until united after the First World War, and the Slovaks' strong sense of separate identity was making itself felt.

Now restlessness was getting out of hand, and Novotny the grudging appeaser was under attack from conservatives as well as progressives within the party. Demands for his resignation coincided with a student protest over poor hostel conditions, and when police used clubs and tear gas on a candelit student procession the entire population was enraged.

With the protest spreading, Leonid Brezhnev visited Prague on 8 December 1967, and concluded that Novotny might be safely retired. Novotny tried to save himself with public promises of a better deal for Slovakia, and 'socialist democracy' for everyone, but it did him no good. After a hectic two-day Central committee meeting,

the Czechoslovak Communist Party - and therefore the country - found itself with a new leader on 4 January 1968. His name was Alexander Dubcek.

## Dubcek's Reforms

Brezhnev cabled his 'hearty congratulations', and the Czechoslovak news agency *Ceteka* recorded Dubcek's 'faithfulness to the spirit of proletarian internationalism'. Dubcek was forty-six, and largely unknown outside the country. Spindly and ungainly, he did not have the manner of one likely to give offence. His Communist background was impeccable: schooldays spent in the Soviet Union; a heroic war record with the Czechoslovak partisans; graduation with honours from an elite political finishing school in Moscow. Yet as party boss in Slovakia, he had lately come to sympathize with those who sought to set limits to Communist power. 'The party does not live outside, nor above society,' he argued.

Novotny was down, but not out, for he still retained the largely ceremonial office of

---

# Alexander Dubcek

Alexander Dubcek was a second-generation Communist who was born in Slovakia but brought up in Kirghizia. He rose through the ranks of the party while it was infected with Stalinism without contracting the disease himself, becoming chief secretary of the regional committee in Bratislava in 1958. He became a full member of the Central Committee's Praesidium in 1962.

In October 1967, the Committee split into two factions, with Dubcek leading the group which opposed the Stalinist First Secretary Novotny. After he was elected to this post on 5 January, Dubcek seemed bemused at first and some weeks elapsed before the steps were taken which led to the Soviet invasion. After the invasion he was gradually eased out of power and for the first six months of 1970 he was ambassador to Turkey. But in June he was expelled from the party and ended up back in Bratislava as a forestry inspector.

A picture of Alexander Dubcek is carried through the streets of Prague. He tried to rule by consent rather than by dictatorship.

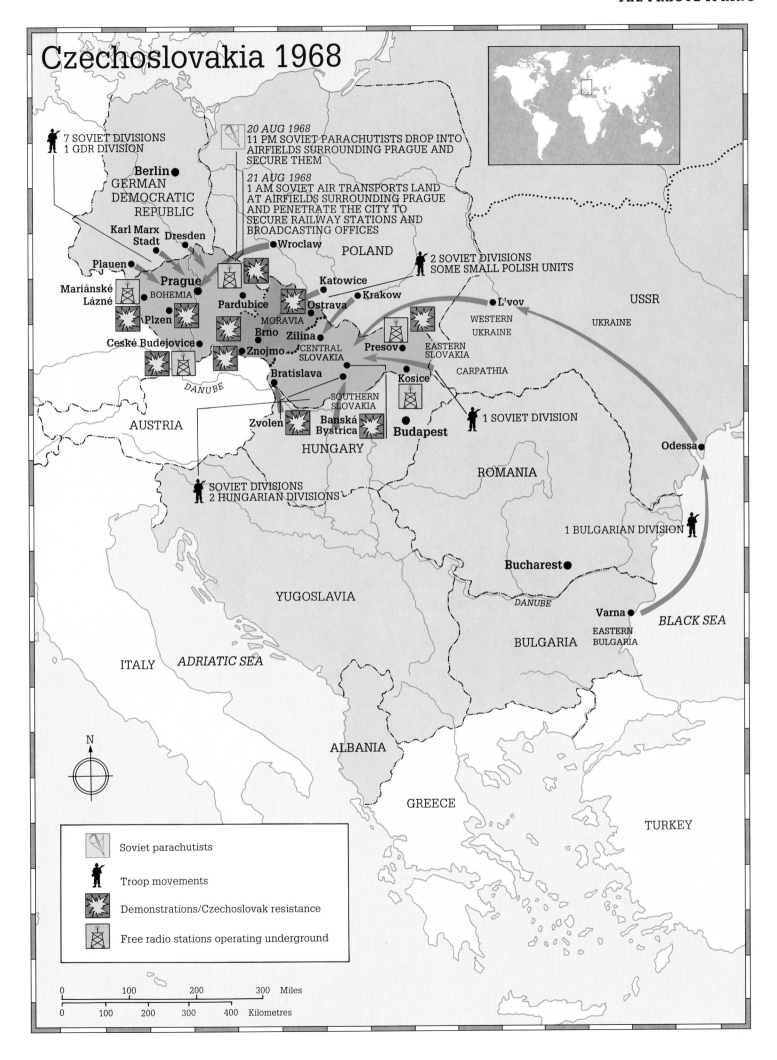

# Czechoslovakia 1968

**7 SOVIET DIVISIONS
1 GDR DIVISION**

**Berlin** ●
GERMAN
DEMOCRATIC
REPUBLIC

*20 AUG 1968*
11 PM SOVIET PARACHUTISTS DROP INTO
AIRFIELDS SURROUNDING PRAGUE AND
SECURE THEM

*21 AUG 1968*
1 AM SOVIET AIR TRANSPORTS LAND
AT AIRFIELDS SURROUNDING PRAGUE
AND PENETRATE THE CITY TO
SECURE RAILWAY STATIONS AND
BROADCASTING OFFICES

Karl Marx
Stadt ● Dresden ●
● Wroclaw    POLAND

Plauen ●

Prague ●    **2 SOVIET DIVISIONS
SOME SMALL POLISH UNITS**

Mariánské
Lázné    BOHEMIA    Katowice ●

Pardubice    Ostrava    ● Krakow    ● L'vov    USSR

Plzen    MORAVIA    Zilina    Presov    WESTERN
UKRAINE    UKRAINE

Brno    Zilina    EASTERN
SLOVAKIA

Ceské Budejovice ●    Znojmo ●    CENTRAL
SLOVAKIA    CARPATHIA

DANUBE    Bratislava ●    Kosice ●

AUSTRIA    SOUTHERN
SLOVAKIA    **1 SOVIET DIVISION**

Zvolen    Banská    ● Budapest    Odessa ●
Bystrica

HUNGARY    ROMANIA

**SOVIET DIVISIONS
2 HUNGARIAN DIVISIONS**

**1 BULGARIAN DIVISION**

YUGOSLAVIA    **Bucharest** ●

ITALY    ADRIATIC SEA    DANUBE    Varna ●    *BLACK SEA*

BULGARIA    EASTERN
BULGARIA

ALBANIA

N

GREECE

TURKEY

Soviet parachutists

Troop movements

Demonstrations/Czechoslovak resistance

Free radio stations operating underground

0    100    200    300    Miles

0    100    200    300    400    Kilometres

Physical resistance to the occupying Red Army in the streets of Prague as young Czechoslovaks set fire to the invaders' tanks.

President, and the hard-liners who had acquiesced in Dubcek's election clearly hoped to be able to control this first Slovak to hold the all-powerful post of Party First Secretary. Now it was Dubcek's move, and he cunningly let others make the running.

Throughout January, Dubcek maintained a silence that threw the system of thought control into confusion, and left the censors so afraid of being proved wrong that they were loath to censor anything. It was just the opportunity that bold spirits had been waiting for. Liberal reformers controlled much of the press, radio and television, which took up the new theme of democraticized Communism, and an enthralled population was entertained to heady talk of a Marxist democracy enjoying 'more freedom than any bourgeois country'. Now Dubcek found his voice. In simple, warm tones he spoke of a need to encourage individualism, and to let everyone have a say in affairs. Friendly and approachable, he drew to himself the sort of popularity more associated with a Western politician. More than this, he put his views directly and in public to Brezhnev and the Warsaw Pact leaders when they came to celebrate twenty years of Communist rule in Czechoslovakia.

The hard-liners were alarmed, but were still well entrenched within the secret police, the army and party organizations, and they still had Novotny installed in the presidential castle overlooking Prague. Concentrating on the factories and mines, they spread dire warnings of the chaos that might result from

any tampering with the system, and they even had Novotny try to emulate Dubcek by appearing in workers' cafeterias and buying beer all round. They were making some headway when suddenly their cause was destroyed from within. On 1 March, it was disclosed that General Jan Sejna, a key figure in the Novotny camp, had fled to the West with his eighteen-year-old son and twenty-one-year-old mistress. Though censorship theoretically still existed, it was ignored, and a startled population got their first taste of unbridled press freedom. To Czechoslovaks, it was like Watergate and the Profumo scandal rolled into one, as each day produced more startling revelations of corruption and deceit. It seemed that Sejna, a one-time farm labourer, had a highly lucrative relationship with Novotny's son and that his life had been a round of wild parties, embezzlement and theft of government property. The most beautiful women, the most exotic Western sports cars, the most splendid country homes - whatever the luxury, Sejna could provide it. At the height of the storm, it was revealed that he had been behind a thwarted military coup on Novotny's behalf. Mass demonstrations demanded the President's resignation; on 22 March he obliged, giving health as his reason. Other resignations followed. The Novotny machine had self-destructed.

To succeed him as President the National Assembly elected Ludvik Svoboda, a seventy-two-year-old retired general who had fought alongside the Red Army in the

Second World War. Svoboda was acceptable to Moscow, yet he was also symbolic of the new spirit. This smiling father figure stirred feelings of national pride by laying a wreath at the grave of Tomas Masaryk, the founder of the Czechoslovak republic, who had been reviled by the previous regime.

A reformist Action Programme - subtitled 'The Czechoslovak Road to Socialism' - was adopted by the party on 5 April. The goal remained a one-party system, but with power dispersed widely throughout the community. Energy and talent were to be rewarded, and people encouraged 'to think for themselves and to express their opinions'. There was to be freedom of speech and freedom to travel. The courts were to be independent of politics. Industrial enterprises were to be free to take their own decisions, and trade was to be pursued on a competitive, worldwide basis. There was something in it for everyone: improved pension systems, an expanded housing programme, facelifts for Prague and for Bratislava, the Slovak capital. To cater for Slovak aspirations, the republic was to be reconstituted along federal lines, with Slovakia and the Czech lands each having their own legislative bodies.

### Daring Moscow

The first day of May in Prague was remarkable, even by the standards set by previous May Days. The marching throngs ranged from People's Militia units rededicating themselves to the cause of proletarian solidarity to groups jauntily carrying the American and Israeli flags. Recently unbanned organizations such as the Boy Scouts strode out in their fresh uniforms, as did motley groups of persons brandishing banners with slogans like 'Make Love Not War'. The police were required only to save Dubcek from a crush of well-wishers and autograph-seekers. That evening, the Polish Embassy was assailed by demonstrators protesting over the treatment of students in that country, and two days later a large student rally went all the way in assailing Communism and calling for the legalization of opposition parties. Late that night, Dubcek and his closest associates flew to Moscow to try to explain what was going on.

The warning was clear when tens of thousands of Warsaw Pact troops with tanks and aircraft poured into Czechoslovakia for 'signal exercises', and took their time in leaving. But although Dubcek dutifully spoke out against 'anti-socialist tendencies' and attacked some would-be opposition groups, he did nothing to stop the spate of liberal ideas and freewheeling comment, which intensified with the formal abolition of censorship on 26 June. The hard-liners and the Kremlin were outraged.

The mood did not improve when Dubcek politely declined to attend a meeting in Warsaw of the Pact leadership, so the Kremlin now determined on a face-to-face showdown between the entire Soviet and Czechoslovak party leaderships. From 29 July to 1 August, the two sides met in a railwaymen's club in the tiny border town of Cierna-nad-Tisou. The discussions were heated, and a banquet was cancelled at the last moment, but Dubcek emerged from the ordeal expressing satisfaction, and Svoboda sounded almost victorious. When cheeks were kissed and flowers exchanged at a follow-up Warsaw Pact summit, people began to talk of the 'miracle of Cierna'. In fact, the Kremlin was no more ready to compromise than Dubcek was to halt the reform process. When the two Communist heretics, Tito of Yugoslavia and Ceausescu of Romania, visited Prague to great popular acclaim, Moscow had already decided that enough was enough.

As crowds relaxed in Myslbek Park and thousands of Western tourists drifted around the sites of Prague, Soviet KGB agents flew in secretly and made contact with deputy Interior Minister, Vilian Salgovic, one of the anti-reformists. At 4 pm on 20 August, Salgovic gathered a group of confederates, told them what was to happen, and assigned them tasks. At 11 pm Czechoslovakia was invaded from the east, north and south by the armies of the Soviet Union, East Germany, Poland, Hungary and Bulgaria.

## Invasion

There was no resistance at the score of entry points, or at the airports, where dozens of Antonov-24 turboprop transports landed thousands more troops. Dubcek, the Prime Minister, Oldrich Cernik, the National Assembly Chairman, Josef Smrkovsky, and other reform leaders were seized and bundled off to Moscow by Soviet troops, but not before they had issued a proclamation condemning the invasion and appealing for calm - there was to be 'no resistance to the troops on the march'. This was broadcast by Radio Prague at 1.50 am on 21 August, after an anti-reformist communications director had failed in an attempt to shut down the transmitters. Since Czechoslovak communications workers refused to broadcast the 'invitation' that a handful of hard-liners had issued for outside intervention, *Tass*, the Soviet news agency, settled for reporting that unidentified 'party and government' leaders had asked for 'urgent assistance'. This led to Czechoslovak jokes about the Soviets needing so many troops 'to look for the people who sent for them'. The Czechoslovak army did not fire a shot, and sporadic resistance came mainly from angry teenagers - as in the Wedneday morning 'Battle of Prague Radio Centre', in which a crowd armed with stones and Molotov cocktails tried to take on the tanks. The troops had been instructed to perform their 'sacred international duty...in a dignified and honourable way' - and not to shoot first. Most obeyed. In a country of almost 14 million, casualties totalled about seventy dead and a thousand wounded.

Dubcek might have suffered the fate of Hungary's Imre Nagy, but for the obstinacy of the old warrior Svoboda, who refused to give his presidential sanction to what had happened. A policy of passive resistance was put into telling effect. On 22 August, more than a thousand delegates disguised in workers' clothes managed to assemble in a Prague factory for a one-day congress of the Czechoslovak Communist Party; they elected a reformist leadership under Dubcek, and threatened a general strike if the troops were not withdrawn and their kidnapped leaders restored to them. The next morning Svoboda was flown to Moscow, but resolutely refused to negotiate without Dubcek. Moscow, chastened by the extent of its isolation, with almost every Communist Party outside its immediate grasp joining in the global protest, finally allowed a haggard Dubcek and his colleagues to return to Prague on 27 August. The price was a humiliating agreement that provided for the permanent stationing of Soviet forces in Czechoslovakia, and for a return to 'normality', Soviet-style.

## Aftermath

The defiant mood changed to depression as the mirage of reform faded. Travel was once more severely restricted, and the occupation forces resorted to intimidatory arrests to restrict protest. On 16 January 1969, a twenty-one-year-old student named Jan Palach doused himself with petrol and set himself alight in Wenceslas Square, in what was seen as a re-enactment of the martyrdom at the stake of Jan Hus, the fifteenth-century national hero. Palach took three days to die, and his death caused national grief and guilt. He was given a state funeral which was attended by half a million people; bells tolled, and public transport was halted as a mark of respect. The Soviets bided their time.

On 28 March, the Czechoslovak ice hockey team scored another victory over the Russians, and the celebrations extended to attacks on Soviet property. Warsaw Pact manoeuvres were once more announced, and in the wake of protest meetings and a wave of arrests Dubcek was finally ousted. Within a few months he had been expelled from the Communist Party itself, as were virtually all the reformists who had led the movement now known as the Prague Spring. So were three hundred thousand others, in a massive purge that extended beyond politics to every corner of Czechoslovak society. A friendship treaty was signed with the Soviet Union, and under the new Brezhnev doctrine of limited sovereignty strict limits were placed on Czechoslovakia's right to determine its own policies. The courageous Svoboda died in 1975, aged seventy-nine. In April 1976, a Party Congress declared itself well satisfied with what had been accomplished. It was not until 1989 that the Czechoslovaks were once again given the opportunity to chart their own future. By this time, however, their demands had extended well beyond the ideological confines of the 'Prague Spring'.

This anti-occupation poster shows the Soviet Army as liberator in 1945 and oppressor in 1968. One of the most popular slogans of the occupation was 'Wake up Lenin, Brezhnev has gone mad'.

# Reform in Eastern Europe

Scattered discontent in Romania over severe consumer and energy shortages did not loosen Nicolae Ceausescu's iron grip on his people.

Despite the brutality of the crackdown in Hungary, the Soviet leadership recognized that force and repression were no longer the way to motivate people or to encourage social and economic growth. Once the dust had settled after the tumultuous events of 1956, the Kremlin decided to revise its relationship with its satellites.

The problem to be solved was how to destalinize the system without destabilizing it. After he had overcome his conflicts with the 'anti-party' group, Khrushchev resumed the attack on Stalin and his methods at the Twenty-second Party Congress which was held at the end of 1961. His attack signalled to the leaders of eastern Europe a greater latitude in political and economic options in future. Many reformers believed that Communism could still work if Stalinism could be removed. They hoped to bring ideology into line with the needs of eastern Europe, while maintaining social and economic stability, and such aims were far from impossible to achieve.

## Hungary

When János Kádár returned to Budapest on 7 November and faced an embittered and divided people, he was the head of a virtually non-existent party. Tens of thousands of Hungarians were being arrested and many were executed; the workers' councils were refusing to concede defeat, and their passive resistance was only finally overcome a year after the revolution. Despite this situation and the street-fighting which had preceded it, Hungary made the greatest progress among the countries of eastern Europe in resolving the tensions inherent in destalinization and ultimately in making reformist Communism palatable.

## The Demands of Charter 77

During the early 1970s, a group of intellectuals challenged the Czech authorities by sending open letters to various ministers. Karel Kosik published a letter to Jean-Paul Sartre complaining that the police had confiscated a manuscript of his new book during a routine raid. Perhaps, he suggested, authors should in future 'phone the police to come and collect their freshly completed works?'

After the Czech Federal Assembly ratified the United Nations International Covenant of Civil and Political Rights in November 1975, a group of protesters got together to expose their government's flagrant and cynical disregard for the measure which they had just signed.

The Czechoslovak playwright, Vaclav Havel, was one of the signatories of Charter 77.

The Charter listed the infractions of human rights in Czechoslovakia under such headings as 'Freedom of Expression' and 'Right to Education'. It was signed by 243 people and delivered to the government, the Federal Assembly and the Czech Press Agency in December 1976. Those carrying the envelopes were arrested despite Article 29 of the constitution which guarantees the right of every citizen to submit petitions. By the end of 1977, nearly 800 people had signed. All were questioned by the police and most suffered police harassment. In the autumn, members of the Polish group KOR and Charter signatories exchanged messages of support.

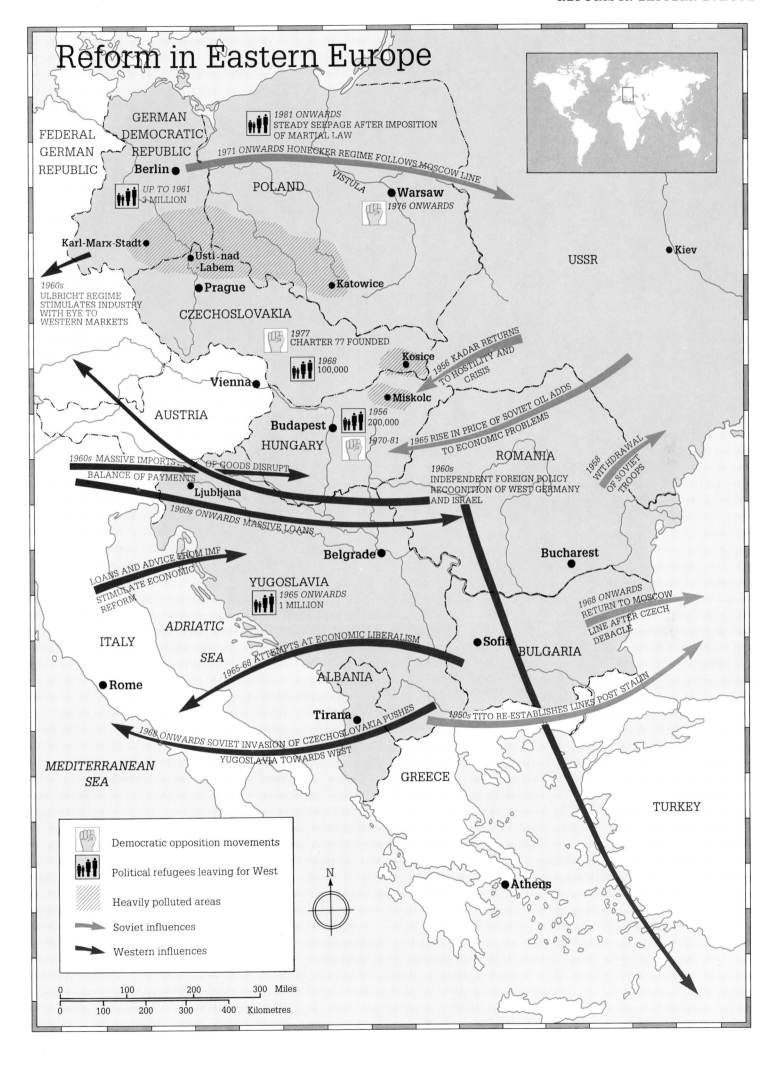

# Reform in Eastern Europe

FEDERAL
GERMAN
REPUBLIC

GERMAN
DEMOCRATIC
REPUBLIC

*1981 ONWARDS*
STEADY SEEPAGE AFTER IMPOSITION
OF MARTIAL LAW

**Berlin** ●

*1971 ONWARDS HONECKER REGIME FOLLOWS MOSCOW LINE*

POLAND

VISTULA

● **Warsaw**

*1976 ONWARDS*

*UP TO 1961*
3 MILLION

Karl-Marx-Stadt ●

USSR

● **Kiev**

● **Usti -nad
-Labem**

● **Katowice**

*1960s*
ULBRICHT REGIME
STIMULATES INDUSTRY
WITH EYE TO
WESTERN MARKETS

● **Prague**

CZECHOSLOVAKIA

*1977*
CHARTER 77 FOUNDED

*1968*
100,000

● **Kosice**

*1956 KADAR RETURNS*
TO HOSTILITY AND
CRISIS

● **Vienna**

AUSTRIA

● **Miskolc**

*1965 RISE IN PRICE OF SOVIET OIL ADDS*

**Budapest** ●

*1956*
200,000

*1970-81*

TO ECONOMIC PROBLEMS

ROMANIA

*1958
WITHDRAWAL
OF SOVIET
TROOPS*

HUNGARY

*1960s* MASSIVE IMPORTS OF GOODS DISRUPT
BALANCE OF PAYMENTS

*1960s*
INDEPENDENT FOREIGN POLICY
RECOGNITION OF WEST GERMANY
AND ISRAEL

● **Ljubljana**

*1960s ONWARDS MASSIVE LOANS*

LOANS AND ADVICE FROM IMF
STIMULATE ECONOMIC
REFORM

**Belgrade** ●

● **Bucharest**

YUGOSLAVIA

*1965 ONWARDS*
1 MILLION

*1968 ONWARDS
RETURN TO MOSCOW
LINE AFTER CZECH
DEBACLE*

*ADRIATIC*

ITALY

*SEA*

*1965-68* ATTEMPTS AT ECONOMIC LIBERALISM

● **Rome**

ALBANIA

● **Sofia** BULGARIA

*1950s TITO RE-ESTABLISHES LINKS POST STALIN*

**Tirana** ●

*1968 ONWARDS SOVIET INVASION OF CZECHOSLOVAKIA PUSHES
YUGOSLAVIA TOWARDS WEST*

*MEDITERRANEAN
SEA*

GREECE

TURKEY

Democratic opposition movements

Political refugees leaving for West

Heavily polluted areas

N

Soviet influences

Western influences

● **Athens**

| 0 | 100 | 200 | 300 | Miles |
| 0 | 100 | 200 | 300 | 400 | Kilometres |

To surmount his immediate problems, Kádár removed the hard-line supporters of the former party boss, Mátyás Rákosi, and those reformers in senior positions within the party who had been allied to Imre Nagy. Then, in January 1959, he launched a drive towards the collectivization of agriculture which relied for its success not on coercion but on financial incentives and persuasion. Within three years 75 per cent of the country's farms had been collectivized, but the peasants refused to work willingly and yields remained low. Despite massive levels of state investment the situation failed to change at first, but the programme did bear fruit some years later. The basic tenets of Kádár's 'alliance policy', of co-operation rather than coercion, had been established.

A year after the Twenty-second Party Congress in Moscow, the Hungarian party's Eighth Congress made its own contribution towards liberalization: it introduced a secret ballot for internal matters. Amnesties for the 'counter-revolutionaries' of 1956 were proclaimed, while some non-party members were selected for senior positions within the civil service. But the real turning point came in December 1963, when a plenum of the party's Central Committee approved the setting up of an investigation, supervised by the Minister of Finance, Rezso Nyers, into the opportunities for economic reform. His report was submitted two years later and approved in May 1966. His proposed New Economic Mechanism, which freed state enterprises from petty interference, was inaugurated on 1 January 1968.

The reforms unleashed the potential of the agricultural modernization programme of the early 1960s, and shelves in shops began to fill with food. Hungary, however, was still short of raw materials, and as the economy took flight imports began to mount. This combined with large imports of Western machinery and consumer goods to create balance of payments difficulties for the country. Hungary's biggest economic shock came in January 1975 after negotiations with the Soviet Union had set a new price for its oil purchases. Until that time, Hungary had been protected from the sudden rise in oil prices initiated by OPEC (the Organization of Petroleum Exporting Countries). But the new agreement made a dramatic difference to the size of its import bill.

The success of the New Economic Mechanism silenced the conservative opposition to Kádár within the party during the late 1960s, and allowed him to co-opt more reformers into the leadership. By the early 1970s, however, this success was leading to the growth of social inequalities as some people benefited more than others - a development which encouraged trade union leaders to become more vocal in defence of the lower paid. After two large wage rises had been forced on the Central Committee, the more orthodox party members gained the upper hand and were able to impose stiffer taxes on the emerging middle class and to oust the reformist 'Budapest School' from

their jobs and from the party. There was, however, no return to the brutality which the Rákosi regime had employed before 1956.

As economic pressure on Hungary eased towards the end of the 1970s, the more conservative elements in the party began to lose heart and the reformers were given fresh encouragement. The New Economic Mechanism was revived at the Twelfth Congress in March 1980, and the country entered the 1980s as one of the most tolerant Communist regimes.

The example of Hungary had repercussions in the Soviet Union, where, as Brezhnev's health failed, Yuri Andropov was manoeuvring his way towards a takeover. Andropov had gone to Budapest as a diplomat in 1953 and been made ambassador in 1954. His key role in the events of 1956 had not gone unnoticed in the Kremlin, and his skill was rewarded in 1957 when he was brought back to Moscow to head the Central Committee's Foreign Affairs department dealing with socialist countries. From this vantage point he was able to observe the success of his protégé János Kádár and the Hungarian reforms; the similarity between measures undertaken in Moscow in the 1980s and Budapest in the 1960s and 1970s is no coincidence.

## The German Democratic Republic

The building of the Berlin Wall was a watershed in the history of East Germany. Since its citizens no longer had the opportunity to slip across the border to a friendly regime and make a new life, they were forced to re-examine their attitudes to the state. The leadership under Walter Ulbricht, for its part, was forced to face the fact that its programmes were not converting the people to socialism.

The confrontation with these unpalatable truths changed the emphasis of party policy,

which now rediscovered its own heroes, such as Rosa Luxemburg, and began to rely less on Soviet models. A new economic policy was adopted; it placed emphasis on science and technology in an attempt to increase the country's productivity after the loss of so many skilled workers to the West.

The new policy was adopted in 1963, but was not accompanied - as it had been in Hungary - by a change in attitude to party interference in the day-to-day running of industry. On the other hand, the New Economic System laid the groundwork for the economic 'miracle' that was eventually to transform the country from an economic backwater to a Communist showcase, attracting shoppers and tourists from all over the Soviet bloc. For Ulbricht, however, the political and economic health of the country depended on the maintenance of East-West tensions and on restrictions on the West German presence in eastern Europe. When he tried to sabotage the process of detente in the early 1970s, the Kremlin had him replaced by the more pliable Erich Honecker. For the next fifteen years, the new leadership's response to any problem would be loyally to follow Moscow's lead.

As the 1970s progressed, Honecker gradually accumulated power and took control of the party machine; at the Ninth Party Congress in May 1976 he was named General Secretary. During the previous months, there had been rising expectations that improvements in working hours and pensions would be declared at the congress. When these hopes were confounded and no announcement was made, the general disappointment was so intense that the leadership hastily reconsidered; five days after the congress had closed, improvements in pensions and wages were announced.

Despite these changes, standards of living stagnated during the late 1970s and early 1980s as the international economic

Tito (standing, second from right), receives the North Vietnamese Prime Minister Nan Dong at his private villa in Bugojno, 1974, while the war between North and South Vietnam continued.

The Estonia Cement Plant in Kunda. For many years, ecological movements in eastern Europe had tried, unsuccessfully, to campaign against the widespread industrial pollution of their homelands.

recession caused by the sudden change in the price of oil hit the GDR. Price increases on imports rose twice as fast as exports, and the country began to accumulate a foreign debt. Even though the economy was growing and productivity improving, this new wealth was absorbed by the interest payments on the country's foreign debt. Unable to reverse the economic tide, the party attracted considerable dissatisfaction; this was to contribute in no small measure to the revolution which eventually swept away Mr Honecker and the Wall whose construction he had personally supervized.

## The Balkans

Although the Bulgarian party leadership was very dependent on the Soviet Union, in the mid-1960s it made a sudden and unexpected move towards reforming its economic system - in a manner which echoed the experiments of Hungary and East Germany. It managed to divorce these attempts at change from any reshaping of the party, however, and after the Czech debacle of 1968 conservative policies returned: during the 1970s the regime became one of the most repressive in eastern Europe.

Bulgaria's relationship with the Soviet Union was more relaxed than that of its neighbours, not least because Russia had been a traditional ally against Bulgaria's enemies in the region: the Turks and the Greeks. The same was not true of Romania, which had suffered as a consequence of its relationship with Nazi Germany and had lost Moldavia to the Soviet Union at the end of the Second World War. Nevertheless, the Romanian leadership managed to persuade the Kremlin to withdraw Soviet forces in 1958, perhaps as a reward for backing the suppression of the Hungarian uprising.

The Sino-Soviet split of the early 1960s gave the Romanians some leverage in their relationship with Moscow. Their price for

supporting the Kremlin was increased freedom for the country to pursue its own interests, and an end to Soviet interference. Romanian nationalism was now to be the guiding light in the country's foreign and domestic policies. This strategy of independence demanded an increase in the size of the army and investment in heavy industry; both were to have disastrous consequences for Nicolae Ceausescu, who had taken over as First Secretary on the death of Gheorghiu-Dej in 1965.

This new direction was very popular with Romanians at first and captured the energies of the people. By the mid-1970s, however, it was becoming obvious that the headlong rush to industrialize and to channel all investment in one direction was creating such serious imbalances within the system that it was in danger of collapsing. For example, a considerable investment had been made in oil-refining capacity; but domestic production failed to match expectations and by 1981 a third of the plant, which had been bought with expensive Western loans, was lying idle.

Ceausescu's foreign policy also showed a degree of independence: in 1967 he broke ranks with his Warsaw Pact allies by opening diplomatic relations with West Germany and upgrading his links with Israel, when the rest of the alliance closed their embassies in Tel Aviv after the Six-Day War. In 1968 he added to his domestic popularity by standing up to the Soviet Union during the Czechoslovakia crisis, refusing to participate in the invasion. But in 1971 Ceausescu visited North Korea and was deeply impressed by Kim Il Sung's repressive regime, which he did his best to emulate in Romania, replicating its emphasis on the cult of personality as well as its totalitarian methods.

During the immediate post-war years, Yugoslavia was unique among the Communist states of eastern Europe in the ideological distance it maintained between

itself and its neighbours - both economically and politically. Once Khrushchev came to power, however, the links between Belgrade and Moscow were revived; for example, the Kremlin took care to warn Tito that the Red Army was about to attack Budapest before the tanks moved in in 1956. In 1964, during a visit to Moscow, Tito was accorded the honour of addressing the Supreme Soviet. And in 1967 Tito even attended two meetings of the Warsaw Pact as an unofficial observer. Only the crushing of the Prague Spring of 1968 disrupted this improvement in relations as most Yugoslavs were very sympathetic to the liberalization under Dubcek.

Economically, Yugoslavia had struck out on its own path far earlier than its neighbours; during the 1950s, for instance, the party allowed workers' councils to share in the management of the factories. But without any central organization or market mechanism, the country's economy grew chaotically as the government printed money without restraint. This caused rampant inflation, and Yugoslavia's only course was to appeal to the International Monetary Fund and to Western governments for help.

The price demanded by the West for this aid was the liberalization of the economy, some price control and the abolition of subsidies. These changes fitted in with the increasing relaxation of political control, as Yugoslavia's constituent republics were given greater autonomy and the country moved towards a federal structure. The sacking of Alexander Rankovic, the head of the secret police, was Tito's demonstration to the West of his new liberal credentials.

After Tito's death in 1980, there was little to hold the force of regional nationalism in check. Yet none of the republics was strong enough to dominate the others, creating instability. Yugoslavia had to sustain opposing republics which seemed trapped in a welter of economic and political problems, threatening the Yugoslav state.

# The Dragon Bites its Tail

The 'Great Proletarian Cultural Revolution' was Mao's swansong: a paroxysm of blood-letting and a power play with over 30 million pawns which was afterwards seen by the party as 'a great catastrophe'. It was formally initiated at the May Day celebrations of 1966 by Zhou Enlai and though technically it continued till Mao's death in September 1976, it was virtually wound up at the Ninth Party Congress in April 1969.

At its height, the Cultural Revolution inspired millions of idealistic young people to mount fanatical attacks on the 'Four Olds' - old culture, old ideas, old customs and old habits. On the pretext of eradicating the 'olds', young zealots turned against more recent innovations, generally from abroad. Youths in stove-pipe trousers, a fashion introduced into China by students who had studied overseas, were stopped in the street and the offending garments were ripped open at the seams. Young women with their hair in plaits were stopped and warned that only short hair was 'correct'.

All of these acts were committed in the name of Chairman Mao's idealism. But from the very outset, these young men and women were mere pawns in a power struggle within the Politburo for the hearts and minds of the Chinese people. Even after the party had begun to banish this disruptive element to the countryside in 1968, China lurched along, swaying from one power ploy to the next as factional in-fighting consumed those at the top. By the time Mao died, the country was in a sorry state. The economy was lopsided; China's infrastructure and social services, such as housing, had been woefully neglected; the education system, which had collapsed completely in the late 1960s, was in a mess. Above all, the mortar which held the edifice in place - the Communist Party itself - was close to disintegration and confronting a population whose younger members in particular had lost faith in it and its ideology.

## The Need for Surgery

Mao launched the Cultural Revolution 'to prevent China from changing colour' and to pre-empt 'a capitalist restoration' similar to that which had happened in the Soviet Union under Khrushchev. In Mao's view, it had taken place because Stalin had over-emphasized the technocratic dimensions of economic development under bureaucratic leadership and had neglected the cultural domain. Mao believed that it was necessary to revitalize the class struggle in the realm of ideas and culture, and to activate the vast masses of the young against the bourgeois ideology which had resurfaced both within the party and outside it. Above all, he feared those of his colleagues who were 'nestling beside' him, as Khrushchev had 'nestled beside Stalin', only to turn against him after his death. Taking a look at some aspects of Chinese society in the early 1960s, it is possible to see why Mao was worried.

During the 1950s, the party had expanded and modernized the school system. But the system was based on Western models, and examinations became a mania among the teaching staff. With academic success considered all-important, the teachers managed to bypass the party's exhortations to integrate knowledge and practical experience; they concentrated, instead, on learning by rote. Furthermore, the system was increasingly weighted towards the children of privileged party officials and members of the bureaucracy who could provide the home conditions conducive to study. Despite Mao's appeal that 'workers and peasants and their children should enjoy priority in education', their numbers were falling at Beijing University.

One of Mao's first attacks on this process of embourgeoisement was made at the tenth plenum of the Central Committee in August and September 1962, during a discussion on agricultural policy. Mao carried the day, and his ideas were adopted the following year as official policy. Within four months, however, Deng Xiaoping, who was then Party Secretary and an ally of Liu Shaoqi, was chairing a committee that adopted proposals which subtly but effectively subverted Mao's purpose. Checkmated, Mao returned to the attack in January 1965 with an onslaught on revisionism, which was known as the 23-Article Document.

It was at this point that Mao realized he had to remove Liu, whom he had nominated as his successor in 1945. During the early 1960s Mao had made many attacks on revisionism and the 'Four Olds'; but his commentaries had been toned down by Liu's followers, who controlled the Ministries of Culture and Education, the Hsinhua news agency, the *People's Daily* and local government in Beijing and Shanghai. Top party officials were aware of the conflict, but the people

Eating out in Canton. The ubiquitous poster of Chairman Mao reminds the people of his revolutionary drive for victory in the Great Cultural Revolution.

# The Cultural Revolution

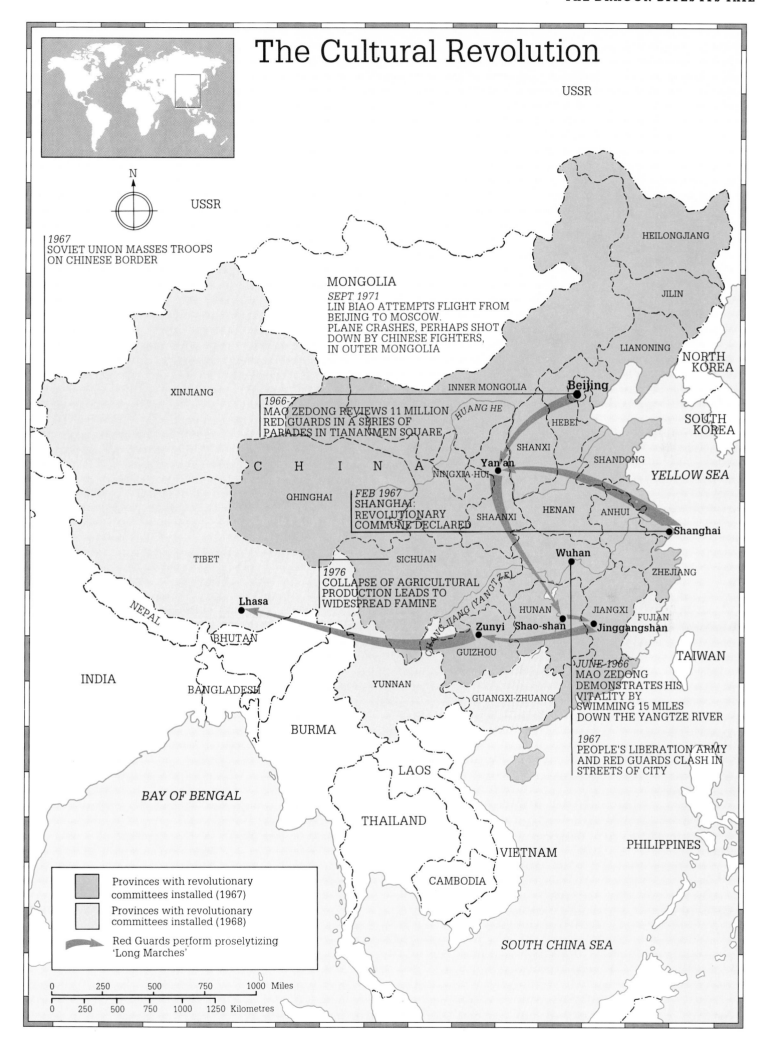

USSR

USSR

N

*1967*
SOVIET UNION MASSES TROOPS
ON CHINESE BORDER

MONGOLIA

*SEPT 1971*
LIN BIAO ATTEMPTS FLIGHT FROM
BEIJING TO MOSCOW.
PLANE CRASHES, PERHAPS SHOT
DOWN BY CHINESE FIGHTERS,
IN OUTER MONGOLIA

HEILONGJIANG

JILIN

LIANONING

NORTH
KOREA

SOUTH
KOREA

XINJIANG

INNER MONGOLIA

**Beijing**

*1966-*
MAO ZEDONG REVIEWS 11 MILLION
RED GUARDS IN A SERIES OF
PARADES IN TIANANMEN SQUARE

*HUANG HE*

HEBEI

SHANXI

SHANDONG

C H I N A

**Yan'an**

NINGXIA-HUI

YELLOW SEA

QHINGHAI

*FEB 1967*
SHANGHAI:
REVOLUTIONARY
COMMUNE DECLARED

SHAANXI

HENAN

ANHUI

**Shanghai**

TIBET

SICHUAN

*1976*
COLLAPSE OF AGRICULTURAL
PRODUCTION LEADS TO
WIDESPREAD FAMINE

**Wuhan**

ZHEJIANG

*CHANG JIANG (YANGTZE)*

**Lhasa**

NEPAL

BHUTAN

HUNAN

**Zunyi** **Shao-shan**

JIANGXI

FUJIAN

**Jinggangshan**

TAIWAN

INDIA

BANGLADESH

GUIZHOU

YUNNAN

GUANGXI-ZHUANG

*JUNE 1966*
MAO ZEDONG
DEMONSTRATES HIS
VITALITY BY
SWIMMING 15 MILES
DOWN THE YANGTZE RIVER

*1967*
PEOPLE'S LIBERATION ARMY
AND RED GUARDS CLASH IN
STREETS OF CITY

BURMA

LAOS

BAY OF BENGAL

THAILAND

VIETNAM

PHILIPPINES

CAMBODIA

Provinces with revolutionary
committees installed (1967)

Provinces with revolutionary
committees installed (1968)

Red Guards perform proselytizing
'Long Marches'

SOUTH CHINA SEA

| 0 | 250 | 500 | 750 | 1000 Miles |

| 0 | 250 | 500 | 750 | 1000 | 1250 Kilometres |

# The Little Red Book

The Red Guards, brandishing their Little Red Books, proclaim 'Hail the defeat of revisionism in our China'. The poster dates from 1967, a year after the Cultural Revolution began.

*Quotations from Chairman Mao Zedong*, the famous little red book brandished throughout the Cultural Revolution, is the prayer book of the guerilla. Each aphoristic paragraph is designed to guide the true believer in Maoism down the right path to the revolution. Whereas Marx and Lenin sustained their arguments with analysis and saw themselves as promoting a 'scientific' dialectic, Mao's best remembered work is a compendium of recipes without reasons 312 pages long.

It first appeared in Chinese in May 1964 and was destined for use by the People's Liberation Army. Most of the quotations were selected by Hsiao Hua, who was then the Director of the General Political Department of the PLS, from the four-volume set of Mao's *Selected Works*. The second edition appeared in 1966, just in time to be clasped to the collective bosom of the Red Guards as they swarmed through Tiananmen Square.

The 5 x 3 inch volume was bound in paper and supplied with a red plastic cover - hence its nickname. Its 33 chapters are organized under such inspiring headings as 'Leadership of Party Committees' and 'Democracy in the Three Main Fields'. 'All reactionaries are paper tigers,' it vigorously proclaims.

knew very little; and it is for this reason that Mao was driven to go above the heads of the party and to rely on the young to scour the Augean stable.

## Bombarding the Headquarters

Mao later traced the start of the Cultural Revolution to a piece of dramatic criticism which he had authorized. Wu Han, vice-mayor of Beijing and a scholar and historian, had published a play that was seen by some as an oblique criticism of Mao's dismissal of his Minister of Defence in 1959.

Beijing was viewed by Mao as a hotbed of revisionism under the control of its mayor, Peng Zhen, the Politburo member responsible for propaganda and fifth in the party hierarchy. Mao became more and more irritated by the inability of the party machine to defend him against what he saw as a veiled attack. At a Politburo meeting in September 1965, he lost his patience and insisted that Peng Zhen organize a committee to prepare a report criticizing Wu's play. This put Peng in a difficult position, since Wu was a member of his own faction. He decided to do nothing.

In the meantime, however, Mao had authorized his wife to commission a criticism of Wu's play from Yao Wenyuan, a radical who was subsequently linked with Jiang as one of the infamous 'Gang of Four'. On 10 November Yao's article was published at Mao's insistence in two Shanghai papers controlled by a radical faction. Peng, unaware of Mao's involvement, was furious and demanded that the radicals in Shanghai be disciplined for publishing the article without proper authorization from the leadership. To counteract Yao's plea for censorship, in February 1966 Peng persuaded the Politburo to approve a document allowing members the right of criticism. Meanwhile one of the leading radicals, the Minister of Defence, Lin Biao, had commissioned Jiang Qing to organize a forum that would prepare a document on literature and art for the army. This pamphlet directly contradicted Peng's liberal position, and both papers circulated in the party. Then, in March, while Liu Shaoqi was abroad, Mao moved directly against Peng at a Politburo meeting. At a meeting of the Party Secretariat a few weeks later, with Peng on the defensive, Mao attacked again, helping to

loosen the revisionists' hold on the party's Propaganda Department, which Peng had run. The way was now open for Mao to spread his message unhindered.

The first shot in the campaign against revisionism was fired by Zhou Enlai in his May Day speech proclaiming the Cultural Revolution. On 7 May, Mao sent Lin a directive announcing that the army was 'a great school' teaching the people how 'to criticize the bourgeoisie'. On the 16th the Politburo issued a circular which clearly defined the enemy within: 'Those representatives of the bourgeoisie who have sneaked into the party, the government, the army and various cultural circles are a bunch of counter-revolutionary revisionists.' Two days later, Lin Biao intensified the attack by naming, in a secret speech, the army's Chief of Staff, two other revisionists and Peng as conspirators in a planned *coup d'état*. Now that Peng had lost control of the paper, the *People's Daily* was publishing photographs of Mao with Lin Biao, Deng Xiaoping and Zhou Enlai - but never with Liu Shaoqi, who had been isolated. And, towards the end of the month, a new phase began in the battle between the radicals behind Mao and the revisionists behind Liu: now the struggle was broadcast beyond the enclaves of party cadres to the whole nation.

On 25 May, a poster entitled 'Bombard the Headquarters' was pasted on a wall of Beijing University by a small group from the Philosophy Department (it later transpired that they had been prompted by Mao's wife). The poster attacked the university president, a nominee of Peng's, with unrestrained vigour, accusing him of preventing the revolutionary intellectuals from defending Mao against 'the attacks of a sinister reactionary gang'. News of this act of defiance raced through the city's student community, and within hours thousands of posters were being produced.

Liu Shaoqi, still Mao's deputy, responded by despatching some four hundred teams of party cadres to restrain the enthusiasm of students throughout the country. But Mao had no intention of being thwarted; and on 1 June, at his insistence, Beijing Radio broadcast the text of the first poster.

Mao's solidarity with the students was further underlined by one of the most spectacular public relations stunts of the twentieth century. On 16 June, assisted by the fast-flowing current and accompanied by hundreds of young people, the leader swam the Yangzi River at Hankou, covering fifteen kilometres in an hour. The next day, the exploit was emblazoned in red ink across the front pages of China's newspapers. All school and university classes were closed so that students could devote themselves to the Cultural Revolution.

On 29 May a group of students at the Middle School attached to Tsinghua University in Beijing had begun wearing armbands labelling themselves 'Red Guards'. The idea caught on, and such units started to appear all over the capital. On 1 August Mao convened a plenary session of the Central Committee and simultaneously published an open letter praising the students, in which he used the phrase 'Red Guards'. On 5 August Mao nailed his own poster entitled 'Bombard the Headquarters' to the door of the room in which the Central Committee met.

### The Devil Wore Red

On 18 August 1966, in the early light of morning, Mao and Lin Biao left the seclusion of their compound in the old Imperial Palace and entered the adjacent Tiananmen Square. Confronting them were a million eager faces; the Red Guards were on the move. Later Mao had to admit that 'nobody - not even I - expected that all the provinces and cities would be thrown into confusion'. That first benign gathering was soon the exception rather than the rule, as gangs of Red Guards terrorized the streets of urban China. Only those at the top seemed safe from physical abuse, and even they were called to account for their 'mistakes'.

Soon several factions of Red Guards developed in Beijing as different elements within the party hierarchy launched their own Red Guard units to protect their interests. At first they fought each other with sticks and stones, but later they used guns stolen from the army.

By autumn 1966 Mao was alarmed by the chaos he had unleashed. He was satisfied that Liu Shaoqi and Deng Xiaoping had been stigmatized as 'number one and number two capitalist roaders', but he realized that the extremists had to be controlled.

Early in 1967 revolutionary factions took over twenty ministries, including that of foreign affairs, and the Soviet Embassy was surrounded. Moscow responded by issuing a threatening communiqué and moving its

The moderate Maoist, Zhou Enlai, in Beijing, 1971. He was Prime Minister of China from 1949 until his death in 1976.

troops up to the border with China. Meanwhile, workers in Shanghai had divided into two warring factions; in January, the radicals emerged on top. The following month they proclaimed the Shanghai Commune, in commemoration of its Parisian predecessor. This was too much for Mao, who summoned the leaders to Beijing where he called them anarchists; instead of their proposed system, he insisted on 'the three-way revolutionary committee' in which Red Guards, approved party officials and military representatives would balance one another.

By September 1967, on a tour of China,

Mao was calling the Red Guards 'politically immature' and 'incompetent'. He allowed Zhou to attempt to reimpose party discipline, but this was now extremely difficult - particularly since Mao could not bear to dismiss the radicals close to him, who included his own wife. By summer 1968 open warfare had broken out in parts of the south. There was no alternative but to use the People's Liberation Army to restore order.

### The Last Act

The army's first move was to disarm the warring factions. They then sent small groups into the schools that were still open in order to keep discipline. However, it soon became apparent that the only way to close down the Red Guards was to send them to the country.

The Ninth Party Congress was convened in considerable secrecy in April 1969. This was the high-water mark of Lin Biao's career, and he was proclaimed as Mao's successor. At the time, Liu Shaoqi was being held under guard in the provinces, and Deng Xiaoping was working as a labourer in a tractor factory. The Congress also witnessed Zhou Enlai's return to favour and he began reinstating those who had suffered in the early months of the Cultural Revolution.

Meanwhile, China was suffering on account of isolationism as skirmishes were fought on the north-eastern border with the Soviet Union. Beijing had no obvious ally and, since America was beginning to withdraw from Vietnam, moves were made to bring the two countries together. This undermined the position of Lin Biao, in effect the apostle of isolation, and enhanced that of the much more pragmatic and conciliatory Zhou. According to Beijing, Lin panicked and tried to assassinate Mao, but failed; he then fled to Moscow but his plane crashed, killing all on board, in September 1971. The truth of this story, which is impossible to verify, tainted Mao, for Lin was his protégé.

Zhou continued to rebuild the party, even managing to get Deng reinstated. But Zhou was suffering from cancer and his death in January 1976 left a power vacuum in Beijing. The people were incensed by the perfunctory official mourning, for Zhou was one of the best-loved leaders in Chinese history; and on 5 April, China's day for remembering the dead, a spontaneous demonstration in Tiananmen Square caught the leadership off guard. It gave the radicals another excuse to attack Deng, whom they once again forced out of power.

Mao, however, did not turn to them for a new leader but promoted a relative nonentity, Hua Guofeng. But even Mao's days were numbered, and less than six months later he too had died. Within weeks the party moved to deal with his widow and her radical clique once and for all. On 4 October 1976 the infamous 'Gang of Four' were arrested, and when the people heard the news they celebrated in the streets.

'Spring Hoeing' painted by Li Feng-Lan, who was a member of the people's commune in Huhsien county. The painting, which is a celebration of Chairman Mao's proletarian revolutionary line, extols the virtues of the 'socialist new countryside'.

# The Vietnam War

Vietnam is where the United States determined to stem the tide of radicalism in the developing world. It was a fateful choice. The Vietnamese had struggled successfully for two thousand years against absorption by the Chinese, and they had just thrown off a century of French rule when the Americans moved in, as alien as they were ignorant of local ways: and they did not comprehend the degree to which nationalism and Communism had become synonymous in the years of fighting the French.

## Origins

The history of Vietnamese Communism is dominated by the personality of Ho Chi Minh, the party founder and inspirational figure in its war of independence against the French. In 1920 he became a founder-member of the French Communist Party, having embraced Lenin's theory that national liberation could only be achieved through social revolution.

Ho studied revolutionary strategies in Moscow before turning up in Canton (Guangzhou) as an adviser to the Soviet mission to Sun Yat-sen. From Canton, and subsequently Siam (Thailand), he was able to proselytize his countrymen. Ho's efforts led to the creation of the Indochina Communist Party in 1930, at a time of famine and peasant insurrections that the French took almost a year to put down.

The Second World War found the Communists small in numbers, but well organized, and the only serious opposition to the Japanese and the Vichy French (after the fall of France in 1940, all French colonies came under the control of the pro-German Vichy government). Irked by French failure to contain the Viet Minh, the Japanese had assumed direct control of the country by their surrender in August 1945.

## The First Indochina War

At this point the Viet Minh seized the capital, Hanoi, and with the support of other nationalist leaders Ho proclaimed the birth of the Democratic Republic of Vietnam, with himself as head of a provisional government. Ho based his speech on the American Declaration of Independence, but the Americans did not take the hint and offer recognition. The French wanted their colony back, and British and Nationalist Chinese troops occupied parts of the south and north pending their return. In November 1946 French warships bombarded the port of Haiphong, and France set about restoring its authority. The Viet Minh retaliated by attacking French garrisons, and the country was at war.

By 1950 the Viet Minh had control of the countryside, where their land reforms made them popular with the peasantry, while the French were barricaded into the cities and towns. Ho reasserted Vietnamese independence; this time he gained the recognition of the Soviet Union and China, which since the Communist victory in 1949 had been supplying his guerrillas with arms. But he had given up hope of gaining American approval, for they were by now caught up in the Cold War, alarmed by the 'loss' of China and increasinly preoccupied with the Korean War. The US feared Communism more than it opposed colonialism, so it decided to back the French with arms and economic aid.

By 1954, the US was paying for 80 per cent of a faltering French effort. The opening in May of an international conference on Indochina in Geneva coincided with the spectacular French defeat at Dien Bien Phu. The conference put together the Geneva Accord, a ceasefire agreement tied to French withdrawal and the temporary partition of Vietnam at the 17th Parallel, with national reunification elections to follow in 1956. Since it was clear that these elections would bring Ho to power, non-Viet Minh elements feared their consequences. So did the United States, which guaranteed support for the Catholic leader Ngo Dinh Diem when, in October 1955, he seized power in the new southern capital of Saigon and proclaimed a Republic of Vietnam, thus perpetuating the partition. When Diem began to reverse the land reforms and hand back what had been redistributed, Viet Minh activists still in the south became guerrillas once more and set about assassinating government officials.

The Communists were now convinced that the country could only be reunited by force, and in December 1960 they launched the National Liberation Front of South Vietnam (NLF), popularly known as the Viet Cong and closely modelled on the former Viet Minh. As insurrection aid began to trickle down what became known as the Ho Chi Minh Trail - a network of jungle paths through Laos and Cambodia - American support for Diem and his army increased dramatically under the new Kennedy administration.

By 1963 the US was providing the Diem government with over $1000 million a year, and fifteen thousand American military advisers were devising 'pacification' such as the Strategic Hamlets Programme - an attempt to remove the peasants from contact with the Viet Cong by driving them into specially

## Ho Chi Minh: Father of Vietnam

Nguyen That Tank adopted the pseudonym by which he has become known to the world during the Second World War when he slipped back into French Indochina. Much of his life had been spent in Comintern activity outside his homeland from which he was exiled because of his revolutionary views. His leadership of the Viet Minh was undisputed, but he chose to bide his time until the French were ousted by the Japanese in 1945. He then won the support of the OSS, the American secret service group which preceded the CIA, for guerrilla operations against the Japanese. Once the war was over, Ho proclaimed his country's independence at a rally in Hanoi, Vietnam's capital. But the French refused to accept this and the country was soon

President Ho Chi Minh, affectionately known as 'Uncle Ho', talking to the people of North Vietnam during the war.

plunged into war again. Ho spent most of the rest of his life leading his people in the fight against imperialism; first against the French and then the Americans. He was hugely popular with his people and never lost their support. He died in 1969.

constructed and guarded villages. As a consequence Diem became more reviled and the Viet Cong more admired, and when the Buddhists turned against him, and his forces attacked their temples, Washington despaired of the man it had tried to promote as a champion of freedom. On 1 November 1963 Diem was overthrown in a military coup, and shot. The Communists in Hanoi offered to negotiate with his successors, but increased support for the Viet Cong when the offer was not taken up.

By 1964 the Viet Cong controlled 40 per cent of South Vietnam, and regular North Vietnamese army units had begun to infiltrate south of the 17th Parallel. In Saigon the elimination of Diem did nothing to stop the political rot, and a series of inept military juntas quickly succeeded one another.

### US Intervention

Lyndon Johnson, who had succeeded the assassinated President Kennedy in November 1963, was advised that direct American intervention was needed to stop South Vietnam falling to the Communists. In August 1964 he ordered the first US air strikes on the North, on the pretext of a supposed Communist attack on American warships in the Gulf of Tonkin. Sustained bombing was authorized six months later, and intensified to such a degree that in three years of the 'Rolling Thunder' air campaign more bombs were dropped on North Vietnam than were used throughout the Second World War. The South was also pounded in an attempt to flush out the elusive Viet Cong. In five years the two Vietnams received the equivalent of 22 tons of bombs for every square mile, or 300 lb of explosives for every man, woman and child. In the South, waves of giant B-52 strategic bombers were used against areas of suspected Viet Cong activity.

In fact, the B-52s dropping their 30-ton loads from 30,000 feet were grossly inaccurate and ineffective, except in generating terror and hatred. The commitment of American ground forces likewise grew out of all expectations, and by mid-1965 they were engaged in heavy fighting in the Central Highlands and along the coast. In the course of that year, the number of US military personnel in Vietnam jumped from 23,300 to 184,000. In 1966 it exceeded 385,000, and reached a peak of 542,400 in January 1969 when Richard Nixon assumed the presidency.

The American forces had some early successes; but they became disheartened by the resilience and elusiveness of the Viet Cong, who relied on small-scale night raids and disappeared back into the forests by day. So the Americans resorted to search-and-destroy tactics, in which friend was as likely to suffer as foe, and success was measured by a 'body-count' that did not always differentiate between the two. When the search operation moved on, the Viet Cong quickly re-established control, and US patrols would be ambushed as before.

A badly wounded North Vietnamese soldier is carried off by American marines at Hué, 1968. By the end of 1968 the war was costing the United States some $30 billion a year.

The US Chiefs of Staff were convinced that sheer weight of firepower would turn the tide. However, the indiscriminate use of napalm, cluster bombs and corrosive chemicals to eradicate guerrilla cover limited their capacity to win 'hearts and minds'; while the more they propped up dubious regimes in Saigon, the more the Communists were able to appeal successfully to Vietnamese nationalism.

### The Tet Offensive

By January 1968, half a million American troops, supported by massive air power, were caught in the Vietnamese mire, their sophisticated weaponry and tactics ineffective against the invisible enemy. On the 31st, the Communists launched a sustained offensive to coincide with Tet, the New Year festival. The scope of the synchronized attack on all major cities and scores of other towns stunned the Americans, even though most of the terrified inhabitants of these places remained passive and did not respond to the Communist call for a mass uprising. In Saigon parts of the American Embassy itself were occupied, and the massed media in the capital provided the world with an unprecedented armchair view of the battle as the Viet Cong held off US and South Vietnamese forces for several days. Viet Cong troops held Hué, the former imperial capital, until American firepower had reduced the city to rubble. Questioned about the similar destruction of Ben Tre, a provincial capital, the American

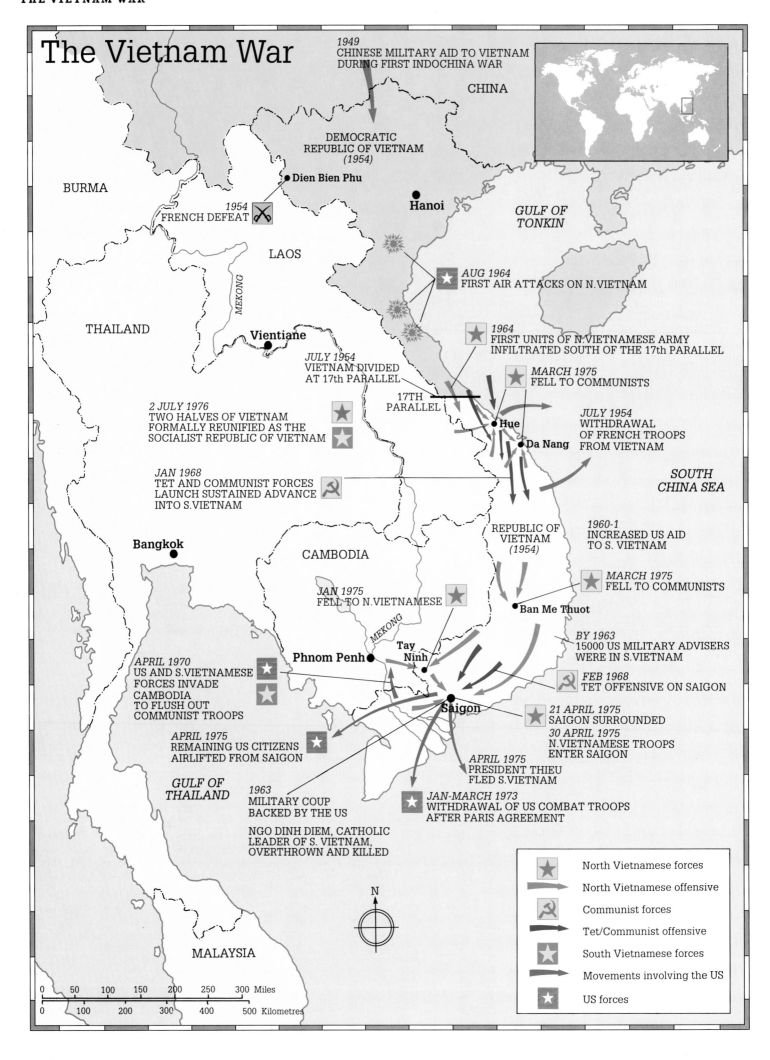

# The Vietnam War

*1949*
CHINESE MILITARY AID TO VIETNAM
DURING FIRST INDOCHINA WAR

CHINA

DEMOCRATIC
REPUBLIC OF VIETNAM
*(1954)*

● Dien Bien Phu

● **Hanoi**

*GULF OF
TONKIN*

BURMA

*1954*
FRENCH DEFEAT ✕

LAOS

MEKONG

THAILAND

**Vientiane** ●

*JULY 1954*
VIETNAM DIVIDED
AT 17th PARALLEL

*AUG 1964*
FIRST AIR ATTACKS ON N.VIETNAM

*1964*
FIRST UNITS OF N.VIETNAMESE ARMY
INFILTRATED SOUTH OF THE 17th PARALLEL

*MARCH 1975*
FELL TO COMMUNISTS

17TH
PARALLEL

*2 JULY 1976*
TWO HALVES OF VIETNAM
FORMALLY REUNIFIED AS THE
SOCIALIST REPUBLIC OF VIETNAM

● **Hue**

● **Da Nang**

*JULY 1954*
WITHDRAWAL
OF FRENCH TROOPS
FROM VIETNAM

*SOUTH
CHINA SEA*

*JAN 1968*
TET AND COMMUNIST FORCES
LAUNCH SUSTAINED ADVANCE
INTO S.VIETNAM

REPUBLIC OF
VIETNAM
*(1954)*

*1960-1*
INCREASED US AID
TO S. VIETNAM

**Bangkok** ●

CAMBODIA

*MARCH 1975*
FELL TO COMMUNISTS

*JAN 1975*
FELL TO N.VIETNAMESE

● **Ban Me Thuot**

*BY 1963*
15000 US MILITARY ADVISERS
WERE IN S.VIETNAM

MEKONG

**Tay
Ninh**

*APRIL 1970*
US AND S.VIETNAMESE
FORCES INVADE
CAMBODIA
TO FLUSH OUT
COMMUNIST TROOPS

**Phnom Penh** ●

*FEB 1968*
TET OFFENSIVE ON SAIGON

● **Saigon**

*21 APRIL 1975*
SAIGON SURROUNDED

*30 APRIL 1975*
N.VIETNAMESE TROOPS
ENTER SAIGON

*APRIL 1975*
REMAINING US CITIZENS
AIRLIFTED FROM SAIGON

*APRIL 1975*
PRESIDENT THIEU
FLED S.VIETNAM

*GULF OF
THAILAND*

*1963*
MILITARY COUP
BACKED BY THE US

NGO DINH DIEM, CATHOLIC
LEADER OF S. VIETNAM,
OVERTHROWN AND KILLED

*JAN-MARCH 1973*
WITHDRAWAL OF US COMBAT TROOPS
AFTER PARIS AGREEMENT

N

MALAYSIA

| 0 | 50 | 100 | 150 | 200 | 250 | 300 Miles |
| 0 | 100 | 200 | 300 | 400 | 500 Kilometres |

★ North Vietnamese forces
→ North Vietnamese offensive
☭ Communist forces
→ Tet/Communist offensive
★ South Vietnamese forces
→ Movements involving the US
★ US forces

As the war dragged on and the number of civilian casualties grew, it became apparant that American military power alone could not impose political solutions on a revolutionary conflict.

colonel responsible was much quoted when he explained: 'We had to destroy the town to save it.'

While Communist losses were heavy, the Tet Offensive represented a profound psychological blow in America, where people had been constantly assured that the war was being won. Now it began to be seen as unwinnable, and the cost of nearly $30 billion a year was straining the dollar and threatening a world economic crisis. Even Johnson's Defence Secretary, Robert McNamara, was seized by doubts and had to be replaced. Johnson himself did not run for re-election, but opened peace talks before being succeeded by Nixon, who set as his aim 'peace with honour'. Under Nixon the US embarked upon a convoluted strategy of extracting itself under cover of increased belligerence. As American troops were gradually withdrawn, military assistance for the South Vietnamese army was stepped up, as was bombing of the North; and, for the first time, secret bombing of Cambodia was carried out, where the Viet Cong had sanctuaries. An invasion of that country followed in April 1970.

Vietnam was the first fully televised war, and the images of napalm victims, wounded GIs and Viet Cong suspects being shot out of hand shocked public opinion, while revelations like the massacre of women and children by American troops in the village of My Lai gave strident voice to an anti-war movement. When soldiers fired a volley into American university students protesting against the Cambodia operation, killing four of them, the shock waves were felt around the world. By the early 1970s huge demonstrations against American involvement in the war were being staged throughout the world, especially in western Europe.

Ho Chi Minh had died in September 1969; in the subsequent 'detente' period of eased East-West tensions Nixon was able to persuade the Soviet Union and China to reduce their aid for the North in order to support the peace talks, which nevertheless dragged on throughout 1972. The morale of American troops declined drastically; drug-taking became widespread, discipline deteriorated and incidents of 'fragging'- murderous attacks on officers by their men - increased, along with racial tension. In a final convulsion, Hanoi and the port of Haiphong were pounded by two hundred B-52s throughout Christmas 1972. The US Congress joined in the worldwide protest, and after eleven days the bombing was stopped. The devastation was great, and bomber losses heavy too.

On 23 January 1973 a ceasefire was finally initialled in Paris, and went into effect five days later. It provided for the complete withdrawal of American forces from Vietnam, and by the end of March the last combat troops had gone. The South Vietnamese President, Nguyen Van Thieu, was left with a well-equipped army a million strong, but of uncertain resolve.

As with the Geneva Accord nineteen years before, the peace did not hold, for negotiations between Saigon and Hanoi got nowhere. In January 1974 Thieu announced that the war had resumed, and his army attacked areas under Viet Cong control. If he had hoped to bring the Americans back, he was disappointed: the US was weary of Vietnam and was embroiled in its own domestic crisis of Watergate. Throughout the latter part of 1974 the Communists built up their strength in the South, and then launched a major offensive early in 1975. Although supplied with the latest American equipment, the South's army disintegrated so fast that by

April Saigon was surrounded. On 30 April, US army helicopters evacuated the last American officials from the rooftops, and the capital fell to the Communists with hardly a shot fired. After more than thirty years of virtually continuous warfare, Vietnam was independent, unified - and Communist.

## Aftermath

The fruits of victory were bitter. An estimated 2.6 million Vietnamese had died since the US intervention, the industrial infrastructure of the North had been shattered by 7 million tons of bombs, and defoliants had stripped bare more than 6000 square miles of the South. Regional rivalries asserted themselves. The heavy Viet Cong losses meant that Northerners played the major role in reconstruction efforts, and many of them resented the relative affluence of the South. Saigon, renamed Ho Chi Minh City, had become a city of bars, brothels and barter - in their eyes, the epitome of Western decadence. 'Re-education centres' were established, where many professionals were consigned and their skills wasted. At a Communist Party Congress in 1976, wildly unrealistic industrialization and socialization plans were adopted. The plans failed, partly because the country was denied the large-scale foreign aid that it desperately needed. And the aid that was forthcoming from the Soviet bloc was inappropriate to the country's rural needs.

In 1978 China cut off its aid, provoked by hostility towards the ethnic Chinese business community in the South and worsening relations with the Chinese-supported Khmer Rouge regime in Cambodia. Vietnam now aligned itself fully with the Soviet Union, signing a friendship treaty, joining Comecon and granting base facilities to the Soviet navy.

# Cambodia and Laos

The exquisite charms of Cambodia were never more apparent than in the 1950s and 1960s, when they seemed miraculously secure from the brutality that had engulfed the rest of Indochina. The country continued to drift in its antique serenity, protected by its Buddhist faith and the deft neutrality of its charismatic ruler Prince Norodom Sihanouk. The Viet Cong and North Vietnamese moved among the mountain tribes of the north-east, and a few bands of indigenous Communist guerrillas, mockingly dubbed by the Prince the 'Khmer Rouge', or Cambodian Reds, operated deep in the forests, but they seemed remote to the bulk of the population.

It was not to last. If the smiling, gentle Cambodians seemed to represent the Oriental ideal to Westerners, there was a dark side to their past. Two thousand years of god-kings and slave empires had bred an unquestioning obedience to authority, and centuries of conflict with their more powerful Vietnamese neighbours had instilled animosities that had not lessened in ninety years as a backwater French protectorate.

It is hardly two hundred miles from Phnom Penh to Saigon, where the United States was being driven to distraction by its elusive Communist enemy. In their exasperation, the American commanders convinced themselves that the Viet Cong and North Vietnamese were operating from a headquarters in Cambodia; the idea became so real in their minds that they gave it the acronym COSVN, for 'Central Office South Vietnam'. In the early morning of 18 March 1969, under secret orders from President Nixon, forty-eight giant B-52 bombers from Anderson Air Force Base on the Pacific island of Guam violated Cambodian neutrality to flatten the suspected headquarters site.

No COSVN was ever found, but the bombers kept on coming, increasing in intensity to reach a climax in 1973. By then, the country had been pulverized and Sihanouk overthrown; and the obscure Khmer Rouge had emerged from the forests with genocidal notions of how to create a better world. A third or more of Cambodia's population was to perish as a consequence of these mad human engineers, and of the actions of those who drove them mad.

### The Roots of Cambodian Communism

There was little political activity in Cambodia until 1930 and the creation of Ho Chi Minh's Communist Party of Indochina (IPC), with its declared intention of struggling 'for the complete independence of Indochina and for

Prince Sihanouk, titular head of the Cambodian government in exile, speaking in New York in 1979.

land for the peasants'. Since the French ran Vietnam, Cambodia and Laos as a single unit there was some sense in this, but the Cambodians remembered the past and never shook free the suspicion that 'Uncle Ho' was bent upon Vietnamese hegemony over Cambodia. The IPC drew most of its recruits from the Vietnamese minority in the country, and as late as 1950 there were reckoned to be only fifty Cambodian members of the party.

While Ho confronted the French in classic revolutionary style, the colourful, crafty Sihanouk found other ways of achieving the liberation of his country. The Prince had spent the Second World War as a meek vassal of the Vichy French and their masters, the Japanese. The French reasserted themselves after the Japanese surrender, but became so pressed by the war with Ho that in 1953 Sihanouk persuaded them to agree to Cambodian independence. International recognition of Cambodian neutrality followed at the 1954 Geneva peace conference, which provided for the withdrawal of all units of Ho's Viet Minh forces then in the country, and the disbanding of the few indigenous Communist groups in the jungle.

Sihanouk retained his personal power by abdicating the throne and forming a political movement, the Sangkum or People's Socialist Community, that was a bundle of contradictions secured by his semi-divine status and immense popularity with the peasantry. He called his policy 'extreme neutrality', and for fifteen years he played his neighbours off against one another, at first accepting American aid and tutelage, but shifting leftward as the US began to lose its grip in South Vietnam. In 1965, suspicious of CIA involvement in plots against him, Sihanouk broke off diplomatic relations with

the US and aligned Cambodia more closely with China and North Vietnam; at the same time he treated his own radical left with increasing harshness, and savagely put down a peasant revolt in 1967 in the western province of Battambang.

A few guerrillas had stayed put in the jungle after the Geneva settlement. They now provided sanctuary to a growing number of disillusioned left-wingers, including a close-knit group of Paris-educated intellectuals whose distrust of the Vietnamese Communists hardened when Sihanouk allied himself with Hanoi. This disaffected group included Saloth Sar (Pol Pot), Ieng Sary, Son Sen and Khieu Samphan - the future leadership of the Khmer Rouge. Unlike the situation in Vietnam, most peasants in Cambodia owned their own land, but many were crippled by debt and there was enough inequality for the Paris group to brood over the iniquities of feudal and colonial exploitation, and endlessly to debate their cure.

### Fateful Coup

Massive American operations in South Vietnam were now pushing more Communist forces over the border. US bombers came in pursuit, driving the Communists deeper into Cambodia to escape the bombardment. Sihanouk's balancing act became ever more precarious. In June 1969 he agreed to restore relations with Washington, and appointed a new government under General Lon Nol, who as his Defence Minister had both harried the Communists and privately profited from their arms traffic.

In March 1970 Lon Nol led a right-wing military coup that ousted Sihanouk while he was on a trip to Moscow and Beijing. Neutralism was abandoned as Lon Nol sided

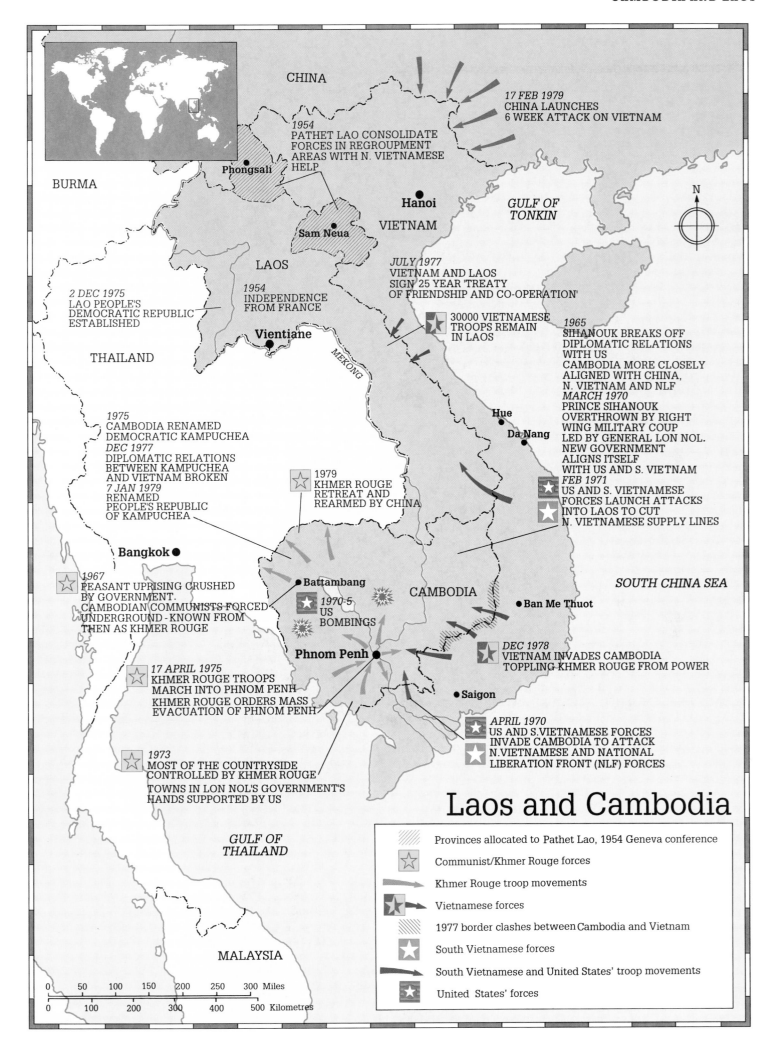

CHINA

17 FEB 1979
CHINA LAUNCHES
6 WEEK ATTACK ON VIETNAM

*1954*
PATHET LAO CONSOLIDATE
FORCES IN REGROUPMENT
AREAS WITH N. VIETNAMESE
HELP

Phongsali

BURMA

**Hanoi**

Sam Neua

*GULF OF
TONKIN*

VIETNAM

LAOS

*JULY 1977*
VIETNAM AND LAOS
SIGN 25 YEAR 'TREATY
OF FRIENDSHIP AND CO-OPERATION'

*2 DEC 1975*
LAO PEOPLE'S
DEMOCRATIC REPUBLIC
ESTABLISHED

*1954*
INDEPENDENCE
FROM FRANCE

30000 VIETNAMESE
TROOPS REMAIN
IN LAOS

*1965*
SIHANOUK BREAKS OFF
DIPLOMATIC RELATIONS
WITH US
CAMBODIA MORE CLOSELY
ALIGNED WITH CHINA,
N. VIETNAM AND NLF
*MARCH 1970*
PRINCE SIHANOUK
OVERTHROWN BY RIGHT
WING MILITARY COUP
LED BY GENERAL LON NOL.
NEW GOVERNMENT
ALIGNS ITSELF
WITH US AND S. VIETNAM
*FEB 1971*
US AND S. VIETNAMESE
FORCES LAUNCH ATTACKS
INTO LAOS TO CUT
N. VIETNAMESE SUPPLY LINES

**Vientiane**

THAILAND

MEKONG

Hue

Da Nang

*1975*
CAMBODIA RENAMED
DEMOCRATIC KAMPUCHEA
*DEC 1977*
DIPLOMATIC RELATIONS
BETWEEN KAMPUCHEA
AND VIETNAM BROKEN
*7 JAN 1979*
RENAMED
PEOPLE'S REPUBLIC
OF KAMPUCHEA

*1979*
KHMER ROUGE
RETREAT AND
REARMED BY CHINA

**Bangkok** ●

*SOUTH CHINA SEA*

*1967*
PEASANT UPRISING CRUSHED
BY GOVERNMENT.
CAMBODIAN COMMUNISTS FORCED
UNDERGROUND - KNOWN FROM
THEN AS KHMER ROUGE

● Battambang

*1970-5*
US
BOMBINGS

CAMBODIA

● Ban Me Thuot

*DEC 1978*
VIETNAM INVADES CAMBODIA
TOPPLING KHMER ROUGE FROM POWER

**Phnom Penh** ●

*17 APRIL 1975*
KHMER ROUGE TROOPS
MARCH INTO PHNOM PENH
KHMER ROUGE ORDERS MASS
EVACUATION OF PHNOM PENH

● Saigon

*APRIL 1970*
US AND S.VIETNAMESE FORCES
INVADE CAMBODIA TO ATTACK
N.VIETNAMESE AND NATIONAL
LIBERATION FRONT (NLF) FORCES

*1973*
MOST OF THE COUNTRYSIDE
CONTROLLED BY KHMER ROUGE
TOWNS IN LON NOL'S GOVERNMENT'S
HANDS SUPPORTED BY US

*GULF OF
THAILAND*

# Laos and Cambodia

| | |
|---|---|
| ▨ | Provinces allocated to Pathet Lao, 1954 Geneva conference |
| ☆ | Communist/Khmer Rouge forces |
| ➤ | Khmer Rouge troop movements |
| ★➤ | Vietnamese forces |
| ▨ | 1977 border clashes between Cambodia and Vietnam |
| ★ | South Vietnamese forces |
| ➤ | South Vietnamese and United States' troop movements |
| ★ | United States' forces |

MALAYSIA

| 0 | 50 | 100 | 150 | 200 | 250 | 300 Miles |
|---|---|---|---|---|---|---|

| 0 | 100 | 200 | 300 | 400 | 500 Kilometres |
|---|---|---|---|---|---|

openly with the US and South Vietnam, and took a hostile attitude towards North Vietnam and the Viet Cong. While the urban elite and officer corps had grown tired of Sihanouk's autocratic antics and intolerance of criticism, the Prince's overthrow was sacrilege to the peasant masses.

In a fit of pique, Sihanouk now allied himself with his former enemies. At a stroke the little band of Khmer Rouge gained national appeal and the backing of the North Vietnamese. The US mounted a two-month invasion of Cambodia that wrought much havoc, but failed to flush out the enemy and further alienated the people from Lon Nol. More and more flocked to support Sihanouk's National United Front and the exile government he set up in Beijing, but as the Front expanded it was the Khmer Rouge who took firm control. Sihanouk's movements were soon restricted, and he was to spend years under house arrest.

The Communists quickly gained half the country, and by mounting an offensive each spring dry season they set about the gradual strangulation of Phnom Penh. By the end of 1972 the Vietnamese role was reduced to the supply and training of the Khmer Rouge, whose endurance and bravery was matched only by their ruthlessness.

Having purged all of its pro-Vietnam elements, the Khmer Rouge was a stridently nationalist party as much as a Communist one, resentful as well as distrustful of the Vietnamese, and now possessed by a maniacal resolve. Throughout the 1973 monsoon Khmer Rouge fighters pressed on with a near suicidal attack under saturation bombing, even though they were aware that the US would shortly be obliged to desist because of opposition to the bombing from its own Congress.

Slowly, Phnom Penh was throttled to death. All roads into the capital were cut, and then the Mekong was blocked: the last river convoy got through just after Christmas 1974. The end came on 17 April 1975, thirteen days before Saigon fell to the Vietnamese Communists. Lines of young, exhausted Khmer Rouge, all in black and wearing checked scarves and sandals, and shouldering AK-47s, strode into Phnom Penh from all sides. Methodically they secured the city and then ordered everyone out, even the dying in the fetid hospitals. That night, more than 2 million people were sent streaming into the countryside with neither food nor possessions. They were told that this was Year Zero, and that Angka - the Organization - ruled and would provide for a new future.

### The Massacre

For the next three years, Cambodia, renamed Democratic Kampuchea, was almost completely cut off from the outside world. Towns were abandoned and formal education abolished. Supporters of the Lon Nol regime, members of the middle classes and Western-educated intellectuals or professionals

('the worthless ones') were exterminated in their thousands; so were ethnic minorities such as the Chinese, Vietnamese and the Muslim Cham. Peasants were rounded up and herded into vast agricultural co-operatives, where all vestiges of individualism, even family life, were discouraged. The urban deportees, known as 'new people', were forced to work under inhuman conditions on huge irrigation sites, risking sudden punishment, including execution, for even minor infractions of stern rules of behaviour. The American bomb craters found a use - as body dumps.

The apparent intention of the Khmer Rouge was to attain a super-pure form of Communist nationalism, through the obliteration of all past associations, allegiances and culture. Between 1 and 3 million Cambodians died in a demented implementation of this policy: hundreds of thousands were butchered in cold blood, while the rest were killed off by the disease and famine that resulted from the total dislocation. It was not until 1977 that Pol Pot emerged as undisputed leader of the grisly regime. Forty-nine and quiet-spoken, he had studied in Paris and worked as a schoolteacher and journalist before fleeing to join the guerrillas in 1963. The influence of Mao Zedong clearly showed in his rhetoric.

The only ally the Khmer Rouge had was China - mainly because, as one exiled Cambodian blandly put it, 'The Khmer Rouge are good Vietnamese killers.' China so

deeply resented Vietnam for aligning itself with the Soviet Union that it was able even to pass over the slaughter of Cambodia's Chinese. The rest of the Communist world refused to recognize Democratic Kampuchea. The West, which was just beginning to enjoy warmer relations with China, stayed largely silent.

Khmer Rouge relations with Vietnam deteriorated steadily. There were territorial disputes and increasingly serious border clashes, and Angka purged itself of thousands of alleged Vietnamese agents - to have any Vietnamese associations at all was a death sentence. In December 1977 Phnom Penh severed diplomatic relations with Hanoi, and the following month Vietnam launched a raid across the border, using tanks and artillery left by the Americans. The Cambodians relied upon tried guerrilla tactics to halt the drive, but a year later a second massive attack succeeded in taking Phnom Penh and toppling Pol Pot. The Khmer Rouge fled back to the jungles, to regroup and wage a new guerrilla war against the Vietnamese and Heng Samrin, a Khmer Rouge defector set up as the nominal ruler.

### Communism in Laos

It has been argued that Cambodia became Communist almost entirely because of American intervention, rather than Communist subversion. This was also largely true of Laos. With their comic opera courts,

## Apprenticeship for Genocide

Pol Pot was born Saloth Sar in the Year of the Dragon, 1928. Although he had every opportunity to get a good education, his academic record was poor. After completing high school, he enroled at a technical college in Phnom Penh and studied carpentry. But through influence he managed to get a scholarship to study in Paris, where he became involved in the activities of the French Communist Party. He stayed in Paris from 1949 to 1952 and then returned to Phnom Penh where he joined a clandestine cell of the Indochinese Communist Party which worked within the nationalist movement. In 1960 the Vietnamese and Cambodian Communists went their separate ways and the Workers Party of Kampuchea was formed. At the Second Party Congress in 1963, Pol Pot became the Party leader.

In 1967, changes to the taxation of rice upset the peasants and the Communists decided to exploit the situation. But Pol Pot got no help from Moscow, which was pursuing peaceful co-existence,

The enigmatic Pol Pot and (right) a grotesque reminder of the thousands butchered during the Khmer Rouge's tyrannical rule.

or Beijing, which threw in its lot with Prince Sihanouk, who christened the Communists the Khmer Rouge. Pol Pot then led them into the hills of the north-east, which were poor in resources and covered in almost inpenetrable jungle. In this environment they turned necessity into virtue and became intensely proud of their self-sufficiency and deeply resentful

of foreign influences, particularly the Vietnamese. Although he had to accept their help between 1970 and 1973, Pol Pot appealed to Khmer nationalism as soon as his forces were strong enough. Any cadres who had been trained by the Vietnamese were marked men and many were murdered even before the 1975 victory. However, this was as nothing to the blood bath to come.

sacred elephants and orange-robed monks, the two countries offered a sharp contrast with Vietnam, where Communism had been a vital force since the 1920s. But while Cambodia played no major role in the war against the French, northern Laos was vital to the war strategy of the Viet Minh, who at times directed the Laotian Communist forces, the Pathet Lao. In the final battle of Dien Bien Phu, the Pathet Lao played an important support role in blocking French attempts to relieve their beleaguered garrison.

The origins of Communism in Laos can be traced to Ho Chi Minh's Indochinese Communist Party of 1930. Support then was lukewarm, but from the very beginning there were such close links with the Vietnamese Communists that experts have debated whether the Communist movement in Laos should be considered as a separate entity. As elsewhere, the Second World War provided a spur to radical endeavour, and a royal prince emerged as leader of an anti-French group. This was Prince Souphanouvong, who after the war took to the jungle and linked up with Ho's Viet Minh. Souphanouvong was exceptional: the rest of the royal family and their officials were content to continue to co-operate with the Vichy French.

When the French withdrew from Vietnam after Dien Bien Phu, they had no interest in maintaining control of Laos but preferred to transfer power to the traditional elite. The problem lay in the north, where the Communists were strong, so a compromise was agreed at Geneva in 1954: the Pathet Lao forces were to be allocated two north eastern provinces as regroupment areas, in the hope that they would eventually be integrated into a national army.

It was an impractical compromise that neither side was eager to implement. When elections in 1958 resulted in a strong swing to the left, a period of political chaos followed in which a centrist Prime Minister, Prince Souvanna Phouma, was ousted by the right. A series of short-lived right-wing coups followed before Phouma was able to return in 1962 and form a broad coalition with the Pathet Lao, the centre and the right.

Over the next decade the Communists pursued a fluid political strategy, participating in or opposing the government in Vientiane, the capital, and resorting to whatever coalition was necessary to maintain Laotian neutrality and so avoid US military intervention. Nevertheless by 1969 Laos had been torn apart by the Vietnam War, its people driven into camps and its society in tatters. That year, US warplanes made 242,000 sorties against Communist-held areas in Laos, including that country's stretch of the Ho Chi Minh Trail; the onslaught had escalated from a mere 136,000 sorties in 1968. The following year President Nixon expanded the 'free fire zone' in Laos and sent B-52s over the heavily populated Plain of Jars for the first time. After an inept invasion of Laos by South Vietnamese forces in February 1971, reliance on bombing increased still further. In Vientiane, the US

*Top:* Helicopters evacuate some of the wounded from the beseiged town of Neak Luong, on the Mekong River, March 1975. Once Neak Luong had fallen, the surrender of Phnom Penh was inevitable. *Above:* The arrival of the Khmer Rouge in the captial in April 1975, after a siege lasting three months.

ambassador and the CIA had greater autonomy than elsewhere and were credited with virtually running their own war.

The Paris agreement of January 1973 provided for strict respect of Laotian sovereignty and political integrity, since peace was seen to depend upon maintaining the country as a neutral buffer between Vietnam and pro-Western Thailand. The following month the various left-wing factions agreed on a unified policy, which so strengthened the Communists' hand that they were able to dominate the new Provisional Government of National Unity. As a sign of changed times, when the fragile coalition peace was threatened by another right-wing coup it was an American diplomat who was able to forestall it.

In contrast to the horrors of Cambodia, non-Communist national leaders remained for some time in the Communist-led

coalition, and it was not until the fall of Saigon in 1975 that the Communists pushed for a takeover in Vientiane. On 2 December 1975 the six-hundred-year-old monarchy was abolished and the Lao People's Democratic Republic was established, with Prince Souphanouvong as President.

The Communist government faced prolonged armed resistance from members of the former Royal Lao army, as well as from disgruntled hill tribes such as the Meo. Private enterprise was severely controlled, and in the countryside there were attempts at collectivization. This alienated a large segment of the moneyed and educated classes, and an estimated two hundred thousand out of a population of 3.4 million fled. In 1977 Laos and Vietnam signed a twenty-five-year friendship treaty, and an estimated thirty thousand Vietnamese troops remained in Laos.

# 1968: The Year of Student Power

Student revolutionary gestures, protests and campaigns of disruption seemed universal in 1968. Inflamed by American conduct in Vietnam, young people in universities around the world took to the streets and occupied their colleges. Parts of Paris and Chicago became battlegrounds. Rome ground to a halt as a battle between students and police produced a monstrous traffic jam. Grosvenor Square in the heart of London's Mayfair, one of the smartest districts in the city and the home of the US Embassy, witnessed another pitched battle which went out live on the nation's early evening television news.

Yet within a few years all this energy seemed to have been dissipated and in most European cities the situation appeared to be 'business as usual'. The same was true of the United States, once President Nixon had evacuated the last troops from Vietnam and 'the boys' were home. It was an illusion, however, for this sudden eruption of energetic protest proved to be a catalyst for a number of radical groups in the years to come, including the women's movement, as well as having a profound effect on American politics and foreign policy for a generation. It also had an important effect on the role of the Communist parties of western Europe.

## Fertile Ground

The movements which led to the street protests of 1968 began to germinate in France and Britain during the late 1950s as a reaction to colonial wars which the Communist Party either colluded in or ignored. In 1956, those British left-wing intellectuals who had been reeling from revelations about Stalin had to watch helplessly as the Red Army occupied Budapest. The result was a group of radicals who were alienated from the party but nevertheless wished to express their disgust with the world as they found it. They became instrumental in forming the Campaign for Nuclear Disarmament (CND), which managed to mobilize large numbers of young people and involve them in street politics. Discontented with the limited effect of CND, the octogenarian philosopher Bertrand Russell organized the Committee of One Hundred which promoted a campaign of civil disobedience, the first of any importance in Britain since that of the suffragettes before the First World War. Although both these campaigns failed to change British policy, they were to have an inspirational effect on young German and American radicals a few years later.

The Algerian War was the catalyst for radical action in France after the Communist Party had been very slow to condemn this act of colonial suppression, which started in November 1954. French citizens who sympathized with the Liberation Front, the FLN, frequently became involved with fund-raising and then smuggled the money abroad. In 1960 the French National Student Union came out openly against the war and began organizing rallies, which were proscribed. These activities were being watched closely from across the border in West Germany, where sympathetic radicals began to collect funds in aid of the FLN, a move which forged links between left-wing radical groups in both countries outside the institutional framework of the Communist Party. Once the war ended in 1962, however, the groups of sympathizers disintegrated.

The 1950s were a time of intense social conformity in the United States and rabid anti-Communism. In Detroit, right-wing campaigners even managed to get the story of Robin Hood removed from the public library system for promoting Communist ideals, and any social dissent was liable to be branded as un-American. Only the black civil rights movement disrupted the bland veneer of the Eisenhower years, which led many white radicals to join its campaigns and learn the tactics of street confrontation.

In the autumn of 1964, on their return from a summer spent campaigning on behalf of black civil rights in the South, activists

studying at the Berkeley campus of the University of California were confronted by an administration which was determined to remove their right to promote radical causes on university property. This repressive move produced a Free Speech Movement which tried to negotiate with the university administration. But after six weeks the authorities announced further repressive measures; these provoked a rally and the occupation of university offices. The administration's response was to send in the police in full riot gear at three in the morning. This over-reaction, which was to be typical of many such confrontations, turned the students into martyrs and resulted in a strike in which the teaching staff sided with the students. A month later, the Chancellor behind the suppression moves was sacked. The following spring the movement was disbanded because it had achieved its aims.

This kind of unrest began to grow in Europe, the United States and Japan during the mid-1960s as wealth spread through the developed world and gave young people the economic enfranchisement which their parents had lacked. For those learning to make their own choices in the marketplace, the authoritarian attitudes of the older generation were no longer acceptable. Architectural students at Turin University sustained an occupation for several weeks in 1963 and won their point about more flexible staff attitudes, only to see their victory eroded by national and local politicians. Women students in Pisa protested at being

Tariq Ali, leader of the Vietnam Solidarity Committee, which protested against US action.

Daniel Cohn-Bendit, of the University of Nanterre, who was known as 'Danny the Red'.

treated as second-class citizens, and won concessions. In Britain, trouble was boiling up at the London School of Economics over the appointment of a Rhodesian as the new director during the autumn of 1966. When the chairman of the governors tried to stop a letter being sent to *The Times*, a demonstration ensued and the student representatives were not punished. It was in this excited atmosphere that the Vietnam War appeared over the political horizon.

### The Tet Offensive

The decision by the newly elected President Johnson to begin the systematic bombing of North Vietnam in February 1965 raised awareness of the conflict in the minds of the American public. Although the Free Speech Movement at Berkeley had disbanded, those who had participated in it were very prominent in the Vietnam Day Committee, which organized a massive campus teach-in during May. They went on to set up a nationwide demonstration in October 1965, which was angrily denounced by politicians in Washington. These demonstrations intimidated the older elements of the left, and the young activists became largely self-sustaining. The London School of Economics and Oxford University held their first Vietnam teach-ins during 1965. Similar protests built up during 1966 and 1967, but the turning point really came early in 1968.

On 30 January the American Defence Secretary, Robert McNamara, told the Senate Armed Services Committee that the 'combat efficiency and morale' of the National Liberation Front in South Vietnam, the Viet Cong, was falling. Such assertions were typical of the illusions fostered by the Pentagon, which was used to success in its affairs and to conducting them with a John Wayne swagger. Unfortunately, that same day - which marked the Vietnamese New Year, or Tet - the Viet Cong launched a massive offensive, backed by conventional North Vietnamese forces, against thirty-six of the forty-four large provincial towns in the south of their country. In Saigon, they even penetrated the US Embassy.

In a matter of days the credibility of the Pentagon was in tatters, and McNamara resigned a few weeks later. Claims that the Viet Cong had been thoroughly defeated during the Offensive were treated with scepticism; and because of the damage to the image of the American military reports which cast doubts on their behaviour in Vietnam surfaced in the media - previously newspaper owners had discouraged such stories, regarding them as unpatriotic. Tales of routine torture of prisoners of war and massacres of civilians were now printed. Criticism about the American aerial bombing of the North began to mount. Television networks began showing programmes which catalogued the devastation of South Vietnam and the suffering of its people. In August 1965, only 14 per cent of Americans between the ages of twenty-one and twenty-nine

The Night of the Barricades, Paris, May 1968. A spectacular show of fire and destruction in the Latin Quarter marks the transformation of the students' revolt from noisy marches to a mass insurrection.

regarded the war as a mistake. By October 1969 that number had risen to 58 per cent. News reports which used the new geostationary communications satellites to transmit their pictures across the world and into the homes of Americans and Europeans now began to have an impact. Reactions to these images became a common experience which crossed national boundaries and mortified a rising generation. The United States was becoming stigmatized as a vicious bully.

### Street-Fighting Man

The first manifestation of the changing mood provoked by the American humiliation was seen in Berlin just two weeks after the Tet Offensive began. A West German who attended the International Vietnam Congress

on 17 February, Peter Tautfest, described how the vision of a poor Third World country taking on the might of America affected delegates. 'Next to the American Embassy in Saigon the battle was raging from house to house, the NLF's flag was flying over Hué. It was said that students were mainly holding the city. There was no doubt now - the world revolution was dawning....'

Delegates to the Congress, who came from Italy, France and Britain, included the leader of the Vietnam Solidarity Committee, Tariq Ali, who was based in London, and Daniel Cohn-Bendit from the University of Nanterre on the edge of Paris. All these left-wing groups were organized outside the traditional Communist Party framework.

The lead taken in Berlin was soon followed by actions elsewhere. A demonstration in London less than four weeks later shocked

# Student Power

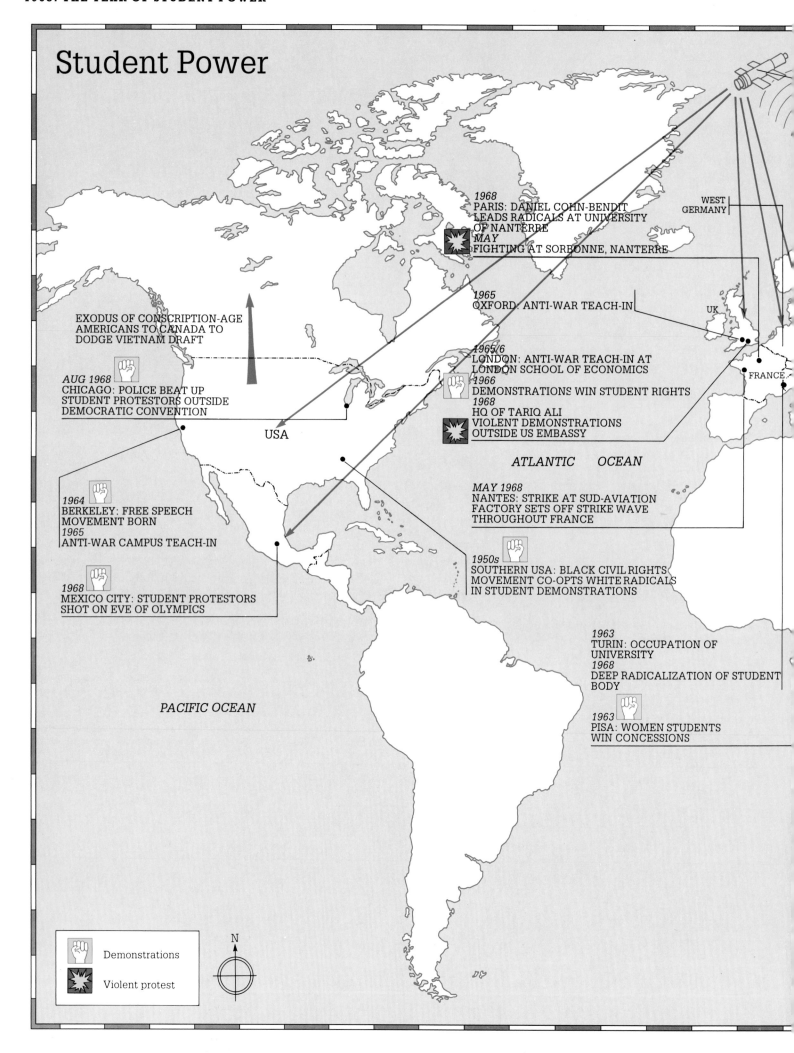

EXODUS OF CONSCRIPTION-AGE
AMERICANS TO CANADA TO
DODGE VIETNAM DRAFT

*AUG 1968*
CHICAGO: POLICE BEAT UP
STUDENT PROTESTORS OUTSIDE
DEMOCRATIC CONVENTION

USA

*1964*
BERKELEY: FREE SPEECH
MOVEMENT BORN
*1965*
ANTI-WAR CAMPUS TEACH-IN

*1968*
MEXICO CITY: STUDENT PROTESTORS
SHOT ON EVE OF OLYMPICS

*1968*
PARIS: DANIEL COHN-BENDIT
LEADS RADICALS AT UNIVERSITY
OF NANTERRE
*MAY*
FIGHTING AT SORBONNE, NANTERRE

*1965*
OXFORD: ANTI-WAR TEACH-IN

WEST
GERMANY

UK

*1965/6*
LONDON: ANTI-WAR TEACH-IN AT
LONDON SCHOOL OF ECONOMICS
*1966*
DEMONSTRATIONS WIN STUDENT RIGHTS
*1968*
HQ OF TARIQ ALI
VIOLENT DEMONSTRATIONS
OUTSIDE US EMBASSY

FRANCE

*ATLANTIC OCEAN*

*MAY 1968*
NANTES: STRIKE AT SUD-AVIATION
FACTORY SETS OFF STRIKE WAVE
THROUGHOUT FRANCE

*1950s*
SOUTHERN USA: BLACK CIVIL RIGHTS
MOVEMENT CO-OPTS WHITE RADICALS
IN STUDENT DEMONSTRATIONS

*1963*
TURIN: OCCUPATION OF
UNIVERSITY
*1968*
DEEP RADICALIZATION OF STUDENT
BODY

*1963*
PISA: WOMEN STUDENTS
WIN CONCESSIONS

*PACIFIC OCEAN*

Demonstrations

Violent protest

N

GEOSTATIONARY COMMUNICATIONS
SATELLITES BEAM REALITY OF
VIETNAM WAR INTO AMERICAN
AND EUROPEAN HOMES

*FEB 1968*
BERLIN: INTERNATIONAL
VIETNAM CONGRESS

*AUG 1968*
PRAGUE: STUDENTS ATTEMPT
TO PERSUADE SOVIET SOLDIERS
TO GO HOME

CZECHOSLOVAKIA

*MAY 1968*
DE GAULLE VISITS FRENCH ARMY ON
THE RHINE TO CONFIRM ITS LOYALTY

LY

JAPAN

*1968*
TOKYO: POLICE TEAR-GAS JAPANESE
PEACE PROTESTORS

NORTH
VIETNAM
SOUTH
VIETNAM

*1968*
TET OFFENSIVE BY VIET-CONG
UNDERMINES CREDIBILITY OF
PENTAGON'S CLAIMS TO BE
WINNING THE WAR

*1965*
US CARPET-BOMBING OF N. VIETNAM
RAISES US CONSCIOUSNESS OF WAR

*INDIAN      OCEAN*

# The Terrorist Connection

The revolutionary terrorist groups of the 1970s - the Italian Red Brigades, the Japanese Red Army group, the Baader-Meinhof Gang in West Germany, the Angry Brigade in Britain, Action Directe in France and the Weathermen and the Symbionese Liberation Army in America - all had their origins in the student protests of 1968.

The most successful and durable of these groups were the Italian Red Brigades, which originated in the north of the country in the late 1960s and carried out their first attacks in 1971. They specialized in kidnapping and assassinating prominent members of the establishment. They were at their most potent in 1978 when they abducted Aldo Moro, the leader of Italy's Christian Democrats, and a former Prime Minister. He was in the middle of a campaign urging co-operation between his party and the Communists and his capture compromised those negotiations. The Red Brigades showed their disdain for this alliance by holding Moro for fifty-five days, and then executing him.

The equivalent organization in West Germany was the Red Army Faction, dubbed the Baader-Meinhof Gang from the names of its two leaders, Andreas Baader and Ulrike Meinhof. They first came to public notice with a dramatic armed raid in May 1969 which freed Baader from the prison where he was being held after an arson attack on a department store. They followed this with a series of bombing raids, which focussed on NATO bases in West Germany. Baader and Meinhof were captured in 1972 but both committed suicide in prison: Meinhof in 1976 and Baader the following year.

the public, because the police lost control and then resorted to violence as their horses charged into the crowd under the eyes of television cameras.

A considerable momentum had already been established in Italy; here students were more concerned with the way in which their universities were run, and with social problems which they felt were being ignored by the Communist Party.

## Tear Gas in the Latin Quarter

The climax to the disturbances in western Europe came in Paris. Student militants were already active at the Sorbonne, which is situated in the Latin Quarter, not far from Notre Dame. They were also well entrenched at the University of Nanterre on the outskirts of the city. On 2 May leaflets appeared saying that the right wing were going to 'exterminate the leftist vermin' at Nanterre. A group of some two to three hundred highly organized Maoists went to the campus to protect it. When the Dean of the Faculty of Letters saw the group the following day he immediately closed the campus. Later that day, rumours circulated that right-wing groups were about to attack the Sorbonne. Students posted guards at entrances, but when the Chancellor saw these preparations he called for the police, a move unprecedented in the university's seven-hundred-year history.

The police surrounded the building and then allowed students to leave after being checked. But once the women had left, they reneged on the arrangement and bundled the men into police vans. To the astonishment of everyone, including those just arrested, the departing vans were spontaneously attacked by students outside, who had realized what had happened. The police responded by viciously attacking anyone they found in the area. The next morning's newspapers were full of stories of police brutality, and a large section of public opinion swung behind the students.

A demonstration was called for 6 May, and was backed by the university staff. But when the students tried to reach the Sorbonne, they found the area had been sealed by the police. After wandering around for some hours, the students made another attempt to reach the university and found their way blocked by French riot police, the CRS. When the police attacked they responded by tearing up cobblestones, and battle commenced. As the CRS was hated by many French people, 80 per cent of Paris was now behind the students, according to an opinion poll. The battle lasted until ten in the evening.

Another rally was called for the evening of 10 May. A crowd of twenty thousand assembled, but with no organization to direct them the students were hesitant. Then Cohn-Bendit suggested that they surround the area controlled by the police. This put the onus on

the police to attack, which would give the government more bad press coverage. The police hesitated until 2 am, but the order was finally given. By now, radio commentators were in the area and most of France listened to a blow-by-blow description as the struggle continued until dawn.

Until this point the Communist Party and the trade union organization it controlled, the CGT, had been dragging its feet. Now Cohn-Bendit called a radio station and issued a challenge: if the CGT did not call a general strike, everyone would know 'they were no longer on the people's side'. A one-day strike was called for 13 May, the tenth anniversary of President de Gaulle's accession to power, and up to a million people marched through Paris. As the day drew to a close, news reached the marchers that the CRS were leaving the Sorbonne and four students held by the police had been released. This government capitulation transformed the Latin Quarter and the party lasted all night.

Meanwhile, a group of university students and workers at the Sud Aviation factory in Nantes in western France had combined their efforts during the day of action. The next day the workers announced they were going on indefinite strike. Within three days, they had been joined by 2 million all over France; after another three days, the number had swollen to 9 million. The greatest strike in French history had erupted spontaneously, but the CGT were determined to end it.

On 24 May, de Gaulle made a speech on the radio which only seemed to confirm that he was out of touch and had lost control of the situation. That night witnessed another bloody battle with the police. Behind the scenes the Prime Minister, Pompidou, negotiated a 35 per cent rise in the minimum wage with the CGT; but this was rejected by the strikers. The climax came at the end of the month when a massive march went off peacefully in Paris. While this was in progress, de Gaulle made a secret trip to West Germany to confirm that the French army units stationed there were loyal. The next day, the 30th, he made another broadcast on radio and television to announce a general election for the end of June. The workers, meanwhile, were bought off with wage rises, a reduction in working hours and an extension of collective bargaining rights.

The election proved to be a decisive victory for the right, but their hold on France had been shaken. De Gaulle's triumph was illusory, and a year later he resigned. The Communist Party suffered heavily in the short term at the election, and in the long term because many union activists had been dismayed by its timidity - as were the left-wing intellectuals who in earlier generations had automatically aligned themselves with it.

The student revolt of 1968 was largely a rebellion of the left; but it was also against the left, the old left of the Communist Party and the Social Democrats. For the first time in a hundred years, Communism had lost the high ground of radical political thought.

The student revoluionaries of Berkeley University, California, make their anti-war protest.

# Chile's Marxist Experiment

Chile's strongly Marxist Socialist Party was quite clear about how it would one day seize power, and keep it - by revolution, and by revolution alone. 'Revolutionary violence is inevitable and legitimate,' the Socialists proclaimed after a party convention in 1967. 'It is the necessary result of the repressive and violent character of the class-state. It constitutes the only way that leads to the seizure of political and economic power and its subsequent defence.' Yet three years later the Chilean Socialists were part of the world's first Marxist-led government outside Europe to gain power democratically through the polls, rather than by force and insurrection.

In 1970 the Socialist Salvador Allende Gossens, heading a coalition dominated by Communists and Socialists (many of the latter standing well to the left of the Communists), won Chile's presidential election. It was a dramatic event, and the whole world took note. For much of the previous decade rural guerrilla insurgencies, backed by Castro's Cuba, had been active in Latin America. But none of the continent's regimes had fallen to insurgents. The Cuban-inspired 'liberation movements' were beginning to collapse.

Now, where the guerrillas had failed, Allende's Unidad Popular (Popular Unity) coalition in Chile had succeeded. There had been no armed uprising, no blood-letting. The victory won by the urbane, sixty-two-year-old Allende and his allies - it was his fourth attempt at the presidency - seemed to herald a promising new departure for the Latin American left. Observers in countries farther afield, such as France and Italy, with Communists in their national parliaments, also watched with interest.

### The England of South America

Chile is a long, narrow, ribbon-like country stretching down the western flank of the Andes from the mineral-rich deserts of Atacama in the north to the cold, wet, blustery Cape Horn in the south. It is 2610 miles (4200 km) long, and never more than 250 miles (400 km) wide.

In contrast to its neighbouring republics, it had had, until the 1970s, a history of relative political stability - Chile was sometimes known as 'the England of South America'. Power usually passed in orderly fashion from one elected president to the next.

But beneath the smooth surface were acute and growing social and economic problems. In the first place there were vast social inequalities. As late as 1965, 25 per cent of Chile's national wealth was in the hands of just 5 per cent of the population. A tiny oligarchy owned vast estates comprising the bulk of the country's best agricultural land; they also controlled most of Chile's industry and its banking system. In the country, landless *campesinos* (peasants) lived in desperate poverty, and miserable *callampa* (literally, mushroom) shanty towns sprawled around the cities.

On top of this was a continuing record of high inflation, and a dangerous economic dependence on one major export - copper mined in the deserts of the north. When world copper prices slumped - as they were to do in the early part of Allende's presidency - the whole economy suffered. The mining industry was, moreover, almost entirely controlled by a handful of large American companies, which creamed off enormous profits and gave little to Chile in return - a fact resented by most Chileans.

Allende had stood in every presidential election since 1952, as candidate first for a straight Communist-Socialist alliance, then for a broader left-wing front. For the 1970 election, the left formed itself into the still broader Unidad Popular (UP) coalition, which included the non-Marxist Radical Party and a breakaway group of left-wing former Christian Democrats. It was the Communists who were largely responsible for creating the UP coalition, persuading the generally more extreme Socialists to drop, for the time being at least, their commitment to gaining power by armed struggle alone. They also secured for Allende (against considerable pressure from within his own party) his fourth nomination as presidential candidate. In the year to come, the Communists were to be Allende's closest allies in pursuing what he came to call the *vía pacífica* (peaceful way) to socialism.

Allende and his UP partners fought a skilful election campaign, promising to turn Chilean society upside down. They would break, once and for all, the power of the oligarchy and of 'foreign monopolistic capitalism'. UP's aim, as the Communist Americo Zorrilla - to become Allende's first Finance Minister - later put it, was 'to defeat definitively the dominant class in Chile'. They intended to redistribute irreversibly all wealth and power in Chilean society.

### A Close Run for the Election

The election was scheduled for 4 September. Everyone knew the results would be close - and they were. Allende came first, with just over 36 per cent of the vote. Alessandri Rodríguez, standing for the right, came second with nearly 35 per cent; and the Christian Democrat Radimiro Tomic trailed third with under 28 per cent. Allende had attracted the

## Pablo Neruda: The Voice of a Nation

The Chilean poet and Communist Pablo Neruda, who won the Nobel Prize for Poetry in 1971, became the voice of the Chilean people. His democratic and articulate concern for the nobility of people, in particular the poor and those who were voiceless themselves, rained down over nearly four decades on the ears of Chile's governors.

He was born in 1904, and by the age of twenty had a national reputation as a poet. From 1927 he worked as a diplomat in the Far East, and in 1934 was sent as Consul first to Barcelona and then to Madrid. In Spain he met a group of writers and artists who were deeply committed to the ideals of common justice and equality and their example, together with the experience of

The Chilean poet Pablo Neruda at a political rally in 1973.

the Spanish Civil War, changed the course of his life.

His anti-Franco activities lost him his post. From 1938 to 1950 he worked on his Chilean epic, *Canto general,* and in 1945 he joined the Communist Party.

During Allende's campaign for the presidency, Neruda travelled the country explaining Allende's 'New Deal'. Allende appointed him Ambassador to Paris, and not surprisingly, Neruda was near the top the hit-list of the Pinochet regime. Only days after the coup, while he lay dying of cancer, his house in Santiago was attacked, the plumbing smashed so that water flooded through it destroying his books and unpublished manuscripts. Three days later he died. At first his death went unreported, but as news filtered out his funeral attracted thousands of mourners and developed into the first mass demonstration against the Junta.

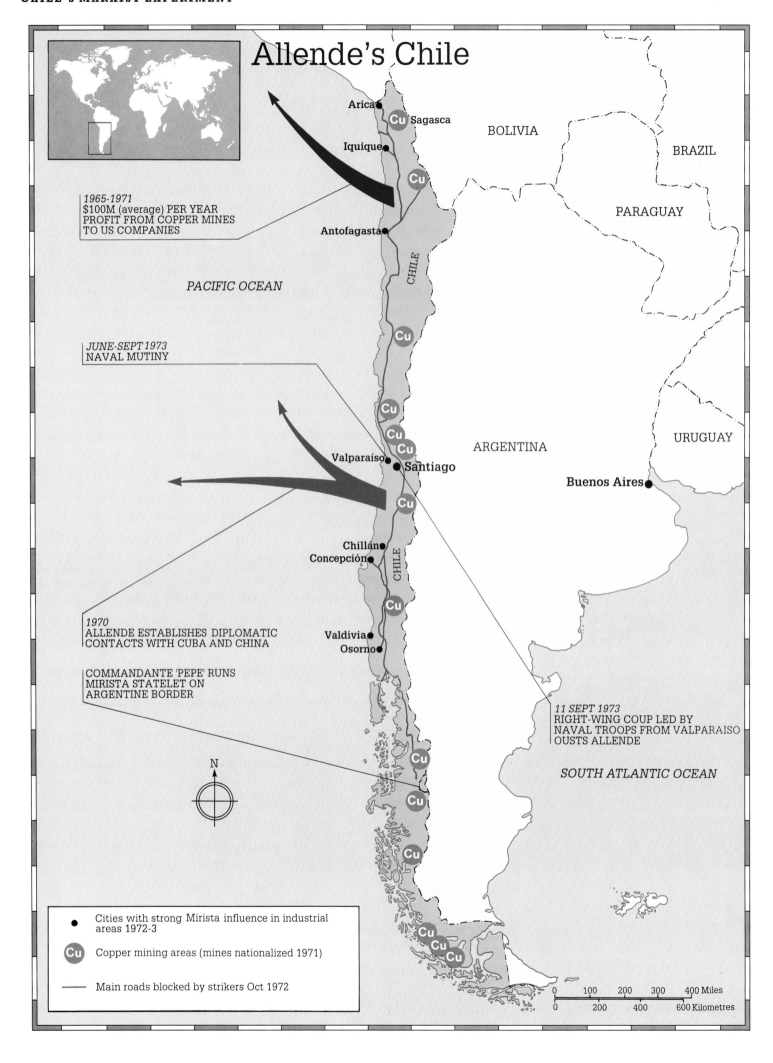

# Allende's Chile

BOLIVIA

BRAZIL

PARAGUAY

Arica
Cu Sagasca

Iquique
Cu

**1965-1971**
$100M (average) PER YEAR
PROFIT FROM COPPER MINES
TO US COMPANIES

Antofagasta
Cu

CHILE

*PACIFIC OCEAN*

**JUNE-SEPT 1973**
NAVAL MUTINY

Cu

Cu
Cu
Cu

ARGENTINA

URUGUAY

Valparaíso
Santiago
Cu

**Buenos Aires**

**1970**
ALLENDE ESTABLISHES DIPLOMATIC
CONTACTS WITH CUBA AND CHINA

Chillán
Concepción
CHILE

Cu

COMMANDANTE 'PEPE' RUNS
MIRISTA STATELET ON
ARGENTINE BORDER

Valdivia
Osorno

**11 SEPT 1973**
RIGHT-WING COUP LED BY
NAVAL TROOPS FROM VALPARAISO
OUSTS ALLENDE

Cu

*SOUTH ATLANTIC OCEAN*

N

Cu

Cu
Cu
Cu

- Cities with strong Mirista influence in industrial
  areas 1972-3

Cu Copper mining areas (mines nationalized 1971)

—— Main roads blocked by strikers Oct 1972

| 0 | 100 | 200 | 300 | 400 Miles |

| 0 | 200 | 400 | 600 Kilometres |

largest number of votes, but not enough to win the presidency outright. For that he would have needed an absolute majority. According to the constitution it was now up to Parliament to decide who the next President would be.

Tensions rose high. Allende himself predicted that while Parliament made its mind up, Chile would 'feel like a football being kicked about by Pelé'. There was a run on the banks; many of the rich began to flee the country. Rumours spread that the military were plotting a coup. Behind the scenes the American telecommunications corporation ITT, which had large investments in Chile, conspired actively against Allende, offering considerable sums of money to those prepared to help prevent a Marxist victory. The CIA, it was later reported, was also involved. Then came a profound shock - on the morning of 22 October the army's Commander-in-Chief, General René Schneider, was shot while driving to his office. It was Chile's first political assassination in over 130 years. Blame was later put on right-wing extremists, apparently disgusted at Schneider's refusal to countenance a military putsch. After this there were fears of a military backlash.

It never came. In the event the transition of power went relatively smoothly - the military remained faithful to their tradition of political neutrality. The Christian Democrats offered Allende their backing in return for an agreement guaranteeing certain democratic rights, such as the freedom of the press. Two days after Schneider's shooting, Parliament voted Allende President.

## The Peaceful Way

From the very first days of his presidency, Allende made it clear that he was leading the people of Chile in a unique and unprecedented experiment. He had come to power committed to laying the foundations of a socialist state, but also to achieve this peacefully, without armed confrontation and without straying beyond the bounds of the constitution and the multi-party system.

But if Allende was committed to following a peaceful path to socialism, he was not committed to pursuing a slow one. Once in office, he and his ministers moved with astonishing speed. Within weeks of coming to power they had ordered wage rises for all workers (up to 65 per cent in some cases) and had made clear their international allegiances by restoring diplomatic relations with Cuba and Mao's China. The United Nations-trained Agriculture Minister, Jacques Chonchol, had launched a sweeping campaign of land reform that was, within two years, to bring 35,000 farms (amounting to nearly 20,000 square miles) into state control.

The UP ministers also set about a massive and ruthless programme of nationalization of industry and commerce - which they saw as the key to breaking the power of the oligarchy. By the end of Allende's second year in office, the country's banking system

*Left:* President Salvador Allende, Chile's moderate Marxist leader, relaxing at home.
*Right:* Allende's successor General Pinochet, inspecting troops on National Independence Day.

and some 80 per cent of its industrial production were state-controlled. In some cases Parliament opposed nationalization. But the government showed that, while committed to respecting the constitution, it was also prepared to push it to its limits. One favourite ploy was to use a little-known law from the 1930s which allowed the state to intervene in certain 'industries producing basic necessities' that failed to meet government-set production targets. A firm which the government wished to nationalize would be accused of failing to meet its targets, and a state *interventor* (administrator) would be sent in to investigate. The *interventor* might then set further - impossible - targets. When the management protested, the authorities would announce that the firm had been expropriated.

A further target for nationalization was the copper industry. This move had near-unanimous support across the political spectrum. On 16 July 1971 Parliament passed, without a dissenting vote, a constitutional amendment that permitted the country to take over full ownership and control of the industry. The government duly did so, offering the foreign copper companies no compensation for loss of future profits, and presenting them with a bill of $775 million for the 'excess' profits they had taken out of Chile over the years. The infuriated companies had no redress.

## Problems Set In

Initially Allende's reforms, though naturally opposed by the right, were highly popular in the country as a whole, including sections of the middle classes. In municipal elections in April 1971, UP won nearly 50 per cent of the vote. From then on, however, problems multiplied. The nationalization programme resulted in a widespread loss of productivity in both industry and agriculture. Prices began to rise dramatically. People had to queue for food. In December 1971, crowds of housewives staged a demonstration

in the streets of Santiago, protesting at the food shortages. Then, in January 1972, the government suffered a major reverse in the loss of two parliamentary by-elections. The economic news grew still more grim. By mid-1972, Chile had accumulated a massive $3.5 million foreign debt. Foreign capital, put off by the experience of American copper corporations, was reluctant to invest in the country. World copper prices were down. Chilean inflation had risen to a catastrophic 163 per cent.

At the same time, extremist forces on the left - the far-left Socialists within the governing coalition, and outside it a former guerrilla organization, the Movimiento de Izquierda Revolucionaria (Movement of the Revolutionary Left, or MIR) - were becoming more and more impatient with the constraints imposed by Allende's *vía pacífica*. Increasingly, they took matters into their own hands. In the country, members of MIR organized bands of peasants and members of Chile's most grossly underpriviledged group, the Mapuches or Indians, in illegal land seizures. In many cases they had the tacit approval of local UP authorities.

The extremists also went to work in the poverty-stricken industrial belts that surround Chile's major cities. They would organize squads of workers to move in, often at night, to take over empty building lots, which they then fenced off. Here they would build streets of wooden houses and set up *commandos communales* (community commands), which ran everything from food distribution and health care to Marxist political education. The *commandos* also set up armed self-defence forces. Political indoctrination was heavy in these *campamentos* (encampments), but living conditions were undoubtedly better than in the workers' previous homes.

As 1972 progressed, so the opposition of those sectors of Chilean society hardest hit by Allende's reforms - the middle classes - intensified and grew more focussed. The military, following the example of the army Commander-in-Chief, General Carlos

# Salvador Allende: Man of Paradoxes

'We set foot on a new road; we march without a guide through unknown terrain, having for a compass only our fidelity to the humanism of the ages - especially Marxist humanism - and having as our guiding star the design of the society we desire, inspired by the deepest longings of the people of Chile.' In this way Allende proclaimed his vision of the new Chile he hoped to create 1970.

Salvador Allende was a man of paradoxes. He came from a solidly upper middle-class background (at university he trained as a doctor), and throughout his life preserved a marked fondness for bourgeois high-living: good wine and food - and women. In appearance (always neatly groomed and besuited) he presented a distinct contrast to his shaggier contemporaries of the Latin American revolutionary left - Fidel Castro, for example.

But he was a dedicated Marxist, all the same. At the age of 25, he was a founder member of Chile's Socialist party, and while still in his early thirties (1939-42) he served as Minister of Health in the left-wing government of President Pedro Aguirre Cerda. Three attempts on the presidency during the 1950s and 60s brought little success, but showed Allende's capacity for survival and intelligent pragmatism that led to his eventual success in 1970.

Not even Allende's political skills, however, could contain the forces of left- and right-wing extremism unleashed after his election. Bereft of moderate support, he became at the last the victim of the fatal clash between the extremes.

Prats, a committed constitutionalist, remained largely loyal to the government. But other middle-class groups - from small businessmen to professionals - increasingly formed themselves into *gremios*, or associations, dedicated to defending their interests against, in particular, threats of further nationalization and the attacks of the far left. In July the opposition parties, hitherto divided, came together in a formal coalition.

## The October Strikes

Then came the worst crisis of Allende's administration so far. In October the *gremio* of the truck drivers, who plied the vital arteries of communication along Chile's vast length, called a national strike in protest at government proposals to nationalize their industry. The strike was promptly joined by swathes of the middle ranks of Chilean society: doctors, nurses, lawyers, some teachers and students, small factory owners whose firms had so far escaped nationalization, better-off workers and shopkeepers. At the same time, extremist groups on the left seized the opportunity to take control of businesses closed down by their striking owners and managers.

Allende, facing a dangerous threat to law and order, turned to the one apparently neutral force in Chilean society: the military. In November, with the support of the Communists - but against the horrified protests of the far-left Socialists - he brought three leading members of the armed forces into the cabinet. To Prats he gave the key post of Minister of the Interior. The armed forces duly pacified the country, and the strikes came to an end. This, the so-called *autogolpe* (self-inflicted coup), was a turning point for Allende. From now on, as political activity on right and left intensified, he would find himself ever more dependent on the armed forces to keep at least some semblance of peace and order in Chile.

The strikes were over - but the economic crisis continued to worsen. In January 1973 the government was obliged to introduce food rationing. Then in March came better news, when UP managed to win just over 43 per cent of the vote in parliamentary elections. On the strength of this result, Allende felt able to accept the resignation of the military ministers. But this optimism was short-lived. By the middle of that year inflation had risen to 323.6 per cent, the highest in the world. There were more strikes. Left-wing groups were calling for an armed uprising against the right. The opposition parties, too, were becoming ever more aggressive in their attacks on the government; it was strongly suspected on the left that they were being secretly financed by the CIA. Then came evidence that the middle echelons of the armed forces were also now joining with the right.

## Crisis

An uninterrupted period of political, economic and military crisis now followed, with the country on the brink of a bloody civil war. There were widespread industrial strikes and the doctors and nurses joined in. Finally, the navy mutinied in Valparaiso, and Allende's naval aide-de-camp, Commando Arturo Araja Peters, was assassinated.

Once more Allende had to turn to the military, in whose commanders at least he still had some confidence. In August he incorporated the chiefs of the navy, army, air force and police into the cabinet. Shortly afterwards, however, his loyal ally Prats was forced to resign after a string of army wives, egged on by their husbands, surrounded his house and howled for his dismissal. General Augusto Pinochet Ugarte took his place. Despite formal protestations of loyalty to Allende, Pinochet was deeply involved in a now widespread military conspiracy to overthrow the President.

The crisis intensified. Subversion now raged openly in the army. On 4 September came the third anniversary of Allende's victory at the polls. A huge crowd of some seven hundred thousand people gathered in front of La Moneda to listen to his exhortations for unity. While shouts of '*Armas para el pueblo!*' ('Arms for the people') went up, drowning out '*Viva Allende!*', the air force planes circled Constitution Square, photographing the demonstrators.

On 7 September Pinochet reported to the UP Defence Minister, Orlando Letelier, that the naval mutiny at Valparaiso had subsided. It was now clear to most people that a coup was in the offing. But Allende, committed as ever to his *vía pacífica*, hesitated to organize armed resistance. On 8 September extreme left-wing groups decided to break with the government and organize the industrial belts around Santiago for combat against military intervention. The moment had come.

On the night of 10 September, the army and air force led a blitzkrieg on the industrial belts. In an overnight putsch, Admiral Torribio Merino took control of the naval base at Valparaiso. With Pinochet, General Gustavo Leigh of the air force and General Cesar Mendoza, the chief of police, Merino formed a self-appointed junta that planned to take power in the coup. In the early hours of the next day naval troops advanced on Santiago. All but one of the telephone lines to the city were cut off. There was no response when Allende tried to contact Pinochet - it was only when he was informed that the Ministry of Defence was in the hands of the army that he realized the extent of his betrayal.

By 9 am La Moneda was surrounded by tanks. The besieging force demanded the President's surrender, with the promise of free conduct out of the country. He refused, and at 9.30 am made a last declaration to the people on the Communist Radio Magellenes, one of the two government radio stations still broadcasting:

Surely Radio Magellenes will soon by silenced, and the calm timbre of my voice will not reach you. It does not matter. You will continue to hear me. I shall always stand with you. My legacy will remain that of a worthy man, a man who was loyal to his country.... Long live Chile! Long live the people! Long live the workers! These are my last words, and I am sure that my sacrifice will not be in vain. I am sure that this sacrifice will constitute a moral lesson which will punish cowardice, perfidy and treason.

From then on, La Moneda was bombarded with bombs and rockets. By 2 pm troops had broken in, and Allende's bullet-ridden body was discovered in the Red Room on the second floor, his machine gun - a gift from Fidel Castro - and empty shells beside him. Whether he had died fighting, or saved the last round for himself, is not known.

At 4 pm the Junta was installed. The foundations of the socialist state that Allende had so painstakingly laid were about to be swept away, and a regime of terror built in their place. The *vía pacífica* had come to a blood-soaked end.

# Africa: The New Frontier

Many young Africans caught up in the rush to independence from the mid-twentieth century onwards knew this much of Communism: that it was deeply feared by their colonial masters. That was recommendation enough. Instead of struggling on its own against a Western power, even the smallest of independence movements had the benefit of knowing that Moscow or Peking was on call to offer sympathy and encouragement - and should the colonists prove obdurate, arms and guerrilla training as well. This fact undoubtedly quickened the independence process, even as it traumatized the aftermath. In less than twenty years, the African empires of Britain, France, Belgium, Portugal and Spain were replaced by a collection of more than forty independent entities lacking in everything except aspirations; most had only a tiny educated elite to hold together what was more a notion than a nation, for the international borders carried over from colonial rule made mincemeat of ethnic unity by severing traditional tribal ties.

In the first two decades of African independence, there were forty successful coups, and attempted coups beyond count. The record was held by the former French territory of Dahomey which, during a period of ten years, in the process of transforming itself into the People's Republic of Benin, went through six coups, five constitutions, and ten heads of state. In the great post-colonial shake-out, one-party dictatorships became the norm and Stalinist modes of governing commonplace.

Gradually the dream of liberation became a nightmare for many of the continent's 350 million people. They were sucked into a downward spiral of poverty and tyranny, and the situation was not helped either by the client-supporting antics of the major powers - of the United States in confrontation with the Soviet Union, and China against the one and then the other - or the belligerence of the last white bastion, South Africa.

### The Dream of African Socialism

Kwame Nkrumah was more than a pace-setter in the decolonization process when, at midnight on 6 March 1957, he led the Gold Coast, now to be called Ghana, to independence from Britain. He was also the standard-bearer of 'African socialism', a new, peculiarly African ideology that was to cut across the capitalist-Communist divide. It was a heady vision: no less than the transformation of Ghana, and then all Africa, into the world's most thriving and unified

Patrice Lumumba, the former Prime Minister of the Congo returns to Léopodville under arrest, 4 December 1960. He was murdered by his political opponents in January 1961.

## The Marxist Missionary

The most influential Marxist missionary to Africa was a West Indian called George Padmore. He had close ties with a group of black American intellectuals who regarded Africa as their home, and who in 1900 formed a Pan-African movement.

Padmore was so excited by the Russian Revolution of 1917 that he moved to Moscow and became a Comintern agent, recruiting African students and seamen in Europe, and making contacts on clandestine trips to Africa. He was given an office in the Kremlin, and was honoured to the point where he shared the stand with the Soviet hierarchy at a May Day parade. Yet he became disenchanted when Stalin failed to help Abyssinia (or Ethiopia,

as it is now known) as it was being crushed by Mussolini in 1936, and he was discarded when Stalin made common cause with the colonial powers in the face of the Nazi threat.

Padmore absorbed this lesson. He was still a committed Marxist, but he was even more passionately committed to African nationalism, and he expressed 'a desire to be free from the dictation of Europeans, regardless of their ideology'. He moved to London, where his flat became a centre of anti-colonial intrigue. He took under his wing a West African student, Kwame Nkrumah, recommended to him by old associates in New York, and he set about reviving the Pan-African movement in a

much more radical form.

The consequent Pan-African Congress, staged by Padmore and his friends in Manchester, provided a new focus with a hotly worded call on 'colonial workers' to 'battle against imperialism'. Nkrumah drafted the resolution, and the future leader of Kenya, Jomo Kenyatta, and that of Malawi, Dr Hastings Banda, were among the ninety-odd delegates in the hall, which was draped with the flags of Ethiopia, Liberia and Haiti, then the only black-ruled states in the world. It was October 1945. Within a dozen years, several of the delegates were legends in their own lands, and Nkrumah was the most famous man in all of Black Africa.

# Political Change in Black Africa

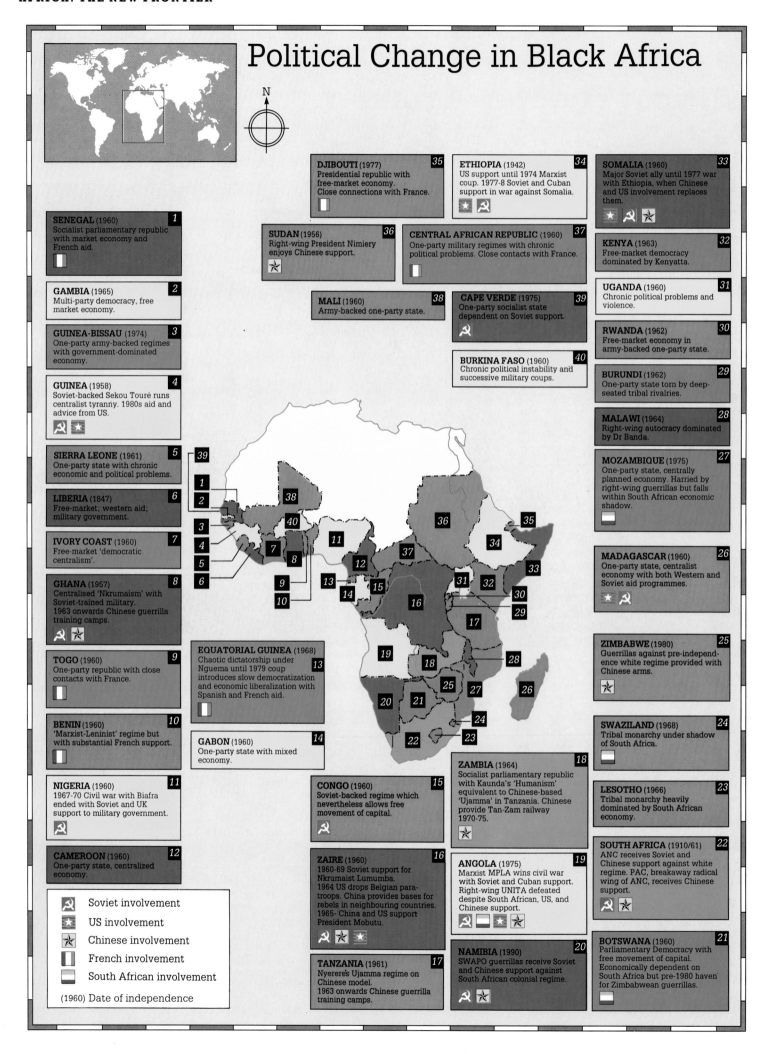

N

**DJIBOUTI** (1977) | 35
Presidential republic with free-market economy. Close connections with France.

**ETHIOPIA** (1942) | 34
US support until 1974 Marxist coup. 1977-8 Soviet and Cuban support in war against Somalia.

**SOMALIA** (1960) | 33
Major Soviet ally until 1977 war with Ethiopia, when Chinese and US involvement replaces them.

**SENEGAL** (1960) | 1
Socialist parliamentary republic with market economy and French aid.

**SUDAN** (1956) | 36
Right-wing President Nimiery enjoys Chinese support.

**CENTRAL AFRICAN REPUBLIC** (1960) | 37
One-party military regimes with chronic political problems. Close contacts with France.

**KENYA** (1963) | 32
Free-market democracy dominated by Kenyatta.

**GAMBIA** (1965) | 2
Multi-party democracy, free market economy.

**MALI** (1960) | 38
Army-backed one-party state.

**CAPE VERDE** (1975) | 39
One-party socialist state dependent on Soviet support.

**UGANDA** (1960) | 31
Chronic political problems and violence.

**GUINEA-BISSAU** (1974) | 3
One-party army-backed regimes with government-dominated economy.

**RWANDA** (1962) | 30
Free-market economy in army-backed one-party state.

**GUINEA** (1958) | 4
Soviet-backed Sekou Touré runs centralist tyranny. 1980s aid and advice from US.

**BURKINA FASO** (1960) | 40
Chronic political instability and successive military coups.

**BURUNDI** (1962) | 29
One-party state torn by deep-seated tribal rivalries.

**MALAWI** (1964) | 28
Right-wing autocracy dominated by Dr Banda.

**SIERRA LEONE** (1961) | 5
One-party state with chronic economic and political problems.

**MOZAMBIQUE** (1975) | 27
One-party state, centrally planned economy. Harried by right-wing guerrillas but falls within South African economic shadow.

**LIBERIA** (1847) | 6
Free-market; western aid; military government.

**IVORY COAST** (1960) | 7
Free-market 'democratic centralism'.

**MADAGASCAR** (1960) | 26
One-party state, centralist economy with both Western and Soviet aid programmes.

**GHANA** (1957) | 8
Centralised 'Nkrumaism' with Soviet-trained military. 1963 onwards Chinese guerrilla training camps.

**TOGO** (1960) | 9
One-party republic with close contacts with France.

**EQUATORIAL GUINEA** (1968) | 13
Chaotic dictatorship under Nguema until 1979 coup introduces slow democratization and economic liberalization with Spanish and French aid.

**ZIMBABWE** (1980) | 25
Guerrillas against pre-independence white regime provided with Chinese arms.

**BENIN** (1960) | 10
'Marxist-Leninist' regime but with substantial French support.

**GABON** (1960) | 14
One-party state with mixed economy.

**SWAZILAND** (1968) | 24
Tribal monarchy under shadow of South Africa.

**NIGERIA** (1960) | 11
1967-70 Civil war with Biafra ended with Soviet and UK support to military government.

**CONGO** (1960) | 15
Soviet-backed regime which nevertheless allows free movement of capital.

**ZAMBIA** (1964) | 18
Socialist parliamentary republic with Kaunda's 'Humanism' equivalent to Chinese-based 'Ujamma' in Tanzania. Chinese provide Tan-Zam railway 1970-75.

**LESOTHO** (1966) | 23
Tribal monarchy heavily dominated by South African economy.

**CAMEROON** (1960) | 12
One-party state, centralized economy.

**ZAIRE** (1960) | 16
1960-69 Soviet support for Nkrumaist Lumumba.
1964 US drops Belgian para-troops. China provides bases for rebels in neighbouring countries.
1965- China and US support President Mobutu.

**ANGOLA** (1975) | 19
Marxist MPLA wins civil war with Soviet and Cuban support. Right-wing UNITA defeated despite South African, US, and Chinese support.

**SOUTH AFRICA** (1910/61) | 22
ANC receives Soviet and Chinese support against white regime. PAC, breakaway radical wing of ANC, receives Chinese support.

Soviet involvement
US involvement
Chinese involvement
French involvement
South African involvement

(1960) Date of independence

**TANZANIA** (1961) | 17
Nyerere's Ujamma regime on Chinese model.
1963 onwards Chinese guerrilla training camps.

**NAMIBIA** (1990) | 20
SWAPO guerrillas receive Soviet and Chinese support against South African colonial regime.

**BOTSWANA** (1960) | 21
Parliamentary Democracy with free movement of capital. Economically dependent on South Africa but pre-1980 haven for Zimbabwean guerrillas.

Chinese Prime Minister Zhou Enlai arrives in Dar-es-Salaam for a four-day state visit to Tanzania. The Chinese offered arms and military training.

# South Africa: Marxism's Promised Land

South Africa, with its large white working class and black proletariat, and its landless peasantry, confirmed an orthodox Marxist vision that existed nowhere else in the continent. It very soon acquired a Communist Party, so motivated by events in Russia in 1917 that it was able to attempt a revolution in March 1922, when armed gold miners hoisted the red flag and seized property around Johannesburg.

But the rebel miners were all white, incensed by the mine-owners' decision to cut costs by opening more jobs to poorly paid blacks, and their slogan was 'Workers of the world unite for a white South Africa'. The government acted ruthlessly to put down the rebellion, and more than 150 miners were killed by troops. The bitterness that resulted helped to entrench white supremacist attitudes in the white labour movement, and blacks were systematically excluded from skilled work.

The Communists, chastened by this lesson in the limitations of class solidarity, now backed the black struggle rather than the white one, and became the epitome of evil in the eyes of the state, which after the Second World War institutionalized racial segregation - apartheid. Under the 1950 Suppression of Communism Act, the government assumed the power to ban any organization, or silence any individual, simply by accusing them of furthering the aims of Communism - whatever their actual intentions and beliefs.

The South African Communist Party went underground and forged ties with the African National Congress (ANC), the major champion of black aspirations, which consequently received support from the Soviet Union. The most celebrated party member was Braam Fischer, a distinguished lawyer who defended Nelson Mandela and other ANC leaders, and participated in the founding of Umkonto We Sizwe (Spear of the Nation), the military wing of the ANC, before being exposed and imprisoned for life.

True to the pattern elsewhere, the Pan-Africanist Congress (PAC), a militant breakaway from the ANC, was adopted by China. While the ANC admitted other races into its ranks, the PAC preached black exclusivity.

The strong ties between the Communmists and the ANC were emphasized on 2 February 1990 when the state president, F.W. de Klerk, announced the release of Nelson Mandela, the unbanning of the ANC, the PAC and the Communist Party. On 27 April, the five ANC leaders returning from exile to participate in negotiations with the government included Joe Slovo, the Patry's Secretary General. Attempts to smear Communists on the negotiating team were countered by strong words from Mandela.

society, drawing its strength and inspiration from traditional African cultural values.

Initial enthusiasm was immense. Although the Colonial Office had branded him 'a thoroughgoing Communist', even Queen Elizabeth warmed to Nkrumah's charm, and American Vice-President Richard Nixon, most ardent of anti-Communists, gushed praise at the independence celebrations, to which the Russians sent a junior minister and the Chinese a general.

Nkrumah lacked a clear programme to achieve his dreams, and hiring his old mentor George Padmore and a squad of social scientists did little to help. 'Nkrumaism' was officially launched in 1960, and soon decayed into a personality cult. Nkrumah assumed the title of Osagyefo, the redeemer, and as he concentrated power within his Convention People's Party opposition was silenced and detention without trial introduced. Grandiose industrialization schemes, and the creation of more than fifty state enterprises, coincided with a decline in earnings from cocoa, the key crop, and the country sank deep in debt.

From 1964, Ghana was a one-party state. Corruption intensified, with government ministers happy to sign overpriced contracts from any quarter, East or West, for a 10 per cent fee. There were assassination attempts, and Nkrumah withdrew behind a Soviet-trained presidential guard. He was overthrown in 1966 by the combined efforts of the police and army, while on a quixotic mission to Hanoi with proposals to end the Vietnam War.

Nkrumaism had many disciples, who reasoned that only a disciplined, centrally directed mass party was able to overcome tribal divisions, inspire a sense of nationhood and mobilize the population for economic development. In practice, the party became the stronghold of a privileged few gathered around a despotic ruler. 'Anything I say is law,' was the honest boast of Malawi's Dr Banda, a super-autocrat who adopted the title Ngwazi, conqueror.

Dr Banda was exceptional in his extreme conservatism, for he even maintained friendly relations with South Africa. More typical was Sekou Touré of Guinea, who made the first African colonial break from France in 1958, and was saved by Soviet aid when the French vindictively departed in a rush, destroying all the equipment they could not take. Sekou Touré enjoyed great popular support, but ruled ruthlessly, constantly putting down real or imagined plots. Touré was convinced that total state control of the economy was the only way to create an egalitarian society freed from external economic domination. A state trading monopoly, agricultural co-operatives and state industries were established. The schemes lacked a coherent plan, or people to run them efficiently - at independence, only a dozen Guineans had university-level education - yet Sekou Touré survived and persevered, eventually to decree the closure of all village markets and their replacement by state stores.

The most acclaimed attempt to define and achieve African socialism centred on East Africa, where Julius Nyerere championed Ujamma, or 'Familyhood', and his neighbour Kenneth Kaunda of Zambia propounded a variant known as 'Humanism'. Nyerere became Africa's most articulate and respected spokesman, his integrity universally admired. He stressed rural development, and borrowed from Chinese collectivism in transplanting more than 10 million peasants from isolated homesteads to small co-operative villages. He also tried to impose Chinese frugality on government and party officials, enforcing a spartan 'Leadership Code' that sought to limit their acquisition of wealth. Although Tanzania made great strides in education, health and social services, the Ujamma programme was poorly handled, and Nyerere's vision of an agrarian utopia became bogged down in massive debts that made a mockery of his vision of self-reliance.

## The Cold War in Africa

Pan-Africa was stillborn, its only memorial being a chronically disunited Organization of African Unity, founded in 1963. By then, disorderly European retreat from the continent had climaxed in the chaos and violence of the Congo, where secessionist

Samora Machel, former leader of Frelimo and head of the Marxist government of Mozambique signed a treaty with the Soviet Union in 1977.

and other crises followed Belgium's hasty granting of independence and brought the Cold War to Africa with a vengeance. This vast and rich territory, what is now called Zaire, became a sprawling tribal and ideological battleground once Patrice Lumumba, a fiery and radical admirer of Nkrumah, gained power in the independence elections.

As the American CIA worked to bring about Lumumba's downfall and death, the Soviet Union stepped in to provide him with air support, and the United Nations mounted a peace-keeping operation which eventually comprised nineteen thousand troops from twenty-six different countries. Lumumba was eventually liquidated, an event which provided radical Africa with a major martyr figure, while rebel groups continued to wage war in his name.

By 1964, American pilots were flying bombing missions and dropping Belgian paratroops on the rebel stronghold, and China joined in the fray by providing the rebels with half a dozen support bases in neighbouring countries. 'If we can take the Congo, we can have all of Africa,' Mao Zedong is reputed to have said. But more to the point, it provided him with the opportunity to divert American attention and energies away from Vietnam and China's frontier for a time.

China had formalized its entry into the African arena with a tour in late 1963 by the Foreign Minister Zhou Enlai, who sent a shiver through the West - and much of the new African leadership - by observing that 'revolutionary prospects are excellent throughout the African continent.' Beijing took a harder line than Moscow, and favoured factions that would rather fight than negotiate; as a result breakaway groups turned to China as their natural patron.

Chinese mortars and bazookas made their appearance in the African bush, and the Chinese version of the Soviet AK-47 Kalashnikov rifle became a standard guerrilla weapon. More important was the meticulous training that China began to provide, initially from a military academy in Nanjing, then in special training camps in Ghana, Tanzania and other sympathetic African countries.

As the Sino-Soviet split widened through the 1960s, Chinese propaganda reviled the Russians as 'revisionists' selling Africa short in the interest of improved relations with the West, but major clients were loath to risk forfeiting Soviet support. Light Chinese weapons were adequate for hit-and-run bush fighting, but the heavier Soviet armaments were needed to clinch victory or to hold territory. Nor could China offer educational facilities such as those of the Lumumba University in Moscow.

So China compensated with an imaginative 'Rainbow of Friendship' aid programme. Where the Soviets usually charged 2 per cent, China provided free loans for a variety of projects. A speciality was sports stadiums, calculated to appeal to the Roman Emperor complex in many emergent leaders. The showpiece was the 1160-mile Tan-Zam railway that provided landlocked Zambia with access to the Indian Ocean, and was intended to trump the Soviets' famous Aswan Dam project in Egypt. The railway was the longest in Africa, and the longest built anywhere since the Second World War. It took five years, twenty-five thousand Chinese technicians, and a hundred thousand local workers, to build it. China's reward for this support was that it was given the opportunity to escape from diplomatic isolation: in 1971 African votes enabled it to gain admittance to the United Nations, despite every effort by the US to prevent it from joining.

## Angola to the Horn

For all the revolutionary fervour and rhetoric, a French study in 1969 found at most four Communist parties in the whole African continent, and all of these were illegal. It was during the next decade, as a policy of increased intervention was pursued by the superpowers, that several regimes professing themselves to be Marxist-Leninist emerged out of the continuing vortex of coups and wars.

First, the US under President Nixon decided on a secret 'tilt' in favour of what was left of colonial and white rule - mostly in the far south; and then Portugal upset all the calculations by suddenly forsaking the African empire it had fought for years to hold. A grim struggle evolved around Luanda, capital of Angola, largest and richest of the Portuguese territories, where three rival liberation movements battled for power aided by an explosive mix of outside support. Soviet arms and a Cuban expeditionary force secured victory in 1975 for the Popular Movement for the Liberation of Mozambique (MPLA), after repulsing a South African armoured column and humiliating a US-backed guerrilla army trained by China.

It was a victory for Moscow, a salutory lesson for Washington and Pretoria, and a disaster for Beijing. South Africa's invasion had provided justification in African eyes for the unprecedented nature of the Soviet bloc intervention, but China could not be forgiven. For Beijing's apostles of revolutionary purity to ally themselves with the Americans might be passed over as an engaging irony, but for them to be caught on the same side as South Africa's 'racist apartheid regime' was intolerable to most black Africans.

The teaming of Soviet firepower with a Cuban strike force now proved its potency in the dusty Horn of Africa, where Somalia had become a major Soviet ally and the Soviet navy had a base. The neighbouring feudal realm of Ethiopia, on the other hand, enjoyed US support, until bloody social revolution in the mid-1970s caused the replacement of the ageing Emperor Haile Selassie by a militant Marxist regime.

Moscow first tried to juggle both sides, and Cuba's Fidel Castro acted as an intermediary in efforts to create a Marxist-Leninist federation on the Red Sea; but local rivalry made this impossible. When Somalia

invaded Ethiopia to enforce a border claim, the Russians decided to hold on to the bigger prize and committed themselves to Ethiopia with such a force of tanks, artillery and Cuban troops that the Somalis were swiftly thrown back. Somalia's defences were replenished with Chinese jet fighters and light arms and it found an obliging alternative ally in the US, which was now partnered with China in their efforts to prevent Soviet influence from spreading even further.

## Somersaults

Other African leaders were bemused to see the Chinese ally themselves with the likes of Sudan's President Nimiery, noted for his slaughter of Communists, and Zaire's corrupt, CIA-sponsored President Mobutu, previously caricatured in the Beijing press as a dog. This was nothing to the surprises dealt them after the death in 1976 of Mao Zedong. The new Chinese leadership began to question the essence of Communist revolutionary beliefs as it set about acquiring Western know-how and technology, and even some Western investment.

Unabashed Chinese diplomats now lectured on the merits of those countries like the Ivory Coast and Kenya, which had kept their free market economies. Peaceful progress was the watchword, and the supply

of arms to guerrillas in Rhodesia was reduced in order to encourage them to take part in the negotiations that shortly led to the birth of Zimbabwe.

A few of Africa's radicals found solace in the appearance of the North Koreans, whose grey-uniformed envoys touting the speeches of Kim Il Sung recalled the Chinese of fifteen years earlier, and who kept gratifyingly clear of the old Sino-Soviet squabble. But Beijing contrived a comeback as champion of African freedom in the 1980s, when a thaw in its relations with Moscow enabled it to offer aid to the African National Congress (ANC) of South Africa and SWAPO of Namibia, both of which were long-time Soviet clients. And it discovered a new role for itself supporting the emerging African economic aspirations against the crushing might of the industrialized world.

## The Legacy

Black Africa was by now exhausted and bankrupt, ground down by all manner of natural as well as man-made disasters. From the Horn to the Kalahari, guerrilla conflict continued even where major warfare had ceased, and famine was becoming endemic. The priorities of survival became more pressing than the dictates of dogma. Sekou Touré, Guinea's self-styled Terror of International Imperialism, disbanded his 'economic police' and in an about turn went to seek investment from Wall Street. 'For the first twenty years, we have concentrated on developing the mentality of the people,' he explained. 'Now we are ready to do business with others.'

So was the Soviet Union, whose relaxed demeanour under Mikhail Gorbachev helped ease the deadly black-white deadlock in the far south, to the extent that South Africa relinquished its hold on Africa's last colony, South West Africa (now to be called Namibia), and the continent's last white regime finally agreed to open negotiations with its Communist-backed liberation movements.

## The Future

Africa went into the 1990s with the landscape dotted with 'people's republics', yet with ideological distinctions assuming less and less importance. Almost all states incorporated some element of centralism, and had toyed with some of the thoughts of Mao, or Stalin, or both.

The results included the anomaly of the Ivory Coast, ardently anti-Communist, yet a one-party state tracing its 'democratic centralism' back to an early alliance with the French Communist Party; 'Marxist-Leninist' Benin, dependent on French assistance and remaining securely in the franc zone; and Brazzaville, capital of the Moscow-backed People's Republic of the Congo, plastered with Marxist slogans - yet providing a safe and profitable haven for capitalist investment.

A military parade in Janba, Angola in 1984 to mark the release of twenty Czechoslovakian nationals held hostage by Jonas Savimbi, the leader of the rebel organization UNITA. In 1988 South Africa, Angola and Cuba signed an agreement which led to the phased withdrawal of Cuban troops.

# Eurocommunism

Clenched fists are raised in solidarity as European Communist and Socialist party leaders assemble for a conference in Madid, 1977. Bettino Craxi, leader of the Italian Socialist Party (far right), and François Mitterrand, later President of France (second from right), are in attendance.

Towards the end of the 1970s, political journalists began flavouring their articles with a new word and a new idea - 'Eurocommunism'. Their theme was a new spirit which appeared to be reviving the Communist movement within those parties which were prepared to assert their independence from Moscow and to adapt their theoretical framework and practical strategies in the light of recent changes in capitalism. The word itself was slightly misleading, for it did not refer to the parties of eastern Europe or that of Greece, for example, whose allegiance to traditional ideas was unimpaired; it referred primarily to the parties of France, Italy and Spain.

It would appear that a Croatian journalist, Frane Barbieri, working for an Italian newspaper, *Il Giornale Nuovo*, coined the word in June 1975. Because the changes in attitudes among the Communist parties had already been noticed by political commentators who lacked a label for the new movement, 'Eurocommunism' soon entered general circulation. Public interest was heightened by the realization

that a number of Communist parties in southern Europe appeared to be on the verge of achieving a share in national political power. For the first time since the 1940s, Communist rule in countries west of the Iron Curtain seemed a possibility.

In Italy the Communists increased their share of the vote in the 1976 general election from 27 per cent to 34 per cent - only 4 per cent less than the governing Christian Democrats. It seemed only a matter of time before their strategy of a 'historic compromise' between Communism and Catholicism would bear fruit and the party would join the governing coalition.

In France the Communist Party had agreed a common programme with François Mitterrand's Socialist Party in 1972. A year later the combined forces of the left won 42 per cent of the national vote, and in 1974 Mitterrand came close to winning the presidential election. Only 1.4 per cent of the vote separated him from the winner, Giscard d'Estaing. The Union of the Left, as the Communist-Socialist alliance was called, seemed destined to win the next national and

presidential elections in 1978 and 1981.

In Spain the death of Franco in November 1975 seemed to hail a bright future for the Spanish Communists - for forty years the most active and consistent opponents of his Fascist regime. The party was legalized in April 1977. Its 10 per cent share of the vote in the general election a couple of months later was disappointing, but an important role in post-Franco Spain still seemed assured.

The Greek and Portuguese dictatorships had collapsed in 1974 and here too the Communists emerged as national political forces, winning 10 per cent and 15 per cent of the vote respectively. These results could not be included in the Eurocommunist wave of successes, however, as the Greek and Portuguese parties remained loyal to Moscow and orthodox in their politics.

## The Growing Split with Moscow

Although the reasons behind the success of individual parties varied from country to country, all of them were affected by a number of common factors. Events in the

# Eurocommunism in the 1970s

*NORWEGIAN SEA*

*ATLANTIC OCEAN*

NORWAY **4%**

SWEDEN **5%**

FINLAND **19%**

Oslo

Stockholm

Helsinki

Goteborg

DENMARK **4%**

BALTIC SEA

Copenhagen

USSR

Glasgow

Dublin

IRELAND

SOUTH WALES

UNITED KINGDOM **1%**

London

BELGIUM **3%**

NETHERLANDS **2%**

Amsterdam

Rotterdam

Brussels

Bonn

RUHR VALLEY

Berlin

POLAND

Warsaw

EAST GERMANY

NORD DEPARTMENT PAS DE CALAIS

Hainaut

Liège

Luxembourg

WEST GERMANY **1%**

Prague

CZECHOSLOVAKIA

Paris

Vienna

Budapest

Basle

Berne

Lucerne

SWITZERLAND

AUSTRIA **1%**

HUNGARY

FRANCE **21%**

MASSIF CENTRAL

Milan

Turin

ROMANIA

Marseilles

Belgrade

Bucharest

YUGOSLAVIA

Oporto

SPAIN **10%**

PORTUGAL **15%**

ALTO ALENTEJO

Madrid

CATALONIA

Barcelona

ITALY **34%**

Rome

ADRIATIC SEA

Sofia

BULGARIA

Lisbon

BAIXO ALENTEJO

Valencia

Tirana

ALBANIA

Thessaloniki

ANDALUSIA

Néapolis

GREECE **10%**

*MEDITERRANEAN*

CALABRIA

Athens

Piraeus

*SEA*

CRETE

| | Eurocommunist orientation |
| | Pro-Soviet orientation |
| ★ | Party strongholds |
| **3%** | Eurocommunist % of national vote mid-1970s |

0   100   200   400   Miles

0   100   200   400   600   Kilometres

Lenin looks down on the people of Portugal. The pro-Moscow Communist Party of Portugal maintained a high profile during the 1970s.

1960s undermined Moscow's prestige and brought criticism from Western parties: the building of the Berlin Wall in 1961 looked like an admission of failure; just over a year later, the split between the Chinese and the Soviet Union became public knowledge and gave other parties an alternative to the model offered by Moscow; and in 1964, Khrushchev was deposed by a palace coup which emphasized the fallibility of the Kremlin. Soviet policy in the Middle East also had its effect as the Foreign Minister, Andrei Gromyko, courted the Arab states, particularly after their war with Israel in 1967. This shift of policy upset many Soviet Jews and increasing numbers sought permission to emigrate to Israel. Since many of them were highly trained the Soviet authorities turned to repressive measures to stem the tide; this provoked criticism in the West which Communists could not ignore.

In 1968, the rumbling undercurrent of dissent heard among Western Communists was transformed into a torrent of abuse when the troops and tanks of the Eastern bloc rolled into Czechoslovakia. The crushing of the Prague Spring dealt a savage blow to morale among the Western parties. Dubcek's 'socialism with a human face' had offered the hope of a democratic Communism which could be presented as a model to the electorates of the capitalist West.

Before the invasion a number of Western Communist parties, led by the Italians, had attempted to forestall Soviet intervention by organizing bilateral meetings and statements in support of the Dubcek government. These independent activities established a pattern of inter-party relations among Western Communists which lent cohesion to the later Eurocommunist phenomenon. In the aftermath of the Soviet invasion seventeen out of the twenty-three Western European Communist parties condemned it, including the traditionally loyal French. This was the first major act of defiance of the USSR by Western Communists.

Such independence of spirit enhanced the appeal of the Western European Communist parties in the eyes of an electorate which began moving to the left as the 1960s drew to a close. The modernization of French and Italian agriculture during the 1950s and 1960s had caused large numbers of peasants to move into the cities to look for work. Their first experience of factories and urban life produced a growing number of citizens who were critical of capitalism. This helped to create the political space for a new initiative from the left. Furthermore, the developing American-Soviet detente made the frenzied anti-Communism of earlier decades look foolish. Not since the 1940s had conditions been so favourable to a Communist advance.

Meanwhile, the United States suffered a series of setbacks during the 1970s which called into question its previous dominance of the Western alliance. The 1973 rise in oil prices, which followed the second Arab-Israeli war, disrupted American supplies and destabilized its banking system as enormous amounts of capital were moved around. In 1975 the United States finally withdrew from Vietnam, humiliated by its defeat at the hands of a Third World Communist power. In 1979 the Shah, the lynchpin of American Middle Eastern policy, was expelled from Iran, which declared itself an Islamic republic. Within months students and Revolutionary Guards had over-run the American Embassy in Teheran and captured the staff.

### The Party of the Future

It was in this general context that Eurocommunism was able to project itself as a modern left-wing movement which was willing and able to assume power in democratic societies. The image was not without substance, for the Eurocommunists did represent a revolution in traditional Communist attitudes. No longer were they Moscow's puppets, and they emphatically resisted all Soviet attempts to reimpose its leadership and discipline.

At the 1976 Conference of European Communist and Workers' Parties, held in East Berlin, the French, Italian and Spanish party leaders defied any suggestion that Communists were united by a single political and ideological line, however broad in character. Their staunch defence of the national independence of each party, supported by a number of the minor players, such as the British, sounded the death knell of a cohesive Communist movement.

The 1976 conference was the last of such international Communist gatherings. The movement's last rites were read at the conference by Santiago Carrillo, the Spanish Communist leader:

For many years Moscow...was our Rome. We spoke of the Great October Socialist Revolution as if it were our Christmas.... This was at a time when we were children. Today we are adults....We are losing more and more the character of a church. The scientific essence of our theories is gaining the upper hand over faith and the mysticism of predestination.

Another feature of the Eurocommunists' contribution to the conference was their elaboration of the idea of socialist pluralism. Indeed, much of the movement's popular appeal stemmed from its wholehearted embrace of what had previously been dismissed as 'bourgeois democracy'. The Marxist-Leninist concept of a dictatorship of the proletariat was abandoned in favour of the idea of multi-party democracy under socialism. In 1976, the French, for example, expunged all references to the dictatorship of the proletariat from their party statutes. The process of alternation of power in government was accepted - Communists would relinquish power following electoral

## Freedom in Berlin

The final stage in the liberation of the Communist parties of Europe from Moscow's domination occurred between 1974 and 1976 during the preparations and holding of an All-European Conference in June 1976. The Spanish party had suggested the assembly, while the Italian and Polish Parties had pressed Moscow into acquiescence. The Soviets then decided to take the opportunity to reassert their leadership of the movement at a preliminary meeting in October 1974; but the Western parties refused to concede the initiative to the Soviet delegation and a way out of this impasse was only found when the Romanians suggested a second meeting, in Decmeber 1974.When this meeting convened, Moscow was still intent on forcing its views. When they failed to get their way, the Soviet delegation tried to blackmail their comrades by saying that if there was no agreement on their terms, there would be no conference and the world would see how disunited they were. At this the Romanian delegation, under orders from Ceausescu, said that if that was the case the meeting would have to be abandoned, thus calling the Soviet bluff. Eventually a deal was struck between the two groups. The conference was finally opened in Berlin on 28 June and was attended by the leaders of the twenty-nine Communist and Workers' Parties of Europe. Although speeches were made, the real work had been done beforehand. The document which was to be the product of the meeting only had to be rubber stamped. The days of Moscow's domination of the movement were at an end.

defeat. The acceptance of this principle predated Eurocommunism but was lent added conviction by, for example, the Italian party's avowal that changes in government were a positive good. Civil liberties and individual freedom should be guaranteed in both theory and practice, said the Eurocommunists, and the existing socialist states should be no exception to this rule.

The Eurocommunist advocacy of pluralism was linked to another crucial feature of their politics: the pursuit of a gradual, democratic road to socialism. The means of achieving socialism had to be as democratic as its end. Indeed, the Eurocommunists criticized the Soviet model of revolutionary change through insurrection and violence as inimical to the aim of democratic socialism.

An important influence on Eurocommunist thinking about a democratic road to socialism were the writings of Antonio Gramsci, the Italian Communist leader imprisoned by Mussolini in the 1920s. From them the Eurocommunists, particularly the Italians, deduced a strategy for socialism based on the concept of a 'hegemonic war of position'. In other words, the road to socialism lay through the construction of an historic alliance or bloc of social, political and class forces which would *progressively* undermine the foundation of capitalist power.

### Outflanked by the Socialists

For a period in the mid-1970s it appeared that this more sophisticated strategy would bring about the long-awaited Communist breakthrough in western Europe. These hopes proved to be very short-lived. By the beginning of the 1980s the Eurocommunist challenge had foundered. Western Communists found themselves once again on the defensive and the initiative passed to their political opponents.

The most disappointing setback for Eurocommunism was the failure of the Italian party to cross the threshold of government power. As part of its strategy of compromise, between 1977 and 1979 the party supported a series of Christian Democrat-led governments of 'national solidarity'. The aim was to enhance Communist legitimacy and support by playing the role of a loyal and constructive opposition. Unfortunately for the Italian Communists, the Christian Democrats could play the political game just as well if not better, and they had the advantage of having been in government for over thirty years. So the main beneficiaries of the Communists' 'historic compromise' turned out to be the Christian Democrats, who took advantage of it to recover and consolidate their own positions.

The Italians also found themselves being outflanked on the left by Bettino Craxi's Socialist Party. In 1979 the Communist share of the vote fell from 34 to 30 per cent - an enormous decline by Italian standards - and by the mid-1980s the Communists were back in the position they had started from in the 1960s, with around a quarter of the vote but condemned to the status of permanent

Communist Party leader Dolores Ibarruri, and the party's Secretary General Carrillo at the Spanish Communist Pary plenary session, 1982.

opposition. Support for the Socialists during the same period, on the other hand, rose by as much as 15 per cent. While the Communists continued to languish in opposition, Craxi joined the coalition government and became, in 1983, Italy's first Socialist Prime Minister.

Communist reverses in France were even more spectacular than those in Italy, although they took a little longer to mature. The scene was set in the autumn of 1977 by the decision of the French Communist Party to break from its alliance with the Socialists, ostensibly because of a turn to the right in the latter's policy. The real reason was Communist concern at Socialist gains within the alliance, which had led to a change in the balance of power on the French left. While socialist support continued to rise, that of the Communists stagnated, albeit at the respectable level of 20 per cent.

As a result of the breakdown of the alliance, the left failed to win the 1978 national elections, although its share of the vote did increase. The French Communists' decision to go it alone also coincided with the party's retreat from its commitment to Eurocommunism. It failed, for example, to join in with the general condemnation of the Soviet invasion of Afghanistan in 1979.

The change of policy by the French finally backfired in 1981 when Mitterrand won the presidency and then led the Socialists to a stunning victory in elections for the French National Assembly. The Communist vote collapsed from 20 to 15 per cent, but worse was to follow. Four Communist ministers served in Mitterrand's administration from 1981 to 1984. However, their departure from office in protest at Socialist austerity

measures was followed by a further weakening of the party's political position. By the mid-1980s, the Communists were barely able to muster the support of 10 per cent of the French electorate and faced the danger of complete marginalization in French political life.

The Communists in Spain ended up in an equally isolated position following a period of continuous electoral and organizational decline. As in France, the Communists found themselves outpaced by the Socialists. Between 1978 and 1982, party membership dropped from over two hundred thousand to under eighty thousand. Then, in the October 1982 general election, the Communists won only 3.8 per cent of the votes and 4 seats. The Socialists, by contrast, increased their vote from 29 to 44 per cent and the triumphant Socialist leader, Felipe Gonzalez, became Prime Minister.

Many of the problems of the Spanish Communists were bound up with internal disputes. The party's failure to make any political headway lead to a number of splits which culminated in 1982 in the resignation of its General Secretary, Carrillo, the architect of the party's Eurocommunist strategy. Carrillo was subsequently expelled from the party and went on to found his own breakaway group.

His successors as party leader were, if anything, even more devoted to Eurocommunism, but they could do little to bring about a change in Communist fortunes. Only in the late 1980s, when a number of the warring factions resolved their differences and formed an alliance with disaffected Socialists did the Spanish Communist Party rise again.

Ironically, the failures of the Eurocommunists contrasted unfavourably with the relative success of the pro-Moscow Communist parties of Portugal and Greece which had emerged from illegality in the mid-1970s. These parties had no prospect of entering government, but they were able to maintain their political position as the focus of militant opposition. Fidelity to Eurocommunism was evidently no guarantee of political success.

Despite its failures in Italy, France and Spain, Eurocommunism continued to inform the politics of most of the western European Communist parties during the 1980s. It remained the best, if increasingly distant, hope for a Communist breakthrough in the West. Indeed, in the mid-1980s it received an unexpected boost from the East with the rise to power of Mikhail Gorbachev.

The new Soviet leader's policies of *glasnost* and *perestroika* borrowed heavily from ideas pioneered by the Eurocommunists in the 1970s. Indeed, the words which were used to rewrite the constitutions of many of the countries of eastern Europe in 1989-90 might easily have been taken from the speeches made in East Berlin in 1976. For the Eurocommunists, however, Gorbachev and the new openness had arrived too late. Their moment in history had already passed.

# Solidarity: The First Phase

To most people in the West, the rise of the Polish trade union Solidarity from its struggles in the Gdansk shipyards to the position in which it began negotiating with the government on behalf of the workers was an overnight sensation in 1980. The Polish people, however, knew better; they knew the years of struggle and false starts which preceded the unprecedented concessions by the country's Communist Party.

Polish workers first asserted their independence in 1970 when three thousand of them assembled in front of the office of the director of the shipyard where Solidarity would eventually emerge. The men met spontaneously on Monday, 14 December to protest against price rises which had been announced over the weekend. Having got no satisfaction from the plant managers, about a third of the crowd marched from the gate towards the city centre and the provincial party headquarters. Again they were frustrated, and when rumours circulated that their delegation had been arrested the workers began fighting with the police and the situation turned ugly. Some of the crowd sought support from other shipyard workers, students at the university and the radio station, but none was forthcoming. Late in the afternoon, the crowd began to attack the party building. Riot police and army units moved in and the crowd retreated. By 10 pm Gdansk was quiet.

Workers from the shipyard took to the streets again the following morning and this time they were joined by people from other enterprises. A crowd of ten thousand returned to the party building and repeated their attack. It was set ablaze and after about an hour the army was authorized to shoot. Tanks were ordered on to the city streets by the Politburo and were stationed outside the shipyard 'to prevent vandals' from damaging public property. A member of the Politburo broadcast that evening, appealing to the strikers to return to work. When the first shift arrived for work the next morning, they were fired on and several were killed.

Despite warnings, protestors assembled the next day at the shipyard and again tried to march to the city centre. They were shot down just a few steps outside Gate Two. However, the Politburo had miscalculated if it thought that such barbarity would intimidate the men: they dragged the bodies of their murdered colleagues back inside the yard and closed the gates. A committee was elected to present demands for wage increases, price cuts and the withdrawal of the army. The strike, meanwhile, began spreading to other yards along the coast and into the industrial zones of Silesia and Poznan. Just as a general strike seemed imminent, Wladyslaw Gomulka, the party leader, received a telephone call from Brezhnev in Moscow telling him to calm down and settle the problem by negotiation. Then Gomulka had a stroke and Edward Gierek became Party Secretary.

## The Road to Ruin

The new leader set out to wheedle the men back to work with speeches such as the one he made at Szczecin early in the new year:

I appeal to you, as I did to the miners in Silesia: help me ... You cannot suspect me of bad faith. I am a worker, the same as you. I worked at the coal face for eighteen years. I don't need lessons from anyone about the problems of the working class. All my family work down the mines. All of them! I have no relatives in high places.

The workers gave him the benefit of the doubt and returned to work. In its turn, the party agreed to refrain from lecturing the people about the advantages of Marxism.

During the following years, Poland took advantage of Western capital and invested large sums in new factories and industrial plant which, it believed, could be paid back out of profits. For a while living standards rose by an annual average of 5 per cent, with some groups, such as the miners and shipyard workers, doing much better. Agriculture was deregulated, and Catholics were given greater freedom of worship.

The first problems surfaced in 1975 when meat shortages led to strikes. These problems arose because better wages had fuelled demand for meat, but little money had been invested in agriculture to increase production, largely because the farms had been left in private hands and never been collectivized. The only answer was to import certain foods using the hard currency which had been loaned to invest in industry.

Unfortunately, even those industrial projects which were completed with Western loans were frequently ill-conceived and their economic promise was never realized. One such was the Katowice steel complex in Silesia. Gierek supported the proposal to build the plant out of loyalty to those in the province who had helped his political career. But the works were to be sited in the wrong place and built at the wrong time. The iron ore was to come by rail from Krivoi Rog in the Soviet Union, a distance of 2000 kilometres (1250 miles), which raised costs

## Lech Walesa - The Early Years

Lech Walesa spent his childhood in a small wooden house in a small village in central Poland. At 16 he left to take a course in mechanized agriculture at a trade school. He qualified two years later and went to work as an electrical engineer at a State Agricultural Machinery Centre. In 1963 he was conscripted into the army. He worked as an electrician after he was demobbed and in 1966 he moved to Gdansk. The following year he was taken on at the Lenin Shipyard.

Two weeks before Christmas 1970, drastic increases in the price of food and fuel were announced. The resulting strikes in Gdansk climaxed in the massacre at the railway station, a catastrophe which changed Walesa's life. He joined the post-strike committee and got his first visit from the secret police.

Lech Walesa at the Lenin Shipyard in Gdansk, 1980.

It was this committment to the men's rights that got him sacked in 1976. He had been discussing problems in the on-site union office and it had not occurred to him that it might be bugged.

He survived by doing odd jobs and repairing cars. In 1978 he came across the first issue of *Robotnik*. He got another job but lost it after trying to lay flowers in memory of the workers killed in 1970. By now he realized that his flat was bugged.

On 14 August 1980, the day the decisive strike broke out at the Lenin Shipyard, he discussed possible action with fellow activists before taking a streetcar to the shipyard. He knew he was being followed by the security police and he thought that he would be stopped before he reached his destination. When he reached the gates he found security guards were checking everyone's identity card and he had to get in by climbing over the wall. A few minutes later he was standing on a tractor and began to speak.

so much that the price of the finished steel was not competitive. Furthermore, serious over-capacity in the world steel market cut demand. The consequence for Poland was a mounting debt, which the country could not repay because it was unable to sell its industrial products in the West, and interest payments so large that they caused a financial crisis. In its desperation to repay the vast loans to the West, scarce foodstuffs, raw materials and fuel were sold abroad - and this caused acute shortages at home.

The political troubles caused by the economic crisis were exacerbated by an initiative from Gierek to amend the country's constitution in 1975. His attempt further to entrench the party's monopoly of power and increase Poland's dependence on the Soviet Union antagonized the newly liberated Church and the country's intellectuals.

## The People Fight Back

By the summer of 1976 the economic crisis had become so acute that the government could no longer afford to continue its massive food subsidies, and on 24 June the Prime Minister proposed price increases of an average of 46 per cent. The following morning, workers at the General Walter Metal Works in Radom in the south-west of Poland called a strike, which was joined by other factories in the city. A crowd attacked the party building and groups of men destroyed shop windows along the city's leading street. The police stood by and took photographs of these 'incidents' and of the 'looting' which followed. Detachments of the Citizens' Militia, a paramilitary police group, then appeared on the streets and began arresting the strikers, using extreme brutality. About two thousand people were detained and many were savagely beaten while in custody. Four people died as a result of the demonstration, including a priest. Similar disturbances occured at Ursus, a small industrial town which sits astride the main railway line to the West. That evening the Prime Minister announced that the price increases were being withdrawn. But the party was not going to allow such humiliation to go unpunished and it sought to take revenge on the workers involved: an action which backfired.

It was during the trial of the workers from Ursus on 17 July 1976 that a critical connection was made. Some of the dissidents who had objected to the attempted revision of the constitution the previous year arrived at the provincial court and, despite police harassment, offered their help and support to the families of the accused. This action effectively founded the Workers' Defence Committee which, although it did not have a formal structure, managed to channel help and funds to those who were normally at the mercy of the state and created a link between workers and intellectuals.

The Committee continued to assist the workers in documenting their ill-treatment. Eventually it called for an independent

# Father Jerzy Popieluszko

As the Polish government tried to grind down Solidarity during the 1980s, the Church of St Stanislaw Kostka in Zoliborz, northern Warsaw, became a haven for the union under its priest, Jerzy Popieluszko. He was particularly detested by the regime, who called him the Savonarola of anti-Communism, and accused him of presiding over 'seances of hatred'.

His activities were being monitored by units of the Ministry of Internal Affairs, who were unsuccessful in their attempts to intimidate him. In their frustration, and encouraged by hard-line elements who were keen to sabotage General Jaruzelski's attempts to build bridges with the opposition movement, the head of an interior ministry sub-department, Colonel Pietruszka, inspired Captain Piotrowski to capture and murder Father Popieluszko on

Father Jerzy Popieluszko, the defender of Solidarity, who was murdered by the secret police.

19 October 1984 with the aid of two lieutenants, and throw his body in the River Vistula. But they allowed the priest's

chauffeur to escape and the whole affair soon became public knowledge.

To everyone's surprise, the Polish government reacted by arresting the four men responsible and putting them on trial in the city of Bydgoszcz at the end of December.

Even more surprising was the verdict of guilty and the sentences of 25 years in jail for the two ringleaders. Such a prosecution of secret policemen was unprecedented in eastern Europe and signalled that Jaruzelski was serious in his attempts at reconciliation. The General immediately assumed control of the Interior Ministry and installed an ex-First Secretary of the party whom he trusted, Andrez Gdula, to forestall any more displays of initiative.

The grave and church of Father Jerzy Popieluszko remain Solidarity shrines.

enquiry into the brutality and for the release of those who had been imprisoned. A year later, all the participants were amnestied: the Committee had scored its first success.

It kept up its pressure on the government by founding a magazine, *Robotnik*, which aimed to forge links between workplaces throughout the country. It achieved this goal by publishing reports from worker-correspondents around Poland, which soon established a sense of solidarity. The first free trade union was founded in Silesia in February 1978, and *Robotnik* ensured that information about this initiative was disseminated throughout Poland. The Free Trade Union of the Coast was founded in Gdansk two months later. It was upon this growing movement that an outside catalyst was to have a profound effect and bring the workers their most powerful ally. On 16 October 1978 the cardinals of the Catholic Church elected a Pole to the papal chair.

The visit of Pope John Paul II to his homeland in June 1979 transformed the mood of the Polish people and gave them a sense of hope, despite their worsening economic plight. The country now owed the West $20 billion, and servicing this debt used up 92 per cent of Poland's hard currency earnings. The government could no longer afford to import raw materials or food to cover shortages at home. During 1979, national income fell by 1.8 per cent.

On 1 July 1980, the government tried again to raise food prices to a realistic level. Sporadic local strikes took place, including a very small one at the Gdansk shipyards, but the government had told local officials to placate militant workers with pay rises and the protests soon fizzled out. Then,

on 9 August, one of the strikers at the Lenin Shipyard who was also an enthusiastic member of the Free Trade Union of the Coast, Anna Walentynowicz, was dismissed. This action provoked protests and a heated meeting ensued. When the director of the shipyard jumped up on to a bulldozer to address the workers, nobody listened. Then he was joined on top of the vehicle by an electrician who had worked at the yard in the past but had suffered repeated dismissals for his free trade union activity. His name was Lech Walesa. Everyone listened to him.

The workers' first move was to insist that all negotiations had to be conducted on the radio so that everyone would know what was going on. The workers' negotiators, who included Walesa, demanded wage increases, free trade unions, the reinstatement of dismissed workers and the release of political prisoners. The yard was occupied for three days before an agreement was concluded. But as the workers finally left, the members of strike committees from other enterprises met them and urged them to keep going. Pandemonium ensued, and two thousand out of the yard's complement of sixteen thousand went back inside.

The strike was now becoming a severe embarrassment to the Polish government, and deputy Prime Minister Tadeusz Pyka was despatched from Warsaw to sort it out. An Inter-factory Strike Committee now represented two hundred enterprises, but Pyka tried to divide them by making individual agreements. The strikers were too shrewd to fall for that manoeuvre, however, so he began offering concessions - which amazed the negotiators. But when he returned to Warsaw, to get them ratified by

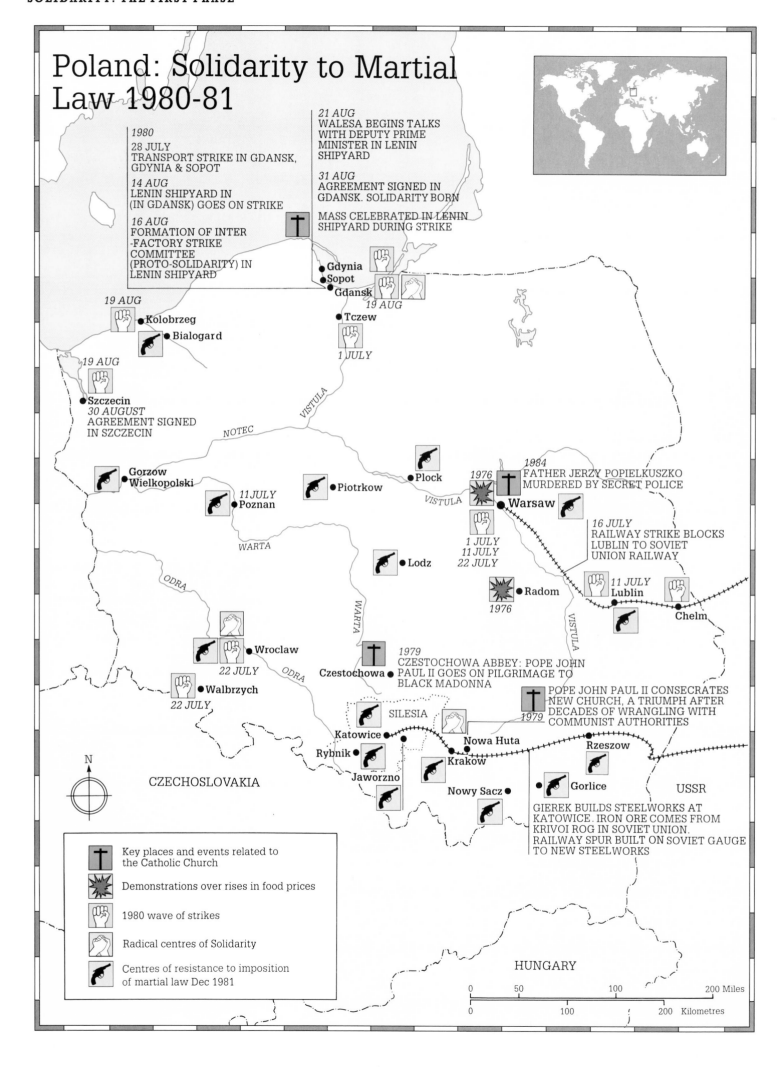

# Poland: Solidarity to Martial Law 1980-81

*1980*
**28 JULY**
TRANSPORT STRIKE IN GDANSK, GDYNIA & SOPOT

*14 AUG*
LENIN SHIPYARD IN (IN GDANSK) GOES ON STRIKE

*16 AUG*
FORMATION OF INTER-FACTORY STRIKE COMMITTEE (PROTO-SOLIDARITY) IN LENIN SHIPYARD

*21 AUG*
WALESA BEGINS TALKS WITH DEPUTY PRIME MINISTER IN LENIN SHIPYARD

*31 AUG*
AGREEMENT SIGNED IN GDANSK. SOLIDARITY BORN

MASS CELEBRATED IN LENIN SHIPYARD DURING STRIKE

**Gdynia**
**Sopot**
**Gdansk**
*19 AUG*

*19 AUG*
**Kolobrzeg**
**Bialogard**

**Tczew**

*1 JULY*

*19 AUG*
**Szczecin**
*30 AUGUST*
AGREEMENT SIGNED IN SZCZECIN

**Gorzow Wielkopolski**

*11 JULY*
**Poznan**

**Piotrkow**
**Plock**

*1976*

*1984*
FATHER JERZY POPIELKUSZKO MURDERED BY SECRET POLICE

**Warsaw**

*1 JULY*
*11 JULY*
*22 JULY*

**16 JULY**
RAILWAY STRIKE BLOCKS LUBLIN TO SOVIET UNION RAILWAY

**Lodz**

*1976*
**Radom**

*11 JULY*
**Lublin**

**Chelm**

**Wroclaw**
*22 JULY*

**Walbrzych**
*22 JULY*

**Czestochowa**
*1979*
CZESTOCHOWA ABBEY: POPE JOHN PAUL II GOES ON PILGRIMAGE TO BLACK MADONNA

POPE JOHN PAUL II CONSECRATES NEW CHURCH, A TRIUMPH AFTER DECADES OF WRANGLING WITH COMMUNIST AUTHORITIES
*1979*

SILESIA
**Katowice**
**Nowa Huta**
**Rybnik**
**Jaworzno**
**Krakow**
**Nowy Sacz**
**Rzeszow**
**Gorlice**

GIEREK BUILDS STEELWORKS AT KATOWICE. IRON ORE COMES FROM KRIVOI ROG IN SOVIET UNION. RAILWAY SPUR BUILT ON SOVIET GAUGE TO NEW STEELWORKS

CZECHOSLOVAKIA

N

USSR

HUNGARY

VISTULA
NOTEC
WARTA
ODRA
WARTA
ODRA
VISTULA
VISTULA

Key places and events related to the Catholic Church

Demonstrations over rises in food prices

1980 wave of strikes

Radical centres of Solidarity

Centres of resistance to imposition of martial law Dec 1981

0   50   100   200 Miles
0   100   200 Kilometres

Three metal crosses outside the Lenin Shipyard in Gdansk symbolize the unsuccessful attempts to bring about changes in Poland in 1956, 1970 and 1976.

the Politburo, only a few minor points were accepted by the government.

The Politburo now changed its tactics. The yard was showered with leaflets which promised wage increases if the strikers returned to work. Party propaganda began vilifying the leaders. The editor of *Robotnik* was arrested and beaten up on 19 August, and many members of the Workers' Defence Committee were also detained. However, the balance of events shifted when Church leaders condemned the party's attitude in a statement issued on 22 August, and urged that honest negotiations be conducted.

Most of the workforce on the Baltic coast was now on strike and the government was on the defensive. A meeting was convened between one of the deputy Prime Ministers, Jagielski, and the strike committee. This was the first of five meetings which took place during the next week and culminated in the signing of an agreement in which both sides made concessions. The government agreed to respect the independence of the new trade union and to allow it to control its own destiny. The union guaranteed to observe the constitution, to accept the 'social ownership of the means of production', to avoid taking on a political role in the country and to leave Poland's 'international alliances' unchallenged.

Jagielski could not, however, cope with the phrase 'free trade union'. So the committee consulted the group of intellectuals which had been advising it. They were led by Tadeusz Mazowiecki, the man who was to become Poland's first non-Communist Prime Minister in a generation. The group pointed out that the strike had been an expression of solidarity, and *Solidarity* was the title of their news bulletin. So why not call the new union by that one word?

### The Party Retaliates

Five days after the Gdansk agreement was signed Gierek had a heart attack and Stanislaw Kania became leader of the Polish Communist Party. Meanwhile, the tide behind Solidarity seemed unstoppable. By the middle of September, over 3 million people had declared their allegiance to the union. But many local groups encountered determined resistance by local officials.

In Warsaw, the Politburo was determined to regain the initiative. The following winter witnessed a smear campaign against the union and the Workers' Defence Committee. However, on 11 February events took an unexpected turn when the Defence Minister, General Wojciech Jaruzelski, was promoted to Prime Minister.

The army had maintained a low political profile and was sympathetically regarded by most Poles. A surge of goodwill towards the new administration encouraged Solidarity to make concessions in its negotiations, and all outstanding grievances were settled within a week. However, Jaruzelski was summoned to the Kremlin and roasted by the most senior members of the Soviet Politburo.

A member of the Workers' Defence Committee who was also a senior adviser to Solidarity was arrested. In the face of continued harassment of Committee members and provocative tactics on the part of the government, union leaders did their best to restrain the members.

The Politburo was, however, determined to succeed whatever the cost, and throughout the summer of 1981 it refused to negotiate with Solidarity, while allowing the economic crisis to simmer and the food shortages to mount. These measures were successful in arousing popular discontent and Solidarity lost a lot of support. Meanwhile, martial law was being planned.

Jaruzelski replaced Kania as party leader, and military operational groups were ordered into the countryside. A month later other groups were stationed in the cities. With his men in place, on 13 December Jaruzelski declared a 'State of War' under which Solidarity leaders and members of the Workers' Defence Committee were immediately interned. The party had regained control of Poland and Solidarity seemed vanquished. But not all the leaders were caught, and some went underground. Solidarity might have lost the first battle, but the war was not yet over.

The Wall begins to fall. In the euphoria of freedom, East and West Germans clamber onto the Berlin Wall, November 1989. The two Germanies were reunited on 3 October 1990.

# REFORM AND REVOLUTION

## 1985 - The Present

# The Demise of Communism?

The election of Mikhail Gorbachev as General Secretary of the Soviet Communist Party on 11 March 1985, less than twenty-four hours after the death of the former incumbant Konstantin Chernenko, was a turning point in world affairs, although few realized it at the time. His radical approach to the massive problems his country faced and his political finesse were to affect the lives of people all over the world within five years. But his greatest impact occurred in eastern Europe, where his refusal to use Soviet power to prop up ageing, discredited regimes unleashed a hurricane of reform which left the Cold War beached like a dead whale, rotting on the ebb tide of history.

## What is to be Done?

Gorbachev represented a new political generation. Unlike his predecessors, he had not held high office under Stalin, and although he had spent thirty years working his way up through the party apparatus under Stalin's former minions, it had been the anti-Stalinism of Khrushchev which had shaped his political thinking. Moreover, as a lawyer with further training in agronomy, a host of acquaintances among the intelligensia and a glancing familiarity with the West - he had toured France and Italy in a hired car and visited Canada as the Politburo member with responsibility for agriculture - he knew that his country was falling behind the West long before he reached the top. The symptoms were all around - absenteeism, alcoholism, worker apathy, nepotism - as well as the inertia of a central planning system which had led the Soviet Union into an industrial cul-de-sac and stifled initiative. Such problems were to be exacerbated by a catastrophic collapse in 1986 of the world price of oil - Moscow's most important source of hard currency - and the continued drain on the exchequer by the country's military rearmament. It was a situation which demanded radical solutions, a call which the new technocratic leadership realized they could no longer evade.

On the debit side, Gorbachev was surrounded by a vast army of party *apparatchiks* with a vested interest in the status quo. Indeed, he was a product of that very system, and for the first few years he proceeded with some caution. Although he pensioned off some of the die-hards, attacked corruption, alcoholism and tried to persuade people to work harder, his economic policies initially reflected traditional planning priorities. Technological modernization was his aim for raising productivity and heavy

East Berlin, October 1989. Gorbachev and Honecker at the parade to mark the fortieth anniversary of the founding of East Germany. That evening, thousands of demonstrators shouted 'Freedom, freedom!'

industry the target. But when, after two years, these exhortations and revisions had made little impact, he moved in to attack the bureaucrats who were trying to protect their lifestyle and the system they knew. Instead of merely wringing his hands in regret, he used the Chernobyl nuclear accident and the attempted cover-up by local officials to expose the urgency of his task of restructuring the system (*perestroika*).

A new era in foreign relations was also far from apparent during Gorbachev's first year in office. His meeting with Ronald Reagan in Geneva in November 1985 produced little more than routine noises of mutual respect from both sides. The real breakthrough came a year later when the two leaders met in Reykjavik, Iceland, during the weekend of 11-12 October 1986. Gorbachev made a series of totally unexpected offers on disarmament which caught the Americans off balance. Limitations on medium-range missiles were agreed, as was a timetable for the reduction of strategic missiles over the following five years. But discussions broke down when the Americans proposed the so-called 'zero option', that is the elimination of all ballistic missiles, and the Soviet side insisted that the Strategic Defense Initiative, or 'Star Wars Programme' had to go.

Many commentators suggested that the US had introduced the 'zero option' in the belief that no Soviet leader could ever accept such a proposal. Washington was, therefore, astonished when talks between the foreign ministers of both sides, George Shultz and Eduard Shevardnadze, held during the autumn of 1987, led to the Intermediate-range Nuclear

Forces agreement, or INF. This unprecedented treaty, which provided for the complete elimination of two classes of weapon systems, the 'double-zero option', was signed in Washington on 8 December 1987 by Reagan and Gorbachev during the first visit by a Soviet leader to the US for fourteen years.

'Hawks' in the American Congress and the Pentagon desperately tried to find objections that would disrupt the ratification process and block the two-thirds majority that the measure needed on Capitol Hill. These manoeuvres failed and the first serious de-escalation of the Cold War went into effect. Cruise and Pershing missiles were taken out of commission on the American side, while the Soviets destroyed their transportable SS12, SS20 and SS23 missiles and their launch vehicles. These measures were verified by mobile teams from the opposing side which could visit any site at forty-eight hours notice, and by permanent teams which were stationed at the plants which had built the weapons in order to ensure that no replacements were manufactured.

## The House of Cards

The same year also saw a major initiative from the Kremlin on eastern Europe after two years of vague remarks by Gorbachev. In January 1987 he addressed the Central Committee with proposals that citizens should demonstrate greater individual and group initiative and that the dead hand of party bureaucracy must be removed if this was going to take place. He followed this with a speech in Prague during April which suggested that eastern European countries should also show more initiative as each country had its own traditions. This rather anodyne message contained the startling implication that Moscow might no longer regard itself as the model which its satellites had to follow. But most of the leaders in his audience were too old to change their spots and events had to wait on a challenge that would test Gorbachev's sincerity.

That trial came in 1988 after the Polish government announced substantial price rises would come into effect on 1 February. Strikes for wages increases that would compensate for these increases in the cost of living began in late April. Although they spread to the Lenin Shipyard in Gdansk, the birthplace of Solidarity, they were not organized by the union. Wage concessions were made by the government and any dissenters were beaten up by the police.

However, the basic economic causes of the troubles could not be dispersed by truncheons and strikes broke out again in August. During a visit to the country in July, Gorbachev had made a speech which dismissed Solidarity as a mistake. But only a month later, in order to contain the disorders, the Polish government had little alternative but to talk to Solidarity if they were to solve their troubles without Soviet help.

The talks finally began in February 1989 and it soon became apparent that if the government wanted Solidarity's support then it would have to make major concessions. The union was relegalized and took part in Poland's first free elections in over 40 years during June 1989. Solidarity was only allowed to contest 35 per cent of the seats for the new parliament but it won all of them. When the new assembly met it promoted the former Prime Minister, General Jarulzelski, to be Poland's first President, but was unable to fill his previous position until Tadeusz Mazowiecki, who had helped end the 1980 strikes, was nominated by Solidarity. He became Poland's first non-Communist

prime minister since the Second World War and the majority of the posts in the government went to his supporters, with the Defence and Interior portfolios being retained by the Communists.

## All Fall Down

By now the rest of the world was watching with amazement as Soviet troops remained resolutely in their barracks. On the other side of the Carpathian Mountains, Hungarians had already enjoyed greater civil liberties than many of their neighbours for some years. Reformers within the Communist Party had already been nibbling away at the old guard and János Kádár, who had been the Party General Secretary since the suppression of the 1956 uprising, was replaced in May 1988. A number of independent parties began to form and the Democratic Union of Scientific Workers, the country's first independent trade union, was tolerated.

With events in Poland apparently unstoppable, reformers within the Hungarian Communist Party led by Imre Pozsgay began to get the upper hand. The leading opposition parties now began to co-ordinate their action and, in the spring of 1989, started negotiations with the government which lasted until the autumn. The government, meanwhile, had removed part of the fence which protected Hungary's border with Austria; a move which proved to have immense consequences for the whole of the Eastern bloc.

Although few East Germans could travel freely to the West, many spent their holidays in neighbouring Warsaw Pact countries. As they saw liberalization gather pace around them, the suffocating grip of Erich Honecker seemed immovable and the people started to take desperate measures. In July, Honecker was taken ill and East Germans took his hospitalization as their cue to act. People began flooding into the embassies in Berlin while others travelled to

Budapest, Warsaw and Prague to seek asylum in a similar fashion. Others headed for Hungary and the risky route through the holes in the fence. Then on 19 August, Hungary opened a border gate and 900 slipped into Austria.

The embassies in Prague were now besieged and a special train to the West had to be organized to relieve the pressure. On 3 October East Germany closed its border with Czechoslovakia to seal off the escape route. But four days later, Gorbachev arrived in Berlin as part of the country's fortieth anniversary celebrations and told Honecker that repression was no longer on the agenda. That night a demonstration on the streets of the capital turned into a running battle with police and the subsequent protests proved unstoppable. Eleven days later Honecker resigned. Only weeks later, the Berlin Wall was opened and free movement became possible between the two Germanies. Millions crossed to take a look at the West, but few stayed.

Czechoslovakia's train to freedom was one of the last to gather momentum, despite the activities of Charter 77 and the unremitting efforts of rebels such as Vaclav Havel. No group of reformers within the party seemed ready to elbow the hard-liners to one side. Suddenly, on 17 November 1989, an over-zealous squad of policemen dispersed a student demonstration with a degree of violence which incensed the public. Two days later a massive but completely peaceful demonstration filled the centre of Prague. At first the government tried to pretend that nothing special was happening, but as people realized that no one was going to open fire on them, their confidence increased and they returned night after night. On 24 November the Prime Minister and the Party General Secretary resigned. A week later, President Husak had gone as well. By now the people could only consider one man as their leader and on 29 December the Czech Parliament elected Vaclav Havel to the post by general acclamation. He seemed almost embarrassed by the fuss.

The Balkans, which had no democratic tradition, did not follow the populist spasms of its neighbours. The political problems of Bulgaria, Romania and Yugoslavia arose because of large minorities residing within their borders. In Bulgaria, 750,000 of the 9 million population were of Turkish origin. But sustained discrimination against them during the previous few years led to nearly half of them departing for their homeland when emigration restrictions were lifted under international pressure during the summer of 1989. That left Bulgarian agriculture paralysed and the harvest rotting in the fields. Two million Hungarians lived in Romania and Ceausescu's unremitting persecution of them led directly to the spark that brought his execution. Yugoslavia was such a melting pot that no one ethnic or religious group exceeded 36 per cent of the population and the country's politics were as much about self-determination as about democratic freedoms. In Albania, ethnically

Going home: Russian troops on the Salang Highway between Kabul and the Soviet border.

The funeral of Armenian nationalist leader Movses Gorgesyan, in Yerevan, Armenia.

# The Demise of Communism?

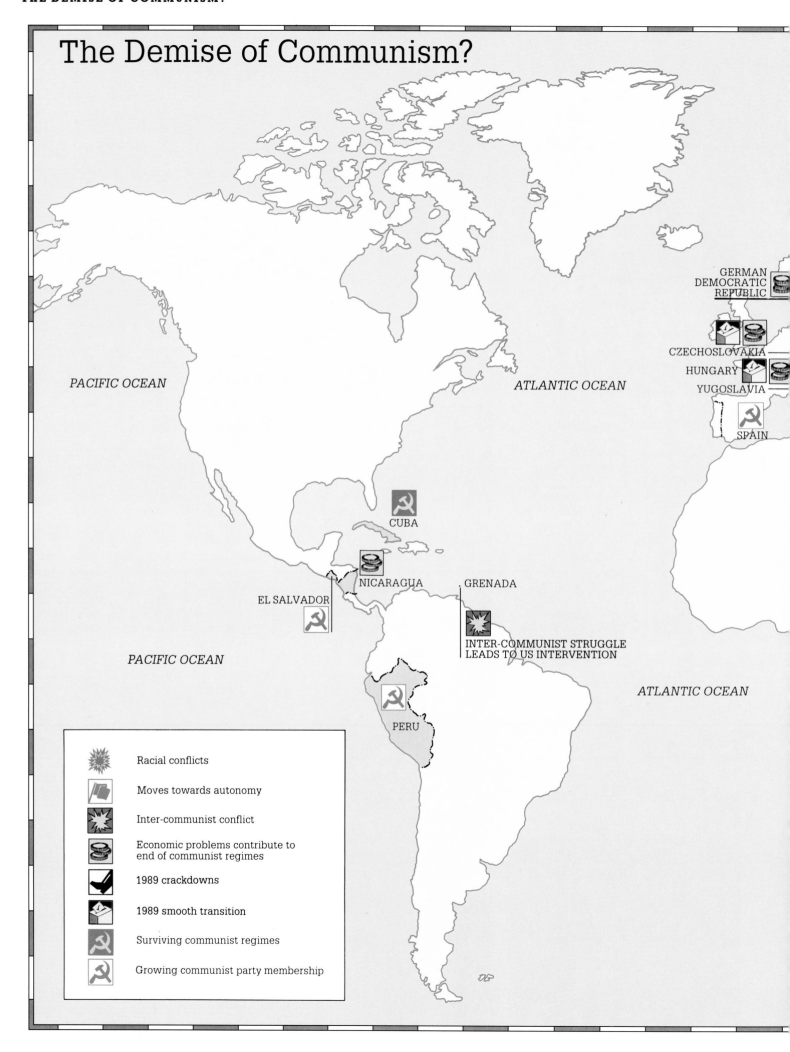

GERMAN
DEMOCRATIC
REPUBLIC

CZECHOSLOVAKIA

HUNGARY

YUGOSLAVIA

SPAIN

PACIFIC OCEAN

ATLANTIC OCEAN

CUBA

NICARAGUA

EL SALVADOR

GRENADA

INTER-COMMUNIST STRUGGLE
LEADS TO US INTERVENTION

PACIFIC OCEAN

ATLANTIC OCEAN

PERU

Racial conflicts

Moves towards autonomy

Inter-communist conflict

Economic problems contribute to
end of communist regimes

1989 crackdowns

1989 smooth transition

Surviving communist regimes

Growing communist party membership

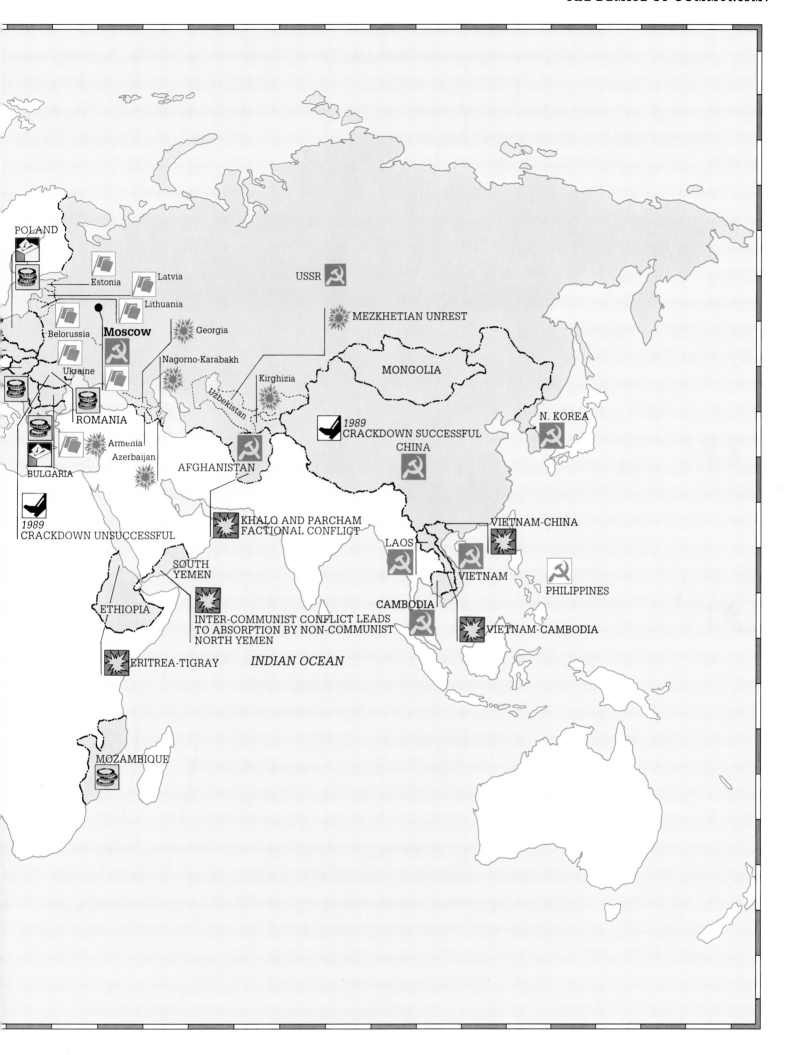

POLAND

Estonia

Latvia

USSR

Lithuania

MEZKHETIAN UNREST

Moscow

Belorussia

Georgia

Nagorno-Karabakh

Ukraine

MONGOLIA

Uzbekistan

Kirghizia

ROMANIA

N. KOREA

1989
CRACKDOWN SUCCESSFUL

Armenia

CHINA

Azerbaijan

BULGARIA

AFGHANISTAN

1989
CRACKDOWN UNSUCCESSFUL

KHALQ AND PARCHAM
FACTIONAL CONFLICT

VIETNAM-CHINA

SOUTH
YEMEN

LAOS

VIETNAM

PHILIPPINES

ETHIOPIA

INTER-COMMUNIST CONFLICT LEADS
TO ABSORPTION BY NON-COMMUNIST
NORTH YEMEN

CAMBODIA

VIETNAM-CAMBODIA

ERITREA-TIGRAY

INDIAN OCEAN

MOZAMBIQUE

# 'Gorbymania' Sweeps the World

Even before he was elevated to the post of General Secretary, Mikhail Gorbachev was the subject of intense curiosity and media attention in the West. When he visited Britain in December 1984, pictures of him and his wife filled the press from *The Times* to the tabloids. A Soviet leader under the age of sixty was a considerable novelty.

However, by October 1985 this first impression was overlaid by something more substantial as he began presenting new arms reduction proposals during his visit to France. People in the West began to feel that their hopes for a more secure, less anxious international atmosphere might be realized. By 1987, Gorbachev's impact on Western public opinion was so great that in France and Britain he was outshining local politicians in the popularity stakes. At the end the year he was named 'Man of the Year' by *Time* magazine.

A year later, during his visit to the United States to sign the treaty abolishing intermediate-range nuclear weapons, one of his impromptu walkabouts brought New York traffic to a standstill. Perhaps the climax to these Western tours came in June 1989 when a visit to a West German factory brought work to a halt as men and women broke into spontaneous applause as the leader of the 'old enemy' appeared. They might not have understood his language but they had no doubts about his intentions.

more homogeneous, the cautious reforms of Ramiz Alia, Hoxha's successor, and the knowledge, widely diffused through television, of the fate of Communism elsewhere in eastern Europe led to a belated mass movement for destalinization.

## Communism's Other Faces

The developing diversity of the Communist world which arose in the 1960s and 1970s was only emphasized by the events of the period which followed. China's change of direction had come with Mao's death in 1976 and Deng Xiaoping's assumption of the reins of power. China's move away from central planning started in the late 1970s as a result of experiments in agricultural production in Sichuan. But at the same time, Deng emphasized that no nonsense about democratic reforms would be tolerated; market mechanisms might be used to boost farming output but the party was still in charge.

Despite the existence of this clearly drawn line, a hard-line faction within the party, worried that anarchy was at hand, did its best to put back the clock. Only Deng's now unchallengeable authority stayed their hand and contained their attacks on western influences. However, when the Tiananmen Square demonstrations flaunted dissent before the cameras of western television crews assembled to cover Gorbachev's visit to Beijing, the diehards got the upper hand and the tanks moved in.

A completely different momentum from that of Eastern Europe was also evident in Central and South America. The success of the Sandinistas in Nicaragua in resisting American intervention in their country and in encouraging guerrilla movements in the surrounding region during the 1980s provided an excuse for the Reagan administrations's interventionist tendencies. That Washington's efforts became entangled with drug trafficking was largely ignored in the American media, despite the mounting weight of evidence. However, when the incoming Bush administration realized that the Maoist guerrillas of Peru, the Sendaro Luminoso or Shining Path, was also financing its fight with drug money, the White House sent military advisers to the Andes, just as it had sent them to Vietnam. Further south, in Brazil, the 1989 election also proved that the left's momentum was far from spent as Marxist administrations took over the running of most of the country's large cities.

On the Pacific rim, the Communist groups in Indonesia and Malaysia which had seemed like a threat in earlier decades showed no signs of resurgence. The story was different, however, in the Philippines where the corruption of the Marcos years encouraged a revolution. Even when Mrs Aquino took power, the influence of the army and the right did not diminish and the Maoist guerrillas exhibited no signs of decline.

On the Asian mainland, the Communist hold on power in Vietnam, Cambodia and North Korea seemed unrelenting, although Indochina had become a battleground for a number of warring Communist factions. Further north in Mongolia the shadowy regime performed a balancing act between its giant neighbours and succeeded in avoiding trouble with either, although as the 1990s opened it began to experiment with free elections.

Further west in Afghanistan, Soviet involvement in the guerrilla war against the mujahidin seemed to be a commitment without end. Only when the new leadership insisted that this bottomless pit had to be sealed were serious negotiations undertaken which would allow the Soviet army to withdraw. To the astonishment of the West, the Kabul regime, benefitting from serious divisions among the Mujahidin, did not collapse.

## The End of a Dream ?

Apart from the drain on men and resources, Moscow was also keen to end its conflict with the Muslim forces of Afghanistan because of the restive state of its own ethnic minorities. The first sign of trouble appeared in December 1986 when one of Brezhnev's cronies, Secretary Kunayev, was retired from the leadership of the Kazakh Communist Party on the sixteenth and replaced by a technocrat, Gennady Kolbin. Unfortunately, whereas Kunayev was a Kazakh, Kolbin was a Russian. Within twenty-four hours, students had taken to the streets of Alma-Ata, the state capital, and were demonstrating against what they regarded as the effects of Moscow's colonial attitudes. The extent of the damage caused was unknown outside the Soviet Union, but even five weeks later Western journalists were being refused admission to the area.

The following summer, other nationalists made their grievances known. Crimean Tartars, seeking a return to their homeland 43 years after their mass deportation on Stalin's orders, demonstrated outside the Kremlin. In the Baltic states, a few thousand people demonstrated in the three capitals for national self-determination. The police made no attempt to interfere in any of the protests.

However, unrest on quite a different scale erupted in February 1988 between the Azeri and Armenian communities which were sandwiched between the Caspian and Black Seas. On 20 February, the regional soviet of Nagorny Karabakh, which was an Armenian enclave within Azerbaijan, passed a resolution requesting that the region be transferred to the control of Armenia. It cannot be a complete coincidence that this vote came forty-eight hours after Gorbachev had made a speech advocating a return of power to the democratically elected soviets as a way of resolving nationalist issues. Rioting broke out within days and reports of pogroms being carried out by mobs against minorities began to filter through to the West. In May the First Secretaries of both local Parties were sacked and suggestions were made that Moscow had discovered that they had been encouraging protests in order to make the implementation of democratic reforms impossible.

More ethnic riots occurred in Georgia during June. Agitation also began to increase in the Baltic republics. By January 1989, the problems surrounding Nagorny Karabakh had become so dangerous that the Praesidium of the Supreme Soviet placed the two republics under the direct control of Moscow. Problems erupted in Georgia in April and the use of troops to quell a peaceful demonstration resulted in many deaths. Five days later the Georgian First Secretary resigned and allegations were heard again that *apparatchiks* were fomenting trouble to protect themselves from reform.

The summer of 1989 saw more riots in Uzbekistan, Kazakhstan and Turkmenia, all of which arose out of minor local incidents. Trouble flared throughout the summer in the southern republics and by the end of the year the Baltic states were in open revolt, while Russians were beginning to insist that their rights should be upheld as well. In a country with 112 recognized languages, government was becoming increasingly difficult to maintain.

# Gorbachev Takes Charge

Making breaches in the walls of the Cold War fortress. Gorbachev and Reagan draw the two superpowers closer together at the Geneva Summit in November 1985. After his first summit as leader of the Soviet Union Gorbachev told a press conference that 'the world has become a safer place'.

*Glasnost* and *perestroika* are the first Russian words to be known the world over, and their remarkable penetration of newspaper headlines everywhere is largely the work of one man: the first charismatic Soviet leader since Lenin. Mikhail Gorbachev was almost unknown in 1980, both in his own country and in the West. Ten years later, he had become a household name from Berlin to Bogota. His meteoric rise was due to both his abilities and the need for radical solutions within the Soviet Union.

The last days of the Brezhnev era were times of sloth and corruption. The desire for consistency and stability which had brought the elderly leader to power had degenerated into stagnation and the avoidance of any move which might rock the domestic boat. He and his cronies were seemingly prepared to tolerate almost any behaviour as long as it did not become public. Increasingly they looked back to the war years and Brezhnev began awarding himself medals

for non-existent 'heroic' deeds. But even they could not halt the passage of time, and eventually disease and old age began to prepare the ground for younger men. And those who were to succeed them were of a generation who did not share many of the memories and attitudes of their predecessors.

**The New Men**

Gorbachev and his generation are the most obvious products of the enormous sums invested in higher education by the Kremlin since the Second World War. When Gorbachev entered Moscow University in September 1950, he joined the most privileged group of the country's 1.2 million students. By the time he was elected General Secretary of the party on 11 March 1985, the number of university students had grown to 5.2 million and graduates were penetrating every aspect of Soviet life.

Gorbachev came to Moscow after growing up in Stavropol, which is situated in the fertile farming lands between the Black and Caspian Seas. His grandfather had organized the local farming collective, while his father was a skilled operator of tractors and combine harvesters and was highly respected within the party. It was probably the esteem felt for his father, who died in the war, which got the fourteen-year-old his first job in the spring of 1945 as an assistant to a combine harvester operator, a much prized job in Soviet agriculture. It says much for the determination of the young Gorbachev that his involvement in the reconstruction of his country did not stop him graduating from secondary school with a silver medal. He also received a medal for his work at the tractor station, a double honour which undoubtedly earned him his place at his country's most prestigious university. His decision to study law also marked him out, for there were few members of that

# The Soviet Union and its Borders

NORWAY

SWEDEN

FINLAND

Taimyr N.O.

Nenets N.O.

Komi A.S.S.R.

Yamal-Nenets N.O.

Evenki N.O.

Khanty-Mansi N.O.

Karelian A.S.S.R.

*BALTIC SEA*

●Leningrad

●**Tallinn**

R U S S I A N

Komi-Permyak N.O.

Mary A.S.S.R.

**ESTONIAN S.S.R.**

**LATVIAN S.S.R.**

●**Riga**

●**Kalinin**

●**Gorkiy**

Udmurt A.S.S.R.

S O V I E T

**LITHUANIAN S.S.R.**

●**Vilnius**

●**Moscow**

Tatar A.S.S.R.

Bashkir A.S.S.R.

F E D E R A T

**Part of the R.S.F.S.R.**

●**Minsk**

●**Tula**

Mordovian A.S.S.R.

●Novosibirsk

POLAND

**BELORUSSIAN S.S.R.**

Chuvash A.S.S.R.

●**Kuybyshev**

Khakass A.O.

CZECHO-SLOVAKIA

●**Kiev**

Gorno-Altai N.O.

HUNGARY

**UKRAINIAN S.S.R.**

●Vologograd

●Karaganda

ROMANIA

●**Odessa**

●**Rostov**

**KAZAKH S.S.R.**

Adyge A.O.

Kara-Kalpak A.S.S.R.

Cherkess A.O.

*ARAL SEA*

**MOLDAVIAN S.S.R.**

Dagestan A.S.S.R.

*BLACK SEA*

Abkhaz A.S.S.R.

North Ossentian A.O.

●Alma-Ata

BULGARIA

South Ossentian A.O.

●**Tbilisi**

●Tashkent

**KIRGIZ S.S.R.**

**GEORGIAN S.S.R.**

Yerevan●

●**Baku**

**UZBEK S.S.R.**

Adzhar A.S.S.R.

*CASPIAN SEA*

**TURKMEN S.S.R.**

●**Dushanbe**

TURKEY

**ARMENIAN S.S.R.**

Nakhichevan A.S.S.R.

Nagorno-Karabakh A.O.

●Ashkhabad

Gorno-Badakhshan A.O.

**AZERBAIJAN S.S.R.**

**TADZHIK S.S.R.**

*MEDITERRANEAN SEA*

AFGHANISTAN

IRAN

PAKISTAN

N

INDIA

| 0 | 200 | 400 | 600 | Miles |
| 0 | 200 | 400 | 600 | 800 | Kilometres |

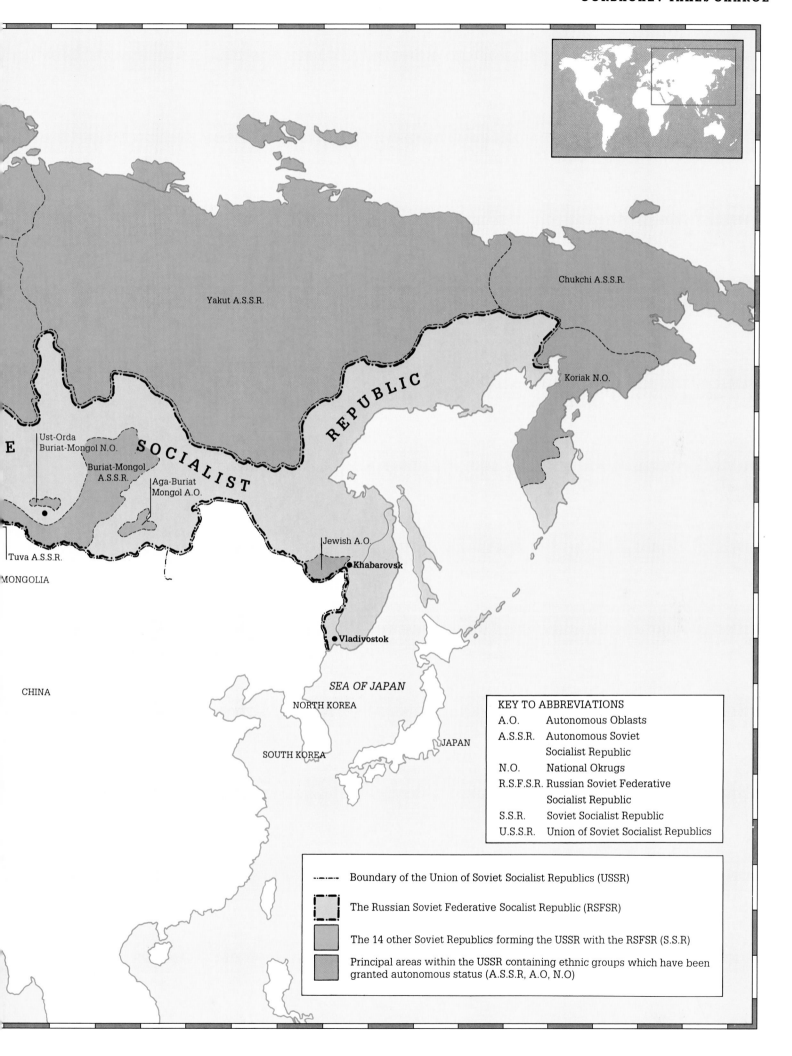

Chukchi A.S.S.R.

Yakut A.S.S.R.

Koriak N.O.

R E P U B L I C

Ust-Orda
Buriat-Mongol N.O.

S O C I A L I S T

Buriat-Mongol
A.S.S.R.

Aga-Buriat
Mongol A.O.

E

Jewish A.O.

●Khabarovsk

Tuva A.S.S.R.

MONGOLIA

●Vladivostok

CHINA

SEA OF JAPAN

NORTH KOREA

JAPAN

SOUTH KOREA

KEY TO ABBREVIATIONS

| | |
|---|---|
| A.O. | Autonomous Oblasts |
| A.S.S.R. | Autonomous Soviet Socialist Republic |
| N.O. | National Okrugs |
| R.S.F.S.R. | Russian Soviet Federative Socialist Republic |
| S.S.R. | Soviet Socialist Republic |
| U.S.S.R. | Union of Soviet Socialist Republics |

— - — - Boundary of the Union of Soviet Socialist Republics (USSR)

The Russian Soviet Federative Socialist Republic (RSFSR)

The 14 other Soviet Republics forming the USSR with the RSFSR (S.S.R)

Principal areas within the USSR containing ethnic groups which have been granted autonomous status (A.S.S.R, A.O, N.O)

profession practising in the Soviet Union during Stalin's final years.

After he graduated in 1955, he returned to his home base to become an official of the party's youth wing, the Komsomol, which has always been one route to a high position. He was soon joined by a former fellow student in Moscow who was now studying for her doctorate in sociology, Raisa. The early years of their marriage were spent in Stavropol where Gorbachev proved his organizational ability. In 1962 he was promoted from the Komsomol to a position within the full party as organizer of the administration of the regional state and collective farms.

The following year his career received another substantial boost when he was appointed custodian of the local *nomenklatura*, the catalogue of key jobs in the region and the list of party members deemed suitable to fill them. National politics now took a hand as Khrushchev's fall in 1964 provoked changes within the party hierarchy. Stavropol's First Secretary, Fyodor Kulakov, was promoted to the secretariat of the Central Committee, while Leonid Yefremov, one of Khrushchev's men in Moscow, was demoted and allowed to serve out the remainder of his career in the southern agricultural region. When he retired in 1970, he was replaced by Gorbachev and at the Twenty-fourth Party Congress in 1971 the rising star of Stavropol was elected to the Central Committee.

Apart from its primary role as an agricultural producer, the region which Gorbachev was now running was the site of holiday resorts and spas to which Yuri Andropov, the director of the KGB, made an annual visit. One of Gorbachev's functions as the regional First Secretary was to pay a courtesy call on any visiting party dignitary, and during the 1970s he got to know Andropov very well. Indeed, Gorbachev became a family friend whom the senior man sought out at Central Committee meetings and invited back to his home.

### Getting Results

In the Stavropol farmlands Gorbachev's fresh approach was producing impressive yields as he used financial incentives to increase output. However, party conservatives managed to have this policy condemned and a number of those who promoted its use were sacked. Gorbachev had moved on, however, to a system of large pools of mechanized units to harvest the crops. The results were so spectacular that he received a personal letter of congratulation from Brezhnev and a summons to Moscow to become the new Secretary for Agriculture on the Central Committee.

Brezhnev was by now a sick man. His poor health provoked increased speculation about his successor, although Andropov was rarely mentioned. However, President Carter unwittingly improved his chances by putting so much emphasis on human rights issues, which was a KGB matter.

His hand was further strengthened during 1980 by the exposure of massive corruption in the Polish government; and the Soviet Central Committee passed a resolution in September of that year condemning official corruption and authorizing the removal and exposure of guilty parties 'regardless of their position'. Such motions threatened the very inner circle of the leadership if the KGB and Andropov were given an opening.

Their chance came at the beginning of 1982, when a case involving the smuggling of massive quantities of diamonds and currency came to light among people closely associated with Brezhnev's daughter, Galina. Details of the case were leaked to Western journalists and reports appeared in the London press. The scandal also touched Semyon Tsvigun, one of Brezhnev's aides and an immediate subordinate of Andropov in the KGB. When Mikhail Suslov, the party's ageing chief theoretician, saw the file on the case, he confronted Tsvigun - who committed suicide that night. Suslov suffered a stroke a few hours after the confrontation and died a few days later. In the atmosphere of the moment Andropov became Suslov's natural successor, particularly as he was supported by the undeniably honest Marshal Ustinov, the head of the armed forces.

While these manoeuvres were underway, Gorbachev was consolidating his position in charge of agriculture. He returned to the idea of incentives, but failed to convert the Politburo completely to his ideas and a compromise package was agreed in 1982.

### The End of an Era

The pace of events speeded up in April of that year when Brezhnev suffered another major heart attack and had to be carried off a plane on a stretcher. Andropov used his

absence to reinforce his own position and by the time the failing leader could attend another Politburo meeting in May the die was cast. The Brezhnev faction was unable to prevent Andropov being named as the party's chief theoretician, a post which commands a powerful bureaucracy. He was now recognized within the Soviet Union as the country's number two politician.

Leonid Brezhnev finally died of a heart attack on the morning of 10 November. The Central Committee plenum called to elect a new leader was held the following day, giving the conservative local party secretaries, who form the largest voting block within the Committee, no opportunity to organize opposition to Andropov, whose anti-corruption drive threatened them and their followers. He was proposed by Konstantin Chernenko, Brezhnev's closest crony and the man whom many people had expected to succeed him.

In one of Andropov's first speeches as party leader he proposed 'a wider independence and autonomy for industrial associations and farms', which was a coded reference to the sort of incentive schemes which Gorbachev had championed. It was one thing to make such proposals, however, and quite another to make them work in the Soviet Union.

Nevertheless, Gorbachev had managed to get the money into the pockets of the farm labourers. But they found little to spend it on as quality consumer goods were in short supply in the USSR. Furthermore, improved grain yields required the administration to invest in more storage facilities and to reorganize the transport system in order to move the produce. But only the labourers earned the incentives, so administrators began returning to the land to earn more money, and the distribution system was

# The Still, Small Voice

The young Andrei Sakharov made an immense contribution to the Soviet programme to develop a hydrogen bomb after the Second World War and through his work came into contact with his country's leaders. This experience caused him acute misgivings about allowing such people to control potentially catastrophic weapons. His position as a member of the Soviet Academy of Sciences during the late 1950s gave him a voice in his country's policies, but neither side in the Cold War was interested in controlling weapons production. By 1961 he was speaking out in public against testing the very bomb he had helped to create.

As the Brezhnev era opened, Sakharov's criticism of Soviet

Andrei Sakharov (right) at a conference in Moscow, 1987.

policies became more general and he signed a joint letter to the Twenty-third Party Congress in 1966 which warned against the

resurrection of Stalinism. Despite his dissent, he retained his professorship at the Lebedev Institute of Physics in Moscow until 1980, when he attacked the invasion of Afghanistan. He and his wife were sent into internal exile in Gorky. Only the personal intervention of Gorbachev in 1986 and his phone call to the ageing scientist brought him back to Moscow. Through his respect for Sakharov, the General Secretary signalled to the world that a new age had dawned in the Communist heartland.

When Sakharov died in December 1989 hundreds of thousands of people attended his funeral. As they filed past the grave, many dropped letters saying 'Forgive us'.

here he saw only his family, his personal physician and Gorbachev.

Yet the old clique was not completely finished, and when Andropov finally succumbed on 9 February 1984 they managed to get Brezhnev's old friend, Chernenko, elected as General Secretary. The price that the new men exacted for their agreement was that Gorbachev be designated Second Secretary. It was the good fortune of the Soviet people, and perhaps the world, that Chernenko was as sick as his predecessors. Mikhail Gorbachev was able to become General Secretary just over a year later.

## The New Broom

It was not long before Muscovites realized that their new leader was rather different from his predecessors. In an unprecedented walkabout he asked a cleaner on a hospital ward about her life and how she managed on her poor wages. When a local official tried to interfere, Gorbachev rounded on him and made it abundantly clear that it was the job of officials to help citizens, and not vice versa. Muscovites knew that the *vlasti*, the leaders, did not do things like that and news of the incident was soon all over the city. The legend of 'Lemonade Joe', the nickname that the citizens gave their leader, was born.

However, the new leaders understood that a fresh approach had to be more than skin deep and that old attitudes and backsliding could no longer be tolerated. In his report to the Twenty-seventh Congress of the Communist Party of the Soviet Union on 25 February 1986, Gorbachev made this clear:

Every readjustment of the economic mechanism begins with a readjustment of thinking, with a rejection of old stereotypes of thought and actions, with a clear understanding of the new tasks. This refers primarily to the activity of our economic personnel, to the functionaries of the central links of the administration. Most of them have a clear idea of the party's initiatives, and seek and find the best ways of carrying them out.... It is hard, however, to understand those who take a wait-and-see policy, or those who do not actually do anything or change anything. There will be no reconciliation with the stance taken by functionaries of that kind. We will simply have to part company with them. All the more so do we have to part company with those who hope that everything will settle down and return to the old lines. That will not happen, comrades!

The direction in which the party leaders were now heading was clear to everyone. The real question was whether they could drag the rest of the party and the people of the Soviet Union with them. The 'old lines' were habits which were hard to break. Perhaps something even more radical than *perestroika* would be necessary. That was where *glasnost*, or openness, would make its contribution. From 1986 onwards, everything in Soviet society would be open to question.

Anniversary parade in Moscow in 1987. Earlier that year Gorbachev and Reagan had signed the first ever treaty to reduce the size of their countries' nuclear arsenals.

disrupted. Such piecemeal solutions, many of which had been tried during the late 1960s and 1970s in various industrial units, were clearly not going to work in isolation. The leadership was clearly going to have to bite the bullet: the whole system needed *perestroika*, or restructuring.

However, this was a task that required time - a commodity which Andropov possessed in limited quantity. For many years he had suffered from kidney disease, and even before he became General Secretary he must have known that the end was close. His solution was to cut his public appearances to the bone and concentrate on replacing the incompetent and corrupt members of the leadership he had inherited with a new generation committed to his own ideas on how to make the Soviet system work.

One of his first moves was to promote Nikolai Ryzhkov to the job of creating a new department of the Central Committee dedicated to co-ordinating industrial production and promoting better management. Andropov promoted Geidar Aliyev, the Muslim from Azerbaijan who had directed the KGB campaign against corruption there. He was made a full member of the Politburo with special responsibility for improving the country's transport.

However, perhaps Andropov's most important move was to give overall control of the economy to Gorbachev - on whom, as his condition deteriorated, he became more and more dependent. Eventually, in order to conceal the true state of his health from the remnants of the Brezhnev faction in the Politburo, he moved into the Kuntsevo Hospital and worked in a special study which was fitted with a dialysis machine;

# The Challenge of Islam

The intense enthusiasm which greeted Ayatollah Ruhollah Mousavi Khomeini when he returned to Tehran on 1 February 1979 came as a shock to most Marxists. Conditioned by their own definitions of revolution, they had not expected to be confronted by a popular uprising which derived inspiration from an ancient religious system and which appeared to embody almost everything they opposed. Yet they could not ignore the most important experiment in the application of Islam for centuries, particularly as it was attracting the allegiance of radical youth in the Middle East - a recruiting ground which they had anticipated would be theirs alone. Furthermore, the Soviet Union itself was the home of over 50 million Muslims in its southern republics, and the prospect that they might be infected by this revolution was profoundly worrying to the Kremlin.

### The Rise of Fundamentalism

The Iranian revolution which overthrew Muhammed Reza Pahlavi Shah and the Western ways which he had sponsored in his country had roots which lay deep in the past. The differences between the *ulema*, or Islamic clerics, and the rulers of Iran can be traced to the late eighteenth century, but the conflict only became acute in the 1920s under the Shah's father, Reza. His drive to modernize Iran antagonized the *ulema*, who formed a coherent political group trusted by both peasants and urban workers.

Khomeini was the latest in a series of militant *ulema* who had opposed the secularization of Iran. He had first come to public notice in 1941 with the publication of his book *The Secrets Revealed*, which attacked Reza Shah. When the shiite faith's leading ayatollah, Ayatollah Borujerdi, died in March 1961, Khomeini became a contender for his mantle. His opposition to the Shah's renewed modernization drive landed him in jail in the spring of 1963. Although he was soon released, he was then rearrested, but the government could do little to silence him. After being released yet again, he was arrested once more on 4 November and put on a plane bound for Turkey. After living for nearly a year near Istanbul, he moved to Najaf in Iraq, which is a leading shiite theological centre and a shrine.

Meanwhile, the Shah was co-operating with American oil exploration companies; as a result petroleum revenues rose from $450 million in 1963 to $4400 million ten years later. Large sums were invested in

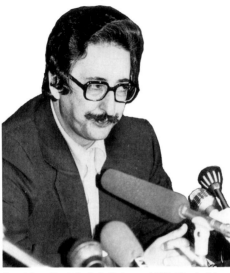

President Bani-Sadr in Tehran, 1981. Ousted by his clerical colleagues later that year, he formed a government in exile with Masoud Rajavi.

industry, which was soon growing at the rate of 20 per cent a year. Education and health services improved dramatically, while land reform redistributed the property of absentee landlords among the peasants.

These radical changes to the Iranian way of life were accompanied by other decrees which gave great offence to the traditional beliefs of the devout majority of the population. Not only did the Shah transfer adjudication on family matters from religious to secular courts; he also gave women the vote and discouraged the wearing of their all-enveloping black *chador*.

All these changes provoked widespread opposition, and the Shah took great care to vet all army promotions above the rank of major to ensure that it remained loyal. He also gave his civilian intelligence service, Savak, *carte blanche* to act as they saw fit, so that torture and political murders became a part of Iranian life. The censorship of books was introduced in 1966, which led to Savak raids on mosque libraries and interference in university life.

By the mid-1970s, as standards of living rose swiftly, the Shah was becoming increasingly confident that his modernization drive was working. In this more secure frame of mind, he ended his support to the Kurdish uprising in northern Iraq in return for a treaty with Baghdad which settled a series of long-running border disputes between the two countries. The treaty also stipulated that travel between the two countries should be eased, and this played into Khomeini's hands.

## Islam Under *Perestroika*

As the Soviet Union edges closer to the West and Gorbachev looks to a 'common European home', the second largest group in the country feels increasingly out of place. The 60 million or so Muslims look to Mecca rather than Moscow and have local traditions that emphasize a separate cultural heritage from their more dominant northern neighbours. Furthermore, while European Soviets are an ageing, static population, their Muslim counterparts are young and expanding. By the opening of the 1988-89 academic year, half of all the children in Soviet primary schools were Muslims.

Although the example of Iran galvanized many of these Soviet Muslims during the 1980s, the majority are Sunnis and do not belong to the Ayatollah's sect. Another large group are Sufis, an ancient mystic sect of great sophistication and learning

Two war veterans, a Russian and a Tajik, at a parade in Tajikistan where 90 per cent of the people are Muslims.

which is the antithesis of militant fundamentalism. There is, therefore, little desire among Soviet Muslims to follow the Iranian path. Instead, it would appear that national traditions are the dominant political force in the southern Soviet republics. Given the dynamic growth of these areas, it is going to become increasingly difficult to control them from Moscow.

For he could now exert considerable influence over Iranian visitors to Najaf, and this was to have a knock-on effect inside Iran.

A second unrelated event - the election of Jimmy Carter to the White House at the end of 1976 - combined with the opening of the border to create suitable conditions for Khomeini's takeover. Carter insisted that, if the Shah was to continue to receive American support, he must demonstrate a more tolerant attitude towards his critics within Iran. The first political prisoners were released within weeks of Carter's inauguration, but each concession only brought greater demands from the opposition. Large street demonstrations became regular events, and on 18 February 1978 one in Tabriz turned into a riot in which a hundred people died. Cries of 'Death to the Shah' were soon heard on the streets.

Demonstrations now began to increase in size, culminating in a rally of half a million people in Tehran on 7 September. Next morning, the army decided to act. It surrounded a group of fifteen thousand protesters crowded into a square, and slaughtered sixteen hundred of them using machine guns and helicopter gunships. The outrage felt by the majority of Iranians was now so great that no act by the army could intimidate them, and it was only a matter of time before the Shah lost power.

## The Left in Iran

Most shades of opinion within Iran objected to the Shah's reign of terror, which had become increasingly associated with American penetration of the region; this was particularly so after the Shah had, in the early 1960s acceded to pressure from the White House to grant immunity from prosecution to all US military advisers working in Iran. The sudden expansion of higher education had created a fertile recruiting ground for the left in the middle of this upheaval. But in the volatile mood of Iran in the 1970s the traditional Communist Party, the Tudeh (masses), was soon joined by other splinter groups.

The Tudeh's leaders misunderstood the anti-Americanism of the *ulema* and underestimated Khomeini's authoritarian attitude. Instead of emphasizing the anti-democratic nature of many of the Ayatollah's pronouncements and the repressive attitude towards women, they were quite content to establish a niche within the new political order after February 1979 and to align themselves with the clerics.

It was the Tudeh who incited students to storm the American Embassy and to take its staff hostage. They spied for the new political police on the activities of other parties, and urged the clerics to exclude liberals from the government. This strategy, which may have been urged on them by Moscow, earned the Tudeh only a temporary reprieve. Even though they were the last independent political party to be banned, they were eventually hauled before the television cameras in 1983 to confess their sins against

Iranian women wearing the Islamic *Hijab* at a pro-Khomeini demostration in Tehran. Khomeini's revolution in Iran was the beginning of his attempt to unite all Muslims under one universal republic.

the revolution: that they had been 'traitors working for the Soviet Union' all along. Only those Tudeh leaders who managed to slip away to eastern Europe have remained at large, and most languished in the regime's jails throughout the 1980s.

Two new leftist groups emerged from the ferment in the colleges and universities during the early 1970s: the Marxist Fedaii, or People's Sacrificial Guerrillas, and the Islamic Mujahidin, or Holy Warriors. Both were full of enthusiastic but inexperienced youngsters who were easy prey for the Savak. The survivors were ill-prepared for the realities of the Ayatollah's rule.

The Fedaii were hamstrung by internal conflicts and by their lack of a consensus on almost every important issue. In June 1980 these conflicts came to a head and split the organization, fatally damaging its work within the workers' councils and the women's movement. The fragmented groups which remained fell victim to the regime's increasing intolerance during the early1980s.

Although they had been formed in 1965, the Mujahidin first came to prominence in August 1971 when they initiated urban guerrilla attacks on the Shah's security forces. Almost all the founder members died in these actions or in subsequent executions. In 1975 the group split into two factions, one of which, Peyker moved further to the left and has been described as Maoist or Trotskyist. By 1979 Peyker was uncompromisingly hostile to the *ulema* and the Ayatollah.

The second group retained its original name and tried to reconcile Marxism with Islam. When the provisional government took power in February 1979 the Mujahidin and its leader, Masoud Rajavi, criticized Khomeini for his 'petty bourgeois and right-

wing approach to Islam', but befriended other clerical leaders. During the summer of 1979, however, conflict between the government and the Mujahidin grew as the latter first refused to surrender the weapons which they had plundered from the Shah's armouries and then demanded the abolition of the national army.

In February 1980, the liberal Paris-educated economist, Abol Bani-Sadr was elected President of the new republic by an overwhelming majority. As a respected Muslim intellectual his faith was unchallengeable, although he frequently disagreed with the Ayatollah on important matters. He formed an informal alliance with the Mujahidin, which was to their advantage in the coming months. The United States was increasing its pressure on the regime in an effort to get its Embassy staff released. This pressure intensified Iranian nationalist sentiments, which Khomeini manipulated in order to compromise his enemies. The prayer leader of Tehran was instructed to tell the faithful that pictures of Lenin or the hammer and sickle would no longer be tolerated on university campuses. The same day, the Islamic Revolutionary Council announced that all political parties should leave the university precincts. The Mujahidin obeyed the call, to the annoyance of the clerics, and Bani-Sadr was able to lead a march of militant Islamic students against the remaining parties without compromising his allies.

Throughout the summer of 1980 the clerics increased their pressure on the left and then, in the third week of September, an outside influence altered the balance within the Iranian regime. The Iraqi President, Saddam Hussein, launched an attack on Iran after relations between the two countries had

# The Challenge of Islam

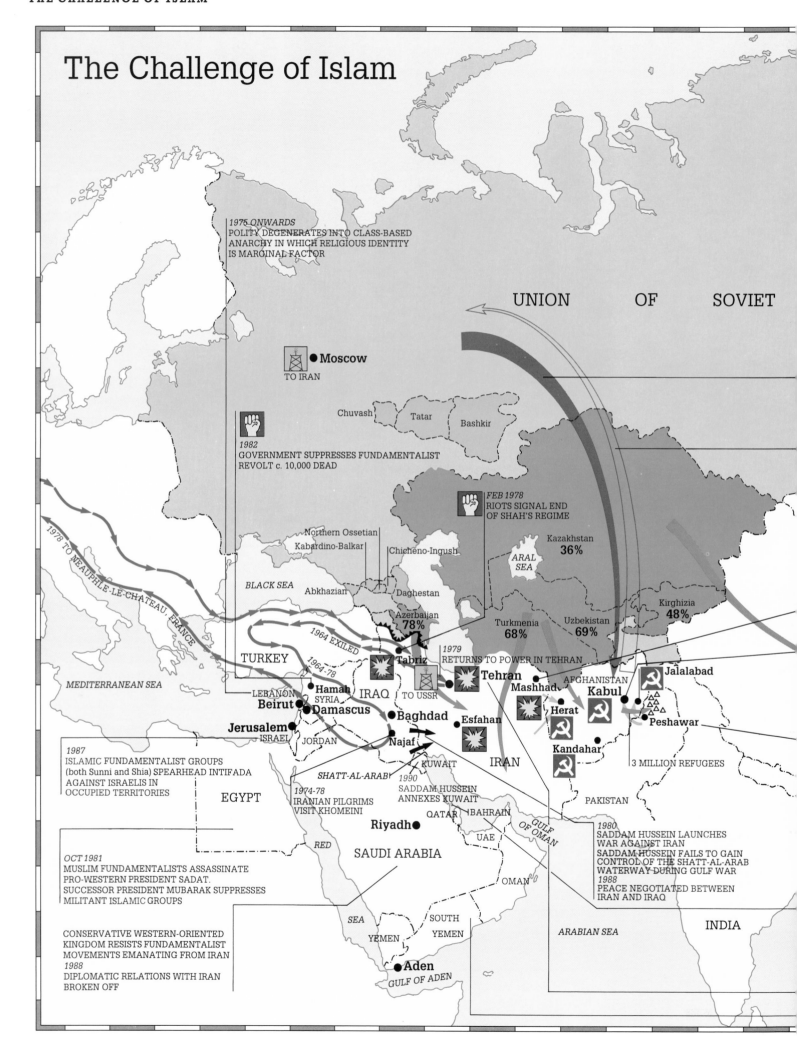

*1975 ONWARDS*
POLITY DEGENERATES INTO CLASS-BASED
ANARCHY IN WHICH RELIGIOUS IDENTITY
IS MARGINAL FACTOR

UNION          OF          SOVIET

● Moscow
TO IRAN

Chuvash     Tatar     Bashkir

*1982*
GOVERNMENT SUPPRESSES FUNDAMENTALIST
REVOLT c. 10,000 DEAD

*FEB 1978*
RIOTS SIGNAL END
OF SHAH'S REGIME

Kazakhstan
**36%**

Northern Ossetian
Kabardino-Balkar

Chicheno-Ingush

*ARAL
SEA*

*1978 TO NEAUPHLE-LE-CHATEAU, FRANCE*

*BLACK SEA*     Abkhazian

Daghestan

Kirghizia
**48%**

Azerbaijan
**78%**

Turkmenia
**68%**

Uzbekistan
**69%**

*1964 EXILED*

*1979*
RETURNS TO POWER IN TEHRAN

TURKEY

*1964-78*

Tabriz

● Tehran

AFGHANISTAN     ■ Jalalabad

Mashhad
■

Kabul
■

LEBANON
Beirut     ● Hamah     IRAQ
SYRIA
● Damascus     TO USSR

● Baghdad     Esfahan

Herat
■

Peshawar

MEDITERRANEAN SEA

Jerusalem ●
ISRAEL
JORDAN     Najaf

Kandahar
■

3 MILLION REFUGEES

IRAN

*1987*
ISLAMIC FUNDAMENTALIST GROUPS
(both Sunni and Shia) SPEARHEAD INTIFADA
AGAINST ISRAELIS IN
OCCUPIED TERRITORIES

KUWAIT

EGYPT

*SHATT-AL-ARAB*

*1974-78*
IRANIAN PILGRIMS
VISIT KHOMEINI

*1990*
SADDAM HUSSEIN
ANNEXES KUWAIT

PAKISTAN

QATAR     BAHRAIN

Riyadh ●

UAE

*GULF
OF OMAN*

*1980*
SADDAM HUSSEIN LAUNCHES
WAR AGAINST IRAN
SADDAM HUSSEIN FAILS TO GAIN
CONTROL OF THE SHATT-AL-ARAB
WATERWAY DURING GULF WAR

*RED*

SAUDI ARABIA

*OCT 1981*
MUSLIM FUNDAMENTALISTS ASSASSINATE
PRO-WESTERN PRESIDENT SADAT.
SUCCESSOR PRESIDENT MUBARAK SUPPRESSES
MILITANT ISLAMIC GROUPS

OMAN

*1988*
PEACE NEGOTIATED BETWEEN
IRAN AND IRAQ

*SEA*     SOUTH
YEMEN

*ARABIAN SEA*     INDIA

YEMEN

CONSERVATIVE WESTERN-ORIENTED
KINGDOM RESISTS FUNDAMENTALIST
MOVEMENTS EMANATING FROM IRAN
*1988*
DIPLOMATIC RELATIONS WITH IRAN
BROKEN OFF

● Aden
*GULF OF ADEN*

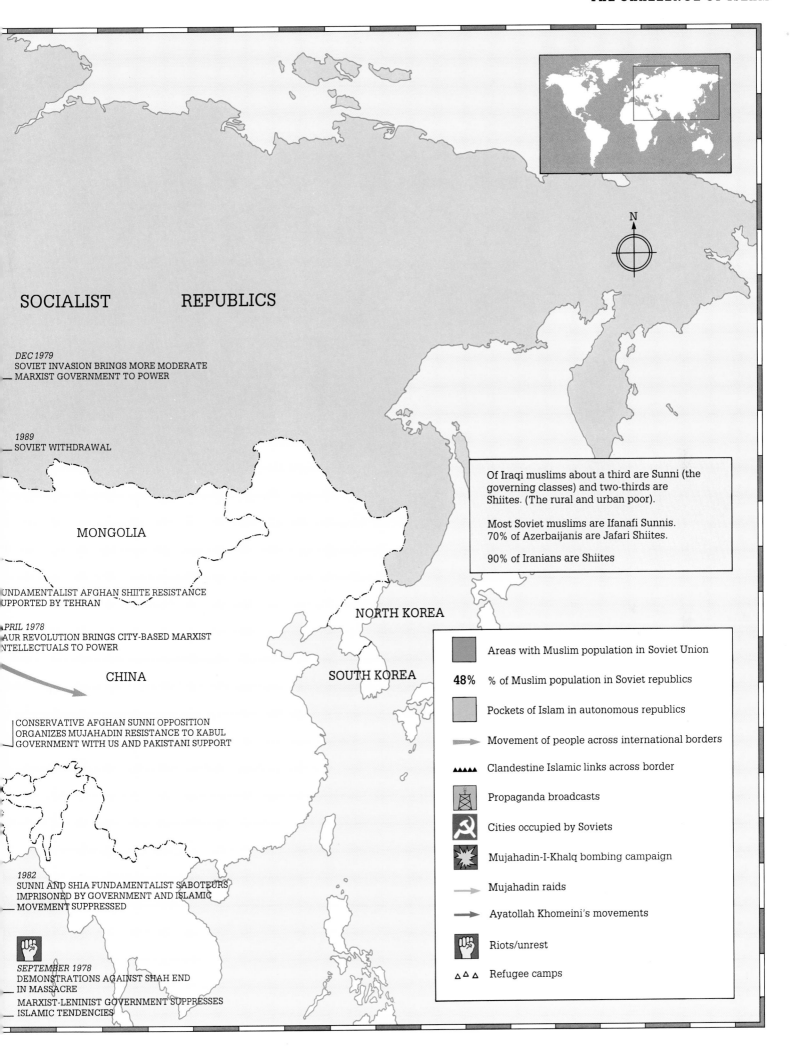

SOCIALIST        REPUBLICS

*DEC 1979*
SOVIET INVASION BRINGS MORE MODERATE
MARXIST GOVERNMENT TO POWER

*1989*
SOVIET WITHDRAWAL

MONGOLIA

UNDAMENTALIST AFGHAN SHIITE RESISTANCE
UPPORTED BY TEHRAN

*APRIL 1978*
AUR REVOLUTION BRINGS CITY-BASED MARXIST
NTELLECTUALS TO POWER

CHINA

CONSERVATIVE AFGHAN SUNNI OPPOSITION
ORGANIZES MUJAHADIN RESISTANCE TO KABUL
GOVERNMENT WITH US AND PAKISTANI SUPPORT

*1982*
SUNNI AND SHIA FUNDAMENTALIST SABOTEURS
IMPRISONED BY GOVERNMENT AND ISLAMIC
MOVEMENT SUPPRESSED

*SEPTEMBER 1978*
DEMONSTRATIONS AGAINST SHAH END
IN MASSACRE

MARXIST-LENINIST GOVERNMENT SUPPRESSES
ISLAMIC TENDENCIES

NORTH KOREA

SOUTH KOREA

Of Iraqi muslims about a third are Sunni (the
governing classes) and two-thirds are
Shiites. (The rural and urban poor).

Most Soviet muslims are Ifanafi Sunnis.
70% of Azerbaijanis are Jafari Shiites.

90% of Iranians are Shiites

| | |
|---|---|
| | Areas with Muslim population in Soviet Union |
| **48%** | % of Muslim population in Soviet republics |
| | Pockets of Islam in autonomous republics |
| | Movement of people across international borders |
| | Clandestine Islamic links across border |
| | Propaganda broadcasts |
| | Cities occupied by Soviets |
| | Mujahadin-I-Khalq bombing campaign |
| | Mujahadin raids |
| | Ayatollah Khomeini's movements |
| | Riots/unrest |
| △△△ | Refugee camps |

Mullahs watch the shelling of Iraq, 1983. By this time the border clashes between Iran and Iraq had escalated to a full-scale war. The Iranian forces, largely hastily trained revolutionary guards, faced a disciplined Iraqi army equipped with Russian weapons.

deteriorated over some months. This was a political windfall for the Ayatollah, for it aligned virtually the entire nation behind him. For a while the home front was quiet, but in November Bani-Sadr used the newspaper that he owned to mount attacks on the behaviour of the fundamentalists' Islamic Revolutionary Party, which was succeeding in marginalizing him.

This provoked a war of words between the President's supporters and the militant fundamentalists. Prominent among the latter were the Hezbollah, the Party of God, who mounted violent attacks on unveiled women and political groups opposed to the clerics' monopoly of power, including the Mujahidin.

Meanwhile, the students who had occupied the American Embassy succeeded in decoding papers which they had seized, and discovered that the CIA had, albeit unsuccessfully, tried to recruit Bani-Sadr; the information provoked Khomeini into a concerted campaign to oust the President. This was finally achieved on 21 June. A week later, a meeting of radical Islamic leaders was bombed and about seventy people died, including Ayatollah Muhammad Beheshti, the leader of the radical clergy in Iran.

The Ayatollah immediately blamed the Mujahidin, although evidence suggests that an obscure group of the Shah's supporters was responsible. Rather than wait to be attacked, the Mujahidin went on the offensive: during August a wave of assassinations, bomb attacks and armed assaults was

perpetrated. Their most sensational outrage was the bombing of the National Security Council on 30 August, which killed the new President, the Prime Minister, the chief of police and the heads of all the intelligence services. Khomeini's response was to execute anyone in jail who was linked with the Mujahidin, and over a thousand people were either shot or hanged.

A new presidential election was announced for 2 October, which the Mujahidin claimed that it could stop. When it failed to do so and Khomeini carried the day, its morale collapsed and the guerrilla campaign came to an end.

### Muslim Expansionism

The fate of Marxist groups in Iran is an indication of the diminishing effectiveness of Communism as a revolutionary guide, and illustrates the way in which it has become trapped within concepts which leave it vulnerable to a militant enemy. In Indonesia, the largest Muslim nation in the world, the local Communist Party met an even more bloody fate in 1965.

For the previous twenty years President Sukarno had ruled the country by balancing the physical power of the army against the political power of the Communists, who had a long tradition as a parliamentary party which had renounced guerrilla tactics or insurrection. But an attempted military coup on 1 October 1965, by a group which claimed to have detected CIA penetration of

the highest ranks of the military, backfired after six generals had been murdered. Once General Suharto had proclaimed himself the 'temporary' head of the army, evidence was discovered that linked the murderers with the Communist Party.

Within days, the army decided to rid itself of its opponents forever. It encouraged the civilian opponents of the Communists to attack them and then stood aside to enjoy the carnage. Between five hundred thousand and a million people died, and by the end of 1965 a party with 20 million members had been destroyed. *Le Monde* described it as 'the most costly defeat in the history of international Communism', and the Indonesian party has never recovered.

An inadequate response to the threat from Islam has also characterized the Soviet approach in central Asia, and no new ideas have been demonstrated which might counter the appeal of Islam. Local and national leaders, including Gorbachev, have merely reiterated ancient prescriptions which ultimately assume that the superiority of atheism will become self-evident if there is enough anti-religious education.

Despite this lack of a new approach, Soviet analysts were quick to realize that modern Islam has become closely entwined with nationalism and that many believers are unable to separate the two. Until the party can offer more potent ideas and draw adherents away from Islam, this powerful combination will prove a destabilizing factor among the Muslims of Soviet Central Asia.

# China: The Slippery Slope of Reform

The students occupy Tiananmen Square on the day of Hu Yaobang's funeral, and refuse to leave when police and soldiers surround the Square.

Mao Zedong's death in September 1976 heralded a new era in Chinese history. Although the nation went about its business much as before, its most important beacon had been extinguished. However, many were not sorry that Mao's guiding light had failed at last, for doubts about his ability to lead China down the road towards the Communist millennium were widespread. Over the previous twenty years the Party Chairman had repeatedly used his power to provoke the nation into a paroxysm of confusion and self-destruction.

The Cultural Revolution, Mao's last convulsive joust with the dead weight of Chinese tradition, had left his country in chaos. All those institutions that China needed to create the future lay maimed by the late Chairman's repugnance for the past. The education system was in tatters, and the training of scientists, technicians and managers had been ignored for a decade. Agricultural production was disorganized and people were starving in potentially rich farming areas such as the province of Sichuan. Most of China's finest administrators had been purged from the party, which remained more concerned with factional in-fighting than with the needs of the people.

There was a faint light of hope in the distance, however. Although Deng Xiaoping had been ousted for a second time in April 1976, many of those party cadres that he had helped to rehabilitate after their humiliation during the Cultural Revolution remained at their desks. The nation's leading mischief-makers, those radicals who had remained closest to Mao, the infamous Gang of Four - Mao's wife Jiang Qing, Wang Hongwen, Zhang Chunqiao and Yao Wenyuan - had been slapped in Qincheng Prison within weeks of the Chairman's death, before they

## Carnage in Beijing

Tension was high in the Chinese capital on Saturday 3 June 1989 after a traffic accident in which four civilians had been killed by an army jeep, and by midnight there were about 30,000 people in Tiananmen Square.

A few minutes into Sunday, two armoured personnel carriers which entered the Square were attacked. One was set alight and when a man emerged he was beaten to death by the crowd. His colleagues were rescued by the students who were camping in the Square's centre. By 1 am, shooting could be heard and the crowd became alarmed. Troops began appearing on the edge of

Hu Yaobang's portrait is held aloft in front of the People's Monument, 22 April 1989.

the Square, some of whom fired into the air. At 4 am one of the students announced that a deal had been struck with the army and that everyone should leave

peacefully. Meanwhile, a line of tanks had formed along the north side. At 5 am they swept south, by which time the students' tents had been evacuated.

As the crowd moved away, armoured personel carriers were driven at them at speed and 11 people died. Troop trucks moving through the city sprayed the streets with automatic fire. People were shot in the back as they ran from trouble. Even ambulances were shot up. Although no one seems to have died in the Square, at least 1000 fatalities occurred in the surrounding districts during the following week.

# Reform and Rebellion 1976-1990

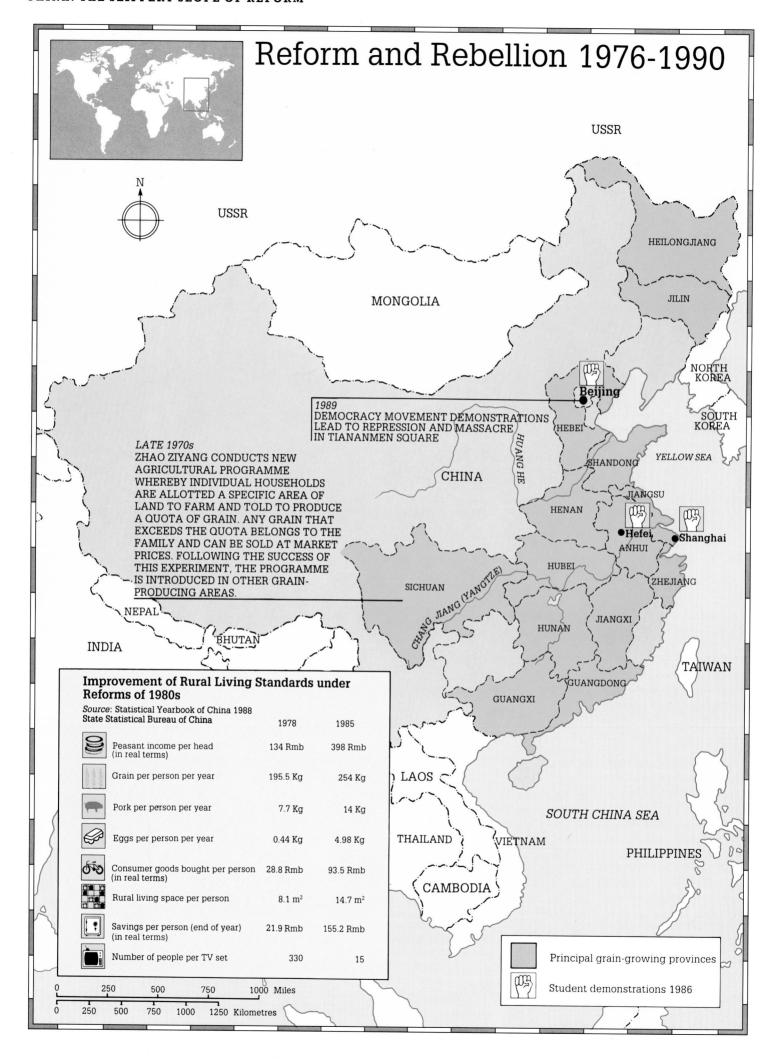

USSR

USSR

MONGOLIA

HEILONGJIANG

JILIN

NORTH KOREA

Beijing

SOUTH KOREA

**1989**
DEMOCRACY MOVEMENT DEMONSTRATIONS
LEAD TO REPRESSION AND MASSACRE
IN TIANANMEN SQUARE

HEBEI

HUANG HE

SHANDONG

YELLOW SEA

CHINA

JIANGSU

HENAN

*LATE 1970s*
ZHAO ZIYANG CONDUCTS NEW
AGRICULTURAL PROGRAMME
WHEREBY INDIVIDUAL HOUSEHOLDS
ARE ALLOTTED A SPECIFIC AREA OF
LAND TO FARM AND TOLD TO PRODUCE
A QUOTA OF GRAIN. ANY GRAIN THAT
EXCEEDS THE QUOTA BELONGS TO THE
FAMILY AND CAN BE SOLD AT MARKET
PRICES. FOLLOWING THE SUCCESS OF
THIS EXPERIMENT, THE PROGRAMME
IS INTRODUCED IN OTHER GRAIN-
PRODUCING AREAS.

Hefei

Shanghai

ANHUI

HUBEI

ZHEJIANG

SICHUAN

CHANG JIANG (YANGTZE)

JIANGXI

NEPAL

HUNAN

BHUTAN

INDIA

TAIWAN

GUANGDONG

GUANGXI

## Improvement of Rural Living Standards under Reforms of 1980s

*Source*: Statistical Yearbook of China 1988
State Statistical Bureau of China

| | | 1978 | 1985 |
|---|---|---|---|
| | Peasant income per head (in real terms) | 134 Rmb | 398 Rmb |
| | Grain per person per year | 195.5 Kg | 254 Kg |
| | Pork per person per year | 7.7 Kg | 14 Kg |
| | Eggs per person per year | 0.44 Kg | 4.98 Kg |
| | Consumer goods bought per person (in real terms) | 28.8 Rmb | 93.5 Rmb |
| | Rural living space per person | 8.1 m² | 14.7 m² |
| | Savings per person (end of year) (in real terms) | 21.9 Rmb | 155.2 Rmb |
| | Number of people per TV set | 330 | 15 |

LAOS

SOUTH CHINA SEA

THAILAND

VIETNAM

PHILIPPINES

CAMBODIA

| | |
|---|---|
| | Principal grain-growing provinces |
| | Student demonstrations 1986 |

0  250  500  750  1000 Miles

0  250  500  750  1000  1250 Kilometres

could do any more harm. When the people were told of the arrests at a huge rally in Tiananmen Square on 21 October, the streets of China's major cities turned into one big party which resulted in the 'three empties' - empty liquor stores, empty fireworks stores and empty hospital beds.

However, although the nation was exhilarated, it took more than a few arrests to reorientate 800 million people. The party's first step was to find a leader to replace Mao, if only on a temporary basis. On 24 October, Hua Guofeng was presented to the people as the new chairman at another huge rally. Yet Hua was in a tricky position. He was a relatively unknown provincial leader, without a secure power base in Beijing. Many in the party resented him because he had been 'helicoptered' to the top at Mao's behest, ignoring both the law of the land and party discipline. Hua's only chance of holding on to power was to draw close to the radical faction. Unfortunately, he chose the wrong bedfellows at the wrong moment.

Deng Xiaoping was a popular leader within the party and among the people. Only weeks after the fall of the Gang of Four rumours about his imminent return to power began to circulate in Beijing. In the minds of many people, Deng's name was strongly associated with Zhou Enlai and, on the first anniversary of the latter's death in January 1977, a demonstration supporting Deng took place in Beijing. In March 1977 he was reinstated by the party leadership.

Hua, meanwhile, concluded that his most effective ploy would be to embrace Mao's closest followers. His response to China's economic plight was to exhort the workers to greater efforts in typically Maoist phrases: 'Let us go all out, aim high, and achieve greater, faster, better and more economical results in building socialism.' Given the failure of Mao's Great Leap Forward in 1959, such slogans were not likely to impress either the people or the party, and the campaign failed.

### The Writing on the Wall

Deng, meanwhile, was nibbling away at the foundations of Hua's position. In July 1977 the Central Committee expelled the jailed Gang of Four from the party, a move which inevitably damaged Hua's situation. A month later the Eleventh Party Congress declared the Cultural Revolution over and reappointed Deng as party vice-chairman, vice-premier and vice-chairman of the crucial Military Affairs Commission. His speech concluding the Congress was the antithesis of Hua's Maoist exhortations and contained more than one side-swipe at his rival.

During the remainder of 1977 and 1978, many of those who had 'helicoptered' to power during the Cultural Revolution through their association with Mao were quietly winkled out of their positions of authority and replaced by Deng's supporters. One of the most prominent was Chen Xilian, the Beijing Military District Commander.

Gorbachev meets Deng Xiaoping in the Great Hall of the People, May 1989. It was the first Sino-Soviet summit for thirty years. Outside, in Tiananmen Square Gorbachev's portrait had replaced Hu's.

Chen Yun, Hu Yaobang and two more of Deng's closest associates were elected to the Politburo. By the start of the Third Plenary Session of the Eleventh Party Congress in December 1978, Deng had the majority of the leadership behind him. It was at this point that those outside the tight-knit circles of the party hierarchy were allowed to make their presence felt.

Fly-posting had always been a weapon in the armoury of the party factions. Outsiders now started to adopt the same tactics. Posters attacking government corruption, and even Mao himself, appeared on the wall opposite Beijing's municipal bus station in the Changan Road - and, to everyone's amazement, they were not torn down. Since the targets of this public invective were Deng's enemies, the vice-chairman was clearly turning a blind eye towards what became known as the 'Democracy Wall'. The young people who used this wall to call for political and social change, and the editors of dissident magazines that sprang up at the same time, were generally designated as workers. But most of them were educated youngsters whose parents were influential party members. Their privileged positions also gave them access to information and documents unavailable to the people. Furthermore, having endured the Cultural Revolution and witnessed the poverty that was still endemic to many parts of China, they were intensely critical of the party's ability to govern their country. Despite differences of opinion among the poster writers, certain common themes recurred on the wall. These included calls for democracy, civil liberties, more jobs and better economic conditions. At the same time, tens of thousands of peasants and other people who had been harmed by the injustices of the Cultural Revolution surged to Beijing to seek redress for their grievances.

In the midst of all this popular activity, the realities of power were being exercised at the Party Congress. More of Hua's followers were demoted or lost their jobs and, although their leader appeared to retain his position, it was Deng who now called the shots. The ten-year plan initiated by Hua was postponed, because it had triggered a spate of industrial investment that was beyond China's means. By the middle of 1979, Hua was forced to admit in public that his plan was unworkable and that the country needed three years of 'adjustment, reconstruction, consolidation and improvement'. Investment was redirected towards agriculture and consumer goods. China's 'Second Revolution' could now begin.

Once Deng had got his way, the poster writers were suppressed. The most prominent were jailed and the Democracy Wall was scrubbed clean, although the party had been shrewd enough to stage an out-of-town event to lure the foreign press corps away from Beijing for the day. Deng had no love for democracy, and he set out the limits for independent political initiatives by establishing the 'Four Cardinal Principles'. These required adherence to Mao Zedong Thought, to the leadership of the party, to the socialist road and to the people's democratic dictatorship. Deng wanted to make it quite clear that economic pragmatism and political indulgence did not go hand in hand.

In practice, economic pragmatism meant a drive for increased production and efficiency through the use of market forces to dictate prices and the availability of goods. It also rearranged the balance of the economy so as to discourage blind investment in heavy industry to the detriment of other sectors. Agriculture was the first economic sector to benefit from these reforms. Prices were raised, street markets were encouraged and a return to family farming was allowed.

The essence of the new arrangement was a long-term contract between the production teams (the villages) and individual households, in which the latter were allowed a specific area of land and told to produce a quota of grain on it. Any produce that exceeded the quota belonged to the family. Rural specialization and various light industrial sidelines were encouraged. The effect of these reforms was dramatic, with grain production up by a third in six years. In the same period, rural incomes doubled. Since this new wealth could not be channelled into the acquisition of land, a housing boom overtook the countryside, followed swiftly by a boom in household equipment sales.

Emboldened by these spectacular successes, Beijing tried to extend the reforms to industry. The principal object of the October 1984 reforms was to encourage factory managers to show some initiative. Under the old system, the state extracted any profits and handed back what was deemed necessary for the payment of wages and investment; under the new system, individual enterprises were to pay a fixed tax and keep the rest, spending it as local circumstances demanded. The pricing structure was also made less rigid: now only a proportion of the output had to be sold at low, state-determined prices, while the remainder could be sold at what the market dictated.

## The Problem with Democracy

From the very start of his 'Second Revolution', Deng Xiaoping emphasized the separation of economics from ideology and his 'Four Cardinal Principles' very clearly circumscribed the limits to political discussion. Yet, there were those within the party who saw even these tight limits as dangerously liberal. In 1982, this conservative group, determined to weed out any ideas from abroad that they felt were

infecting the young, launched a campaign against 'spiritual pollution'. Then, in December 1986, a challenge appeared from a very different quarter.

University students in Hefei demonstrated for the rights to nominate and elect their own representatives. When their claims were met students in Shanghai took up the cry. With thirty thousand demonstrators involved, some violence inevitably occurred; but the students' demands were generally restrained and the party looked on benignly. The same attitudes prevailed at first when the movement reached Beijing. However, when the demands of the demonstrators started to stray to non-campus issues such as press freedom, the *People's Daily* sounded words of warning, reminding the students of the 'Four Cardinal Principles'. These warnings were repeated in the first days of 1987, when the newspapers announced that military leaders had taken a strong stand against 'bourgeois liberalization'. Student leaders decided that discretion was the better part of valour, and the unrest died down.

The most prominent victim of the conservative backlash was Hu Yaobang, who resigned as Secretary-General of the party. Other prominent liberals also lost their jobs. At first, Deng managed the situation so that these token sacrifices appeased the forces of opposition. Within a year, however, Hu was back in favour and Deng's move to create a liberal succession seemed back on course. What he could not have foreseen was the reaction to Hu's death. Announced on

15 April 1989, it sparked off the Tiananmen Square explosion of June that year.

Student demonstrators demanded greater freedom of expression, an end to corruption, an open dialogue with the party leadership and the public declaration of the assets of their sons and daughters. Although warning shots were fired in the press, the civic authorities seemed reluctant to clear the streets forcibly in front of the world's television cameras - assembled to cover the imminent arrival of Mikhail Gorbachev. That the Soviet leader's schedule had to be curtailed was a public embarrassment which only intensified the party's reaction. The day after he left, martial law was declared; but the people of Beijing took to the streets to protect the students, and the columns of troops were halted in their tracks. Again the party stalled while the hard-liners struggled for power within the party. With the hard-liners in control and fresh troops from remote regions primed for action, the carnage began. In the darkness of the night of 3-4 June, the tanks advanced on the children of hope as they lay sleeping in Tiananmen Square. Even casual bystanders in the surrounding streets were slaughtered. Every justification for China's first revolution seemed bankrupted by the need to keep Deng's second revolution on course. It is one of Communism's more barbaric ironies that this night of blood and its aftermath transformed China under Deng Xiaoping from its role as a pioneering model of reform into a prime example of repression.

'The Goddess of Democracy' appeared on 30 May, looking across Tiananmen Square to the portrait of Mao hanging over the entrance to the Forbidden City. Because of her resemblance to the Statue of Liberty, she was later used as evidence of an American inspired rebellion.

# America's Back Yard

When the Marxist Sandinistas swept suddenly to power in Nicaragua in 1979 after a cruel civil war, conservatives in the United States and left-wingers in Latin America were, for once, in full agreement. Both forecast a wave of revolution in what had traditionally been considered Washington's back yard: the Caribbean Basin, an area that includes Mexico, Central America, the island states of the Caribbean itself, and the northern states of South America - Panama, Colombia, Venezuela, Guyana, Surinam and French Guiana.

A decade later the prediction had yet to be fulfilled. The region was indeed far from stable. The small Central American state of El Salvador, in particular, was locked in a seemingly endless civil war, and the Sandinistas still held sway in Nicaragua, despite a costly campaign by the United States to dislodge them. But Nicaragua's Marxists presided over a regime that had little in common with those of the older-style Communist states of, say, eastern Europe, and were in any case soon to lose power in

democratic elections. Elsewhere in the region, non-Marxist regimes - some democratic, some quasi-democratic, others blatantly undemocratic - still clung, though often precariously, to power.

The Frente Sandinista de Liberación Nacional (Sandinista Front of National Liberation or FSLN) emerged in 1962 as part of the 'first wave' of 'national liberation movements', sponsored throughout Latin America by Cuba's revolutionaries. The founders of the Nicaraguan Front were a young intellectual, Carlos Fonseca Amador, and a small group from the left. They were dedicated to the overthrow of the Somoza family, who had ruled Nicaragua with corruption and brutality - and American backing - since 1937.

## The Early Years

The Sandinistas had a patchy record in their early years. During the 1960s their activities were limited to sporadic guerrilla forays, mostly in the mountainous north of

Nicaragua. They received no support from the local Communists, who, in fact, periodically condemned them as extreme left-wing adventurers, and the Somoza regime seemed well able to contain them. They had a period of better fortunes in the early 1970s, on one occasion taking hostage Nicaragua's Foreign Minister and members of the Somoza family. But by the middle of the decade they had reached another low point, with their front splintered into three rival factions, each holding widely differing views on how to topple the Somoza regime. In 1976 Carlos Fonseca Amador, the one person with any hope of reuniting the Front, was killed in a shoot-out with members of the Somozas' combined army and police force, the National Guard. Just three years before they were to sweep so dramatically to power, ousting the current Somoza dictator, General Anastasio Somoza Debayle, the Sandinistas seemed set for oblivion as a unified guerrilla force.

The turning point in the anti-Somoza struggle came in January 1978, and was the

Voting is compulsory in El Salvador. People queue to cast their vote in the presidential election of March 1984, beneath a poster proclaiming: 'Your right to live in peace - decide it with your vote'.  José Napoleón Duarte won the election, but the civil war raged on.

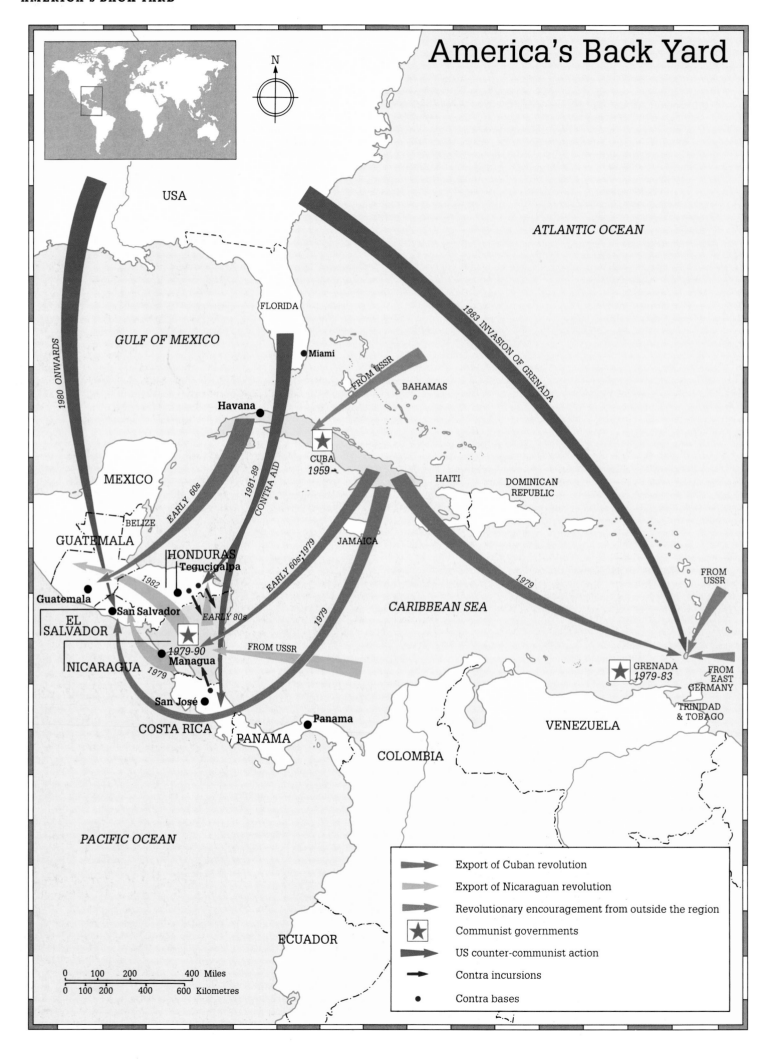

# America's Back Yard

ATLANTIC OCEAN

USA

*1983 INVASION OF GRENADA*

*1980 ONWARDS*

FLORIDA

GULF OF MEXICO

•Miami

*FROM USSR*

BAHAMAS

**Havana** •

*EARLY 60s*

*1981-89*

*CONTRA AID*

★
CUBA
*1959*

HAITI

DOMINICAN
REPUBLIC

MEXICO

BELIZE

GUATEMALA

**HONDURAS**
**Tegucigalpa**

*1982*

JAMAICA

*EARLY 60s;1979*

*1979*

FROM
USSR

**Guatemala** •

*EARLY 80s*

CARIBBEAN SEA

**San Salvador** •

EL
SALVADOR

*1979*

★
*1979-90*
**Managua**

*FROM USSR*

NICARAGUA

*1979*

★ GRENADA
*1979-83*

FROM
EAST
GERMANY

**San José** •

TRINIDAD
& TOBAGO

COSTA RICA

**Panama** •

VENEZUELA

PANAMA

COLOMBIA

PACIFIC OCEAN

ECUADOR

0   100   200        400  Miles
0  100 200    400      600  Kilometres

| | |
|---|---|
| ➤ | Export of Cuban revolution |
| ➤ | Export of Nicaraguan revolution |
| ➤ | Revolutionary encouragement from outside the region |
| ★ | Communist governments |
| ➤ | US counter-communist action |
| → | Contra incursions |
| • | Contra bases |

Daniel Ortega gives a speech at a rally during the 1990 election campaign in Nicaragua. Ortega's Sandinistas were beaten in the polls by Violeta Chamorro's UNO coalition.

result of an outrage against Nicaragua's increasingly active non-Marxist opposition. In that month Pedro Joaquín Chamorro, the widely respected owner-editor of Nicaragua's leading opposition newspaper, *La Prensa*, was shot (almost certainly by hit men working for General Somoza) while driving to his office in the capital, Managua. He was a long-established foe of the regime, the most important leader of the moderate opposition, who had been jailed five times and exiled twice for his anti-Somoza activities. At the news of his death, Nicaragua erupted in grief and fury. Crowds some thirty-thousand-strong poured into Managua for his funeral, and rampaged through the streets, chanting: 'Who killed Chamorro? - Somoza', setting cars and buildings ablaze, and attacking businesses known to belong to members of the Somoza dynasty. Shortly afterwards, a twenty-four-hour general strike brought the country to a temporary halt.

## Civil War and Victory

Conditions were clearly ripe for insurrection - and now at last the Sandinistas (thanks partly to initiatives by the non-Marxist opposition, partly to proddings from Fidel Castro) began to move once more towards unity. For some time the moderate opposition leaders had been seeking an alliance with them. This approach was welcomed by the Front's pragmatic Tercerista faction (led by, among others, the brothers Daniel and Humberto Ortega), who favoured just such an alliance as a means towards launching a swift anti-government revolt. But the idea of an alliance was opposed by the other two, harder-line factions, who believed in a prolonged struggle exclusively among Nicaragua's urban and rural working classes. Only under considerable pressure from Castro did they drop their objections to the

alliance, and start working in co-operation with the Terceristas.

Events moved swiftly. In August Tercerista guerrillas scored an eye-catching success when they seized the building in Managua that housed the National Congress and two government ministries. They took a thousand hostages, among them the Interior Minister and members of the Somoza family. After three days of high suspense the government agreed to most of the guerrillas' demands, including a $500,000 ransom and the release of several political prisoners. Then in September outright civil war set in, with the newly united Sandinistas seizing control of several provincial towns.

At first Somoza's National Guard kept the upper hand. In a campaign of indiscriminate brutality, they drove the Sandinistas from areas the guerrillas had taken. Whole streets under Sandinista control were strafed from helicopter gunships, and thousands of rockets and bombs were used against entire towns: hundreds of civilians were killed. By early 1979, however, the battle was beginning to turn. The Sandinistas' alliance with the moderate opposition brought them wide international support, and various Latin American states, together with the Carter administration in Washington, put increasing pressure on Somoza to quit. He refused. But by the summer it was clear even to him that the end had come. On 17 July he left the bunker in Managua's National Guard headquarters from which he had directed the war, and flew to exile in Miami. He was later assassinated in Paraguay - probably by a left-wing Sandinista sympathizer.

In Washington, meanwhile, President Carter, alarmed at the prospect of a Marxist-dominated government coming to power so close to home, had attempted to orchestrate a transition of power that would exclude the Sandinistas from office; but international

support for the Front was now too great. On 19 July Sandinista units took control of Managua. The next day vast crowds of Nicaraguans, waving the Sandinistas' red and black colours, greeted the arrival in Managua of the new 'Government Junta of National Reconstruction' - officially a coalition administration that included Chamorro's widow, but effectively controlled by the Sandinistas.

## El Salvador and Guatemala

The Sandinista front had become the spearhead of a 'second wave' of liberation movements. Action now turned to neighbouring El Salvador, where, as earlier in Somoza's Nicaragua, conditions were ripe for insurrection. In El Salvador, as in most of the countries of the region, political and economic power were monopolized by the wealthy landed few, while landless peasants and poverty-stricken urban workers lived in unrelieved squalor. Left-wing guerrilla bands, with their power base among the poor, had been active since 1973, provoking a backlash by terrorist squads who were closely associated with far right elements in the military. Both groups engaged in campaigns of bombings, kidnappings and assassinations. Since 1977 the dictator General Carlos Humberto Romero had ruled the country with a brutal disregard for opposition akin to Somoza's. His namesake Oscar Romero, the Archbishop of San Salvador, led a mounting opposition on behalf of the poor.

Then in 1979, just three months after the Sandinistas had come to power in Managua, a group of middle-ranking military officers, with civilian backing, ousted Romero in a coup. At first the civil-military government that emerged promised important reforms - land redistribution in favour of the poor, and an increased respect for human rights. But chaos continued to engulf El Salvador, driving the new junta into ever more repressive action as it struggled to maintain law and order. The reform programme came largely to a halt - and at this point the Sandinistas stepped in. Together with the Cubans they helped to weld El Salvador's left-wing guerrilla groups into a single force the Frente Farabundo Martí de Liberación Nacional (Farabundo Martí Front for National Liberation or FFMLN), named after a Salvadorean Communist leader who had led an unsuccessful left-wing uprising in the 1930s. This became the second liberation movement of the 'second wave'.

From this point on El Salvador was plunged into full-scale civil war, as guerrillas, government forces and right-wing death squads - manned in many cases by the sons of some of the country's wealthiest families - fought it out with ever greater brutality. In 1980 an estimated nine thousand people lost their lives in the violence, the most prominent victim being Archbishop Romero, shot through the heart as he raised the chalice during late afternoon mass in San

# The People's Priests

The Second Vatican Council, which began in October 1962, created a spirit of hope in the Catholic Church. The Second Conference for the Latin-American Hierarchy, held in Medellin, Colombia in 1968, crystallized those hopes in a South-American context. No longer was the Church merely to encourage stoicism among the poor and bless the status quo without reservation. The conference urged the clergy to witness the harm poverty represents and a solidarity with 'the exploited ones'. In 1971 Gustavo Gutiérrez's *A Theology of Liberation* was published which christened the movement.

Before long, the first meeting of Christians for Socialism was underway in Santiago, Chile and the new gospel was being taken up by clergy throughout South

**Mourners surround the coffin of Archbishop Romero in the Cathedral of San Salvador. An outspoken critic of El Salvador's government, Romero was assassinated by right-wing guerrillas while he was taking mass.**

America. From the favelas of Rio to the rubber plantations of Amazonia or the poverty-stricken Andean villages of Peru, young priests and nuns began to preach change and act to put

it into effect, despite the frequent opposition of conservative bishops.

During the 1970s, Catholicism tolerated both points of view, but in 1979, with the election of John Paul II, the Curia in Rome headed in a conservative direction. This lead to ecclesiastical fragmentation in Latin America as some bishops, particularly in Brazil, sided with their clergy and opposed their governments. This theological conflict reach its apotheosis in Nicaragua under the Sandanistas, when Father Miguel D'Escolo became Foreign Minister, Father Cardenal was Minister of Culture and Father Parrales was Minister of Social Welfare. This provoked the Nicaraguan hierarchy and all three were suspended from the exercise of their priestly functions in January 1985.

---

Salvador cathedral. His assassins were right-wing terrorists. And there were foreign casualties as well: in December a squad of right-wing soldiers kidnapped, raped, tortured and then murdered three American nuns. President Carter, in the dying days of his administration, sent a team to investigate the outrage. 'My emissaries said they could hear hand grenades and automatic rifles going off all during each night as people were killed,' he noted in his diary on the team's return. 'They don't have anybody in the jails; they're all dead. It's their accepted way of enforcing the so-called laws.'

In January 1981 the FFMLN guerrillas, backed by the Sandinistas and Cubans, launched what they described as a 'final offensive' from their bases, mostly in the northern mountains of El Salvador. The previous November Ronald Reagan, with an open commitment to roll back the 'red wave' in the Caribbean basin, had won the American presidential election, and he was due to take office that month. The Salvadorean guerrillas and their allies, who poured in increasing amounts of arms and other supplies, were anxious to place a second revolutionary government in power before Reagan was able to launch his anti-Communist crusade. They never achieved their ambition, but neither did the Salvadorean government succeed in suppressing them. The government received huge amounts of economic and military aid from the Reagan administration to help them to suppress the FFMLN insurgency. But still the violence spiralled on. The guerrillas kept up a murderous campaign from their bases in important areas of the north, and the right-wing squads continued their brutal activities.

Another Central American country, meanwhile, was also clearly ready for Sandinista intervention. In Guatemala, as in Nicaragua, left-wing guerrilla groups had been active since the early 1960s. A ruthless 'pacification' campaign by a military-dominated government had more or less silenced the guerrillas in the early 1970s. But violence by both left- and right-wing groups flared up again in the second half of the decade and in the early 1980s. In 1982 the Sandinistas stepped in once more, helping to merge the left-wing guerrilla bands into the Unión Revolucionaria Nacional Guatemalteca (Guatemalan Revolutionary National Union or URNG) - the third liberation movement of the 'second wave'. The Guatemalan military, however, proved more effective than their Salvadorean counterparts in dealing with this threat - even without US backing. They launched another 'pacification' drive and by the mid-1980s, at the cost of more than seventy thousand lives, had decimated the URNG. The guerrillas were left holding out in only a few isolated pockets.

### Launching the Contras

By this time the Sandinistas were themselves fighting for their lives, having become a prime target for President Reagan's anti-Communist campaign. Within weeks of taking office the new President had stopped all US aid to Nicaragua, and in November 1981 he authorized a 'covert' campaign against the Sandinistas - the administration, mindful of the international support the Nicaraguan government still enjoyed, was reluctant to commit itself to overt action. This was to be a war fought with US involvement, but by proxies: the Contras (*contra revolucionarios* -

counter-revolutionaries), as the Sandinistas dubbed them. The Contras were anti-Sandinista Nicaraguans, mostly former members of Somoza's National Guard, but including some disenchanted ex-Sandinistas. Argentina's unsavoury military regime initially organized and trained them; Reagan authorized just under $20 million of aid. The Contras were based largely in Honduras to Nicaragua's north (where the government was sympathetic), though a more moderate group operated from Costa Rica to the south. They also had headquarters in Florida.

The first major Contra offensive began in March 1982 with a push from Honduras down Nicaragua's Atlantic coast. The Sandinista government - headed by the former Tercerista leader Daniel Ortega declared an immediate state of emergency and sent in troops to contain the invaders. From now on war waged unremittingly to and fro over Nicaragua's border regions. The Contras launched offensive after offensive, but Sandinista forces, receiving increasing military and economic aid from Cuba and the Soviet Union, denied their enemies the foothold they were seeking. In 1983 US and Honduran forces carried out manoeuvres on Nicaragua's northern border, aimed at intimid-ating the Sandinistas. They failed, and the revolutionaries fought on. Later that year the Contras, with CIA support, carried the attack to Nicaragua's largest port, Corinto on the Pacific coast, blowing up important oil reserves. Early in 1984 they mined a number of Nicaraguan ports, again with CIA back-up. Several foreign ships were hit.

As the war continued, so positions became more entrenched. In the United States President Reagan, facing mounting criticism both at home and abroad for his administration's increasingly transparent involvement in the war, was adamant in his support for the Contras. 'They are our brothers, these freedom fighters,' he proclaimed in March 1985, 'and we owe them our help.... They are the moral equivalent of the Founding Fathers and the brave men and women of the French Resistance. We cannot turn away from them. For the struggle here is not right versus left, but right versus wrong.' In Nicaragua, meanwhile, the Sandinista authorities were themselves becoming ever more heavy-handed in their response to the Contra threat - evacuating thousands of peasant farmers from Nueva Segovia province, partly to prevent them from joining the Contras, and arbitrarily jailing often innocent people suspected of anti-Sandinista sympathies, no matter how flimsy the grounds.

At the same time, the Contras hardly merited the glowing picture drawn of them by Reagan. The Honduran-based former National Guardsmen, in particular, were frequently brutal and were prone to violent rivalries. A Florida-based Contra, interviewed in Honduras by the American journalist Christopher Dickey, described the leaders of his movement: 'They have, like, double personalities. Very tender, very cruel.'

He went on to give a vivid picture of one leader nicknamed *El Tigrillo* (Little Tiger):

He is lively and quick. I've seen him this side of the border and he plays the idiot. 'Mi commandante' this and 'mi commandante' that. But you cross the [border] with him and he becomes a tiger. He hangs people. He rapes. He shoots people who don't obey him. Whatever is necessary in the jungle. I once saw one of his soldiers challenge him and he pulled out his pistol and shot him. He doesn't have any doubts about killing. But he is also tender with his troops, caring for them and watching over them.

Representing a more moderate face of the Contra movement were the Costa Rican-based forces of the former Sandinista hero Edén Pastora, *Commandante Zero*. Pastora had been one of the most daring leaders in the fight against Somoza, and in the celebrations for the Sandinistas' triumph he was the star attraction with the crowds. He was '*the* revolutionary', commented Christopher Dickey:

A Nicaraguan man - the Nicaráguan man. With his coarse language, his bragging, his bravery and his womanizing, his kindness and his many, many children, he was everything Nicaraguan men grew up laughing about and loving in themselves.

But he had never been comfortable with, or trusted by, the more extreme elements in the Sandinista movement and grew disillusioned with the new government's increasingly leftward tilt as well as what he saw as the decadent lifestyle of its leaders. He slipped out of the country, tried (but failed) to join the guerrillas fighting in Guatemala, and then was contacted by the CIA. With American backing he took over the leadership of an internationally more acceptable wing of the Contra movement (largely composed of other disillusioned former Sandinistas), vowing to 'take [the Nicaraguan leaders] out at gunpoint from their mansions and their Mercedes-Benzes'. In fact, he had no more success than the Honduran-based Contras in ousting the Ortega government.

## Grenada's New Jewel

Action by Marxist groups and their enemies had not been confined to Central America during this time. The Commonwealth islands of the Caribbean, though enduring severe social and economic problems of their own, had none of the traditions of violent dictatorship, coup and counter-coup endemic in their Latin American neighbours. In 1979, however, in the tiny east Caribbean island of Grenada, an overtly Marxist group, the New Jewel Movement, came to power in a bloodless coup, ousting an elected, although increasingly corrupt and dictatorial, government. The New Jewel Prime Minister, Maurice Bishop, a British-trained barrister, soon made his allegiances clear. He established close links with Cuba and the Soviet bloc, and Cuban troops, together with East German advisers, arrived on the island to help train the new regime's People's Revolutionary Army. Workers also arrived from Cuba to assist in building a new airport which, the government claimed, would help the important tourist trade, but which was widely believed outside Grenada to be a potential Soviet military base. Fears arose not only in Washington, but also among Grenada's pro-Western neighbours, that the island was being turned in a launching pad for Marxist revolution throughout the region.

Then dissension broke out between extremist and more moderate members of the New Jewel Movement. In October 1983 Bishop was ousted and murdered in a further coup led by the extremist faction. Alarm among Grenada's neighbours rose yet higher, and on the morning of 25 October the world woke up to the news that US troops, along with a contingent of soldiers and police from other Commonwealth Caribbean states, had landed on Grenada. New Jewel's soldiers and their Cuban comrades resisted, but had little hope against the overwhelming strength of the invasion force. In mid-December Reagan was able to withdraw US troops. An interim administration was set up to hold power until elections were called.

## Peace, but ...

In the late 1980s and early 1990s the scene began to change in parts of the Caribbean region. In Nicaragua in particular events took a new turn. In August 1987 the Central American presidents, meeting in Guatemala City, signed a ten-point peace plan proposed by the Costa Rican President, Oscar Arias. This plan committed the Sandinistas to seeking a negotiated end to the Contra war, and to liberalizing their country's political system. Negotiations with the Contras duly started, and in March 1988 major hostilities ceased. In 1985 Mikhail Gorbachev had arrived in power, and in 1989, in a letter to the new US President, George Bush, he stated that the Soviet Union had ceased shipping arms to Nicaragua. Finally, in a dramatic turnaround, the Sandinistas lost power in presidential elections held, under close international scrutiny, in early 1990. The Ortega government accepted its defeat at the hands of an albeit fragmentary coalition led by Chamorro's widow Violeta Barrios, who had long since broken with her former allies in the Sandinista movement.

Elsewhere, however, the outlook seemed as bleak as ever. In El Salvador the civil war raged on. There had been hopes for peace after democratic elections in 1984 when the moderate Christian Democrat José Napoleón Duarte became President. Duarte was committed to a programme of reform and to negotiating with the FFMLN guerrillas, but when he instigated negotiations he failed to achieve peace. Then, in 1989, the election of the right-wing Alfredo Cristiani (though he too sought negotiations with the FFMLN) resulted only in an intensification of violence. In Cuba, meanwhile, Castro made it clear during a visit to the island in 1989 by President Gorbachev that there would be no *glasnost*-style liberalization of his regime.

Moreover, a further menace to order in the Caribbean states was emerging - not a political ideology this time, but drugs. Violence escalated in Colombia especially, as an embattled government sought to bring to heel the cocaine 'barons' of the 'Medellín cartel'. To some extent at least the 'red menace' so feared by former President Reagan had been contained, but the seeds of violence remained. Poverty and social deprivation - the root cause of so many of the region's conflicts - remained a problem in most countries, and democracy even in many of the most stable countries of the region remained a fragile plant.

Contras in northern Nicaragua in 1983, the year that President Reagan and the American government openly backed the rebels' fight to overthrow the Marxist Sandinista government.

# East Asia and the Pacific

The domino theory at the forefront of American strategic thinking in the Far East can be traced to a remark made by former President Eisenhower, who in April 1965 warned that 'the loss of Indochina will cause the fall of Southeast Asia like a set of dominoes'. The loss of Indochina was completed in 1975, when the Communists were able to consolidate their control in Laos a few months after the conquest of Cambodia and Vietnam had been accomplished. No dominoes dropped.

Apart from the Soviet Union and China, and the Indochina trio, there continued to be just two Communist regimes in this region of 3 billion people: the Mongolian People's Republic and the Democratic People's Republic of Korea - North Korea.

### Early Defeats

The nationalist fervour fomented by the Japanese humbling of the old colonial masters during the Second World War burst right across East Asia. As fast as Ho Chi Minh moved in 1945 to try to rid Indochina of the French, he was no quicker than the Indonesians, who declared their vast archipelago independent from the Dutch. By 1948 the Dutch 'police action' against their rebellious colonies was faltering. That September the Communists attempted a takeover of the independence movement, but they were thwarted by elite forces of the revolutionary army, who wiped out the Communists' base at Madiun in east Java.

The Dutch departed in 1949, and support for the Communists grew once more under the populist President Sukarno, until in 1965 - 'The Year of Living Dangerously', as Sukarno dubbed it - the army was able to stamp its authority after a failed coup. Anarchy reigned as Muslim and army elements exacted a terrible vengeance on their rivals. Under General Suharto, the new ruler, the Communist Party and Marxist-Leninist teaching were outlawed.

In Malaya, sole opposition to the Japanese occupation had come from a group of Chinese Communist guerrillas, who from 1943 operated in conjunction with a small British force. When the British administration returned after the war, the Malayan Communist Party decided on military confrontation to hasten independence. So the same guerrillas returned to the thick jungle that covered much of the Malay peninsula and provided ideal cover for raids on such vulnerable targets as isolated police stations, plantation bungalows and tin mines.

Schoolgirls march past the statue of Kim Il Sung during an obligatory visit to the Revolutionary Museum to absorb more of the Great Leader's revolutionary thoughts.

The British were thrown into confusion at first, but under General Sir Gerald Templer they devised an effective strategy to isolate the insurgents, who never numbered more than nine thousand and were mostly recruited from Chinese squatter camps. The rebels depended upon the camps for their food supplies; so when these were cleared and nearly half a million people relocated in 'new villages' they were left without a support base, and could be weeded out of their jungle retreats. The 'Emergency' officially lasted twelve years, but the threat was largely eliminated by 1954.

The defeat of the Communists in Malaya was hailed as a triumph, and Templer's methods (it was he who coined the phrase 'winning hearts and minds') became an example to be copied elsewhere. However, the majority were fearful of Chinese domination, and were content peacefully to await independence, which was achieved in any case in 1957.

### Mongolia: The First Satellite

With a population of under 2 million, and a land area three times the size of France, this obscure, vulnerable, land-locked state had been under Chinese domination since the seventeenth century when the fall of the Manchu dynasty in Beijing in 1912 provided an opportunity of escape. For a time Chinese, Japanese, Russian and Mongolian tribesmen of various political hues jockeyed for power, but the end of Russia's civil war freed Soviet troops for duty in support of a small band of Mongolian revolutionaries and

in 1924, the Mongolian People's Republic was proclaimed in what had been Outer Mongolia. It was the first Socialist base outside the Soviet Union, and the ever-present threat of China kept Mongolia so firmly in Moscow's grip that it became the most reliable ally in the entire Communist bloc. In return, it was rewarded with substantial economic assistance.

Every major development of Soviet history was duly reflected. Stalin's purges and collectivization, for example, were mirrored in the brutal suppression of the Mongols' traditional Lamaist Buddhism, carried out by Stalin's local henchman, Marshal Chiobalsan. Whether over the Sino-Soviet split of the 1960s, the invasions of Hungary, Czechoslovakia and Afghanistan, or Vietnam's intervention in Cambodia, Mongolia dutifully followed the Moscow line.

With the rise of Gorbachev, Mongolia set about implementing *perestroika* and unpopular anti-alcohol campaigns, and in line with Moscow's improving relations with Beijing, Mongolia even discovered areas of agreement with the old oppressor. Meanwhile, Soviet troops stationed in Mongolia under the 1966 Treaty of Friendship and Co-operation were being gradually reduced.

### North Korea: The Communist Kingdom

The Korean War was suspended in 1953, but never officially ended. The 151-mile-long demilitarized zone (DMZ) remained one of the world's most dangerous flashpoints, with nearly 2 million heavily armed troops confronting one another, and splitting

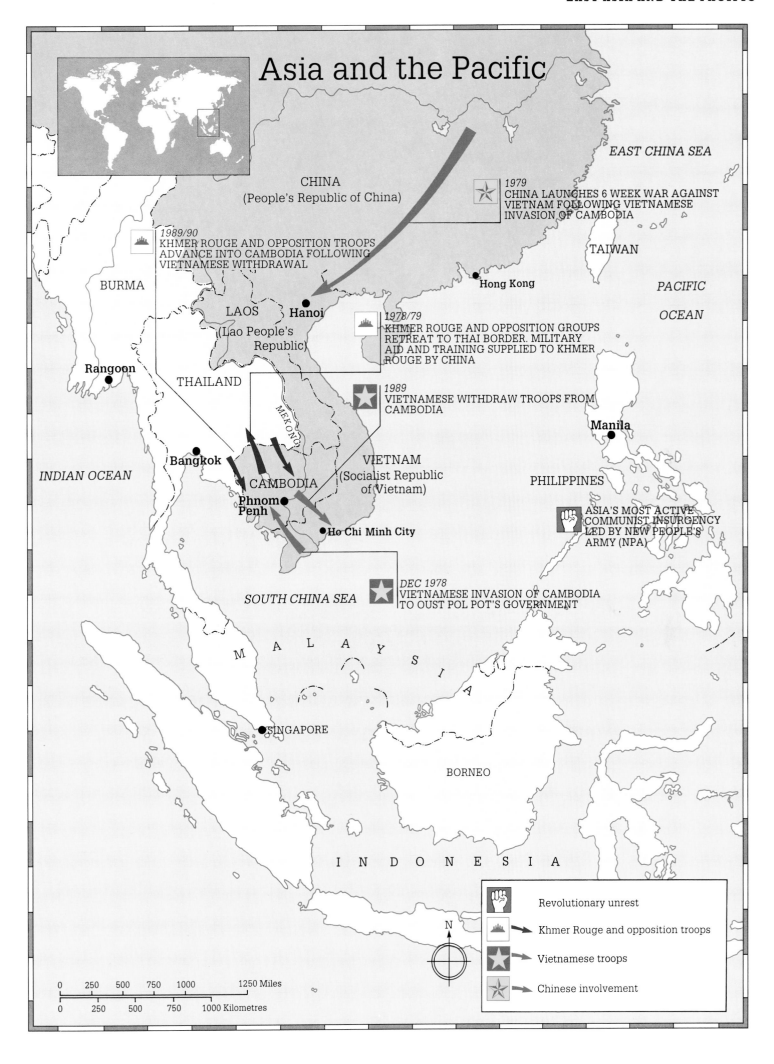

# Asia and the Pacific

CHINA
(People's Republic of China)

EAST CHINA SEA

*1979*
CHINA LAUNCHES 6 WEEK WAR AGAINST VIETNAM FOLLOWING VIETNAMESE INVASION OF CAMBODIA

TAIWAN

*1989/90*
KHMER ROUGE AND OPPOSITION TROOPS ADVANCE INTO CAMBODIA FOLLOWING VIETNAMESE WITHDRAWAL

BURMA

● Hong Kong

PACIFIC

OCEAN

LAOS
(Lao People's
Republic)

**Hanoi** ●

*1978/79*
KHMER ROUGE AND OPPOSITION GROUPS RETREAT TO THAI BORDER. MILITARY AID AND TRAINING SUPPLIED TO KHMER ROUGE BY CHINA

**Rangoon** ●

THAILAND

*1989*
VIETNAMESE WITHDRAW TROOPS FROM CAMBODIA

MEKONG

**Manila**

INDIAN OCEAN

**Bangkok** ●

CAMBODIA

VIETNAM
(Socialist Republic
of Vietnam)

PHILIPPINES

**Phnom
Penh** ●

● **Ho Chi Minh City**

ASIA'S MOST ACTIVE COMMUNIST INSURGENCY LED BY NEW PEOPLE'S ARMY (NPA)

*DEC 1978*
VIETNAMESE INVASION OF CAMBODIA TO OUST POL POT'S GOVERNMENT

SOUTH CHINA SEA

M A L A Y S I A

● SINGAPORE

BORNEO

I N D O N E S I A

N

| | | |
|---|---|---|
| ✊ | | Revolutionary unrest |
| 🏯�➤ | | Khmer Rouge and opposition troops |
| ★➤ | | Vietnamese troops |
| ✴➤ | | Chinese involvement |

0   250   500   750   1000        1250 Miles

0   250   500   750   1000 Kilometres

60 million Koreans between a xenophobic Communist dictatorship and a pro-Western oligarchy, neither of which had much regard for human rights. A shared desire for reunification found expression in periodic moves towards talks, but the political stakes of the rival leaderships and their sponsors were too high for even postal or telecommunications links to be tolerated.

North of the DMZ, the Democratic People's Republic vied with Albania as the most isolated and introverted of Communist states. After the fighting had stopped, strong man Kim Il Sung embarked on an ambitious, largely successful programme of economic reconstruction along classic Stalinist industrialization lines. By 1980, however, there were signs that the country was running into serious economic difficulties: it had been outpaced by capitalist South Korea and had a rising foreign debt. No serious attempt was made at political or economic reform. Instead, Kim Il Sung remained obsessed with reunification on his terms, attempting subversion and occasional acts of terrorism. In 1983, North Korean army officers planted a bomb in the Burmese capital, Rangoon, that killed four visiting South Korean ministers and narrowly missed injuring the President.

As he endured to become the world's longest-serving ruler, Kim Il Sung, the 'great leader', and increasingly his son Kim Il Jong, the 'dear leader', became objects of a personality cult that was extraordinary even within the pantheon of Communist autocrats and exceeded in fervour even the cults of Stalin and Mao.

North Korea exploited the Sino-Soviet split of the early 1960s more effectively than any other Communist state, though from the mid-1980s it appeared to be siding more with the Soviets, in order to register disapproval of China's growing trade relations with South Korea. North Korean ties with various Third World radicals such as Libya and Iran were also strengthened.

The 1990s dawned with Korea still the most likely trouble spot in Asia, if only because of the uncertainty of the Kim dynasty's reaction to the Soviet Union's warming relations with the South, and evidence that the North has been working on a nuclear device, expected to be operative by the middle of the decade.

**The Philippines: Enduring Revolt**

The roots of radical revolt in the Philippines go back to the 1930s. The Communists gained respect during the Second World War, when their Hukbalahap (Huk) movement waged a limited but effective guerrilla campaign against the Japanese on the major island of Luzon. When the Huks successfully contested seven seats in the 1946 independence elections, advocating a programme of radical land reform, the ruling elite became alarmed and the seven elected delegates were denied their places in the Philippines Congress.

The Huks resorted to rebellion, and became in effect an alternative government in areas of Luzon where they had operated during the war. They reached their zenith in 1950, but were crippled by the action of an informer, who directed government forces to a rendezvous in Manila where almost the entire Huk leadership was captured. The movement was unable to recover from this blow, nor was it able to spread revolution to the other Philippines islands, where the rich landowners maintained a firm grip on a submissive peasantry steeped in Catholicism, or, in the case of the southernmost island of Mindanao, Islam.

Small Communist groups, mostly Maoist, continued to persevere, and in the early 1970s President Ferdinand Marcos used the excuse of Communist insurrection to declare martial law after large demonstrations had demanded a fundamental restructuring of political power. But this only led to a resurgence of the radical left. Skirmishes involving the New People's Army (NPA), the military wing of the outlawed Philippine Communist Party, increased from 1979. The NPA was active in northern Luzon,

on Samar, and Mindanao, where government forces also fought Muslim militants of the Moro National Liberation Front.

The NPA drew its support from students and intellectuals, and its ideological inspiration from Maoist China. It was vehemently anti-Soviet. As China drew closer to the West with its 'open door' policy, Beijing withdrew its backing - which, far from hampering the NPA, only strengthened its credentials as an independent, national movement. With the authoritarian government failing to address chronic political and social problems, the NPA was able to exploit labour unrest and to stir resentment against the powerful American military and business presence.

The assassination of opposition leader Benigno Aquino in 1983 further darkened the image of the Marcos regime. Government instability increased, and demonstrations in Manila became a familiar sight. In February 1986 Marcos felt able to call a general election, but clumsily rigged the results in his favour. He had misread the mood of the country and the extent of American embarrassment. The army rallied around Aquino's widow Corazon and the Marcos family fled into

The first big parade in Ho Chi Minh city, May 1975. Saigon surrendered on 31 April, 1975 when the Communist North Vietnamese forces entered the city and the Americans left Vietnam after a fifteen-year involvement.

# Burma: Poppy Power

If ethnic considerations and oligarchic allegiances appear to have influenced the fate of Far Eastern Communism more than have the degree of ideological commitment or social deprivation, the case of Burma demonstrates how complex things can get.

This stewpot of 33 million people achieved independence from Britain in 1948 in a state of ethnic turmoil that has never abated. Rangoon was able to exert only tenuous control over the Shans, Kachins, Karens and other minorities.

Following a military coup in 1962, Burma became a one-party republic dedicated to finding a 'Burmese route to

socialism', based upon self-reliance and the discourage-ment of foreign investment.

While this slowed economic growth to a crawl and isolated the country, it had no impact on activities in the interior; here all kinds of nationalists and various strains of Communists, plus a sprinkling of old-fashioned bandits, waged a continuous drug war with strong political overtones. Here, among the remote, jungle-covered mountains, is the Golden Triangle, where growing poppies is easy and opium trading a way of life. The haphazard war of the smugglers dates back at least to the Second World War. Forces involved have included

Burmese Communist rebels who turned to the drug business, Chinese Nationalist Guomindang remnants who failed to escape to Taiwan after the Communist victory, Laotian royalists who fled the Communist Pathet Lao takeover in Vientiane, and some Pathet Lao.

As drug addiction reached crisis proportions in America in the late 1980s, the US stepped up its pressure on the Burmese and Thai governments to launch a campaign against the major drug smugglers of whatever political complexion, but the complexity of political sponsorship and the huge pay-offs involved have made success difficult to achieve.

exile in the US, to be pursued by law suits seeking recovery of $2 billion bled from the Philippines' economy.

The restoration of democracy and civil liberties did not mollify either the radical left or the radical right, and the death of Marcos in 1989 demonstrated the precarious nature of peace. So much support for the Marcos faction remained that President Aquino denied permission for the return of the body, fearing its 'malignant influence'. In such an atmosphere, the Communists continued to present a substantial challenge.

### Indochina Under Communism

Through the 1980s the USA led an embargo on aid and investment in Indochina, citing as reasons the Vietnamese invasion and continued military presence in Cambodia. The boycott, observed by all Western countries except Sweden, helped cause a severe economic crisis, which only served to further increase the region's dependence on the Soviet Union.

Vietnam experienced particular difficulties, compounded by the fast growth rate of its population. Widespread black marketeering and corruption were described by Le Duc Tho, Hanoi's Paris peace negotiator, as 'tainting every level of society'. As the economic difficulties escalated, so did the exodus of refugees.

In 1985 tentative moves towards economic reform - reducing the level of subsidies and granting a greater level of autonomy to enterprises - only worsened the situation, and inflation soared to a staggering 700 per cent annually. In May 1986, Le Duc Tho openly attacked the party's shortcomings, saying that they had led to sycophancy, opportunism and demoralization. That December the party adopted a reform programme, and the following year party and government ranks were purged of those deemed to be 'corrupt and degraded'. The party newspaper, *Nhan Dan* (People's Daily), acknowledged that never before had 'morale been so eroded, confidence so low, or justice so abused'. Even by the standards of *glasnost*, which was then just beginning to have an impact in the Soviet Union, that editorial was striking.

It became clear that the accelerated pace of reform was being encouraged by pressure from Moscow when a senior member of the Soviet Politburo, Yegor Ligachev, revealed that Soviet aid to Vietnam was running at $2.5 billion a year, and the Soviet press increasingly criticized the uses to which the aid was being put.

### The ASEAN Shield

One consequence of the Communist conquest of Indochina was the strengthening of ASEAN, the Association of Southeast Asian Nations - Malaysia, the Philippines, Singapore and Thailand, joined in 1984 by Brunei. ASEAN was formed in 1967, with the declared purpose of promoting economic

The exodus of refugees from Vietnam grew to unmanageable proportions when the boat people, in their fragile craft, began to arrive in Hong Kong in huge numbers.

co-operation. Yet it was not until 1976 that it staged its first leadership summit, when the need for a co-ordinated policy towards the changed strategic situation had become a priority. Vietnam's invasion of Cambodia in December 1978 further heightened ASEAN concerns over the emergence of a Vietnam-dominated Indochina. Burma alone in the region disdained alliances of any kind.

Although the Vietnamese had toppled the infamous Khmer Rouge from power, the client government they installed in Phnom Penh in January 1979 was to be recognized only by the Soviet bloc and India. As a result the Khmer Rouge were able to retain the country's seat at the United Nations and the legitimacy that this conferred. After mounting a six-week war along Vietnam's northern borders, and suffering much heavier losses than it inflicted, China settled into helping the Khmer Rouge regroup in refugee sancturies along the Thai border. Here the Thai government passed on Chinese arms and obliged international relief agencies caring for hundreds of thousands of Cambodian refugees also to feed and care for the Khmer Rouge. Above all else, the Thais wanted the Vietnamese driven back.

By early 1981 the Khmer Rouge were again a fighting force, an estimated forty thousand strong and able to tie down the two hundred thousand Vietnamese troops in Cambodia. At the same time, a Beijing-inspired diplomatic effort was directed at refurbishing their image. It was declared that Pol Pot was no longer leader, and a remarkable policy switch was proclaimed - from Communist to Social Democrat! Prince Sihanouk was reactivated to lead a shaky national front of royalists, elements from the right, and the sanitized Khmer Rouge, which received its funding from China and Thailand. The Vietnamese continued to rule from Phnom Penh, obdurate and intractable,

until in May 1988 Hanoi announced that the security situation had improved, and troop withdrawals began. Late in 1989 all Vietnam's troops had been withdrawn, and Laos reported the departure of all Vietnamese troops from that country. As a mass of refugees straggled back across the devastated Cambodian countryside, Western policy was to seek a government in Phnom Penh that limited Vietnamese influence, and if possible excluded the Khmer Rouge. In 1990 fears of the Khmer Rouge regaining power prompted the US to open discussions with Hanoi for the first time since the war in Vietnam.

### Pacific *Perestroika*

Forty years of American 'containment' left the East Asian landmass with a garland of big American bases, from Subic Bay in the Philippines through Okinawa, South Korea and Japan. While attention in the late 1980s was all on the changes within the Soviet Union, and the sudden self-destruction of entrenched Marxism in eastern Europe, the zephyrs of *perestroika* and *glasnost* were blowing sufficiently briskly through Asia to raise questions about the future disposition of such American might.

By 1990, Moscow had begun to withdraw 200,000 troops from its border with China and to cut back elsewhere in the east, both in military hardware and aid to old clients. Soviet relations with South Korea had improved to such an extent that Moscow's Korean-language broadcasts openly mocked North Korean leader Kim Il Sung's cult of personality, and no major arms delivery to the North had been detected in more than a year. With a few strategists reasoning that the Soviet threat no longer existed, history threatened to come full circle when some US concerns began to be redirected towards Japan, owner in the early 1990s of one of the largest military budgets in the world.

# Empires May Crumble

On 17 January 1969, Jan Palach set light to himself in the centre of Prague as a protest against censorship and the occupation of Czechoslovakia by Soviet troops. Twenty year later, on 16 January 1989, eight Czech dissidents were arrested as they tried to lay flowers on the site of his suicide. One of them was the playright and founder member of Charter 77, Vaclav Havel. He was tried on 21 February and found guilty of incitement to anti-state and anti-social activities and obstructing an official. He received a nine-month prison sentence. His colleagues were tried separately. Five received suspended sentences, one got nine months and the other twelve months. Nothing seemed to have changed in 20 years.

But just ten months later, on Friday 29 December 1989, a special session of the Czech parliament was held in the fifteenth-century Vladisav Hall of Hradcany Castle in Prague. There was only one item of business on the agenda, yet the proceedings were being televized live to the country. The 323 members were electing a new president and only one man had been put forward as a candidate - Vaclav Havel.

### The Anti-socialist Chip

Many factors burst the Communist bubble in Eastern Europe in 1989. The fact that all the economies in the bloc were in bad shape certainly prompted some of the governing elites to look more closely at the causes behind this phenomena. One answer that their enquiries uncovered was that the planning process had long ceased to be efficient. There were too many transactions for a central office to control and many small or complex deals were left out of the equation, which misled those who were trying to make decisions.

Furthermore, many of the original economic choices made in the 1950s promoted an industrial structure which was unable to reorientate itself a generation later. By concentrating on a few, high profile industries based on late nineteenth-century technology, and calling them 'socialist', it invested them with the sanctity of ideology and made it virtually impossible to question the need for coal, steel, heavy engineering and large-scale construction.

The West, meanwhile, was developing the electronic control systems which steadily enhanced industrial productivity during the 1960s and 1970s and kept costs under control, allowing wages to rise in real terms so that the mass of people were able to afford a range of goods which had been far beyond the reach of their parents. The industries producing these luxury goods in their turn became major employers, as did the manufacturers of the control systems as the West became totally computerized.

This electronics-led industrial revolution posed a particular problem for eastern Europe because it put a premium on the fluent dissemination of information as the end result, an idea which was an anathema to the Soviet Union and its satellites. It also led manufacturing towards cleaner production processes and to the development of sufficient profits for some of the surplus to be used to combat the pollution created by older processes after being put under pressure by the 'green' lobby.

The failures of the system were all too apparent to the intelligentsia on whom the Communist hierarchies had depended to run their countries once they had realized that ideological purity was not enough to organize a modern nation. This educated elite might have been duped in Stalin's time because they were ill-informed about the West, and the differences in living standards and opportunities between the Communist and non-Communist countries of Europe were not so great. But the growth of tourism, which the East needed as a source of hard currency, and the pervasive penetration of television broadcasting broke down the barriers of awareness and demoralized those whom the Communist leaders desperately needed to motivate.

### Gorby's Magic Flute

Yet all these undercurrents had failed to develop any momentum before the new Soviet leadership revealed that it was no longer prepared to coerce its neighbours into following the Moscow line. That change of position was revealed by Mikhail Gorbachev on a visit to Prague on 10 April 1987. He insisted that Soviet solutions were right for Soviet problems, but that these solutions were not to be considered as obligatory by the rest of the Eastern bloc.

This stone fell for a long time into the darkness of eastern Europe before the splash of reform was heard. After so many dashed hopes and promises that came to nothing the people's confidence in their ability to command their own destiny seemed moribund. This was particularly evident in Poland where the government, taking its lead from Moscow, held a referendum on 29 November 1987 in which it asked the people if they favoured radical but drastic changes in the economy. The people were also asked if they wanted a 'Polish model' of democratization.

## Albania: The Last Stronghold

Enver Hoxha died of a heart attack on 11 April 1985, having been his country's leader longer than any other Communist. He was succeeded as First Secretary by Ramiz Alia, who joined the Communist-led National Liberation Movement during the Second World War. After the war, he spent some time in Moscow, and was elected to the Central Committee on his return to Tirana. His progress was slow but steady and he became a Politburo member in 1961. Twenty years later, Hoxha promoted him to Chairman of the Praesidium; a move which gave the impression that Alia was the heir-apparent.

Once Alia took over he was quick to quash any notion that change might be on the way.

Nevertheless, on 6 August 1986 Albania was linked to the outside world by rail for the first time in its history when a track was opened to Titograd, Yugoslavia. Further contact with the rest of the world was increased when ambassadors were exchanged with Spain, Singapore and Mozambique in 1986 and Canada and West Germany in 1987. The same year saw a treaty signed with Greece that officially ended the Second World War. In February 1988, Albania participated in the Balkan Conference for the first time since 1961.

Any outside influences were rigorously excluded from everyday life at first, but a break with the past did occur on 15 November 1989, when the Praesidium declared an amnesty, which included some political prisoners, to mark the forty-fifth anniversary of the country's liberation from Nazi occupation . Then, quite unexpectedly, reports of social unrest began to filter through to the West in the spring of 1990. These were followed by a series of reforms passed by the People's Assembly on 7-8 May, which marked a liberalization of the penal code and an end to religious suppression. It was also announced that passport restrictions on Albanians would be lifted. This precipitated a major invasion of foreign embassies; a situation which was only resolved when the government allowed the refugees to leave for the West.

# The Collapse of
# Communism 1988-90

BALTIC SEA

*APRIL, AUG 1988*
MAJOR STRIKE WAVE THROUGHOUT COUNTRY

*LATE 1988*
GORBACHEV ACCEPTS DISCUSSIONS BETWEEN
SOLIDARITY AND JARUZELSKI GOVERNMENT

*4 JUNE 1989*
SOLIDARITY WINS SEMI-FREE ELECTIONS
*MAY 1990*
SOLIDARITY TRIUMPHS IN LOCAL ELECTIONS

WEST
GERMANY

ELBE

**Berlin**

EAST

GERMANY

NEISSE

ODER

WARTA

**Warsaw**

POLAND

VISTULA

BUG

AUSTRIAN BROADCASTS TO SOUTH-WESTERN
CZECHOSLOVAKIA

*NOV 1989*
EAST GERMAN, POLISH, AUSTRIAN AND
WEST GERMAN TELEVISION SHOWING
DEMONSTRATIONS IN EAST GERMANY
ALL RECEIVED IN CZECHOSLOVAKIA

*JAN, AUG. OCT, NOV 1989*
ANTI-GOVERNMENT DEMONSTRATIONS IN
PRAGUE

*NOV 1989*
KGB POSSIBLY ENCOURAGES DEMONSTRATIONS
AGAINST ORTHODOX GOVERNMENT

*DEC 1989*
CZECHOSLOVAKIA BEGINS TO DISMANTLE IRON
CURTAIN WITH AUSTRIA AND WEST GERMANY

*9 JUNE 1990*
WON BY CIVIC FORUM

**Prague**

CZECHOSLOVAKIA

DANUBE

**Vienna**

AUSTRIA

**Budapest**

HUNGARY

ROMANIA

USSR

HUNGARIAN, YUGOSLAV, BULGARIAN, SOVIET
MOLDAVIAN BROADCASTS HEARD IN ROMANIA

*1987 ONWARDS*
HUNGARIANS FROM TRANSYLVANIA TO HUNGARY

*DEC 1989*
DEMONSTRATION IN TIMISOARA FIRED ON BY
SECURITAT

*DEC 1989*
DEMONSTRATION IN BUCHAREST

*25 MAY 1990*
WON BY NATIONAL SALVATION FRONT

WEST GERMAN BROADCASTS
TO EAST GERMANY (EXCEPT FAR
SOUTH-EAST OF COUNTRY)

*JULY-NOV 1989*
120,000 EAST GERMAN REFUGEES FLEE TO THE
WEST VIA CZECHOSLOVAKIA AND HUNGARY AND
VIA WEST GERMAN EMBASSIES IN PRAGUE AND
WARSAW

*OCT 1989*
GORBACHEV VISITS BERLIN AND CRITICIZES
HONECKER IN PUBLIC

*NOV 1989*
BERLIN WALL AND BORDER BETWEEN THE TWO
GERMANIES DISMANTLED

*18 MARCH 1990*
WON BY CHRISTIAN DEMOCRATS

TISA

**Belgrade**

**Bucharest**

YUGOSLAVIA

BULGARIA

BLACK SEA

**Sofia**

ADRIATIC SEA

AUSTRIAN BROADCASTS TO
WESTERN HUNGARY
(NOT AS FAR AS BUDAPEST)

*LATE 1988*
GORBACHEV ACCEPTS
MULTI-PARTY SYSTEM

*MARCH 1989*
DEMONSTRATIONS IN BUDAPEST

*MAY 1989*
HUNGARY BEGINS TO DISMANTLE
IRON CURTAIN WITH AUSTRIA

*JUNE 1989*
DEMONSTRATIONS ACCOMPANY
REBURIAL OF IMRE NAGY

*25 MARCH/8 APRIL 1990*
WON BY DEMOCRATIC FORUM

ITALY

ALBANIA

GREECE

*JUNE-AUG 1989*
300,000 ETHNIC TURKS EXPELLED BY BULGARIA
TO TURKEY; 50,000 EVENTUALLY RETURN TO
BULGARIA

*NOV 1989*
DEMONSTRATIONS IN SOFIA

*NOV 1989*
GORBACHEV REFUSES TO SUPPORT ZHIVKOV IN
POLITBURO STRUGGLE WITH REFORMERS

*9 JUNE 1990*
WON BY SOCIALIST PARTY

MEDITERRANEAN SEA

0     100     200     300 Miles

0   100   200   300   400 Kilometres

Withdrawal of Soviet support

Popular expressions of discontent

Borders open

Refugees

Cross-border influences: television
and radio

Free elections

So pervasive was the apathy that only 67 per cent of the population bothered to vote and only 66 per cent of them voted for economic reform, that is 44 per cent of the total electorate. A slightly greater number wanted political reform. Solidarity, meanwhile, although refused official recognition, held its own May Day parades which were broken up by the police, while various underground activities kept bubbling up.

The spark which lit the fuse of the 1989 revolution was the announcement by the Polish government of price increases. This move was in line with the views expressed by the people in the referendum and there were few immediate protests. The first signs of trouble came in late April when bus and tram drivers in the city of Bydgoszcz abandoned their vehicles in the streets on the twenty-fifth and caused chaos. This was followed by a wave of strikes at the Lenin steel works in Nowa Huta, the Stalowa Wola works near Krakow, and the Lenin Shipyard in Gdansk.

On 15 August, coalminers in Jastrzebic in southern Poland struck for better pay and the reinstatement of Solidarity. The strike spread rapidly to other coalfields, and north to the Baltic port of Szczecin. The Lenin Shipyard came out again and the wave of strikes was getting out of hand. Curfews were declared but the church intervened and arranged a meeting between Lech Walesa and the Interior Minister Lieutenant-

General Kiszczak on 31 August. The strikers returned to work after guarantees were given that the government would involve Solidarity in discussions designed to resolve the country's economic and political crisis.

The government spent the next five months prevaricating and making life difficult for Solidarity. The round table discussions were scheduled for October and then postponed by the government. Only on 18 January 1989 did the Party's Central Committee approve the negotiations with Solidarity after the First Secretary, General Jaruzelski, had insisted that Solidarity had to be accommodated. The talks began on 6 February at the Palace of the Council of Ministers in Warsaw with 57 participants from all sides, including the Church and a number of dissidents. Solidarity was offered legal recognition and the opportunity to take part in 'non-confrontational' elections.

The elections were set for June and divided into two rounds. Only 35 per cent of the seats in the Sejm, or lower house, could be contested by the Solidarity Citizens Committee at the first free election but they won all 161 of them. The Senate, or upper house, consisted of 100 seats, all of which could be contested by any party, and Solidarity won 99. Sixty-two per cent of the electorate voted in the first round and only 25 per cent in the second.

Solidarity's moral victory now created a nice political problem for, although the

Communist Party and its allies possessed an overwhelming majority in the Sejm, they clearly lacked a mandate to govern. A compromise was reached in which Solidarity acquiesed in General Jaruzelski's election as president on 19 July in order to avoid a constitutional crisis. However, all attempts by the Communists to form a government that was acceptable failed because their former allies, the Peasants' Party, had changed sides. This situation dragged on until September when Solidarity put forward their own candidate, the Catholic intellectual Tadeusz Mazowiecki, who had helped Solidarity to negotiate with the government in August 1980. By doing a deal in which the Defence and Interior ministries were retained by the Communists, Mazowiecki became Poland's first non-Communist Prime Minister in a generation on 12 September.

Clearly, many members of the new government expected the West to rush in with offers of massive aid to support the nascent democracy. Unfortunately, they were sadly mistaken and all that the West offered was shipments of food and a relatively small amount of financial support. The government, which was primarily a coalition of Solidarity and the Peasants' Party, was left to confront the same problems that had defeated the Communists: a lack of natural resources, serious underinvestment, poor industrial plant and a limp productivity record. By early 1990 the government's popularity was waning while Lech Walesa was living in a large villa in the country having sold his life story to Hollywood.

# Never Forgotten

On the mornig of 16 June 1989, a vast, silent crowd filled Heroes' Square in Budapest. At their heart was a giant black catafalque and on it lay six coffins. One, which was empty, symbolized 400 citizens who had been executed as counter-revolutionaries after the 1956 uprising. Four contained the remains of leading members of the government. And the last contained the remains of Imre Nagy himself, who had been hanged on 16 June 1958 after being convicted of high treason for his part in the 1956 uprising. For years they had lain disregarded in unmarked graves, and now they were honoured as heroes. Six giant candlesticks from the Budapest Opera House stood guard over them. Even the Corinthian columns on the edge of the square were swathed in black.

The officials attending included Miklos Nemeth, Imre Poszgay, representatives of Charter 77 from Czechoslovakia and the leader of the Italian Communist Party. Of the Warsaw Pact countries, only Romanian representatives were absent.

The state funeral of Imre Nagy in Heroes' Square, Budapest, on 16 June 1989, thirty-one years after his death.

Two days later the Ceaucescu regime complained of 'hostile manifestations' in Budapest which were 'clearly fascist, irredentist in nature, and aimed against ... socialism and communism'.

The reburial was also attended by those who had fled the country after the Soviet tanks crushed the rising, as well as the young and old from throughout Hungary. For hours they filed past, dropping flowers in a gesture of respect for the past and hope for the future.

On 1 November 1956, Nagy had broadcast a declaration to the Hungarian people: 'People of Hungary! The Hungarian National Government, imbued with profound responsibility towards the Hungarian people and it history ... declares the neutrality of the Hungarian People's Republic. The Hungarian people ... wish to live in true friendship with their neighbours.' On 16 June 1989 that wish seemed about to be fulfilled. On his coffin lay the legend, 'Never Forgotten'.

## Hungary Springs a Leak

The Hungarian Communist Party had shown a degree of flexibility unusual in eastern Europe during the 1980s. It was not surprising, therefore, that they were among the first to respond to the Gorbachev initiative of April 1987 with the appointment in June of a new Prime Minister, Karoly Grosz, who set about rebuilding the government. A year later he became General Secretary, and several leading conservatives on the Politburo retired. Imre Pozsgay, the leader of the Patriotic People's Front, was one replacement who would figure prominently in the reforms to come.

It was Pozsgay who, on 28 January 1989, leaked the findings of the Central Committee's Historical Commission, which had concluded that the 1956 uprising could not be dismissed as 'counter-revolutionary'. Instead, it should be described as a 'popular uprising against the existing state power' which was transformed by the intervention of Soviet troops into 'a national independence struggle'. Six days later a government spokesman announced that the country would no longer celebrate the Russian Revolution. The anniversary of the 1848 Hungarian uprising against the house of Habsburg would be substituted instead on 15 March every year.

*Top:* Demonstrations in Central Square, Bucharest, Christmas Eve 1989. Tanks and armoured personnel carriers littered the centre of Bucharest. *Above:* Demonstrations in Prague, 1989. Unlike Romania, the old regime in Czechoslovakia fell without bloodshed.

During the first eight months of 1989, 50,000 East Germans had left legally for the West, but this turned into a torrent in July as everyone tried to take advantage of the government's paralysis while Honecker went into hospital for an operation. Groups of 100 or more slipped through the holes in the Austro-Hungarian border during August. Any that were caught were given an initial warning. The failure of a second attempt would lead to their name being reported to the East German authorities and a note being entered on their papers. But even these measures were abandoned by the end of August and the only punishment was a reprimand. On 10 September, the government announced that even if East Germans entering Hungary did not possess legal travel documents, they would not be refused admission. By the end of September, 24,000 East Germans had escaped into Austria across the open border.

Meanwhile, the West German embassies in Budapest, Prague and Warsaw were being overwhelmed by thousands of East German refugees claiming asylum. On 1 October the Honecker government agreed to allow them to go to the West by train as long as they surrendered their documents on the way. But when the trains stopped in East Germany to do this, another 2000 jumped aboard.

However, not everyone was determined to leave and several hundred civil rights protesters gathered in Leipzig on the evening of Monday 4 September. Although they were attacked by police and many were arrested, another crowd gathered in the same place on the following three Mondays. By 25 September the crowd had swollen to 8000 and the police did little to interfere. The protests had spead to Dresden, where between 5000 and 10,000 people were demonstrating every day.

Gorbachev arrived on 6 October to take part in East Germany's fortieth anniversary celebrations. Hours after his departure on the seventh, 5000 to 7000 people gathered in East Berlin's Alexanderplatz and marched on the Palace of the Republic. They were attacked by the police and many were arrested, but this was the last time that the police interfered. The following day, 30,000 people took to the streets of Dresden and the local party chief, the reformer Hans Modrow, agreed to meet a delegation. The weekly demonstrations in Leipzig increased to more than 100,000 citizens. On the eighteenth Honecker resigned and his place was taken by former security chief, Egon Krenz.

On 19 September, a group of civil rights and political protesters had joined forces and applied for official recognition under the title New Forum and had been refused. But on 26 October the East Berlin party leader, Gunter Schabowski, met two of the leaders of New Forum.

Early in November, the reformer Modrow was appointed Prime Minister and free elections were promised. But the most sensational change of policy occurred on the ninth when Krenz announced that East

A meeting of the Central Committee in April 1989 removed all but one of the remaining conservatives on the Politburo and gave more power to the reformers. Soviet troops, meanwhile, began moving out as a result of Gorbachev's unilateral declaration of troop cuts at the United Nations General Assembly on 7 December 1988.

On 2 May 1989, work began on dismantling the fence along the 260-kilometre border with Austria. It was estimated that the job would take 18 months but its effect was to alarm the more intransigent parties in East Germany, Czechoslovakia and Romania. An extraordinary Party congress led to a new name, the Hungarian Socialist Party, amendments to the constitution and a date

for free elections in March 1990. When those elections were held, the Socialist Party received just 10 per cent of the vote, which was about the same level of support as the Communists polled in the last free elections back in 1947. The centre-right Hungarian Democratic Forum won 164 seats out of 386 and formed the next government.

### Riding the Freedom Train

Many East Germans spent their holidays in Hungary and some of them began to think of making this but the first stage in a longer journey after Erich Honecker showed no signs of making any serious political changes during the first half of 1989.

# The People's Choice

Vaclav Havel was the son of a civil engineer and because of his father's professional status he was denied the opportunity to go to college. He went, instead, to work as a laboratory technician and completed his education at night school. In 1955, at the age of nineteen, he published his first article, but after failing to get a place at drama school, he took a job as a stage hand. However, his talent was soon obvious and he began writing scripts and working as the assistant to a leading producer. His first play, *The Garden Party,* was performed in December 1963. This and his many other plays were translated into numerous languages and seen throughout Europe and in New York, where he won a number of awards.

His criticisms of the regime led to surveillance by the police during 1969 in the wake of the Soviet invasion and from that time his plays were only rarely performed in Czechoslovakia, although they were widely seen abroad. His actions on behalf of human rights issues culminated in an open letter to the Czech president, Gustav Husak, which was also published abroad, in which he attacked the insidious pressures exerted on citizens, pressures which he called a 'hideous spider whose invisible web runs right through the whole of society'.

Late in 1976 he became

The people's choice: playwright, co-founder of Charter 77 and President of Czechoslovakia, Vaclav Havel at home.

involved in the discussions which led to the creation of the Charter 77 group, of which he was one of the three spokesmen. This led to his arrest and detention for four months at the beginning of 1977. He was tried in October and received a fourteen-month suspended sentence which was conditional on refraining from public statements. But Havel refused to give in and in April 1978 he helped organize the Committee for the Defence of the Unjustly Prosecuted. He was arrested for this in May 1979 and charged with 'criminal subversion of the republic'. He was sentenced to four and a half years in jail. In January 1983, he developed pneumonia and the illness was so serious that he was transferred to hospital and released.

Despite this harrassment, he refused to give an inch and resumed his work for the Charter 77 group as soon as he was fit. This lead to a series of brief detentions in police custody but the regime was clearly reluctant to provoke the adverse foreign publicity that another jail sentence would bring. Until, that is, they were frightened by a bunch of flowers.

Germans would be allowed to travel abroad freely. On the weekend of 10-11 November, millions flooded through the Berlin Wall to take their first look at the West, but less than 2000 chose to stay.

In December, details began to emerge of the way in which the former East German leaders had lined their own pockets and enjoyed luxurious lifestyles. Within days, nine former members of the Politburo were charged and only Honecker, because of his poor health, was not arrested. Krenz was forced to resign as General Secretary.

### Two Into One Will Go

A round table discussion between the party and the various opposition groups which were now beginning to emerge was held on 7 December. On the fifteenth, the Christian Democrats held their first conference in East Berlin. On 22 December, the West German Chancellor Helmut Kohl met Modrow to open the Brandenburg Gate in the centre of Berlin as a crossing. At this point, all the major politicians were studiously ignoring the issue of German reunification.

On 17 January 1990 the whole German agenda was thrown into question when Kohl made a speech at the French Institute on International Relations in Paris and insisted that the post-war Oder-Neise line between East Germany and Poland would not be altered whatever happened, which implied that open discussion of reunification was about to occur. In view of the unstable situation, the East German elections were brought forward to 18 March.

By February, Modrow was prepared to talk about a proposal for 'overcoming the division of the German nation'. On the sixth, Kohl announced his readiness 'to open immediate negotiations on economic and monetary union'. In East Berlin, eight opposition leaders had joined the government. In the run up to the March election, these fledgling groups were swamped by the West German party machines of the Christian and Social Democrats, who overwhelmed them with expertise and money. A grand coalition was formed by the victorious parties in the aftermath of the election to set the timetable for reunification, which was now being almost entirely

dictated by Bonn. On 31 May, the East German government introduced legislation to determine the value of assets of political parties with a view to expropriating any held on 7 October 1989. As the Communists were the only party existing at that time, the measure was clearly a vindictive attack on them and an attempt by the West Germans to see that if anything went wrong, the Communists would be in no position to exploit the situation. Gregor Gysi, their chairman, protested but few in the West were interested. East Germany would soon disappear from the map.

### A More Modest Marriage

This headlong rush into the arms of the West was not repeated in the Balkans. Albania remained almost completely isolated from the process until the spring of 1990, when the Party's First Secretary, Ramiz Alia, announced 'we want friendly relations with all countries, irrespective of their social systems' at a plenum of the Central Committee on 17 April, a statement which seemed to imply that diplomatic ties might be resumed with both Moscow and Washington. Three weeks later, some liberalization was announced on religious matters and foreign travel, but the party remained firmly in control.

Yugoslavia was more concerned with reconciling internal differences between its constituent states and holding the country together. These differences were reflected in political changes as elections in Slovenia and Croatia, the two northern states which were physically close to the West, brought non-Communist administrations to power after the first multi-party elections for 51 years.

The Bulgarian Communist Party appeared almost as immoveable as the Albanian until Todor Zhivkov, the 78-year-old General Secretary, was forced to resign on 10 November 1989. He was replaced by Petar Mladenov, who moved swiftly to remove the former leader's cronies. Opposition groups soon began to appear in public and on 7 December formed the Union of Democratic Forces and called for political pluralism. Three weeks later the Politburo agreed to hold negotiations with the new alliance.

At an extraordinary congress, held between 30 January and 2 February, the party adopted a new constitution and many of the old guard were pushed to one side. At the same time the party affirmed its allegiance to Marxism and refused to follow the Social Democratic path adopted in other eastern European Parties. On 3 April, nevertheless, it adopted a new name, the Bulgarian Socialist Party.

The Bulgarian electorate, meanwhile, was beginning to realize that the Polish experience and the probable economic traumas in East Germany meant that the adoption of Western models did not bring Western-style affluence with it automatically. And, to the astonishment of the West,

At the Wall, November 1989. The Berlin Wall begins to crumble, at first in small pieces hacked out and taken away as souvenirs. By 22 December, the Brandenburg Gate, in the centre of Berlin, was open. Before long the first tentative proposals were made for German reunification.

the BSP won 211 out of 400 parliamentary seats at the general election of 10 and 17 June, which was judged reasonably fair by Western observers.

### Fighting Over Television

Of all the Eastern European rulers, Nicolae Ceausescu seemed the least vulnerable at the beginning of 1989, not least because he was entirely independent of Soviet troops and hence direct Kremlin pressure. However, his rural resettlement programme, which violated all codes of internationally agreed human rights, had created an enormous reservoir of resentment among the Romanians as he tried to obliterate almost half of the nation's villages in a drive for economic 'systematization'. In addition, his desire to pay off Romania's debt to the West had succeeded at the cost of reducing most of the people to abject poverty.

This supressed hatred boiled over in December 1989, when large crowds protested over the attempted deportation of Laszlo Tökes, a Protestant pastor. The Securitate, and perhaps some troops, opened fire. This only provoked greater protests which spilled over into other towns. When Ceausescu addressed a large rally on 21 December, he was heckled and booed, a reaction which could not be concealed because it was broadcast live on television.

The following morning, huge crowds gathered in Bucharest and a national state of emergency was declared. The state radio announced that the Defence Minister, Colonel-General Vasile Milea, had committed suicide, but his murder by a member of the presidential guard was later exposed. This act was the result of Milea's refusal to instruct his troops to fire on the people and it was the final straw for the army, who turned against the regime. They formed an alliance with opposition groups under the name of the National Salvation Front. The new group took control of the radio and television stations. That evening, the Securitate launched a well-planned attack on the television station and succeeded in gaining entry. But soldiers inside fought them off and by the 25th the worst of the fighting was over. The Front was in control.

Ceausescu, meanwhile, had escaped from the presidential palace in Bucharest by helicopter on 22 December. But he was captured the same day and imprisoned in a military barracks in Tirgoviste. On Christmas Day he and his wife were placed on trial, found guilty of genocide and executed. Their bodies were shown on Romanian television the same day.

The Council of National Unity was formed on 1 February 1990 to serve as a transitional government. This move did not succeed in calming the unrest which was evident in Bucharest as different groups tried to oust those formerly associated with Ceausescu. Even the holding of elections of 20 May, which were won with a landslide by the Front, was not enough to bring the chaos to an end. The defeated parties, particularly of the right, tried to cast doubt on the result but the presence of Western observers undermined this manoeuvre. On 20 June 1990, a new government was announced by the newly elected President Ion Iliescu and contained only three ministers who had served in the former interim administration.

### The Gentle Touch

The Czechs were proud that their revolution had avoided such disorder and brutality. Vaclav Havel had come to power because the twelve opposition groups under the banner of Civic Forum had been determined to pursue their action peacefully. The conciliatory attitude of the Prime Minister, Ladislaw Adamec, was crucial in accommodating the demands of the protestors and on 26 November he joined Havel and Dubcek in addressing a crowd of almost half a million. There he promised to present the demands of Civic Forum to the Central Committee.

On 1 December, the Praesidium announced the reversal of its position on events in 1968 and described the Soviet intervention as 'unjustified and mistaken'. A new government was announced two days later but it was denounced by Civic Forum as cosmetic. Finally, on 9 December, President Husak resigned and it rapidly became clear that only one candidate would be acceptable to the Czechoslovak people. On 20 February 1990, President Havel was received by President Bush at the White House.

# Glasnost and Perestroika

The new openness or *glasnost* which was to be Mikhail Gorbachev's watchword began in earnest in February 1986, at the opening of the Twenty-seventh Congress of the Soviet Communist Party, when the General Secretary made a frank six-hour report. It continued with changes to the party's rule book which made members and officials much more accountable. Admission to membership would henceforth take place at open meetings which could be attended by ordinary citizens. Nominations to the all-important *nomenklatura* lists of those worthy of promotion could be made by local party groups and were no longer the preserve of individual officials. The right of individual members to criticize officials was strengthened by the provision that officials had to 'inform party organizations of their work on the realization of critical remarks and Communists' suggestions in the interim between party congresses'.

These changes were necessary if the new men at the top - Gorbachev, Ryzhkov, Shevardnadze and Ligachev - were to shake the inert mass of Soviet bureaucracy sufficiently to wake it from its slumber of the last years of Brezhnev's rule. The whole economy needed restructuring, or *perestroika*, and had to be more flexible in its response to changing conditions, as Gorbachev pointed out in his opening address to the Congress:

Price levels must be linked not only to the cost of production, but also with the degree to which they meet the needs of society and consumer demand.

It is high time to put an end to the practice of ministries and departments exercising petty tutelage over industrial enterprises.

Farms will be given the opportunity to use as they see fit all the produce harvested over and above the plan.

It is essential that the government's wage policy should ensure that incomes strictly correspond to the quantity and quality of work done.

## The State of the Union

Unfortunately, these comments and similar speeches over the years have been misinterpreted by many in the West as an admission that Soviet economic planning and its industries are in a state of collapse - which would be overly pessimistic. Production goals set in the 1960s, which aimed for Soviet industry to surpass its American counterpart, were largely met. By the late 1980s the country claimed to be producing 80 per cent more steel than the Americans, 78 per cent more cement, 42 per cent more oil and five times as many tractors. However, an industrial revolution had taken place in the West during the intervening twenty-five years and the economic goal posts had been moved. Heavy industry was no longer the criterion by which advanced economies were measured. New materials, sophisticated service industries and, above all, electronics were the new engines of the industrial machine. What the Soviet leaders were saying was that their planning system had been unable to respond to these changes

and the system had to be restructured to make it more flexible.

One mechanism through which the Politburo tried to create a more responsive system was to introduce agreements whereby the state would buy half of the output of a particular industry and leave it to find customers for the other half. Industries would also be permitted to choose their own suppliers. Enterprise directors would be elected by the workforce, who would have to ensure that the individual business was self-financing. They would also be able to decide how to spend their profits, choosing from options which could include increasing wages or reinvestment, for example.

Changes were introduced into foreign trade by which individual businesses were allowed to negotiate directly with their partners abroad, rather than work through a central organization. New regulations were drafted, designed to encourage foreign companies to invest in the Soviet Union through joint ventures with local businesses. At first the foreign partners were limited to a 49 per cent holding in the jointly owned company, but when this proved insufficiently attractive the restriction was relaxed.

Another important objective was to legalize many small-scale ventures which, up till then, had no alternative but to operate on the edge of the black market because supplies were so difficult to obtain on a reliable basis from state enterprises. Many of these businesses were providing a genuine service, such as car maintenance or small construction jobs which the state was unable to organize effectively. Such businesses would be able to expand and be drawn into the tax system, for they would no longer be liable to prosecution for illegal trading if they declared the source of their income. It was envisaged that many of these small businesses would be family co-operatives in which there would no employees at first, but that once they were established, the hiring of employees might be permitted.

Further radical changes to the agricultural system were proposed, by which individual farmers and their families could lease land and equipment from state and collective farms. They would then contract to sell a certain amount of produce to the state; the excess they would sell privately. Those around the large cities were able to sell their produce in markets provided by the state and during the winter fresh fruit and vegetables can command extraordinary prices from a growing middle class which is

## The Question of Baltic Secession

Nationalists in the three Baltic republics of Estonia, Latvia and Lithuania first came to Western notice when an unofficial demonstration took place in the Latvian captial Riga on 18 November 1987. Confronted by strong local feelings, the party officials approved rallies in all three Baltic republics on 23 August 1988, the anniversary of the Nazi-Soviet Pact, which had led to their loss of sovereignty.

Local elections in March 1989 changed the balance of power within each soviet but many party members retained their popularity because of the

support for Baltic autonomy. Encouraged by their success at the ballot box, the nationalists organized their own demonstration for 23 August 1989, a human chain 600 kilometres long which linked all three Baltic capitals. On 19 September, Gorbachev spoke publicly in favour of greater autonomy for the republics; a sentiment endorsed by the country's Supreme Soviet which granted greater economic independence to the Baltic states from 1 January 1990. This seemed to go to the heads of the inexperienced nationalist politicians and on

11 March 1990 the Lithuanian Supreme Council declared its independence from Moscow. Vytautas Landsbergis, the new president, called for 'fraternal solidarity and support' from the international community and clearly thought that the West would come to their aid when Moscow imposed an economic blockade. But as the measures began to bite, the Lithuanians realized that they had gone to far and a face-saving formula had to be found. On 29 June 1990 the Lithuanians suspended their declaration while Moscow resume trade.

Lenin watches over Muslim nationalist Azeris in Baku, Azerbaijan as they demand independence from Moscow in the move to self-determination.

# The New Russia

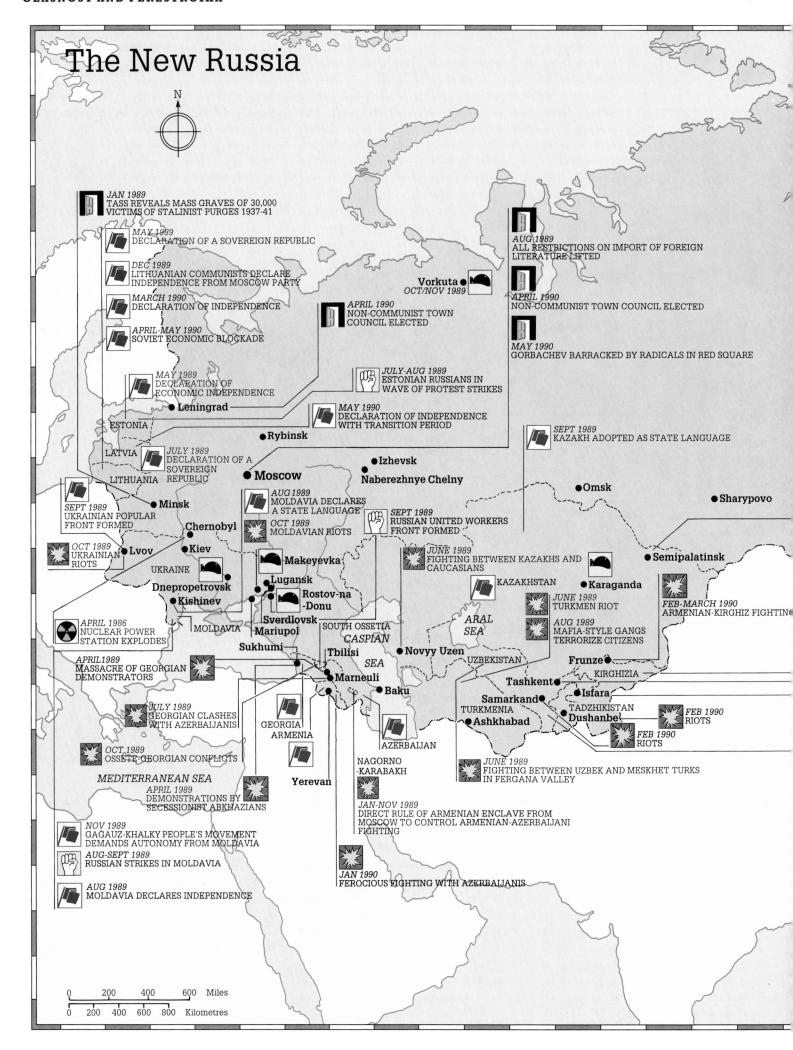

N

*JAN 1989*
TASS REVEALS MASS GRAVES OF 30,000
VICTIMS OF STALINIST PURGES 1937-41

*MAY 1989*
DECLARATION OF A SOVEREIGN REPUBLIC

*DEC 1989*
LITHUANIAN COMMUNISTS DECLARE
INDEPENDENCE FROM MOSCOW PARTY

*MARCH 1990*
DECLARATION OF INDEPENDENCE

*APRIL-MAY 1990*
SOVIET ECONOMIC BLOCKADE

*MAY 1989*
DECLARATION OF
ECONOMIC INDEPENDENCE

**Vorkuta**
*OCT/NOV 1989*

*AUG 1989*
ALL RESTRICTIONS ON IMPORT OF FOREIGN
LITERATURE LIFTED

*APRIL 1990*
NON-COMMUNIST TOWN COUNCIL ELECTED

*MAY 1990*
GORBACHEV BARRACKED BY RADICALS IN RED SQUARE

*APRIL 1990*
NON-COMMUNIST TOWN
COUNCIL ELECTED

*JULY-AUG 1989*
ESTONIAN RUSSIANS IN
WAVE OF PROTEST STRIKES

**Leningrad**

*MAY 1990*
DECLARATION OF INDEPENDENCE
WITH TRANSITION PERIOD

ESTONIA

**Rybinsk**

*SEPT 1989*
KAZAKH ADOPTED AS STATE LANGUAGE

LATVIA

*JULY 1989*
DECLARATION OF A
SOVEREIGN
REPUBLIC

**Izhevsk**
**Naberezhnye Chelny**

LITHUANIA

**Moscow**

**Omsk**

**Sharypovo**

*SEPT 1989*
UKRAINIAN POPULAR
FRONT FORMED

**Minsk**

*AUG 1989*
MOLDAVIA DECLARES
A STATE LANGUAGE

*OCT 1989*
MOLDAVIAN RIOTS

*SEPT 1989*
RUSSIAN UNITED WORKERS
FRONT FORMED

**Chernobyl**

*OCT 1989*
UKRAINIAN
RIOTS

**Lvov**

**Kiev**

**Makeyevka**

*JUNE 1989*
FIGHTING BETWEEN KAZAKHS AND
CAUCASIANS

**Semipalatinsk**

UKRAINE

**Lugansk**

KAZAKHSTAN

**Karaganda**

*FEB-MARCH 1990*
ARMENIAN-KIRGHIZ FIGHTING

**Dnepropetrovsk**

**Rostov-na
-Donu**

*JUNE 1989*
TURKMEN RIOT

**Kishinev**

**Sverdlovsk**

*ARAL
SEA*

*AUG 1989*
MAFIA-STYLE GANGS
TERRORIZE CITIZENS

*APRIL 1986*
NUCLEAR POWER
STATION EXPLODES

MOLDAVIA

**Mariupol**

SOUTH OSSETIA

*CASPIAN*

**Novyy Uzen**

UZBEKISTAN

**Frunze**

*APRIL 1989*
MASSACRE OF GEORGIAN
DEMONSTRATORS

**Sukhumi**

**Tbilisi**

*SEA*

KIRGHIZIA

**Tashkent**

**Isfara**

*JULY 1989*
GEORGIAN CLASHES
WITH AZERBAIJANIS

**Marneuli**

**Baku**

**Samarkand**

TADZHIKISTAN

*FEB 1990*
RIOTS

GEORGIA

TURKMENIA

**Dushanbe**

ARMENIA

**Ashkhabad**

*FEB 1990*
RIOTS

*OCT 1989*
OSSÈTE-GEORGIAN CONFLICTS

AZERBAIJAN

*MEDITERRANEAN SEA*

NAGORNO
-KARABAKH

*JUNE 1989*
FIGHTING BETWEEN UZBEK AND MESKHET TURKS
IN FERGANA VALLEY

*APRIL 1989*
DEMONSTRATIONS BY
SECESSIONIST ABKHAZIANS

**Yerevan**

*NOV 1989*
GAGAUZ-KHALKY PEOPLE'S MOVEMENT
DEMANDS AUTONOMY FROM MOLDAVIA

*JAN-NOV 1989*
DIRECT RULE OF ARMENIAN ENCLAVE FROM
MOSCOW TO CONTROL ARMENIAN-AZERBAIJANI
FIGHTING

*AUG-SEPT 1989*
RUSSIAN STRIKES IN MOLDAVIA

*AUG 1989*
MOLDAVIA DECLARES INDEPENDENCE

*JAN 1990*
FEROCIOUS FIGHTING WITH AZERBAIJANIS

0   200   400   600   Miles

0   200   400   600   800   Kilometres

**Renaming of cities:**

| Date | Pre-glasnost name | Old name restored |
|------|-------------------|-------------------|
| June 1987 | Ustinov (Brezhnev Defence Minister) | Izhevsk |
| Jan 1988 | Brezhnev | Naberezhnye Chelny |
| Mar 1988 | Andropov | Rybinsk |
| Dec 1988 | Chernenko | Sharypovo |
| Jan 1989 | Zhdanov (Stalinist minister) | Mariupol |
| Nov 1989 | Voroshilovgrad (Stalinist Marshal) | Lugansk |

*OCT 1989*
POPULAR FRONT FOR RUSSIAN SOVIET FEDERATED SOCIALIST REPUBLIC FORMED

*MAY 1990*
BORIS YELTSIN ELECTED PRESIDENT OF RUSSIAN SUPREME SOVIET

*SEPT 1989*
KAZAKH-RUSSIAN CONFLICT

PACIFIC OCEAN

*SEPT 1989*
KIRGHIZ ADOPTED AS STATE LANGUAGE

*FEB 1990*
UZBEK-KIRGHIZ FIGHTING

*OCT 1989*
UZBEK DEMONSTRATIONS

*JULY 1989*
TADZHIK CLASHES WITH KIRGHIZIS

*SEPT 1989*
UZBEK'S PEOPLE'S MOVEMENT FORMED

| | |
|---|---|
| Resurgent nationalism | |
| Ethnic unrest | |
| Russian nationalist backlash | |
| Miners' strikes July 1989 | |
| Glasnost | |
| Nuclear accident | |

able to afford such luxuries. Enterprising farmers became rouble millionaires.

By the end of the 1980s considerable restructuring had taken place, but if anything the country's overall economic performance had deteriorated, since the changeover disrupted the old system before it was able to deliver the benefits of the new one. The process was also hindered by the sudden drop in the price of oil between the death of Brezhnev and the election of Gorbachev as General Secretary. With 20 per cent of the Soviet Union's foreign earnings coming from oil, the drop from $28 a barrel to $14 was catastrophic and prevented the country from importing some of the Western technology which it needed to renovate its industries.

## Power to the People

To prevent the country slipping back into its old ways through inertia when faced with these initial problems, the new leaders realized that they needed to enlist the people and channel their private criticisms into public action. Gorbachev led from the front. Within a few months of becoming General Secretary he received a visit from Vladimir Karpov, the editor of the leading Soviet literary journal *Novy Mir*. Karpov had submitted verse by Yevgeny Yevtushenko, the Soviet Union's most famous poet, to the state censorship board, which had refused to allow the magazine to publish it. This was not surprising, as the work dealt with a number of sensitive topics, including neo-Nazism and those who still idolized Stalin. The General Secretary glanced at it and said he could see no reason to uphold the board's decision; but he wanted to refer the case to Yegor Ligachev, the party's new chief ideologist, who is widely portrayed as the leader of the conservative faction. Ligachev read it carefully and sent Karpov a note saying that the Central Committee had no objections; publication went ahead. In June 1986 the Central Committee abolished the censorship board completely.

Such decisions were a clear signal to the intelligentsia, which is a large and influential part of Soviet society. For example, *Novy Mir* has a circulation of over 4 million a month, whereas any comparable Western publication would be lucky to sell forty thousand. Soon Boris Pasternak's *Doctor Zhivago*, which had been banned for almost thirty years, was on sale, as was the searing exposé of Stalin's rule, *Let History Judge,* by the dissident Roy Medvedev. Forbidden films, long buried in the archives, were shown and acclaimed.

As the Politburo had hoped, the new ways began to catch on. Soviet newspapers, which had hitherto been dry and predictable, were transformed into essential reading - full of articles critical of those in the bureaucracy who were dragging their heels over reform. By the end of the 1980s the press had become the watchdog of *perestroika* and the mouthpiece of *glasnost*.

In June 1988, at a special Party Congress, another radical proposal was made which

# Boris Yeltsin: The People's Choice?

A portrait of Boris Yeltsin is carried by demonstrators at a democracy rally in Moscow, 1990.

Boris Nikolayevich Yeltsin is a man with his foot permanently on the accelerator of *perestroika*. As the First Party Secretary of Moscow he announced the arrest of hundreds of corrupt trade officials and attacked some by name. Instead of using a chauffeur-driven limosine, he upset the party hierarchy and endeared himself to Moscovites by riding the city's buses and subway, asking commuters what they thought about the system.

But on 21 October 1987, this flamboyant, undisciplined but honest character went too far at a Central Committee meeting by attacking Yegor Ligachev, the darling of the conservatives, and he had to resign.

Yeltsin was too popular to remain in the cold for long. Early in 1989 he was nominated for the election to the Congress of People' Deputies, and was elected with 89 per cent of the vote. He was then nominated to the Supreme Soviet, and elected Chairman of the Russian Supreme Soviet in May 1990.

In a surprising move in summer 1990, Gorbachev supported Yeltsin's proposals for economic reform over those of Prime Minister Ryzhkov.

attempted to revive a pre-war institution that, it was hoped, would encourage reform and thwart the conservatives. Delegates agreed to amend the constitution to provide for a choice of candidates at elections for a new Congress of Deputies, which would choose a genuinely legislative Supreme Soviet. The President of the Congress was to be the party's General Secretary, while the deputies would be limited to two consecutive five-year terms. These amendments were approved in December and the elections took place early in 1989. Among those chosen to sit in the Supreme Soviet were the dissidents Roy Medvedev and Andrei Sakharov, who spoke at the opening sessions which were presided over by Gorbachev and seen on television.

This revolution in attitudes eventually spread into open discussion of perhaps the most embarrassing skeleton in the Soviet closet: Stalin. Although Khrushchev had given the topic an airing and opened the prison camps, Brezhnev had firmly closed the door again and barred any further public discussion. The new leaders now went much further and the full extent of the horror of the purges was at last made known to the Soviet people. The reputations of victims were rehabilitated and an organization called Memorial was set up, dedicated to remembering them. Joint commissions of

Soviet and foreign historians were set up to investigate and report on controversial historical events, while archaeologists probed the mass graves, trying to establish when and how the victims had died.

## Chernobyl

The greatest test of the new openness came in April 1986, when the nuclear power station at Chernobyl, one of the largest in the country and sited just a hundred miles north of Kiev, a city of 3 million people, suffered a catastrophic failure. Even closer to hand was the town of Pripjat, just two miles away, with a population of forty thousand.

The explosion occurred at 1.23 am local time on Saturday, 26 April. The first reports to reach Moscow were confused, partly because the radiation contamination was patchy and partly because the local officials were clearly terrified of what the Kremlin might do to them, because the explosion was the consequence of an unauthorized experiment with the reactor controls. Their immediate reaction was to try to cover up what had happened, just as they might have done under Brezhnev.

The Politburo sent the deputy Prime Minister, Boris Scherbina, to Pripjat to investigate. He arrived on Sunday morning and immediately ordered the evacuation of

At last, the people are free to demonstrate and huge crowds, carrying placards, posters and flags, voice their opinions at a rally in Moscow, 1990.

the town; all but a handful of the inhabitants were bussed out in two hours. Meanwhile, workers at the Swedish reactor in Forsmark, seven hundred miles to the north, were detecting abnormal levels of radiation. Reports from the rest of the country and from Finland over the weekend indicated that the radiation was drifting from the Soviet side of the border, and Swedish officials in Moscow began pressing the Foreign Ministry for a statement. Again the automatic reaction of denial was used, and the spokesmen stonewalled until Monday evening, when a brief report that there had been a nuclear accident at Chernobyl was broadcast on the main Soviet television news.

Back at the disaster area, helicopters were being used to drop thousands of tons of sand, boron and lead on to the gaping reactor to seal it. Beneath the reactor, teams of miners were boring tunnels to drain the ground water and then inject concrete and molten lead to prevent any contamination leaking out. No one had ever dealt with such a disaster before, and many Soviet nuclear scientists were alarmed that sealing the reactor might provoke a second explosion.

Eventually, Gorbachev addressed his people on television on 14 May, using the occasion to point out the dangers of nuclear warfare and the likely after-effects, and how impossible they would be to overcome. Within weeks he was pressing the point and offering unilateral arms cuts, and this time

even the hard-liners in Washington began to listen. People everywhere had seen a demonstration of what their future might be - and they were frightened.

**Disengagement and Disarmament**

Soviet commentators began to insist that national security could not be achieved by military means alone, nor by one country at the expense of others. They insisted that the sheer weight of arms in the world reduced international security.

The Soviet Union, of course, had pressing economic reasons for adopting this stand as well as ideological ones. The defence budget and absorption of many of the country's most capable scientists and technicians into the quest for military hegemony had become an intolerable burden which had to be contained if *perestroika* was to become a reality.

In Washington, the 'Irangate' scandal was beginning to damage the careers and credibility of many of the most aggressive 'hawks' in the Reagan administration, giving the pragmatic Secretary of State, George Shultz, the ear of the President. So Gorbachev's renewed offers on arms reduction at last fell on fertile ground. Little more than eighteen months after Chernobyl the two leaders signed the treaty banning intermediate nuclear weapons.

In 1988 Gorbachev announced a unilateral cut of half a million men from the Soviet

military. A withdrawal from Afghanistan was negotiated and conducted to schedule; the last troops left in February 1989. To the astonishment of Western governments, the Kabul government survived and the Kremlin had extricated itself from an apparently unwinnable war without any loss of face.

Then, towards the end of 1989, the entire balance of power within Europe shifted as reform movements in eastern Europe took their courage into their hands and their protests on to the streets. The Kremlin, meanwhile, continued to emphasize that inter-socialist relations should be based on respect for sovereignty and independence, and refused to shore up unpopular regimes. At an ever-increasing pace, the Eastern bloc dissolved on Western television screens like a grandiose soap opera. Many in the West thought that this opportunity for self-determination might infect the Soviet Union and cause the collapse of Communism there, particularly as racial tensions were raising their ugly head in the southern republics of Azerbaijan, Georgia and Uzbekistan, while secessionist tendencies were manifest in Lithuania, Latvia, Estonia and elsewhere.

Whether this will come to pass is still an open question. One thing is certain, however. Mikhail Gorbachev and his colleagues have tackled a difficult situation head on and, despite dire predictions to the contrary in both East and West, the Soviet system has, with significant modifications, survived.

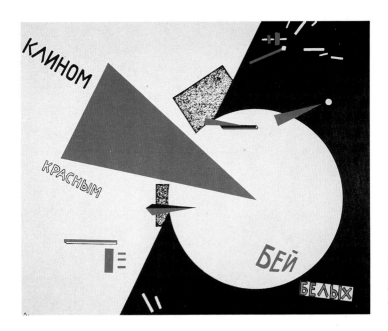

Lissitsky's Civil War poster, 'Beat the Whites with the Red Wedge', 1920.

# COMMUNISM: WHAT NOW?

Has the spectre supposedly haunting the world for nearly 150 years - the spectre of Communism - disappeared for ever? Was it simply the product of the fertile imagination and self-conceit of Marx, Engels, Lenin and their latter-day disciples? Has Communism, the self-proclaimed gravedigger of capitalism, effectively dug its own grave? The recent collapse of Communist rule in one country after another has led to the widespread belief that Communism is finished as a system of rule, a political movement, a tool for economic modernization, a vision of the good life and above all as an ideology. Political forecasting is a notoriously hazardous enterprise: events have an annoying habit of confounding the predictions of even the shrewdest observer, and it is worth noting that many who today write off Communism as a busted flush only yesterday regarded it as a threat to civilization and a menace to mankind. Surely if an 'evil empire' can collapse that easily, does it not not suggest that the original perception of threat was misconceived? Either that, or, to paraphrase Mark Twain, the reports of its demise have been greatly exaggerated.

During the 1970s all the symptoms of demoralization, disillusion, degeneration, division and decay were already evident in the Soviet Union and eastern Europe. These were what Gorbachev has called 'the years of stagnation'. Yet, paradoxically, these were also the years when the Communist 'club' was rapidly expanding its Third World membership. And, although it may have been clear to the astute onlooker that the 'evil empire' had feet of clay, many in the West seemed to take at face value the Communist notion that the 'global correlation of forces' had shifted decisively in favour of Socialism.

If geographical expansion was no indicator of the health of the Communist body politic nor surely is its contraction. For the ultimate fate of an ideology or political movement does not depend on the numbers of those believing or acquiescing in it - or succumbing or submitting to its dictates - at any particular time.

How, it may be objected, after its dismal record, could any sane and decent person want Communism ever again? Communist visionaries (and they still exist) would argue that they have never had Communism in the first place - certainly not as envisaged by Marx and Engels. For the architects of modern Communism would never have given their imprimatur to a bloc of states in which representative institutions are rudimentary, privilege and patronage persist and people continue to put self before society. The 'true' Marxist world of compatible self-administered Communist societies, then, has yet to be created, and for the faithful follower of the Communist ideal, it is still worth striving for.

In any case, if the behaviour of fallible individuals and their institutions were to be the test of a belief system, Christianity would have failed it long ago, especially after the religious wars, the Inquisition, the excesses of the Borgias and the appearance of two, then three, popes simultaneously. Nor would capitalism have survived the test, what with the 'dark satanic mills', the cramped and unhygenic working conditions, the long hours and low pay and, above all, the pervasive sense of 'alienation' that resulted, causing Marx and Engels in the nineteenth century to view capitalism as a system in its death throes.

Yet, despite the most appalling misdemeanors committed in their name, the world's great economic, political and religious systems survive, live down their past and attract new converts. So where are Communism's new converts likely to spring from? In certain Third World countries, such as the Philippines, where there is widespread dissatisfaction both with existing rulers and with the socio-political systems they are pledged to uphold, the Communist Party continues to act as a medium for articulating popular discontent. In a number of Western countries too, the party lives on, if only as a vehicle of protest. And there are signs that in some of those very countries of eastern Europe that so recently threw off the shackles of Communist rule, the party - suitably renamed - may experience something of a revival. After all, in ridding themselves of inefficient, corrupt and often repressive regimes, the peoples of eastern Europe have also lost the 'nanny' state that provided for their basic needs, albeit at a comparatively meagre level.

Apart from anything else, the introduction of market mechanisms has meant cutting government expenditure, squeezing out subsidies and closing inefficient enterprises - which has had two unpalatable, if possibly short-term effects. They have depressed already low living standards still further as prices soar while more and more people lose their jobs, often for the first time. For people who have never experienced unemployment before, and are not used to 'standing on their own feet', and 'taking responsibility for their own actions', the effect can be traumatic.There is, as the psychologist, Erich Fromm pointed out years ago, 'a fear of freedom' among those who stand to lose by it. And with the disappearance of secure employment, minimal rents, free education and health services, cheap and abundant public transport, sports facilities and entertainments, even hardened anti-Communists may hanker for the days when the Communist state took care of you from cradle to grave.

Another unedifying consequence of the collapse of Communist power in eastern Europe has been the reappearance of the kinds of malign force once anaesthetized by Communism - national chauvinism, religious obscurantism and intolerance, anti-Semitism and crypto-fascism. Not for nothing was this region once known as 'the powder keg of Europe', which in the inter-war period resembled much of Africa and Asia today, with its coups and counter-coups, civil strife, economic instability and minority and refugee problems. And if eastern Europe were to descend once more into disorder bordering on anarchy, some, not normally sympathetic to the party, could grow nostalgic for the days of Communist hierarchy, order and discipline.

Finally, of course, since Communist rule has often been thrust upon people rather than freely chosen, are we to assume that this will never happen again, that the days of the party are entirely over, never to return? After all, Communists continue to rule in a handful of countries, and they remain a force to be reckoned with in a number of others. And can we be sure that we have seen the last of the Great Communist Dictator? When, for example, the French Revolution occurred in 1789 no-one anticipated the emergence of a Napoleon within a decade; and when the two revolutions occurred in Russia in 1917 few would have expected a Stalin.

As the turmoil mounts in eastern Europe and people take stock of the new political configurations in the wake of a unified Germany, it would be rash to predict what lies in store. One thing, however, is certain: wherever there is perceived injustice, oppression, exploitation and abuse of power, there will still be a need for an organization of political protest armed with an emotionally reassuring set of action-based theories. In this sense the future of many a Communist party is probably assured, even if the Communist world of Marx's imagination remains in the realms of dreams, conjectures and speculations.

# INDEX

# PICTURE CREDITS

Poster by D. Moor, 'The
Third International', 1921

NOTE: t = top, b = bottom, r = right, l = left

Akademie der Künste der Deutschen Demokratischen Republik, (John Heartfield Archive/A12, Vol XII, no 45, 1933) for page 84; Camera Press Limited, London: 104, 110, 115b, 121b, 123, 126, 132, 134, 135b, 139, 143, 147b, 158t, 158b, 159, 164b, 168, 172, 178l, 180l, 185, 187l, 187r, 199, 228; Colourific: 219t (Peter Turnley/Black Star), 221 (Kenneth Jarecke/Contact); The Communist Picture Library, London: 16, 28l, 57t; The Library of Congress: 81, 90l; Deutsche Akademie der Künste Berlin and the Estate of Kathe Kollwitz/DACS: 65tr; E.T. Archive, London: 256; Foreign Language Press, Peking: 171b (Peasant Painting from Huhsien County); By Courtesy of the Estate of George Grosz/DACS: 69b (Title page Die Pleite, 1919); the Hulton Picture Library, London: 13r, 34l, 35l, 56; IKON: 17, 20t, 59b, 103b, 135t; By Courtesy of the Estate of Vera Inber: 103t (from 'Leningrad Diary', by Vera Inber, published by Hutchinson, 1971); International Centre for Photography, New York: 99t (Zelma); Katz: 202-203 (Tom Stoddart), 222 (Mary Beth Camp/Matrix), 235t (Keith Bernstein), 236 (J. Polleros/JB Pictures), 242 and 243 (Jeremy Nicholl); David King: 1, 3, 6, 25, 40, 41, 44t, 44b, 45, 50-51, 52, 57b, 59t, 60, 61, 64, 65tl, 65b, 66, 68, 71, 75l, 75r, 77t, 77b, 80b, 88, 90r, 95, 99b, 118, 119, 244; Lauros-Girardon: 10-11, 31; Magnum Photos Limited, London: 70 (Collection Aslier), 85t (David Seymour), 85b (Robert Capa), 96 (Walter Bosshard), 98 (Wu Yinxian), 102, 108-109 (Elliott Erwitt), 114 (Elliott Erwitt), 127 (Henri-Cartier-Bresson), 129 (Marc Riboud), 142 (Eric Lessing), 146 (Remi Burri), 147t (Sergio Lorrain), 148-149, 164t (Martine Franck), 160, 162, 163, 171t (Marc Riboud), 166 (Ian Berry), 167 (Fred Mayer), 173 (Don McCullin), 175 (Philip Jones-Griffiths), 178r (Marc Riboud), 180r and 181 (Bruno Barbey), 184 (Wayne Miller), 192 (Susan Meiselas), 194 (Leonard Freed), 196 (A. de Andrade), 198 (Peter Marlow), 201 (Bruno Barbey), 206 (Alberto Venzago), 207l (Franklin), 209, 212 (Inge Morath), 214b (Abbas), 219b (Abbas), 225 (Susan Meiselas), 227 (Natchwey), 234 (Franco Zecchin); The Mansell Collection, London:

12, 13l, 30, 34r; Mary Evans Picture Library, London: 21, 39; Lee Miller Archives: 115t; Network: 223 (Mike Goldwater), 235b (Leighton); Popperfoto: 47, 80t, 93t, 105, 107, 111, 121t, 131, 140, 144, 150, 189, 191, 197, 214t; Museo del Prado, Madrid/DACS: 86; By Courtesy of HM the Queen: 24; Rex Features: 155 (SIPA-Press), 213 (SIPA-Press), 218 (Manoocher/SIPA-Press), 230 (SIPA-Press), 231, 237 (Alfred), 239 (Laski); Museo del Risorgimento, Milan/Scala: 22; Science Photo Library, London: 154; SOLO: 89 (Non-Intervention Poker, cartoon by David Low, Evening Standard, January 13, 1937), 93b (Just in Case There's Any Mistake, cartoon by David Low, Evening Standard, July 3, 1939); Frank Spooner Pictures Ltd: 151 (Gamma), 176 (Gamma), 179t (Sou Vigruth), 179b (Roland Neveu/Gamma), 193 (Pascal Maitre), 215 (Gamma); Sygma, London: 207r (A.Nogues), 226 (P. Chauvel); Topham Picture Source: 20b, 23, 28r, 37t; Ullstein Bilderdienst: 37b, 46, 69t, 76; VAAP, Moscow and London: 74; Victoria and Albert Museum, London: 29; H. Roger Viollet: 35r.